27 FEBRUARY 1900

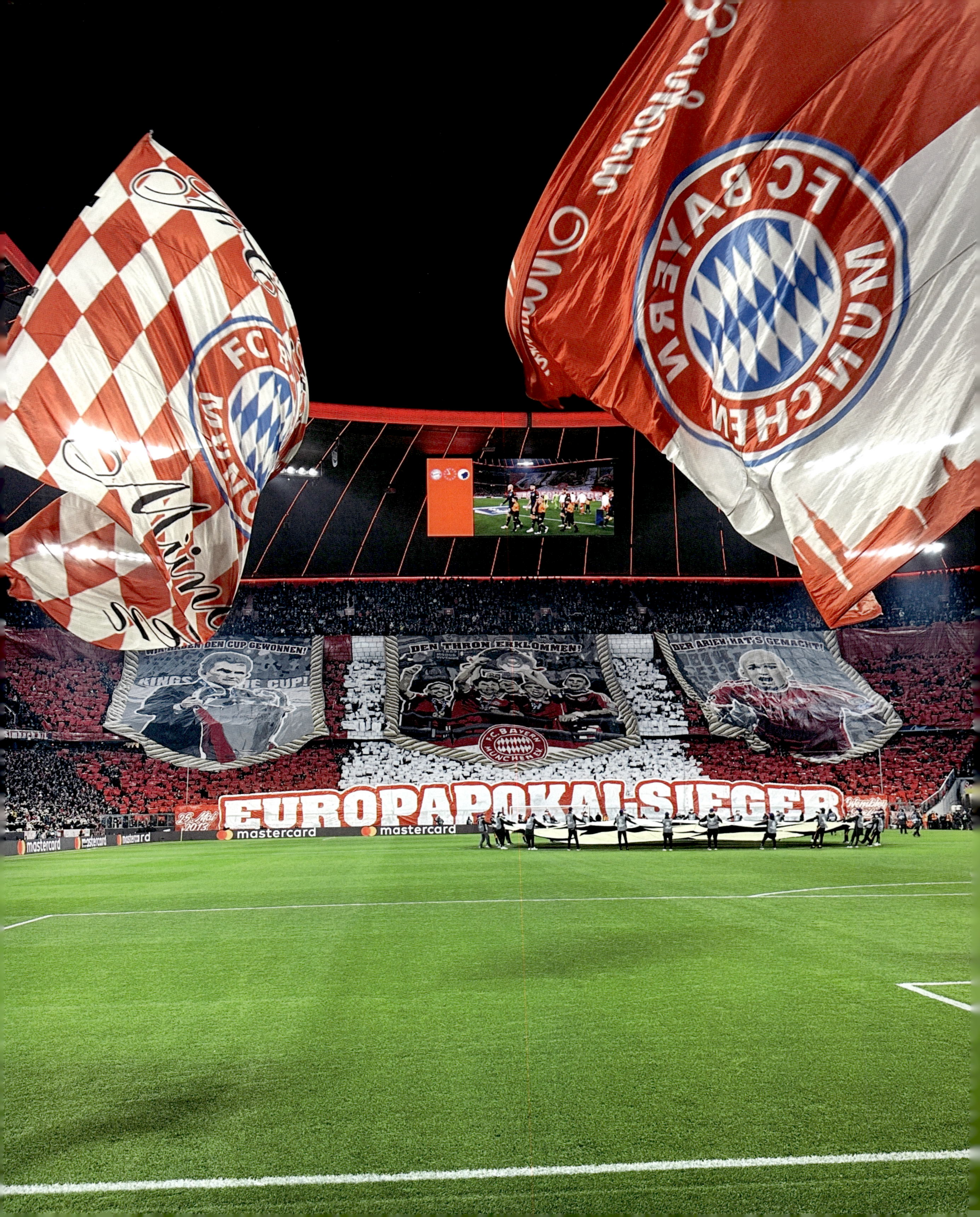
DEN THRON ERKLOMMEN!
EUROPAPOKAL-SIEGER
mastercard

Christian Eichler

FC BAYERN
125 YEARS
MIA SAN MIA

PRESTEL
Munich · London · New York

Einhundert
FünfundZwanzig

DEAR BAYERN!

125 Years of FC Bayern – *Mia san mia* means togetherness

What would the young men who founded FC Bayern in Café Gisela in Schwabing on 27 February 1900 think of this club today? They loved football, wanted to devote themselves to this new sport, left the men's gymnastics club and went their own way – a group of personalities who looked to the future, who wanted to make a difference. Much of what characterises FC Bayern to this day – all of it, in effect – is still marked by the spirit of the meeting in Café Gisela. Our club has constantly developed – and nevertheless succeeded in keeping its core values at all times.

FC Bayern stands on three immovable pillars: sporting success, financial solidity and social responsibility. The basis for all of these pillars are its members, whose numbers are approaching the magic figure of 400,000 in this proud year of the club anniversary. FC Bayern is the sports club with the largest membership in the world, and its enormous support shows that it reaches the hearts of people both here in our home region of Bavaria and also across the whole world by setting benchmarks and guidelines. The decisive point that distinguishes us from international competitors is that FC Bayern has never sold its soul. We can all be proud of that, and we must stay on this path. *Mia san mia* – we are who we are.

FC Bayern is a home, a family. And in this club, with our members, we have everything that we need to grow together. "Mia san mia" means togetherness, and in a world confronted by divisive forces that are enemies of democracy, in which people wonder who is still able to organise togetherness at all, our FC Bayern fulfils precisely this task: connecting people, communicating and living the idea of community.

Our club has always had a good compass. And it has guiding stars that it can follow. It is a task for all of us to continue developing the club in the spirit of personalities such as our Jewish president Kurt Landauer, who returned from exile after the end of the Nazi dictatorship and remains to this day a role model for reconciliation, and of personalities like Franz Beckenbauer, Uli Hoeness or Karl-Heinz Rummenigge – and in the spirit of the young visionaries who took a decision in Café Gisela that led to the unique success story called FC Bayern Munich.

Beneath club president Herbert Hainer (left) and chief executive officer Jan-Christian Dreesen (right) is the founding document of FC Bayern, which initiated a unique success story on 27 February 1900 in Café Gisela in the Schwabing district of Munich.

Herbert Hainer
President

Jan-Christian Dreesen
Chief Executive Officer

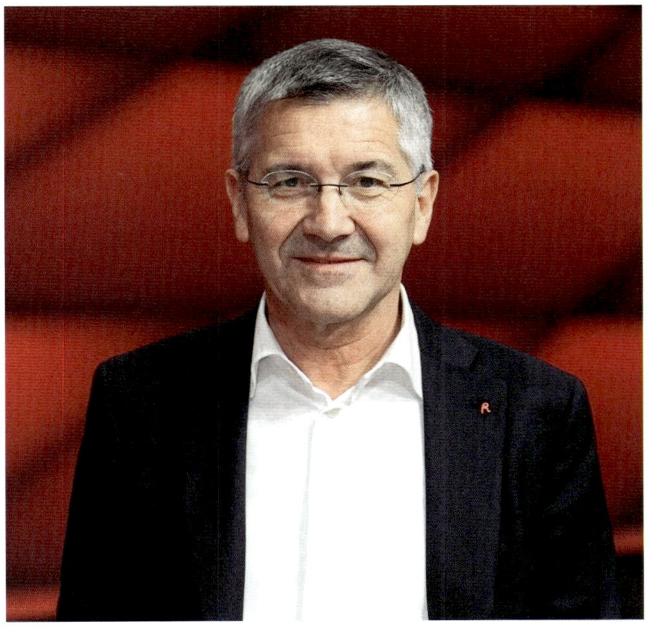

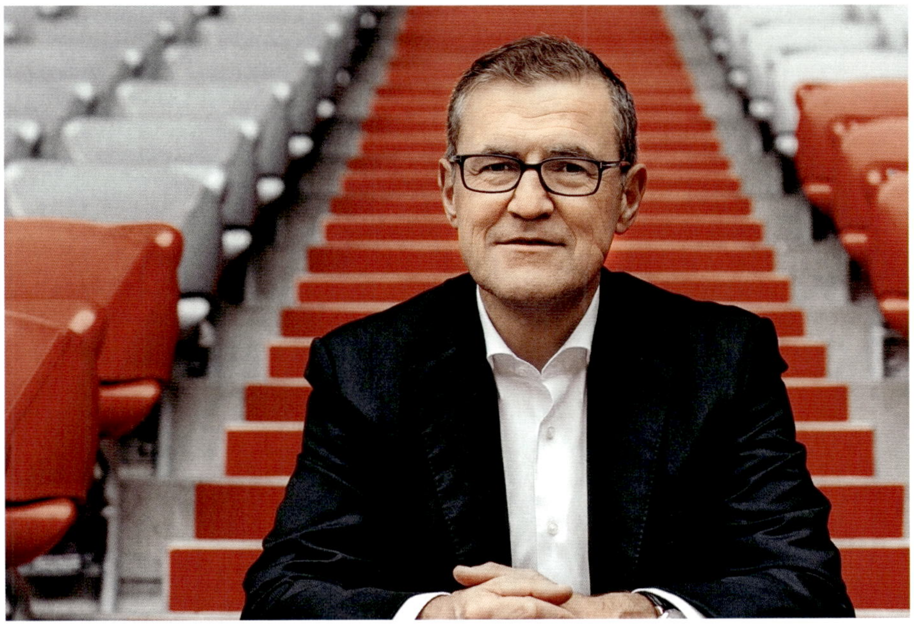

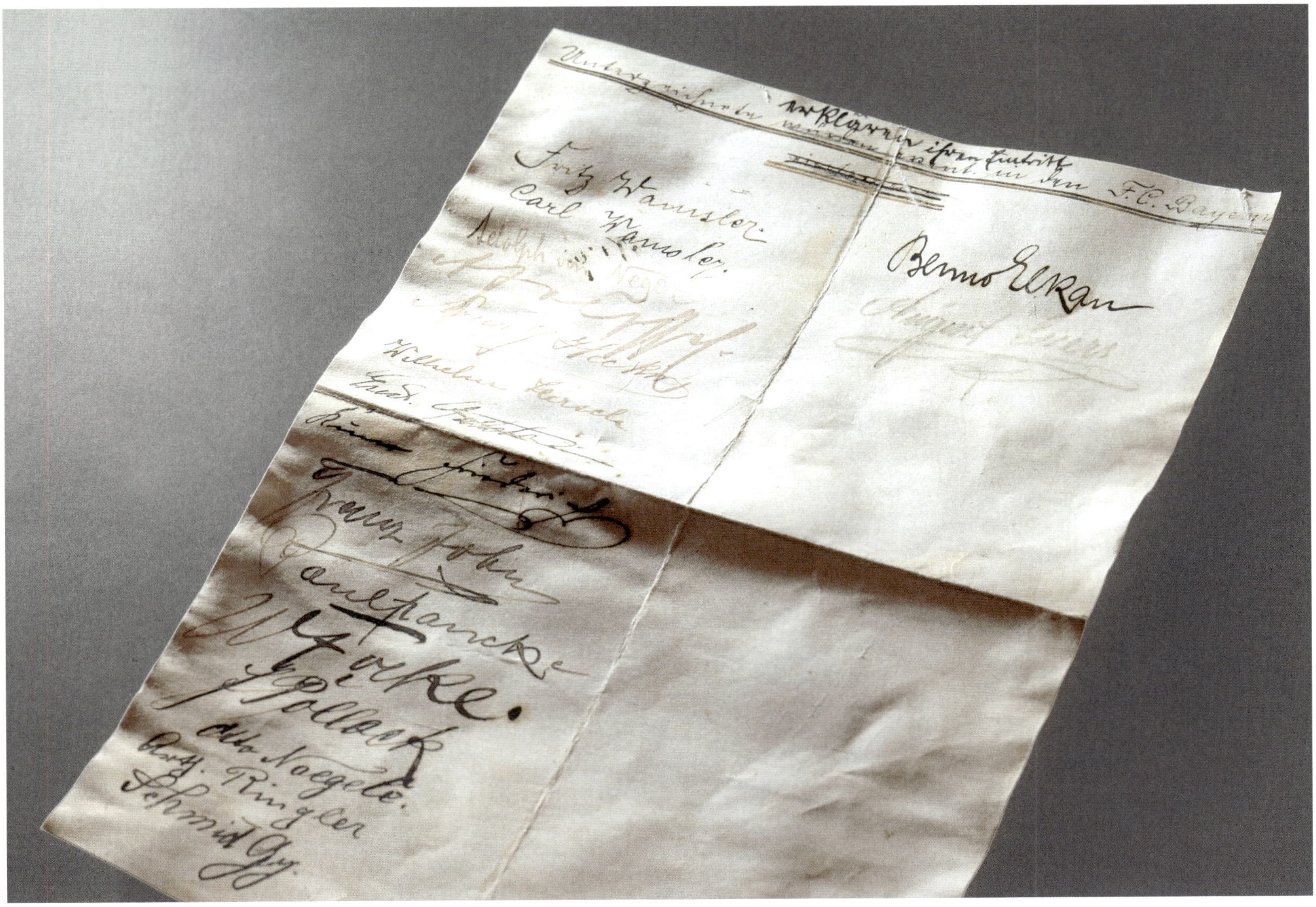
Fritz Wamsler
Carl Wamsler
Benno Elkan

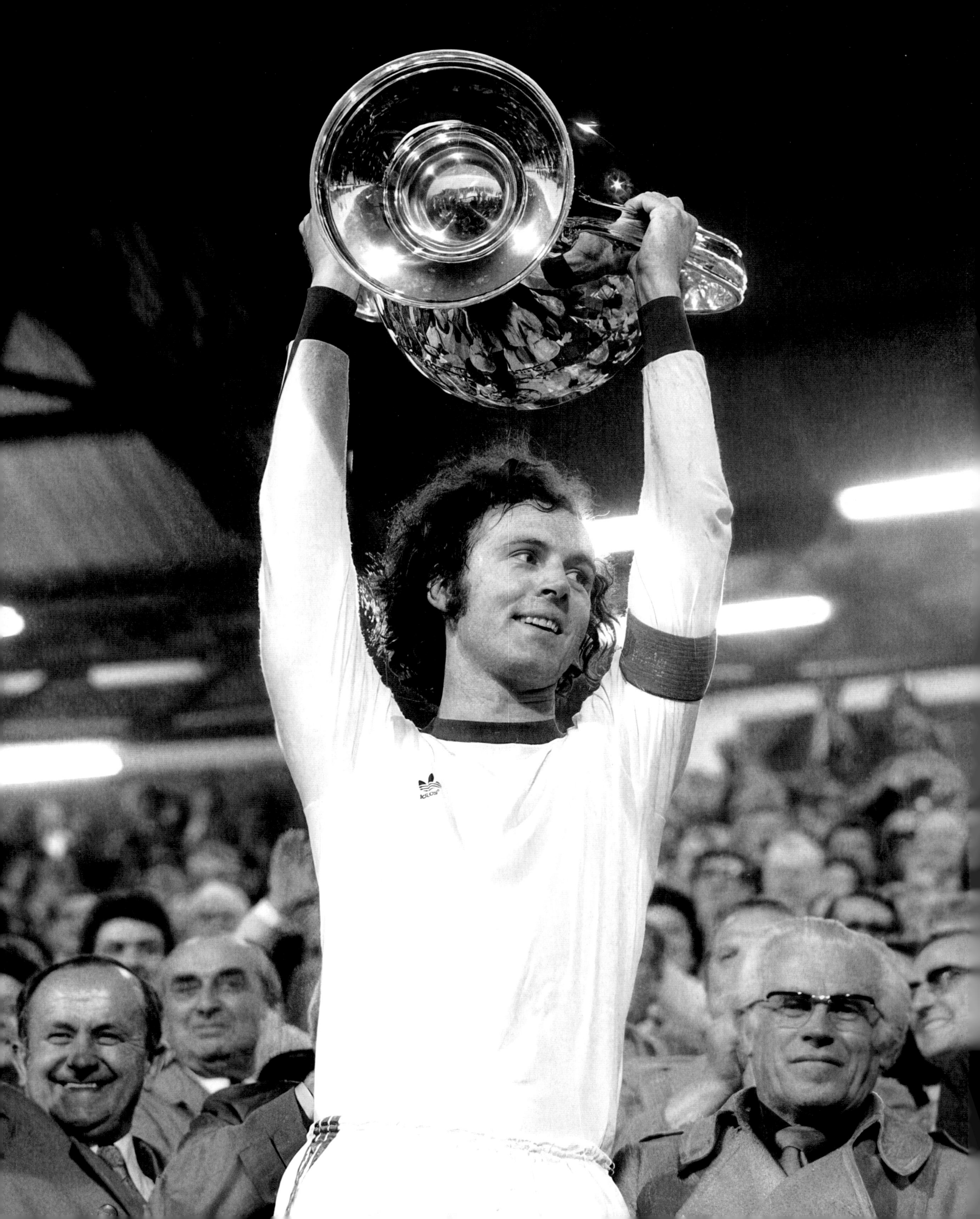

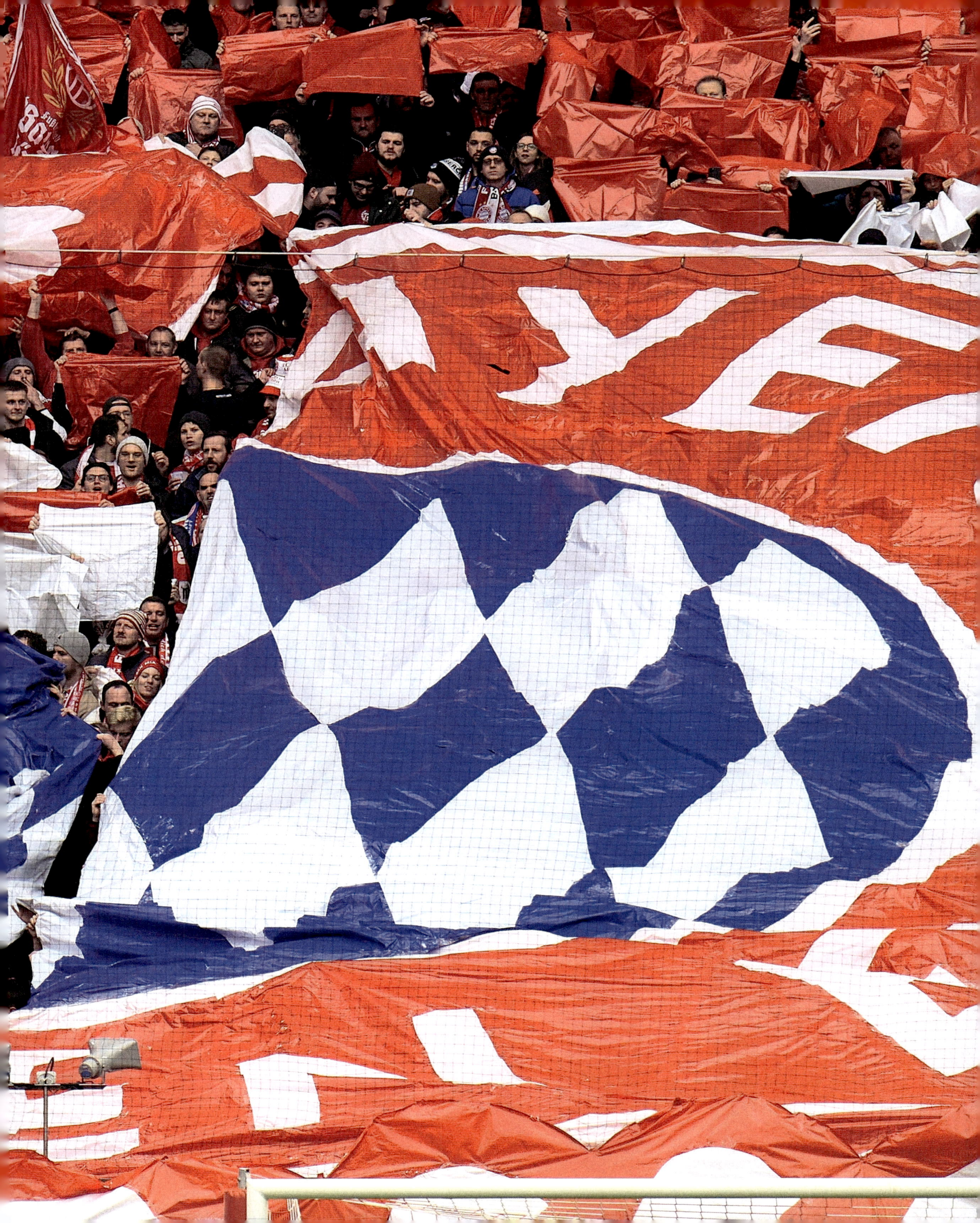

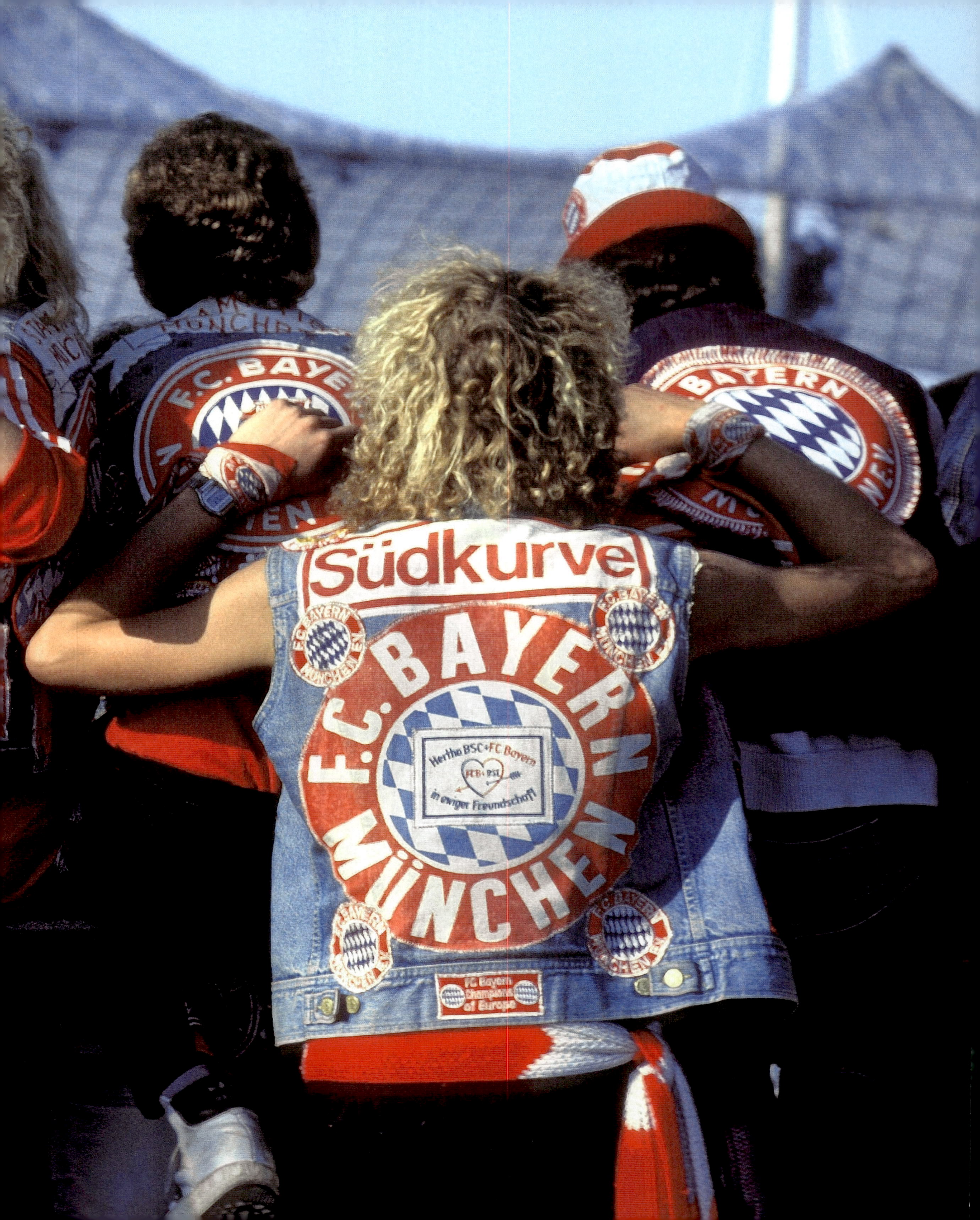
Südkurve
F.C. BAYERN MÜNCHEN
Hertha BSC + FC Bayern
in ewiger Freundschaft
FC Bayern Champions of Europe

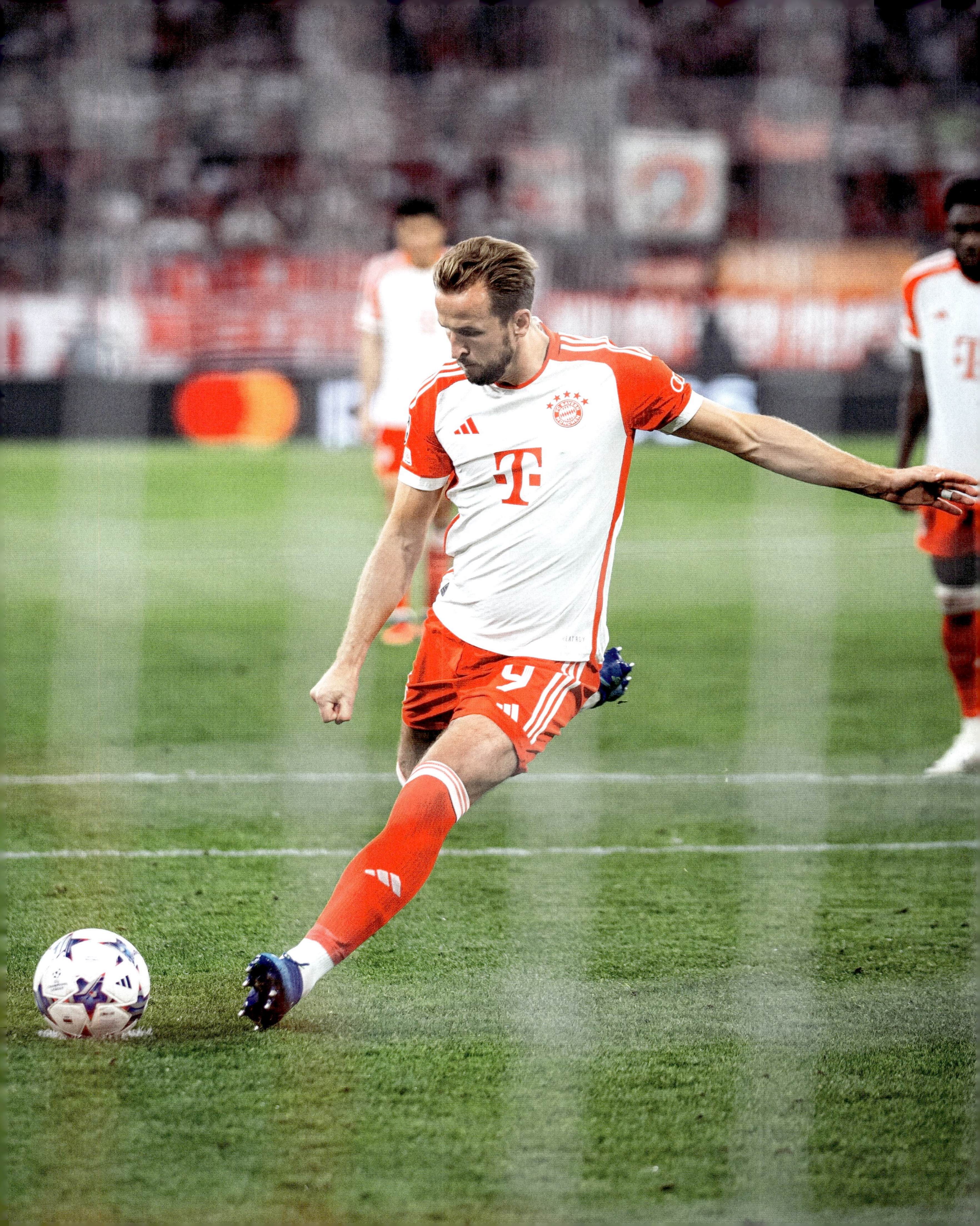

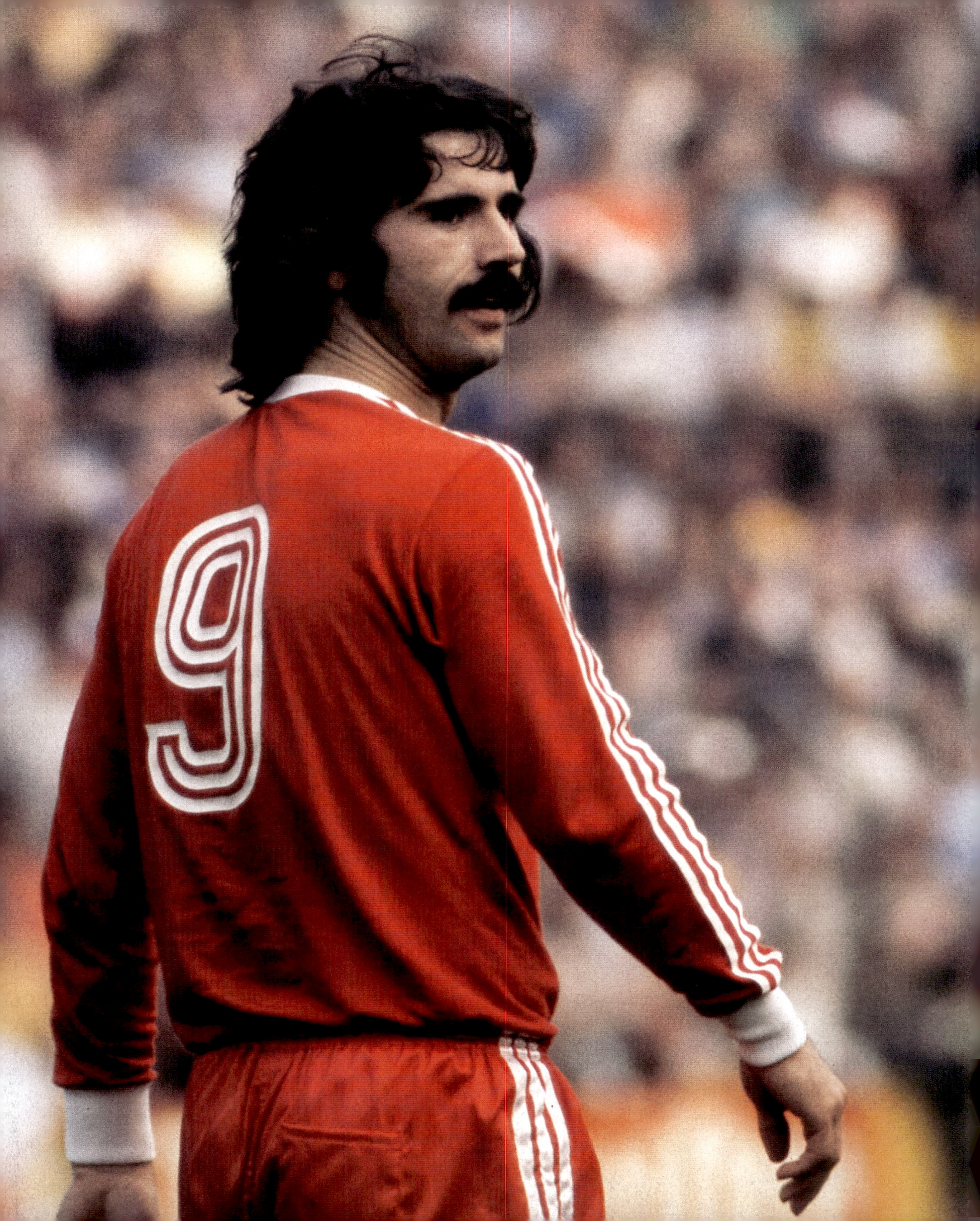

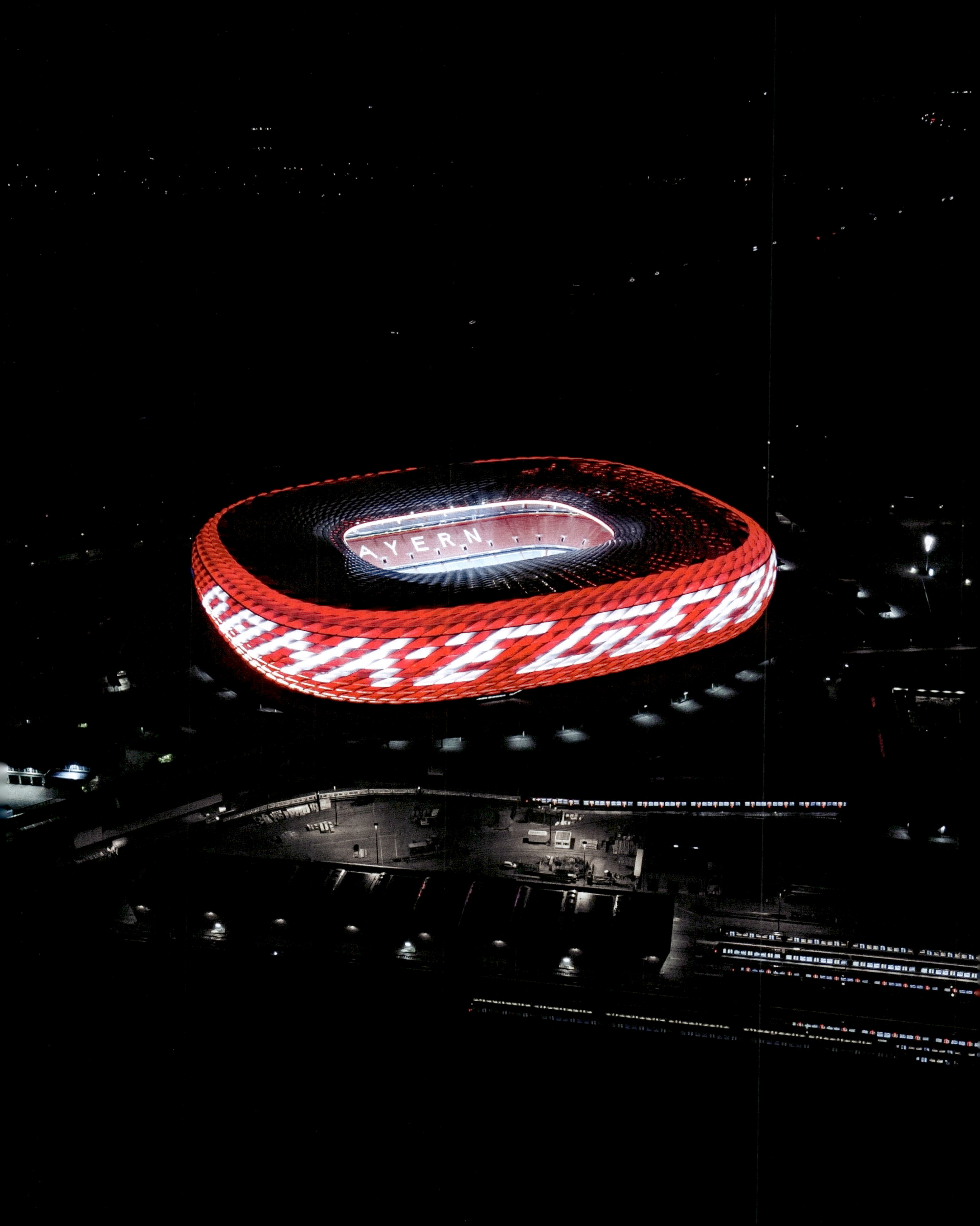
AYERN

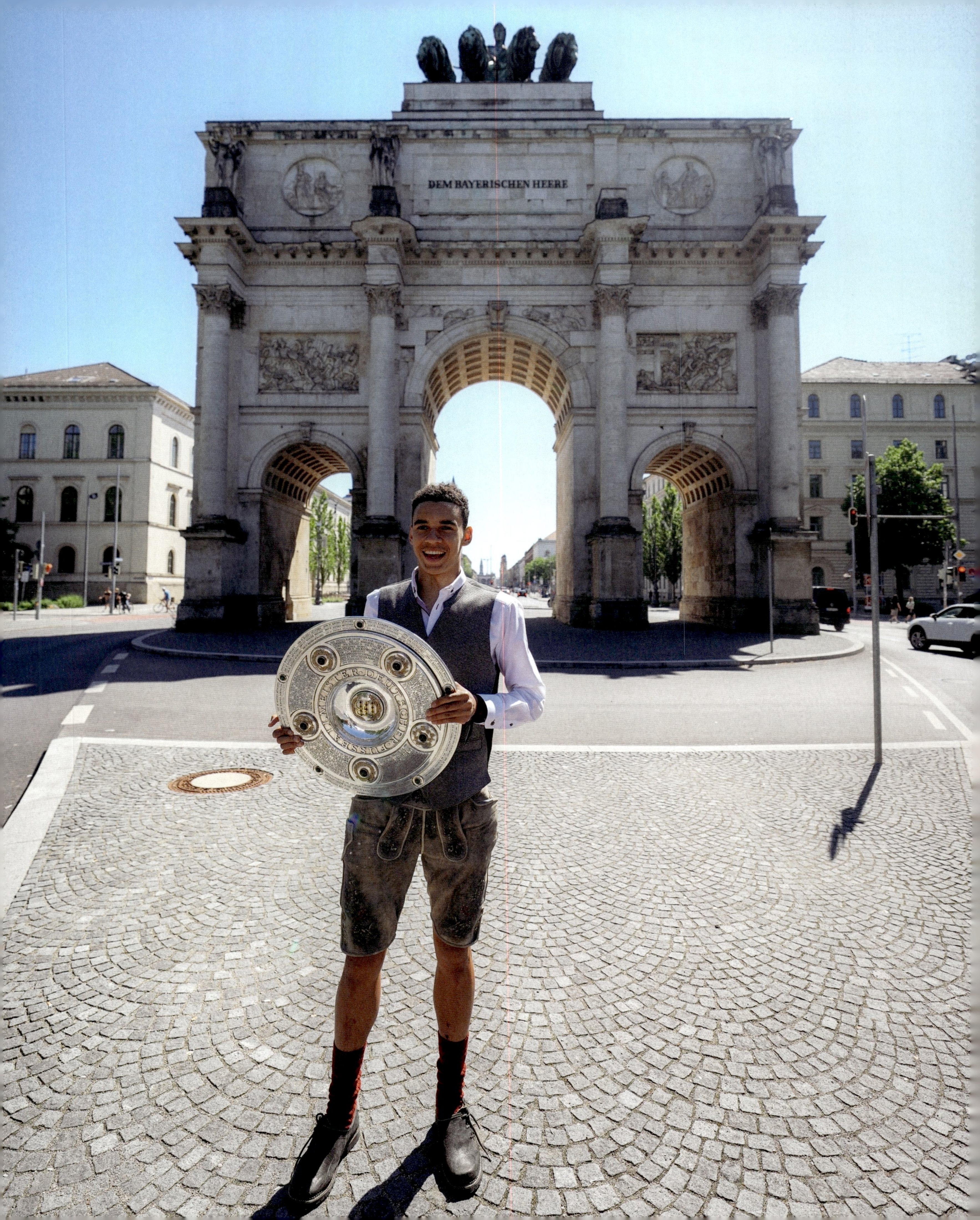
DEM BAYERISCHEN HEERE

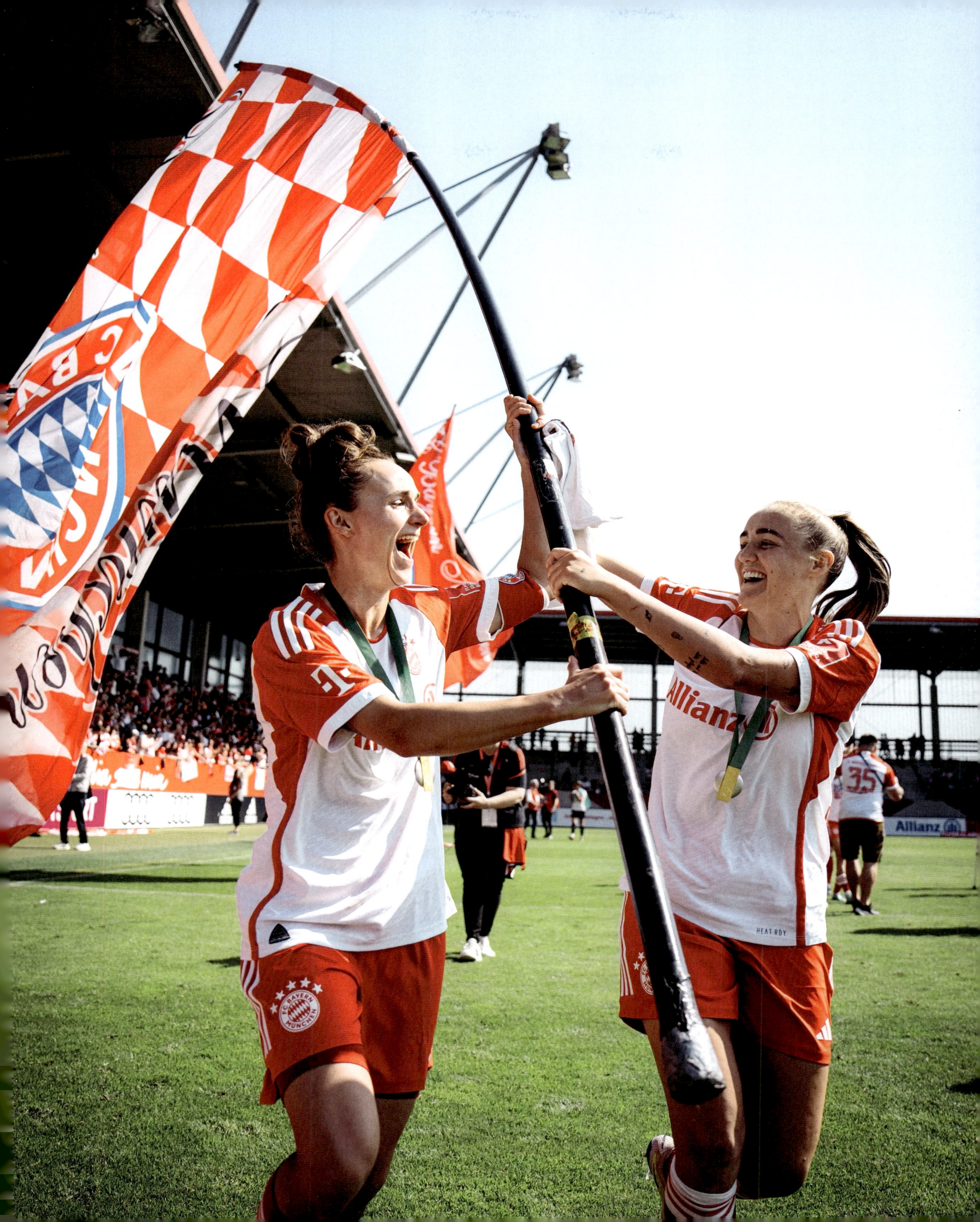
Allianz
35
Allianz

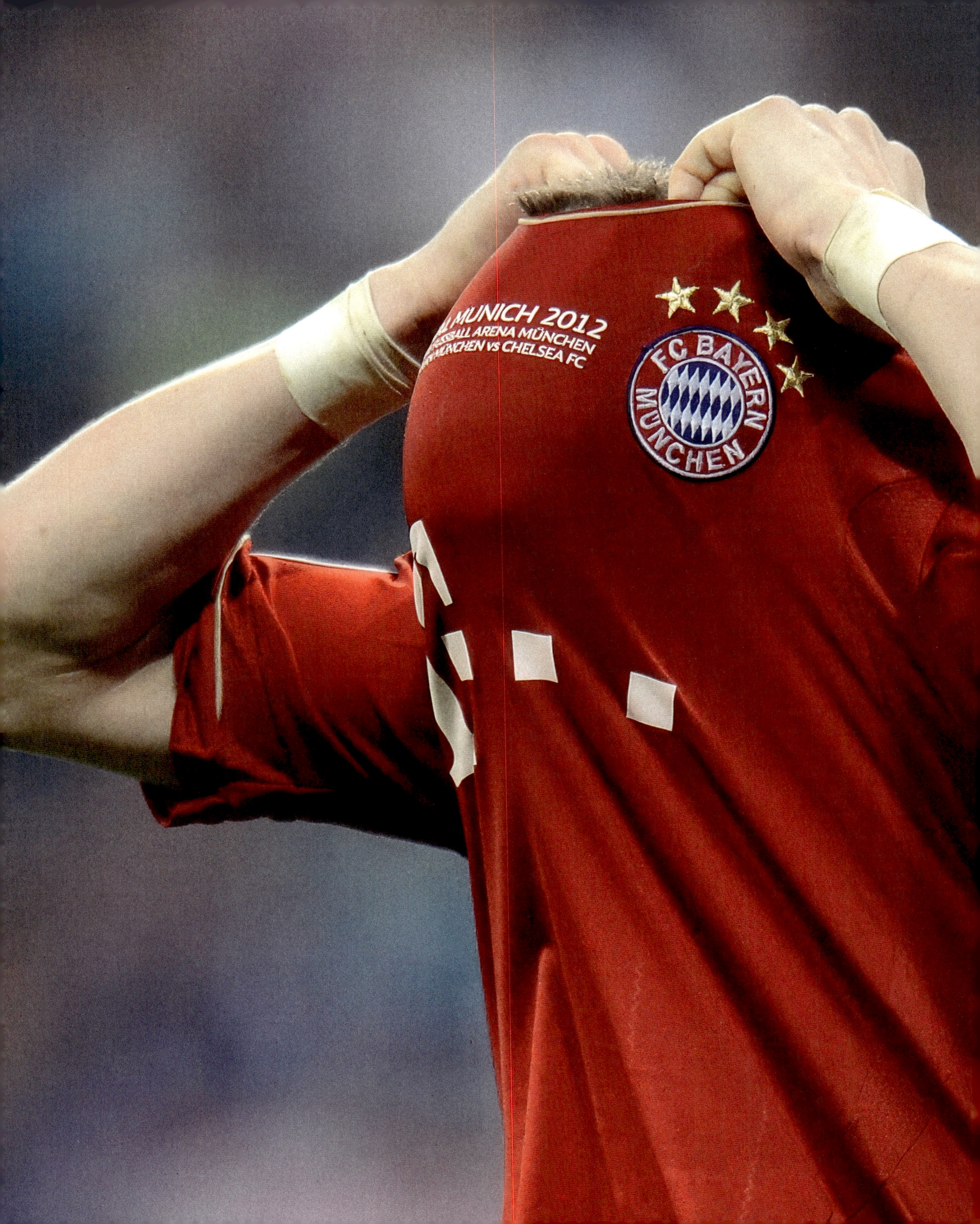
MUNICH 2012
ARENA MÜNCHEN
vs CHELSEA FC
FC BAYERN MÜNCHEN

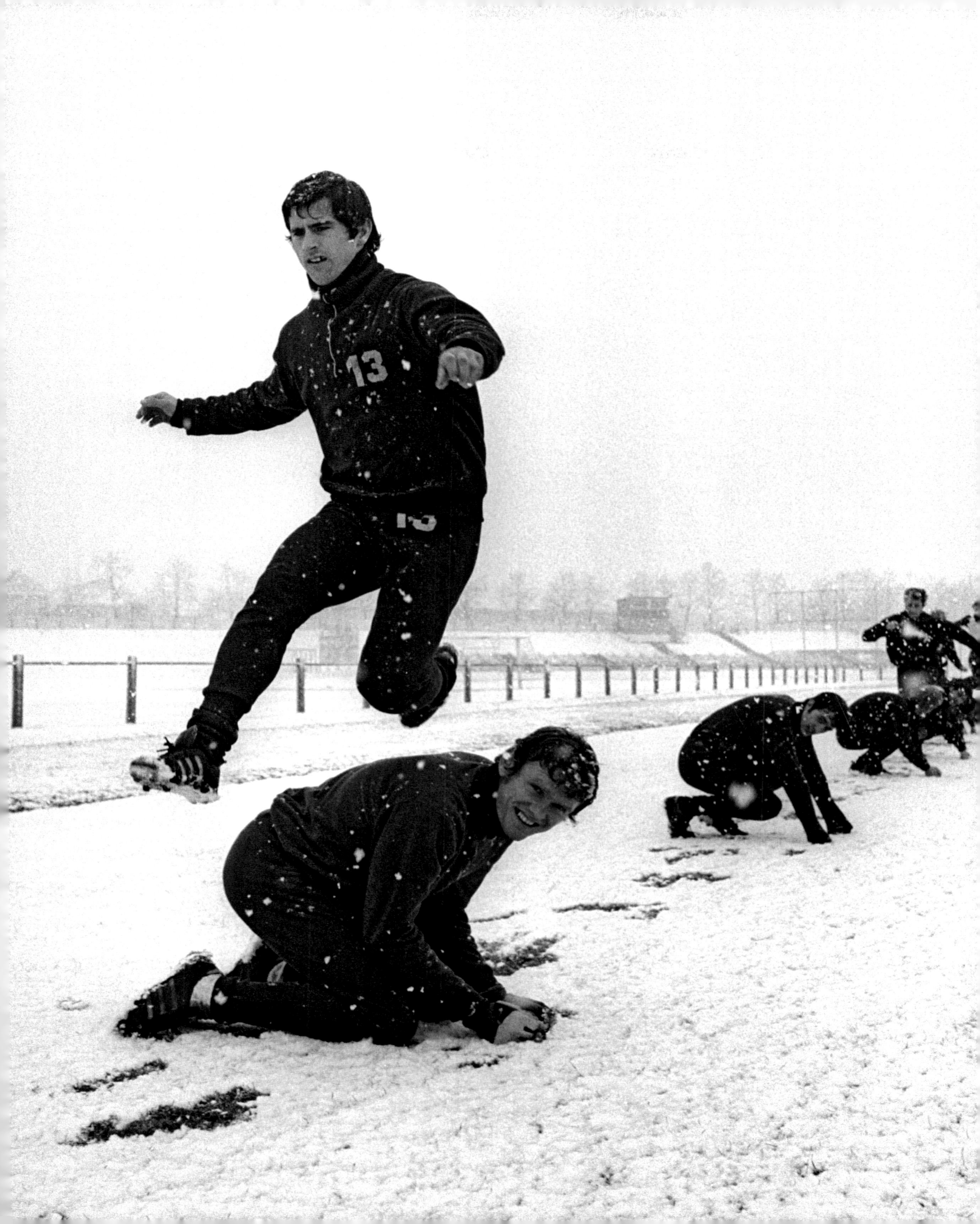

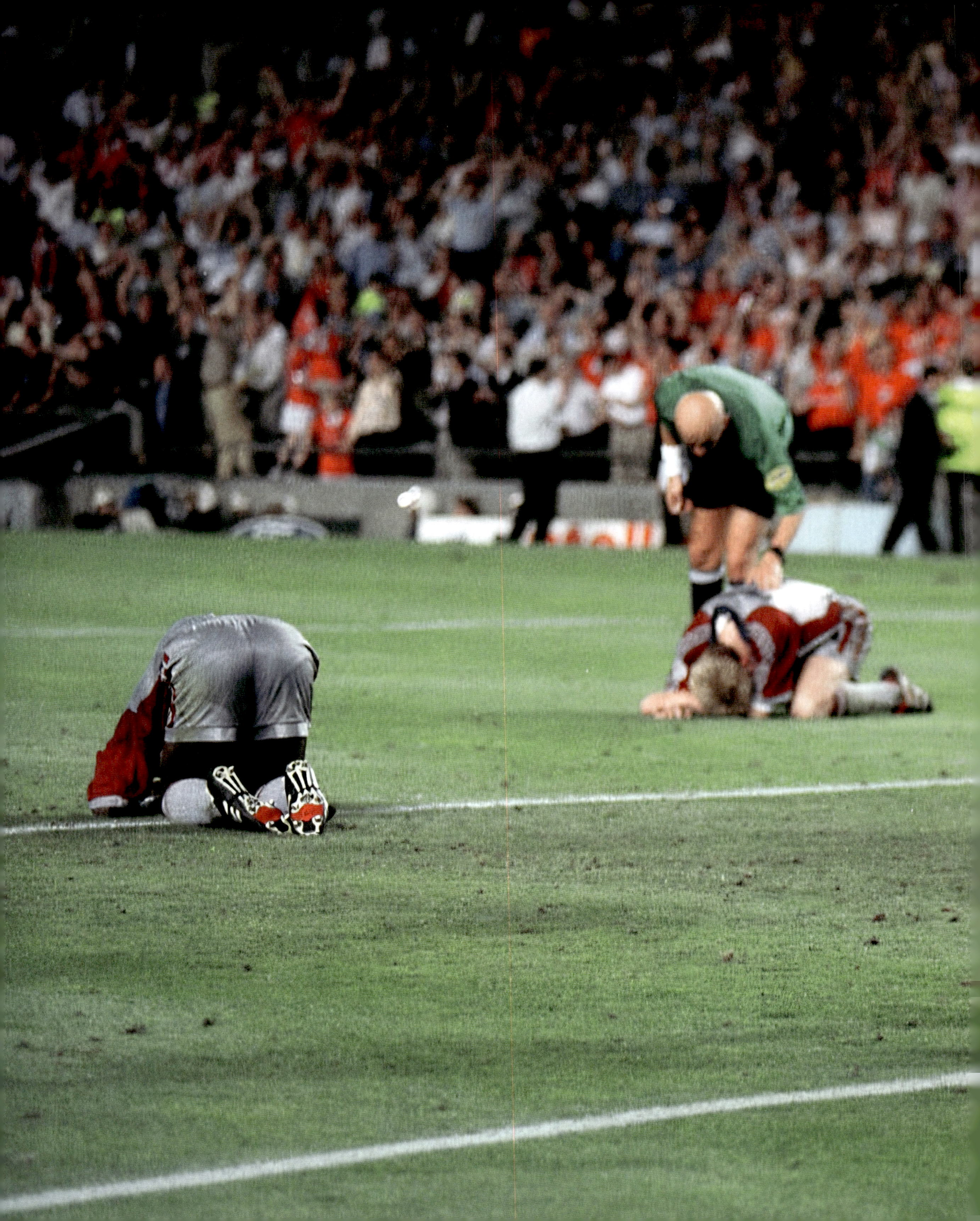

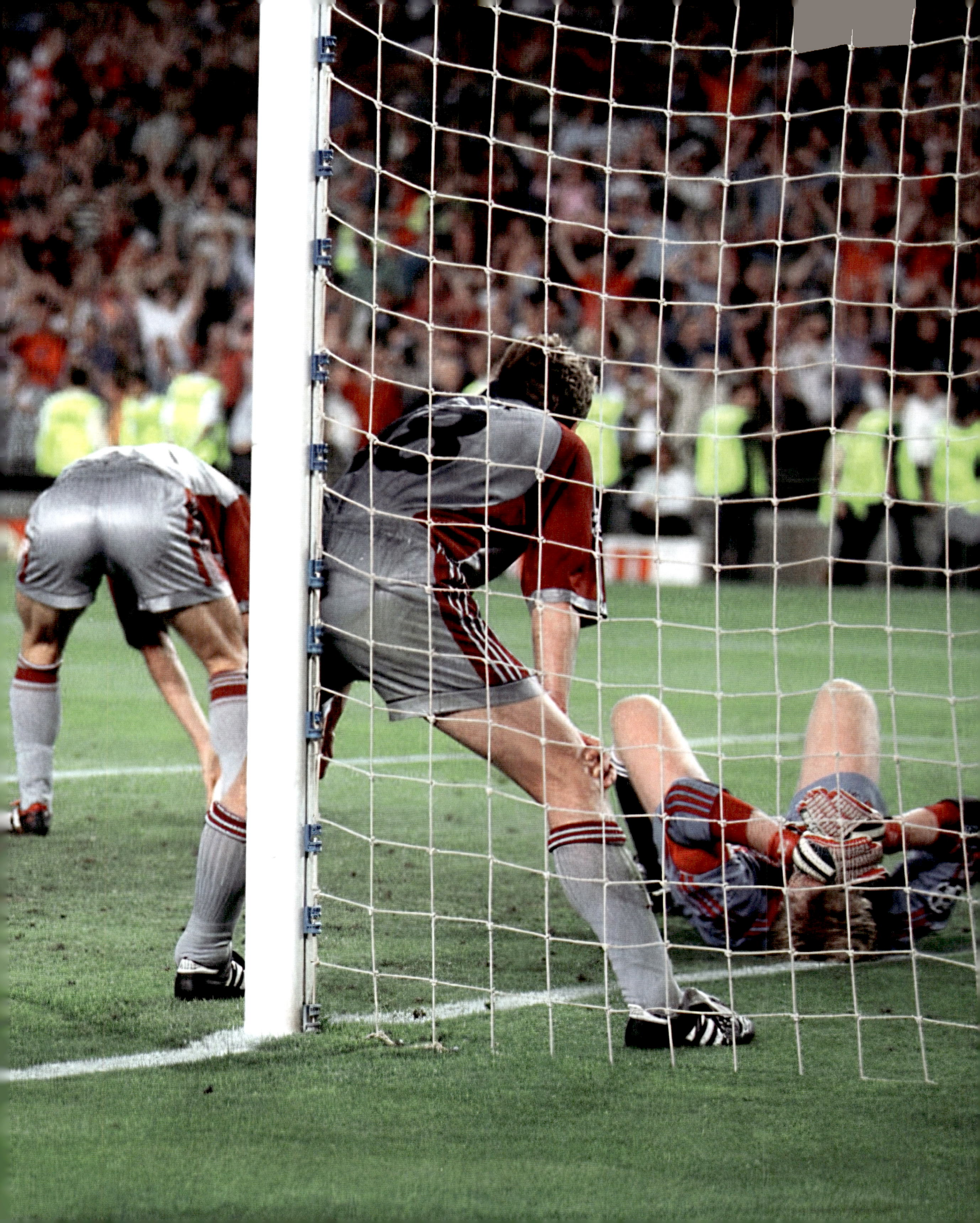

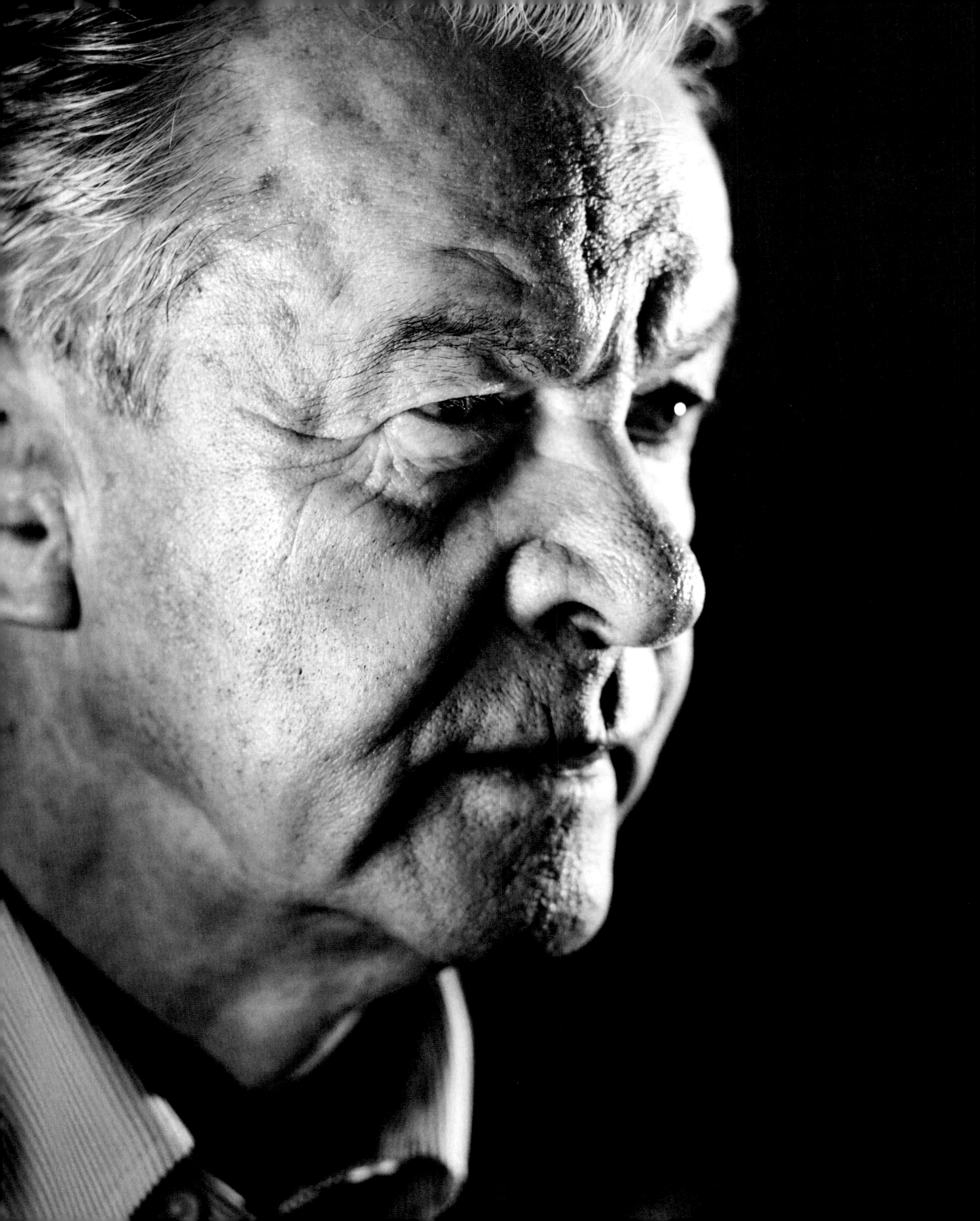

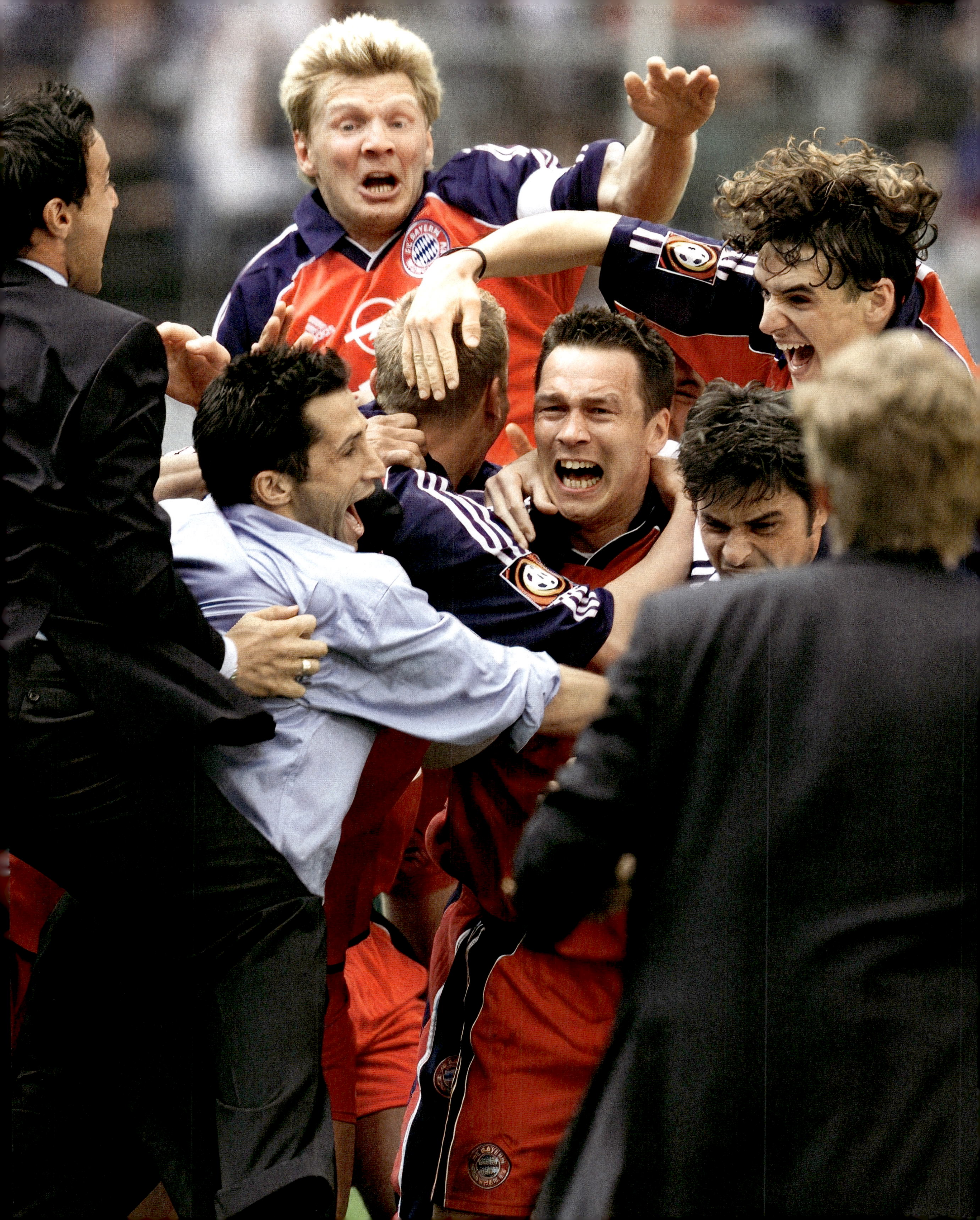

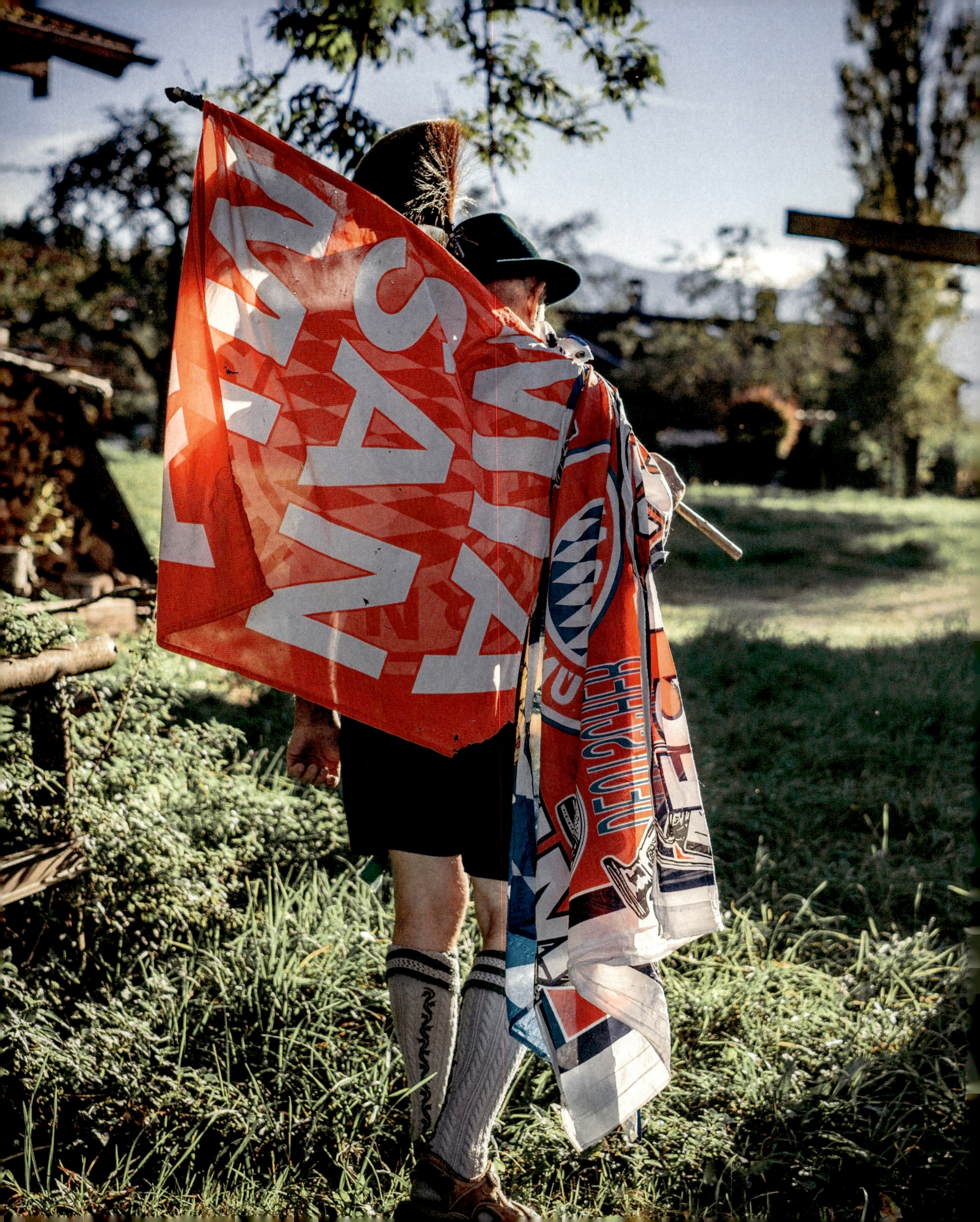

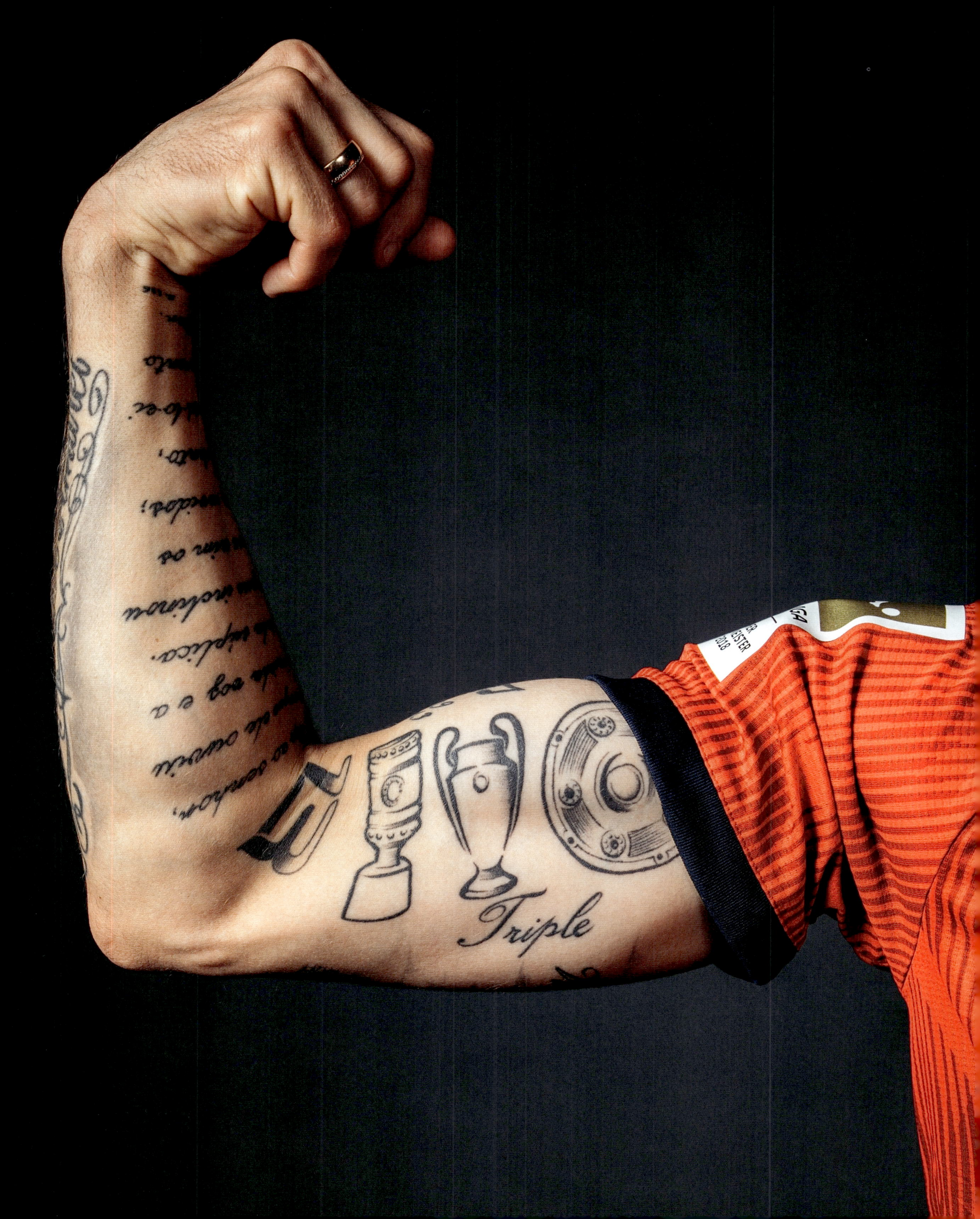
Triple

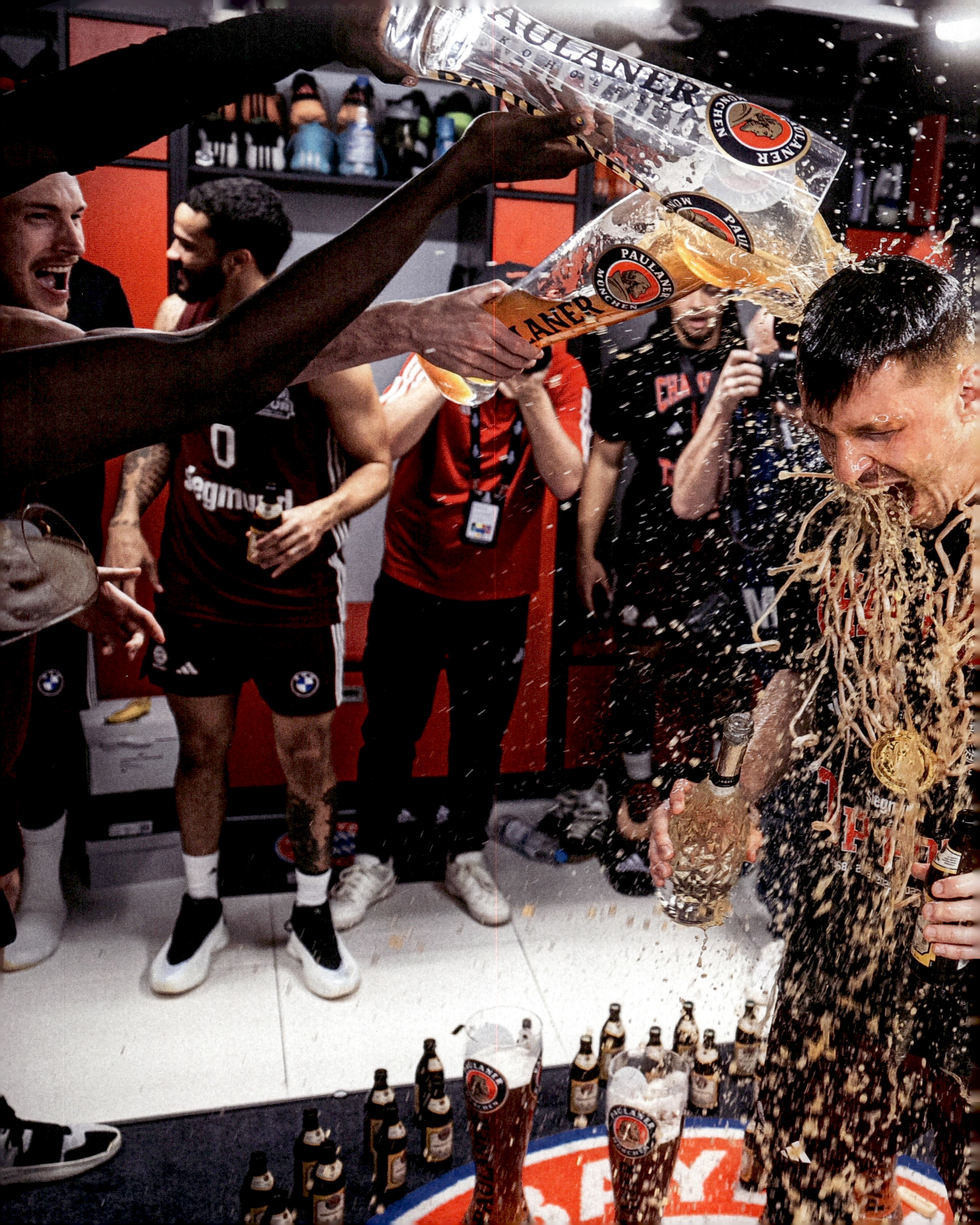
PAULANER

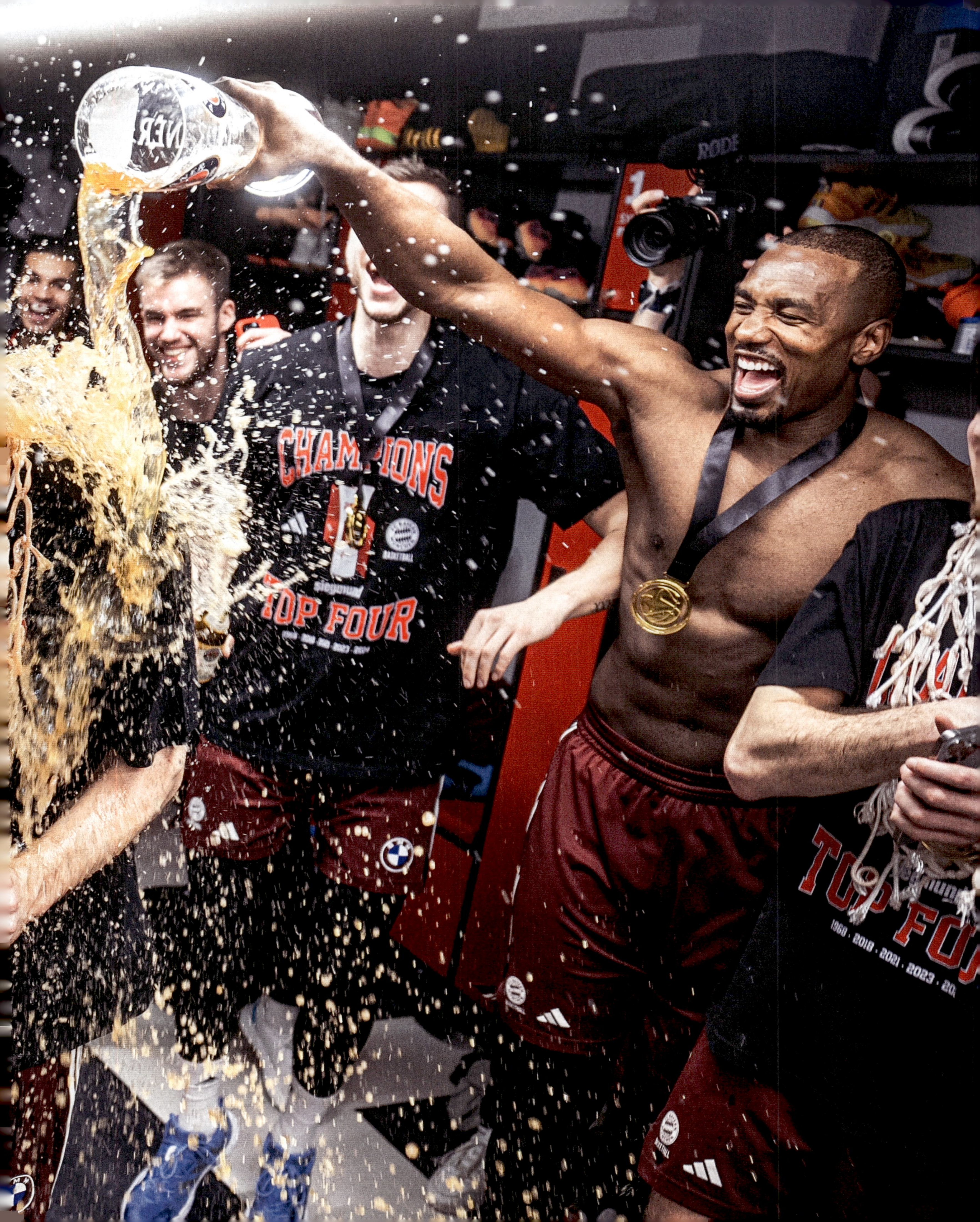
CHAMPIONS
TOP FOUR

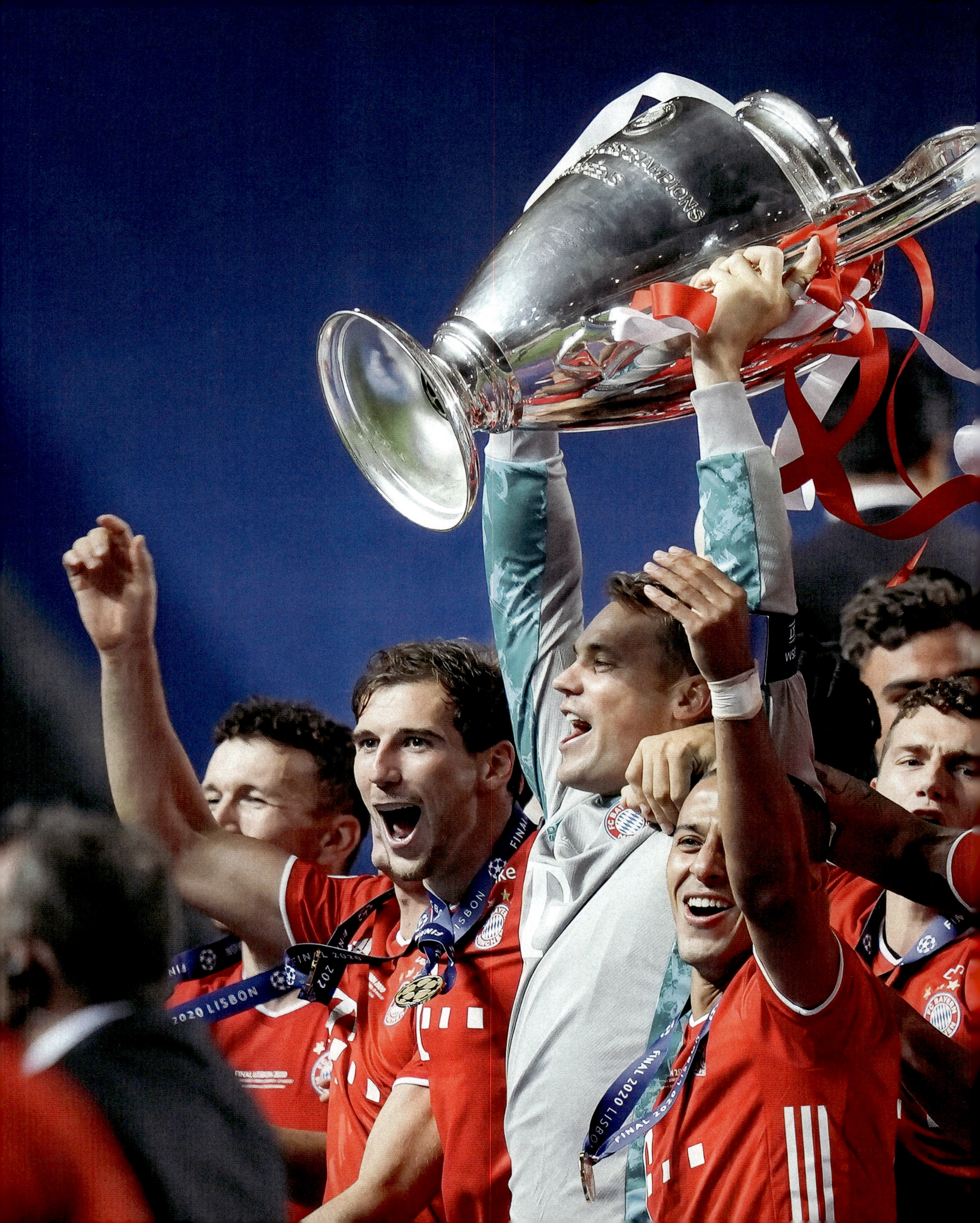
2020 LISBON

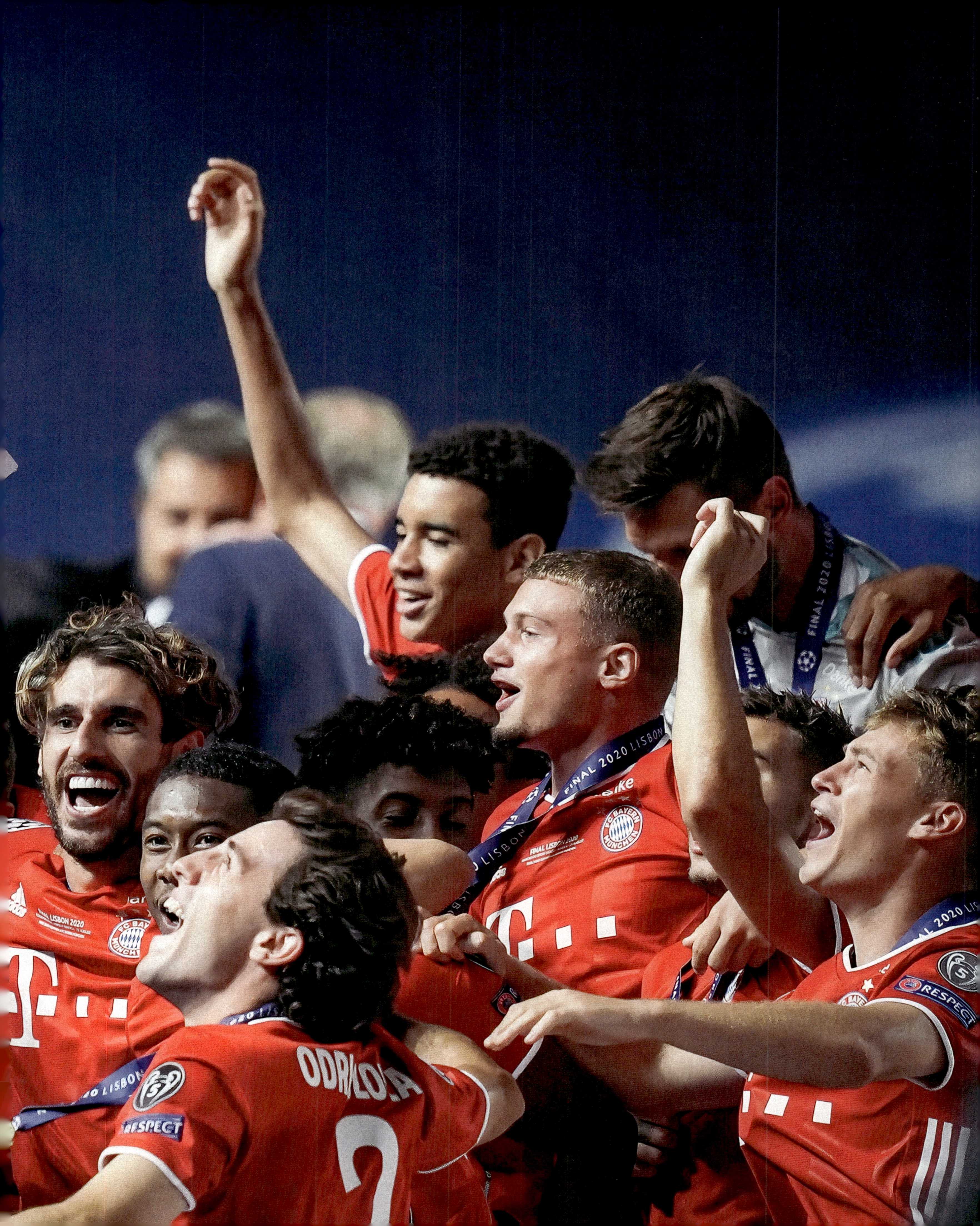
FINAL 2020 LISBON
RESPECT

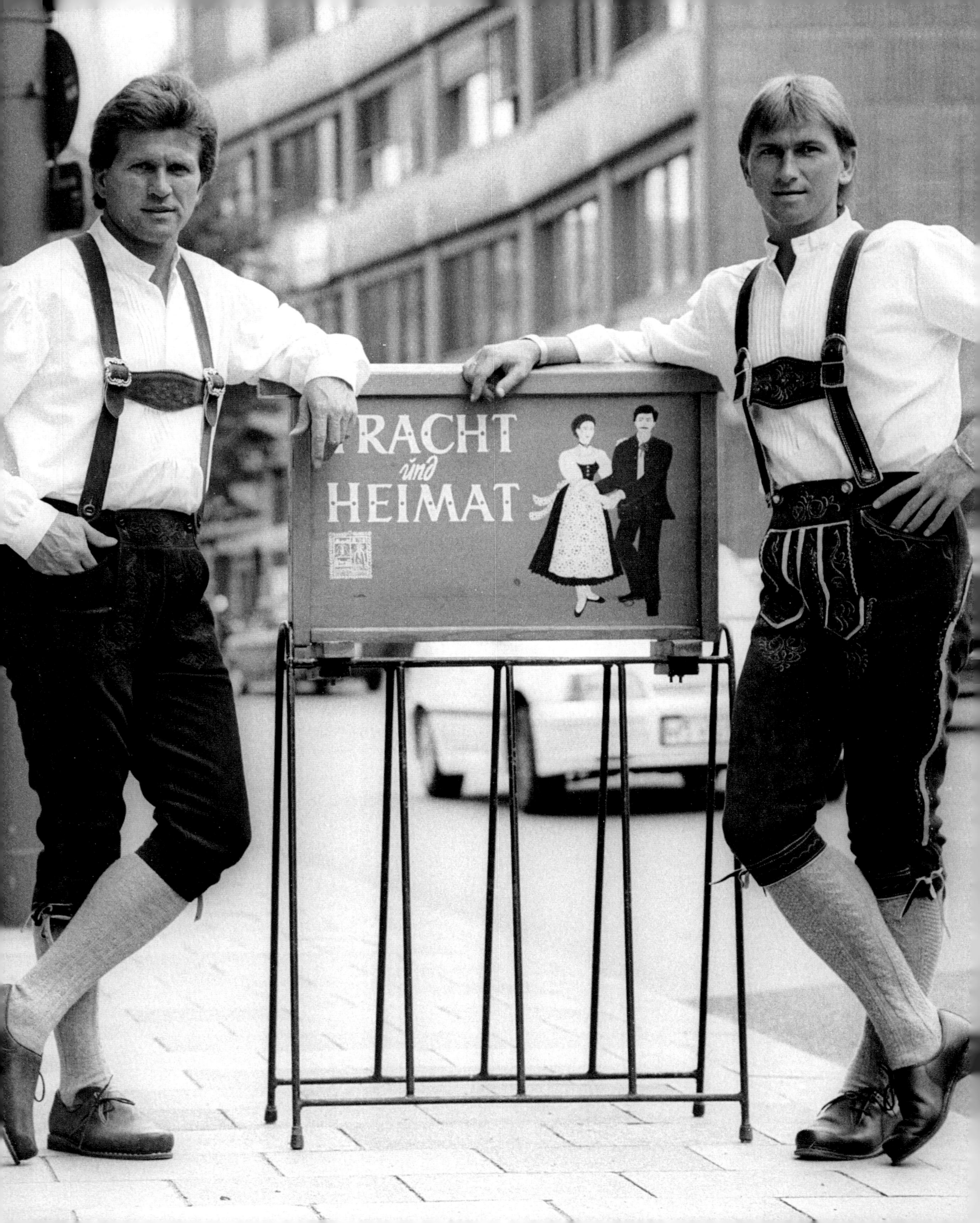
RACHT
und
HEIMAT

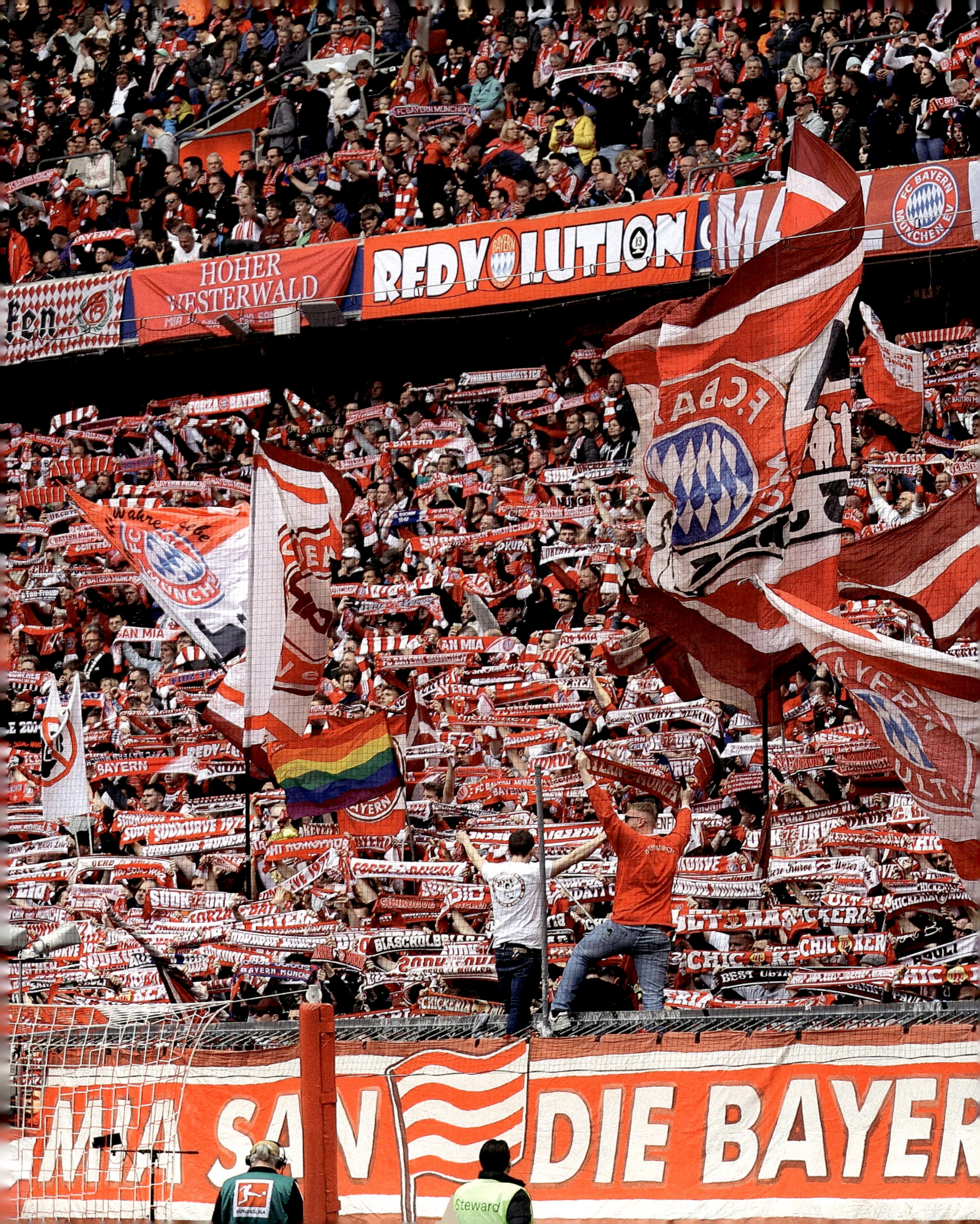
HOHER
WESTERWALD
REDVOLUTION
FC BAYERN MÜNCHEN EV
MIA SAN
DIE BAYER
Steward

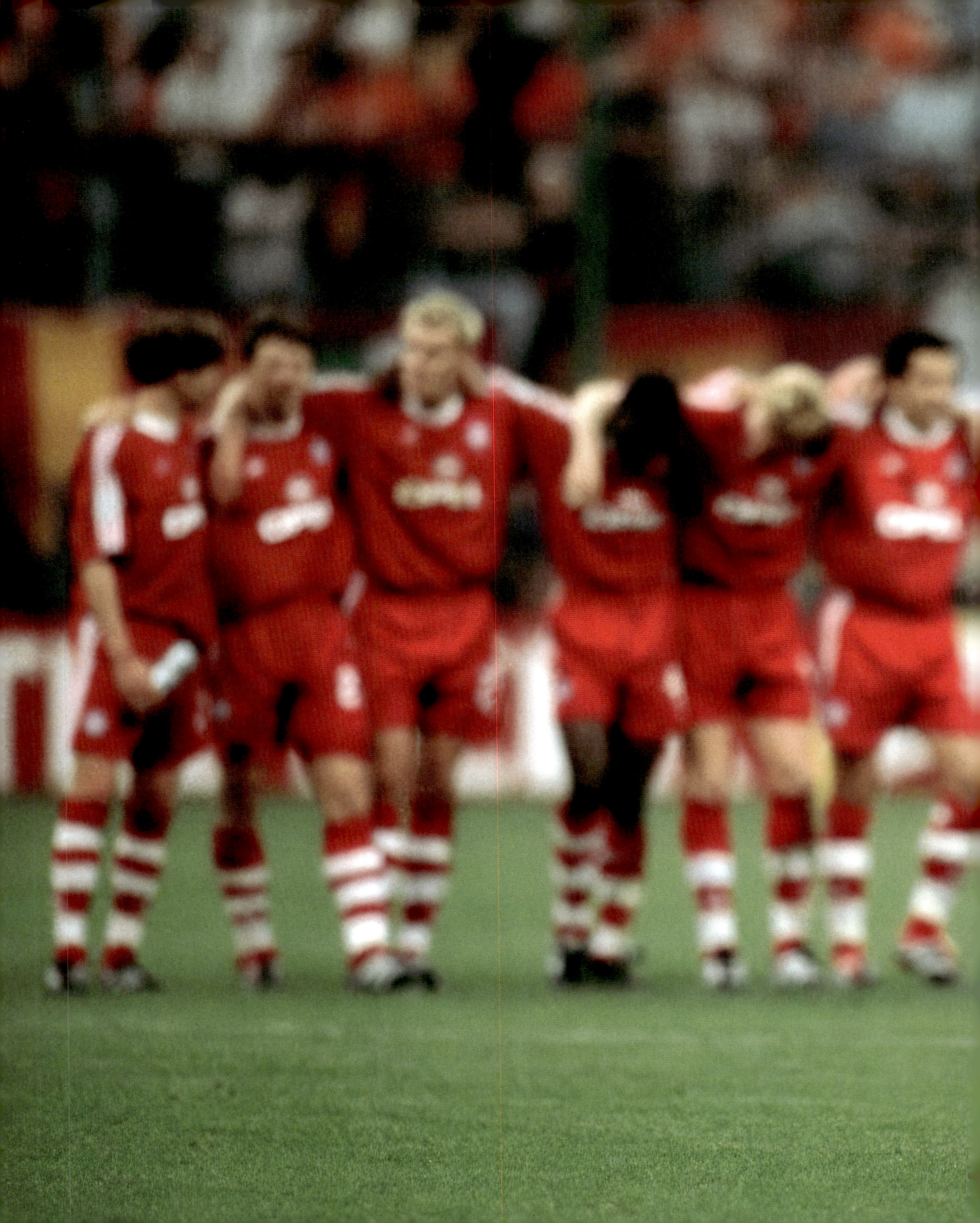

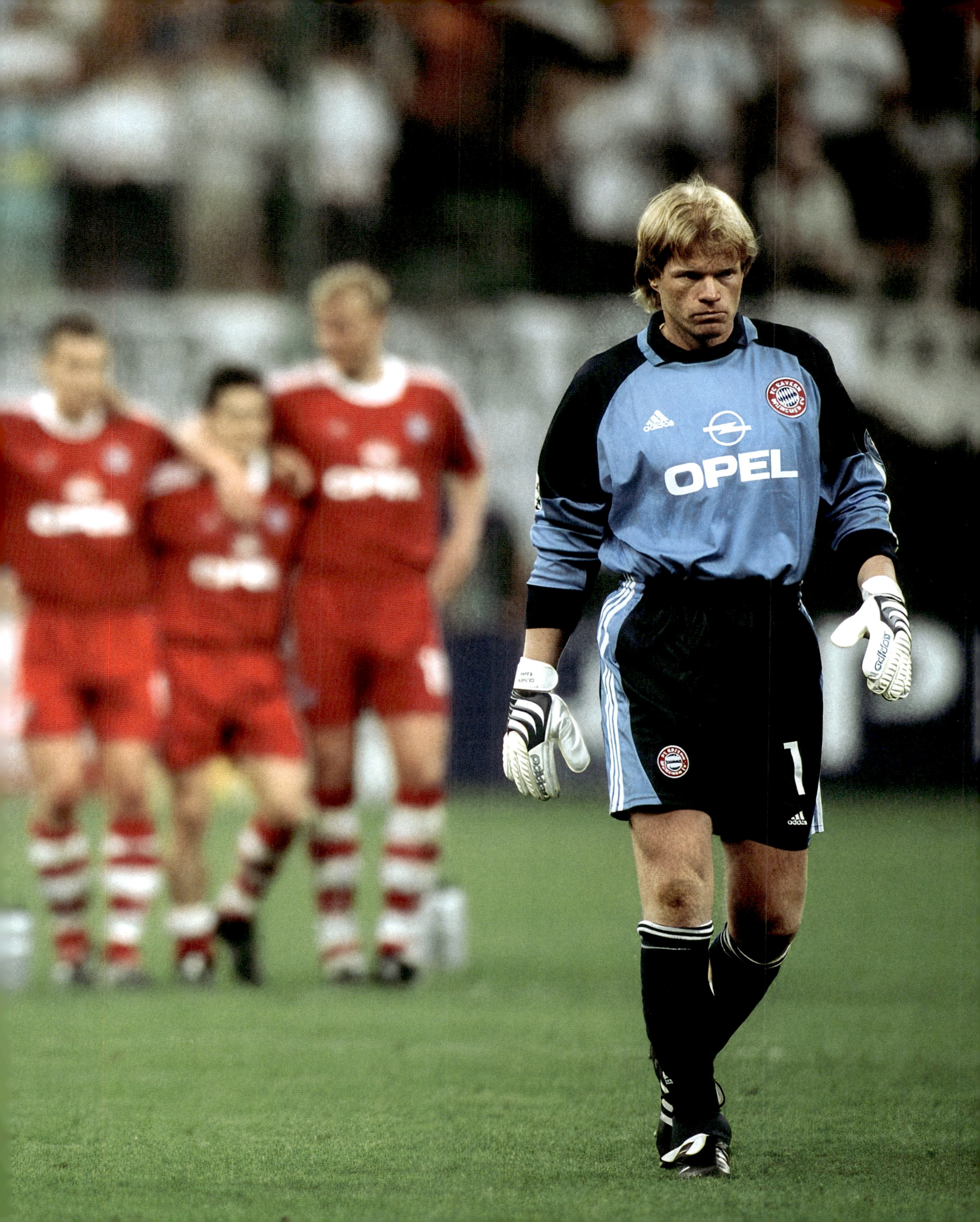
OPEL

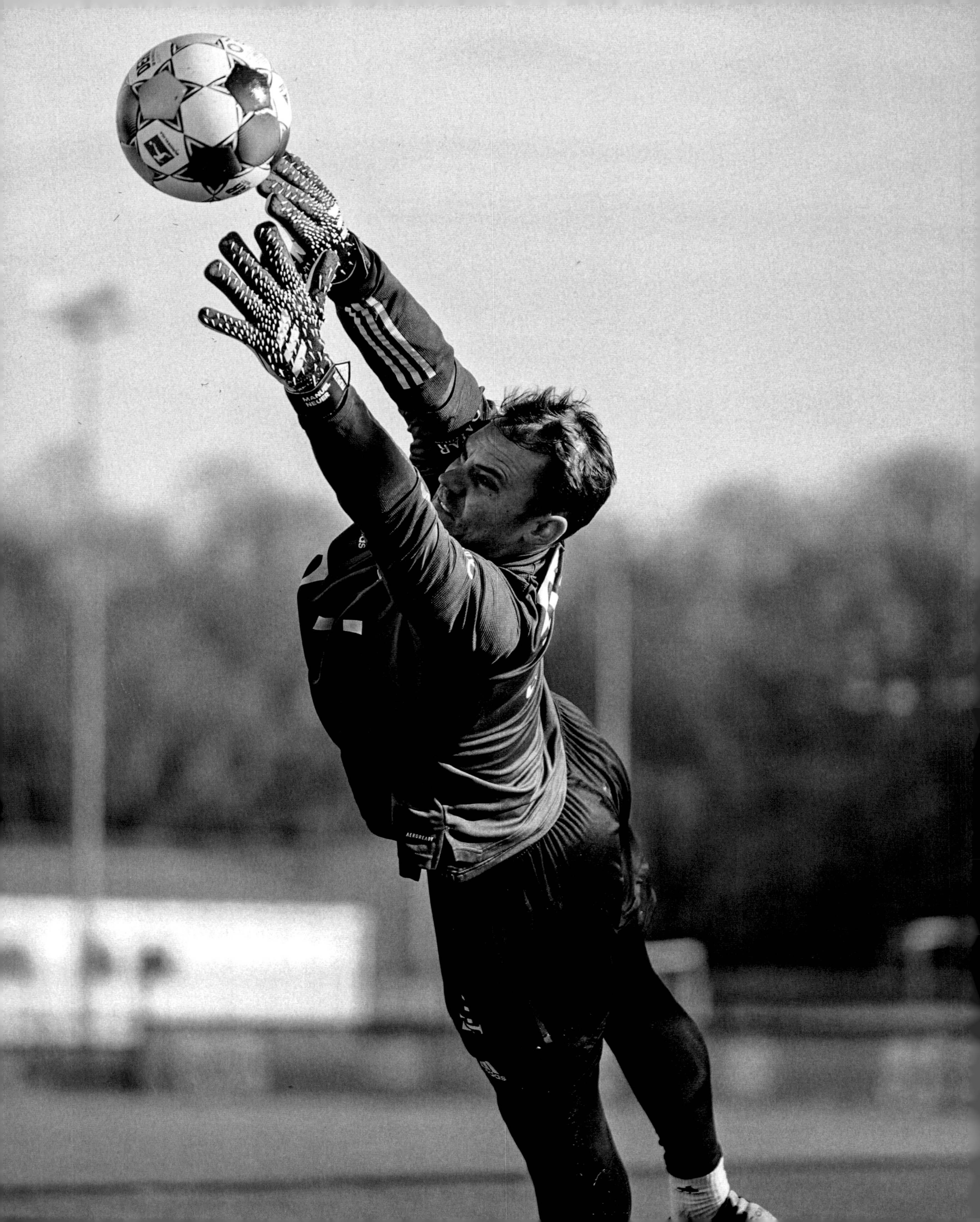

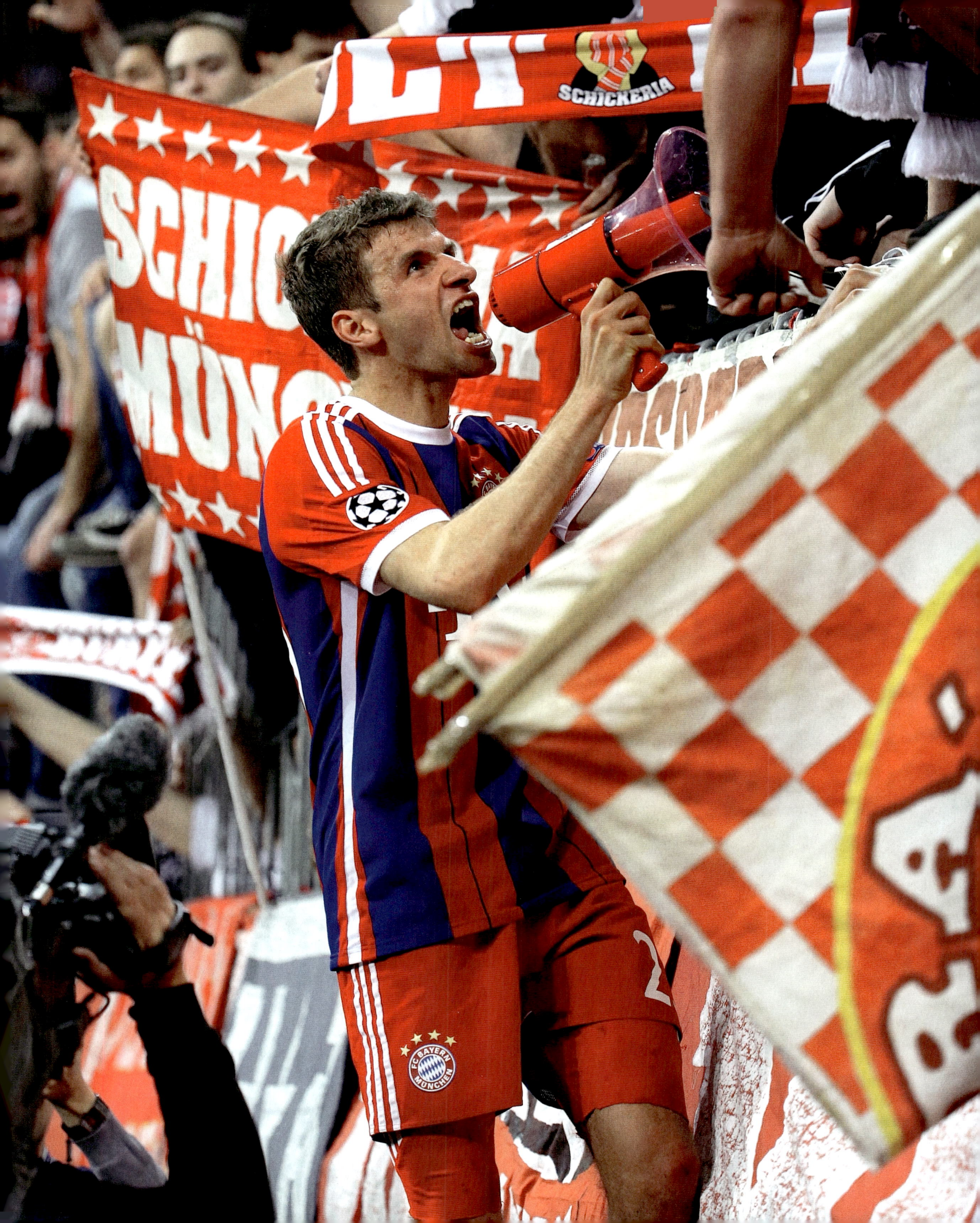
SCHICKERIA

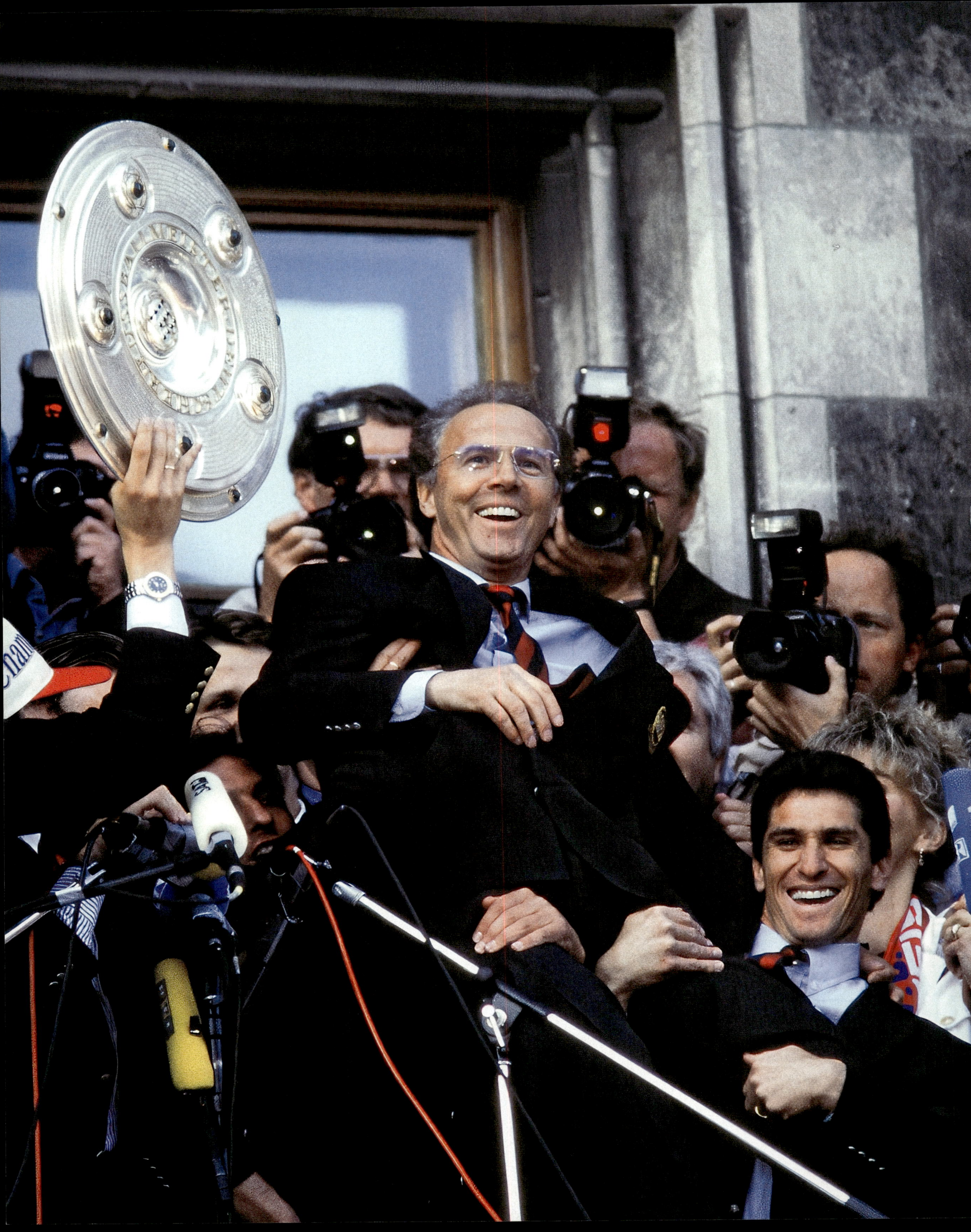

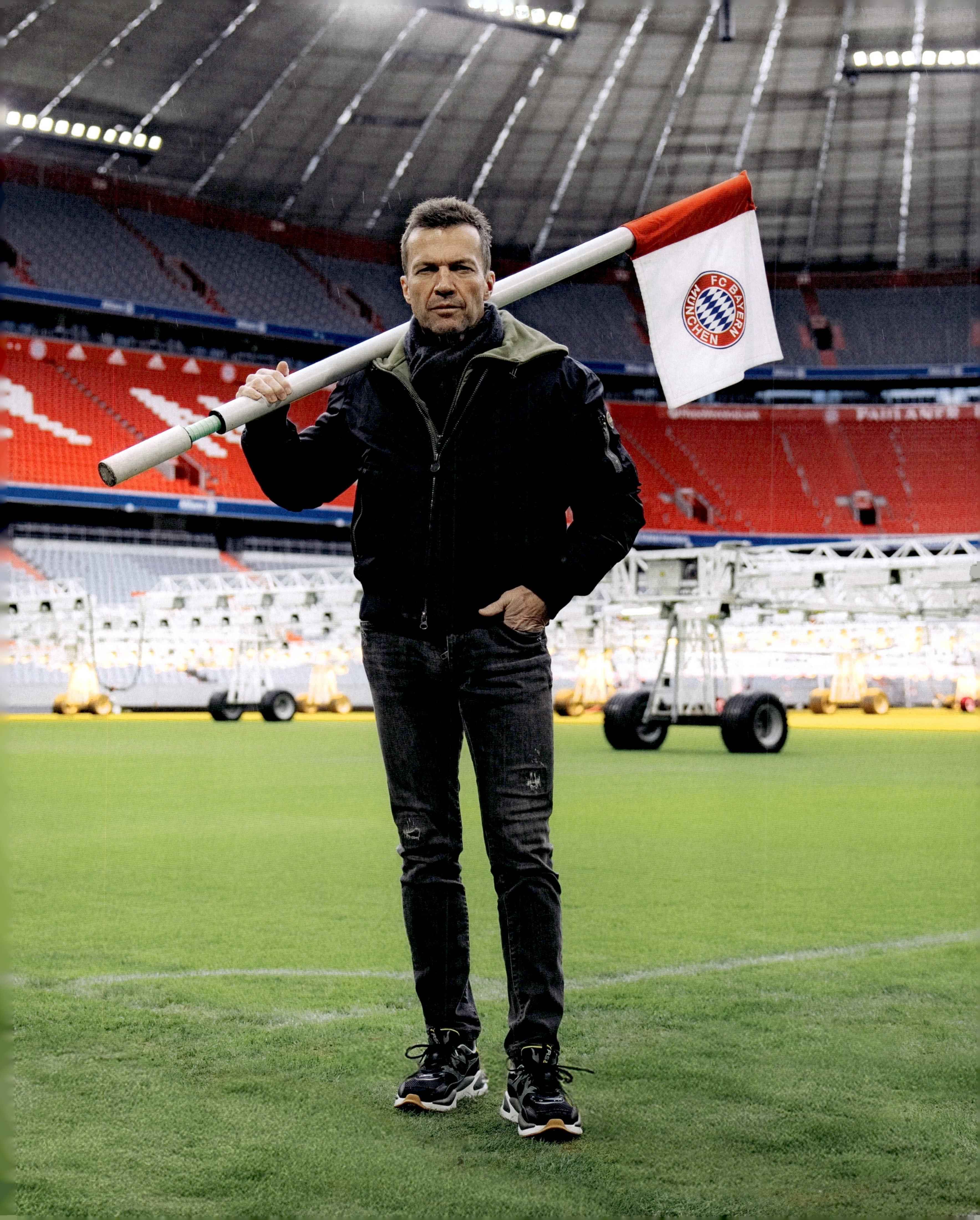
FC BAYERN MÜNCHEN

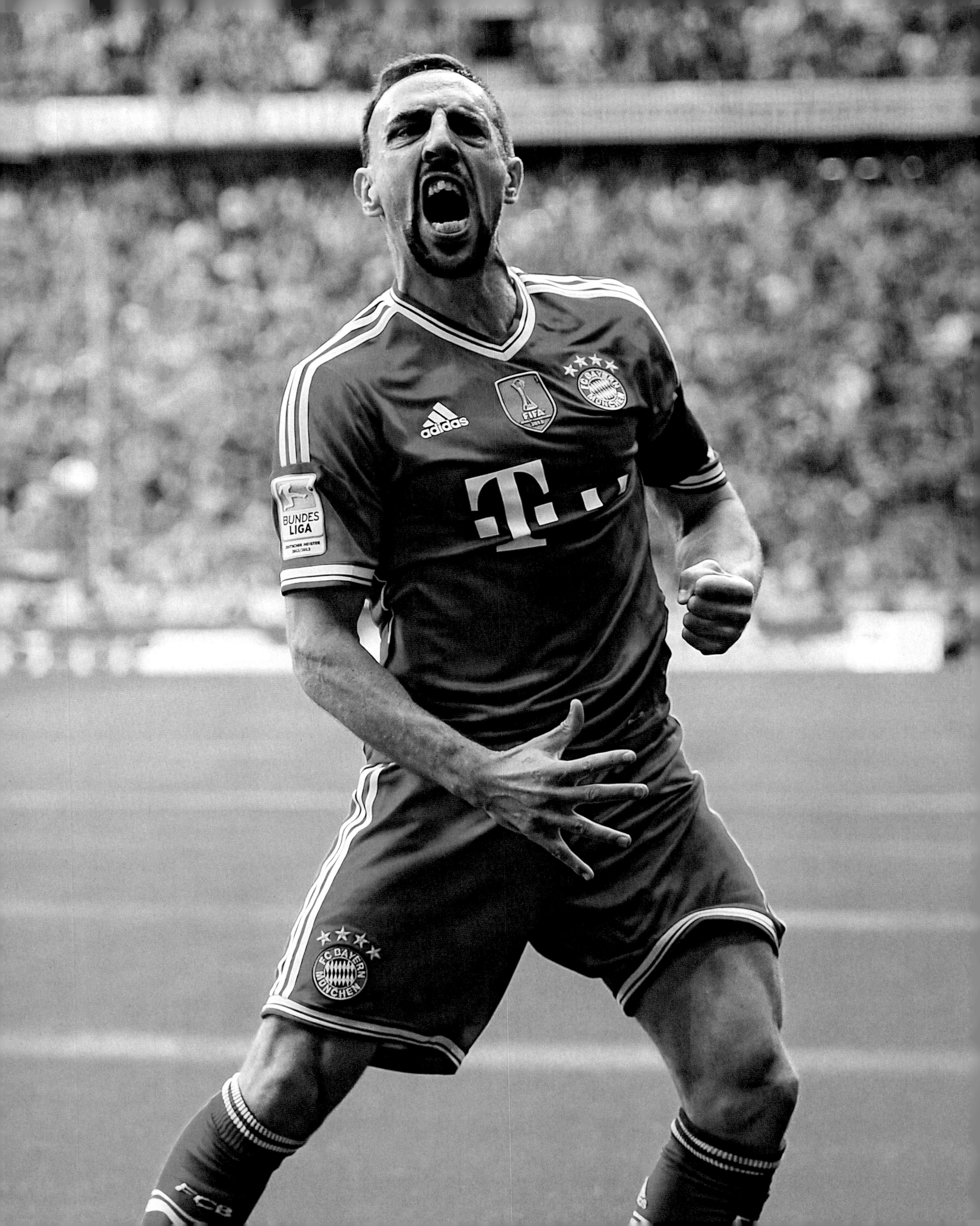
adidas
BUNDES LIGA
FC BAYERN MÜNCHEN

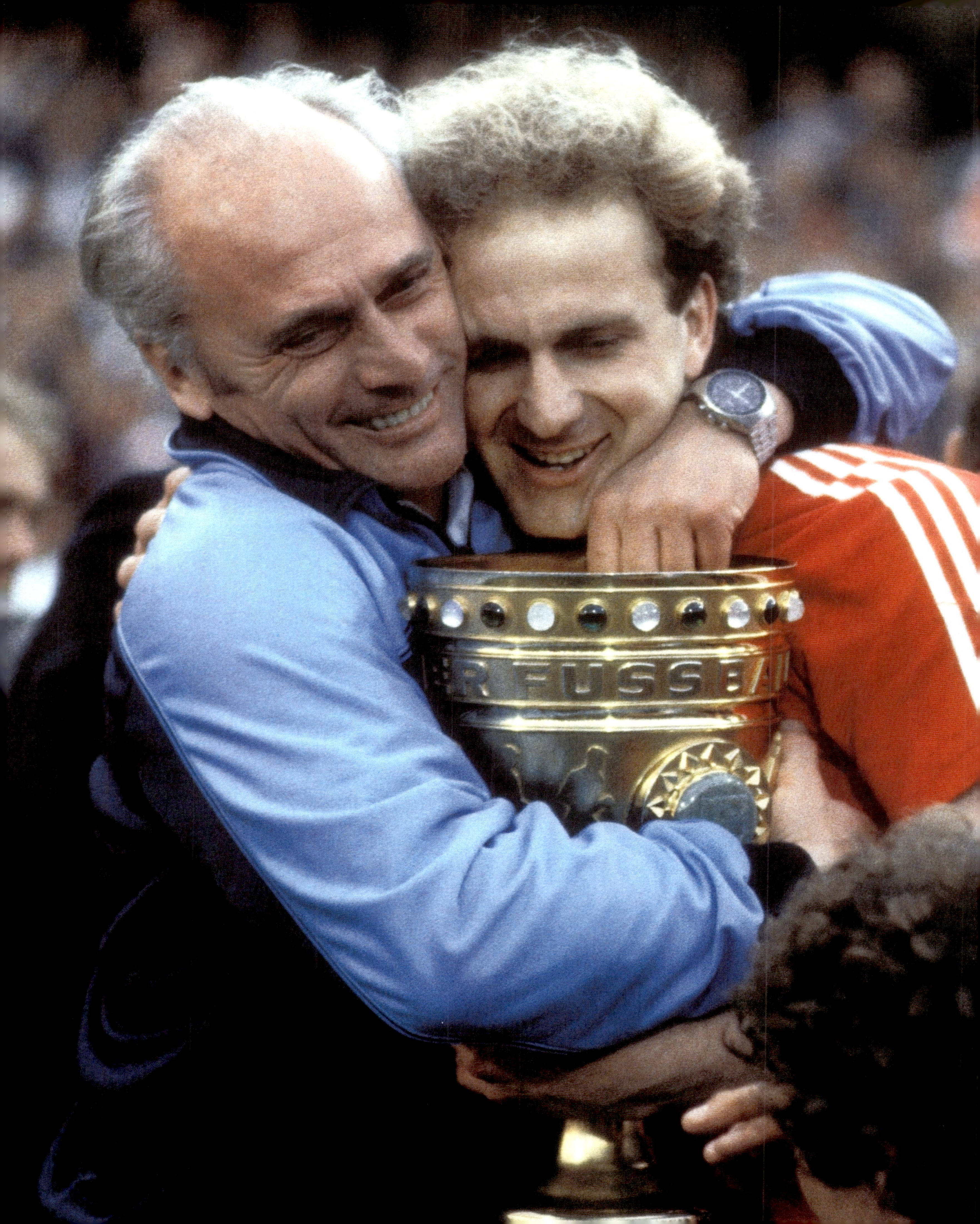

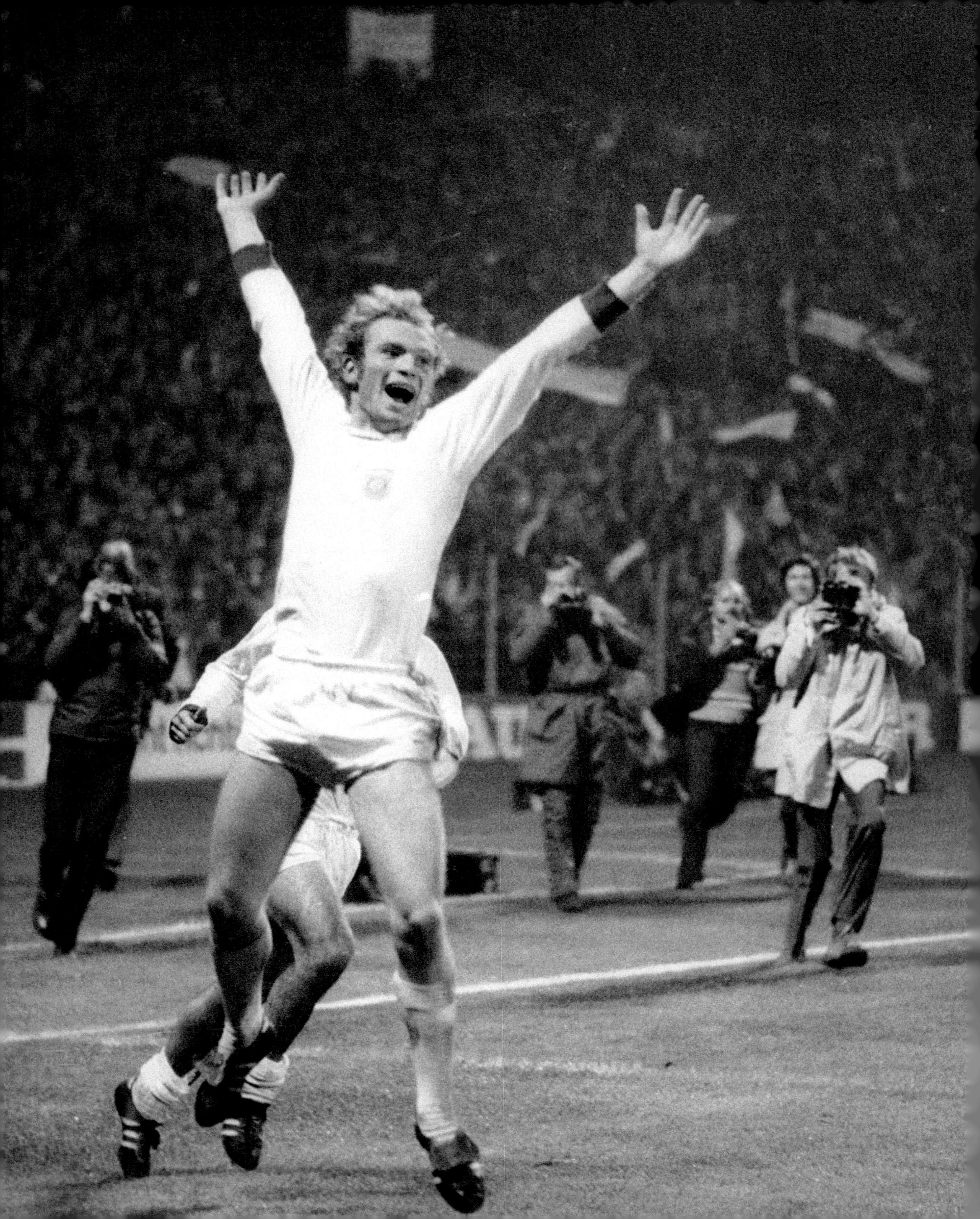

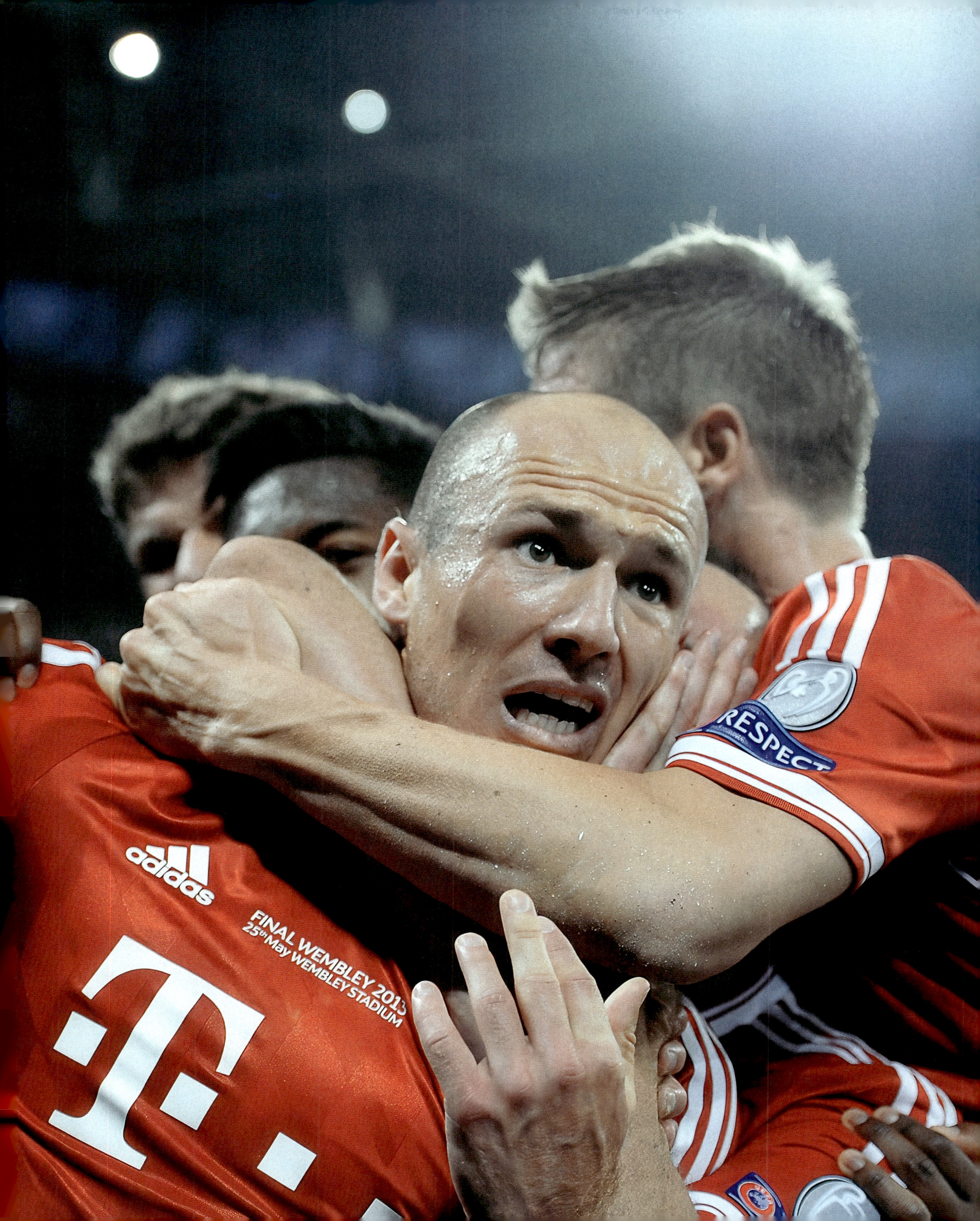
adidas
FINAL WEMBLEY 2013
25th May WEMBLEY STADIUM
T
RESPECT

A club of opposites – the will to win, pain and joy – best wishes, FCB!

MIA SAN MIA

It always starts with the football. The urge to play, the joy that it brings. And so FC Bayern began with eleven young men who liked playing football. Because they were not allowed to do that, they founded their own club. That was 125 years ago, an anniversary when FCB once and for all exceeds the life span even of its longest-lived members. Spanning the time from the imperial Germany of the kaisers to the death of the last German "Kaiser", Franz the First of Giesing in Munich. A spontaneous idea that arose on the last Shrove Tuesday of the nineteenth century has led to something that moves millions of people in the twenty-first century: one of the world's biggest football clubs. The very biggest, going by the number of members. Back then, ten years after FC Bayern was founded, there were some 1,300 football clubs in Germany. Today there are more than 27,000. What was it that turned this particular one among them into an outstanding club? And made the club what it is today? To answer these questions, it is helpful to look back to 1962. In that summer, far away in Chile, the World Cup was played, the last one without live TV broadcasts. From FC Bayern Munich only the defender Willi Giesemann was in the squad, and Germany was knocked out in the quarter-final. The German champion was 1. FC Köln. And FCB? Placed third in the Oberliga Süd, the top south-German league, in the club's best result since the war, FCB just missed the final round of the German championship. But this was a team with a future, with an average age of 23. Money was tight, but the danger of financial ruin had passed. The departing president, Roland Endler, had averted that with subsidies from his own private funds. His successor was Wilhelm Neudecker. And there was something else: the year end was the deadline for applying to join the new Bundesliga. FC Bayern applied, but the Bundesliga started up in August 1963 without FCB, and with its rival club 1860 München.

So why 1962? This is the precise midpoint of Bayern's first 125 years. Summer 1962 was half-time in the jubilee of FC Bayern Munich. Something completely new and epoch-making was emerging then. If we look back from 2025 at the two halves of the story so far, to the first sixty-two and a half years during which FCB steadily grew into a presence on the regional and national stage, winning the championship in 1932, then fighting for survival for a long time in the Nazi period, during the war and in the post-war years and stagnating in sporting terms, and if we then compare that with the second half of the story, when almost everything was a dynamic development of success and growth – then we might almost think that the clubs playing in these two halves were two different clubs.

But it was the same FC Bayern. The club history is reminiscent of the course of one Bundesliga match that will not be forgotten by anyone who watched. On 22 September 2015 in the Allianz Arena, Pep Guardiola's team was 0–1 behind against VfL Wolfsburg at half-time – and then the substitute Robert Lewandowski scored five times inside nine minutes for a 5–1 win. As if this reflected the whole great history of FC Bayern: 0–1 down at the break, but powerfully shooting all the way to the front in a short time, and controlling the

At a club like FC Bayern, success is always about teamwork - on the pitch, in the stands, behind the scenes. Without cooperation, no big win and no big tifo display by the fans is possible.

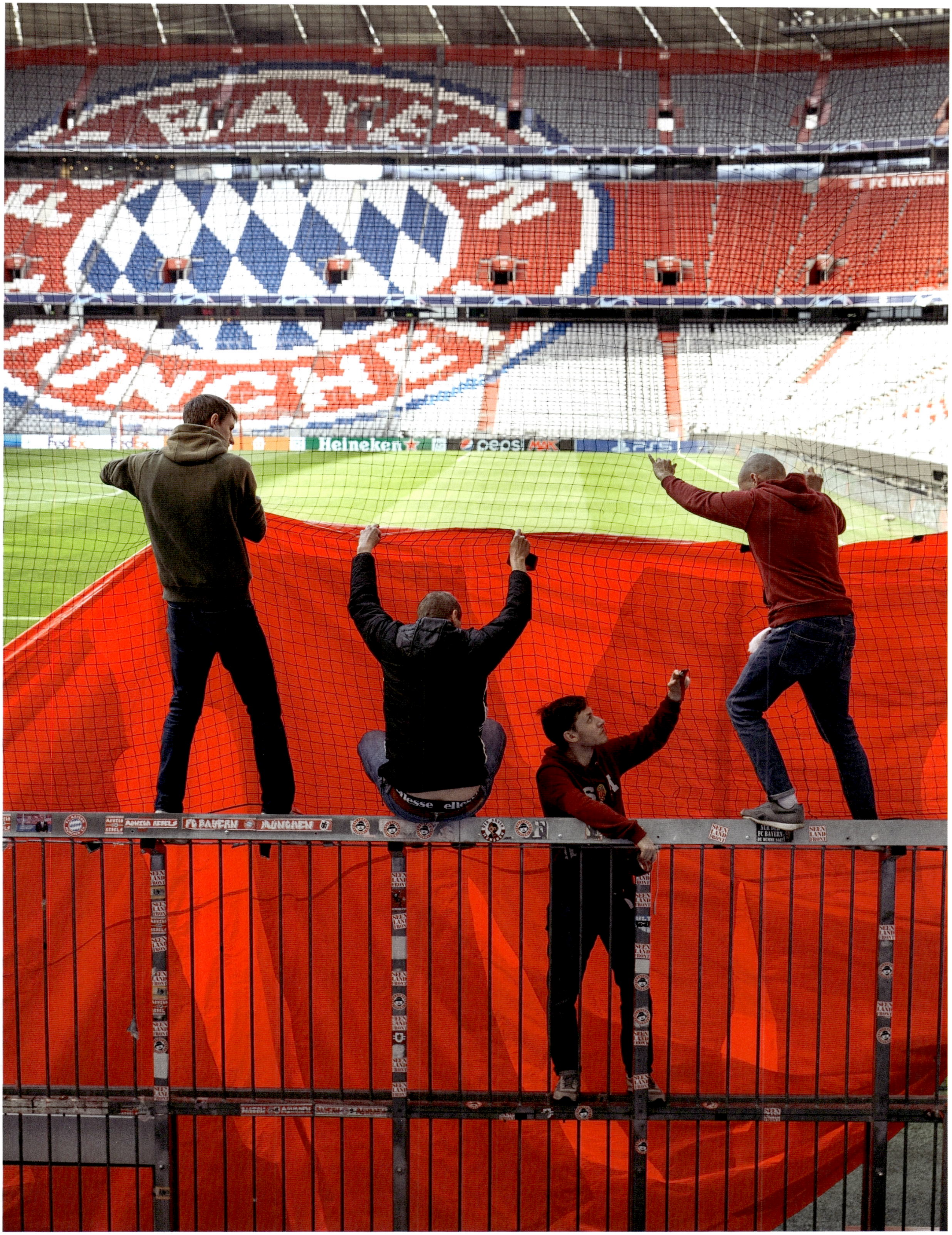
FC BAYERN
Heineken
FC BAYERN MÜNCHEN
ellesse

game from that point onwards. It seems that, as if by magic, everything came together at the right moment on Säbener Strasse to kick off something really big. Something almost like a refounding, but this time, fittingly in the new age of space travel, a rocket take-off. In the two years after 1962 – at the start of the second half, that is – the following things happened. Firstly, Čik Čajkovski became coach. Secondly, Robert Schwan became manager. Thirdly, Sepp Maier, at the age of 19, became the number-one goalkeeper. Fourthly, it was quickly clear that 18-year-old Franz Beckenbauer had what it takes to become a world-class star. And fifthly, Gerd Müller, also aged 18, started a part-time job as a packer in a furniture Munich store, arranged by FCB. And another job as a goalscorer, though only after sitting on the bench for eleven matches until Čajkovski, under pressure from the club president, finally put him in the line-up. An 11–2 win in Freiburg followed straight away. "Little Gerd hit his first goal", as captain Werner Olk recalls, "and after that never stopped again."

All of this resulted in the rise of FC Bayern. Not only into the Bundesliga, in 1965 at the second attempt, but quickly to the top level of German and even European football, and this at record speed. In contrast to the sixteen founding members of the Bundesliga, of whom only four are still playing in the top flight in FCB's jubilee season of 2024–25, FC Bayern has never been relegated from the Bundesliga.

At some stage in these years of success, the phrase "Bayern-Dusel" – Bayern luck – was coined. This usually means being awarded a penalty or scoring a dodgy goal at the right moment. However, first of all, in his twenty-five years coaching young players, Hermann Gerland instilled into Thomas Müller, Philipp Lahm and Bastian Schweinsteiger the tenet "Always lucky – that's skill." And secondly, true luck in football is often found in places where nobody notices it. For example in the legendary story, now known to every schoolchild today, of how 12-year-old Beckenbauer was hit by a player from 1860 München called König (King), and then decided that he would prefer to be Kaiser for FC Bayern.

On 27 February 1900 eleven footballers gathered in Café Gisela to found a new football club. They trained at the Schyrenplatz in the district of Untergiesing, and the first club president was Franz John from Berlin. He guided the club with success: only a few months after it was established, Bayern was number one in Munich.

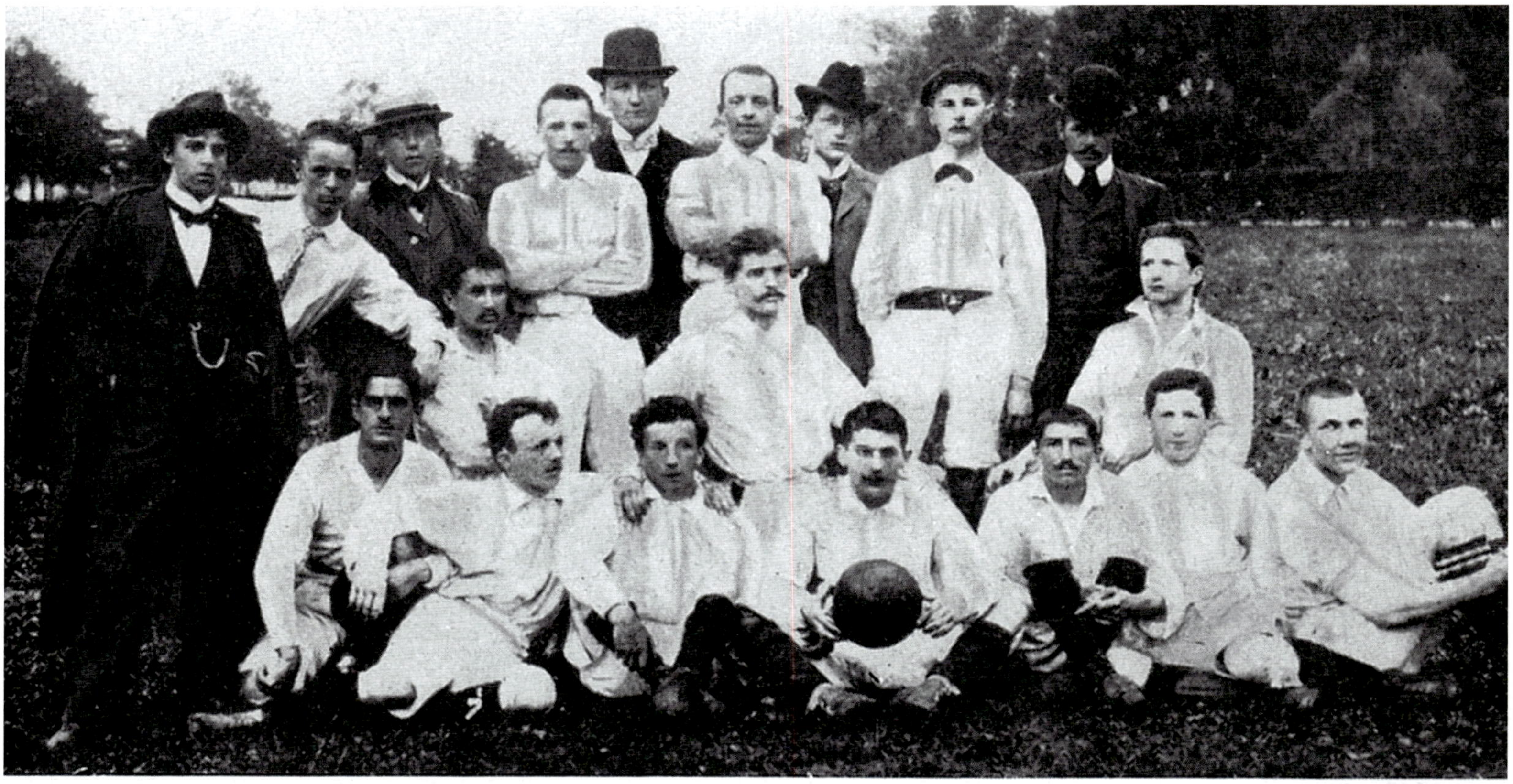

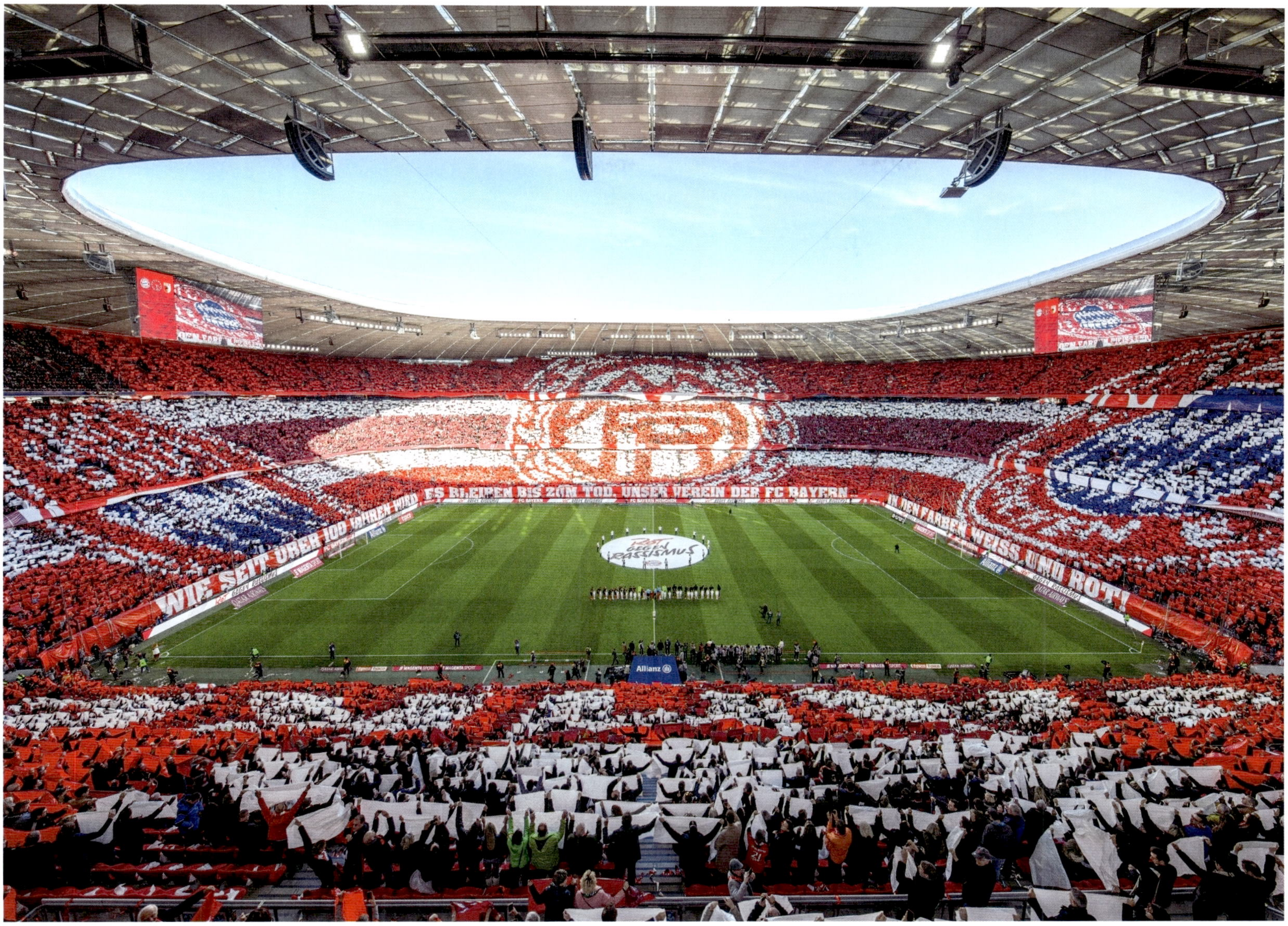

In this photo, showing the panoramic tifo display for the 120th birthday of the club and capturing three of the four stands with an extreme wide-angle lens, the pitch of the Allianz Arena almost looks like a square. In this view from the main stand (where, scarcely visible here, the message "120 years" is displayed), we see the club shield from 1924, made up of thousands of small sheets, at the opposite end, the shield from 1919 on the north side (left); and the present-day logo in the Südkurve, the south end.

An equally momentous event was a goal scored by Pak Doo-ik, a dentist from Pyongyang. This led to a hail of tomatoes, thrown when Italy, the favourites at the 1966 World Cup, had to return home early after an embarrassing defeat by North Korea – and also led to a ban on foreign players in Serie A, preventing Beckenbauer's move, already agreed before the World Cup finals, to Inter Milan for a fairy-tale salary of DM 900,000 per year. So the young Kaiser stayed at home and became "the greatest personality that FC Bayern ever had", as Uli Hoeness said after Beckenbauer's death in 2024. "As a player, coach, president, human being: unforgettable. No one will ever match him."

One of Beckenbauer's great achievements was to guide Udo Lattek to Bayern in 1970 as the new coach – and Lattek in turn persuaded two lads from the German youth team that he managed to sign contracts at FC Bayern: Uli Hoeness and Paul Breitner. Their arrival was the opening of a new, highly professional and self-confident generation for FCB. It was the last piece in the puzzle, making it possible to create the new, great FC Bayern. Hoeness, the lightning-fast striker, became a 27-year-old manager with big ideas following a fine, much-too-short playing career. And Breitner became the footballing leader of the new start in the late 1970s, when Beckenbauer and Müller had left for America.

The rest is history. "I have always led the club as if it were my own family," says Hoeness, looking back on more than fifty years as a player, manager, president, board member and honorary president – and in many more roles, especially as a man who understands players. Countless times he has helped them out of trouble, patted them on the shoulder or kicked them in the behind, listened and found solutions. Without this, the club would not be what it is today.

As a child of the post-war years, from everyday family life in his parents' butcher's shop in Ulm, Hoeness also knew that the German "economic miracle" was in truth no miracle but the result of hard work and thrift – and with these virtues of his youth, accompanied by his old teammates Franz Beckenbauer and Karl-Heinz Rummenigge, from

1991 onwards he created his own economic miracle: a great football club that functioned and prospered entirely from its own means. A club whose growth was entirely organic. Rummenigge, a global star when playing for FC Bayern, quickly took on the role of an indispensable networker. His international contacts gave the club an established place in the international elite – off the football pitch, too. With Rummenigge as chairman of the board, FC Bayern was always in the driving seat when decisive crossroads in world football were reached. FCB now definitively became a global player.

To keep the family atmosphere of a club that had a staff of twenty persons in 1979, excluding the footballers, and has more than one thousand today, is one of the many big opposing elements that FC Bayern had to resolve within itself in the decades of success. Another, more decisive opposite was the transformation of the club – an association of members and thus a social entity – into a flourishing business enterprise, while at the same time retaining an element of local feeling. This is the greatest challenge arising from success that is faced by the city of Munich, as well as the Free State of Bavaria as a whole, and FC Bayern too – and the club overcomes it, one generation after another.

The very first generation at FCB displayed a creative approach to setbacks. Between 1902 and 1904 the young club three times won the city championship in Munich, its first, though still unofficial, titles, but then was defeated by MTV 1879. When the team was unsuccessful again the following year, the members gathered in mourning clothes for a ceremonial "burial" of its championship dreams, with the player Hanne Beyssel lying on a bier to represent the deceased. Then they moved on to the Pschorr-Bräu beer hall for a merry wake.

Humour is when you celebrate in spite of everything – a motto that revived several players almost one hundred years later in the night after the unfathomable 1–2 defeat

Heads together in a circle, shoulder to shoulder, showing their togetherness, the team are amongst themselves in the midst of tens of thousands of people, using this ritual to get into the right competitive spirit one last time before the kick-off.

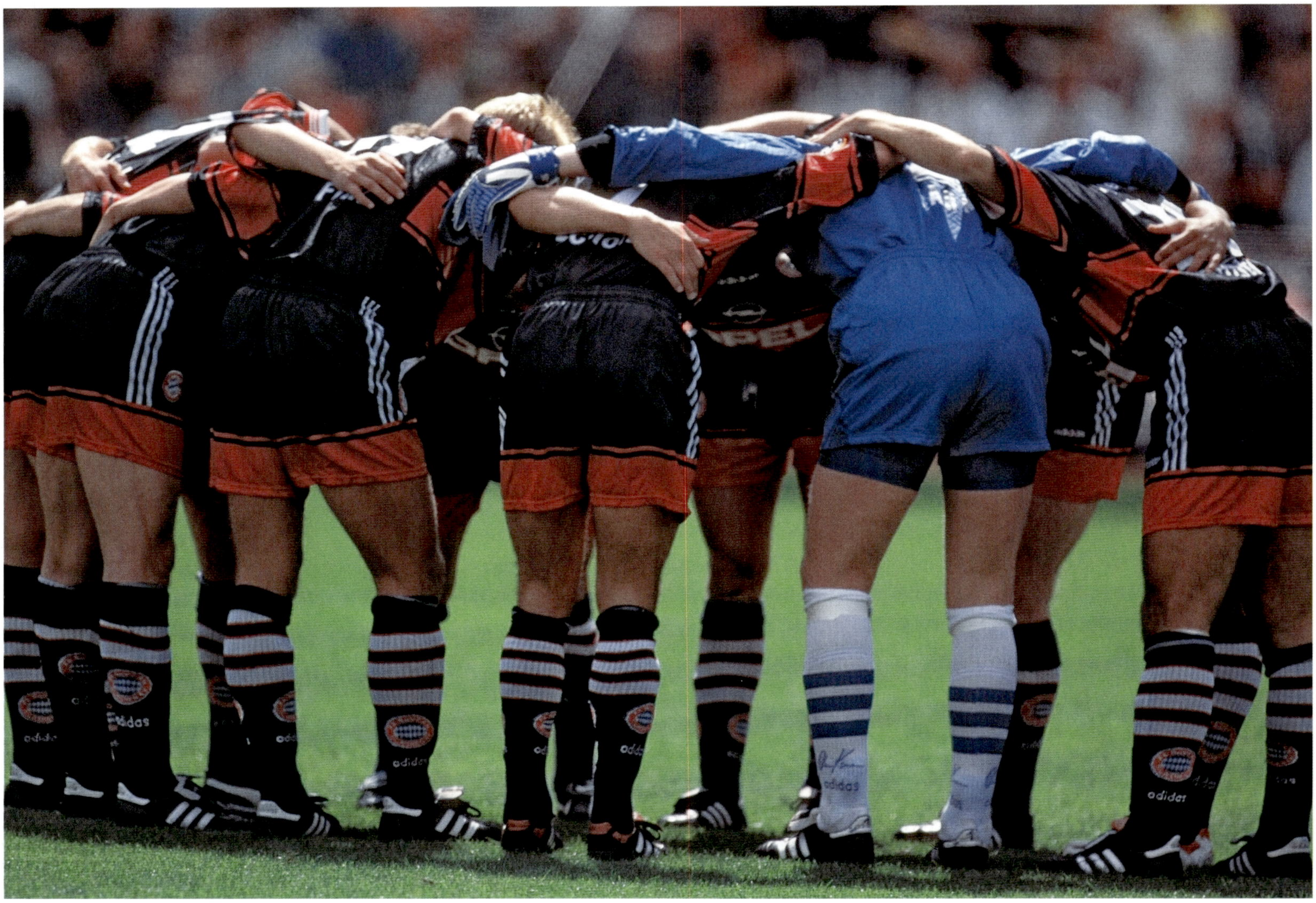

After the match - at least when it was such a dramatic defeat as in the final of the Champions League against Chelsea in 2012 - at first every player is alone in his disappointment. But captain Philipp Lahm is already going from one to another to console them. And the following night, Thomas Müller will post prophetic words in the team chat: "Next year we'll hit back."

to Manchester United in the Champions League final in Barcelona. This was the start of the defiant reaction that led to a victory party in Milan within two years. In 2012–13 Bayern's pattern of defiance – defeat, reaction, triumph – worked once again, but this time it was defeat, reaction, treble. Another tradition at FC Bayern is its entertainment value off the pitch. While still a player, Franz Beckenbauer became one of the most glittering personalities in world football, the first superstar of German football and an icon of the advertising business, who made it acceptable for higher social circles to be seen in a football stadium. As president, he led the club with charming utterances and powerful outbursts of rage, and in the dual roles of president and coach set a seal on the championship celebrations in 1994 by kicking a ball poised atop a wheat-beer glass into a hole in the "goal wall" at the ZDF TV studio. Uli Hoeness, too, often put on a spectacle and battled without restraint for his club in disputes with rivals like Christoph Daum or Willi Lemke.

In this way FC Bayern and its glittering personalities became something more than a football club: an event in society. With a high level of public awareness and constant potential for emotional agitation. A club that almost everyone knows. That is cheered or abused, that people love, or love to see losing. Here something permanent is set against the randomness of the modern entertainment industry: an eternal stimulus, a daily theme that connects people. If you have already exhausted the weather as a topic, the second-best conversational gambit is "So what's going on at Bayern?"

The result of all this is the FC Bayern of the jubilee year 2025, a club that can afford the sporting successes that it achieves. In contrast to some European rivals. And in contrast to the FC Bayern of 1965. In the late 1960s, for example, after promotion to the Bundesliga, when they caused a furore like no other club, winning the German DFB Cup three times, the European Cup Winners' Cup and the

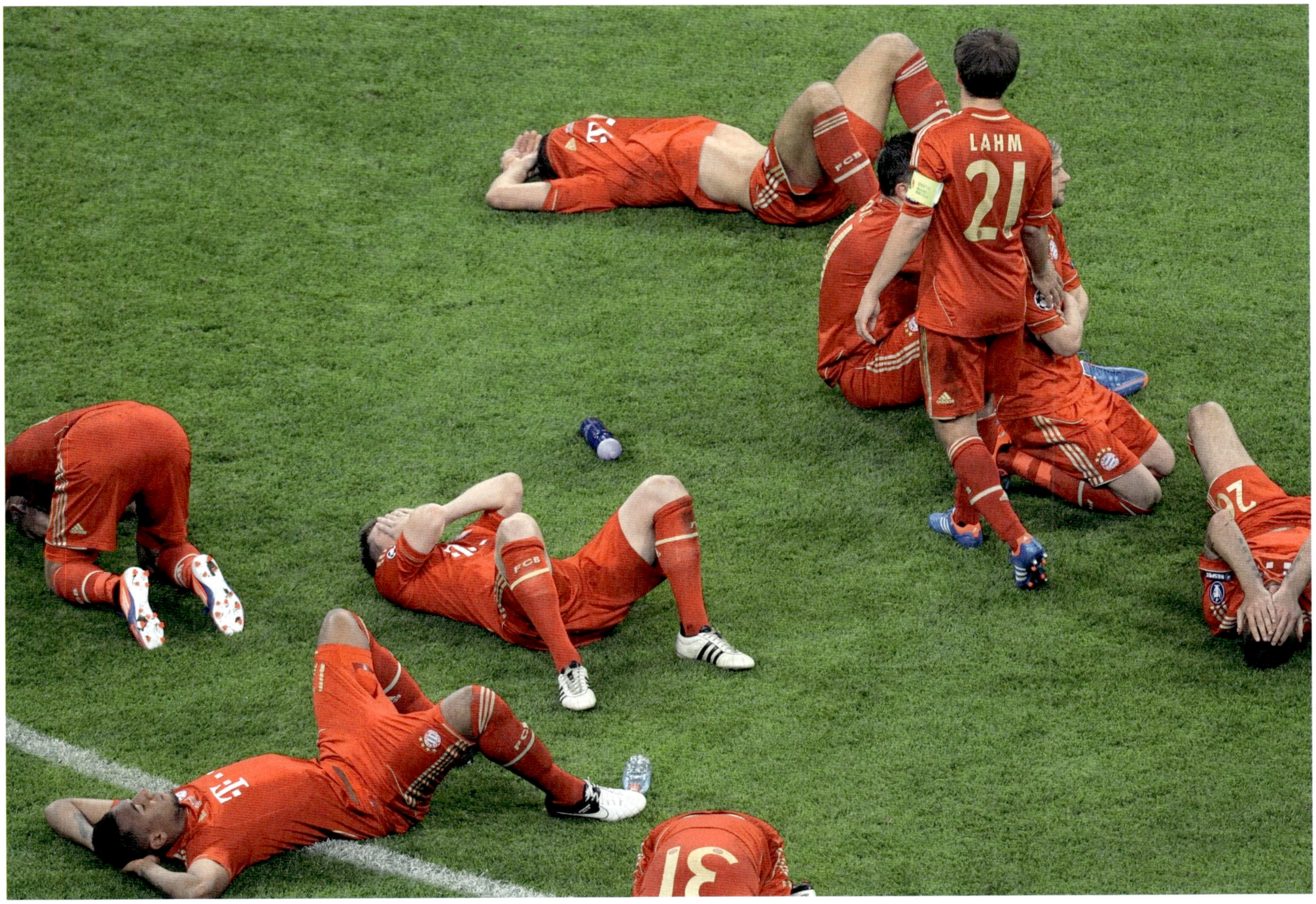

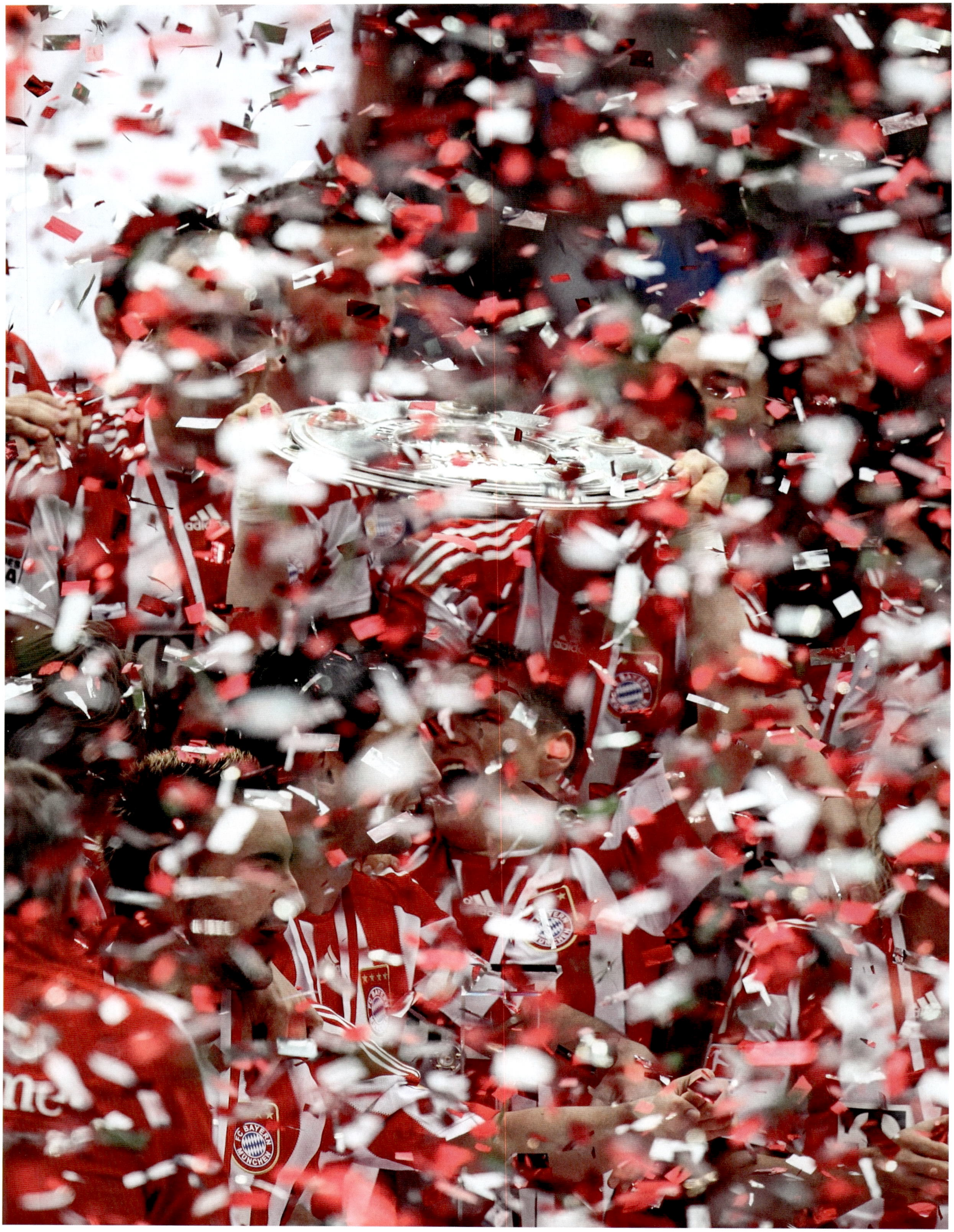
FC BAYERN MÜNCHEN

Nothing can part good friends... not even an ill-fitting wig. Karl-Heinz Rummenigge, Uli Hoeness and Franz Beckenbauer, a winning trio for FCB on the field and later in club management, indulged in a joke in 2001 and put on kits for a photo on their tenth anniversary of working together as club officials – in a retro look to match the occasion.

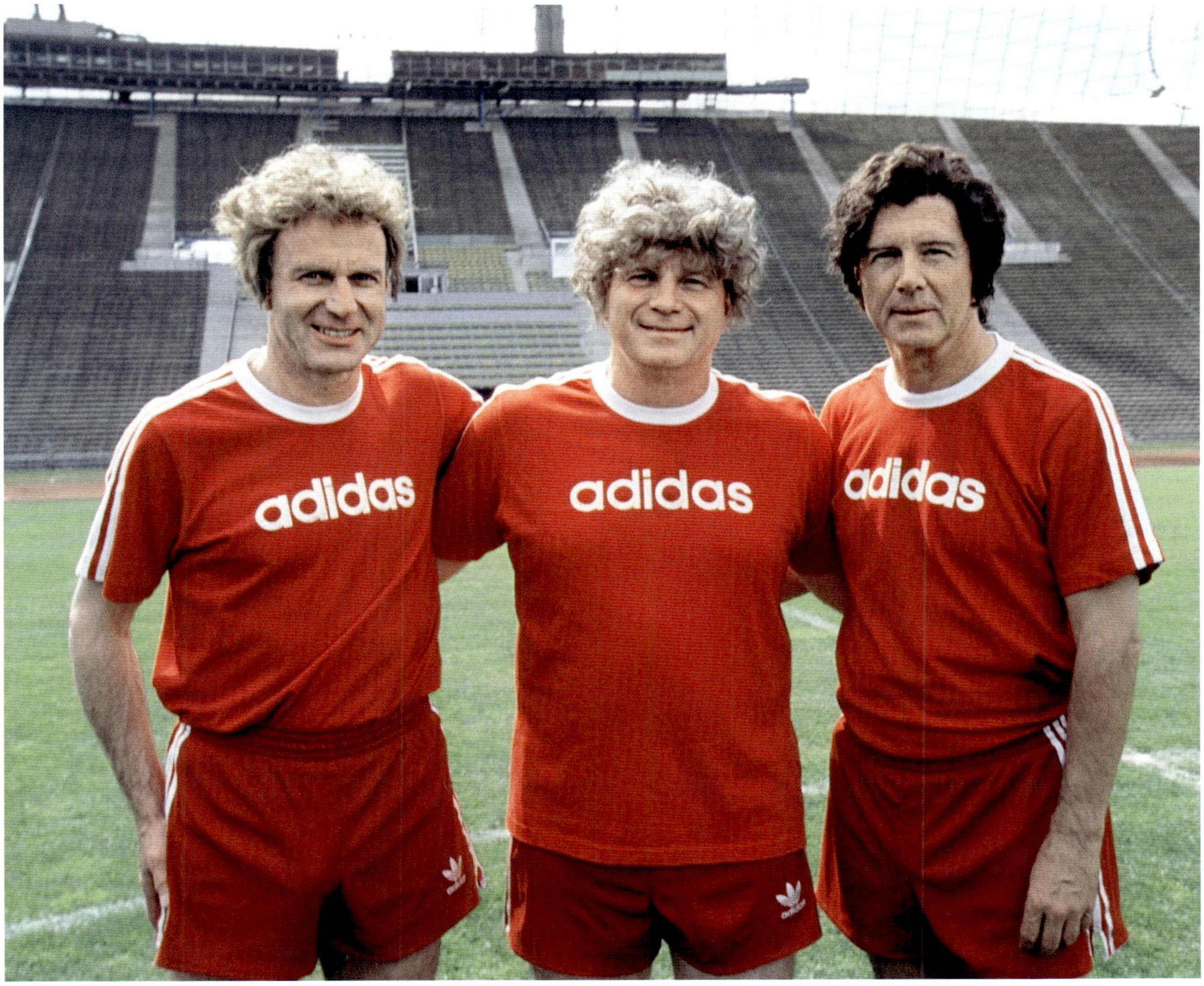

German championship, all within four years, the point was reached when Bayern's success was said to be making the club poor. The fans were euphoric, the officials in a state of alarm. Trophies filled the display cases and emptied the bank accounts as a result of high bonuses. For this reason, the Bayern team around Beckenbauer and Müller had to play private matches for many years against lower-calibre provincial opposition, and by the mid- 1970s this was increasingly wearing the players down.

When Uli Hoeness later took over as manager, he found new and different ways of acquiring capital. Thanks to stable sources of income from sponsors, TV rights and merchandising, the club could allow its players more time to regenerate. The tours for private matches were then replaced by the much more lucrative Audi Summer Tour to Asia or America, for the sake of better global marketing. The contradiction between business and sporting aims constantly has to be rebalanced. For every great football club that is not controlled by an investor, the decisive success is not found on the bottom line of the balance sheet but in the trophy cabinet. Financial success is important but not an end in itself; rather it is a means to sporting success.

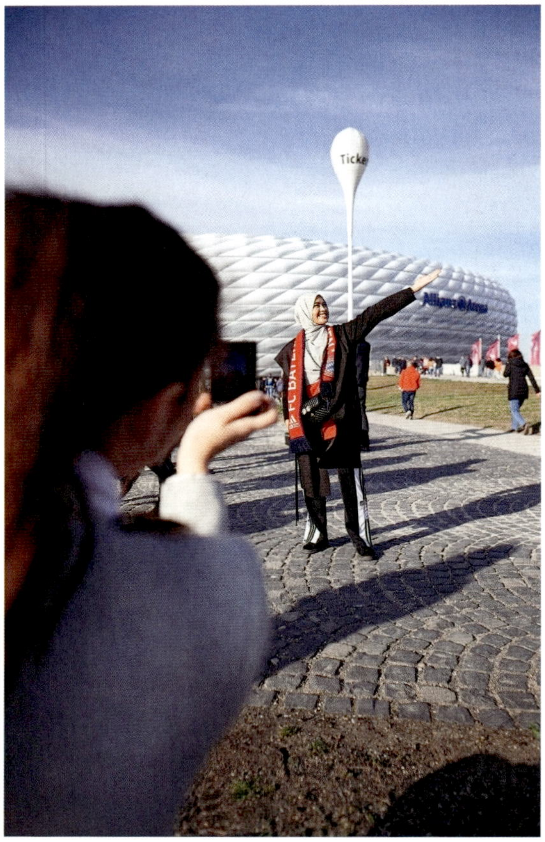

The Allianz Arena has long been more than just a football stadium: it is one of Munich's biggest tourist attractions, like Marienplatz, where FC Bayern's triumphs are celebrated, and where decking out the city hall in red and white on these days has almost become routine.

So many complex opposites – and the trick always consists in not only living with them, but in exploiting them, and even in generating energy from them. The opposition between fan culture and business, for example. Between toughness and tenderness, the global market and local roots, between being cosmopolitan and down-to-earth. Between living the present-day experience and illuminating a history, whose darker aspects during the Third Reich were openly examined by the Institut für Zeitgeschichte (Institute for Contemporary History) in an independent study that was commissioned by FC Bayern and brought to the attention of a wider public by FCB, its fans and its museum.

But there are also opposites in the approach of FC Bayern to its rivals: on the one hand, the club is an opponent, extremely hard to defeat and the yardstick for achievement at the highest level; and on the other, it is a source of solidarity and assistance in times of need, contributing to economic recovery with benefit matches or, for example, lending millions to Borussia Dortmund in 2005. Even people for whom the Reds from Munich are like a red rag to a bull can perceive these contradictions, which do not always fit in with the simple image of FC Bayern as the enemy, the rich club that crushes everything in its path. In his song "Bayern", the musician Campino, a fan of Liverpool FC, sang with his band Die Toten Hosen: "I'd never go to FC Bayern", but later admitted that "With Bayern Munich you can only be a proper enemy if you stay biased. As soon as you stick to the facts, things become difficult."

And then, to conclude the subject of big opposites with the most decisive one of all, the one within the team, its blend, its "chemistry", there is the example of Franck Ribéry and Arjen Robben. Such fantastic players. And such completely different characters. Which club would not have been pulled apart by having two personalities like those in the team – with only one ball to share between them? But it worked. The right treatment was given to Robben's sensitive musculature by Dr Hans-Wilhelm Müller-Wohlfahrt, and to Ribéry's temperament by club president Uli Hoeness on the Tegernsee lake. Until the contrast led to an explosion, in the dressing room of the Allianz Arena, during the half-time break in the first leg of the Champions League semi-final against Real Madrid in 2012. After which Robben's swollen eye needed some cooling ice from the physiotherapist's bag. After which Uli Hoeness and Karl-Heinz Rummenigge had to work hard to cool things down. And to talk Robben out of his intention never to play with Ribéry again. In the following year, at the latest, in their duet for the winning goal at Wembley, the cool-headed Dutchman and the hot-headed Frenchman had become a duo for eternity, for the great portrait gallery of FC Bayern. Why? Because they both became true Bayern players. That means: winners, who find in their mentality the rapport that welds everything together, regardless of whether they already had it or they evolved it in this mentality-driven club. This rapport means success, shared success. After their fight in the dressing room, says Ribéry, they "became true brothers".

There it is again: opposites that attract each other, that do not become a contradiction but lead to energy, strength, success. To "Mia san mia", "We are who we are", the words that bridge all opposites. And thus to FC Bayern. To the greatest and one of the most successful football clubs in the world – and at the same time something that transcends football. In its 125 years, Germany changed from an empire to a republic, from a republic to a dictatorship, from a dictatorship to a country that was destroyed, then rebuilt, then reunified, and to a democracy that has been stable but not free from threats for more than seventy-five years. And from FC Bayern Munich, the glorious idea of eleven young men in the carnival season, arose a Bavarian and also a German institution.

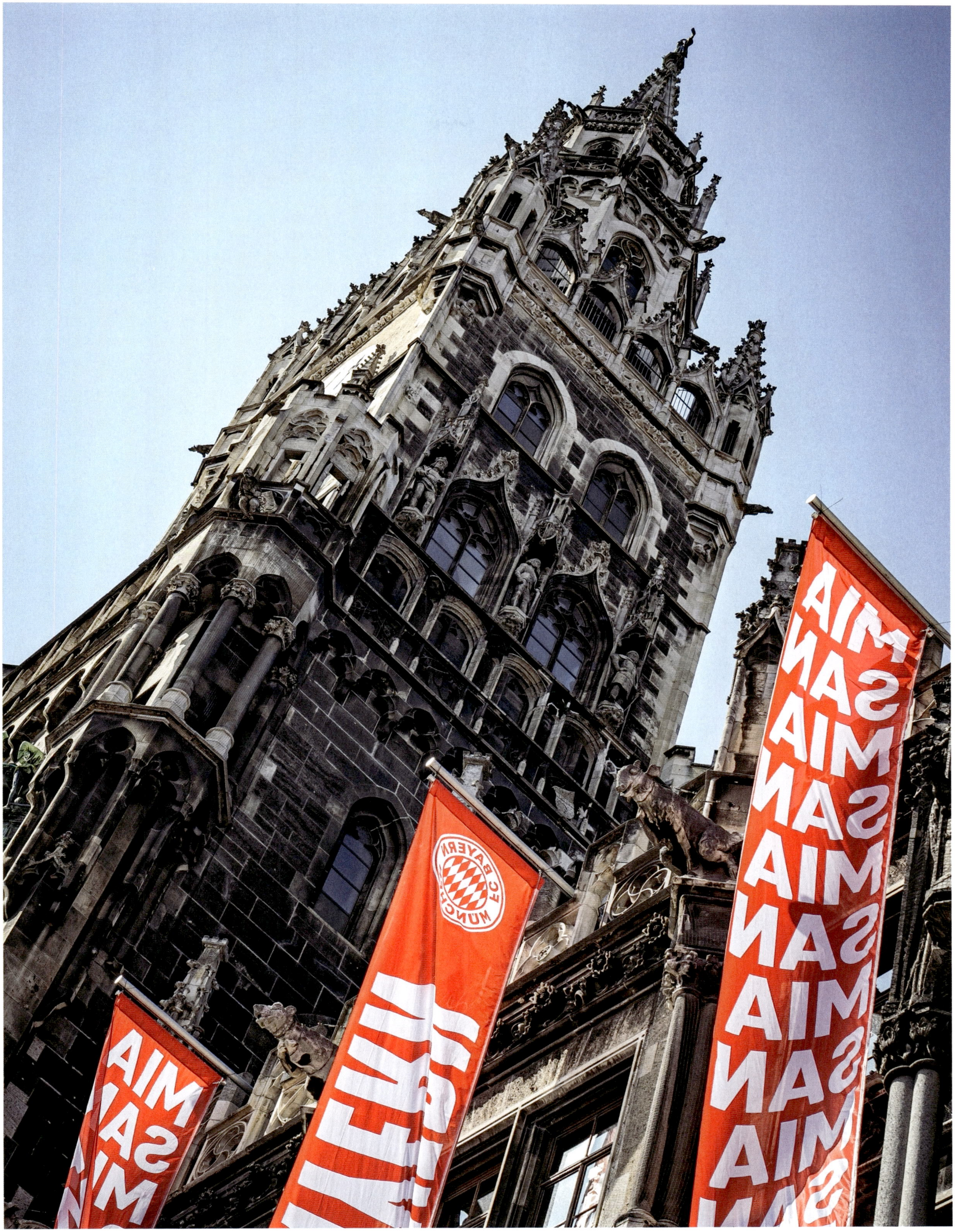
MIA SAN MIA
FC BAYERN MÜNCHEN

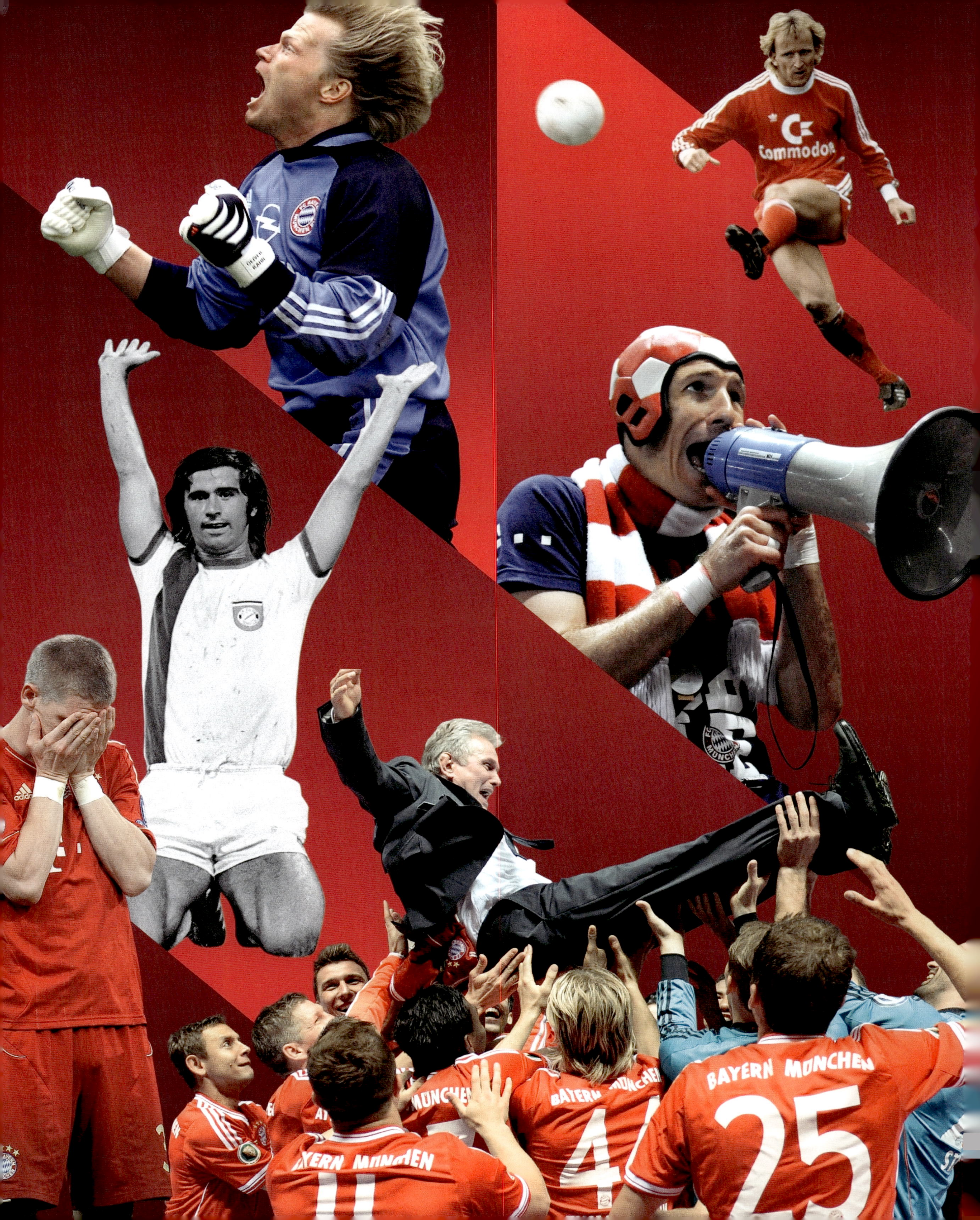
BAYERN MÜNCHEN
25

PASSION

You can't start a fire without a spark. In the stadium that's true for both sides, for the footballers and the fans: they can only fire each other on if they enjoy what they are doing. And show it, too.

125 YEARS OF **PASSION**

It begins with the colour. Red, the colour of passion. What could a club that wears red, a team that is called "the Reds", personify, if not passion? This is the start of everything, in football at least. You don't become a footballer or a fan because it is sensible or useful or healthy, because the doctor or your mother or common sense tells you to. You do it out of enjoyment, enthusiasm. Out of passion.

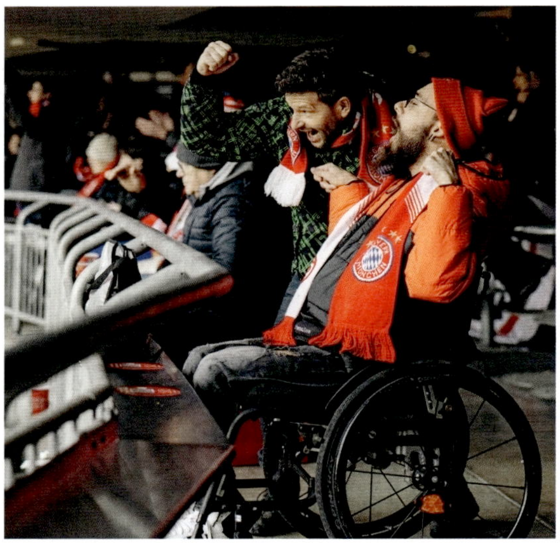

Football is the sport that English gentlemen invented but the common people adopted for themselves. That is why it is not some formal way of passing the time between lunch and tea, but a game that has always belonged to the aspirational and dynamic sections of society. A game that is unimaginable without joy and frustration, without anger and love, without the ego trip and the team feeling.

No other sport can enthuse and involve the fan, the spectator, as strongly as football, and make the fans part of the action – in the stadium, but also in their imagination. At its best moments it gives them a vitality that can take possession of everything. It is what Wikipedia defines as "passion": an emotion that "takes complete hold of the mind, thought, feeling and will".

Passion is the genesis of everything, therefore, but never the whole thing. Perhaps no one in German football has taken this to heart more than FC Bayern. When it mattered, the team always had the ability to win matches with a cool head. And to take far-reaching decisions with an equally cool head. This made FCB the greatest and most successful club in Germany. And the most popular, but also the club that most polarises opinion. Only the world's greatest football clubs are capable of this. It shows that hardly anyone can regard them with indifference, the opposite of passion.

The financial gains that FCB derives from the strength of its brand and its market position are never its *raison d'être*, however, but only a means to an end. It is employed to maximise sporting rather than business success. The success of the Reds. And therefore the pleasure of millions of passionate fans.

Since the pandemic, at the latest, everyone knows what the fans miss when there is no football. But above all, what football lacks without the fans. After those sad kick-abouts in empty stadiums, the game that for far too long was only watched on flickering screens has come back to the centre of our lives. Back to people who show that the virus could not kill their passion.

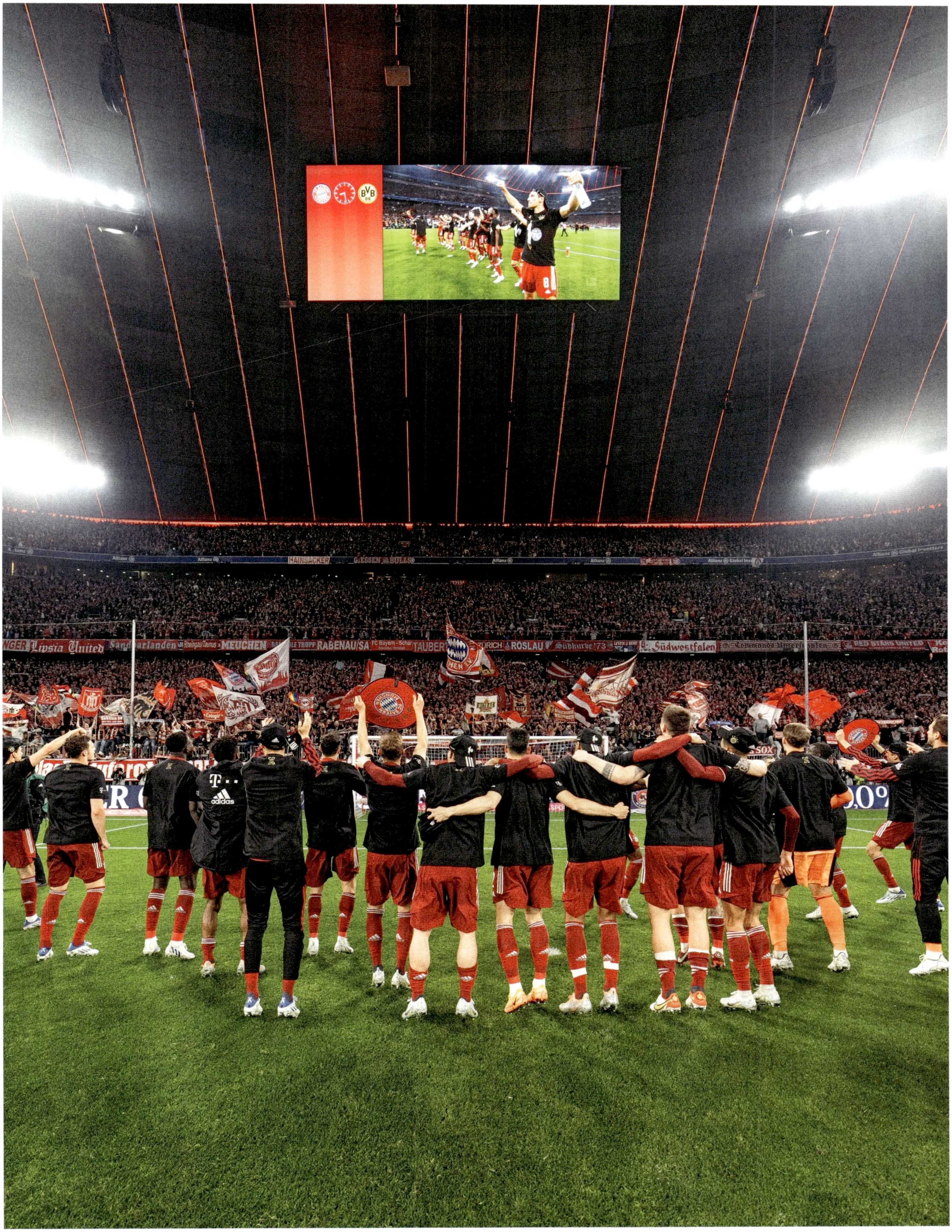
HAINSACKER
MEUCHEN
RABENAUSA
ROSLAU
Südwestfalen

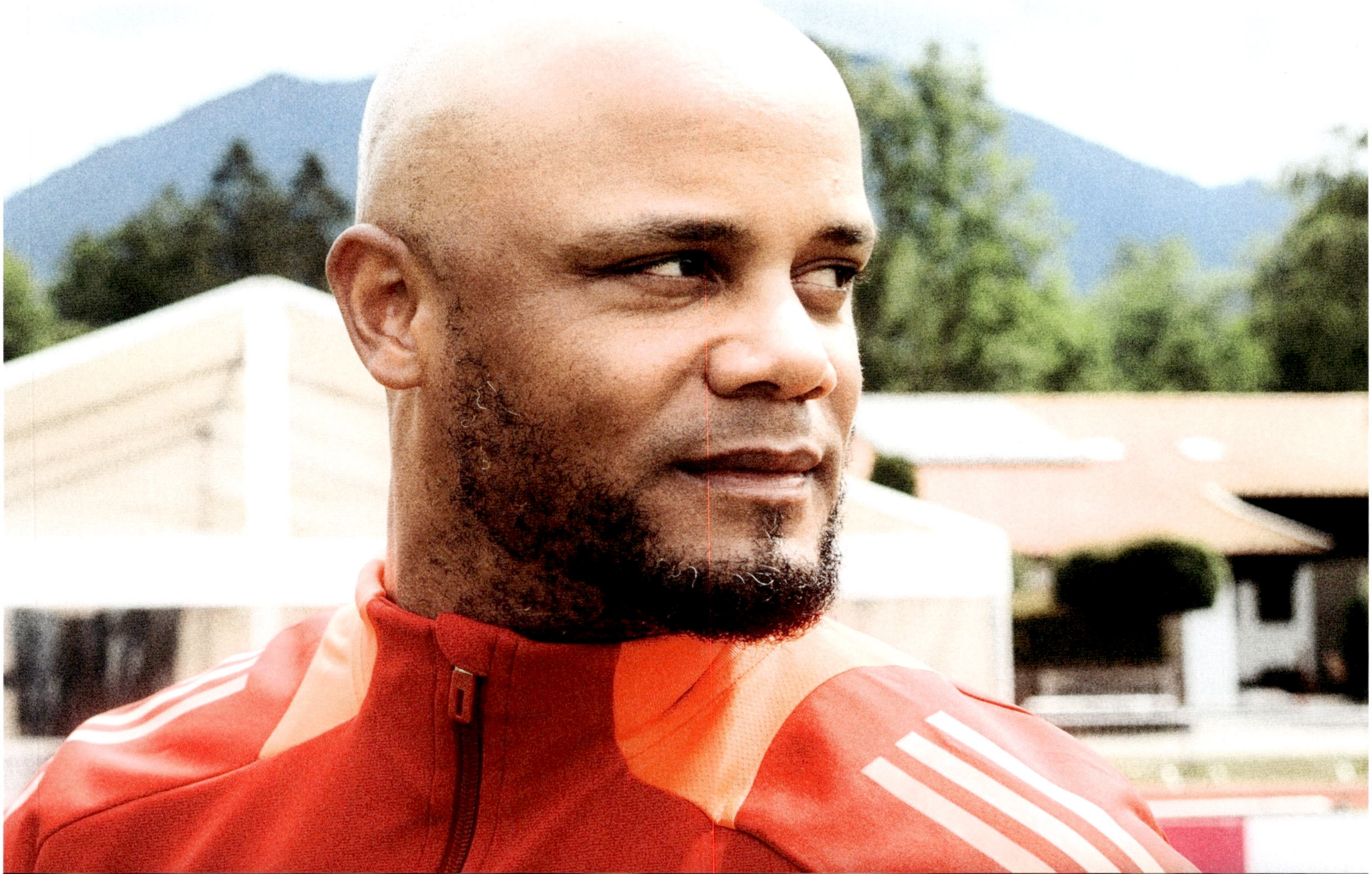

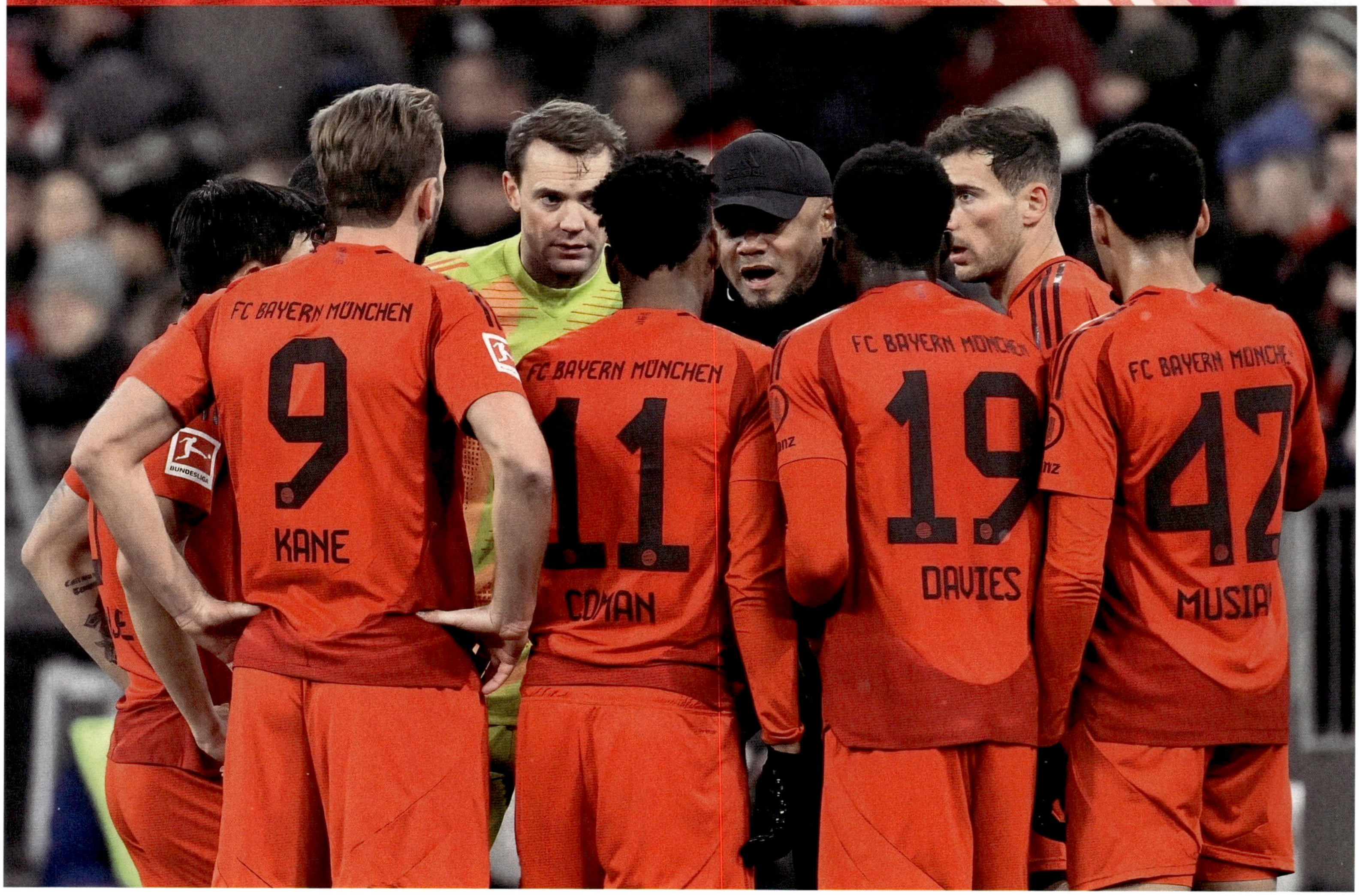
FC BAYERN MÜNCHEN
9
KANE
FC BAYERN MÜNCHEN
11
FC BAYERN MÜNCHEN
19
DAVIES
BUNDESLIGA

"MY PROSPECTS? NOW I'M A COACH."

Taking him on was a big step, not only for FC Bayern but also for the Bundesliga, where Vincent Kompany is the first black trainer – sixty-one years after it was founded. And Bayern took on someone who never stopped believing in himself in the face of other people's prejudices. "My father came to Belgium from a refugee camp in Congo. What were my prospects of playing in the Premier League one day? Of winning a championship? Playing international football? 0.001 per cent, maybe. And now I'm a coach."

And not just any coach, but the coach of FCB. After the 9–2 win against Dynamo Zagreb in the Champions League, Kompany gave a passionate response to the question of whether FC Bayern was too big for him. "The real question is: Do you stop believing in yourself because of what other people say? Because the chances of success are very slim? The right mentality is always to carry on. Whether you fail or not, you will get better every time. That's what matters."

With this mentality he makes a good impression in Munich. He is not a megaphone but an accomplished communicator, in six languages. Empathetic, reflective – a born leader, but in a gentle way. At the age of only 18 he won the title of Footballer of the Year and the championship in Belgium with RSC Anderlecht, then captained Manchester City to winning the Premier League four times. And at the end of his eleven years with the Blues, he learned the kind of football that the Reds know well and now, under Kompany, sometimes recognise: Pep Guardiola's football. Pressing in forward positions, high-percentage possession of the ball, coupled with dominance and impetus towards the goal – the football that the Allianz Arena had seen under the Catalan maestro himself. "Managing the space is the biggest thing that I learned from Pep", says Kompany. It seems as if, eight years after Guardiola, all of this has fallen on fertile ground.

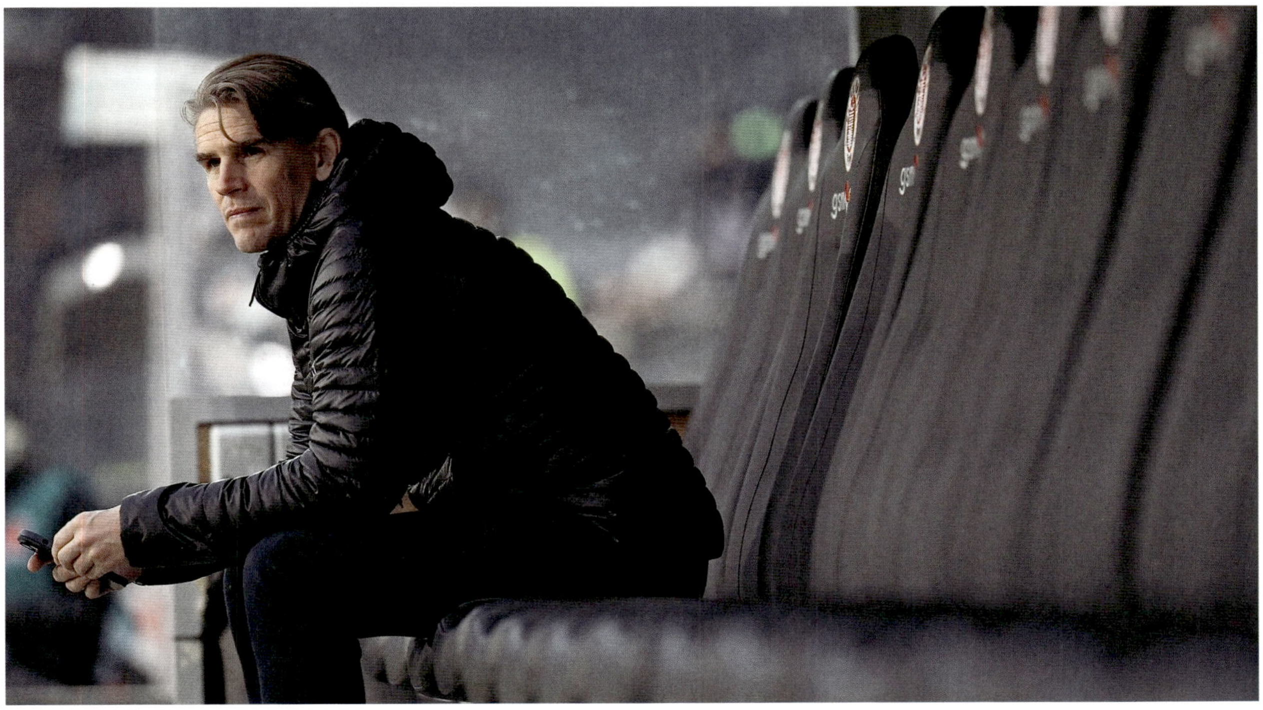

The two men who are closest to the team at FCB were both shaped in young years by taking responsibility. The coach Vincent Kompany, while captain of Manchester City, completed a course of business studies, cared for homeless people and founded a football club for children from poor families. Director of sport Christoph Freund gave up his professional career in the second division in Austria at the age of 24 to manage the family carpentry business following the death of his father.

"A HOME FINAL"
FCB-CHELSEA 3-4 · 2012

The "home final" against Chelsea in 2012 – and no match ever turned all the numbers upside down like this one. Or the mood of every Bayern fan. Shots on goal: 35–9. Corners: 20–1. Penalty kicks: 1–0. One hundred per cent the better team. And the losers.

In their dream final in their own stadium, Bayern had three match balls. Thomas Müller won the first of them when his header overcame Chelsea's fortress after eighty-three minutes. Didier Drogba saved that match ball just before the final whistle, scoring from the English team's only corner to make it 1–1. The second match ball, in extra time, was won by Franck Ribéry, whom Drogba fouled. Arjen Robben missed the penalty. And the third came courtesy of Manuel Neuer, who made a save against Juan Mata in the penalty shoot-out and scored a spot kick himself. But then Petr Čech saved against Ivica Olić and Bastian Schweinsteiger. As the Czech goalkeeper revealed ten years later in the *Generation Wembley* Bayern documentary, before the final he had studied every Bayern penalty since 2007 – and then, when Schweinsteiger paused in his run-up, recognised the pattern that the Bayern player had shown once before, in Basel.

And so Cech dived to the right corner, as he did for all five previous penalties. He finger-tipped the last one onto the post – and then Drogba's winning shot ended the drama. Or rather, raised the curtain on it. On the drama in the mind that goes on for days and nights after an ending like that: How could we have lost this match? Karl-Heinz Rummenigge masochistically declared that he watches the final against Chelsea every year – and still cannot understand it.

Only one thing is certain: that the feeling of defeat does not paralyse FCB, but always sets something in motion. "What should there be in my mind? There's nothing," said Thomas Müller to the reporters in the stadium at the time. "It's hard to put it in words." "Radio Müller" managed to do that after all, of course, the first team member to post in the team chat, before dawn: "Keep your heads up, lads. What happened yesterday really hurts. But next year we'll hit back."

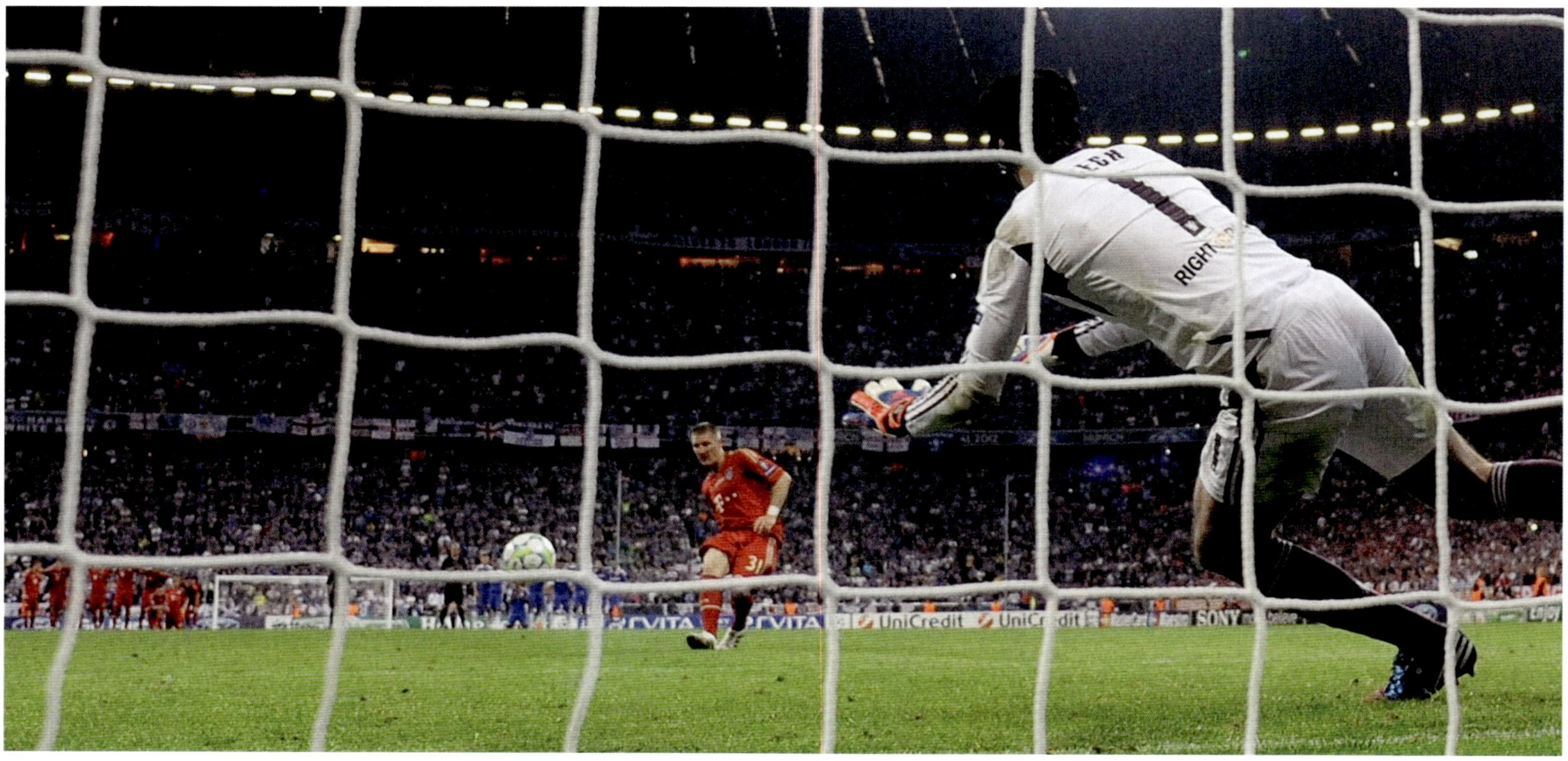

Two images, with only a few seconds between them – and at the same time separated by an abyss in the emotions of every Bayern fan. And above all in Bastian Schweinsteiger's feelings. When the ball left his foot, all seemed to be right with the world. But Petr Čech was already diving.

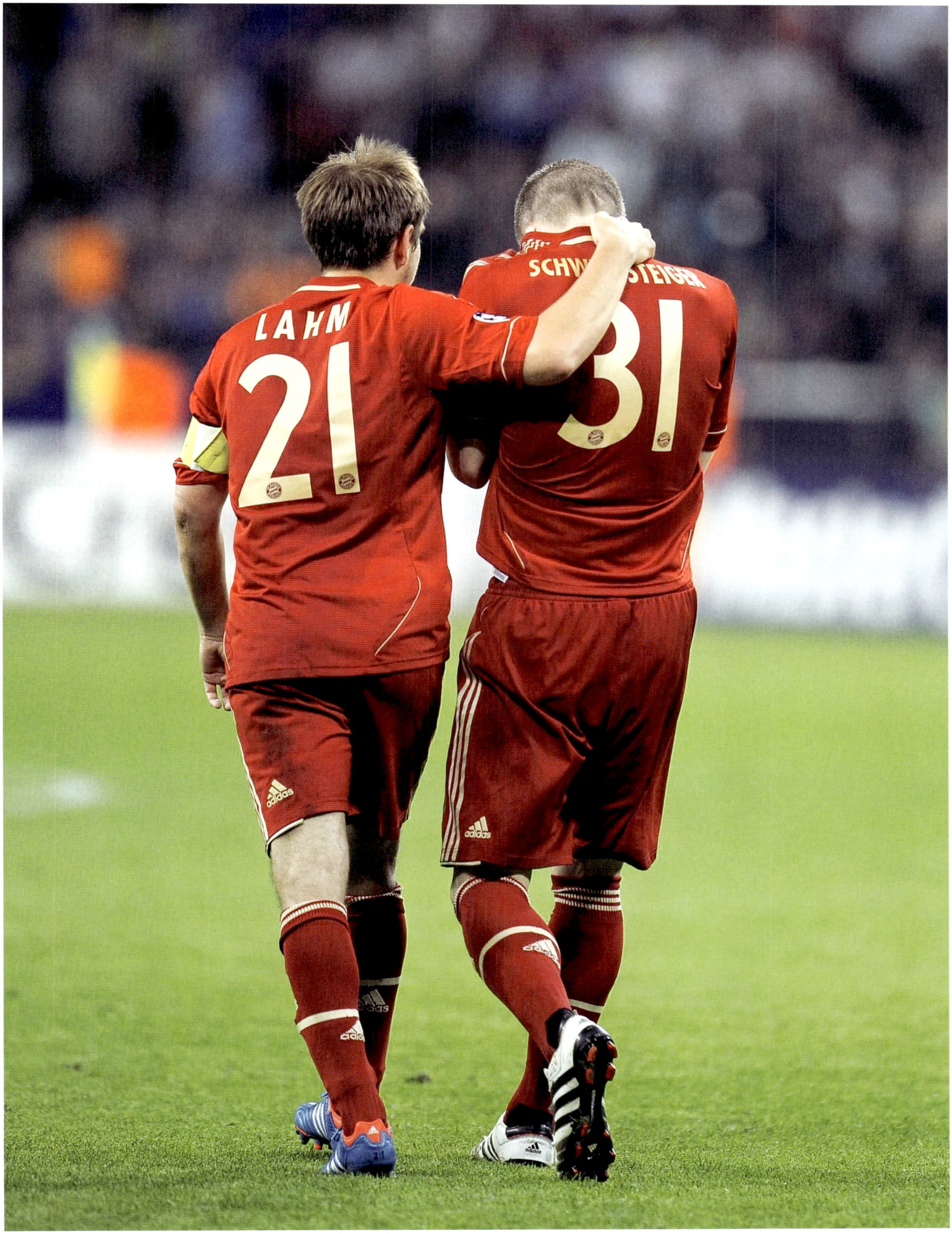
LAHM
21
31

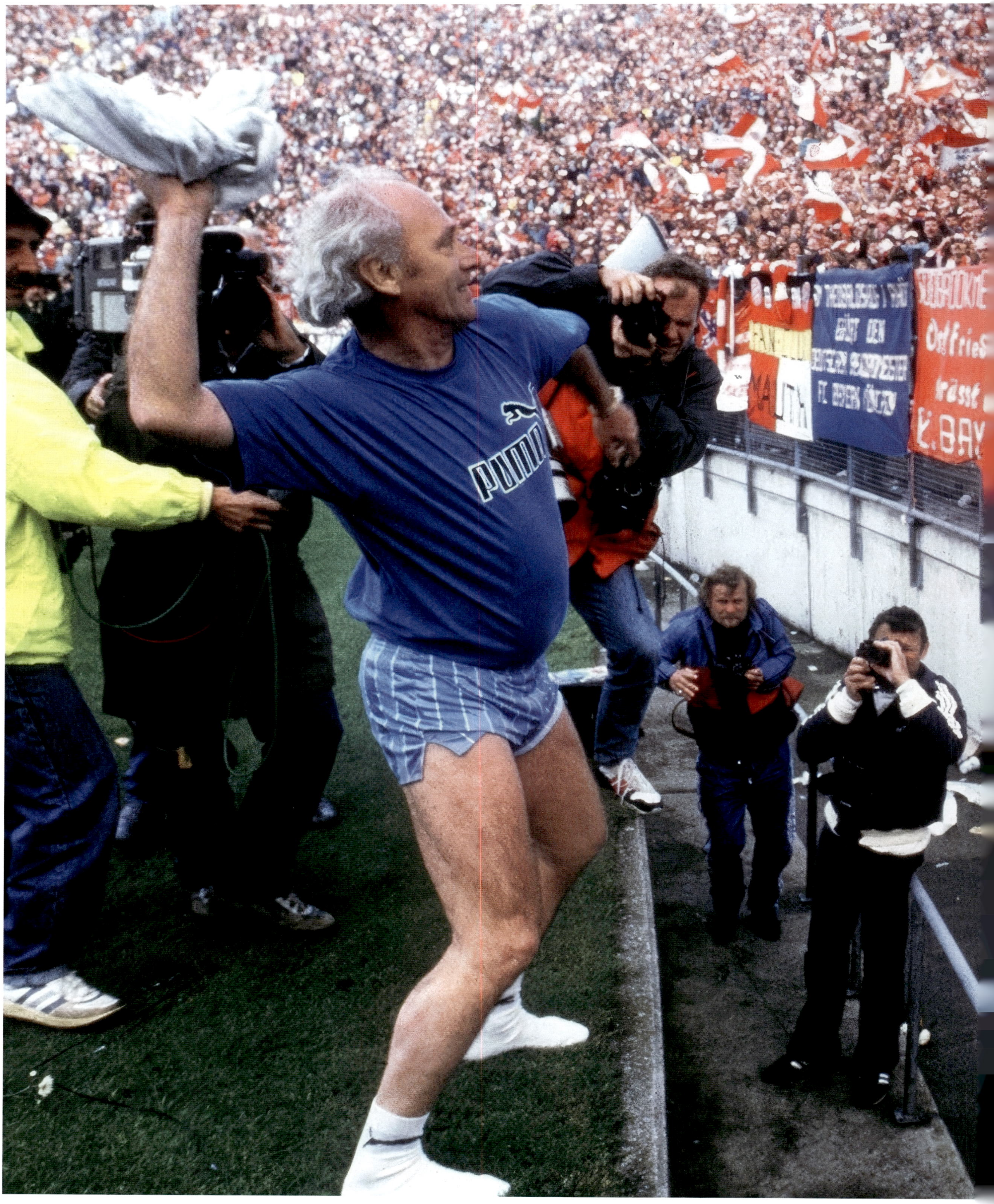
PUMA

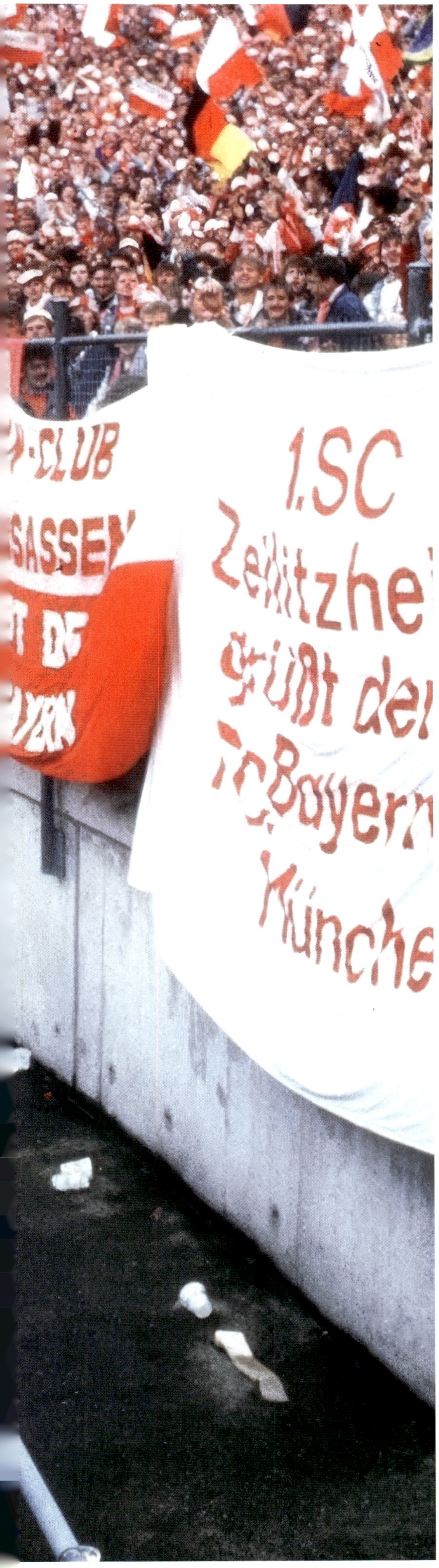

TROUSERS **DOWN!**

Saturday, 17 June 1987, is a special date in the 125-year history of FC Bayern Munich: the day when FCB took the record for the most German championships. And the coach was a hit as a stripper.

To reach this milestone, Udo Lattek did not bet the shirt on his back, but he did part with some clothing. Following a 1–0 victory against Schalke 04 he took his trousers off, threw them to the delirious fans in the Olympic Stadium, and continued his celebrations in pale blue boxer shorts. On a glorious day like this, even underclothes in the colours of the club's local third-division rival can be forgiven. With a tenth championship, the third in succession, Bayern overtook 1. FC Nürnberg as the record holder after sixty-two years – probably forever. It is a mathematical certainty that, at least for the club's 150th birthday on 27 February 2050, FCB will still be able to celebrate its status as the record holder. It would take a few months longer to be overtaken in the number of championship titles. The theoretical calculation for this is that Borussia Dortmund win the title twenty-six times in succession. Or Nürnberg gain promotion and win all twenty-five championships from now until 2050.

If the trophy could talk, it would have a story to tell. All year it lies in a showcase, polished till it gleams brightly - and then suddenly, in May, it is taken out, passed around, celebrated, kissed and embraced by sweaty men in shower rooms. And a year later? The same thing, ever since 1949.

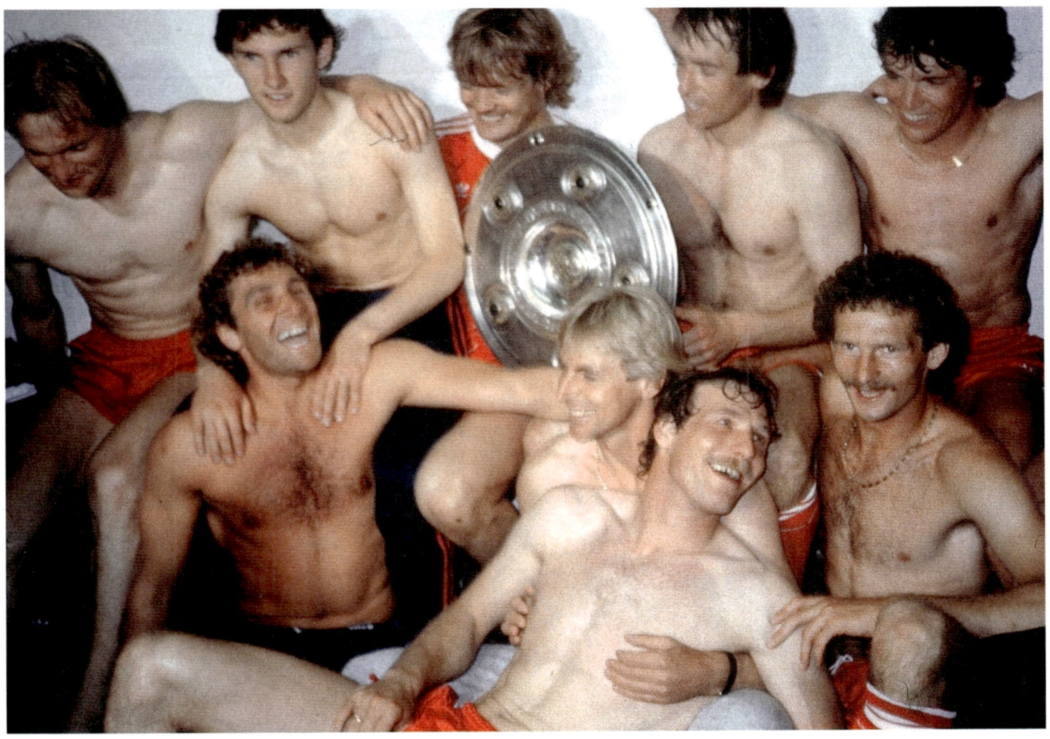

"I DREAMED ABOUT YOU" **BVB-FCB 1-2 · 2013**

What spectacular goals Arjen Robben scored wearing a Bayern Munich shirt. Moving from the right into the centre, with his left foot into the corner – the trademark Robben goal. But the dream goal of every Bayern fan was an unforgettable roll-in.

The ball takes three seconds to get from the centre circle to the Dortmund penalty area, hit with precision over forty metres by Jérôme Boateng to Franck Ribéry, from whose back-heel it luckily passes into Arjen Robben's path. It is the 89th minute of a heated, high-calibre Champions League final, in a world-famous arena at boiling point, and the drama is about to go into extra time. Then suddenly a gap appears in the black-and-yellow wall, and the flying Dutchman glides through just as his namesake flies over the water. Only the goalkeeper, Roman Weidenfeller, stands in the way of a triumph and moves in the direction of Robben's run, but the Dutchman finds the last possible moment to change direction – not his own, but the ball's direction. With his left foot he sends the ball at right angles to his own diagonal path, pushing it inches past the big toe of his right foot, past the leg that is taking his weight – and above all past the wrong-footed keeper, who has no room to manoeuvre from this unexpected angle. Like the other 86,000 spectators in Wembley Stadium, Weidenfeller can only watch as the ball rolls into the goal. One and a half seconds that seem like eternity.

And the rest is jubilation in red. Robben runs towards the corner flag, where his father is somewhere in the crowd and sees him celebrating, before his teammates catch up and almost crush him in their joy. On this evening, his Frisian first name became part of a classic in the treasury of Bayern songs: "I dreamed about you, about our night at Wembley!" That is how the fans in the Südkurve, the south end, updated an old hit by Matthias Reim. "We've won the cup, we've taken the throne, Arjen has done it!" But how he did it at the end was something no one could dream of, not even Robben himself.

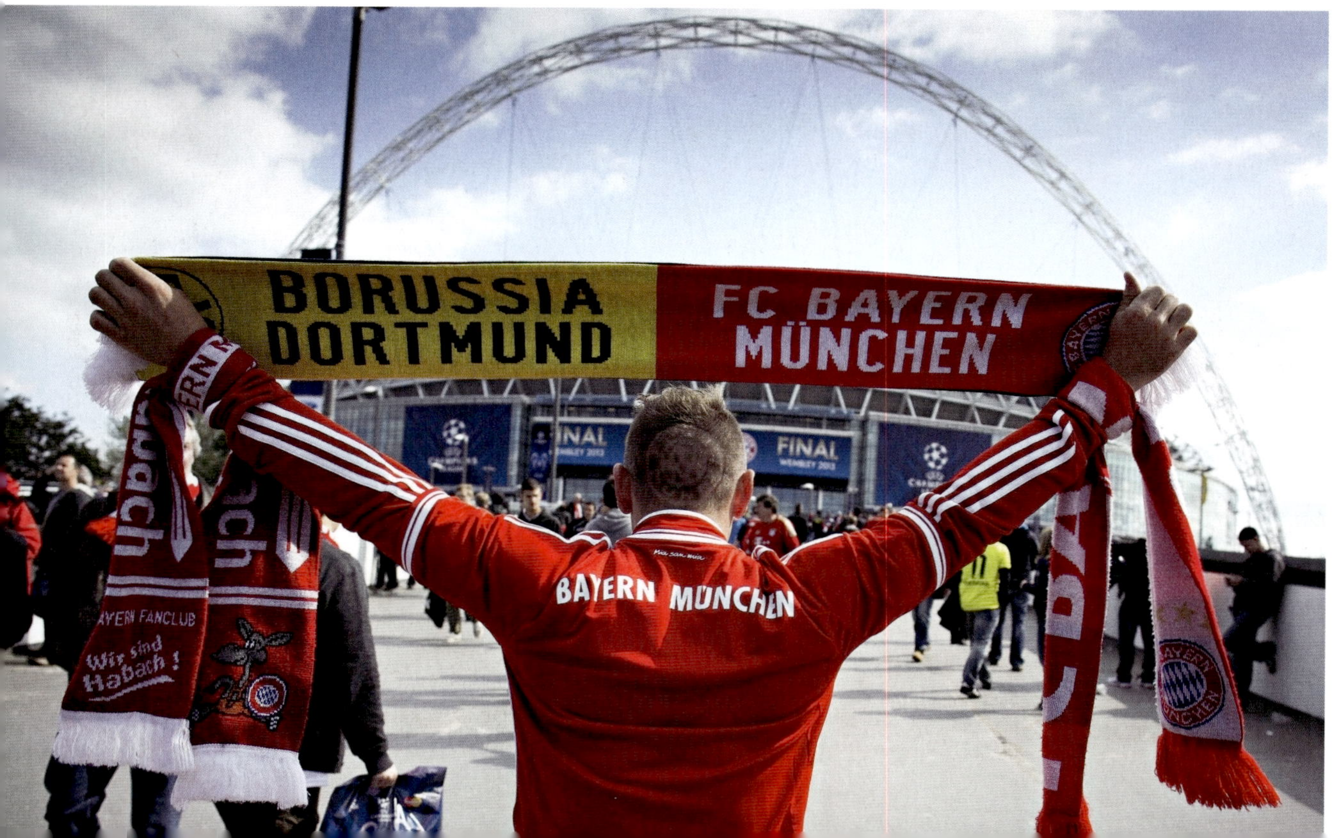

In this great match, emotions soared almost as high as the huge arch over Wembley itself on 25 May 2013 - an occasion that nobody who wore red on that day will forget. Especially not the men who played on the "holy" turf of the world's most famous stadium.

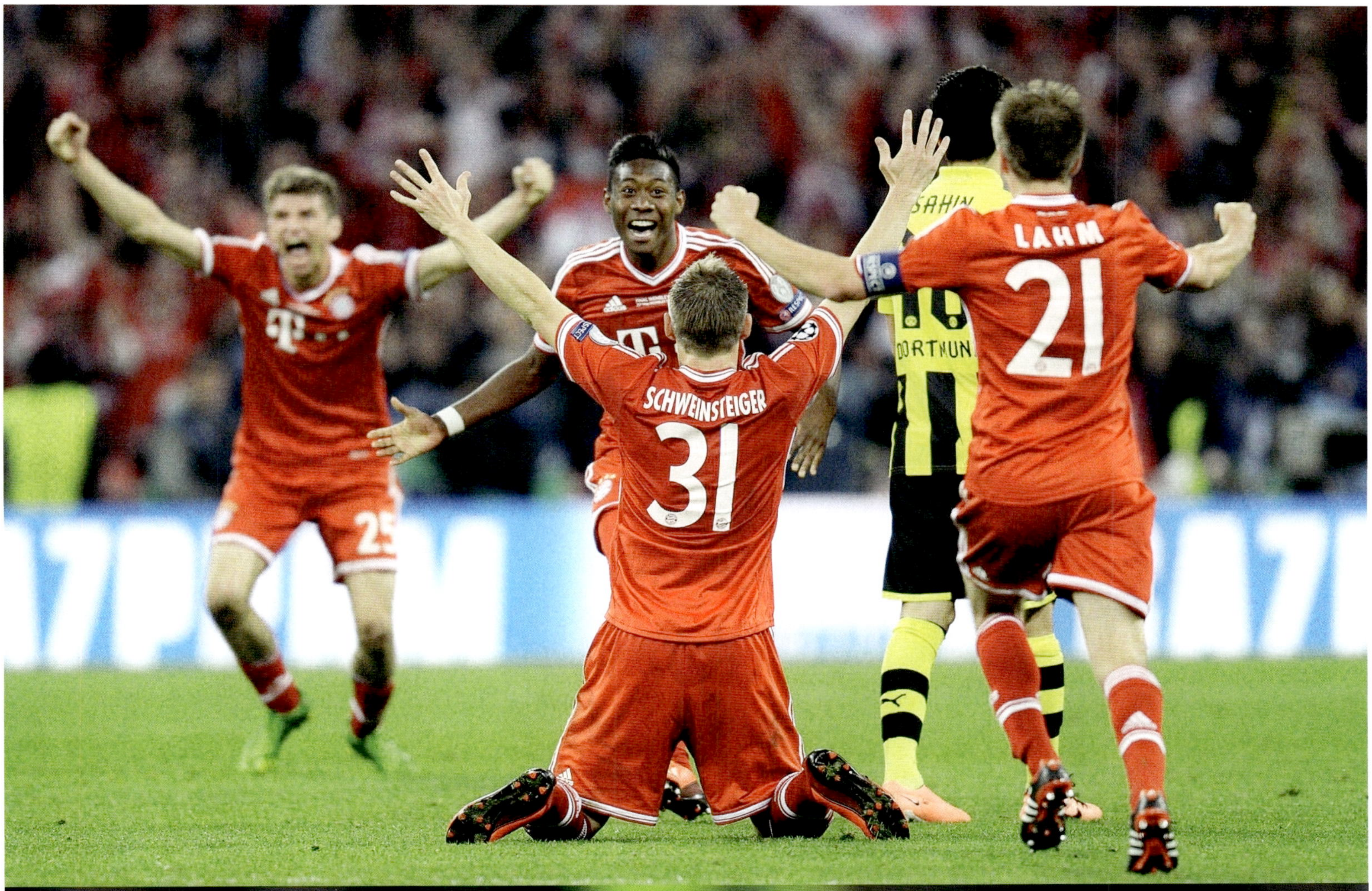
SCHWEINSTEIGER
31
LAHM
21
25

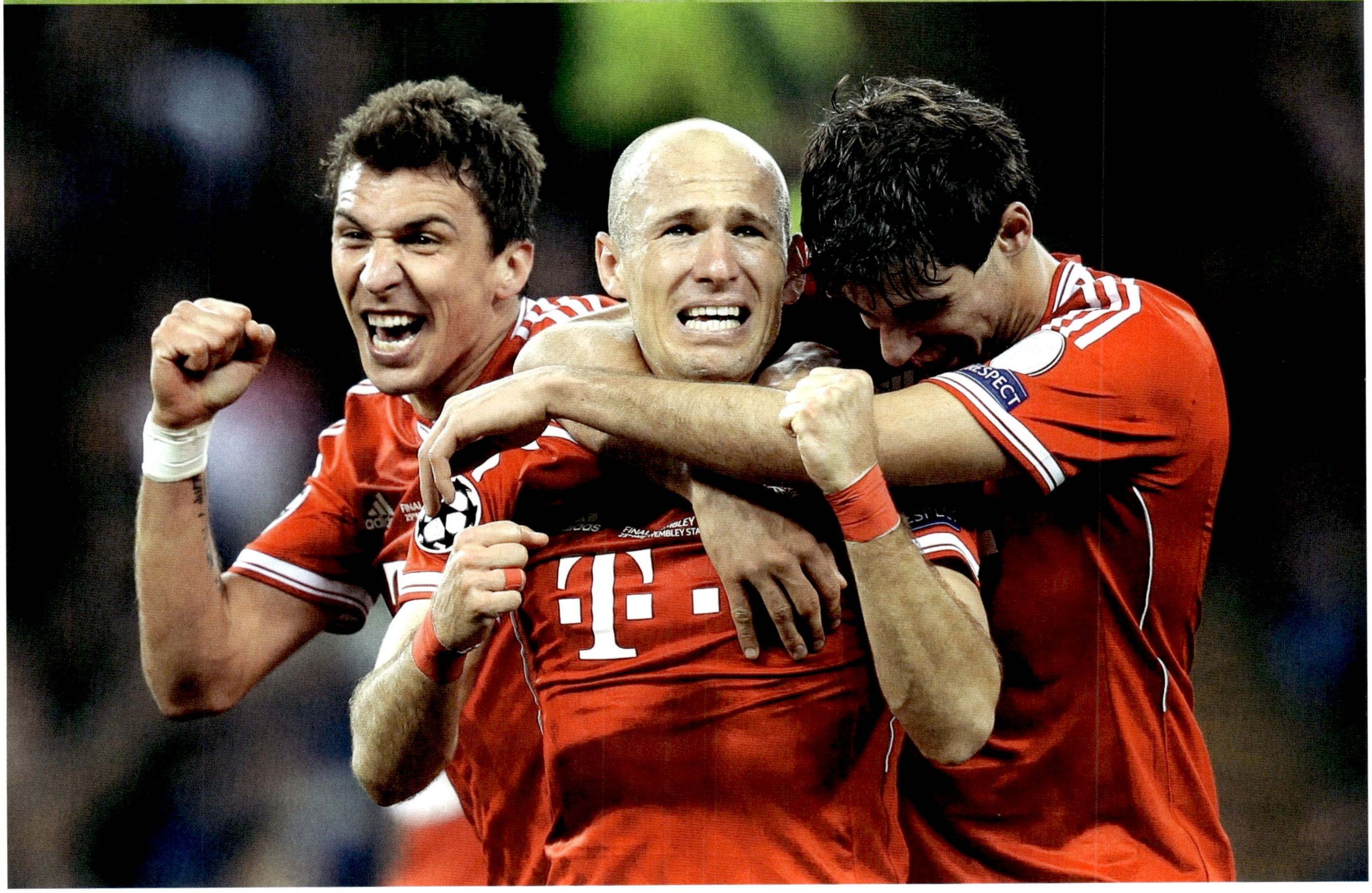

OUR BIG **BAYERN FAMILY –** MORE THAN **JUST FOOTBALL**

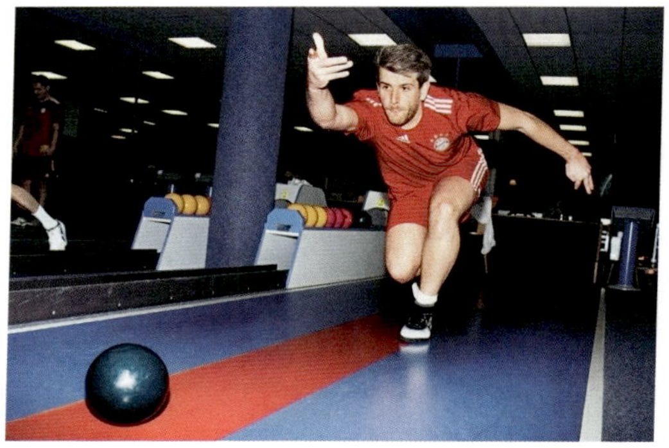

FC Bayern Munich has never seen the words "football club" in its name as excluding other athletes. Ice hockey was part of the programme as early as 1901, then again in 1966, while baseball and gymnastics were temporarily added. Today six different sports are represented at FCB.

For more than a hundred years, FC Bayern has given a home to sports equipment that looks nothing like a football. Players can bowl balls down an alley, move their king across the board, ping a celluloid ball over the net – and in the past they shoved a puck over the ice and their teammates in a rugby scrum.

The first properly established sport alongside football was rugby, from 1922 to 1936. Three times FCB won the Friediger Cup, the trophy for the Munich champions donated by the Jewish hotelier and Bayern club member Markus Friediger. His sons Karl and Leopold, both rugby players, escaped the Holocaust by emigrating to the United States. Markus Friediger and his wife Hedwig were deported in 1941 to the ghetto of Riga and are thought to have been murdered in Auschwitz.

Basketball was introduced to FCB in 1946 by Franz Kronberger, whose war injury prevented him from playing football. In 1954 and 1955 Bayern won the German championship, and repeated this, now with a professional set-up, four times between 2014 and 2024. FC Bayern Baseball, too, won championships – twice in the 1960s. And in gymnastics, which was part of the club until 2014, FCB became German champion four times in the 1980s. The ice-hockey team that was acquired in 1966 only played in the top league for two seasons, as the costs were too high. Today, alongside football, basketball and handball, there is a table-tennis section, whose excellent youth work was rewarded in 2024 with three German titles at junior level; the skittle team, in which Mehmet Scholl knocked over all nine skittles several times; and the chess players, who have been back in the top division since 2019. In one way they have even drawn equal with the great footballers: at lightning chess they hold the record for the most championships.

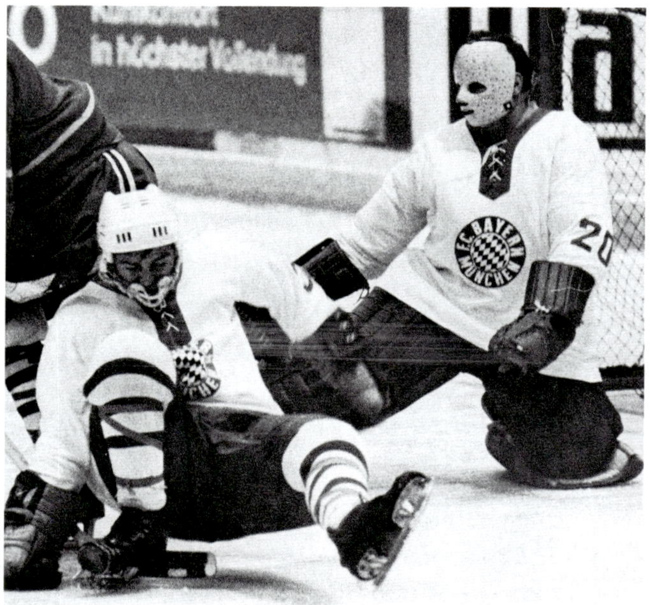

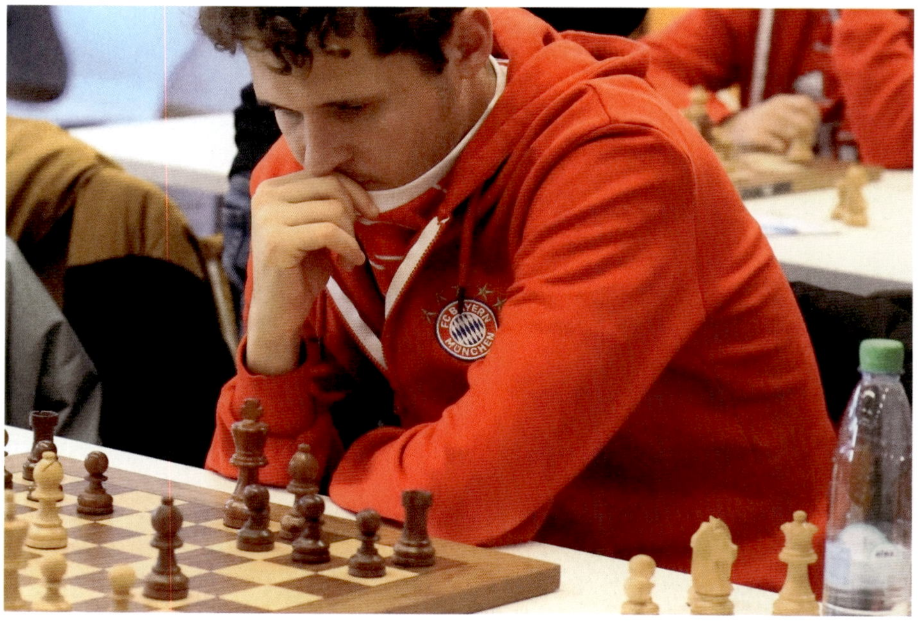

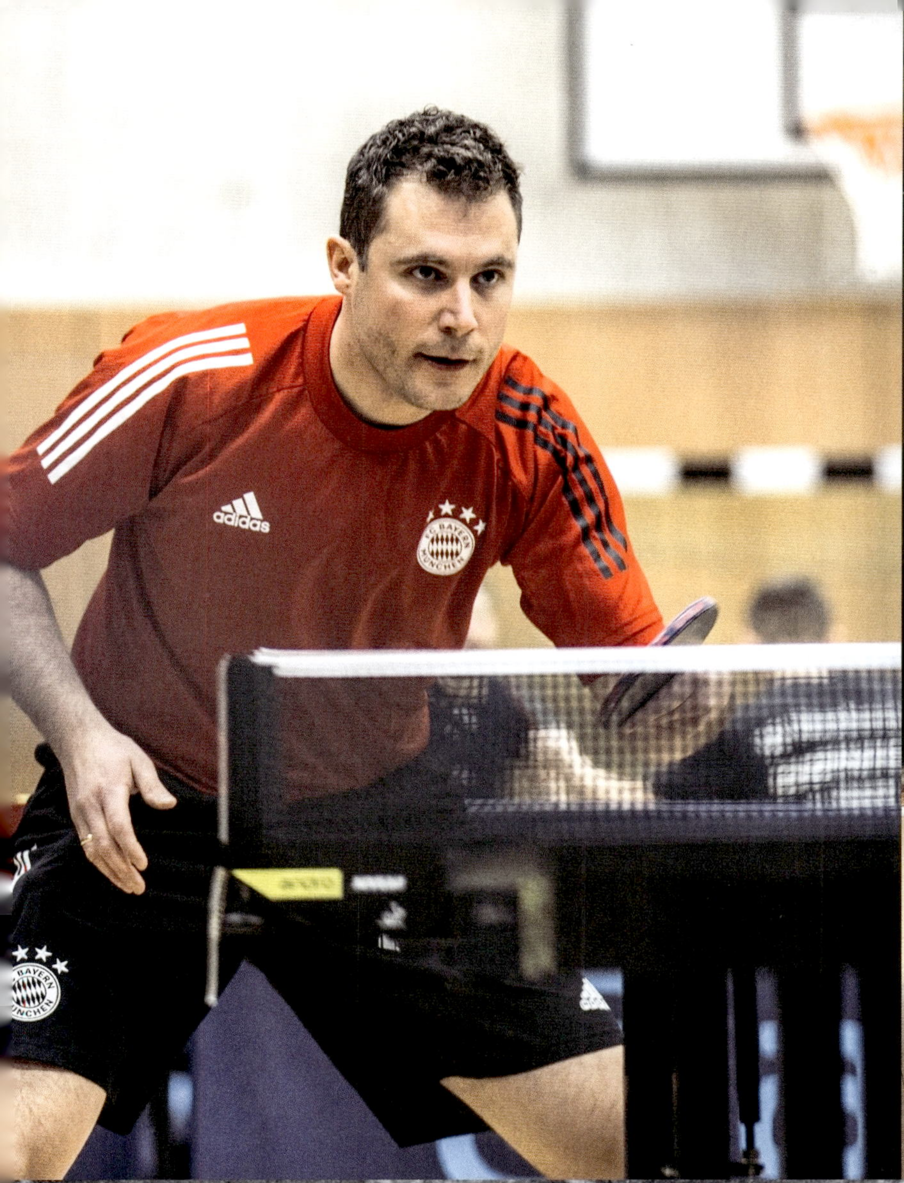
adidas

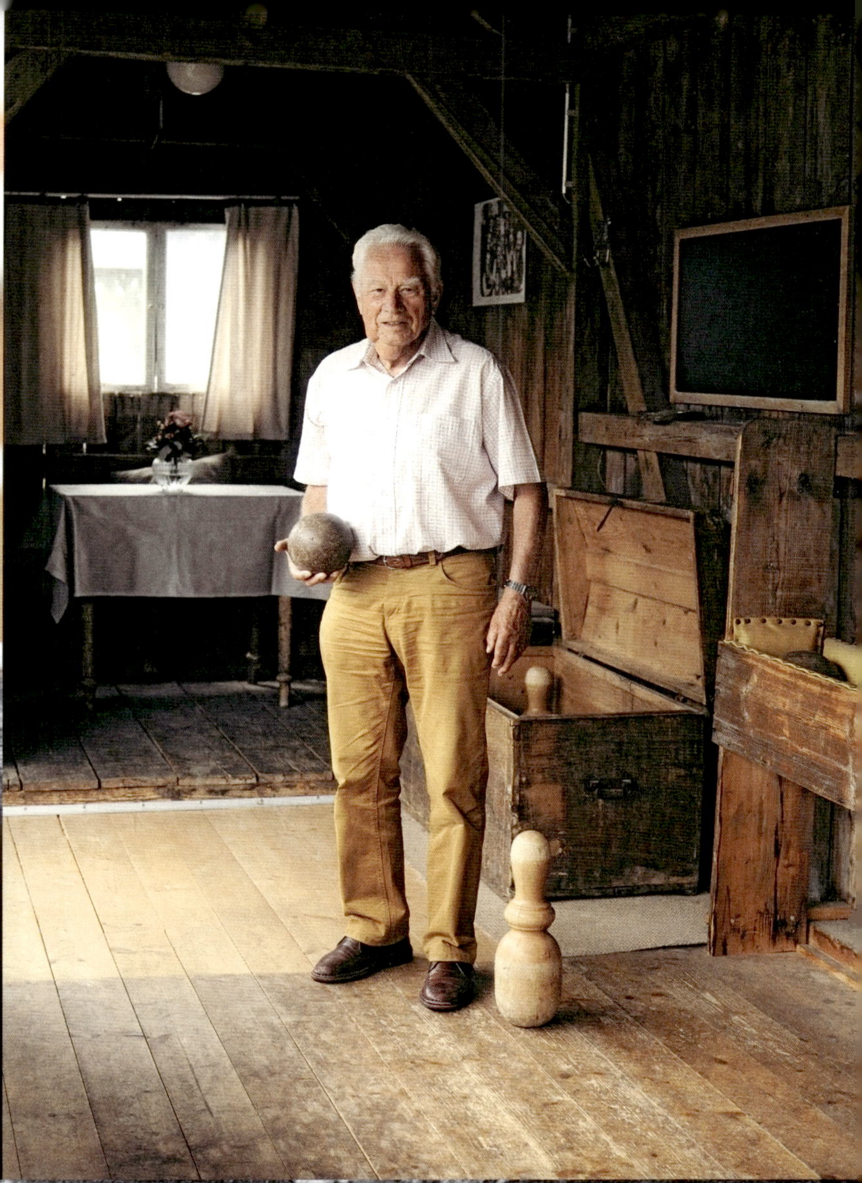

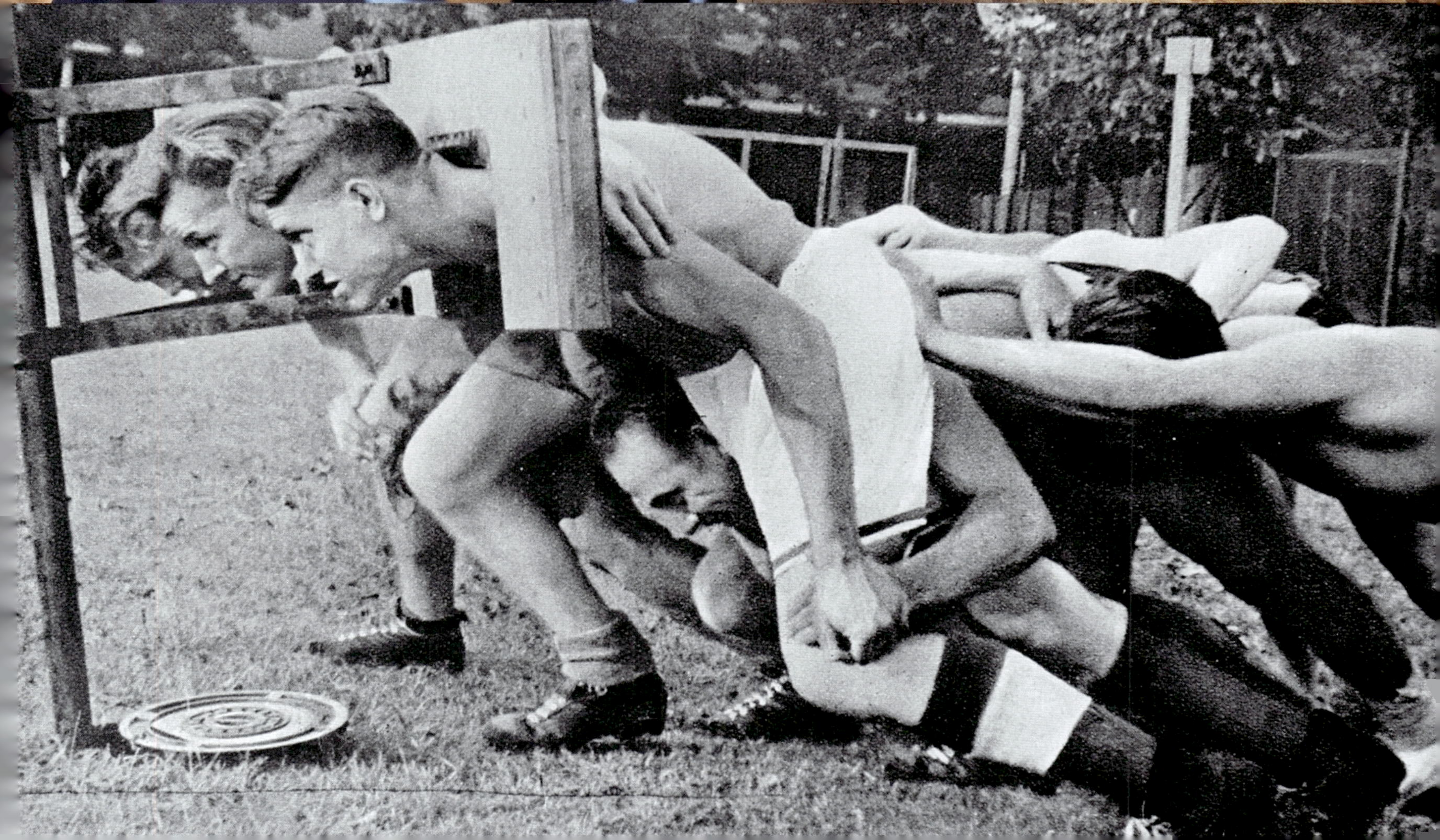

A SHOT TO REMEMBER
A HOLE FOR THE MUSEUM

We've all had a day like that. You labour till you are worn out, nothing goes right, customers shout, the boss complains, and your feelings are dammed up. On 10 May 1997, when the scoreline stood at 0–0 against bottom-of-the-table SC Freiburg and Jürgen Klinsmann, the holder of World Cup and European Cup medals, was taken off the field after a noisy argument with his coach Giovanni Trapattoni to be substituted by Carsten Lakies, a regional league player, his dam burst. And so, after all, a frustrated goal-getter did hit a target that day: a wooden barrel at the edge of the pitch advertising Japanese batteries was the lightning rod for his flash of anger. Klinsmann was fortunate, only getting a few grazes from the metal supports inside the barrel. The matter was soon settled behind closed doors, two weeks later Bayern had the championship title, and Klinsmann was about to move to Italy. But the shot that hit the barrel became famous. And everyone won: the media, the battery maker, a charity for poor children – and visitors to the Bayern Museum, where the hole made by a size 44 boot is a real eye-catcher.

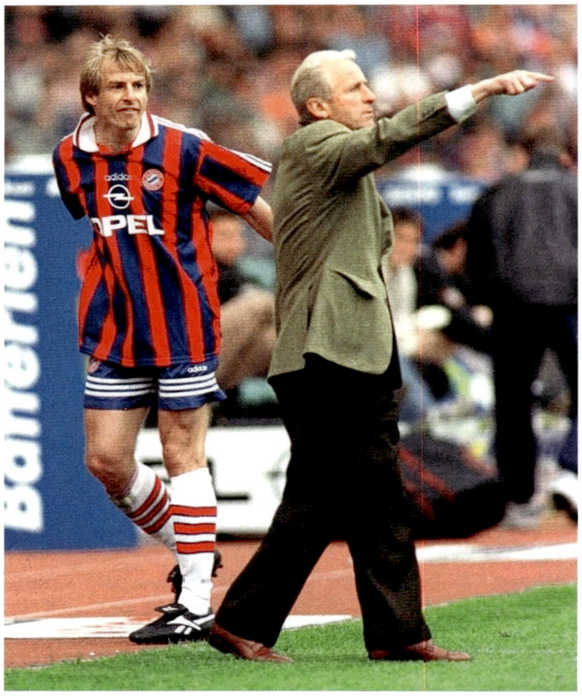

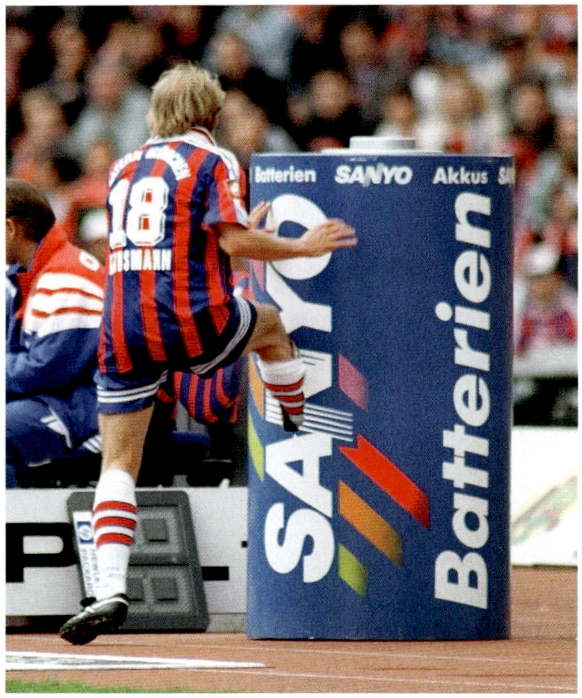

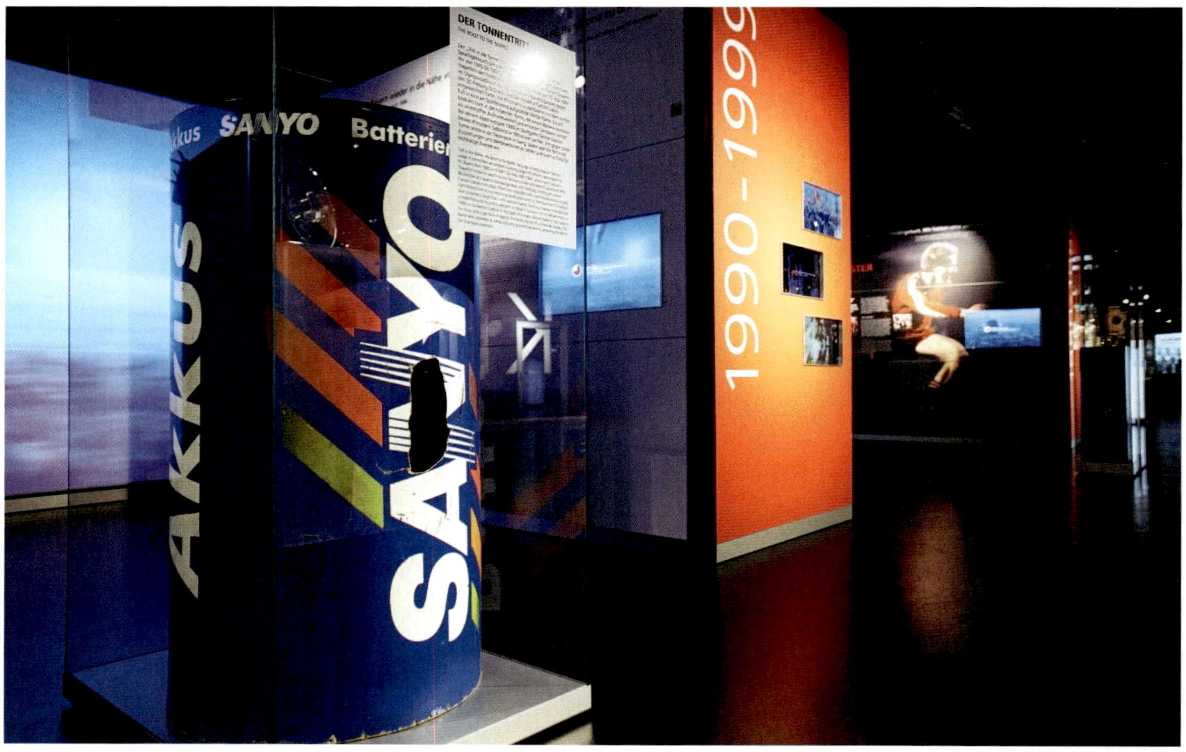

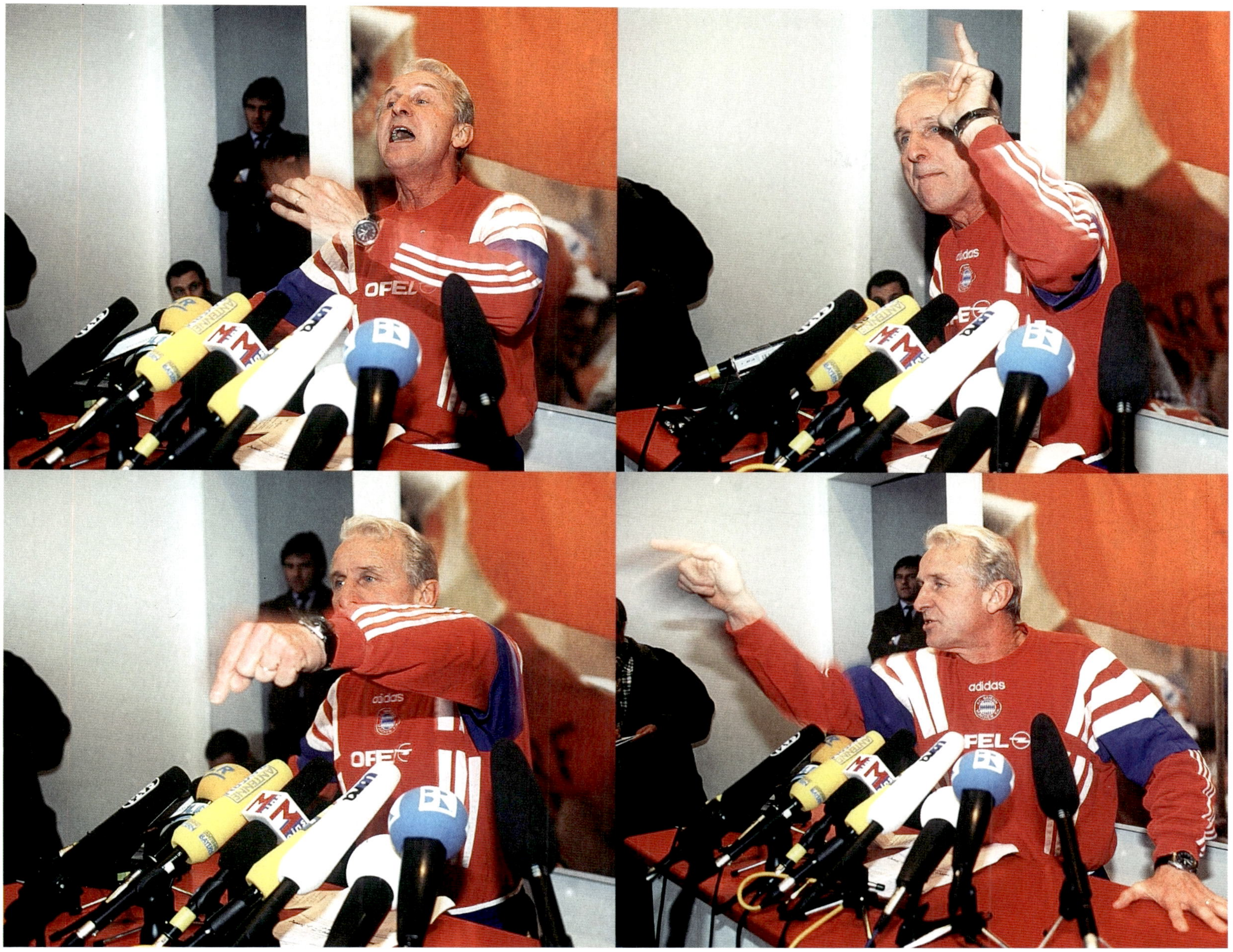

"POOR AS **A BOTTLE EMPTY"**

Media manager Markus Hörwick, in the background, sensed disaster. Trap's verbal cascade was growing into a media avalanche. In the evening it was the lead story on the main television news broadcast.

A "symphony of arbitrarily joined-up syllables", as he later described it to *Der Spiegel* magazine, suggesting that, since John F. ("I am a Berliner") Kennedy, "no other foreigner has so vehemently spoken his way into the hearts of all Germans" as Giovanni Trapattoni did in 1998 when he said, in faulty German, "Ich habe fertig" (something like: "Is finish me"). According to The Times of London, he had invented nothing less than "a completely new kind of German". "Trap" was already in a fury before this. After losing 0–1 in Schalke, the third defeat in a row, he held a first flaming address in the team hotel – and accidentally spilled a bottle of red wine over Uli Hoeness's suit. Three days later the players, "poor as a bottle empty", got a dressing-down. Superbly enigmatic sentences tripped over each other in Trap's staccato delivery: "What Strunz permit?" or "We must not Zickler forget. Zickler is a tip more Mehmet e more Basler. Is clear, this words, is possible understand?" The fans understood and responded in the match against Bochum with "Grazie, Trap". They too voiced their opinion about the players: "Apart from Olli you can all leave."

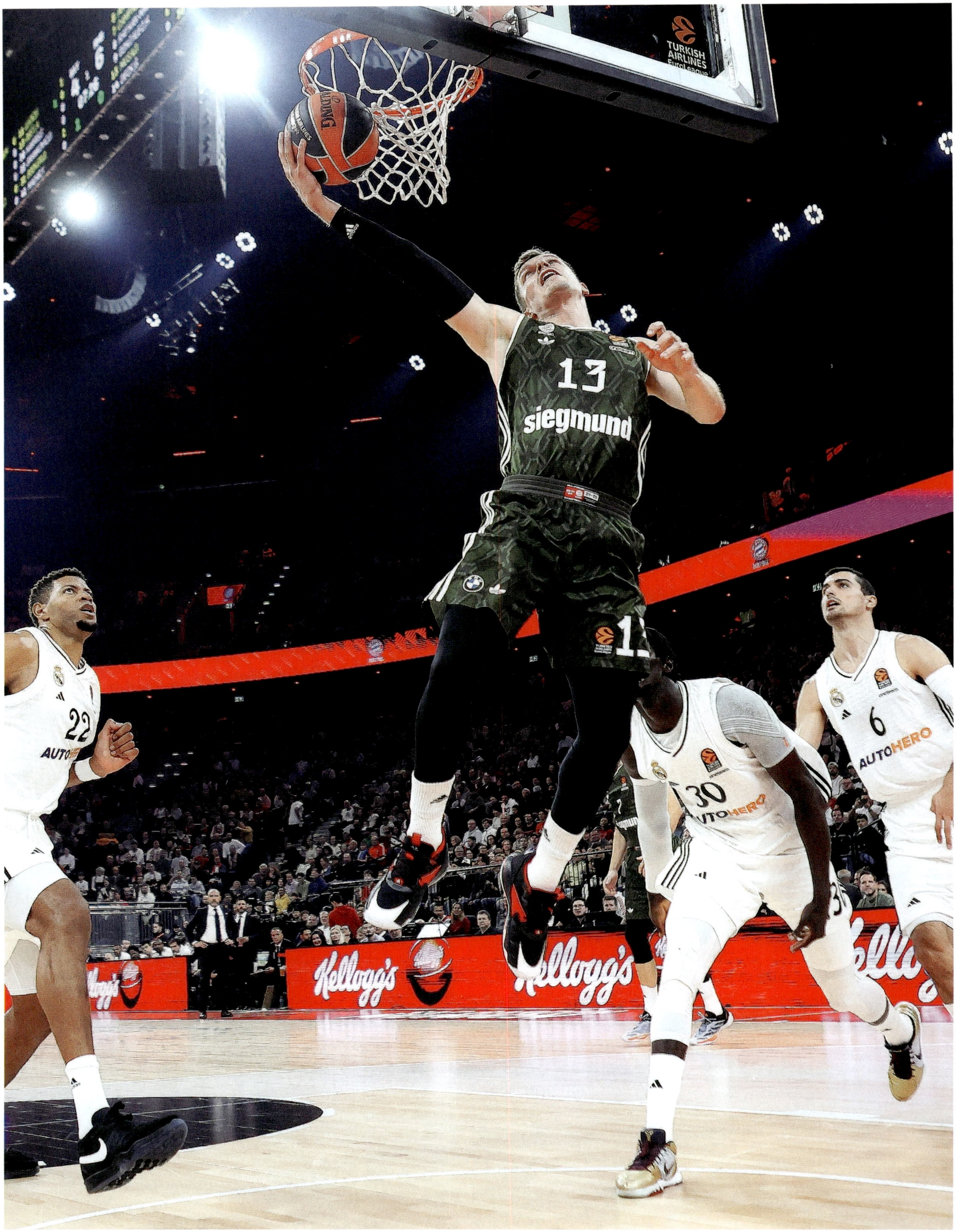

13
siegmund
22
6
AUTOHERO
30
AUTOHERO
Kellogg's
Kellogg's

A TEAM ON ITS **WAY UP**

Three Bayern professionals, Andreas Obst, Niels Giffey and Isaac Bonga, became basketball world champions in 2023. A year later, the world champions' coach, Gordon Herbert, also arrived in Munich and announced ambitious goals: to retain the championship title and to reach the Final Four in the Euro League for the first time. The basketballers were aiming almost as high as their footballing colleagues.

"The best German players outside the NBA have to play for FC Bayern," demanded the new director of sports Dragan Tarlac. However, even in a top squad, the mix has to be right. To illustrate the division of tasks, Gordon Herbert jokingly likes to distinguish between the "racehorses", i.e. the stars, and the "pigs", who do the dirty work. But, he says, a team can only be successful if the racehorses too do the dirty work. And the pigs must never take on the work of the racehorses.

FCB reached the very highest level of German basketball at an early stage, but returning to the top turned into a long-distance race. The championship wins in 1954 and 1955 were followed by decades of mediocrity. Head of department Klaus Schulz, once FCBB's best player, led the team back to the first division in 1987. Then the club ended its support, and the team plummeted down to the third division. Support returned under club president Uli Hoeness, with the approval of 75 per cent of the club members questioned. In 2011 the team returned to the top division, and in 2014 under the legendary trainer Svetislav Pešić gained the first of four championship titles. Big matches in the Euro League, in which FCB was the first German team to reach the playoffs in 2021 and 2022, have been held since October 2024 in the new SAP Garden, whereas most first-division matches are still played in the BMW Park. In both of these arenas, the basketballers are a big draw for Munich spectators. "The identity that has evolved", says managing director Marko Pešić, "appeals to the city."

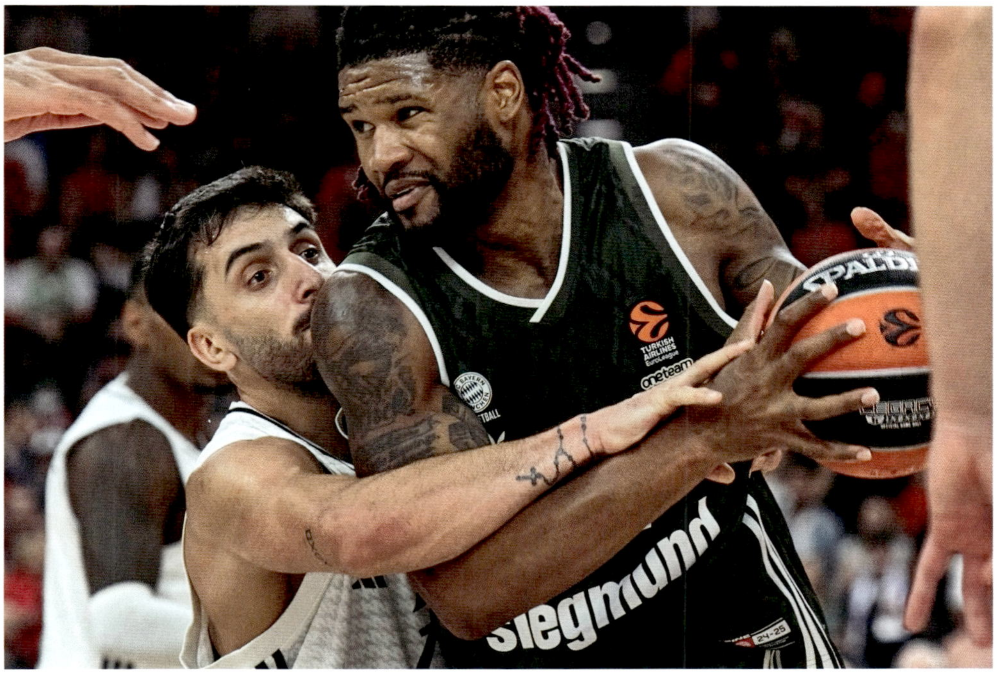

In the best game in world championship history, the sensational 113-111 victory of the German team against the USA in 2023, he was the best player: Andi Obst (left, launching himself at the basket in the 97-89 against Real Madrid at the start of the 2024 Euro League). "He shoots incredibly well," warned LeBron James, the best scorer in NBA history before the US Olympic triumph in 2024: "You always have to know where he is." The fans know where: at FC Bayern.

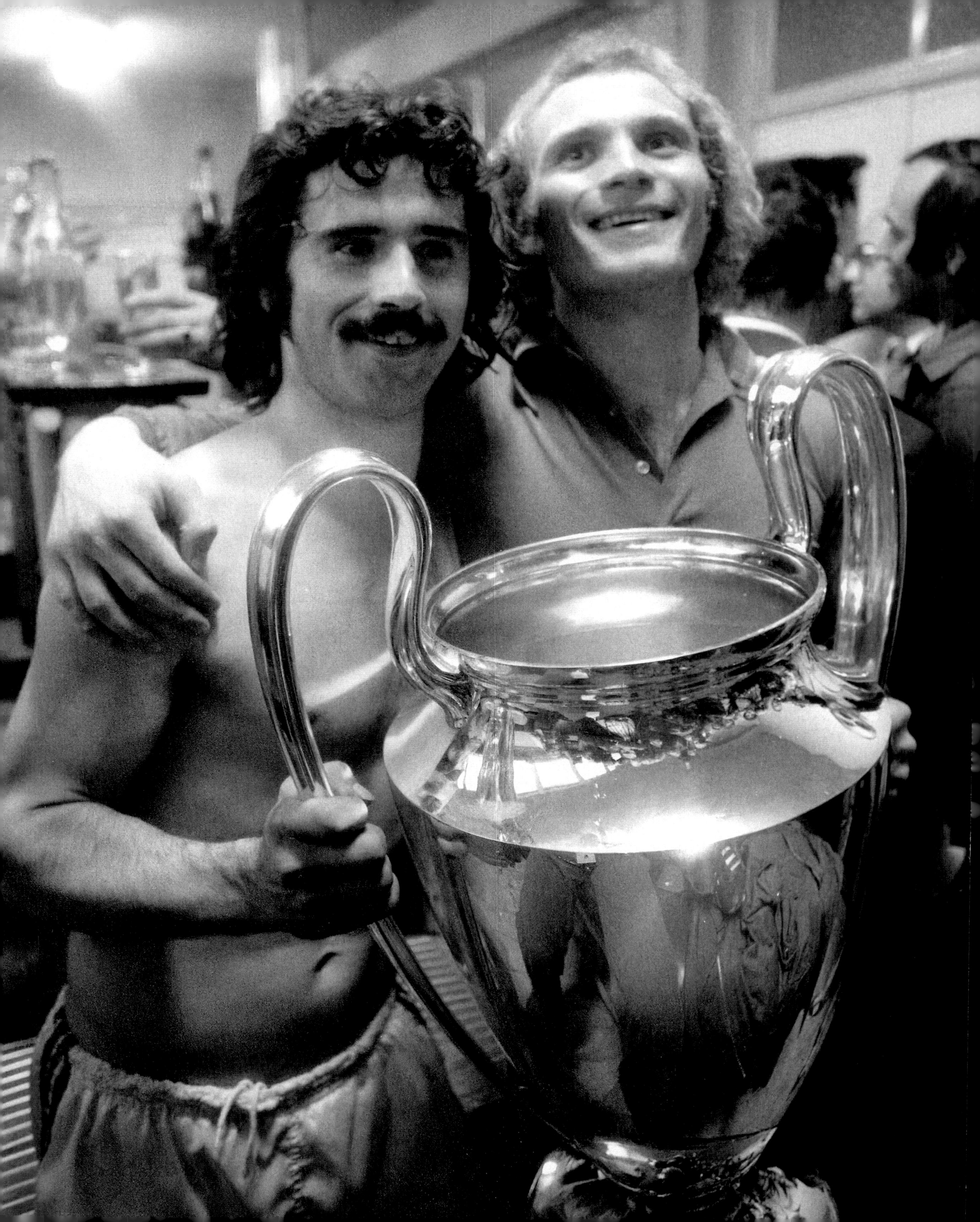

FROM FRONT MAN **TO ATTACK DEPARTMENT**

It was the late 1970s, and both were in trouble: FC Bayern and Uli Hoeness. For Bayern the team was in revolt, for Hoeness it was the knee. Thus, largely by chance, the two came together – creating a historic win-win situation that continues to this day.

When Hoeness was just 23, his cartilage was already damaged, and after that he was "never really free of pain". At 27, now in Nuremberg, he faced a choice: undergo a risky operation, or hang up his boots. He took the doctors' advice and opted out of the operation. But now he needed a job, as his earnings from a few years in professional football would not last until retirement age. Then he got a call from club president Wilhelm Neudecker, offering him the position of Bayern manager. "He wanted me as a buffer," says Hoeness today. "It was my good fortune not to arrive until after the revolution" – by means of which the striking team wanted to keep out Max Merkel as coach. When Hoeness arrived in Munich, Neudecker had already disappeared. Had the job as manager vanished too? Willi O. Hoffmann, Neudecker's successor, reassured him: "We'll do it."

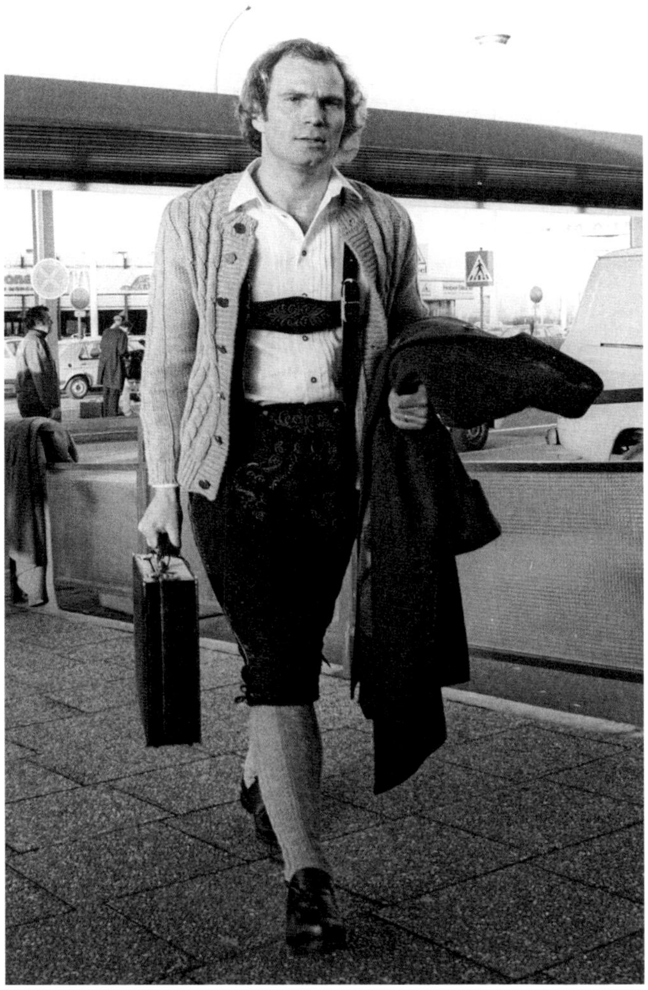

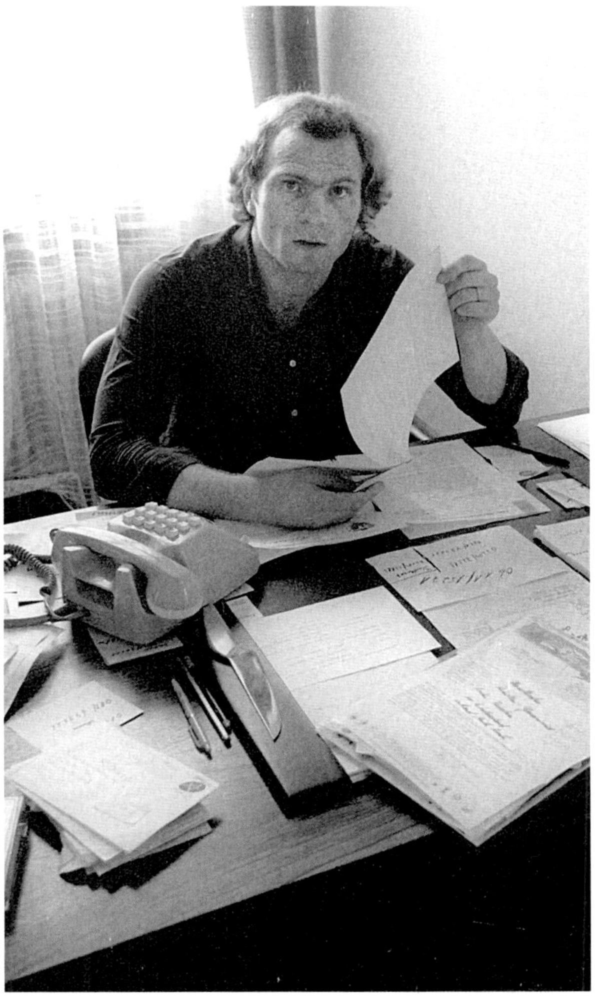

They were the "attack department": Uli Hoeness and Gerd Müller, who scored all four goals in the replay of the final against Atlético and then beamed with joy as they held the trophy in Brussels in 1974. For Hoeness it was "the happiest day", a day when "I would have liked time to stand still." But time has more stamina than even the fittest footballer. It runs on and on, tirelessly. And a mere five years later, Hoeness was no longer a player but the manager, flying to all points of the compass to find good players, helping his team members out of difficulties countless times - and squaring up to anyone who challenged his FCB: the legendary "attack department".

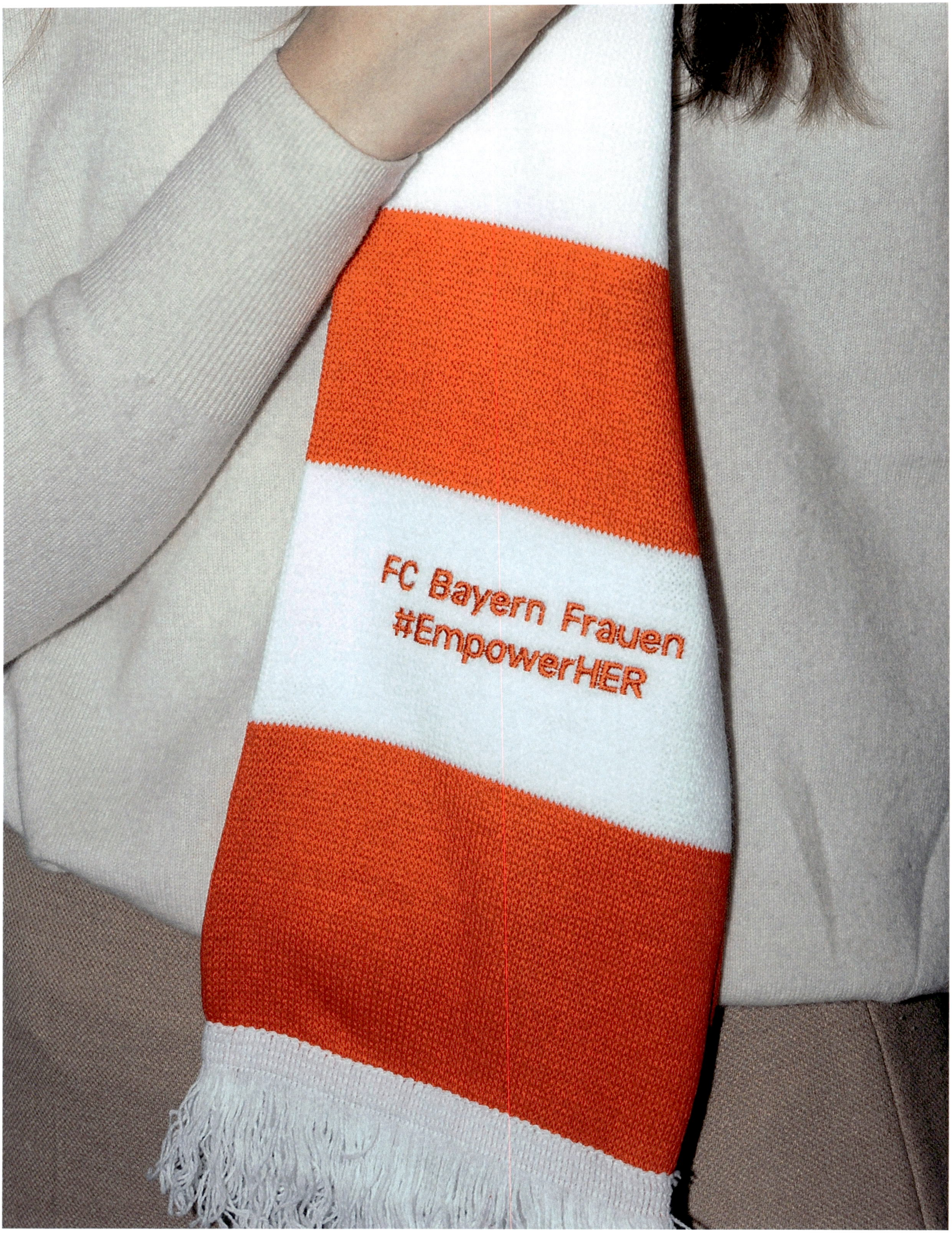
FC Bayern Frauen
#EmpowerHER

WOMEN WITH POWER
FULL SPEED AHEAD

Pep Guardiola was astonished when he arrived at FCB – because the players trained in public. He put one training ground under wraps with a screen and was considered the originator of "secret training" in German football. But this existed much earlier: with Bayern's women footballers.

Back then, in 1970, it was so secret that hardly anyone knew about it: the first women's team at FCB. Because the German football association DFB still prohibited women's football. However, the end of this backward-looking rule was in sight, and FC Bayern was prepared – and thus was the only Bundesliga club that had a women's team from the very start. Karl-Heinz Mainz, coach of the amateurs, took on the job of setting it up in good time. For three months, training took place quietly. The debut match resulted in a 7–1 win against SV Olching, and predictable comments. The newspaper *Bild* reported about "kicking Amazons", who served up "a plain footballing diet" along with "grace and bosoms". Yet this diet satisfied their hunger for goals. In a first season of competitive games, the FCB women scored 114 times in fourteen matches. The pinnacle of these pioneering years was winning the German championship in 1976 after beating TB Berlin 4–2 in the final. However, decades passed before they took the title again – partly thanks to Franz Beckenbauer.

After the national team was knocked out only narrowly at the World Cup in 1999 against the hosts, USA, the club president, impressed by the quality of women's football, increased the budget for the Bayern women to DM 300,000, five times its previous level. In 2000 the team returned to the Bundesliga, gained a place in the Champions League in 2008, won the German cup in 2012, and celebrated winning the championship in 2015. In 2024 the women became German champions for the sixth time – whereas the men, for once, brought no trophy home. You could say that they had emancipated themselves. The days when they had to conceal themselves, as their predecessors did, are long gone. The power of the FCB women ceased to be a secret many years ago.

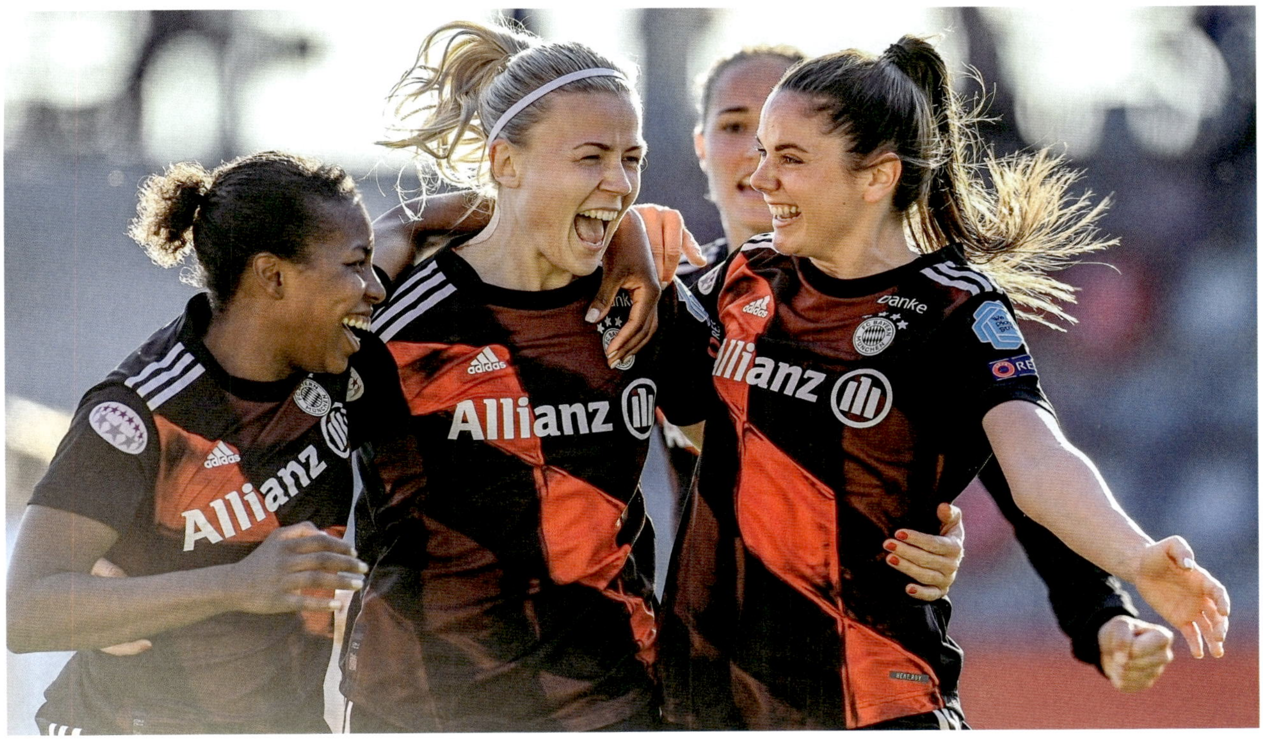

The FC Bayern women are a force to be reckoned with in football: for almost two years, from October 2022 until October 2024, the championship-winning team led by captain Glódís Perla Viggósdóttir (centre) was undefeated in the Bundesliga for forty-four matches in succession.

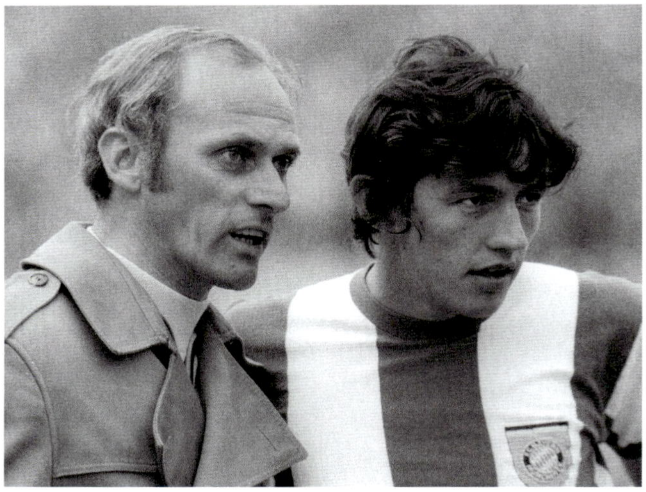

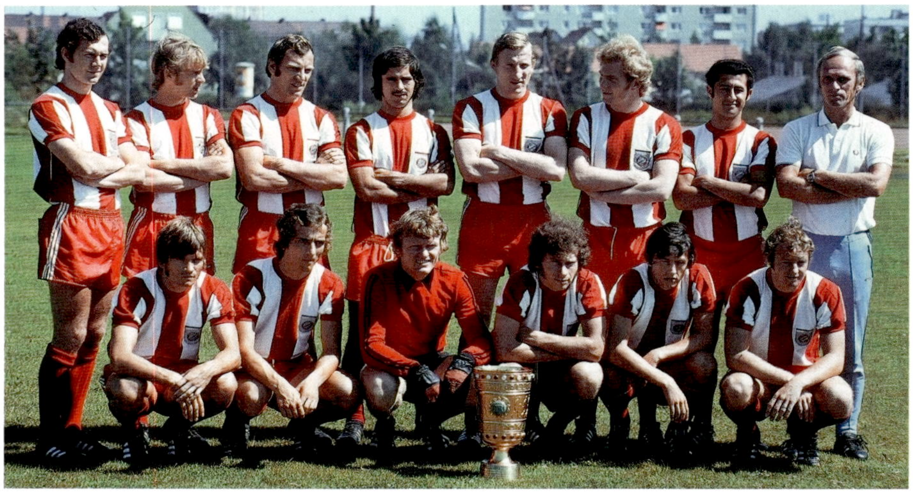

HAMMER-EDE SMASHES IT IN **AND IS A CUP-FINAL HERO**

When Udo Lattek became coach at Bayern in 1970, he brought talented players from the German youth teams with him: Paul Breitner, Uli Hoeness – and Edgar Schneider. The last named did not win a World Cup or European Cup like those two others, but he did become the first cup-winning hero for the Bayern team. In the 1971 final against 1. FC Köln, the situation was not looking good: a goal down early on, Beckenbauer's equaliser, Herward Koppenhöfer sent off after a revenge foul, and one man short for almost fifty minutes – until Schneider, brought on as a substitute in the 118th minute, showed why his nickname was "Hammer-Ede". He lashed the ball into the corner from eighteen metres. "Everyone was unbelievably happy," he recalls. Without his goal there would have been a replay, "and everyone just wanted to go on holiday". It was Lattek's first title. From then on, he hugged Schneider, "my first cup-winner", whenever he saw him. In 1973 Hammer-Ede moved to FC Augsburg and the second division, and after that played for VfB Pforzheim as an amateur in his home town. In 1986 FCB sent its cup-final hero into his retirement from football with a farewell match there.

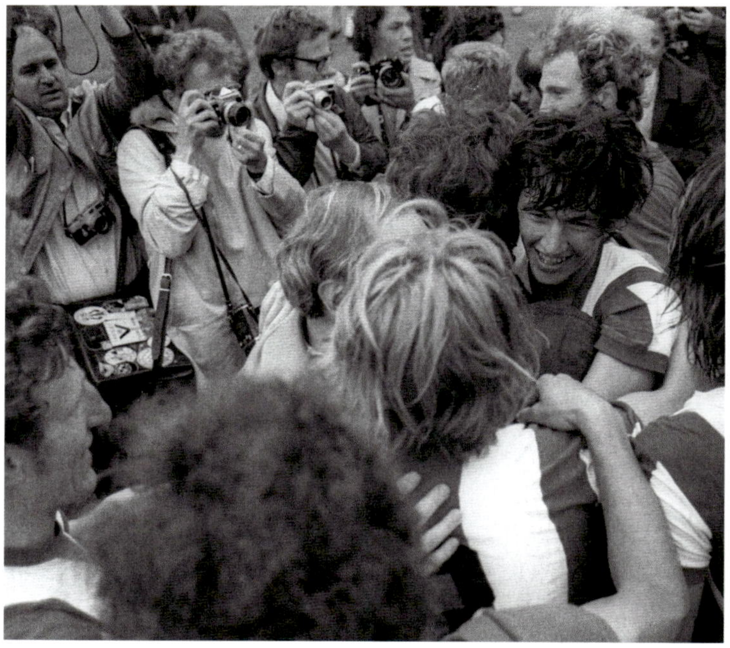

Tips from the coach Lattek before going on as a substitute (above); hugs from teammates after the win (below right). Edgar Schneider's winning goal in between came out of the blue, and no photographer was able to capture it.

A TURBAN GOAL **IN A CUP THRILLER**

1982 was Dieter Hoeness's "best year", not only for winning the cup. He scored two "goals of the month" - not with his head, but on the volley after taking the ball on his chest.

What must be FCB's most spectacular cup-final win owes its continuing popularity to a piece of headwear that did not adequately fulfil its purpose – the bloody "turban" of Dieter Hoeness, who fearlessly rose to head the ball in a 4–2 victory against Nürnberg 1982.

"In a normal match I would have left the field", he says today. "But it was a cup final, and you have so much adrenaline that you don't notice the pain." After a collision early on, a plaster was stuck on, then a bandage, then at half-time four or five stitches without anaesthetic, and a new bandage – and the turban passed into German football folklore. With this bloody headdress Hoeness set up two goals, after going into half-time 0–2 down, then scored the final goal for 4–2 himself – all of this with his head. He worried only at the thought of his wife, who was in the last stages of pregnancy, watching on television, "where the whole thing looked much more dramatic". Everything went well, however. Eleven days later Sebastian, now one of the top coaches in the Bundesliga, was born. And his father is a little bit proud of the turban story: "Next to the business side and all the show, first and foremost it's pure football that counts – showing unconditional commitment for the team."

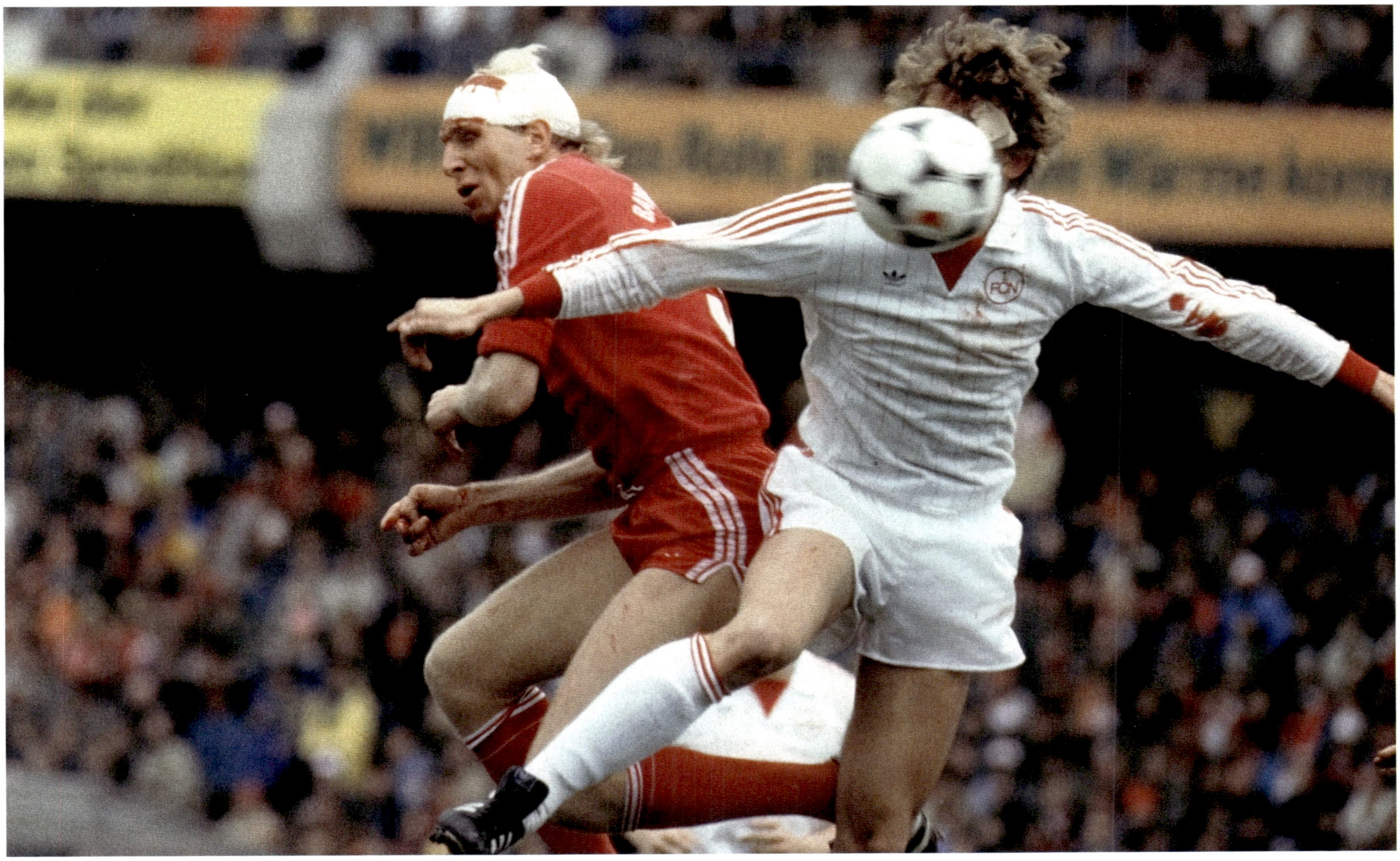

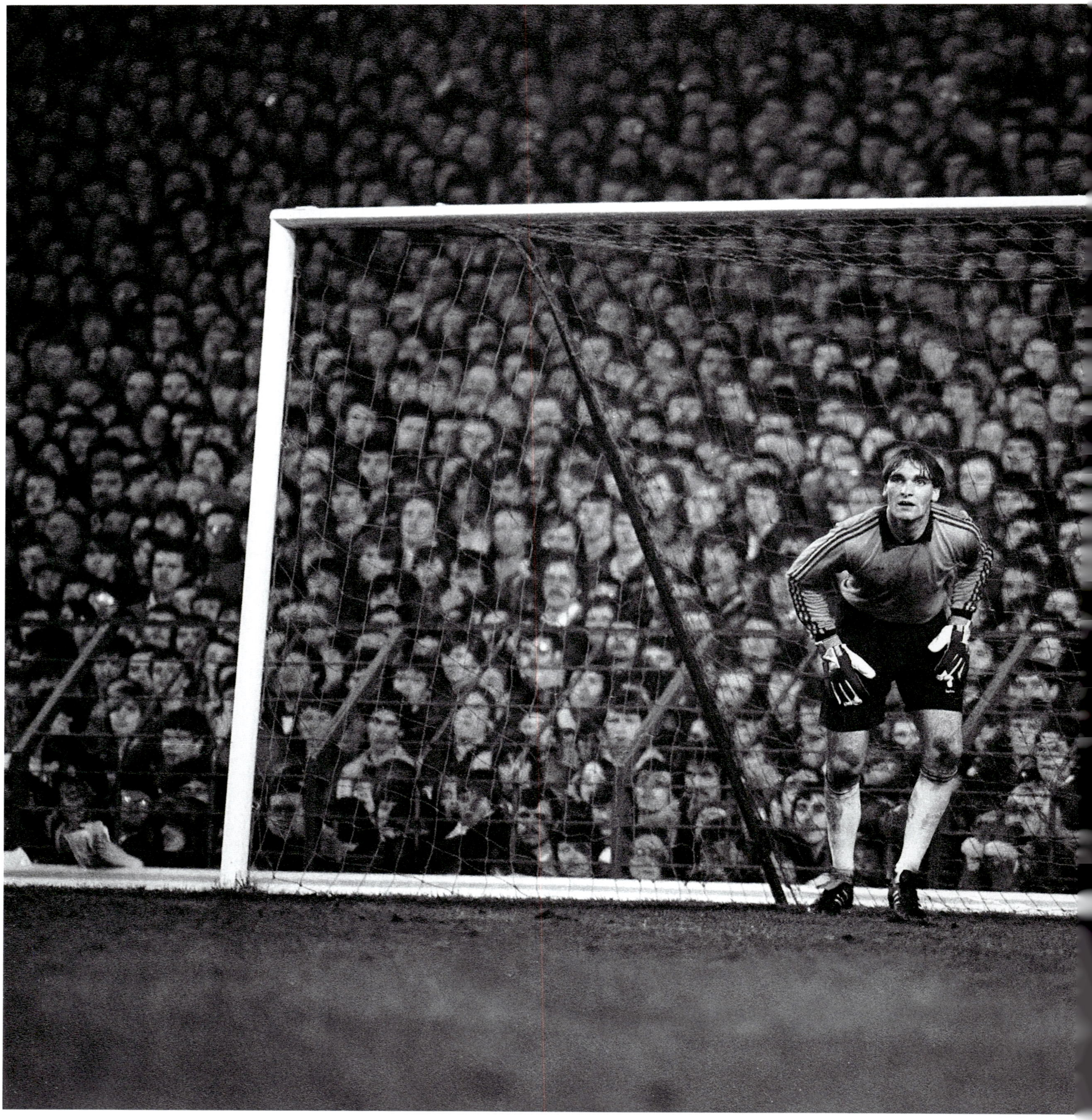

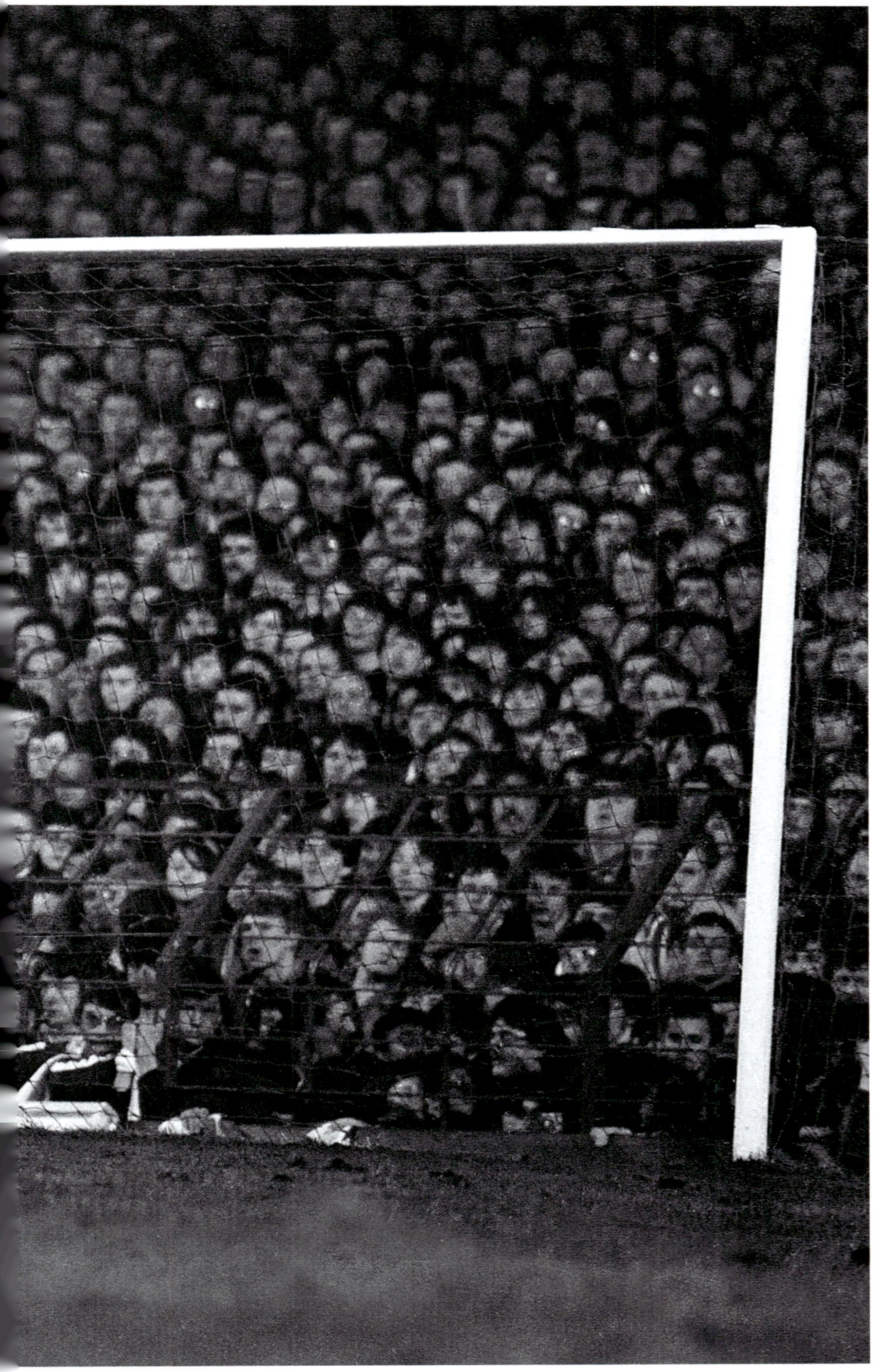

YOU'LL **NEVER** KEEP **ALONE**

Walter Junghans in front of the legendary Kop in Liverpool – this famous photo hangs on the wall in the FCB offices as a print two metres wide. On 8 April 1981, in the semi-final first leg of the European Cup (it finished 0–0, the second leg in Munich 1–1), Hans Rauchensteiner was sitting behind the Bayern goal and keeper Junghans, but from there could not shoot the photo that he envisioned. So he crept to the trainers' benches, where the angle was right. The three minutes that he had until the stewards chased him away sufficed for an iconic football photo. Forty years later, this great sports photographer died while on the job in the Allianz Arena, immediately after FC Bayern's 4–2 win against Borussia Dortmund.

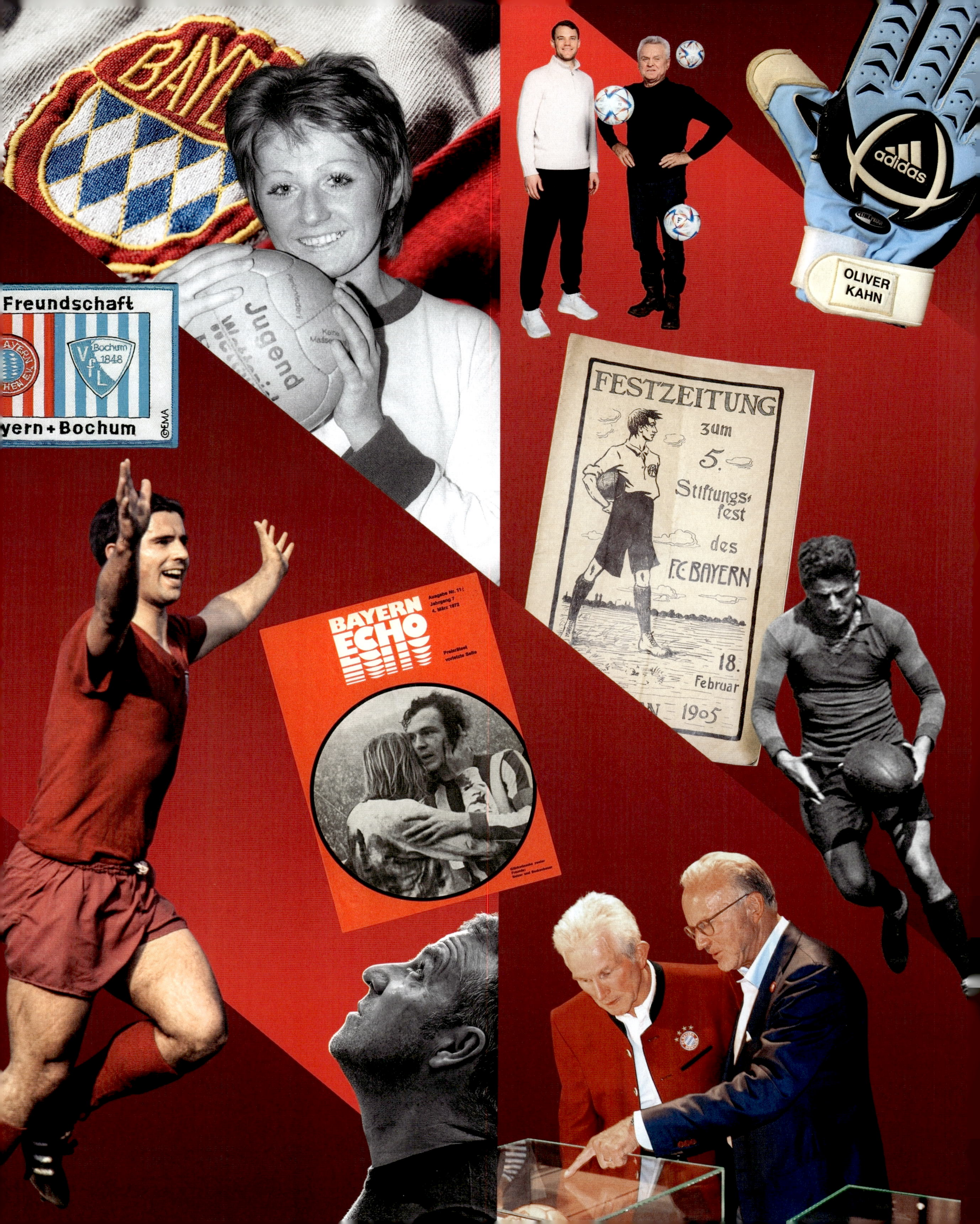
Freundschaft
Bochum 1848
VfL
Jugend
adidas
OLIVER
KAHN
FESTZEITUNG
zum
5.
Stiftungs-
fest
des
F.C. BAYERN
18.
Februar
1905
BAYERN
ECHO

TRADITION

Tradition does not mean that everything used to be better. Tradition means that many things are just as good today. In other words: tradition is yesterday's progress. And today it can still work very well.

125 YEARS **TRADITION**

For a club like FC Bayern, 125 years old and therefore what is called a "club with tradition", one of the most important tasks is to strike a balance between the necessity of modernising of methods and the possibility of maintaining values. Maintaining what constitutes the identity of the club, without standing in the way of its development.

In this balancing act, FC Bayern has always been highly agile, highly accomplished in trying out what is new while retaining the old – not least in the tradition of involving former players in the work of the club at a later date. This is one reason why many who have experienced the club from inside describe it as "like a family". Alongside visible elements that are part of Bayern folklore and its representation to the outside world – lederhosen, visits to the Oktoberfest, showers of wheat beer – this family feeling includes the frequently unseen tradition of giving help to former players and employees in need. But also to rivals, for example matches played for traditional clubs that have fallen on hard times.

At the same time, every competition is determined by the survival of the fittest. Especially in professional football, which is always about performance, about visible, verifiable achievement – every week, every day in training under the eyes of the coach, every match day in the eyes of the rest of the world. FCB has always looked for players who not only stand up to this permanent pressure, but also want it. It is this tradition of choosing people, looking for winners, that explains another tradition, that of winning when under pressure. This is evident historically in, for example, the fact that FC Bayern won every single major final when the club reached that final for the first time: in 1932 the German championship, in 1957 the German cup, in 1966 the European Cup Winners' Cup, in 1974 the European Cup, in 1976 the World Super Cup, in 1996 the UEFA Cup, in 2013 the FIFA Club World Cup. Of course, great triumphs were followed by major defeats, and this is where part two of the Bayern tradition of winning takes effect – namely of learning from defeat. The threefold principle that derives from this is the mother of all sporting traditions for Bayern. Those who arrive at Säbener Strasse soon learn it. The short version is: 1 Win. 2. Don't lose. 3. If no. 2 fails to happen, back to no. 1.

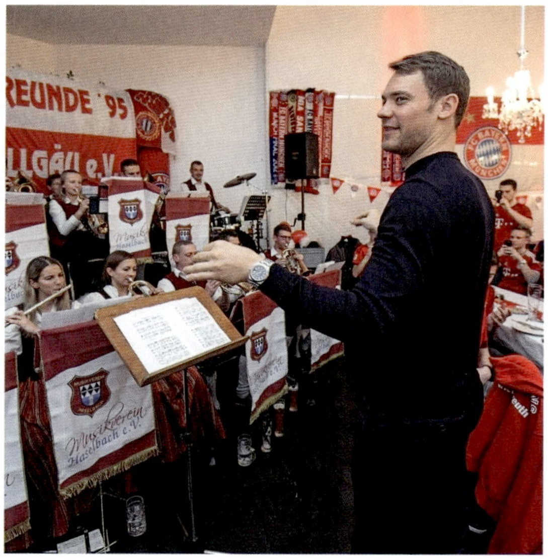

A modern club keeps up traditions – not only the ones inherited from grandfathers, but also those that it creates itself, such as the custom, extremely popular since 1985, of visits to fan clubs by the football stars at Christmastime (here with Manuel Neuer conducting music in the Allgäu). These are traditions that will be inherited one day by grandsons. Or by granddaughters, as in the tradition of women's football that FC Bayern has maintained since 1970.

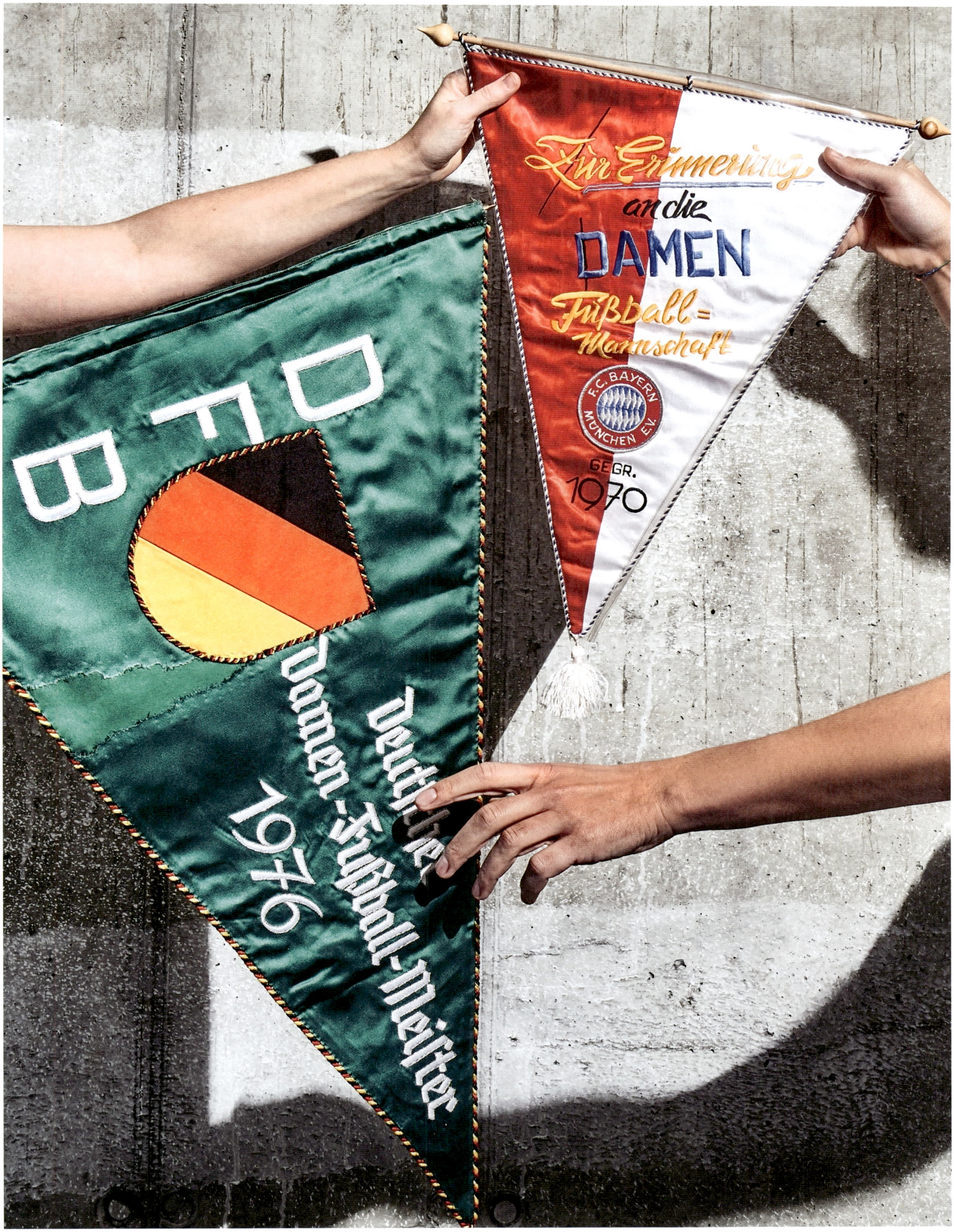

DFB
Deutscher
Damen-Fußball-Meister
1976
Zur Erinnerung
an die
DAMEN
Fußball=
Mannschaft
F.C. BAYERN MÜNCHEN E.V.
GEGR.
1970

"ONWARDS – ON AND ON AND ON!" **HSV-FCB 1-1 · 2001**

Onwards, on and on and on" was the title of episode no. 1,079 of the evergreen TV crime series *Tatort*. A real thriller – but it bears no comparison with a different run of success, with the 1,224th match that FC Bayern played in the Bundesliga. A last-second drama provided the most emotional of all titles. And Oliver Kahn immortalised his mantra of the unbending character of Bayern DNA.

Every good story needs twists and turns, and in the 2000–01 season, the Bundesliga had plenty of them. The league leadership had switched over fifteen times between six clubs – most recently on the thirty-third of thirty-four match days, when Schalke 04 was top of the table until the final minute, then conceded a goal to go 0–1 down in Stuttgart, seven seconds before Bayern took a 2–1 lead against Kaiserslautern. One newspaper called it "death in seven seconds". But the last day of the season surpassed even that. In their last match in their Park Stadium in Gelsenkirchen, Schalke won 5–3 against the relegated team from Unterhaching – and tuned in to Hamburg, hoping for assistance from the home team HSV. Bayern needed a point, having a worse goal difference. The score still stood at 0–0, and in the ninetieth minute Sergej Barbarez scored for HSV – unleashing an earthquake 350 kilometres away in Gelsenkirchen and pure horror on the Bayern bench. The players seemed to have no more to give, but Kahn pushed them forwards. Four minutes of extra time were almost over. One final pass up the field, too far forward, but the HSV keeper Mathias Schober took a back pass from Tomáš Ujfaluši with his hands – conceding an indirect free kick. Kahn couldn't stay in his goal and rushed forwards, wanting to take the free kick, but Stefan Effenberg wouldn't let him. Seventy seconds ticked by before it was taken. Ten metres from the goal, a wall of bodies stood in the way. Effenberg passed to the side, Patrik Andersson shot the ball – and it flew through the wall into the net. "I can't believe it", said Marcel Reif, the TV commentator. "That ball just cannot go in." FCB was champion again, Schalke only the "champion of hearts". The Bayern players celebrated Andersson, who had never scored in two years. They celebrated their luckiest championship win. Kahn ran to the corner and jumped at the flag. Four days later, the Champions League trophy awaited. Onwards, on and on and on.

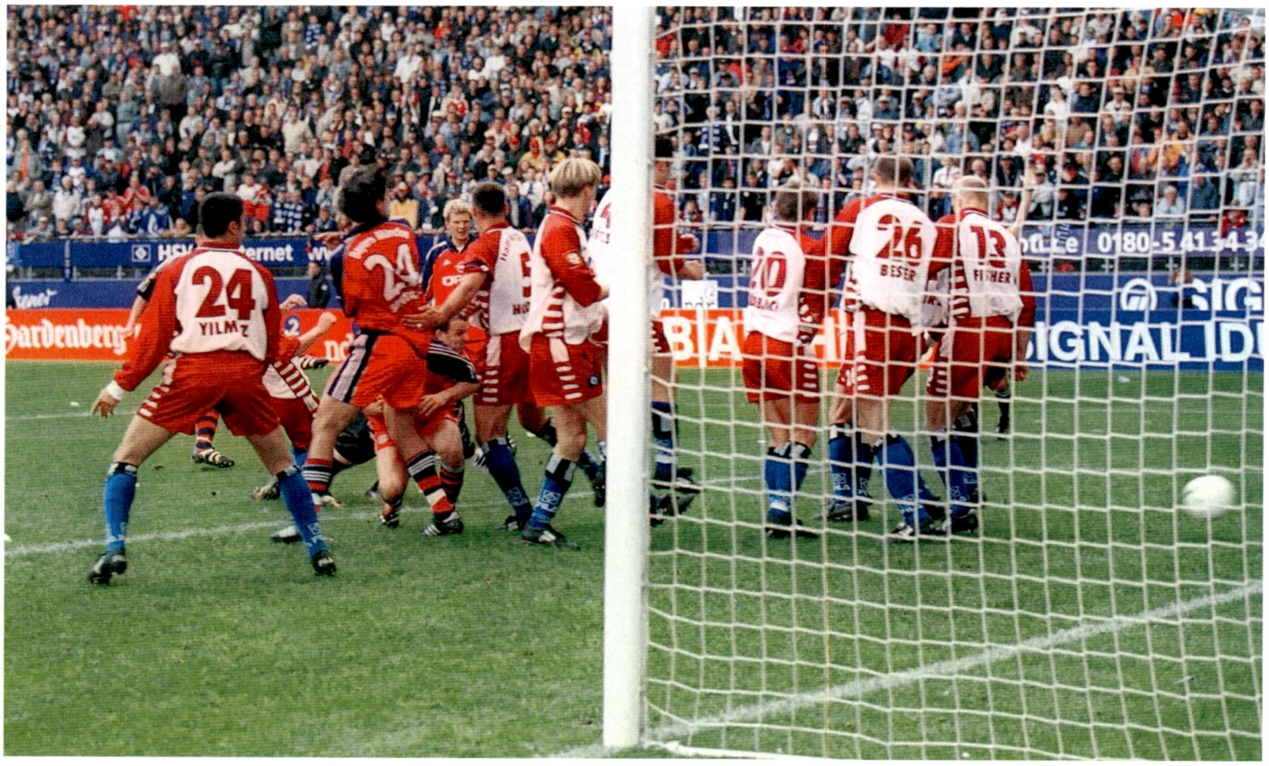

It is the moment that decides everything, with twenty-one players crammed into a small space, but where is the ball? On its path into the goal, even though almost nobody can see that. At a speed of 120 kilometres per hour it will smash into the net, between the outside man in the Hamburg wall, Andreas Fischer (no. 13), and the post, only three-tenths of a second after Patrik Andersson has hit it. Because at the moment when it was kicked, the Hamburg team instinctively hopped forwards, opening up the tiny, decisive gap.

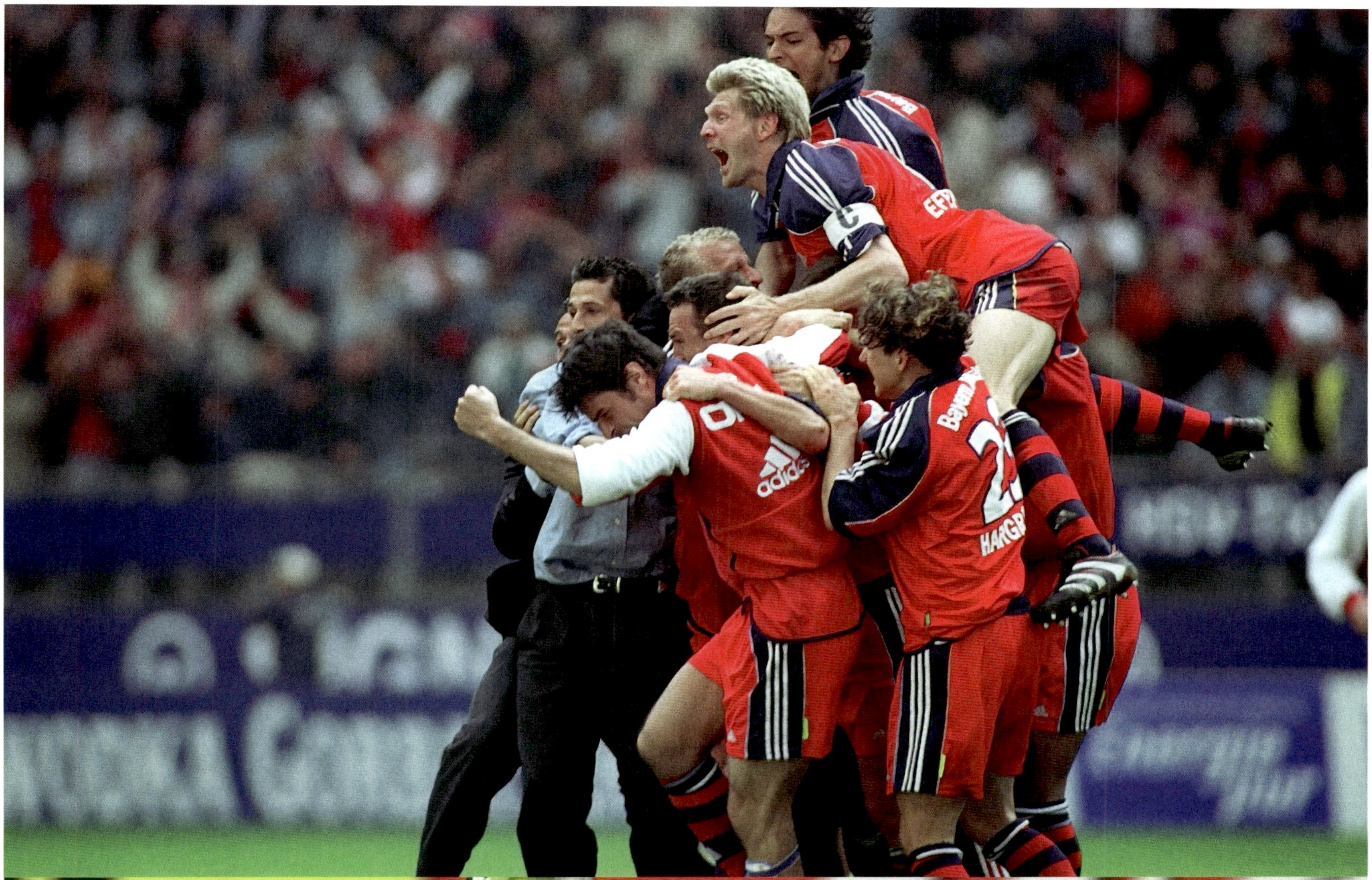
adidas

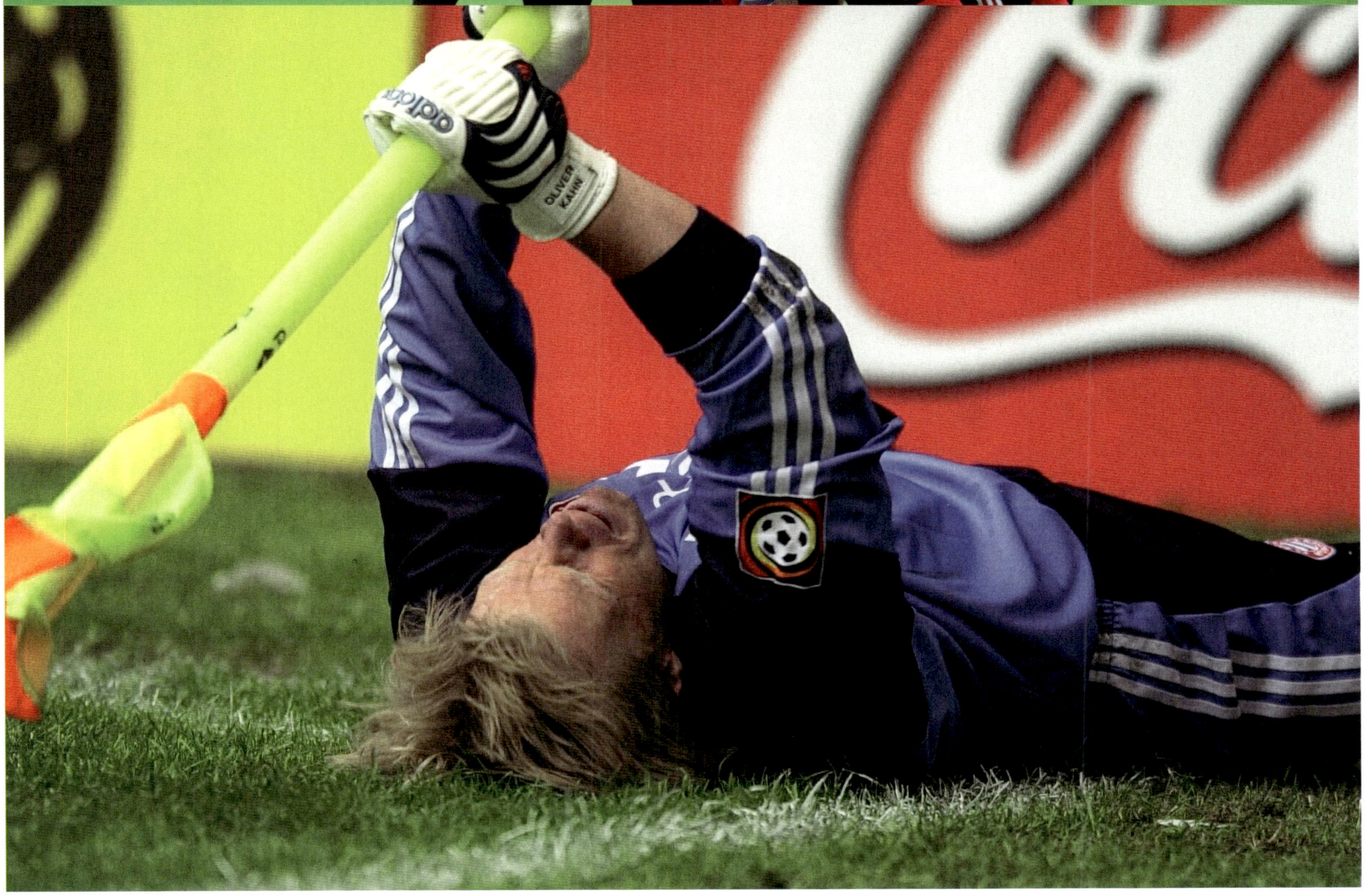

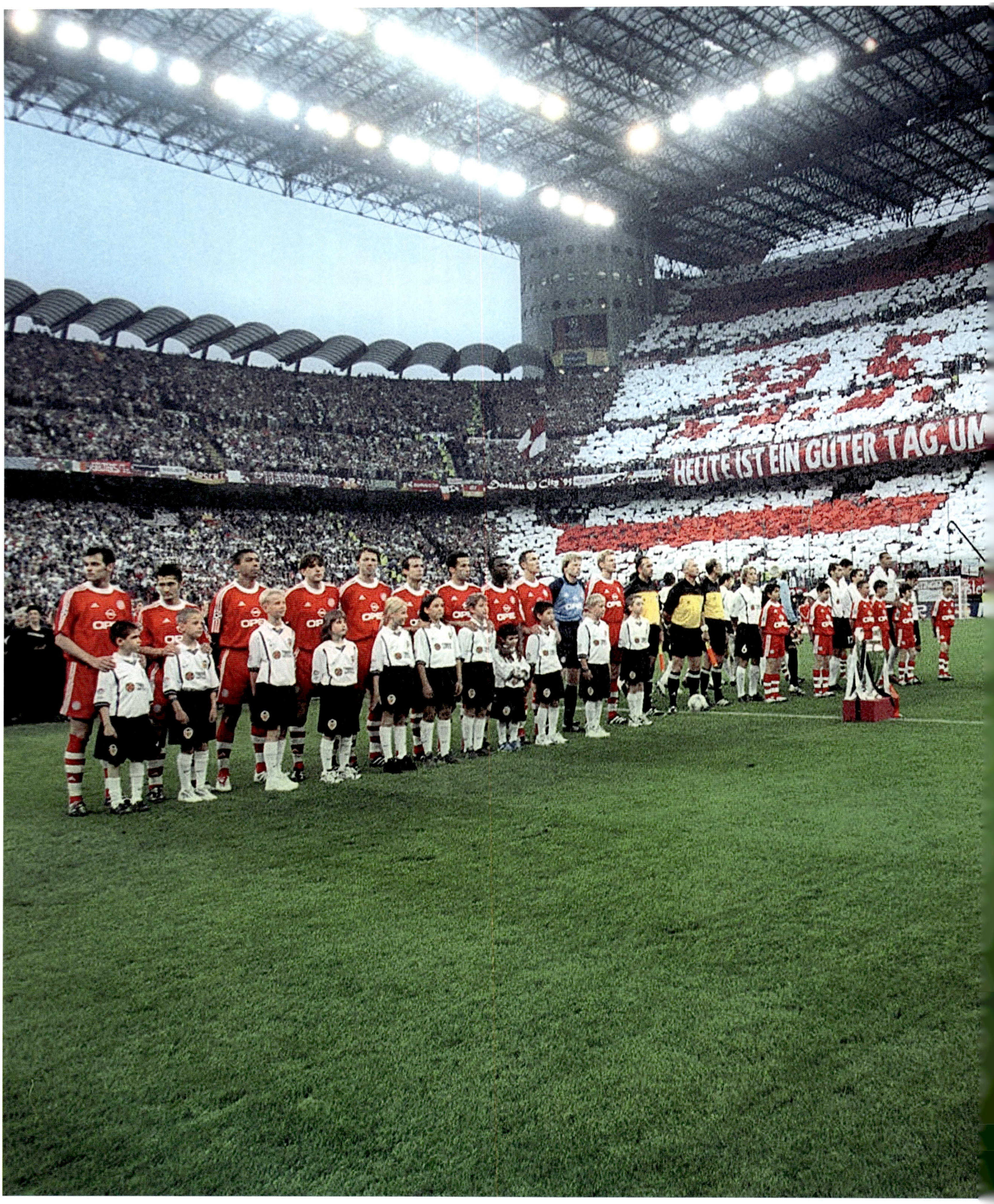
HEUTE IST EIN GUTER TAG,UM

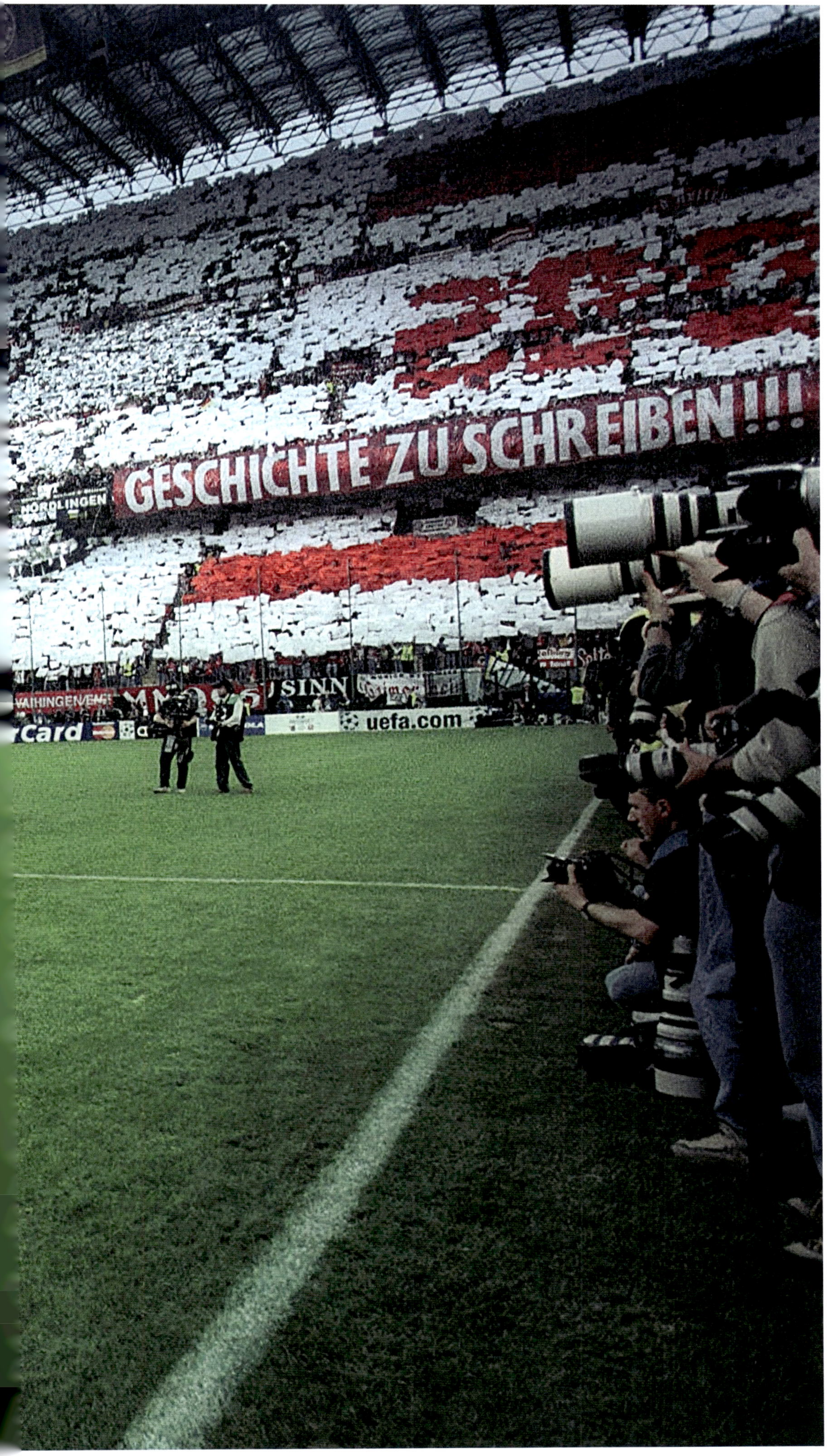

TODAY **IS A** GOOD **DAY**

In the end the twenty-third of May 2001 really was a "good day to make history", as the banner proclaims. When Oliver Kahn's third save in the penalty shoot-out against FC Valencia put an end to a quarter-century without winning that trophy with the handles, part of the triumph was the tifo display which Gregor Weinreich from Club No. 12 sketched with a felt-tip pen and a copied photo of the stand, and which 20,000 fans holding sheets of paper put together in the San Siro. "We wanted to give the team one final push when they ran in," said Weinreich. With success. "The sight of it made us all feel proud," said coach Ottmar Hitzfeld. "The fans go through ups and downs with their club, and moments like that are moments for eternity. The banner, the message, all of that created a connection that was almost magic."

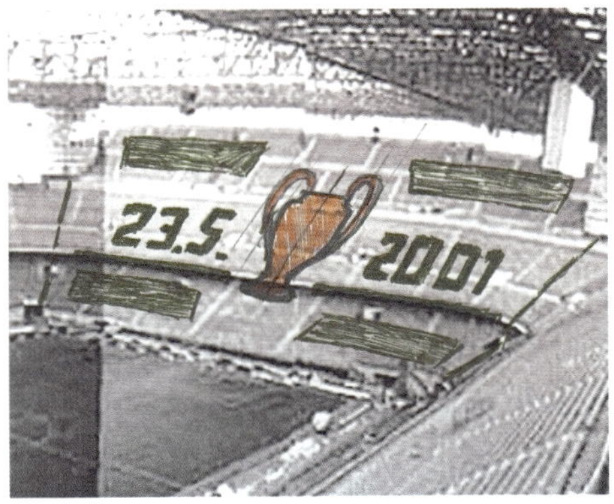

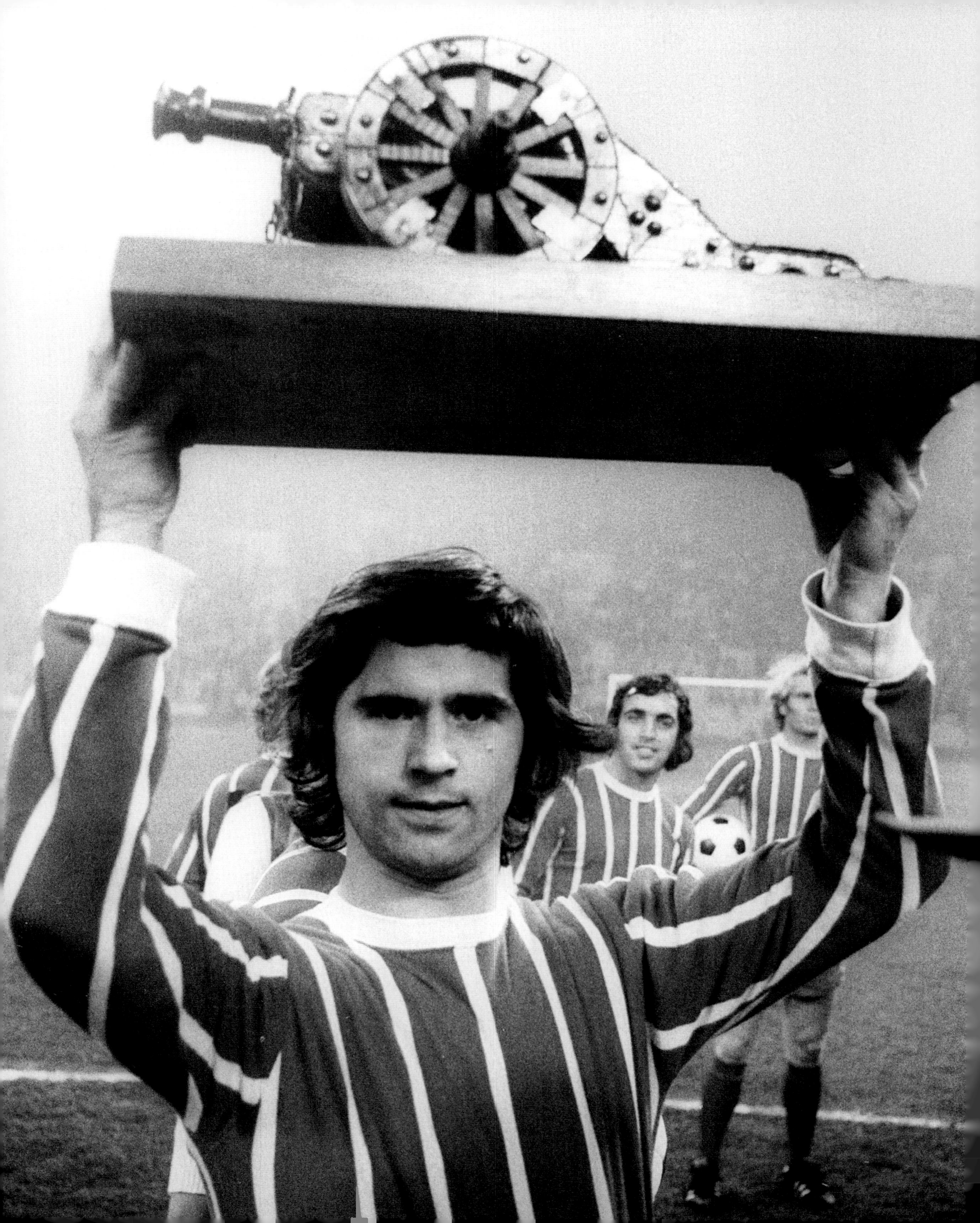

GERD MÜLLER & THE CANNONS: **THEN IT GOES BOOM**

When Gerd Müller made his debut as a singer in 1969, he described what he could do better than anyone else in German football: "Then it goes boom, yes, and then there's a bang." With 365 goals in the Bundesliga and seven Golden Cannons as top scorer, his achievement remains unequalled.

The cover of the vinyl single shows him with a crown, sceptre and royal cloak. To match the sound that the chorus of the hit song reproduced, the magazine *Kicker* has awarded a Golden Cannon (*Torschützenkanone*) to the top scorer, the "goal king", since 1966, the season when Bayern made their debut in the Bundesliga. No one won it more often than the diminutive, powerful forward from Nördlingen. When he first appeared at Säbener Strasse, the coach Čik Čajkovski called out: "What am I supposed to do with a weight-lifter?" Müller gave the answer on the pitch. In only his second season in the Bundesliga he won the cannon at the age of 21, to this day the youngest holder of the award. FC Bayern has provided the leading scorer twenty-two times: Gerd Müller seven times, Robert Lewandowski six times, Karl-Heinz Rummenigge three times, Roland Wohlfarth twice. It has been won once each by Giovane Élber, Luca Toni, Mario Gómez and, with thirty-six goals in his debut season of 2023–24, Harry Kane – the first German king to come from England.

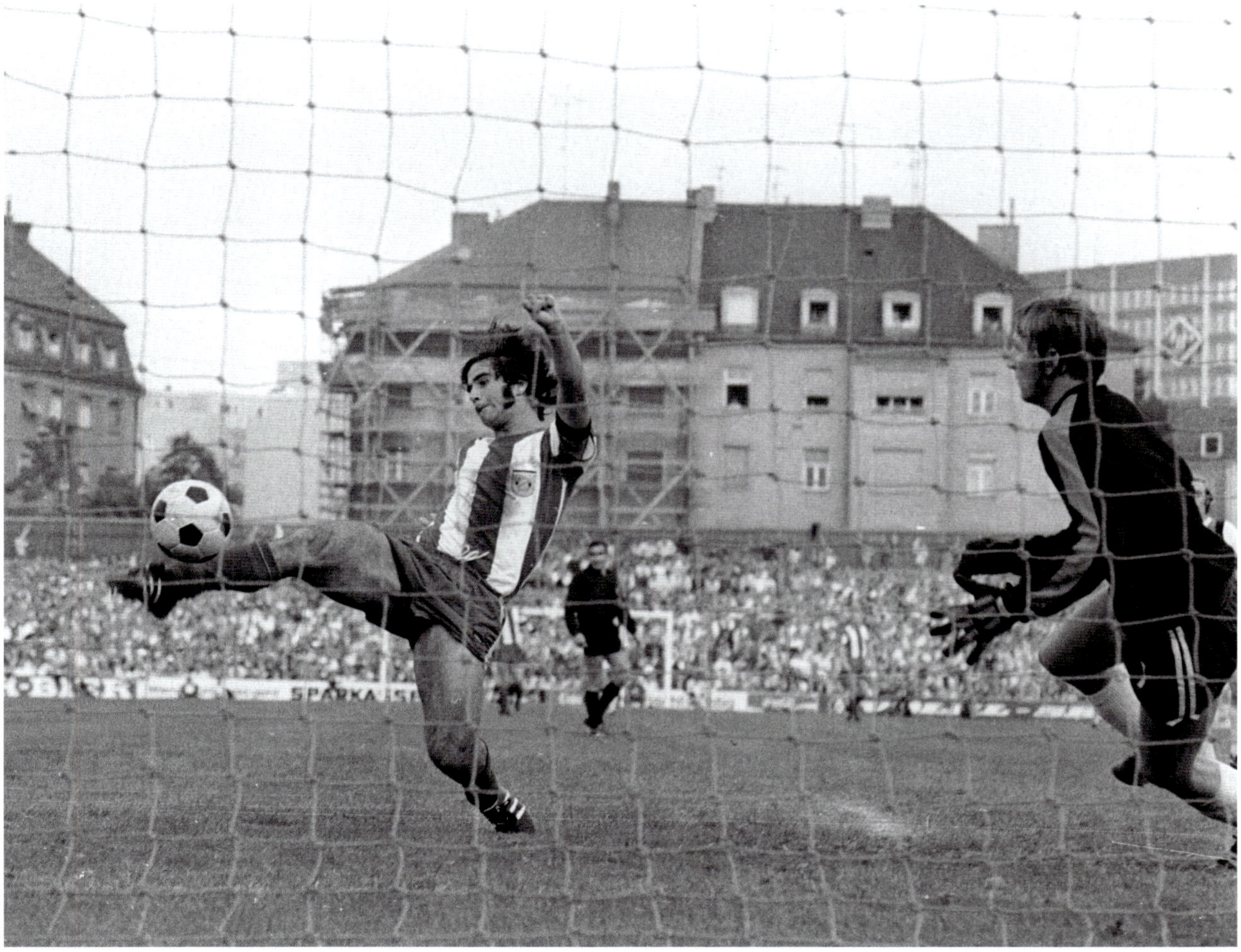

Two months after the 1970 World Cup in Mexico, where, after netting the ball thirty-eight times in the Bundesliga season, Gerd Müller became top scorer with ten goals in five games and became a global star, he presented himself back home again, as goal-hungry as ever. Inimitably, on 19 September 1970 he scored in the Grünwalder Stadium for a 2-1 lead against Borussia Mönchengladbach, the German champions - though his rival goal-getter Jupp Heynckes was to hit an equaliser in the 90th minute.

OUR FIRST PLAYER IN **THE NATIONAL TEAM**

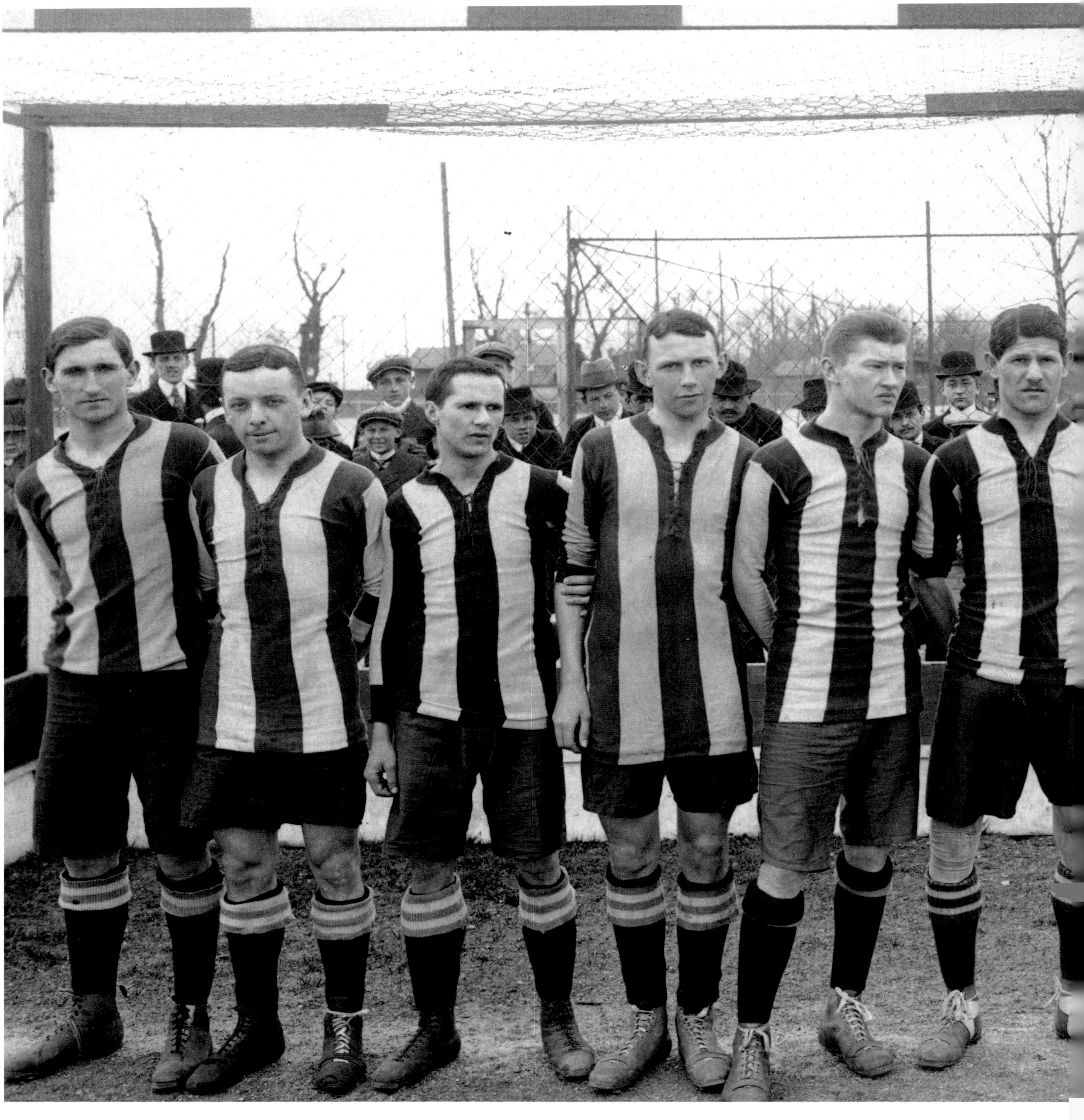

"Gaberl" - that was the name given to the first man from FC Bayern who played for Germany. In the team photo of FCB, local league champion in 1911, he is on the far left. On the pitch he played on the other wing. He made his debut for Germany in 1910 against Belgium, and the 0-3 scoreline was not the fault of the speedy right-winger, but due to the fact that the match was played one day after the final of the German championship between Karlsruher FV and Holstein Kiel. Without the players from the two teams in that final, the German side had to make up its numbers by recruiting four volunteers from among the spectators. Max Gablonsky's second international went better, and he scored in the 6-2 result against Switzerland - though it took the German football association a hundred years to credit the goal to him. Only then did he officially become the first scorer for Germany from FCB.

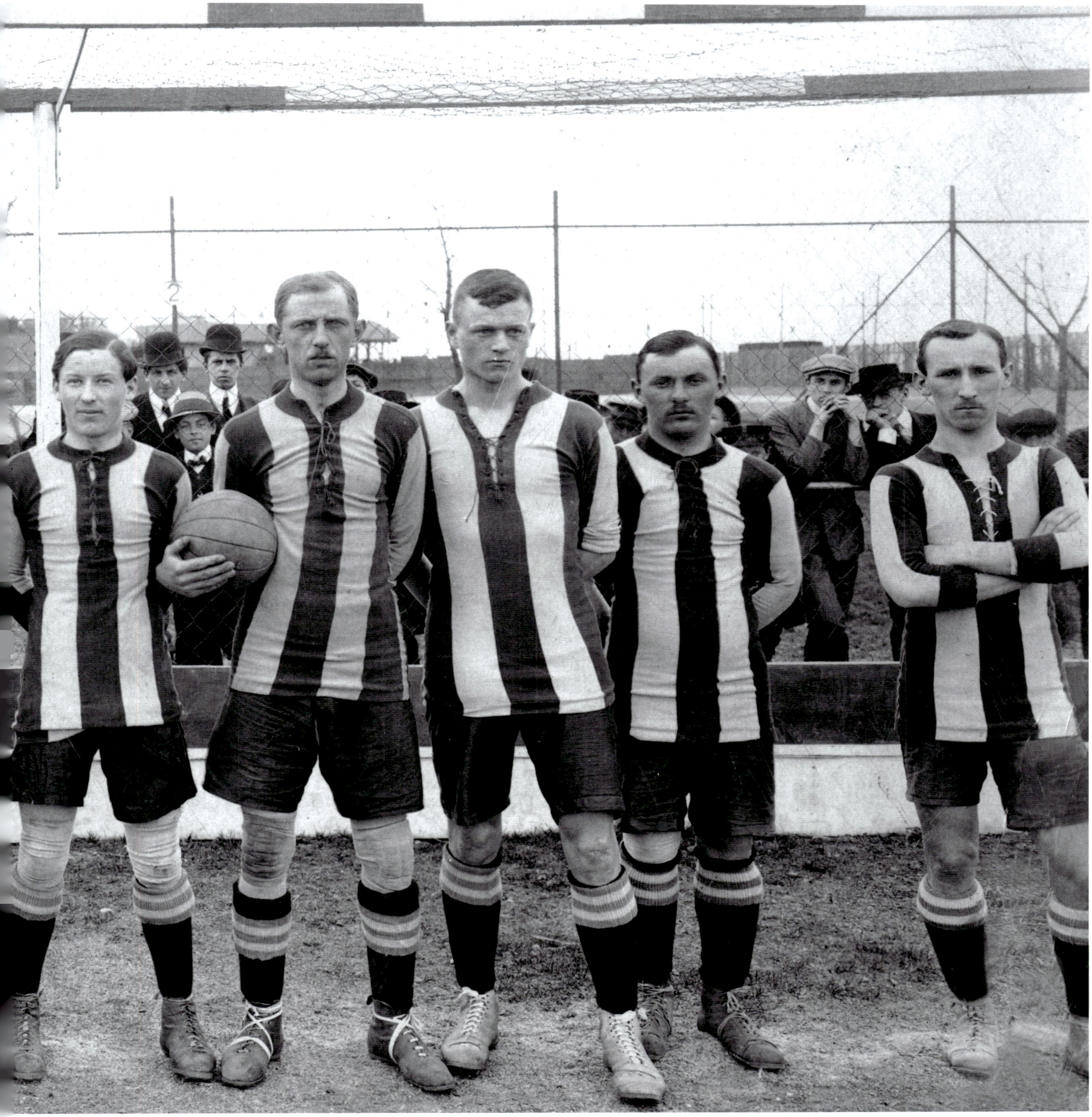

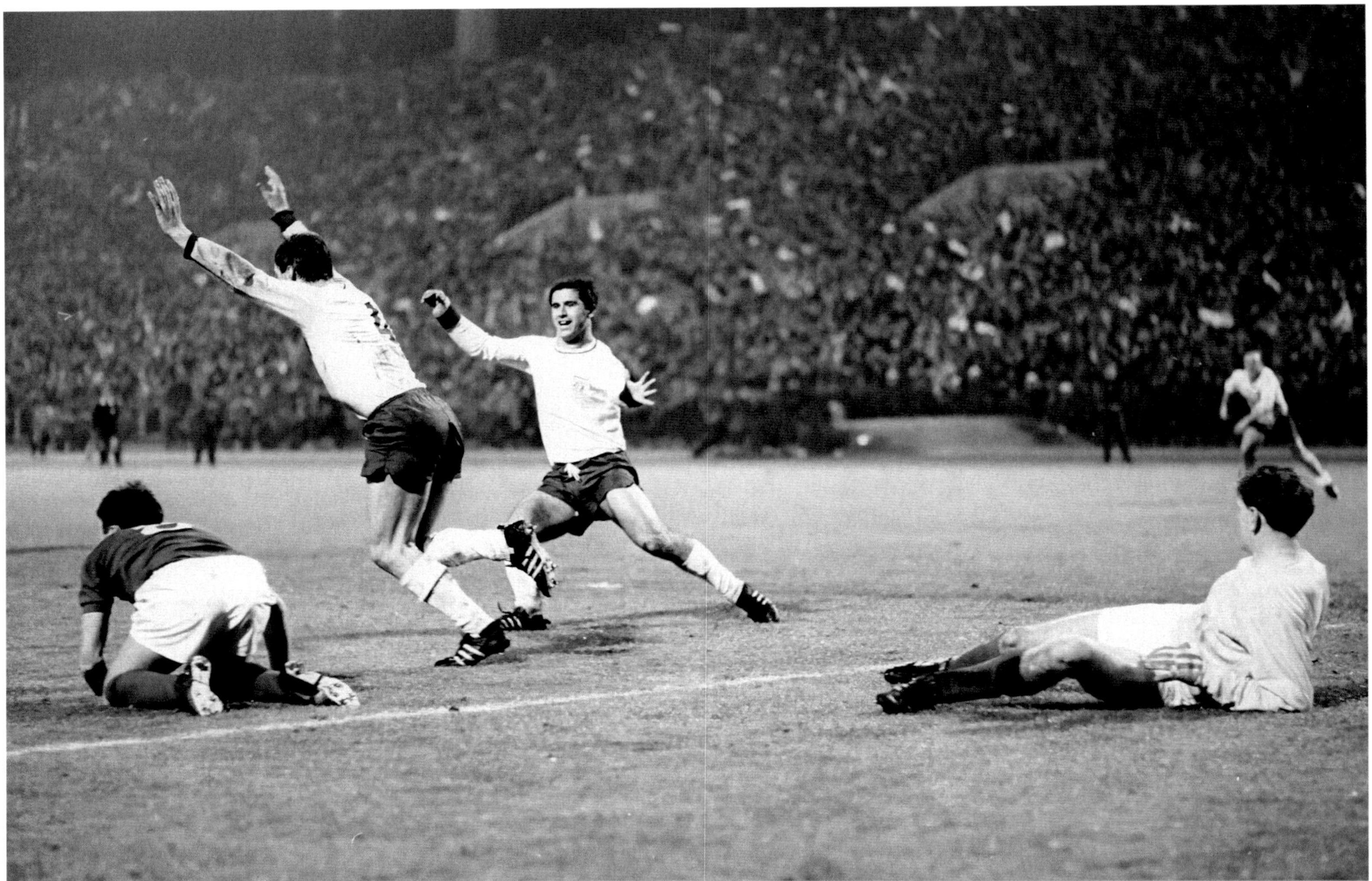

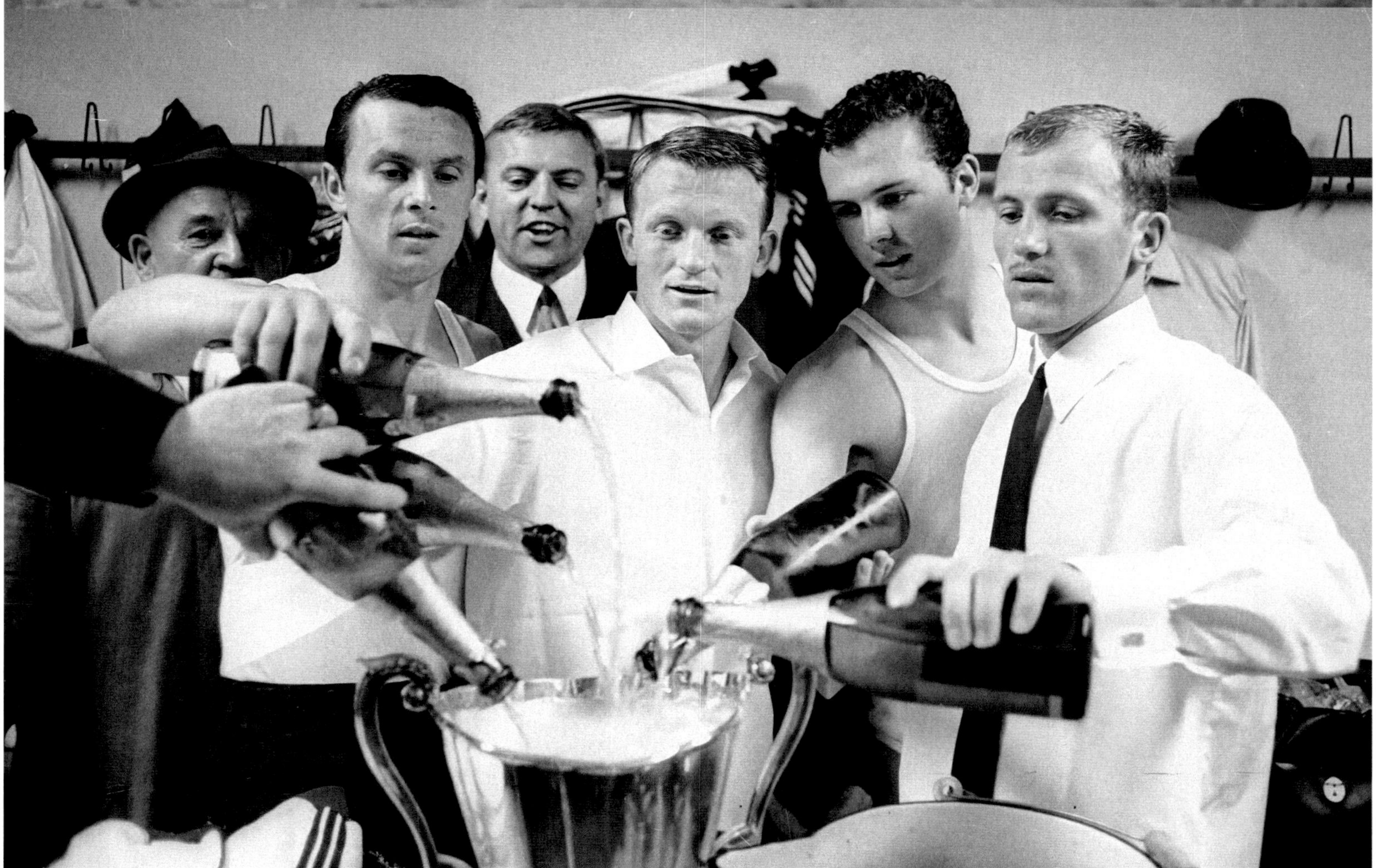

THE START OF AN ERA
FCB-RANGERS 1-0 · 1967

Just as it was thirty-five years earlier, when Bayern Munich won the championship for the first time, on 31 May 1967 tens of thousands made the pilgrimage from Munich to Nuremberg, and Bavaria took firm possession of the Frankenstadion, the stadium of Franconia. Once again, the journey was worthwhile. In pouring rain the fans witnessed the entrance of FCB to the ranks of the great European clubs. And the hero was a farmer's lad from the Allgäu.

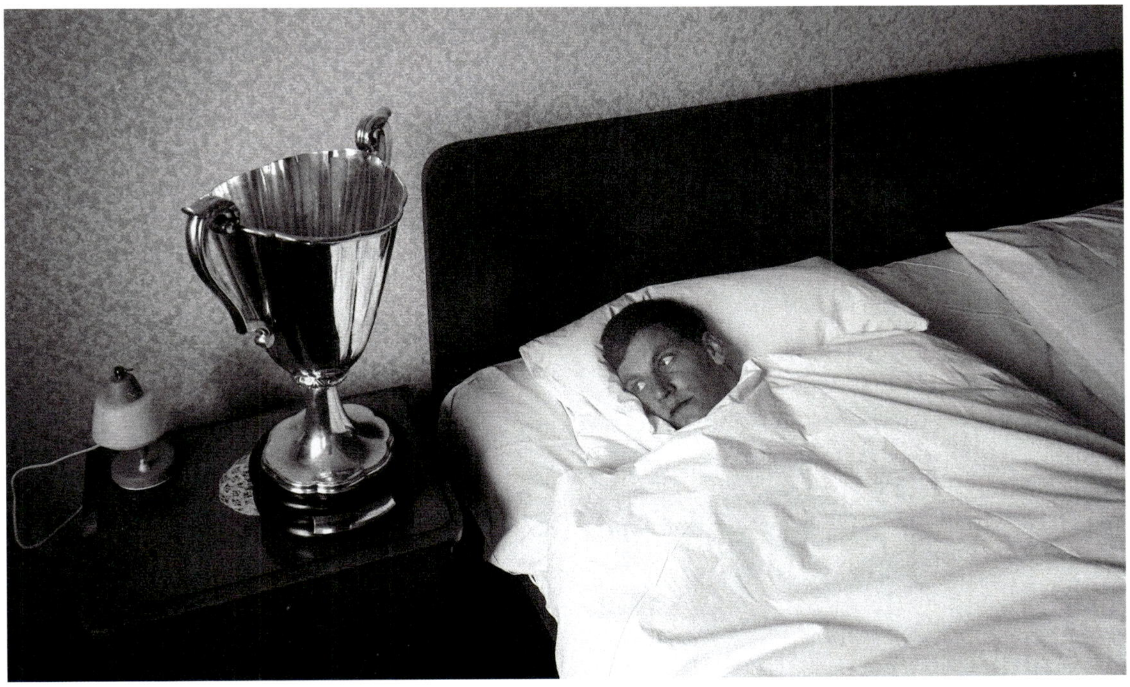

At the age of 17 he played for TSV Bertoldshofen in the C class, the lowest league, from which relegation is not possible. Three years later Franz Roth, called "Bulle", was the man who made the difference at the great FC Bayern in "our international breakthrough", as he describes it today. With his winning goal in the final of the European Cup Winners' Cup against Glasgow Rangers, "the great Bayern era took off". He took off with a powerful sprint from deep, into the Scottish penalty area, where, after 109 goalless minutes, a forty-metre pass from Rainer Ohlhauser descended at exactly the right moment. The defender Dave Smith tried to pull Bulle round. Though not standing straight, he nevertheless hit the ball – so skilfully that it sank into the back of the net with the perfect trajectory behind the advancing keeper.

The match was not wrapped up, and Bayern had to hold on to the 1–0 lead till the end, then escape from charging fans who wanted to tear the shirts from their heroes' backs – and at the final whistle Bulle needed the ball, too. "So I went to the ref, who had it, and laid on the tears – me, the young lad in his first big match," laughs Roth today. "Part true, part fairy tale." This softened the heart of the Italian referee. Today the leather ball, with which one of the great success stories in European football began, is kept in the Bayern Museum.

First you pursue the cup, and then, when you have it, it seems almost spooky. That, at least, is how the otherwise fearless Franz "Bulle" Roth looks, before going to sleep in the team hotel in Nuremberg, as he eyes the gleaming treasure on his bedside table. Three years earlier, Bulle was playing in the lowest amateur league for his local side, TSV Bertoldshofen. Now he is FC Bayern's first big hero in a European competition - and in summer will be back on his parents' farm in the Allgäu to help out with the harvest.

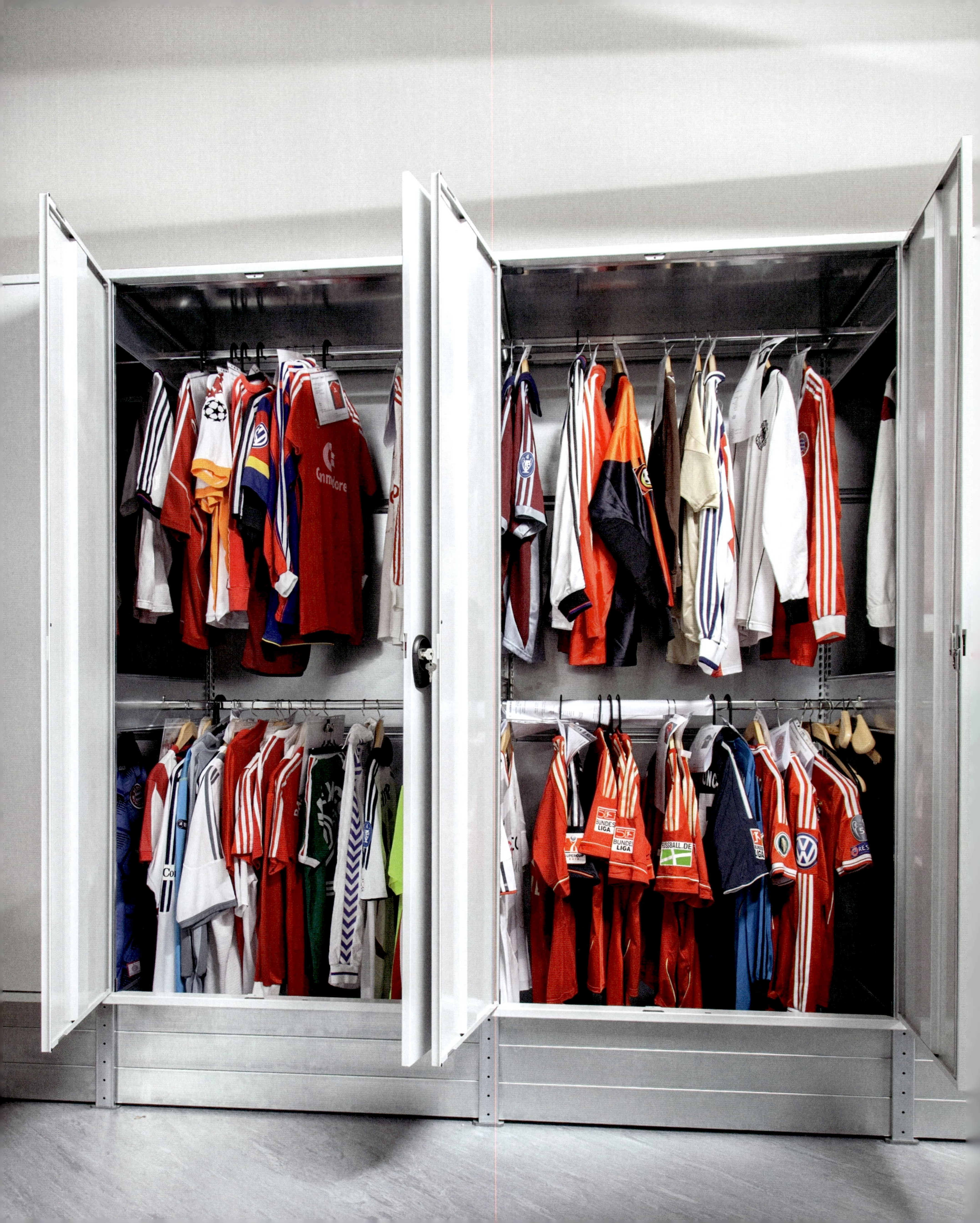
BUNDES
LIGA
BUNDES
LIGA
FUSSBALL.DE

FROM THE PITCH TO THE **MUSEUM AND ARCHIVE**

In June 2024 the FC Bayern Museum in the Allianz Arena welcomed Franziska Ott, its 500,000th guest of the season. Twelve years after opening, Germany's biggest club museum had reached the figure of half a million visitors for the first time.

"This museum has a very important part to play", said Jan-Christian Dreesen, chief executive officer, handing a bouquet of flowers to Franziska Ott. "It displays *Mia san mia* as it is lived, and is the heart and core of FC Bayern." On an area of 3,300 square metres, almost half the size of a football field, visitors experience more than just the club's great history, which gleams at the viewer from the parade of accumulated trophies. It also shows the present day, for example through a guard of honour of the current season's players and coaches, reproduced life-size on aluminium sheets. Showcases and projections illustrate 125 years of club history, while individual eras, events and biographies are presented in temporary special exhibitions.

In addition to the 500 exhibits in the permanent exhibition, more than 7,000 other items are stored in the museum archive: photos and film posters, letters and beer glasses, players' kits, tactical notes, top scorers' cannon trophies and much more – even the furniture from Uli Hoeness's old office. Many exhibits were donated or loaned by Bayern fans.

While the trophies for winning the German championship are replicas – thirty-one shields and the twenty-five-kilogram Viktoria dating from 1932 – visitors to the FC Bayern Museum can admire a historic original of the cup that in sports terms is the most valuable in club football: the trophy awarded for winning the European Cup (today called the Champions League). Until 2008 a club was allowed to keep the genuine original trophy if it won the competition three times in succession – as FC Bayern had in 1976.

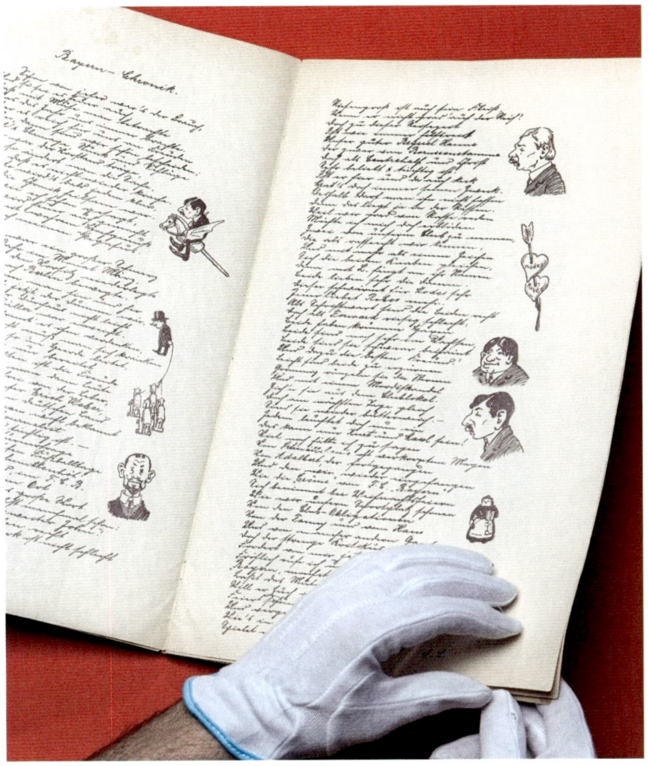

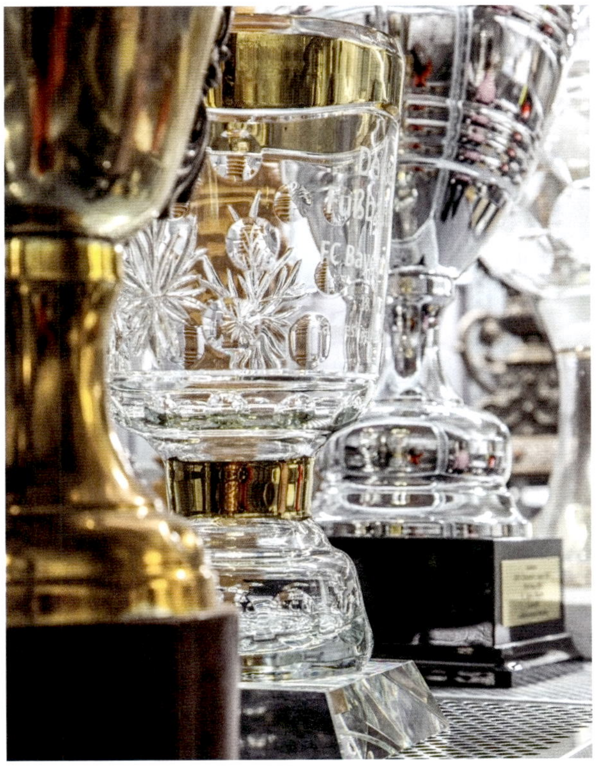

In the archive of the FC Bayern Museum, wardrobes containing playing shirts from past years are well filled - and so too are cupboards and shelves storing thousands of memorabilia from a wealth of club history.

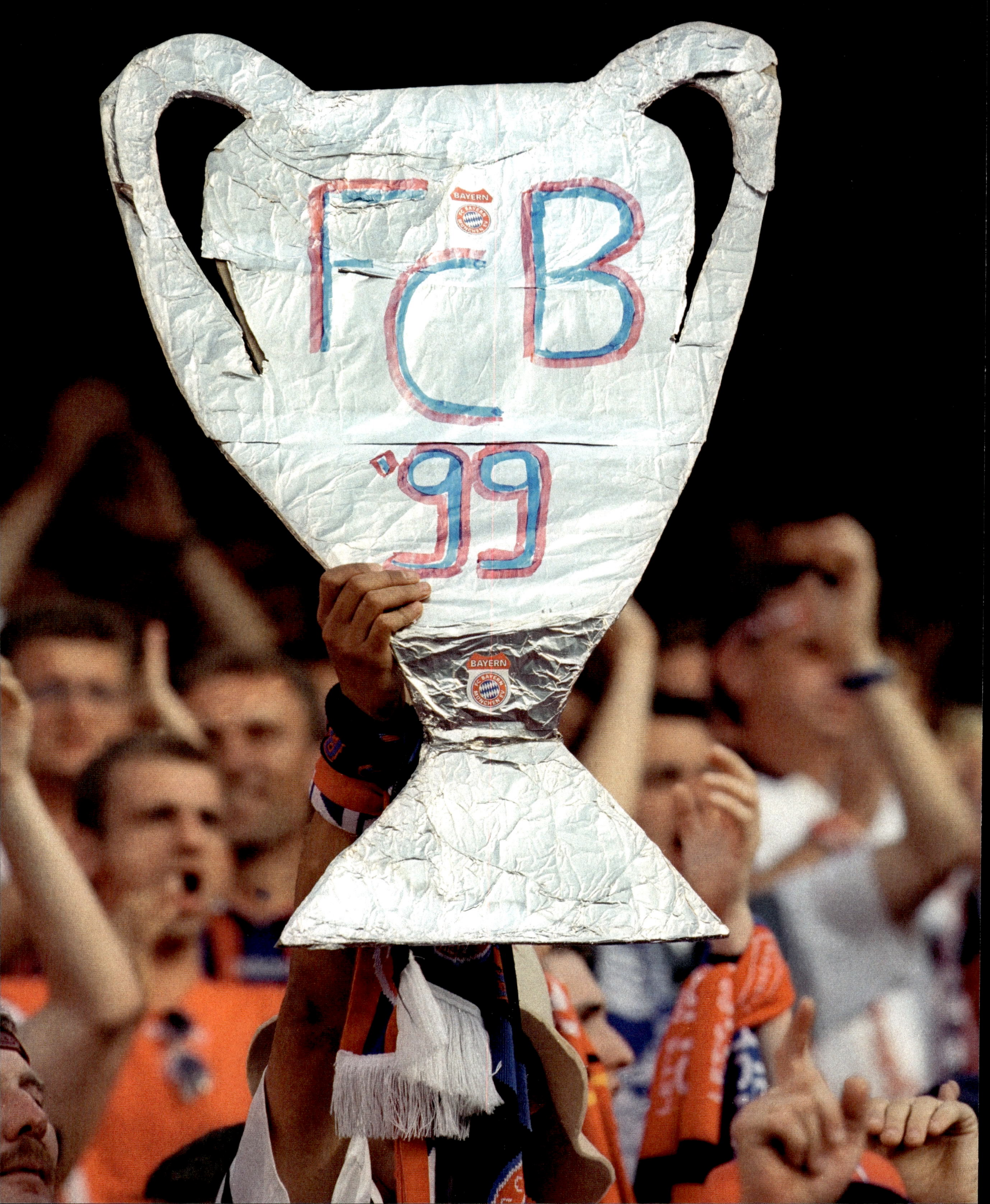
FCB
'99
BAYERN
BAYERN

"THE MOTHER OF ALL DEFEATS"
FCB - MANCHESTER 1-2 · 1999

Camp Nou, in the ninetieth minute of the Champions League final. For eighty-four minutes FCB has been in the lead. Then the sign with the "3" lights up, red like an alarm. "Damn it", thinks Ottmar Hitzfeld, "that's a long one." They will be the longest three minutes in the life of everyone at Bayern.

When they are over, it is too much even for the toughest of the tough guys. Sammy Kuffour shakes in spasms of tears. Carsten Jancker cries without restraint. Kahn stares into empty space, "as if paralysed". For him, this is "the mother of all defeats". Yet in this very night, it will also become the mother of a triumph, two years later. In the dressing room, defiance already mixes with the laments and silence, and something from the FCB tradition happens: in the worst defeats "Mia san mia" translates into "Now we'll show them". At the banquet in the Barceló Sants Hotel, Scholl, Markus Babbel and Mario Basler dance on the tables until the early hours, singing a hit song about unrequited love, a lament that is actually addressed to a woman. But in this case to an equally unfathomable force of destiny, to football: "It's crazy, why are you sending me to hell?" Why? Perhaps to make heaven even more wonderful later.

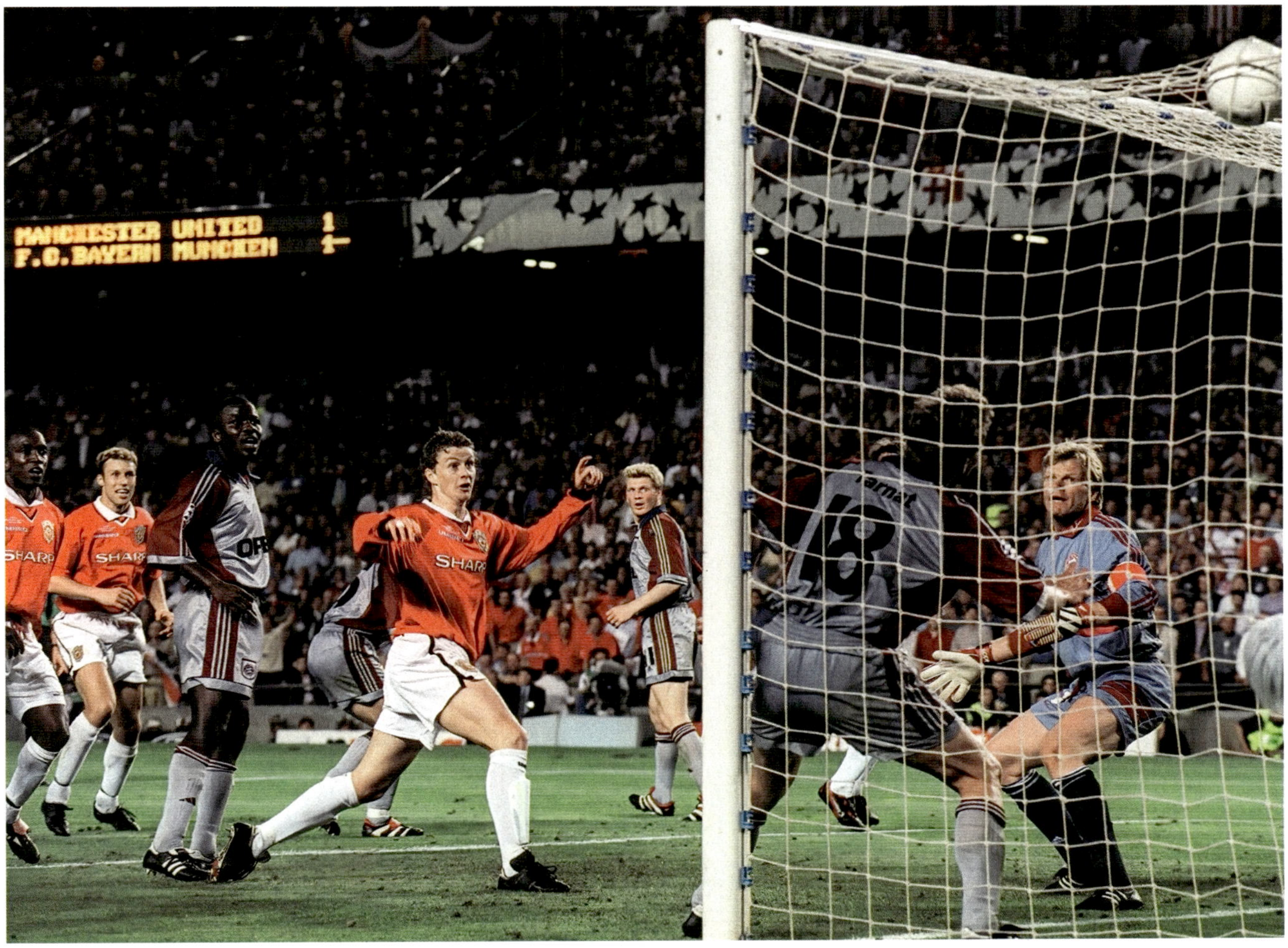

92:37 minutes on the clock: Ole Gunnar Solskjær scores, and the only cup held by Bayern is the one made from cardboard and aluminium foil. One of those moments that Liverpool's coach Rafael Benítez will describe, six years later after another dramatic final: "The way the world splits at this moment into two, into joy and pain - only football does that."

They are not only for real Bavarian men - leder-hosen, janker jackets and *Haferlschuhe*. Italian gentlemen like Giovanni Trapattoni and South American golden boys like Claudio Pizarro and Giovane Élber look good in them, too.

NO ONE PULLS OFF **OUR LEDERHOSEN**

Paul McCartney and John Lennon wrote a song for Ringo Starr for every Beatles album. It had to be catchy, as the drummer didn't have a powerful voice. 'Yellow Submarine', for example, where the refrain consists of only four notes. Udo Scholz listened to it in his car, and that's when the thing with the lederhosen started.

While on holiday in Murnau he had heard a sentence that he liked: "Pull the lederhosen off the lad." Then the Beatles' song was broadcast on the radio, and in his mind the yellow submarine and the Bavarian trousers had already merged to form a stadium hit. 'Zieht den Bayern die Lederhosen aus' (Pull the lederhosen off the Bavarians) rang out from the stands the next time Bayern played in the Betzenberg Stadium in Kaiserslautern, where Scholz was the announcer. And from then onwards it was heard in almost every ground in the Bundesliga. This gave the captain Paul Breitner and the manager Uli Hoeness an idea. The players were fitted out with lederhosen, which they wore on 1 December 1979 when they ran onto the pitch in the Rheinstadion in Düsseldorf. "There was massive cheering", said Breitner. "People thought it was fantastic that we responded so confidently and humorously to the insulting song." Six months later, the championship was celebrated wearing traditional dress. Since 2003 FCB footballers have always worn lederhosen when presenting the championship trophy on the city hall balcony on Marienplatz, and even footballers from South America or southern Europe look good in them. And when the women celebrate, since 2015 they have worn a dirndl dress.

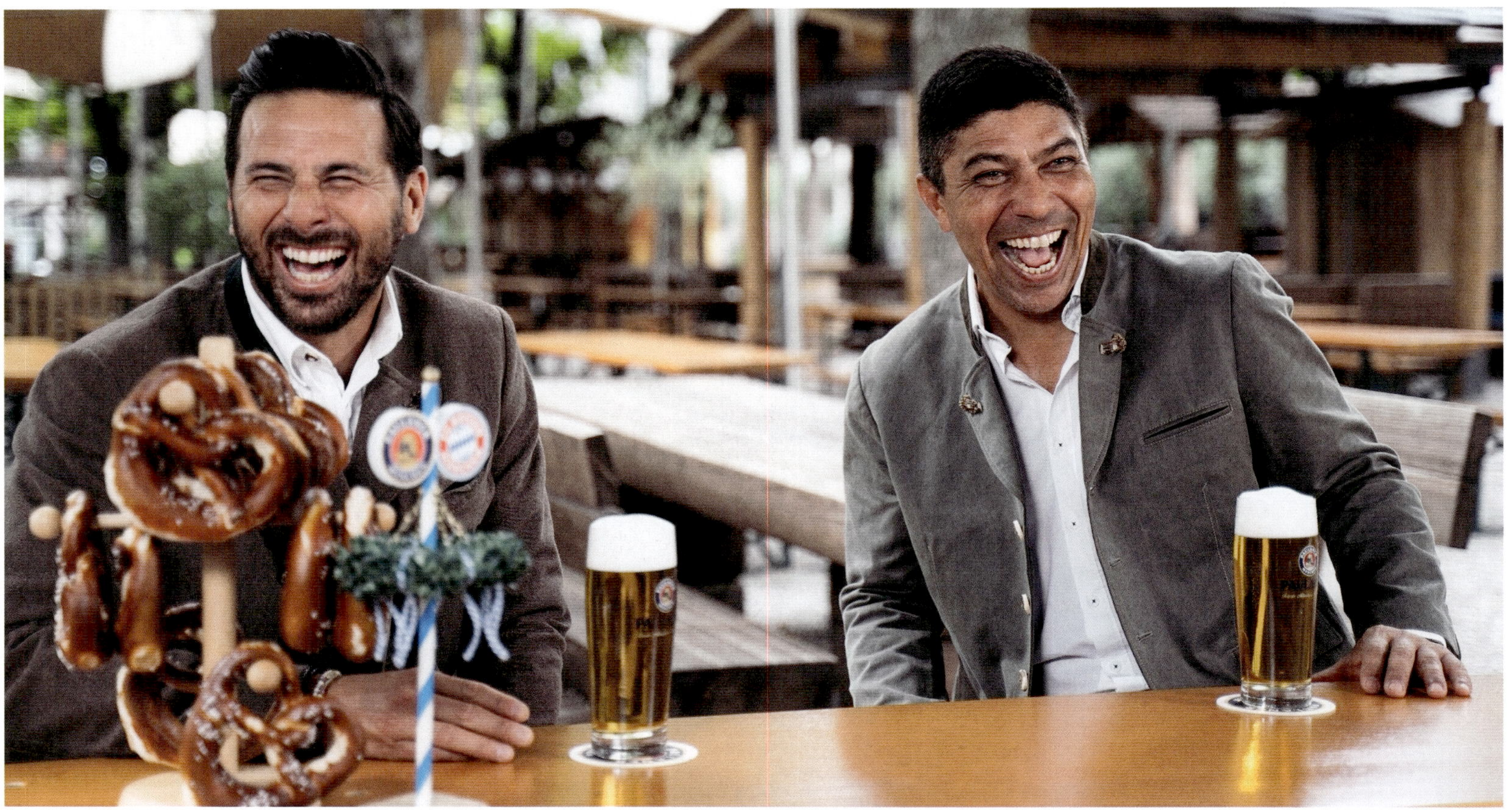

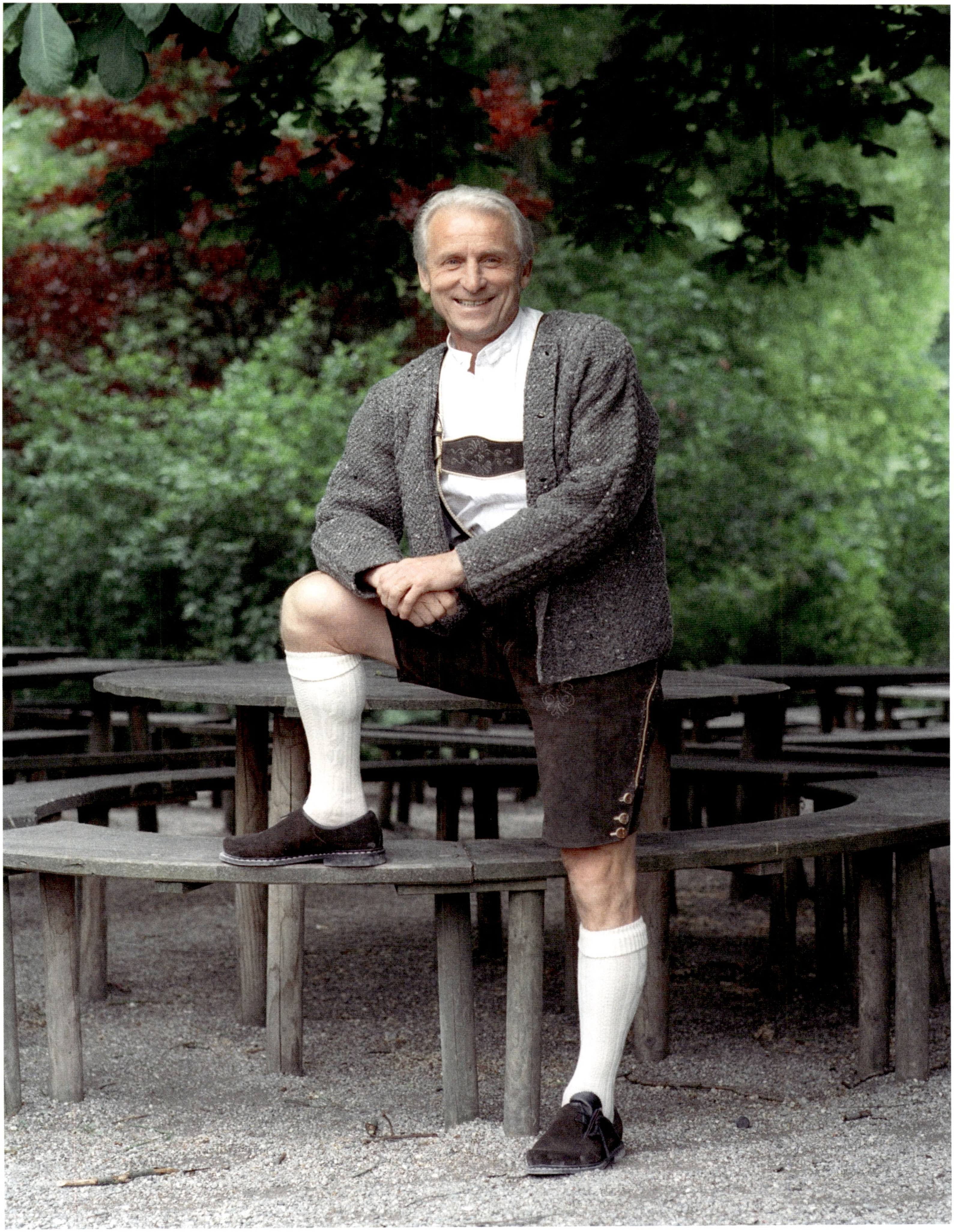

WET **OR** WHAT!

Pep Guardiola couldn't have known – how in Munich you get a cold shower even as league champion. And how cold is a full three-litre glass of alcohol-free Paulaner beer.

The shower of wheat beer is a tradition, celebrated for the 25th time in the 125th anniversary year of FC Bayern. The originator is said to be Giovane Élber, who in unbounded joy poured a glass over his coach Ottmar Hitzfeld after the news of Leverkusen's defeat in Unterhaching that handed Bayern the championship in 2000. Two years before he had already done the same thing to Giovanni Trapattoni after the cup victory in Berlin, but that was not wheat beer. There's no point in running away, as the players are faster. Even Uli Hoeness, once hailed as "the quickest forward in Europe", could not get away from Mehmet Scholl and Hasan Salihamidžić in 2005. He wanted to stay dry, because he still had to go on the ZDF *Sportstudio* TV programme. And he pulled a muscle while trying to flee.

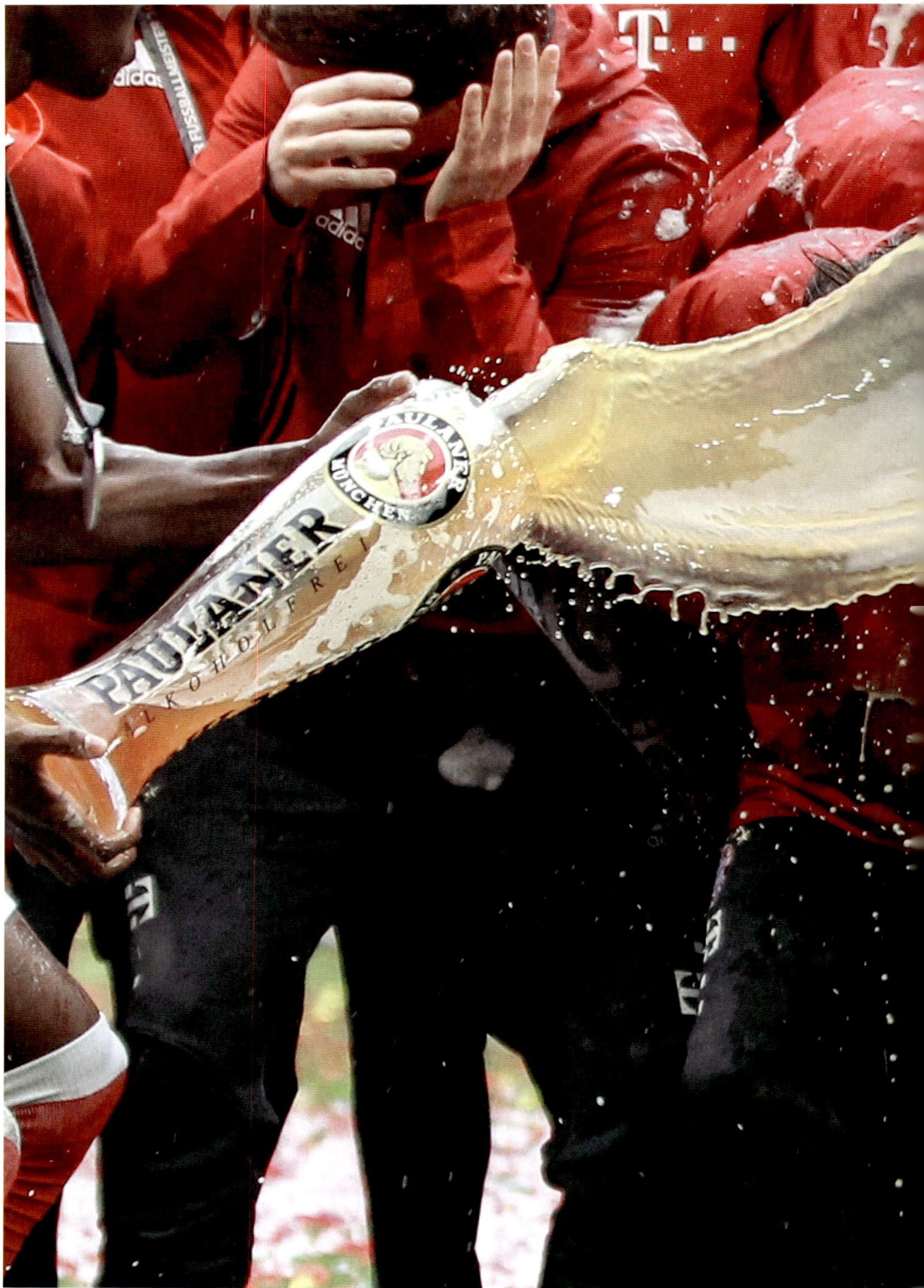

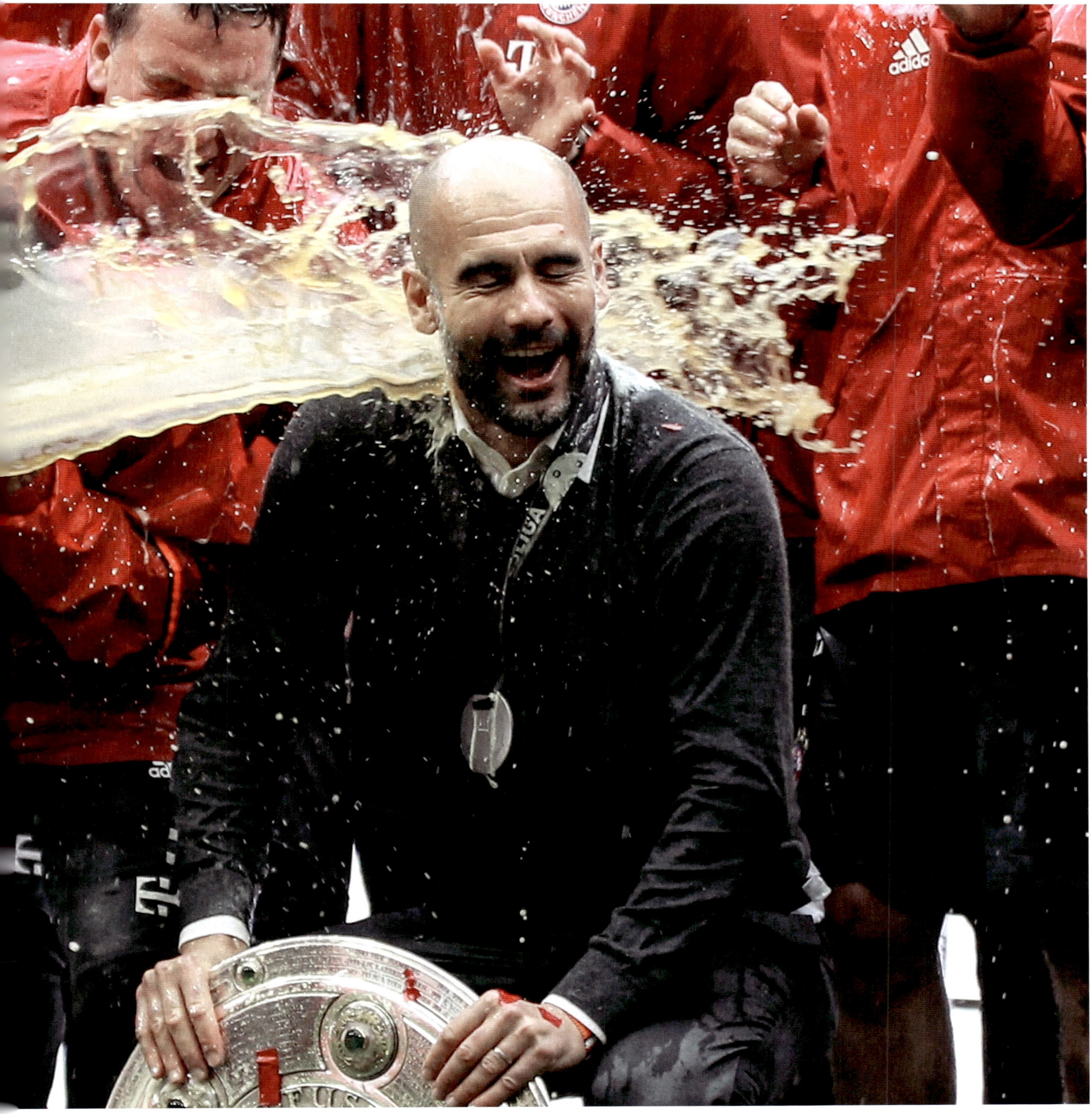

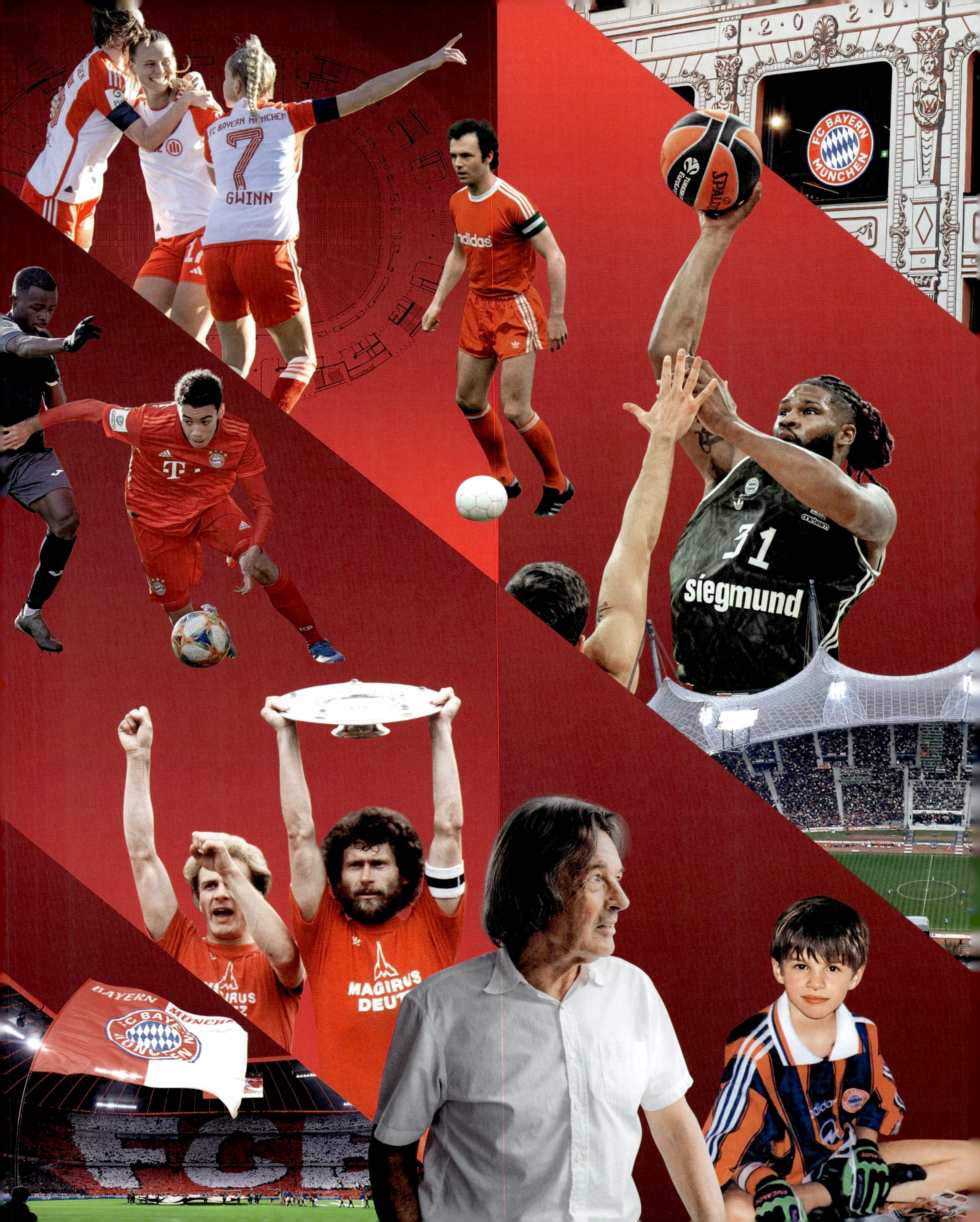
7
GWINN
adidas
FC BAYERN MÜNCHEN
31
siegmund
MAGIRUS
DEUT
BAYERN

FUTURE

You can't start a fire without a spark.
We won't inspire others unless we enjoy
what we do and how we do it.

125 YEARS **FUTURE**

At his first press conference as Bayern coach in July 2024, Vincent Kompany said: "I'm not one to talk much about the past. For me, it's about the future." This was true for the founders of FC Bayern back then. They wanted to play football in competitions, but the male gymnastic club of which they were a small, young section, the Männer-Turn-Verein von 1879, was against this. In many places in Germany, the backward-looking rejected the game that came from England. But the founders of FC Bayern knew that football was the future. They left the meeting and the club, held a constructive pub crawl and founded a new club.

No one could have predicted how glorious its future would be, but as early as 1901 FCB laid the foundations for this: with a youth section. Otto Albert Beer, who led them to be the best in Germany in the 1920s, said, "If you have the youth, you have the future." The team that won the championship in 1932 included four home-grown talents. But the future was bleak for Beer himself, as he was Jewish. In 1941 he and his family were deported to Kaunas in Lithuania and murdered. His youth section was sacrificed to the Nazis' perfidious plan to take control of children, away from their families, churches and clubs. In 1936 all under-14s were removed from their clubs and transferred to the Hitler Youth.

Many years of football youth, the future of the club, were lost. The late 1950s were all about simply surviving for FCB. Roland Endler, an industrialist from the Rhineland, became president and saved the club from bankruptcy, but showed little inclination to invest his money in youth development. Instead he wanted to tempt Pelé to come to Munich. It was only his successor Wilhelm Neudecker who put his faith in youth again, in "provincial footballers who are keen to learn and whose talent holds more promise than big names", and contributed DM 10,000 a year of his own money to the youth section.

The team that gained promotion in 1965 had an average age of 21.8 years. Players from the club's own youth programme around the young Beckenbauer laid the basis for the years of success up to 1976. As in the second great era, the years since 2009, with home-grown youngsters such as Lahm, Schweinsteiger and Müller from Hermann Gerland's tough school of youth development. His motto remains valid for the future of the generation who will emerge from the Campus that opened in 2017: "Ability is always fortune."

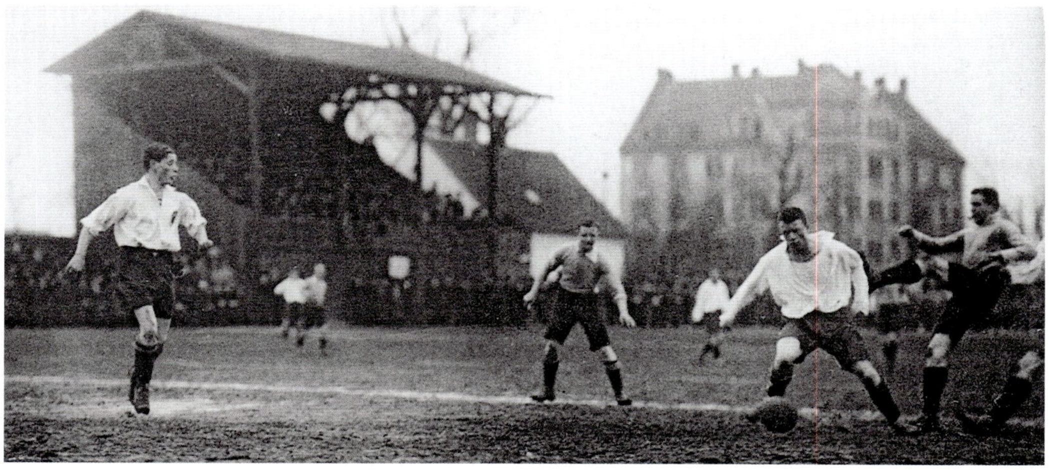

Today and in the past, the future is the same: it was and still is young footballers who love to play and form part of a team.

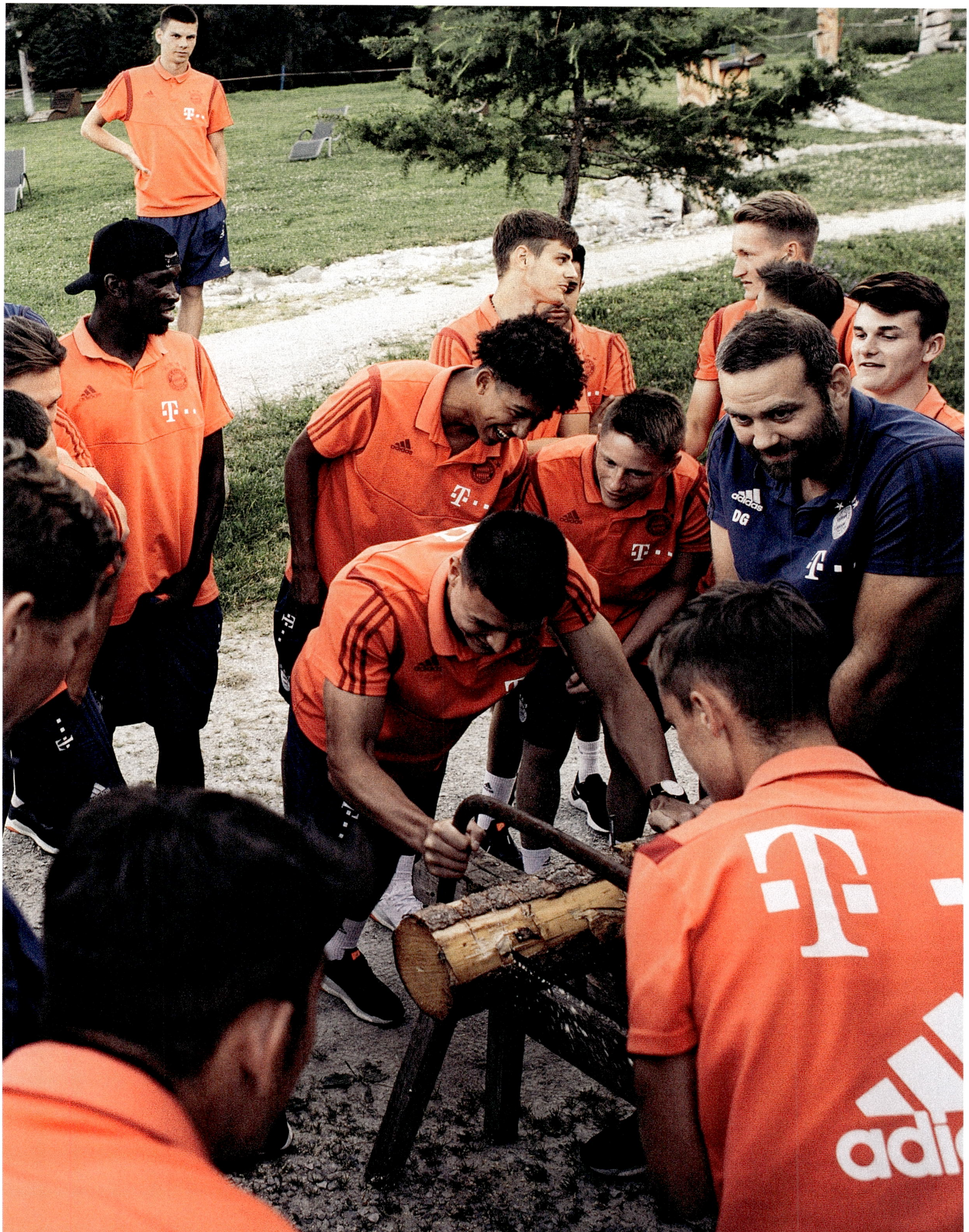

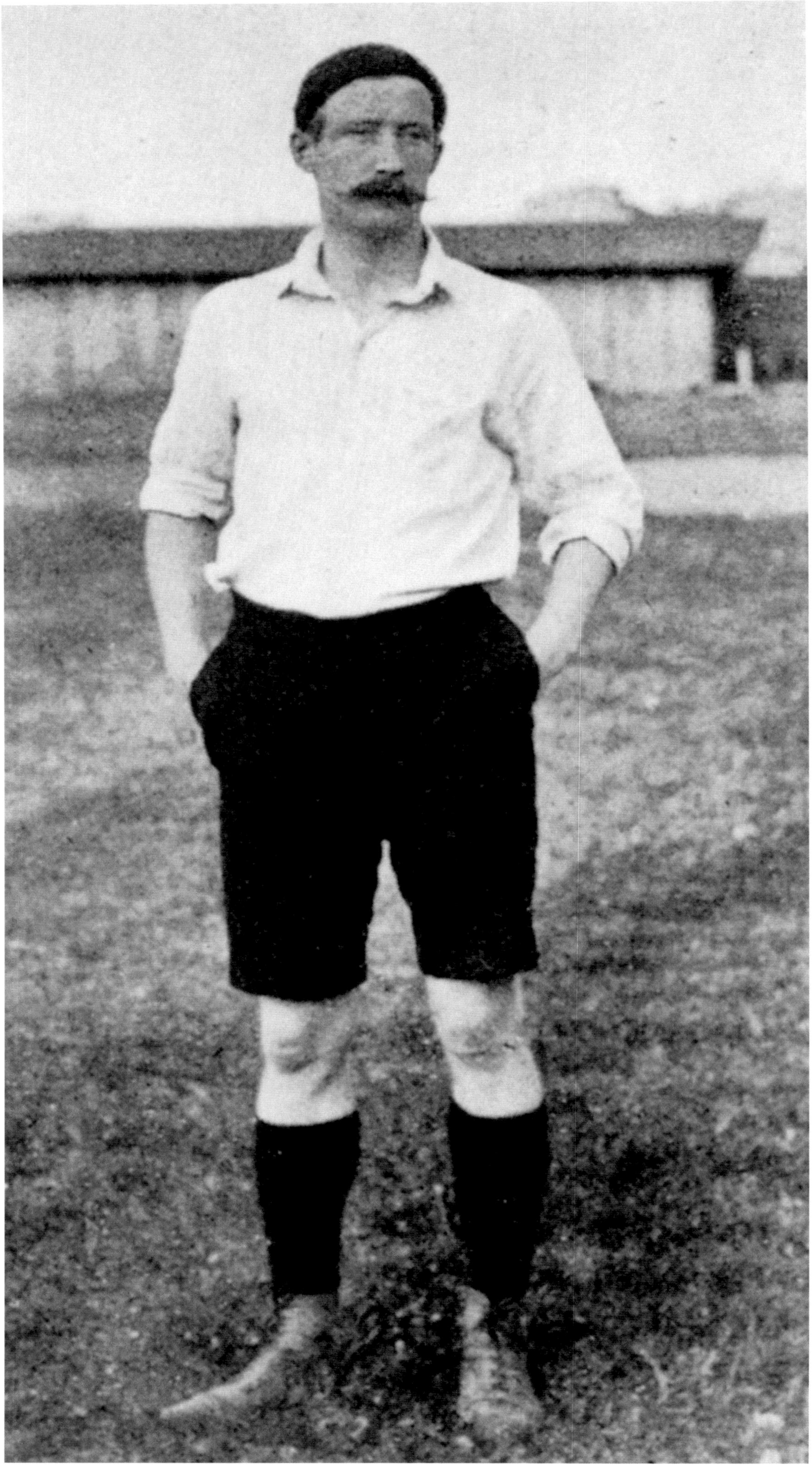

THE ANCES-TOR **OF** FRANZ **AND** LOUIS

Long before Franz Beckenbauer, he too combined everything in one person: player, coach, president. All that at the same time. Willem Hesselink, known in Holland as "Het Kanon" because of his powerful shot, came to Munich to study chemistry and joined FCB in 1903. The man with the blue woolly hat was an all-rounder: he held the Dutch record for the long jump and running a mile, as well as championship medals for tug-of-war and, with HVV Den Haag, football. As player-coach and president, according to a club history, he "constantly tried to include talented youngsters" – just like his compatriot Louis van Gaal, who preferred teenagers such as Thomas Müller and David Alaba over established stars more than a century later. Back in the Netherlands, Hesselink was an expert on blood analysis and fingerprints who played a part in solving several murders. The most versatile of all Bayern pioneers was also the most long-lived: he died in 1973 at the age of 95.

Strictly speaking, he was the first from FC Bayern to play in an international match. While still holding office as president of FCB, in May 1905 Dr Willem Hesselink was a member of the Dutch side that beat Belgium 4-0 in the second game of its history.

TABLE-TENNIS BATS – **A WORLD-FIRST IN GOAL**

An exhibition about Sepp Maier in the Bayern Museum celebrated him as a "goalkeeper, tinkerer, a jack-of-all-trades". The tinkering was about the goalkeeper's gloves that he made for himself from a great variety of materials that he stuck together, from cloth, leather, towelling and rubber.

As recently as 1974 in the World Cup final, one of the two goalkeepers, the Dutch player Jan Jongbloed, played with bare hands. The other, by contrast, wore goalkeeper's gloves that he had developed and marketed himself. Early in his career Sepp Maier had experimented with all kinds of materials, for example with the bumps on table-tennis bats. Until he discovered the foam used by the physiotherapist to protect injured bones as a material for gloves.

But he had to travel a long road before it worked. In 1973, under constant bombardment from Ajax Amsterdam, the glued-on foam flew from his hands. Bayern lost 0–4, and Maier threw everything – his shorts, shirt and gloves – "out of the seventh-floor hotel window into the canal". He declared that he would look for a different job – for which a Munich furniture company offered him work for a salary of DM 2,000. "So I reconsidered", he says. "It was just a joke." A year later, in the final of the European Cup against Atlético Madrid and in the World Cup final against the Dutch, the material was fit to win trophies. "These gloves were my invention," says Maier. "Every goalkeeper today should be grateful to me when they can keep firm hold of the ball." he claims. "Apart from the ones who are beyond help anyway."

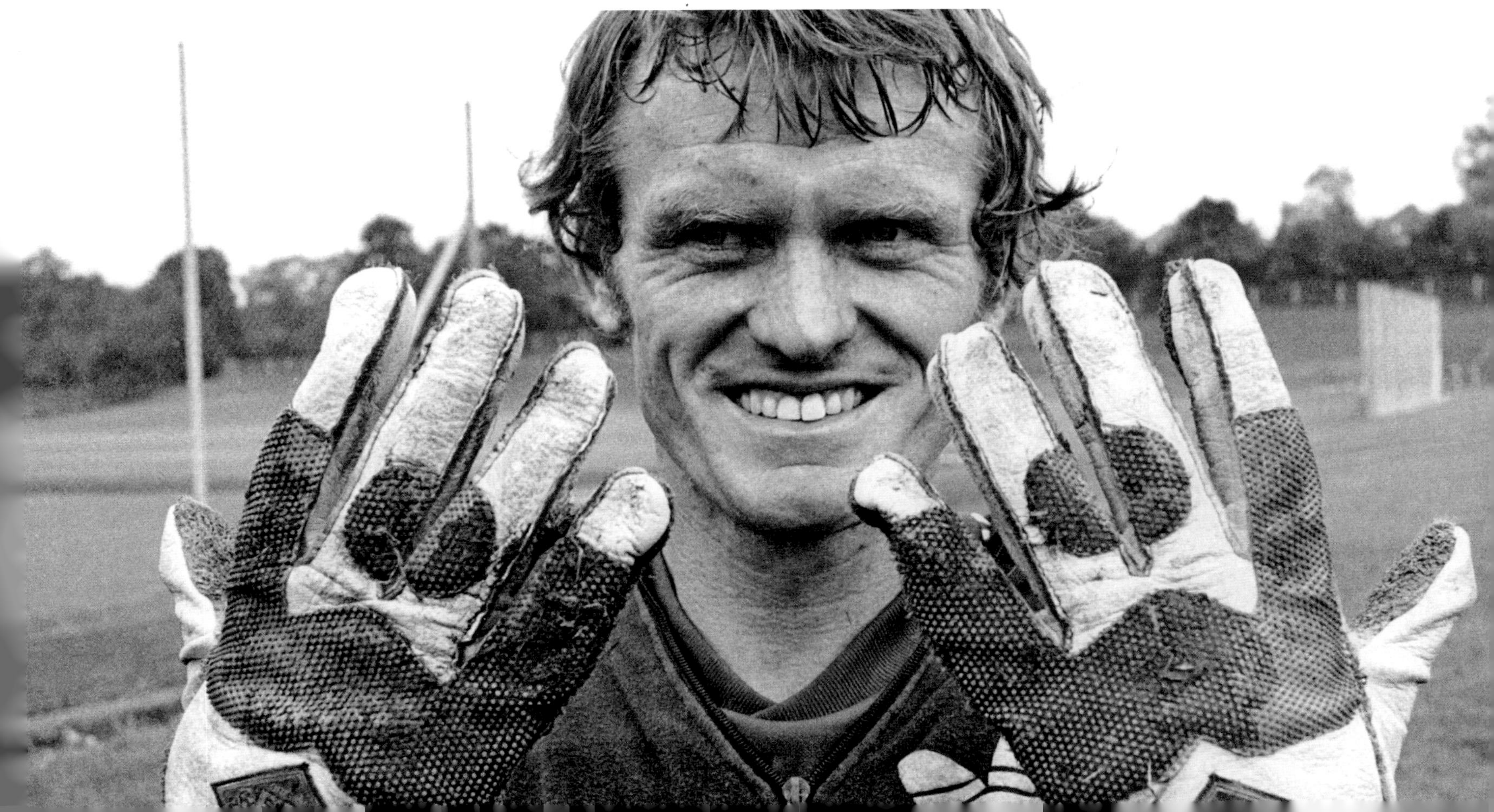

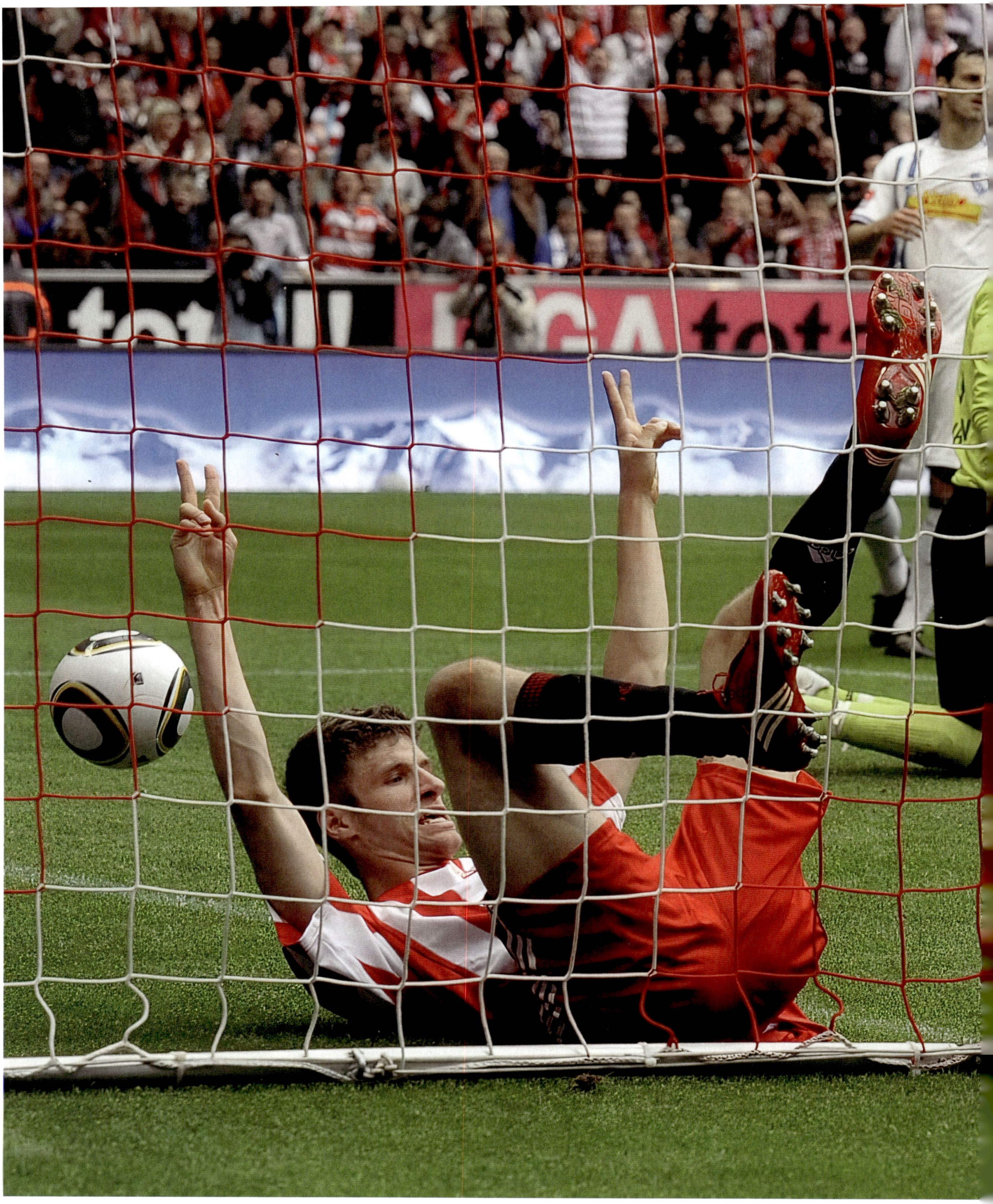

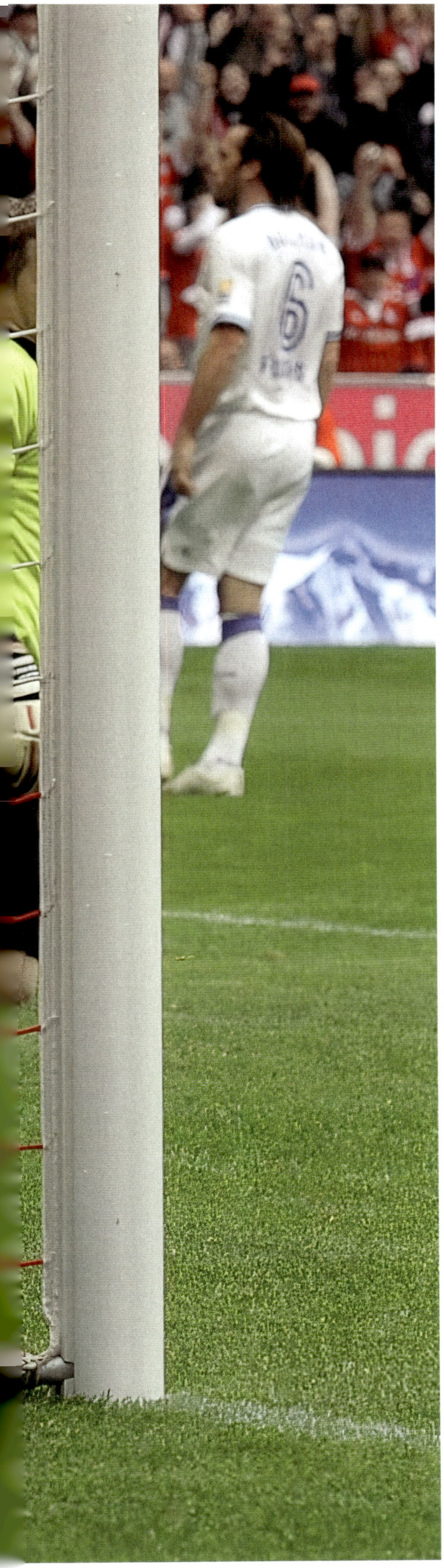

"MÜLLERING" REBORN

Klinsmann did not want him, Hoffenheim offered three million, but Hermann Gerland went up to Uli Hoeness's office and fought for him: "He simply always scores." A year later he scored three, and Bayern won the Bundesliga.

May Day 2010, and truly a holiday. The second-last match of the season, Bayern against Bochum, a tight race with Schalke, a must-win game, and who will play up front? Not Gómez, not Toni, not Klose – no, a Müller. Not a player bought for €35 million, but a youngster on a starting salary of €3,000. After eighteen minutes he makes it 1–0 with his chest, leaps after the ball and lies in the net with a grin on his face, making a V-sign with both hands. Two minutes afterwards it's 2–0, a header. Later the fans stand up and do the Mexican wave, though nothing has just happened in the Allianz Arena – but far away, clearly, at Schalke (who lost against Bremen). Then Müller realises that they have done it. And scores another goal. Championship winners with three goals from Müller – what more could lie ahead? What indeed? The second Müller era at FCB. Fifteen years later, after twelve more Bundesliga championships, it is still not over. And Thomas Müller, as Ottmar Hitzfeld says, "is already a legend".

Victory signs in the goal net, ballet on the ball - not a typical footballer, this lanky man, and that was clear from the start. His rapid rise, then aged 20, did not proceed entirely accident-free. Three weeks after the three goals for the championship, he fell from a bike in the World Cup training camp in South Tyrol and needed stitches in his chin. His knees were merely grazed, and at the World Cup finals he promptly ended up as top scorer. Back in Pähl am Ammersee, his mountain bike was "sold again straight away".

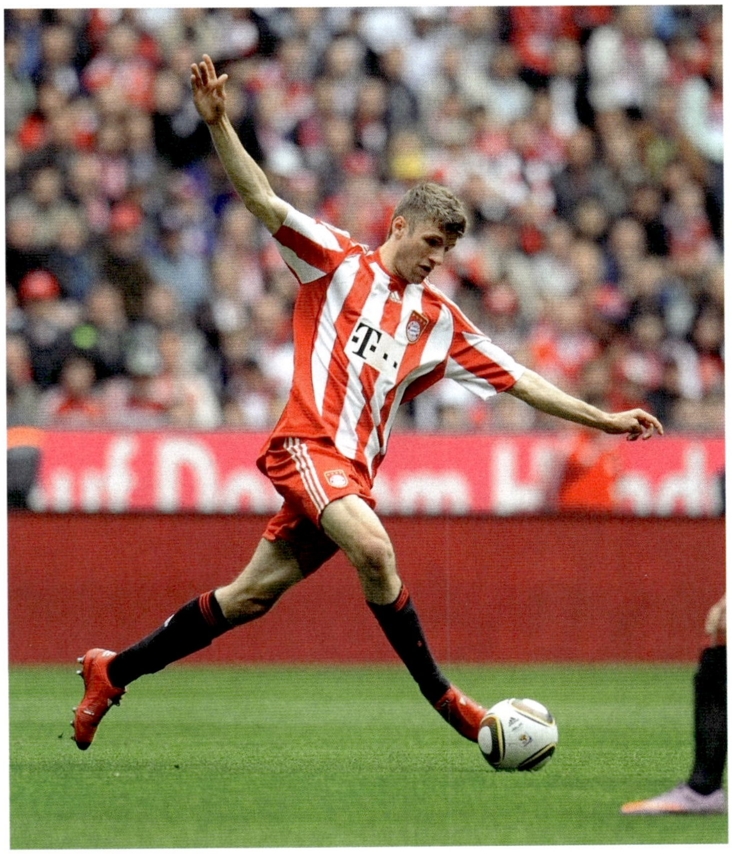

THE WORLD'S **FINEST ROOF**

It has the first heated pitch and the first VIP zone in the Bundesliga. And FC Bayern's bottom line after thirty-three years was no argument against the Olympic Stadium: 17 Bundesliga championships, 5 European Cup wins, 552 victories in 751 matches.

Not everyone warmed to the Olympic Stadium. Literally, because in that open bowl with its world-famous curving tent of a roof, spectators would freeze when the wind blew cold. However, the move there from the small Grünwalder Stadium blew a warm shower of money into the coffers of FCB.

The last match of the season, on 28 June 1972, was a genuine final against second-placed Schalke for the championship. It gave a perfect debut to the most modern stadium of the time, the first in Germany with a heated pitch and VIP boxes. "We played on a carpet in front of 80,000 spectators. It was a show," Franz Beckenbauer enthused. The sold-out Olympic Stadium gave Bayern their first-ever day's take in seven figures, DM 1.2 million. A Bundesliga game was screened live on TV for the first time. And with a 5–1 win, Bayern secured both the championship and a record that stands to this day of 101 goals in a season.

The subsequent 750 matches before the move to the Allianz Arena in 2005 were not always as glorious. A crowd in the low ten thousands often seemed lost in the huge stadium. However, the additional income on big money-spinning days, in a derby or a top match in the league or European Cup, laid the foundations for the club's ascent to lasting domination of German football. Borussia Mönchengladbach, Bayern's great rival in the 1970s, was not able to compensate for the financial discrepancy much longer by sporting means. "We vegetated in our small stadium," Günter Netzer later said, and levelled his accusation at the then manager Helmut Grashoff. "If he had built us a big stadium, perhaps we would have become like Bayern Munich." But of course there could only be one Bayern Munich. When the Reds arrived at the Olympic Stadium they were celebrating their third Bundesliga championship. When they left, thirty-three years later, their nineteenth.

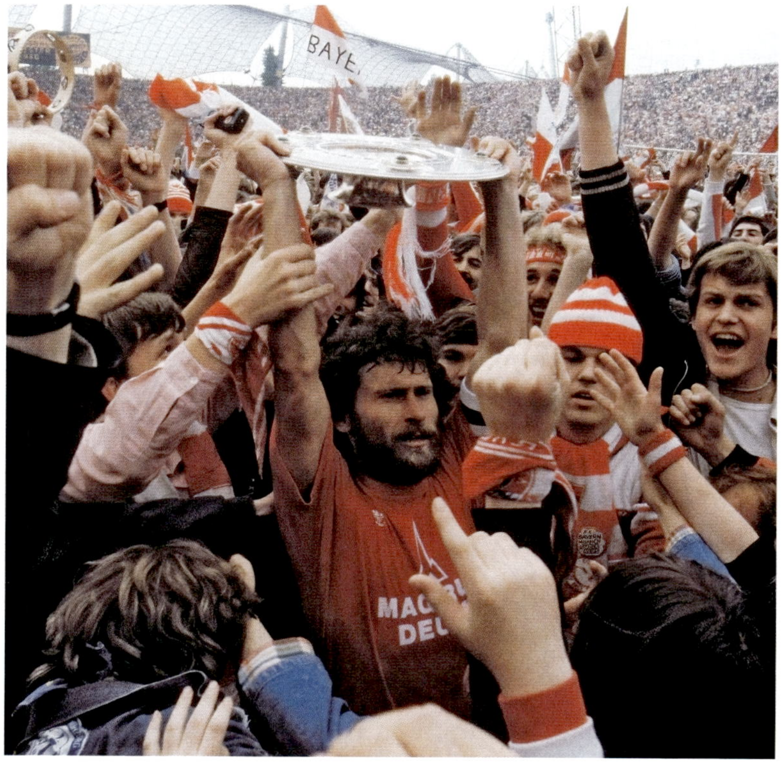

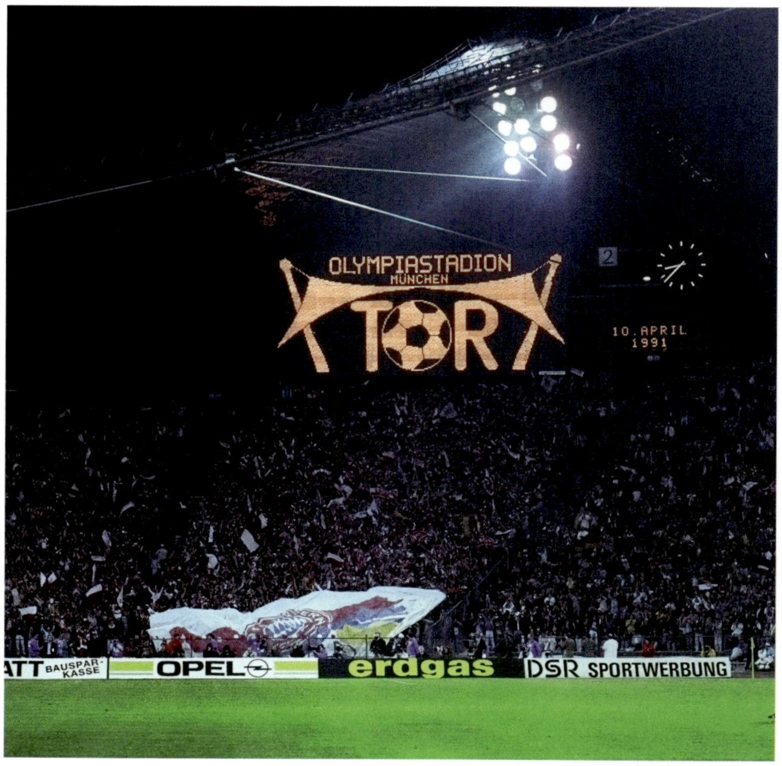

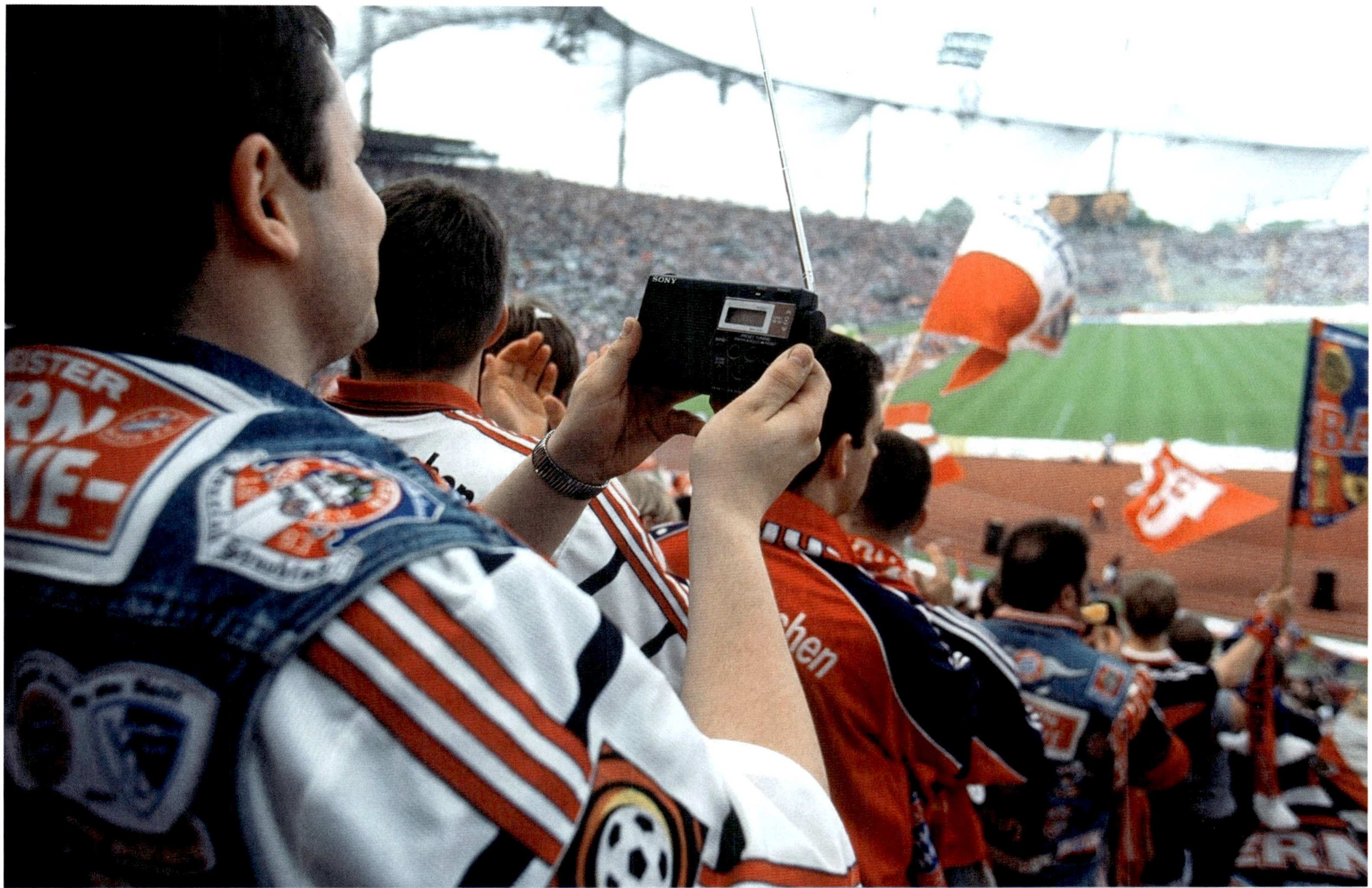

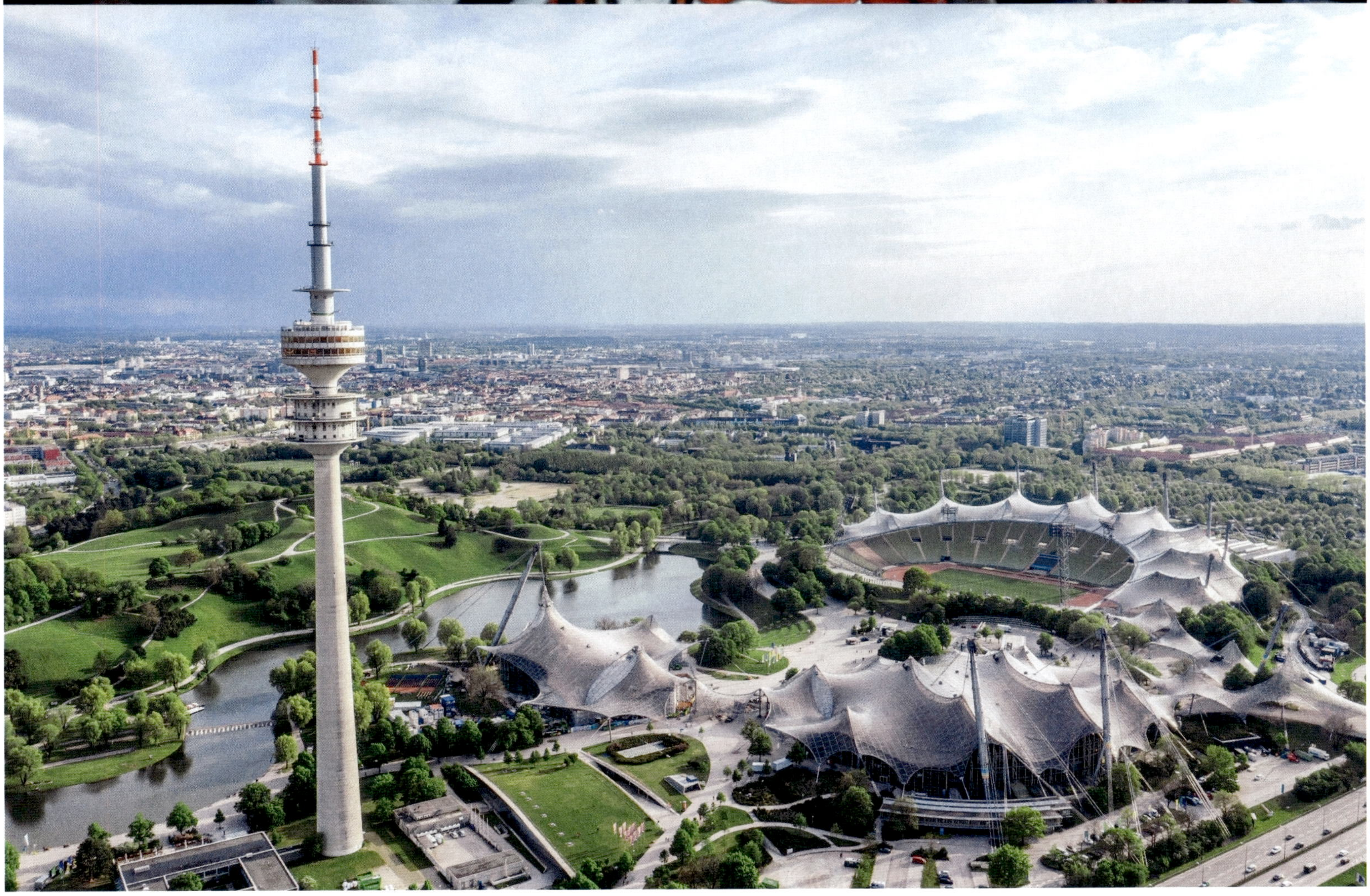

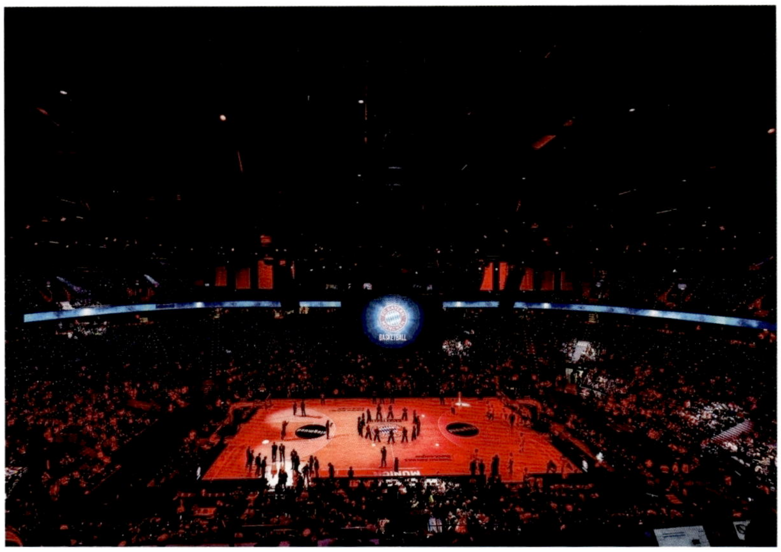

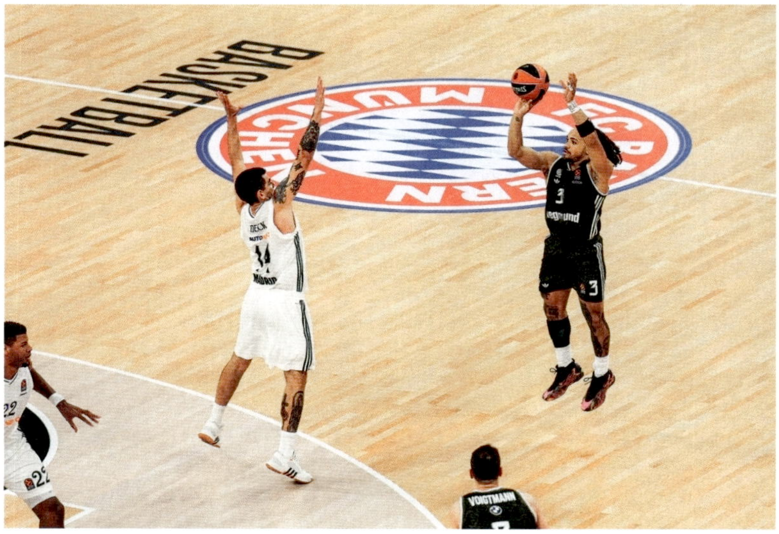
BASKETBALL

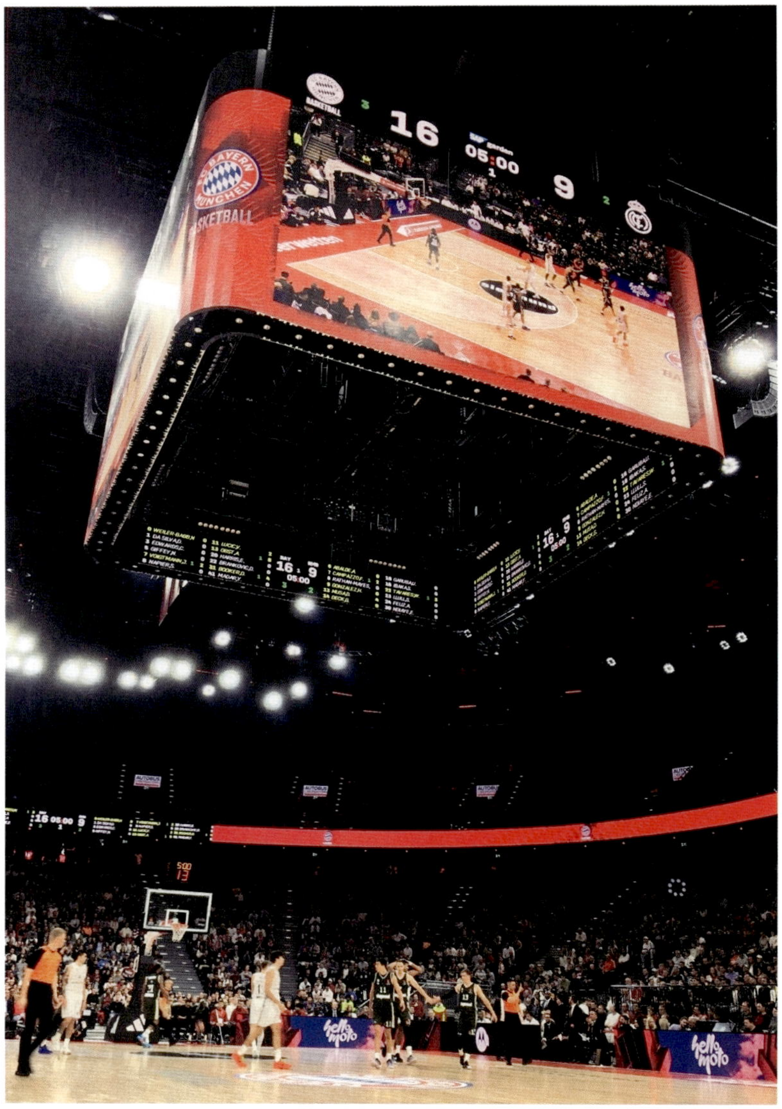
16
05:00
9
BASKETBALL

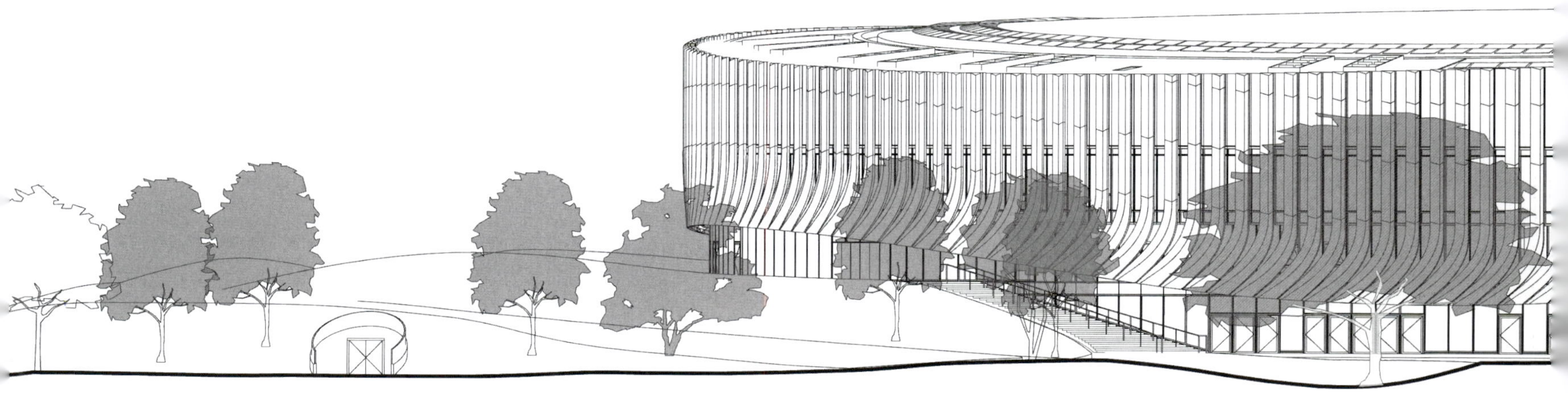

SAP GARDEN – **BACK TO THE FUTURE**

The first sport apart from football at FC Bayern was ice hockey, back in 1901. But only briefly. Then again in 1966. President Wilhelm Neudecker's idea of running a third sport at top-class level alongside football and basketball proved to be a flop. Due to high costs and low income he sold the ice hockey department to Augsburger EV. Since 2024, however, ice hockey and Bayern basketball have been played under one roof.

This is the green roof of the SAP Garden, an out-of-the-ordinary arena that was conceived by Red Bull GmbH for its ice hockey team, EHC Red Bull Munich. This took place in cooperation with two rent-paying parties: FC Bayern, whose basketball team plays Euro League matches and top games in the Bundesliga there, and the City of Munich, which makes almost 8,000 hours of time on ice available for school, club and leisure sports on three underground ice rinks. An innovative system for spectator stands makes it possible to adapt the playing surface to the sport in question within a few hours – from ice to a wooden floor and back again.

In Munich's Olympiapark the SAP Garden occupies the spot where the indoor cyclists competed for medals in 1972. At the opening of the multipurpose arena, EHC Red Bull, four times ice hockey champions, played against the Buffalo Sabres from the National Hockey League (NHL). Six days later, the German basketball champions FC Bayern defeated the star line-up of Real Madrid 97–89 at the opening of the Euro League. "The SAP Garden will be our party room," said Marko Pešić, managing director of the basketball Bayern, who will continue to use BMW Park, formerly the Audi Dome, as their "living room".

The atmosphere and capacity of the SAP Garden, which can hold 11,500 spectators for basketball matches, makes Pešić optimistic "that we will make Munich a hub of European basketball in the coming years." And also that the arena will make his job of looking for top players easier: "The new hall will attract players whom people would not have expected to come to Munich."

The SAP Garden was constructed with an emphasis on sustainability. A circular solar power installation with 799 photovoltaic modules around the almost 8,000-square-metre flower meadow on the roof generates a maximum of 330 kW for the independent energy supply of one of the three subterranean ice rinks.

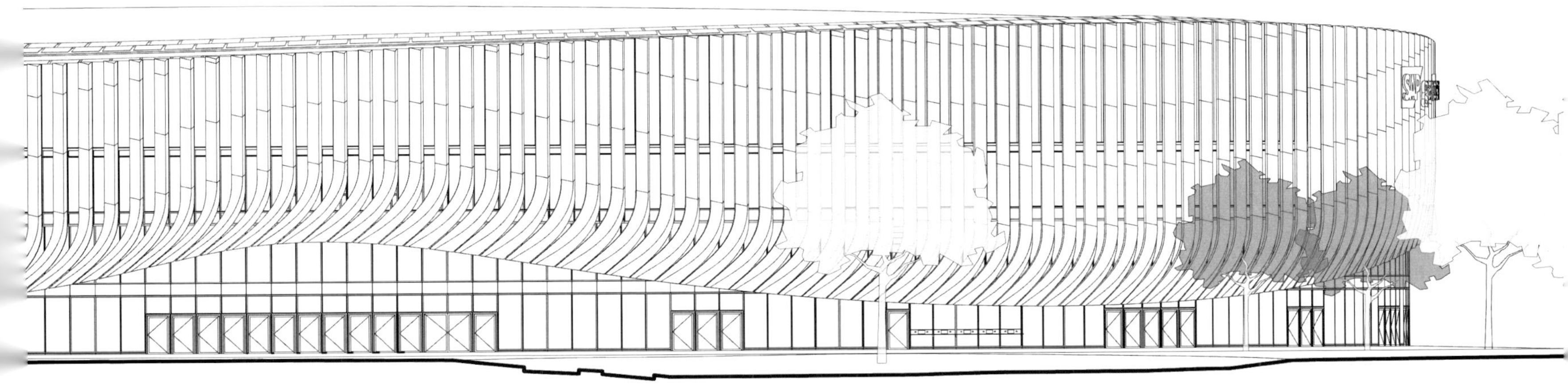

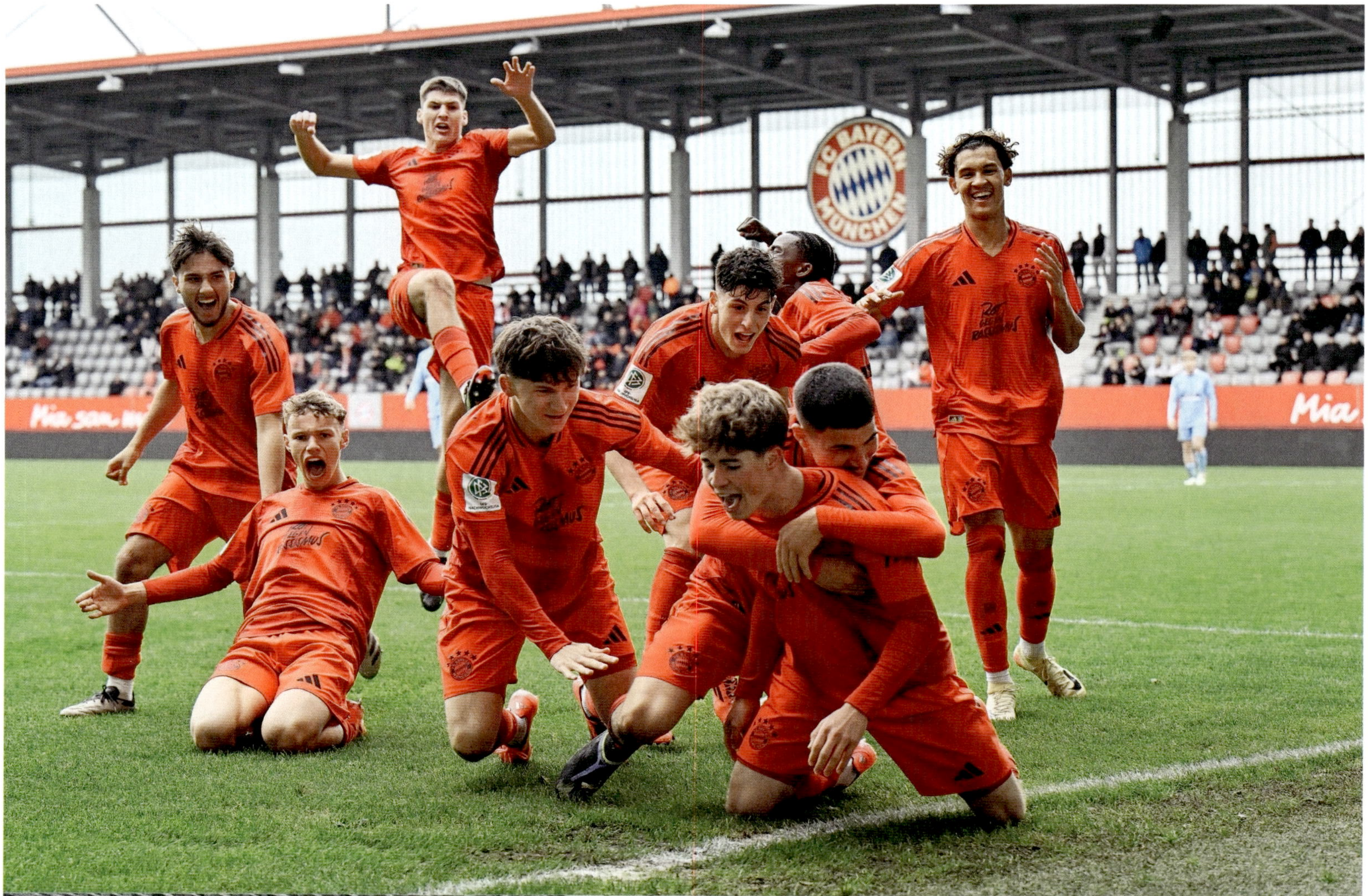

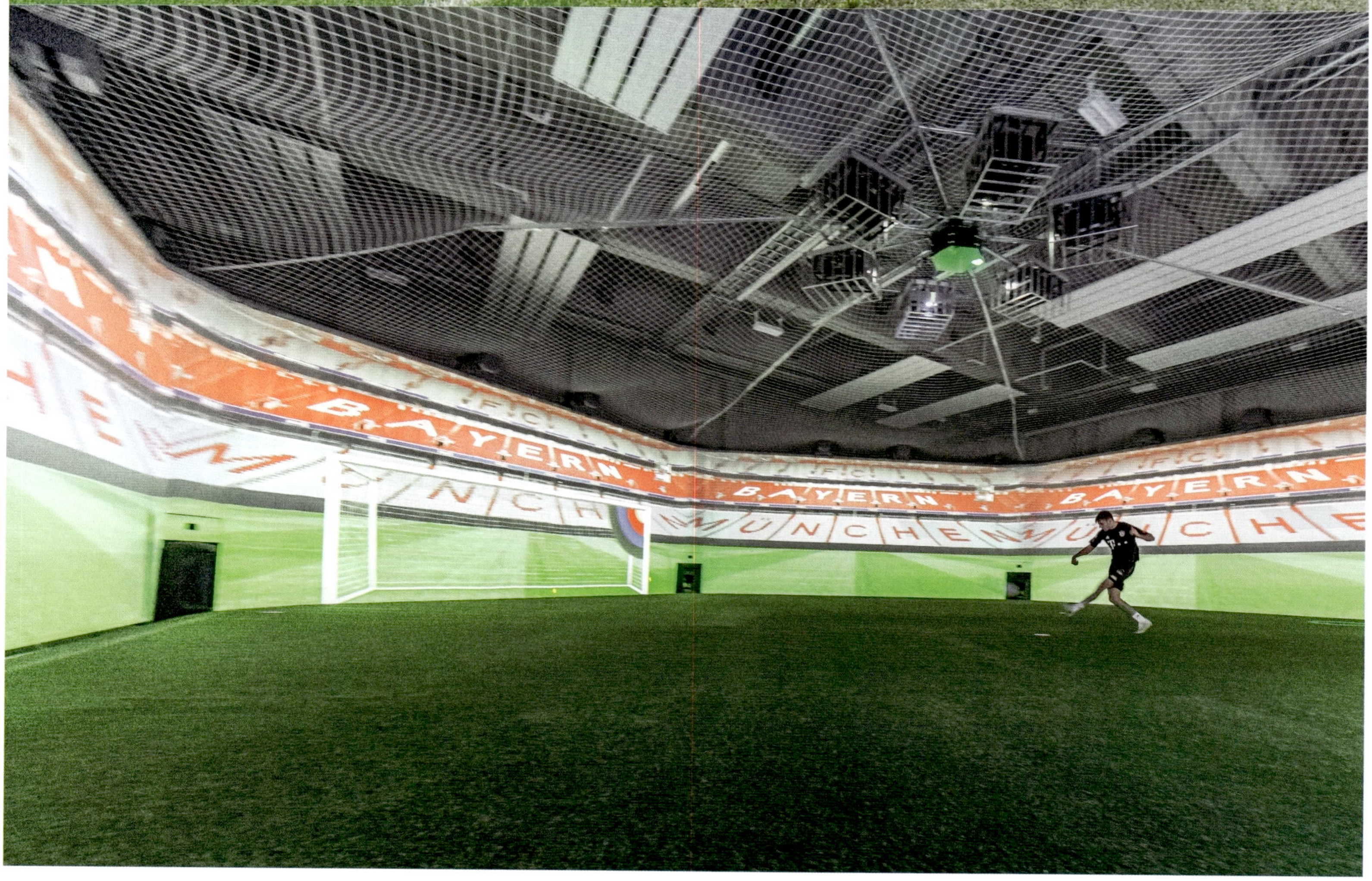
BAYERN

FROM THE CAMPUS TO **GLOBAL STADIUMS**

When the Campus was opened in 2017, Uli Hoeness described the investment of €70 million "FC Bayern's answer to the transfer madness". In its first seven years, twenty-nine players trained by FC Bayern have made their debut in the professional team, more than at any other club in Germany.

Some, like Aleksandar Pavlović, Josip Stanišić and of course Jamal Musiala, who came from Chelsea FC in 2019 as a sixteen-year old, have been given long-term professional contracts by FCB. Others, for example Joshua Zirkzee and Malik Tillman, yielded high transfer fees, which cover part of the costs of developing talent. "Today we are increasingly reaping the rewards of our good youth work," said Campus chief Jochen Sauer in 2024. Among those who completed the training programme in the years 1999 to 2003, he calculates that the proportion who became professionals was 39 per cent.

On an area four times as large as that on Säbener Strasse, the Campus provides perfect training facilities – including the Skills.Lab, a football simulator in which a projector shows changing playing situations and the players have to find solutions with a ball that comes to them from a ball machine. An equally important element is the network of clubs where talented youngsters can take their first steps in professional football after their training course on loan, but still closely monitored by FC Bayern. In the 2024–25 season, the club loaned twenty-two players, five of them in the Bundesliga. Before reaching this stage, however, they are meant to be real FC Bayern players who have internalised the playing philosophy of all teams, emphasising "dominance" and "dynamism". The overarching aim is always the maximum flow from the youth programme to the professional squad.

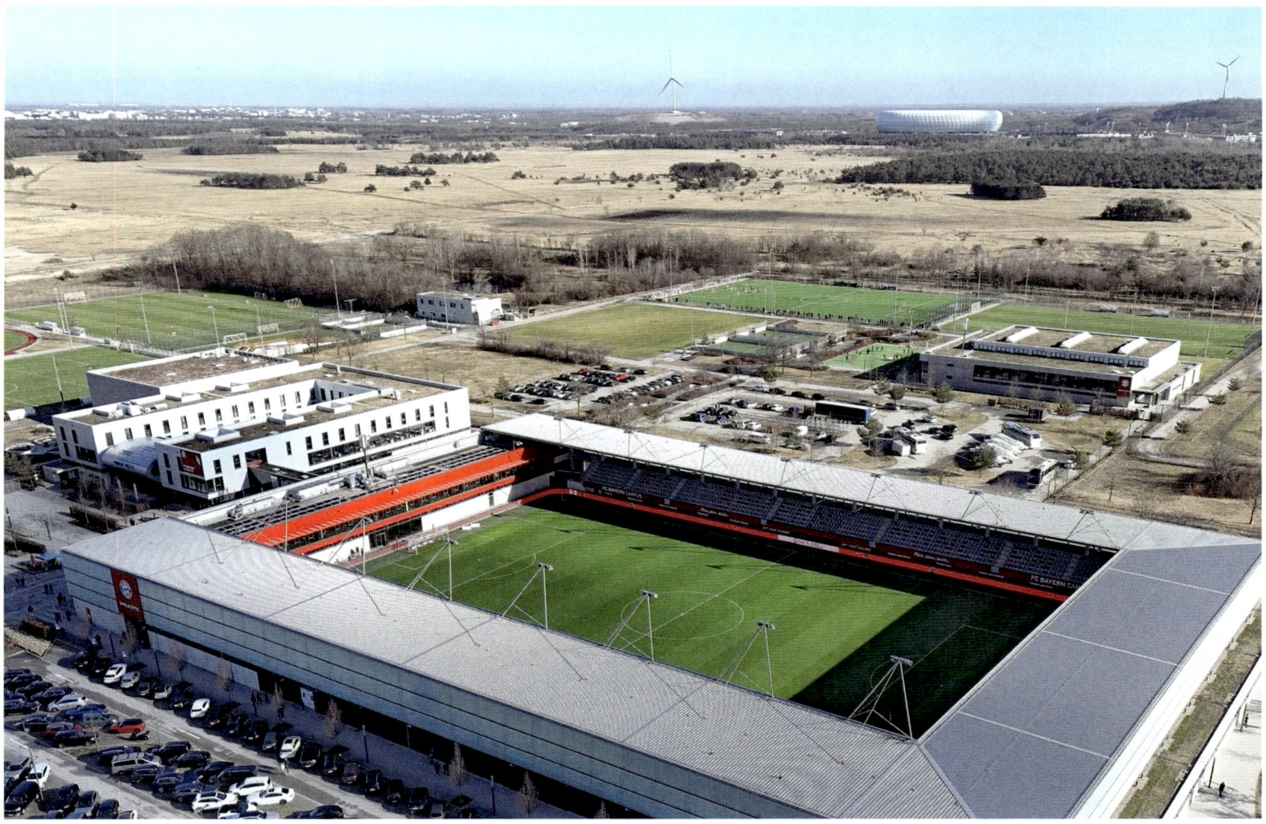

On the eight football pitches and thirty hectares of the FC Bayern Campus, all FCB youth teams train and play, from the under-9s to the under-19s, as do all the women's and girls' teams. In the central playing area, which holds 2,500 spectators, the Bundesliga home games of the under-17s and under-19s, as well as those of the under-19s in the UEFA Youth League, are held.

THE FIRST **CHAMPIONS**

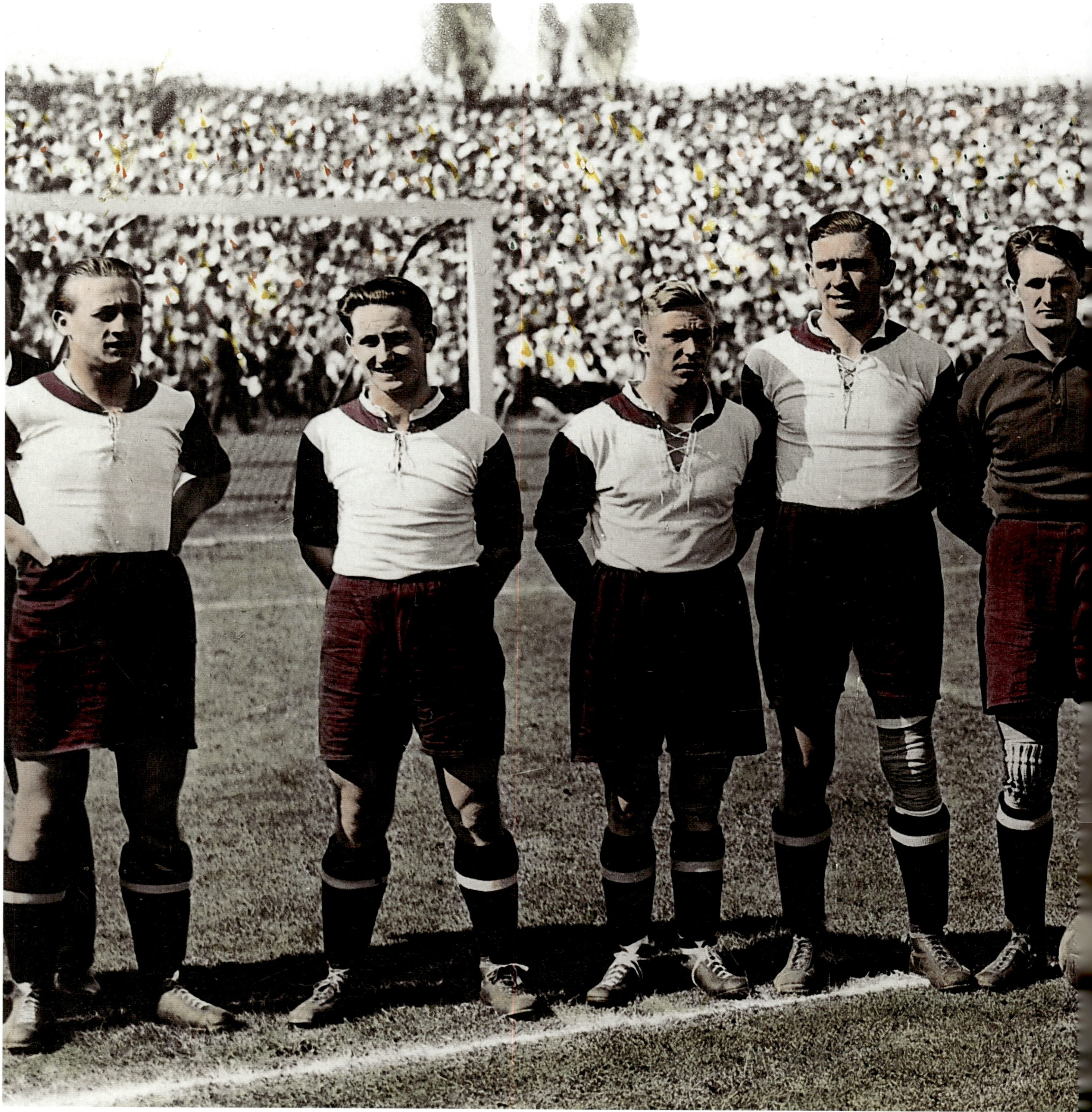

They were the team of the future, who played the most modern football in Germany: the eleven men who won FC Bayern's first championship on 12 June 1932 with a 2-0 win against Eintracht Frankfurt. The future was dark, however. Under the rule of the National Socialists, who came to power six months later, FCB were never able to continue the success that they had under their Jewish coach Richard Dombi, who emigrated to Spain via Switzerland in 1933. Oskar Rohr (far right), who converted the spot kick for 1-0, went to France to turn professional. Franz Krumm (fourth from right), scorer of the goal for 2-0, died as a soldier on the eastern front in 1943, four days after Josef Bergmaier (second from left), the outstanding player in the final, who set up both goals.

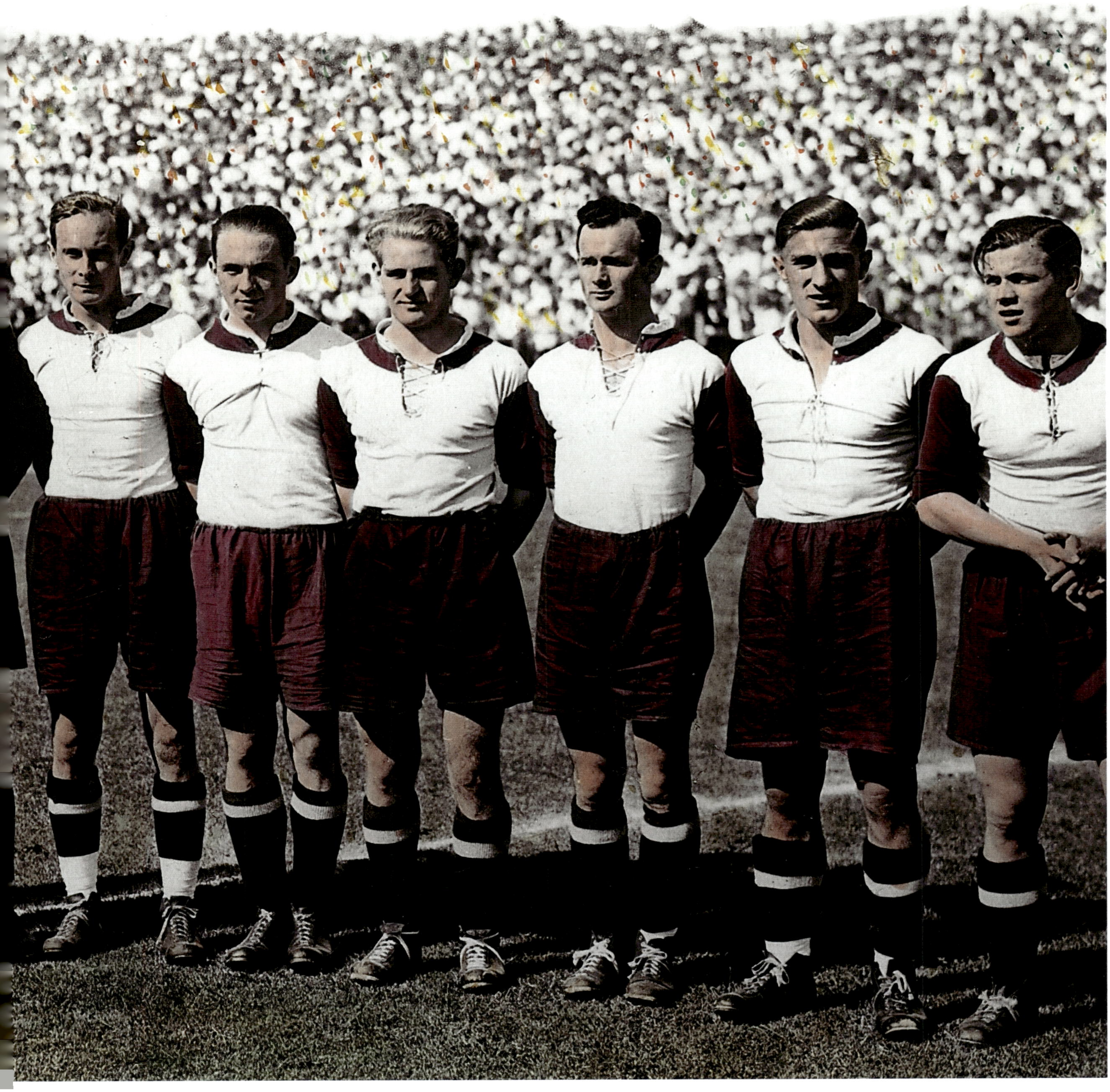

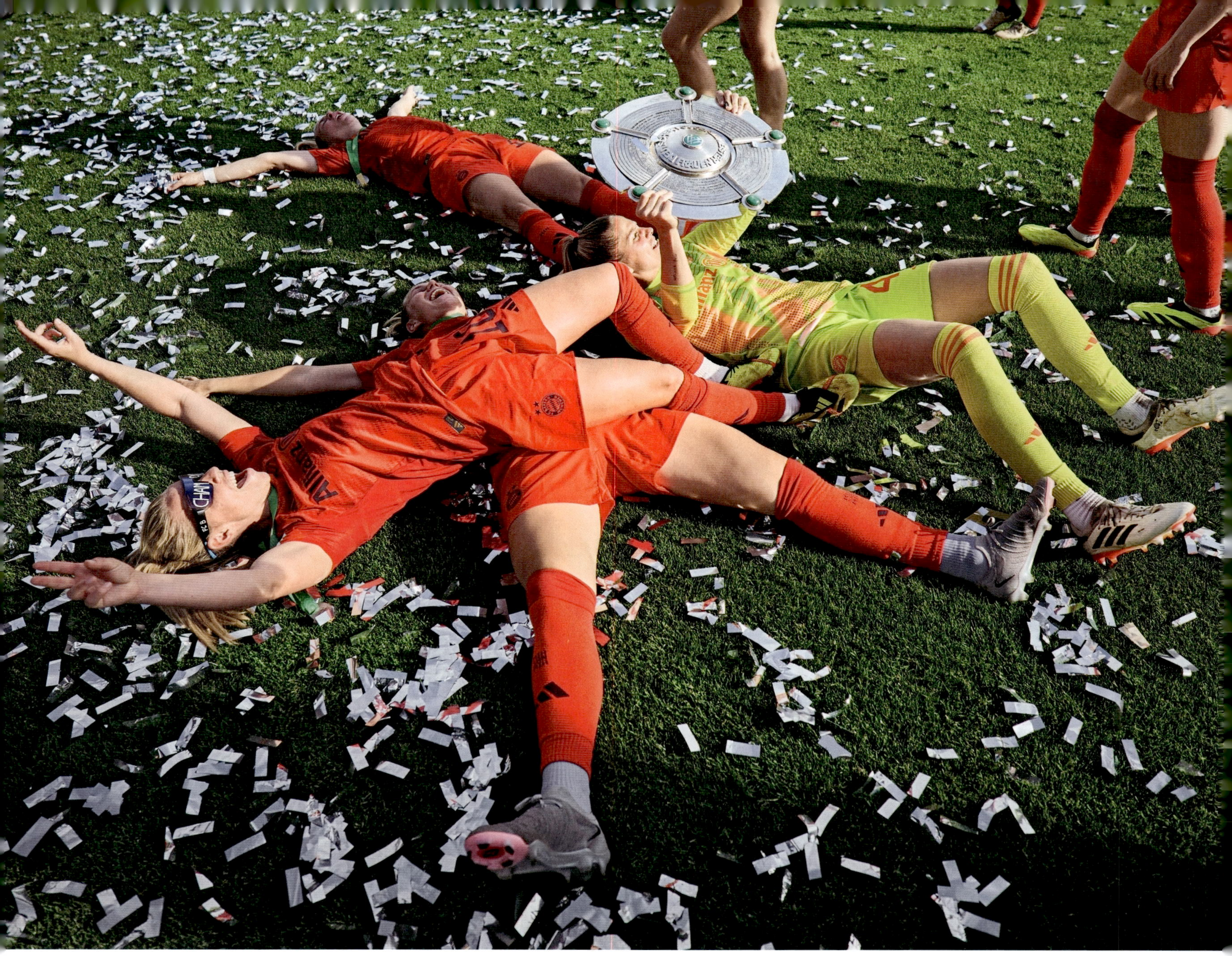

IN SIXTH HEAVEN

It's the last day of the season. For the football women, too, that means that summer has come.

What could be better than simply falling onto the green grass, surrounded by shining snippets of paper, smelling the scent of fresh wheat beer? With the championship shield in your hand – the genuine version this time. Two weeks earlier, with a 2–1 win in Leverkusen, the Bayern women had already clinched their defence of the title, but there they celebrated with a fan's shield made from cardboard. Following the 4–1 victory in Hoffenheim, in May 2024, the real championship shield, the one made of silver, was theirs for the sixth time in the club's history. Following a whole Bundesliga season without defeat. After the summer holidays, the next celebration was due: a first win in the Super Cup thanks to a 1–0 victory against VfL Wolfsburg.

Whether it's Dr Müller-Wohlfahrt (with Franck Ribéry), Dr Hahne (with Harry Kane) or Professor Dr Ueblacker (with Manuel Neuer): team doctors have to be quick. Quick in getting to an injured player, quick in diagnosing. Can he carry on? Do we need a substitute? There on the pitch, far from all medicinal apparatus, they need the skill that Müller-Wohlfahrt named in the title of his autobiography, "seeing with your hands". For the legendary medical check-ups and the team's internal medicine, the cardiologist Prof. Dr Schmidt is responsible.

HEALING HANDS AND **HIGH-END MEDICINE**

When Dr Hans-Wilhelm Müller-Wohlfahrt became team doctor in 1977, this was the medical department: "A bathtub, a sauna, two couches, a masseur, two cupboards, two pots of ointment." Today two orthopaedic doctors, a specialist for internal medicine and seven physiotherapists are equipped with MRT, CT and ultrasound to ensure the best possible medical care of the professional players.

Ahead of almost every training session in Säbener Strasse, Prof. Dr Peter Ueblacker, alternating with Dr Jochen Hahne, who is also the doctor of the German national team, discusses the fitness and robustness of every player with the athletics coaches and physiotherapists. Prof. Dr Roland Schmidt, the club's cardiologist and internal specialist, who is head consultant for internal medicine at the Brothers of Mercy Hospital in Munich, is always involved too. If a problem arises in training, an orthopaedic doctor is always on call in the neighbouring surgery. Just as important as modern radiography equipment is the doctor's skill with which, according to Karl-Heinz Rummenigge, Müller-Wohlfahrt "set a global benchmark in sports medicine" in four decades with FCB, and which is valued by exceptional athletes such as Usain Bolt: feeling injuries with the fingers, including injuries that can be prevented by rest. The consequence was that in 2012–13, the treble-winning season, Müller-Wohlfahrt recorded "only three muscular injuries" in the squad.

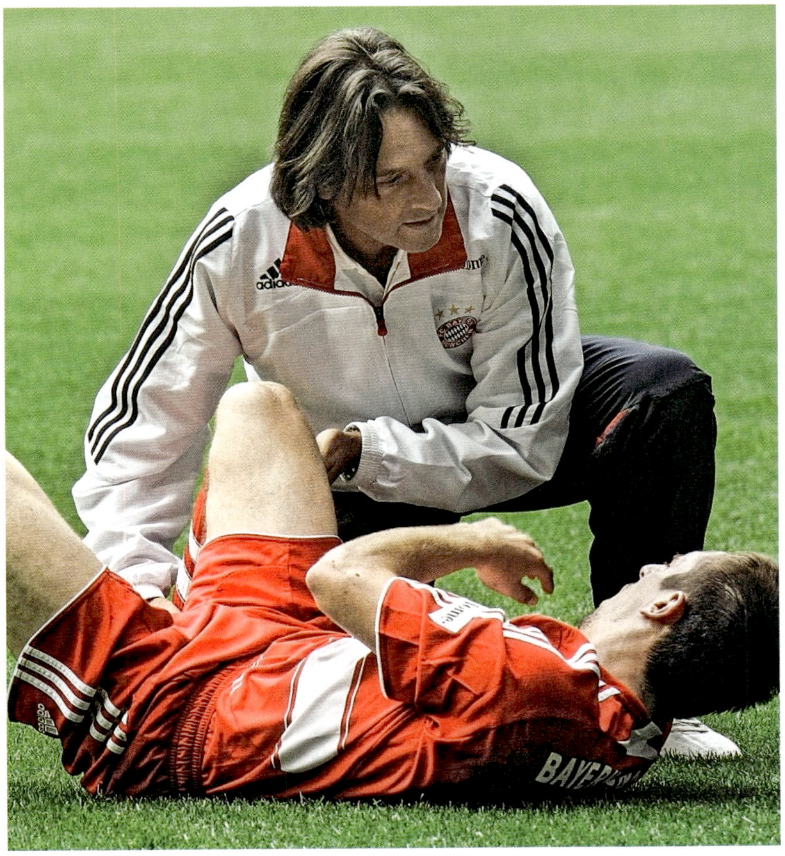

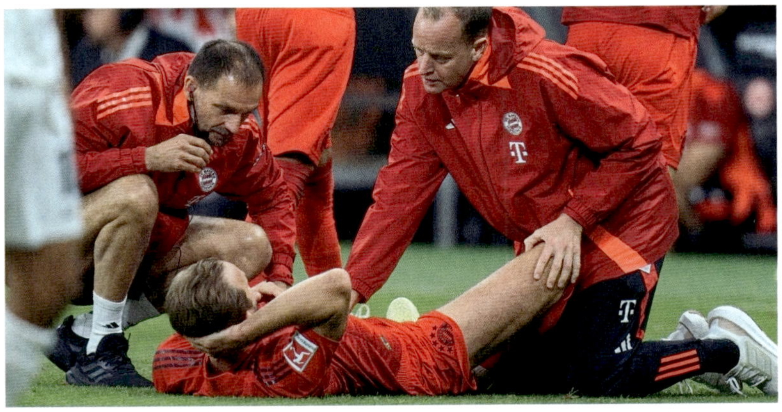

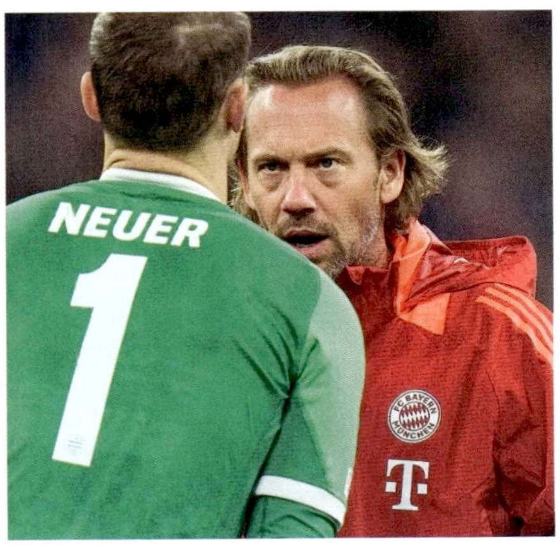

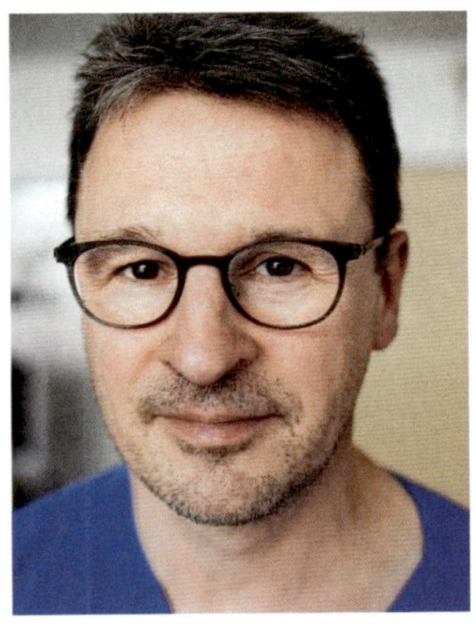

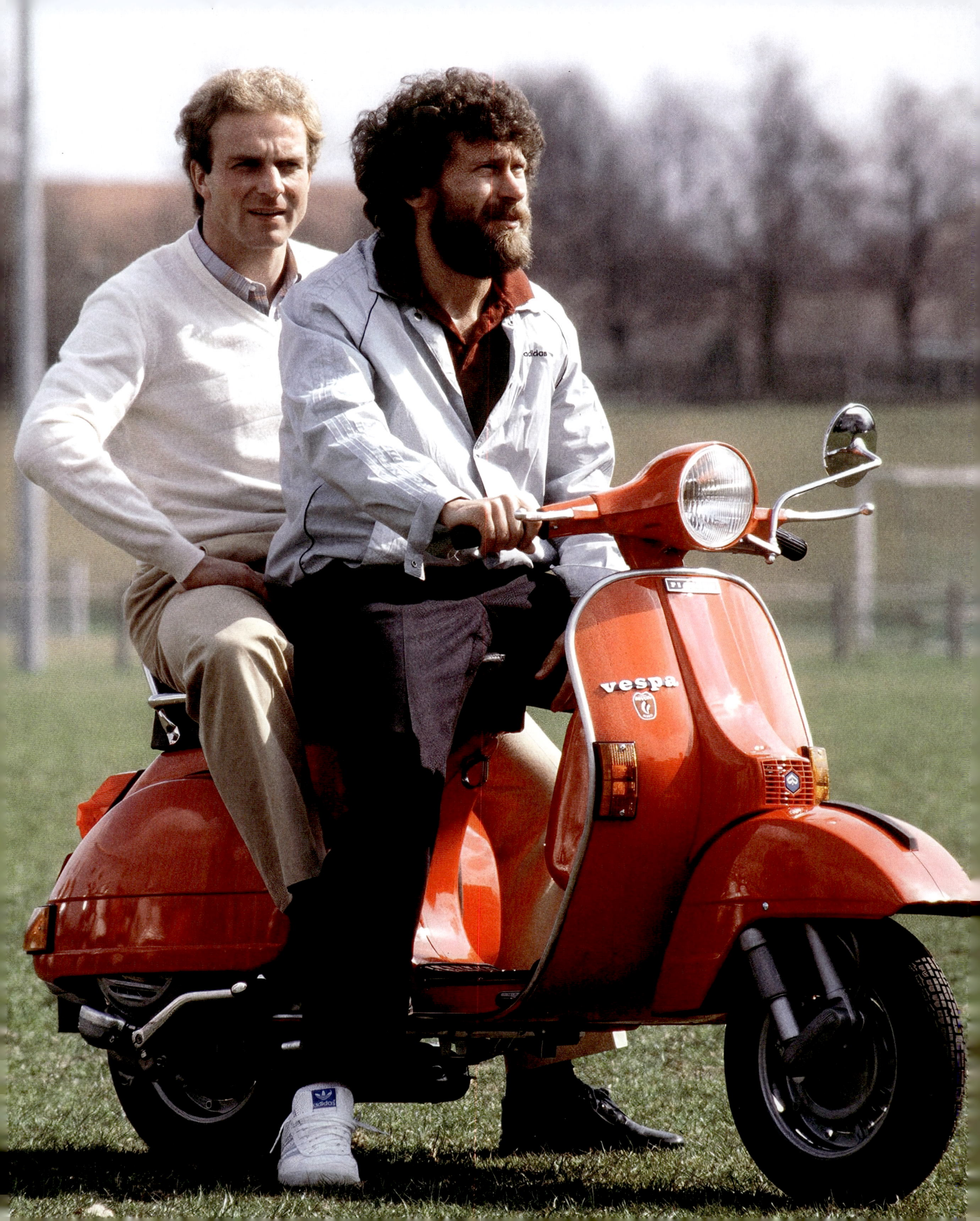
adidas
vespa
adidas

THE NET-
WORKER

The first big game for the trio of Franz, Uli & Kalle in 1974 ended in a 0–6 defeat against Offenbach. In 1991 they came together in new roles – and made their mark on an era of success.

The 1991–92 season was the worst since gaining promotion to the Bundesliga in 1965. In the league, the club were only five points above relegation, in the cup they were knocked out by second-division Homburg, and in the UEFA Cup took a shameful 2–6 hammering from B 1903 Kopenhagen. The manager Hoeness looked for new faces for the club – and found two ex-colleagues for the job. The new vice-presidents meant a “trebling of expertise in the club”, as he later described it. Franz Beckenbauer, soon to be president, a man of the people, was a brilliant club representative – while Karl-Heinz (“Kalle”) Rummenigge busily built up an international network that benefits FCB to this day. In 2002 Rummenigge became president of the board of the spin-off company FC Bayern Fussball AG, and remained in the role until 2021. Working with Hoeness, he increasingly succeeded in striking the difficult balance between financial stability and sporting success – which had tipped the wrong way in 1991, when the club sold the international players Kohler and Reuter and acquired, apart from high transfer earnings, a huge hole in the defence. For all this, Kalle never saw himself as an “official”, a man for finances, balance sheets and political manoeuvres. But as a man for football: “For me, the most important day in every week is match day at the weekend”.

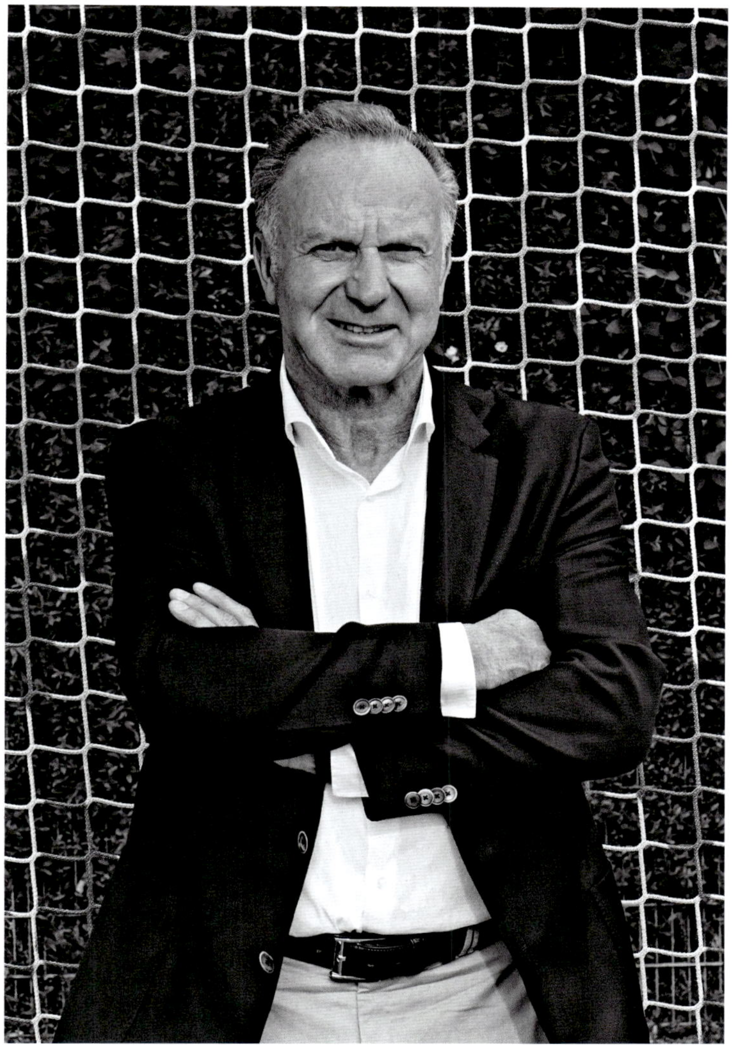

As vice-president and chairman of the board, you have to cut a good figure in many roles: as passenger on Paul Breitner’s scooter, signing your own biography, hugging the Belgian national team goalkeeper and Bayern colleague Jean-Marie Pfaff - and of course, for a former forward, it’s no problem to be in the place that matters in football: in front of goal.

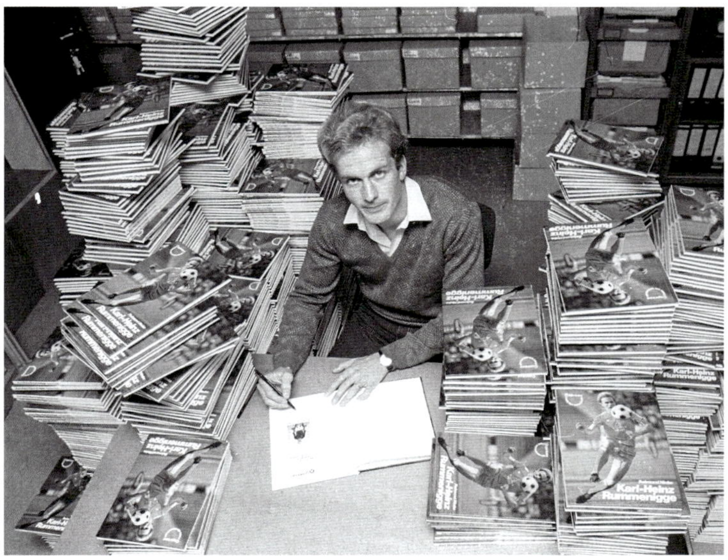

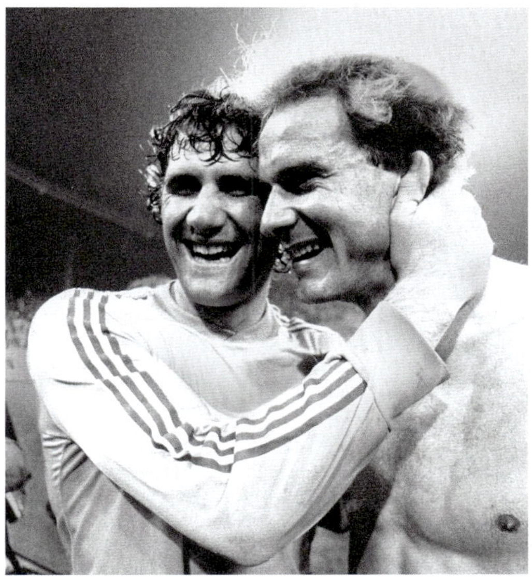

Who doesn't enjoy watching other people work? Especially if they are world-class footballers. The public training sessions presented by FC Bayern to its fans free of charge at regular intervals - something that few top clubs in Europe do - are a great crowd-puller at Säbener Strasse. They attract up to 3,000 spectators.

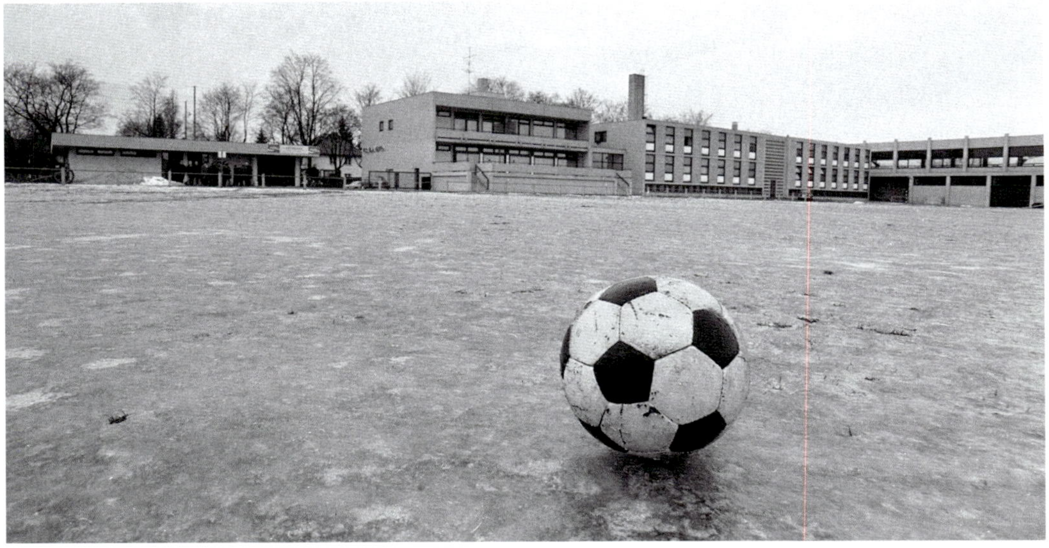

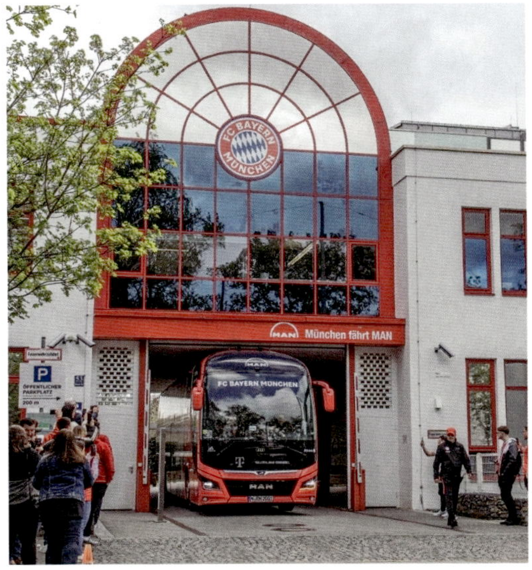

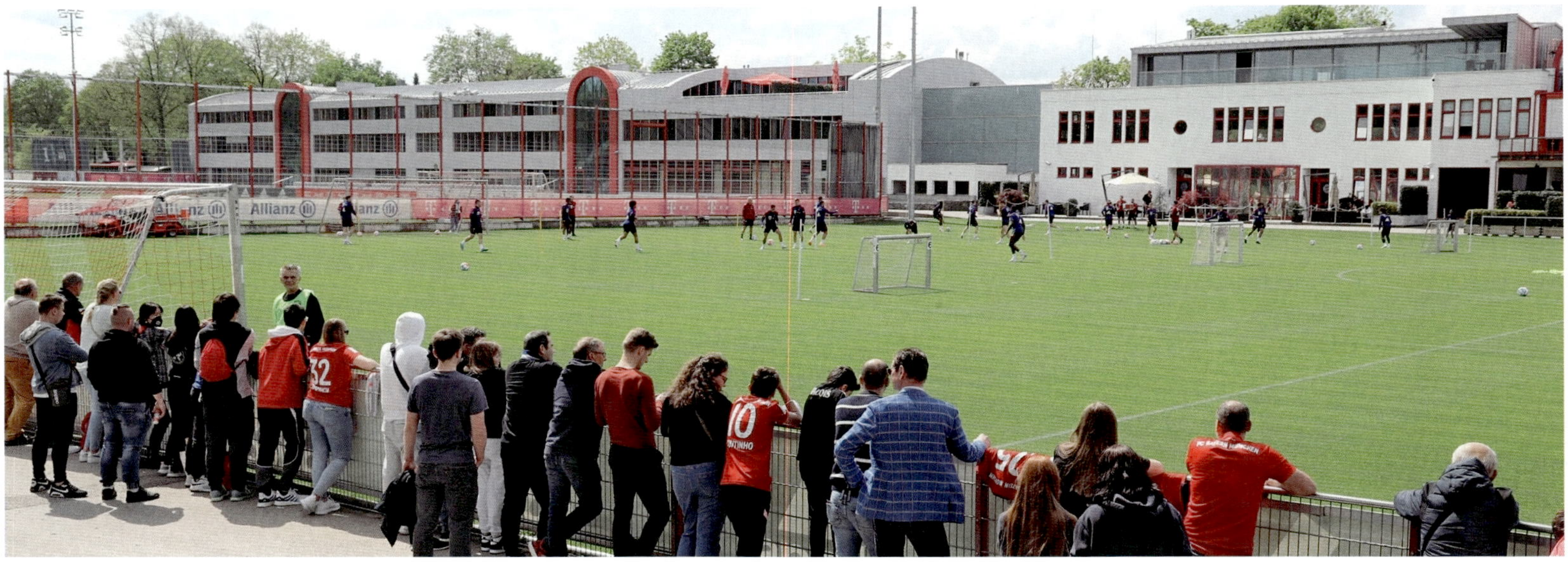

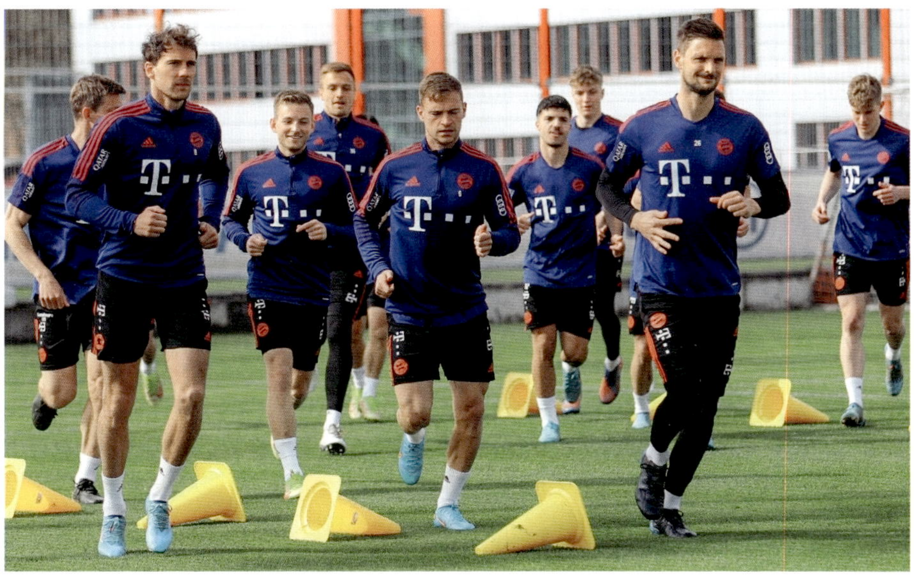

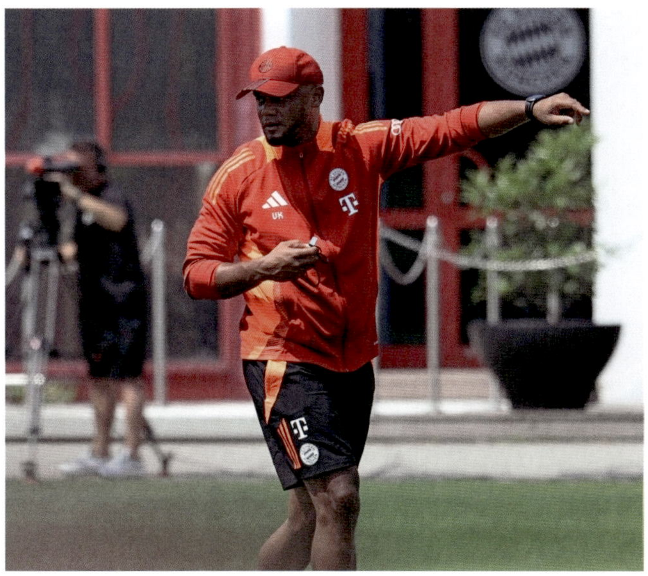

SÄBENER STRASSE – **AT THE FOREFRONT**

If football were a game of Monopoly, the top-ranking street on the board would be Säbener Strasse in Munich, the best address in German football. A field with a wooden hut became a group headquarter with ideal working conditions.

"Without Gerd", said Franz Beckenbauer in 1995 when Gerd Müller reached the age of 50, "we would still have the old wooden shed on Säbener Strasse for a changing room." The importance of Müller's goals was matched by the stubbornness of ex-president Kurt Landauer. Returning home from exile in Switzerland after the war, he lobbied the city authorities for years, until what was once the "Harlaching local sports facility" on Säbener Strasse at last became a permanent training ground for the club. The original rent was DM 1,000 per year, but not until 1971 was there enough money to modernise the training ground and accommodate the club's offices there for the first time. Following the most recent modernisation in 2018, FC Bayern has everything that a leading club needs on an area of 80,000 square metres at Säbener Strasse: five grass pitches, one with artificial grass, a beach volleyball court and a gym, a service centre, fan shop and an office building. Everything except a wooden shed.

The new performance centre – with the building permit already applied for – will house the changing rooms, coaches' offices, players' canteen, fitness and physiotherapy rooms, rehabilitation pool and cold chambers. Moving forward, the infrastructure of the headquarters will occupy a top position among European football clubs. Conversion of the adjacent office buildings is also being considered.

Existing buildings
Planned expansion of the performance centre

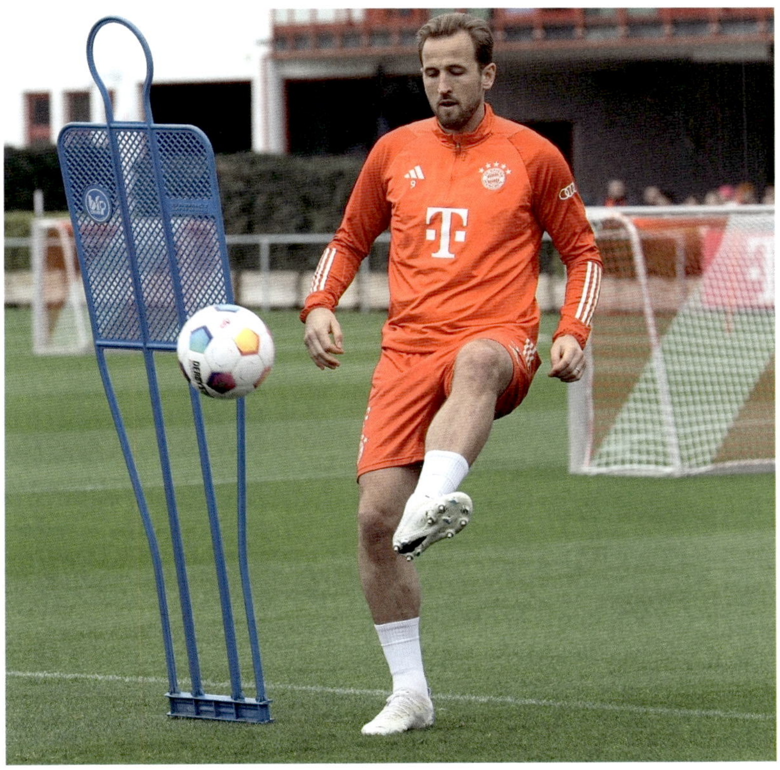

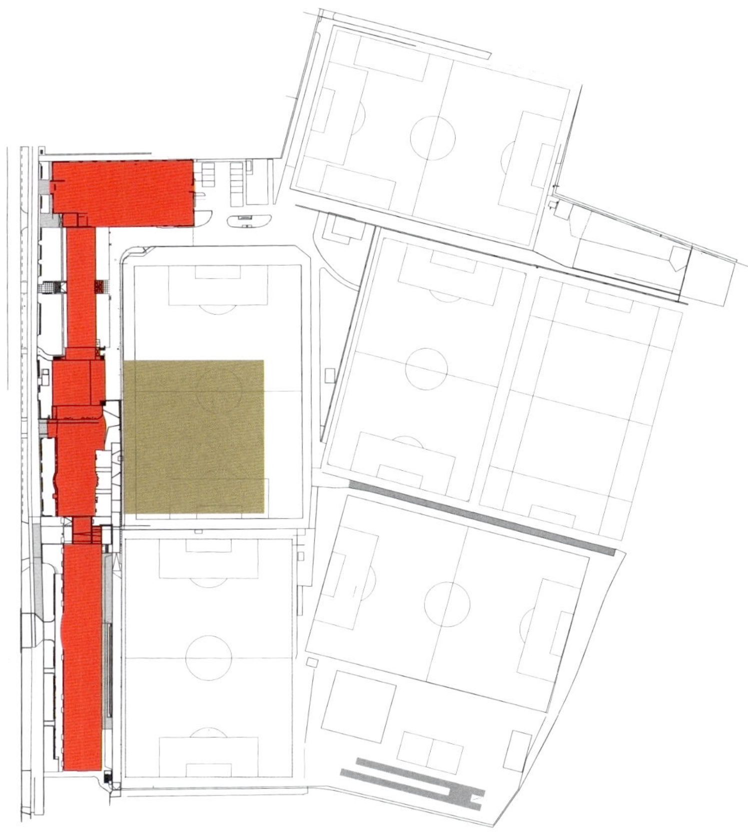

JAMAL **FOREVER**

Leroy Sané christened him “Bambi”. And Joshua Kimmich took him to the gym after training to put more muscle on his slender Bambi body. That clearly made a difference.

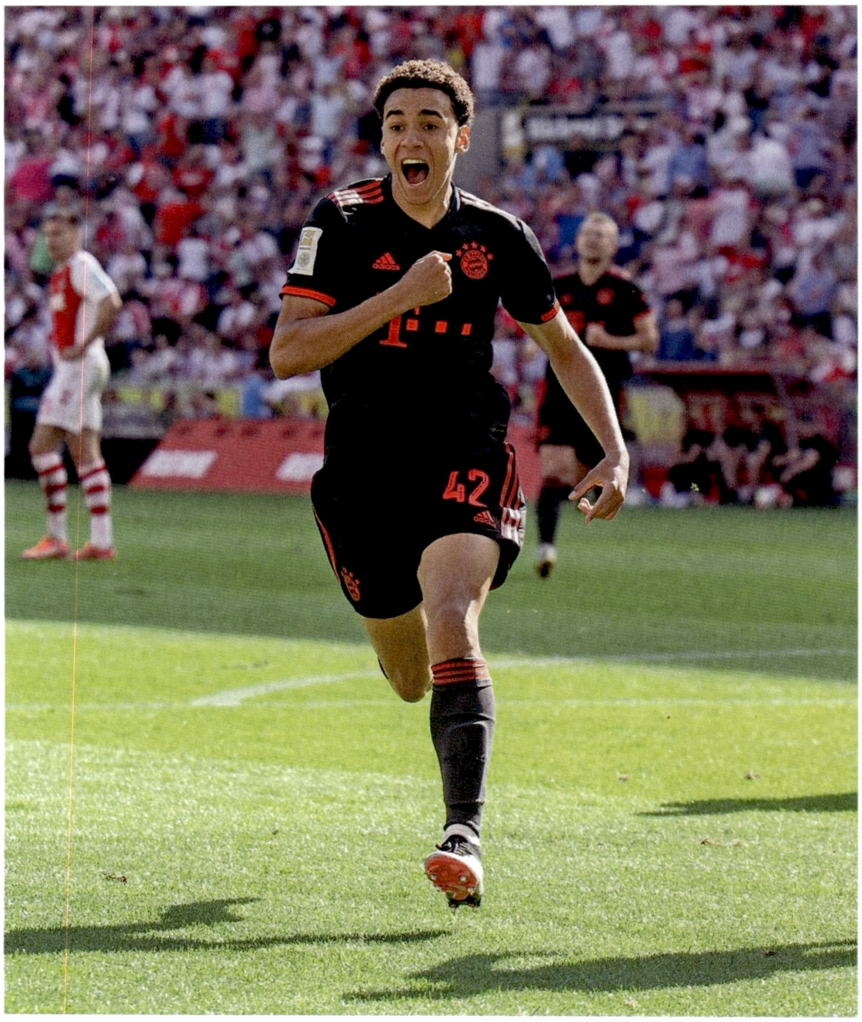

When he was 5 years old, there was only one thing that his coach in Fulda could teach him: not to celebrate when the opposition scored. Little Jamal was delighted at every goal, whoever scored it. In England he was tipped for a professional career at the age of just 7. That career would probably have been in the United Kingdom, but Brexit made his mother want to return to Germany. So Musiala, available from Chelsea at 16 without a transfer fee, was a stroke of good fortune that happens only once in a blue moon, even for a club like FC Bayern. At 17 he played in the Bundesliga and scored goals, played in the Champions League and scored goals, then at 18 got his international cap and scored. At FCB he has been a fixture since 2023 at the latest, when his late winning goal in Cologne sealed the eleventh championship win in succession. At 21, Musiala has seen four Bayern coaches, three national coaches, two European Championship tournaments and a World Cup. And one thing is certain: the best is yet to come.

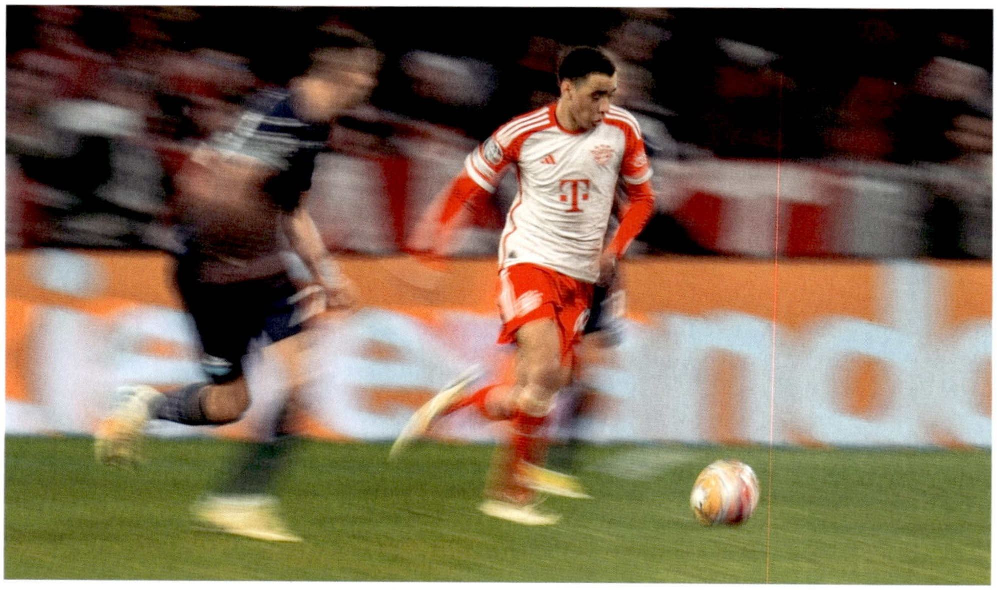

On the ball, Bambi turns into a snake man. Jamal Musiala twists and turns through the smallest gap and has an ability that Lionel Messi brought to perfection: to keep the ball on his foot while dribbling without losing speed. Hardly anyone masters this art as he does - to merge his own motion with that of the ball so that it seems as if opponents are, as they say in German football, “out-played on a beer mat”. But he does not like beer.

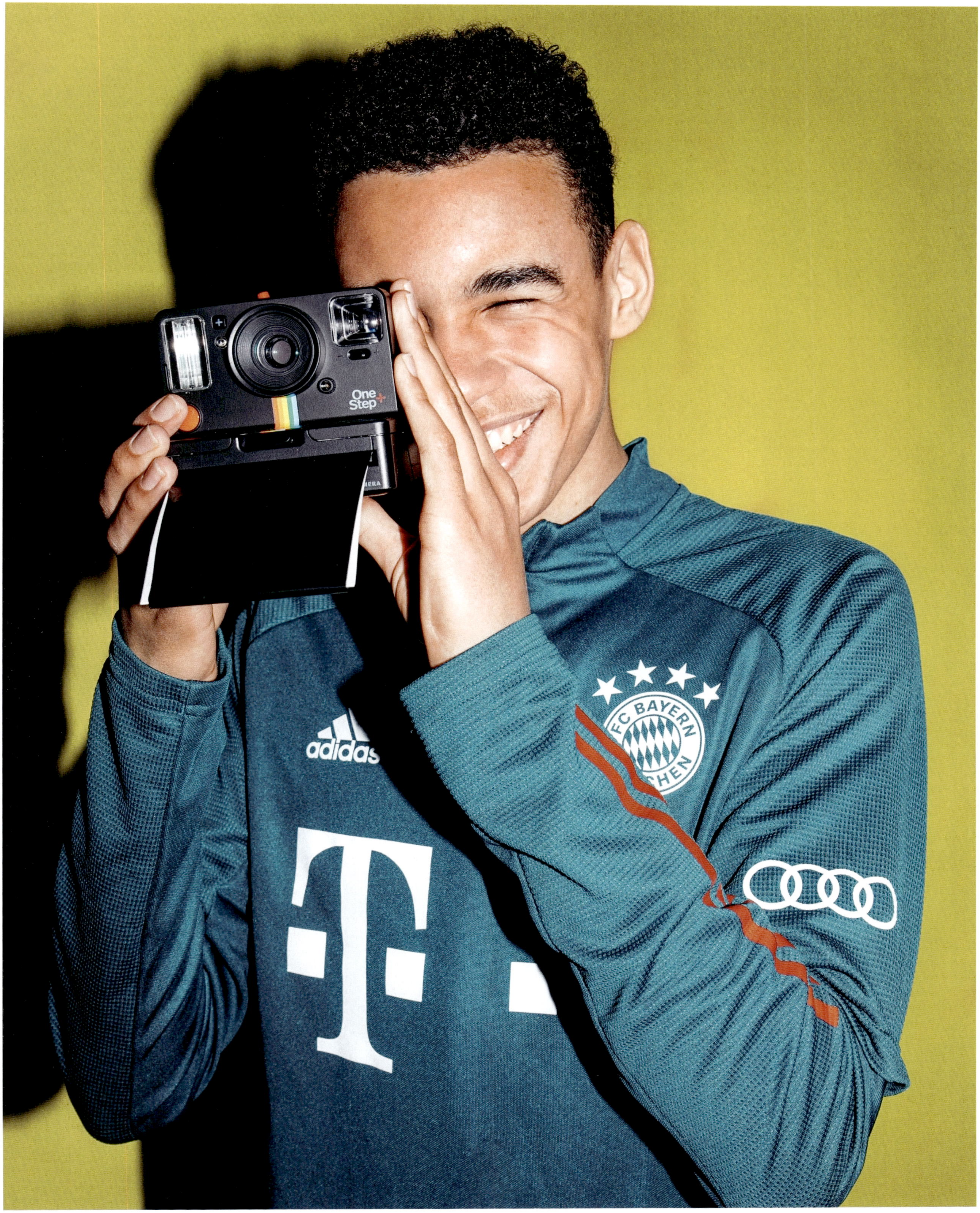
One
Step+
adidas
FC BAYERN

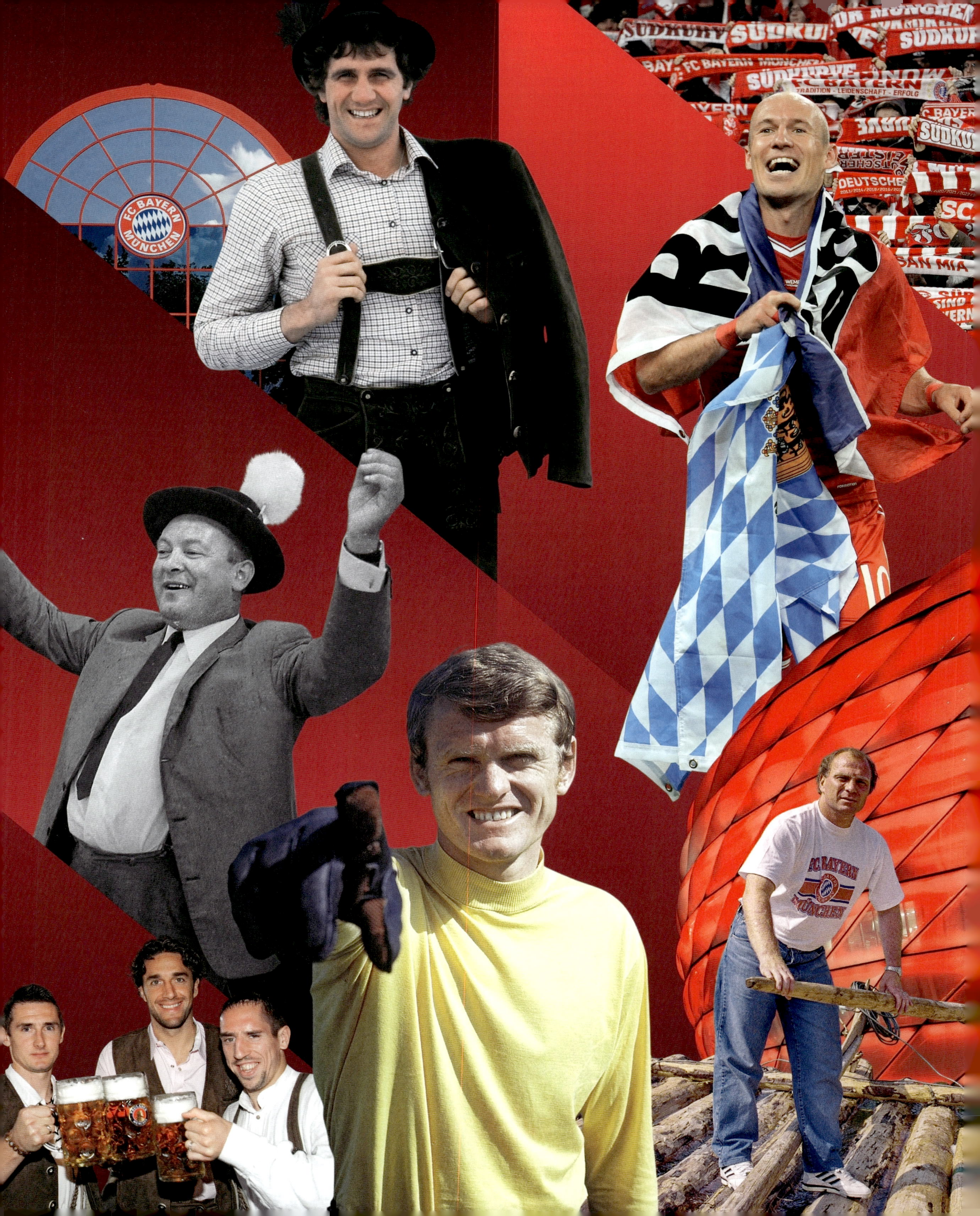
FC BAYERN MÜNCHEN
SÜDKURVE
FC BAYERN
TRADITION · LEIDENSCHAFT · ERFOLG
FC BAYERN MÜNCHEN

HOME

When eleven young men left the Bäckerhöfl tavern on Carnival Tuesday in 1900, they were homeless. In sporting terms. They founded a club that is a home today for the emotions of millions.

125 YEARS OF **HOME**

The Männer-Turn-Verein München von 1879, being a men's gymnastics club, did not want to let its small, recently established football section take part in a regular league. The gymnasts, with their German nationalist roots, regarded the English ball-kicking game with suspicion. So the eleven footballers left, moved to Café Gisela a few blocks away, and founded their own club. And, perhaps because most of them did not originally come from Munich and Bavaria – they were from Saxony, Prussia, the Hanseatic north – they gave the club the most home-sounding name that was possible: FC Bayern München, or Bavaria Munich.

Today FCB has become an emotional home for people far beyond Munich and Bavaria. More than 10 million Germans describe themselves as followers of Bayern. In 2024 some 140 million people around the world followed FCB on social media. The roots of this national and international fame and popularity lie in the 1960s and 1970s, when FC Bayern, not being rich, put its faith in talented youngsters from the region, and thanks to the class of Franz Beckenbauer and Gerd Müller rose in record time from the regional league to become a leading address in German and European football – including a major presence in live broadcasts of football, which were then still infrequent.

However, this global club, established by players without a home, spent a long time looking for its own footballing home. Founded in Schwabing, at first FCB played on different fields in that district, and from 1907 onwards at the wealthy Münchner Sportclub on high-class Leopoldstrasse. In 1925 they moved to the municipal Grünwalder Stadium in proletarian Giesing, and in 1972 to the Olympic Stadium. Each move meant a financial improvement, but still an emotional distance. The club was always a tenant, which means it was a stranger. "We wanted to give our fans a home," said Uli Hoeness of the plan that finally led to the Allianz Arena, which was opened in 2005 and became a world-famous sports ground straight away, visually unmistakable with its 2,760 cushions and 380,000 LED lights. It belongs entirely and without debt to FC Bayern and thus also to its fans.

For more than a hundred years, FC Bayern was no more than a rent-paying guest at its home grounds. At the opening of the Allianz Arena in 2005, the club, the team and the fans got their own home for the first time.

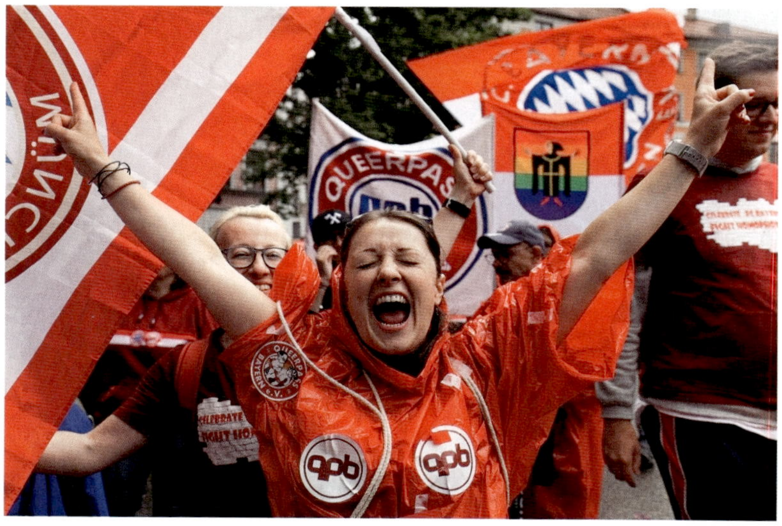

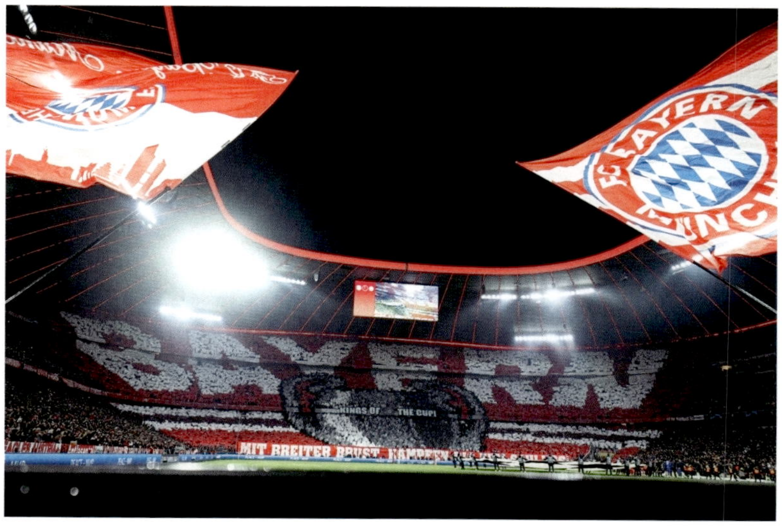

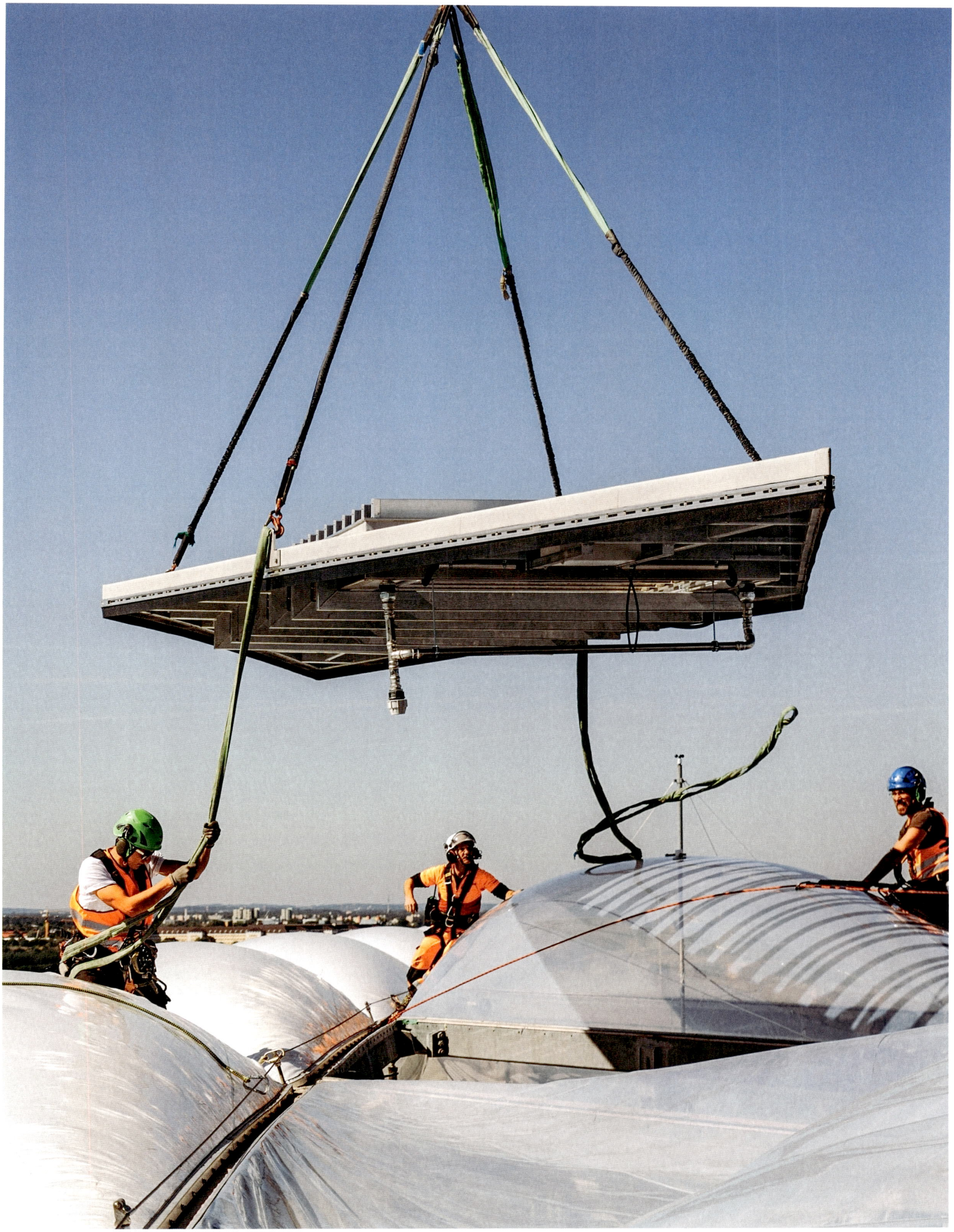

The heads and legs of the Bayern players, loosening up with gymnastics (photo right) before extra time, will feel heavy when Luis Aragonés scores from a free kick to make it 1-0 for Atlético. But then, late on, Katsche Schwarzenbeck will have his moment.

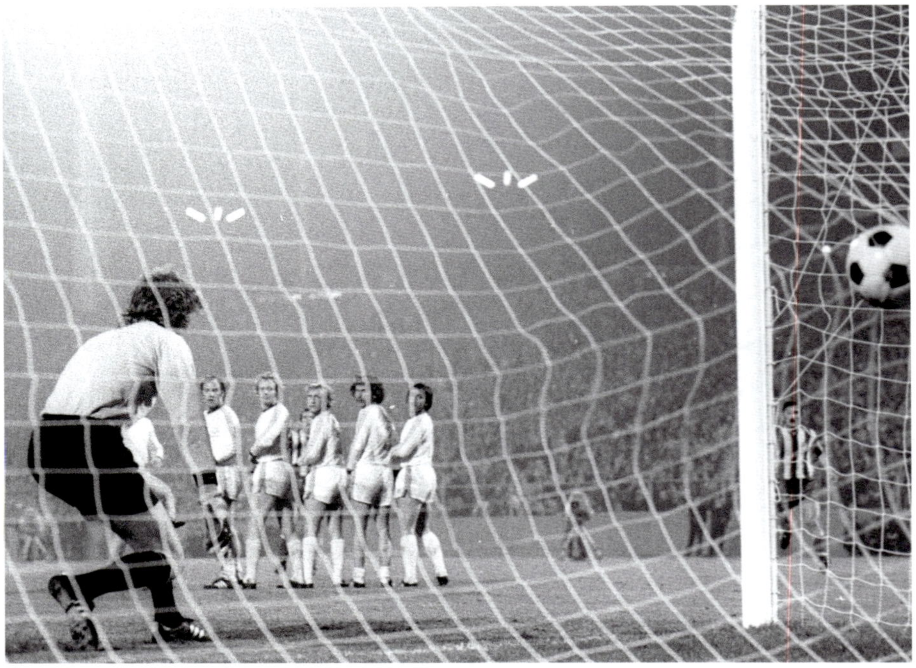

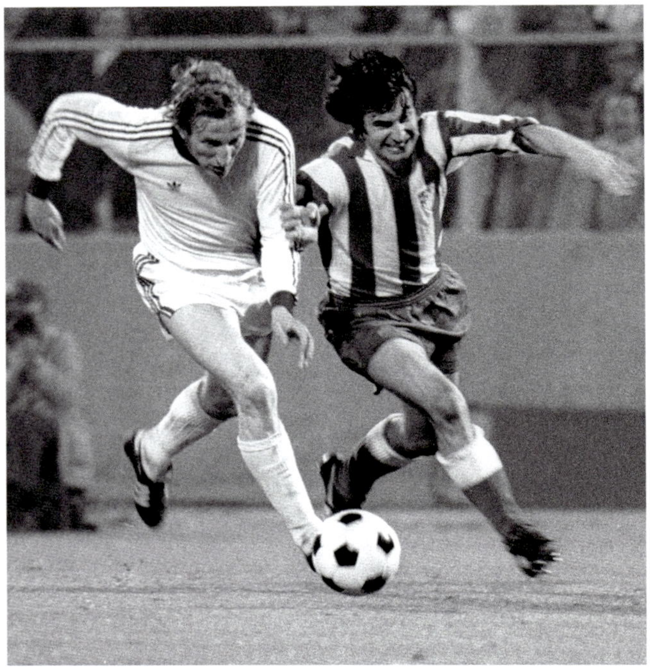

KATSCHE THE TALISMAN
FCB-ATLETICO 1-1 (AET) · 1974

The score is 0–1 in the final of the European Cup. It's the 120th minute, and what does Franz Beckenbauer do? Without knowing it, he takes one of his best decisions. He, the man with the genius touch, leaves the ball to someone whose genius mainly consists of hard work. Or in this case, shooting hard.

Decades later, Hans-Georg "Katsche" Schwarzenbeck is still astonished: "So Franz, who always complained if you passed to the side and said 'the goal is up front', so Franz passes sideways to me." At this moment Kaiser and Katsche, two very different kinds of lads from Giesing, who complement each other perfectly in defence, swap roles just for once. Schwarzenbeck takes the ball, runs off determinedly, not challenged by Atlético – he is only the holding defender, after all, so what could possibly go wrong? He backlifts, hits the ball so powerfully and at the same time so cleanly that it streaks low through a scrum of nine bodies and hurtles into the net. He's hugged and embraced by his teammates, first and foremost by Beckenbauer, like a talisman that brings good fortune.

The replay two days later is the consummation of good fortune, as Bayern win the cup for the first time. Later Uli Hoeness called it his "happiest day" at FC Bayern. The TV reporter Oskar Klose commented on his sixty-metre solo run to make the score 4–0, "Hoeness! Hoeness! Hoeness! One more man, one is still with him, he has to pass him, a second one is coming... now they'll bring him down!", and then corrected himself, "No, he's beaten them all! But Klose was wrong on both counts. They didn't bring him down. And Katsche Schwarzenbeck had already beaten them.

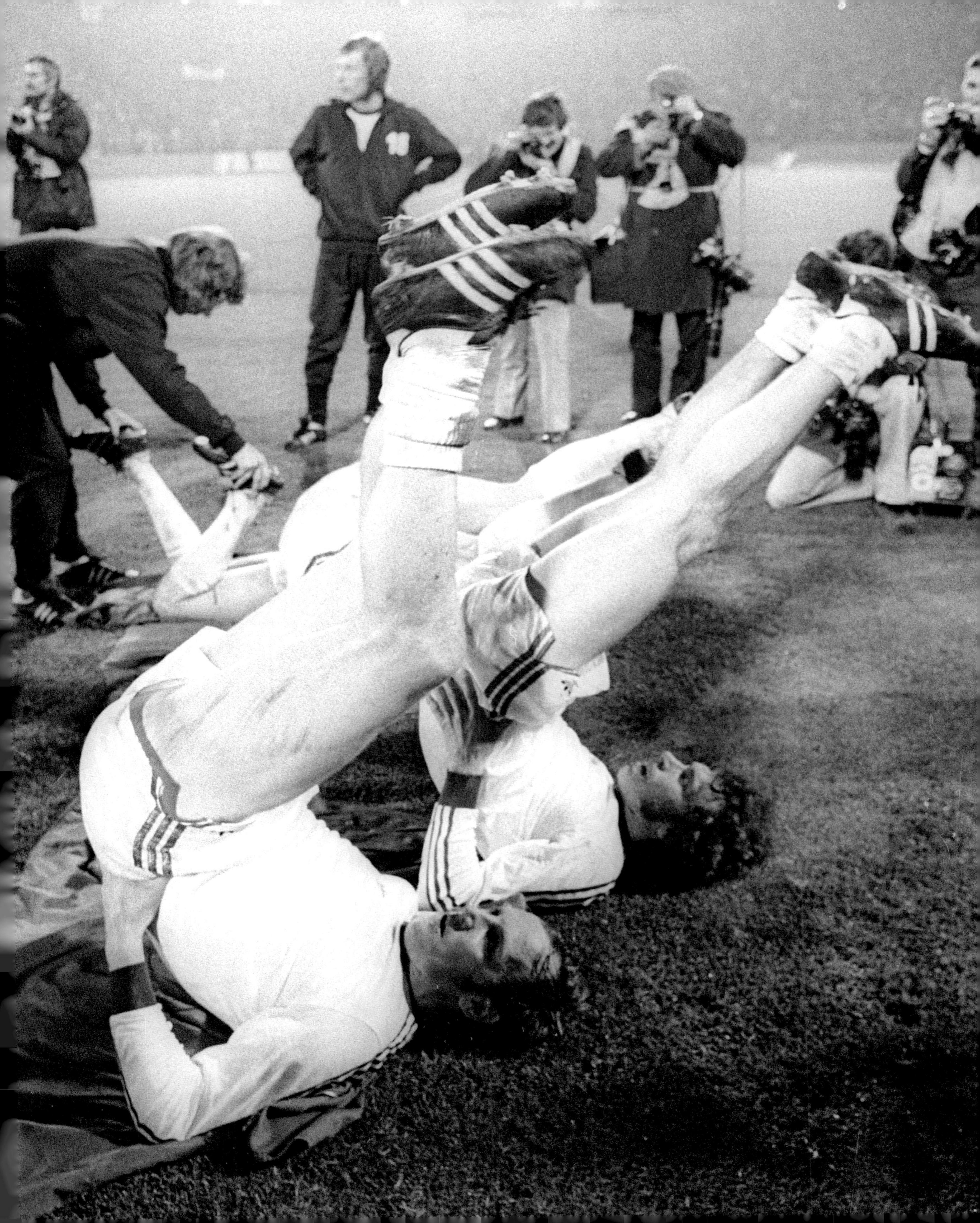

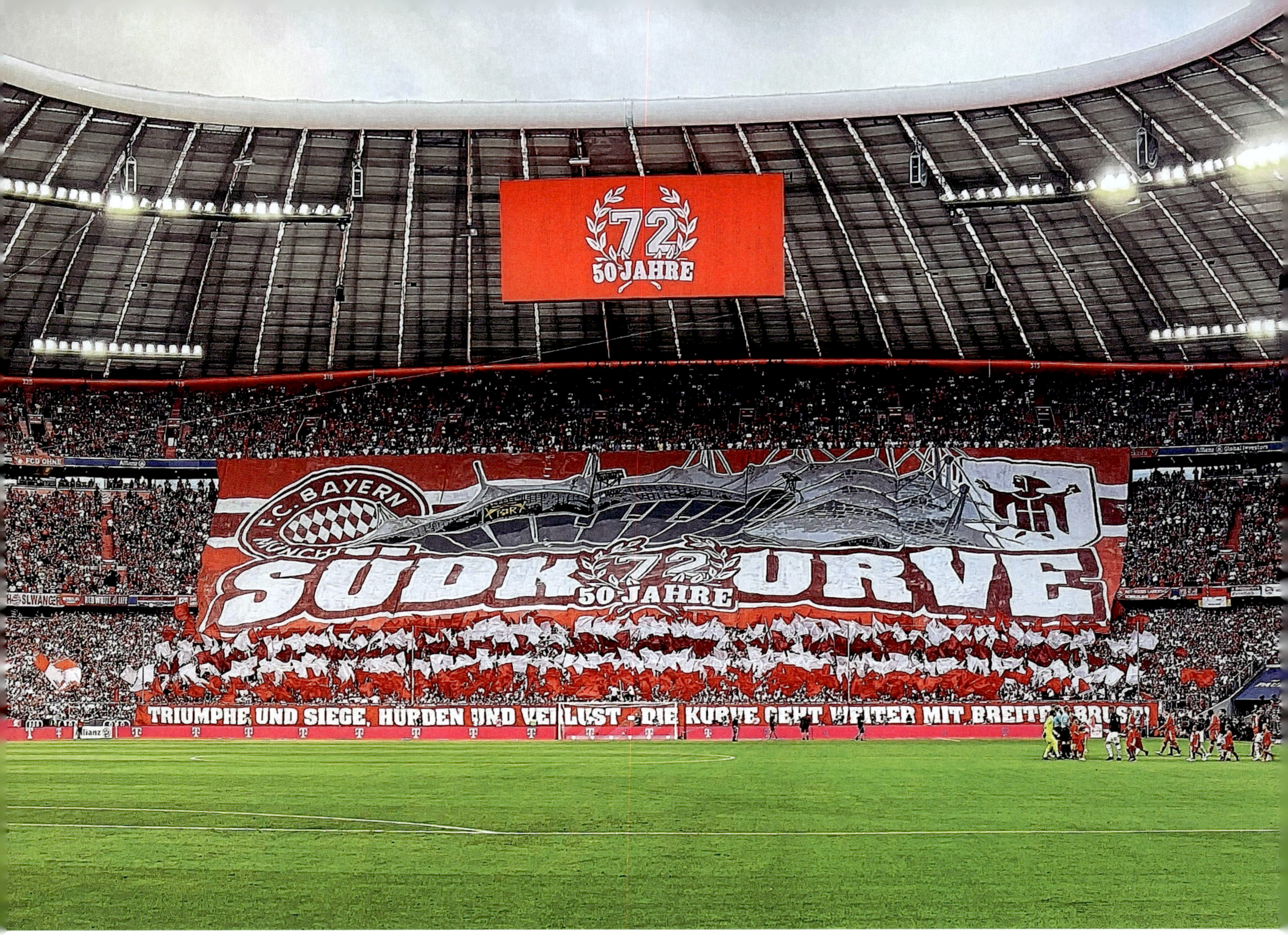

WE ARE FROM MUNICH, **WE ARE BAYERN**

Fifty years after they started up in the Olympic Stadium, the fans in the Südkurve cheer in the Allianz Arena – and "walk on proudly".

You come across curves everywhere: at driving school, in mathematics lessons, when studying beautiful forms. And in the stadium, where the "curve", i.e. the fans' stand behind the goal, can be more than it means anywhere else: a home. The fans of FCB found their home on 2 August 1972. They watched a match in one of the strangest competitions in the history of football: a "league cup" to bridge the gap caused by the Olympic Games, which extended the summer break until mid-September. This was an eleven-month tournament with qualifying groups formed from eighteen Bundesliga and fourteen regional league teams. All the same, the Olympic Stadium was full, as the match was a derby, with Beckenbauer and company seeming better motivated for their 3–1 against 1860 Munich than later against Bayern Hof (when they lost 1–4 and 4–5, and were knocked out). Shortly after the break, Gerd Müller scored the first goal that Bayern fans celebrated beneath the huge screen. During FCB's first game in the stadium, a masterly 5–1 against Schalke five weeks earlier, only the away fans had stood there, making more noise beneath the pinnacle of the tent roof with their shouts than the Bayern fans opposite them. So the fans switched ends, partly because the tickets were cheaper, and the Südkurve, the south end, the home of the most passionate fans, was born. In the Allianz Arena it has kept the name, even though the curve is more like a straight line there. In football a curve is not a bent shape, but a matter of allegiance.

SCHWABING, **OUR FIRST** HOME

The newly founded FC Bayern was a club from Schwabing. It was founded there and played its first matches there. And still exudes something of the libertarian spirit of this district.

In the early twentieth century, this district, incorporated into Munich only recently, in 1890, attracted students, artists and free spirits, as rents were low and it was close to the university and academy of arts. The comedian Karl Valentin performed there, the poet Joachim Ringelnatz wrote his verses, the satirical magazine *Simplicissimus* battled against the establishment. In this milieu of academics and artists, the newly founded FCB found members and grew. By 1906 matches were played at Clemensstrasse and then, following a merger with the Münchner Sportclub and until they took leave of Schwabing in 1924, in the stadium of the sports club on Leopoldstrasse. It was the first in Munich to have a small, covered wooden stand, and could hold 1,000, later up to 8,000 spectators. The all-round fencing was extremely useful. Why? The club could charge an entrance fee. This was the beginning of the business idea called Bayern Munich.

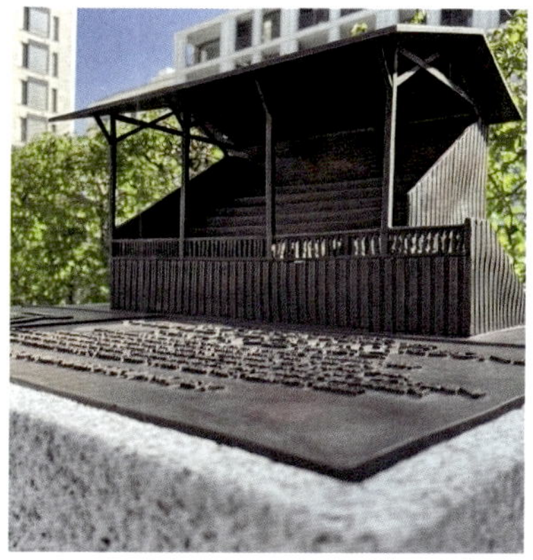

The "shoe box", a wooden stand for 200 spectators, was the pride of the stadium where FCB played from 1907 to 1924. Today a shoe-box-sized artwork in bronze on a memorial stone commemorates it.

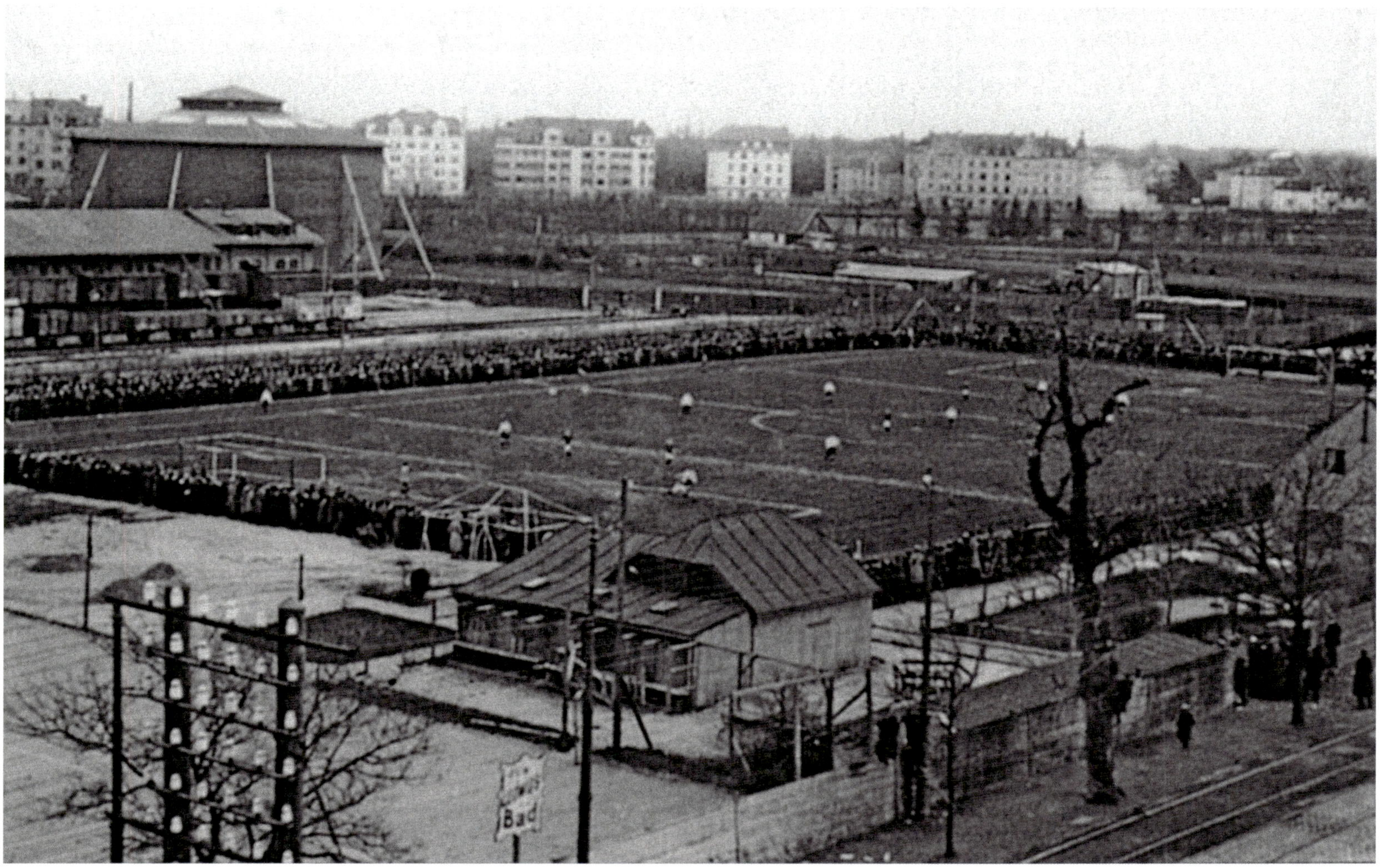

In his parents' house at what is now Zugspitzstrasse no. 6 in Munich-Giesing he was elevated above the ground - with a view from the fourth floor of the football ground of SC 1906, where little Franz and his brother Walter wriggled through the fence of loose posts to play barefoot with the neighbours' children. And then, as head of the organising committee of the 2006 World Cup, he hovered above the Allianz Arena in the north of Munich in a helicopter.

FROM THE HEIGHTS **OF GIESING** TO THE NORTH

FC Bayern is a child of Schwabing. But the club put down roots in Giesing, playing there in the Grünwalder Stadium from 1925 to 1972 and training at Säbener Strasse since 1949. In Giesing, shortly after the war, was born a child who was to transform the club.

"I grew up in the rubble of Giesing. We had almost nothing," Franz Beckenbauer said later. "We were street footballers, playing with bundles of wool because there were no proper balls." He earned money for the first time at the age of 8 and invested it in football immediately. "I collected rags and scrap metal so that I could finally swap our ball of cloth for a real leather one." Later, having lived in genteel Grünwald for some time, he returned to the old working-class area for the photographers, to his parents' house at Zugspitzstrasse no. 6 and to the sports ground opposite, where a global career started with the club SC 1906 München. As a young player he already seemed to hover above the ground, as he really did half a century later, in a helicopter above the Allianz Arena, which was built when he was president at Bayern.

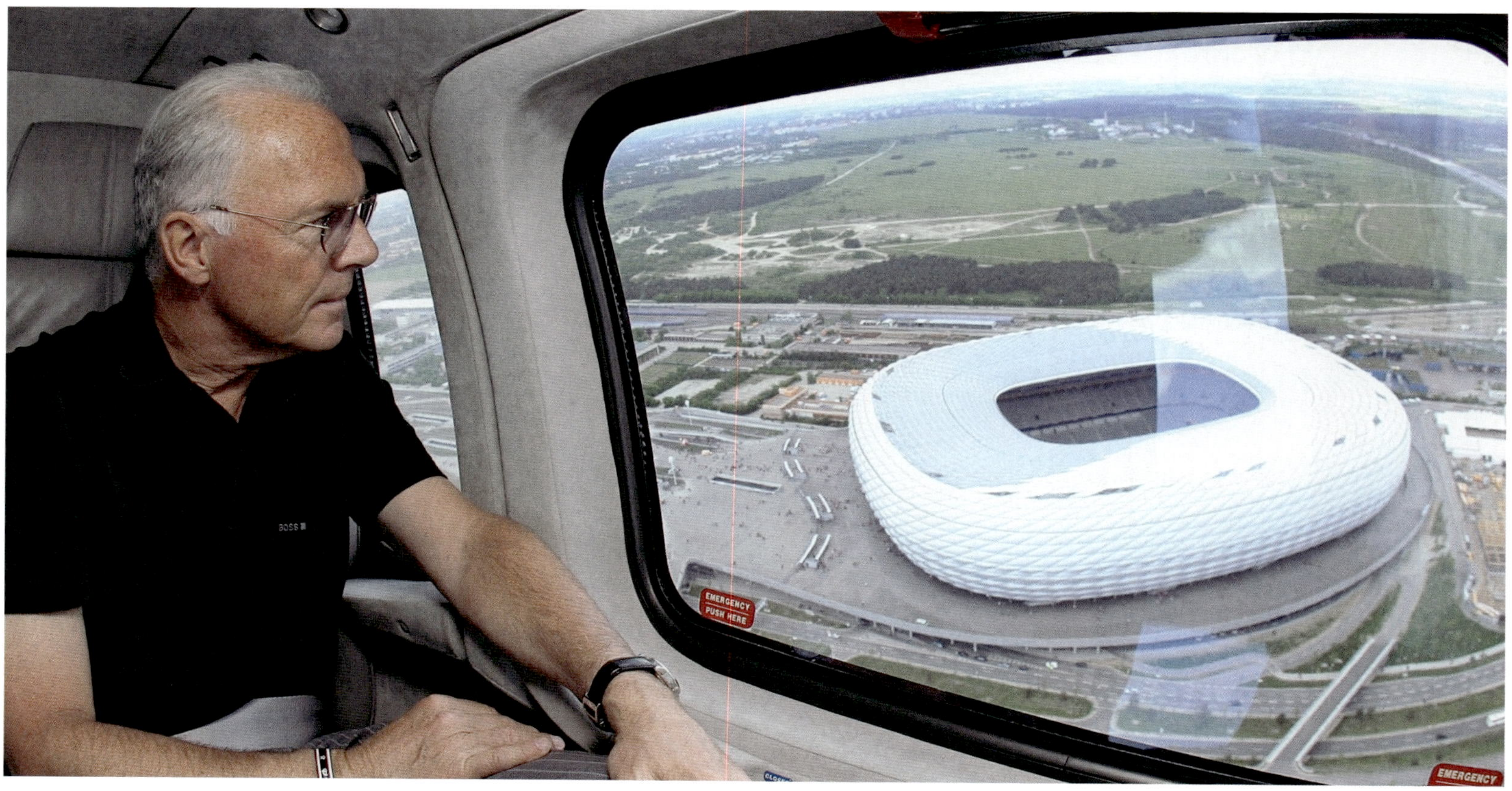

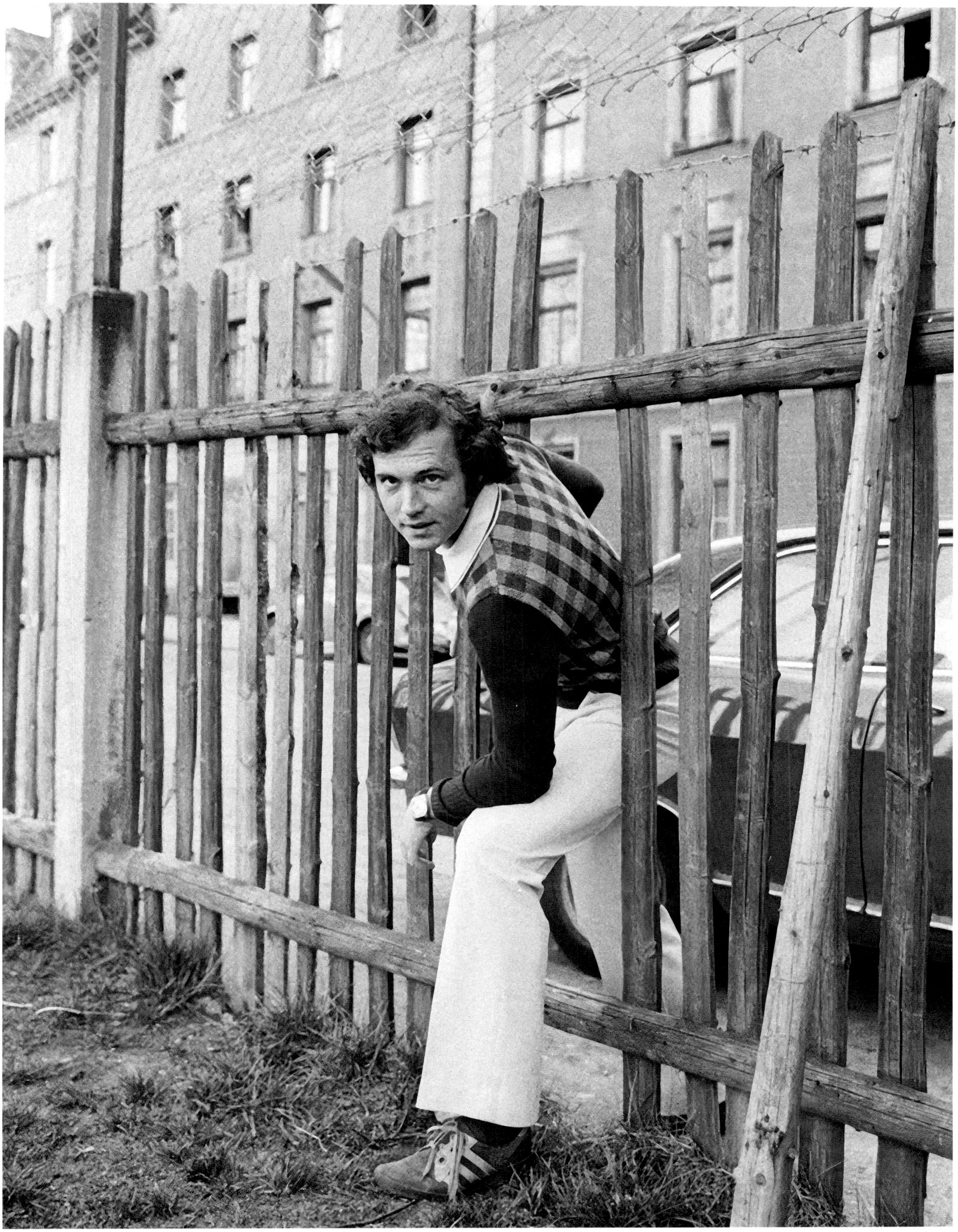

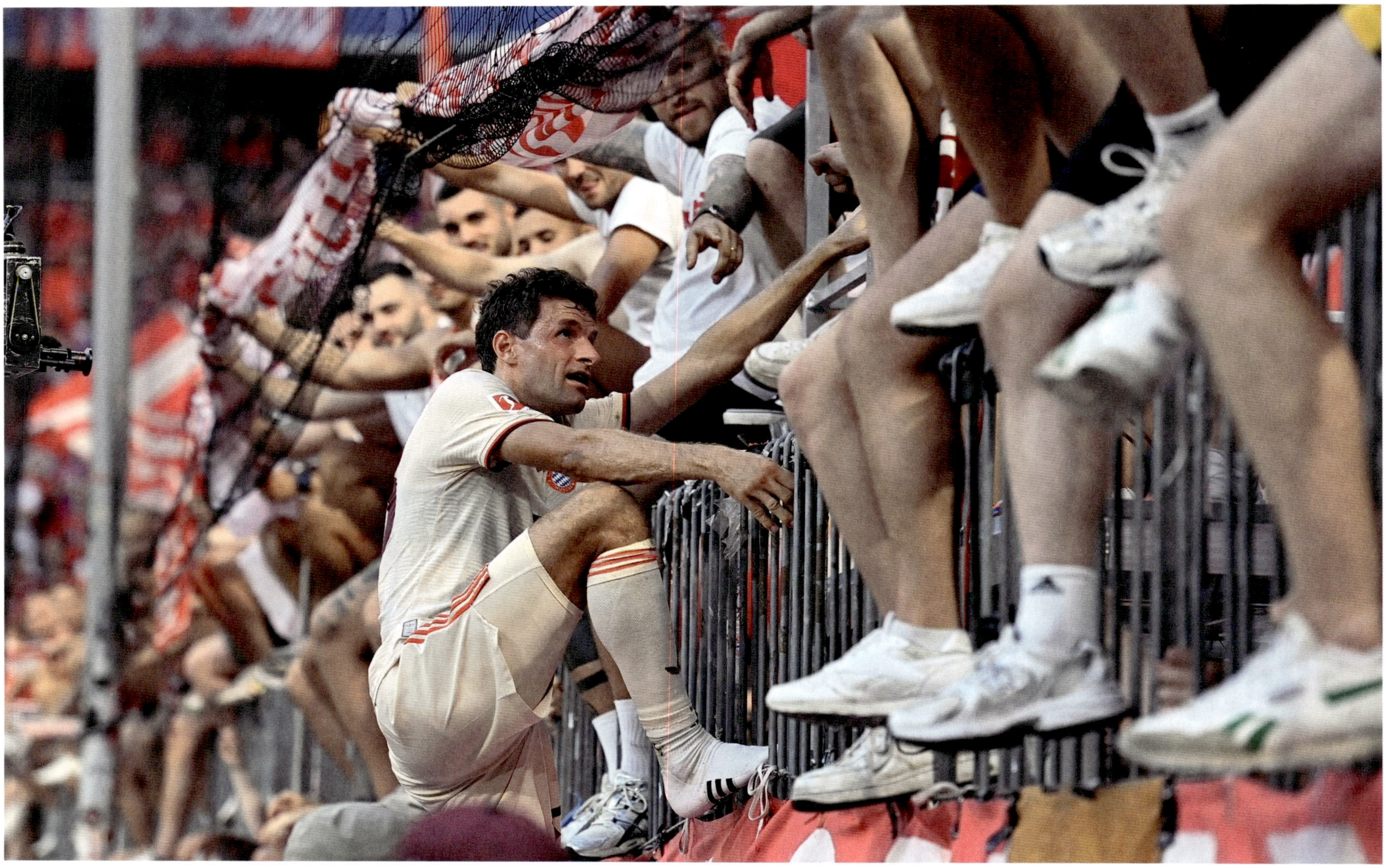

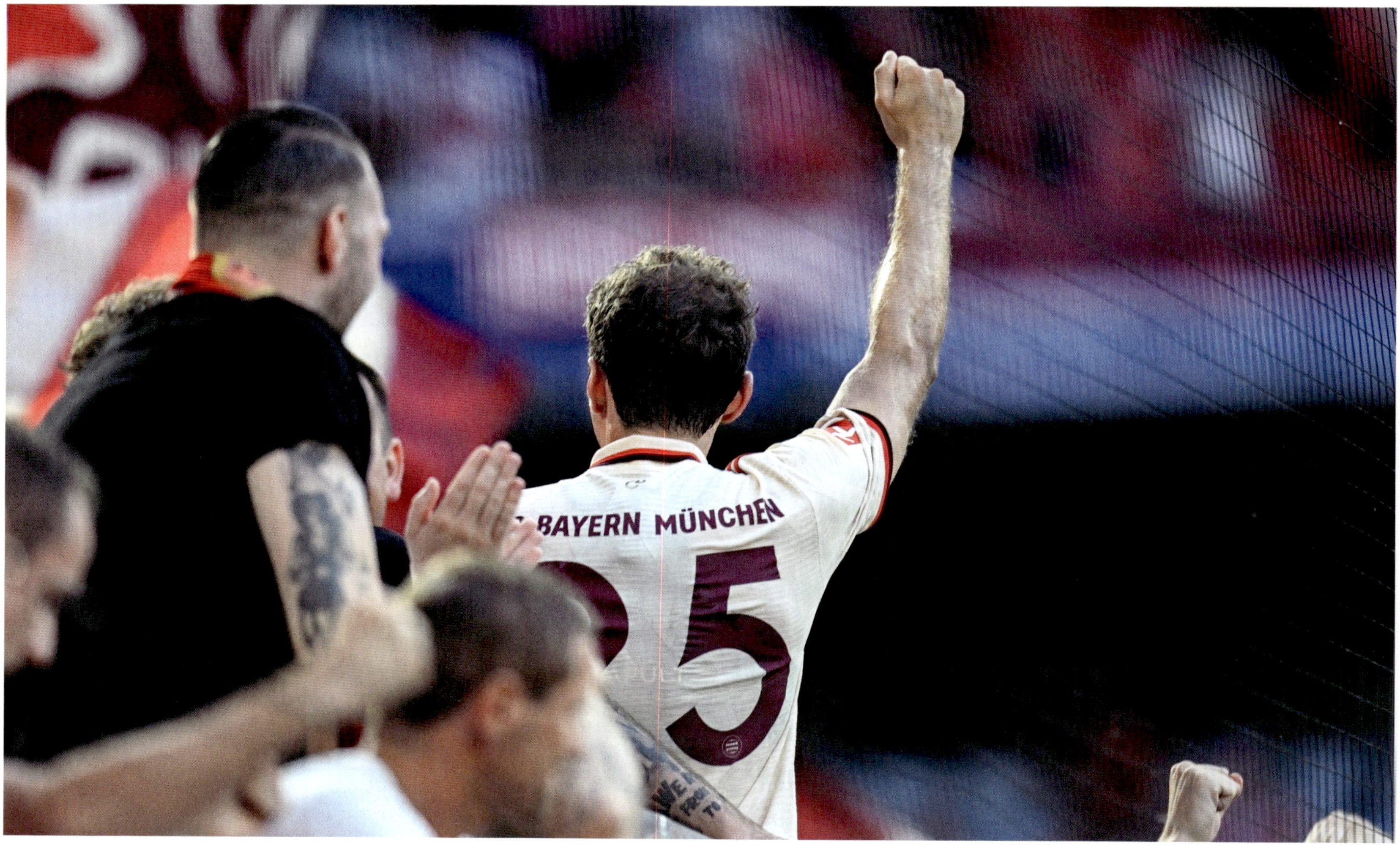
BAYERN MÜNCHEN
25

An important skill for football fans' heroes: climbing. After winning against Freiburg, Thomas Müller climbs up to the Südkurve, while his teammates line up in a row below to honour him. He returns barefooted, giving the boots that were made especially for this match to the fans, who pass them on to the FCB Museum on loan. But his new bosses, coach Vincent Kompany (below left) and sports director Christoph Freund (right), know that Müller himself is by no means ready for a place in the museum.

A RECORD-BREAKER **ON A HOME VISIT**

The jubilee for 125 years of FC Bayern, in Thomas Müller's 25th year at the club, was a record-breaking season from day one. Müller still has a great impact – and at the very start, he set new records week by week.

It started with a 3–2 win in Wolfsburg, Müller's 474th Bundesliga match for Bayern, surpassing Sepp Maier – and repeating the feat a week later with his 710th competitive match for FCB. He marked the occasion with a 2–0 win against Freiburg, and Manuel Neuer sprinted all the way across the pitch to give him a hug. After the final whistle, Müller celebrated in the Südkurve, with the fans who had honoured him with a banner proclaiming "710 times 100 per cent for FCB and no end in sight". Then, in the 9–2 thrashing of Dinamo Zagreb, the biggest win in the history of the Champions League, Müller set his next club record in his 152nd appearance in that league. After a 5–0 win in Bremen, twelve points from four games and a goal difference of 16–3 also meant a new record for the opening of the Bundesliga. How could a jubilee season have a better start?

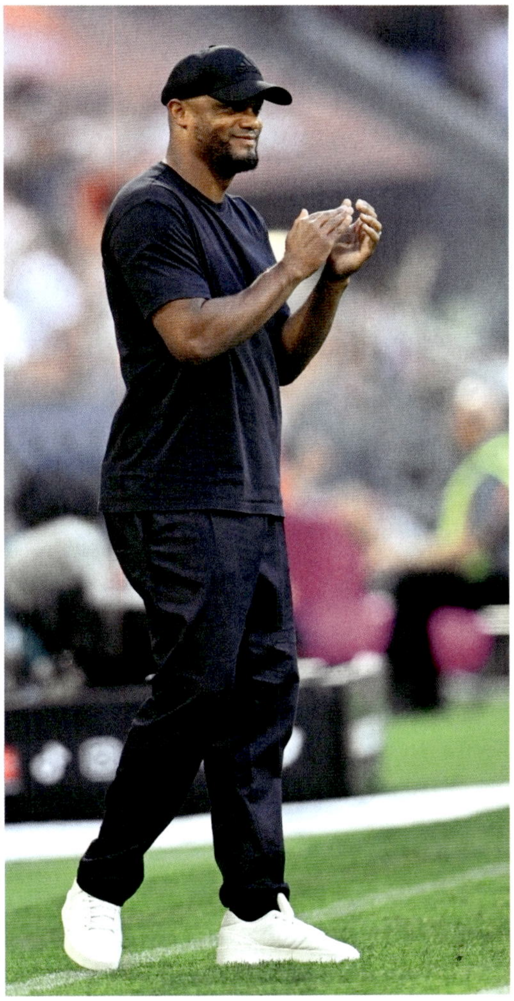

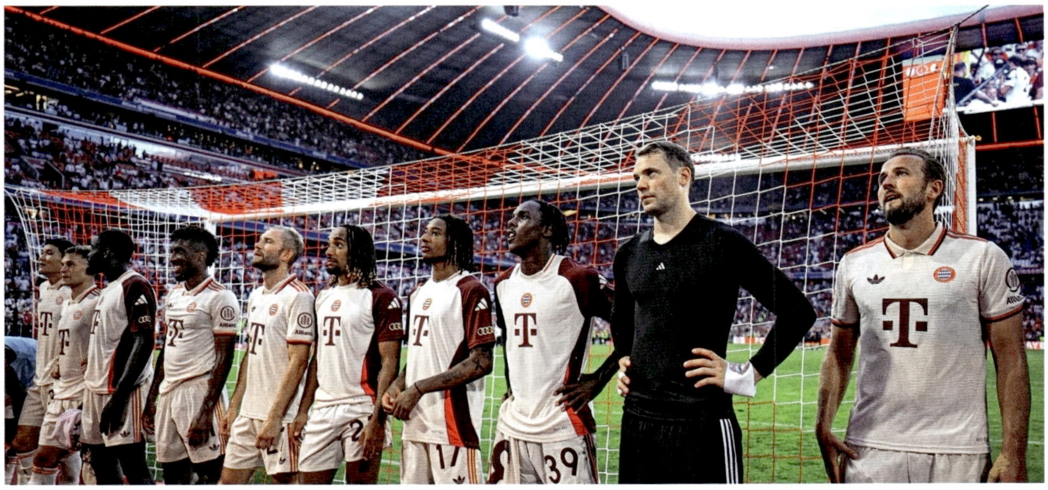

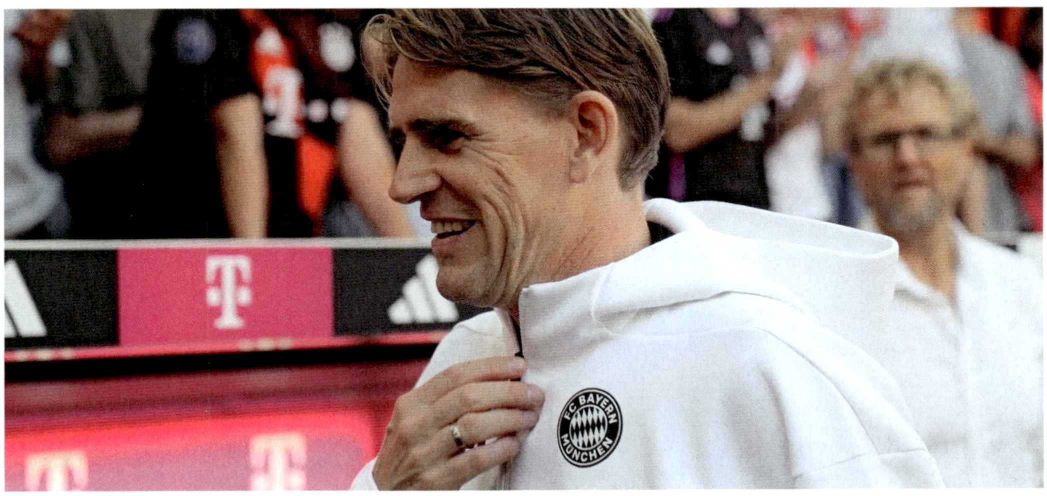

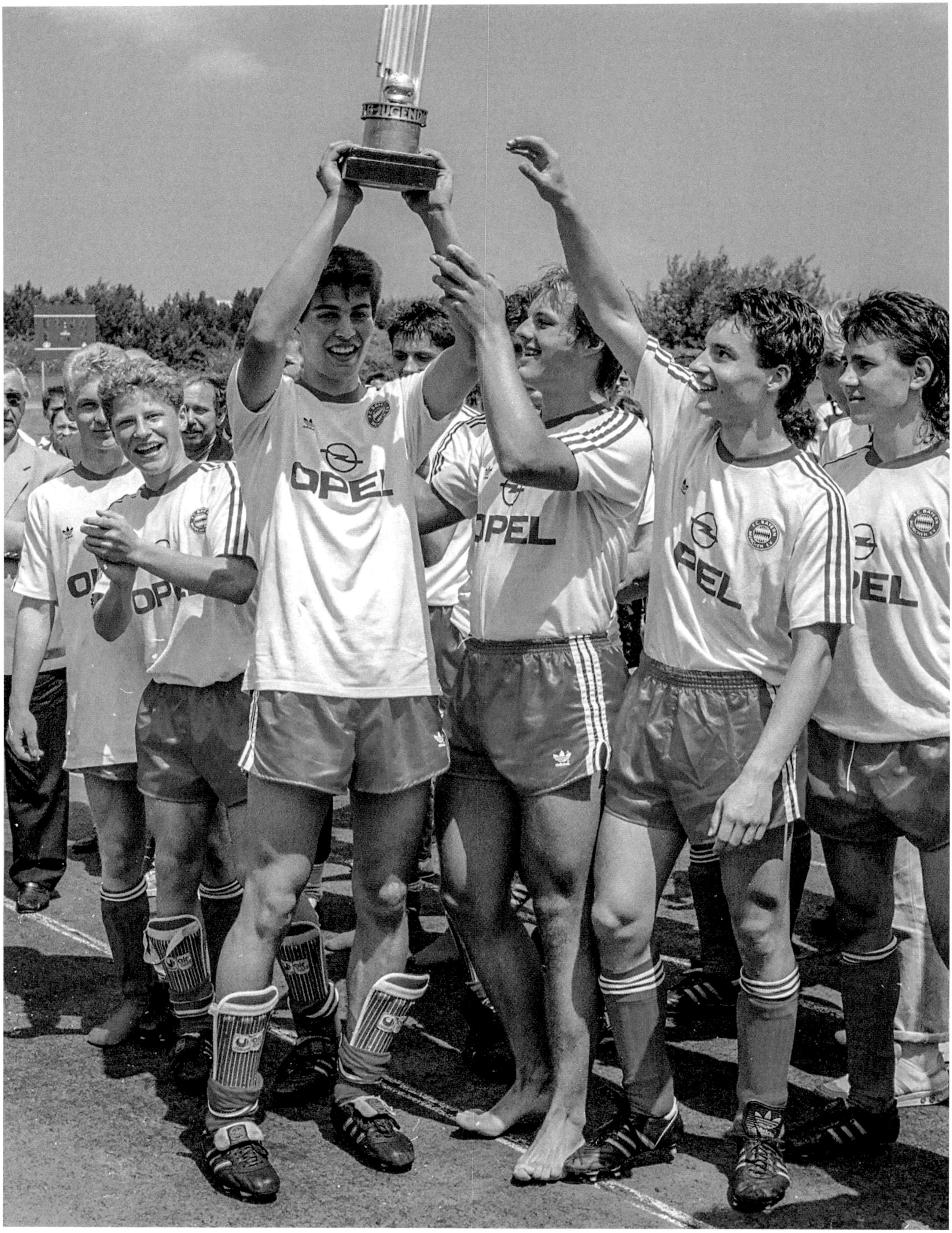
OPEL

WELCOME HOME, MAX!

In 1989 Max Eberl was a member of the first youth team of FCB that won the German championship. In the photo he is standing on the left behind Markus Babbel, who is holding the trophy high. They won the title for the B-category youth in a penalty shoot-out against Hertha Zehlendorf, for whom Robert Kovac, later a professional for FCB, missed the decisive penalty, while Eberl safely converted his.

He played for FCB all the way up from the Bambini to the Bundesliga, then became a highly successful director of sport – and in 2024 a member of the board at Bayern.

In March 2024, something that began for Max Eberl at the age of 5 came full circle: when he arrived at Säbener Strasse as board member for sports for FC Bayern, this was a return to the place where he embarked on his path in the world of football as a 5-year-old player. “For me it is a great joy to come back home after thirty years. FC Bayern was always the club of my heart”, he said when he was introduced. “I feel extremely excited to be able to work at this top level.” Since then he has devoted himself to the development of the club – always taking account of what he was taught back then as a little kid.

Club president Herbert Hainer describes Eberl as a man with “absolutely expert knowledge of the Bundesliga”, adding that “We need people of truly top calibre, not only on the field but also in management, so that we can achieve our ambitious aims.” And Jan Christian Dreesen, chief executive officer, sees in his colleague “someone who comes with a great deal of know-how. Max played for FC Bayern for almost fifteen years, and he knows the club’s DNA. Even though he was in Mönchengladbach for a long time, FC Bayern was always in his heart.”

Max Eberl moved up from the newly formed Bambini, the section for the youngest kids at FC Bayern Munich: at 15 he was in the B-youth, the first Bayern junior team to win the German championship. An outside defender who ran and tackled hard, he developed in Hermann Gerland’s youth A-team into a player in the German national youth team and was the first footballer at FC Bayern to pass through every level from the Bambini to the professional side. For FCB, Bochum, SpVgg Greuther Fürth and Borussia Mönchengladbach he played 215 matches as a professional, 104 of them in the Bundesliga. In 2008 Eberl became sports director at Mönchengladbach, leading them out of the Bundesliga relegation struggle and into the Champions League. After gaining more than fifteen years of experience, the time was ripe for a return to his roots.

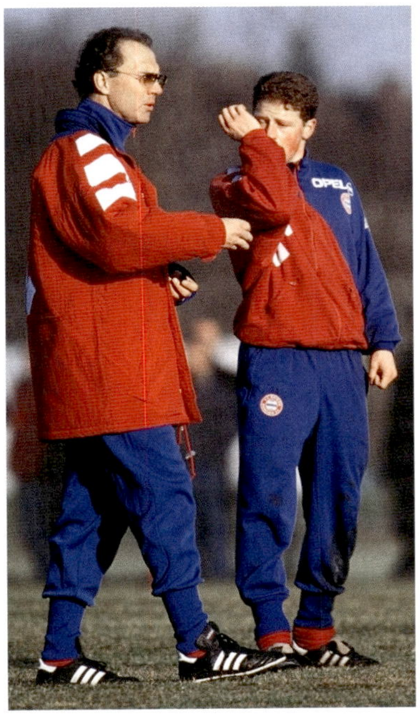

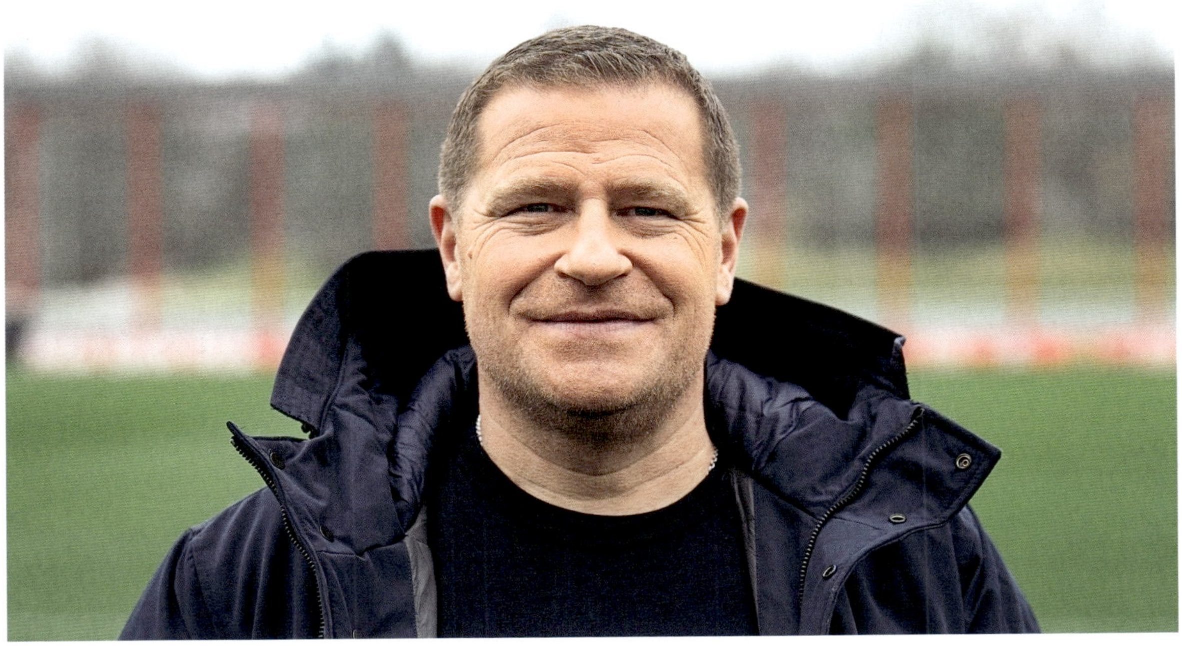

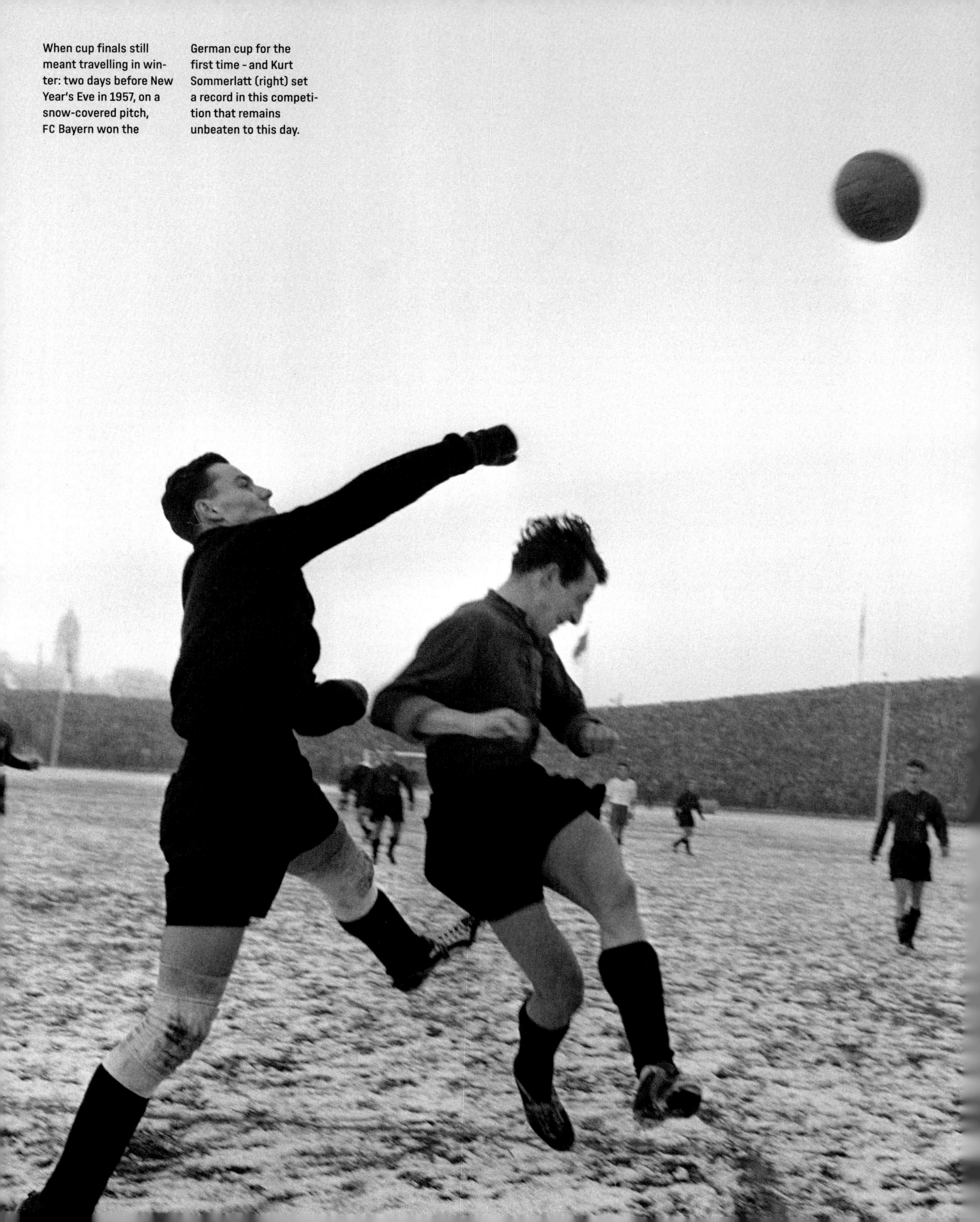

When cup finals still meant travelling in winter: two days before New Year's Eve in 1957, on a snow-covered pitch, FC Bayern won the German cup for the first time – and Kurt Sommerlatt (right) set a record in this competition that remains unbeaten to this day.

CUP VICTORY IN THE SNOW
FCB-FORTUNA 1-0 · 1957

FC Bayern's first win in the German cup was almost sacrificed to save money. In the 1950s the club's coffers were constantly empty, and the board considered giving the competition a miss. They feared that the earnings from the cup would not cover the travel costs. The coach, Willibald Hahn, persuaded the board to participate. And the journey to the final only had a minimal impact on the expense account – sixty kilometres to Augsburg.

Bayern were considered the outsiders against Fortuna Düsseldorf. It turned out differently, probably in part because of the season – winter. The cup competition was spread over the whole calendar year at that time, with the first round in January and the final in December. In the night, two days before New Year's Eve, it snowed and the Düsseldorf players could not cope with the slippery surface. By contrast the Bayern team, who had to fight their way through the rounds all year, going into extra time four times and to a replay twice, now dominated the game. "The attacking élan, the tempestuous vigour", enthused *Sportmagazin*, "the cup-final fire that burned untamed in the whole team, cast Fortuna into a hopeless losing role." The winning goal was scored twelve minutes before the close on the rebound by Rudolf Jobst, the midfield general who, according to the coach of the national team, Sepp Herberger, had "an outstanding game". Two years later he retired from football at the age of 24 with a knee injury. The captain, Hans Bauer, the first winner of the World Cup from FCB, whom Herberger deployed in 1954 in two matches in the qualifying round, received the trophy, the so-called Golden Pheasant Cup, which was replaced in 1965 by the present DFB Cup.

On that winter's day in Augsburg, Kurt Sommerlatt, the engine in midfield, earned an honour that he did not see until fifty-seven years later in Berlin – when his footprints, cast in bronze, were displayed on the Walk of Fame of the DFB cup competition at the Olympic Stadium. Sommerlatt, on the winning side in the cup finals of 1955 and 1956 with Karlsruher SC, remains to this day the only player in Germany who has a hat-trick of cup victories.

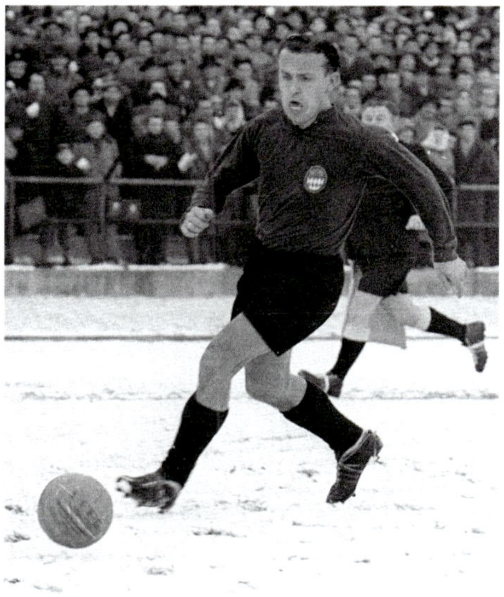

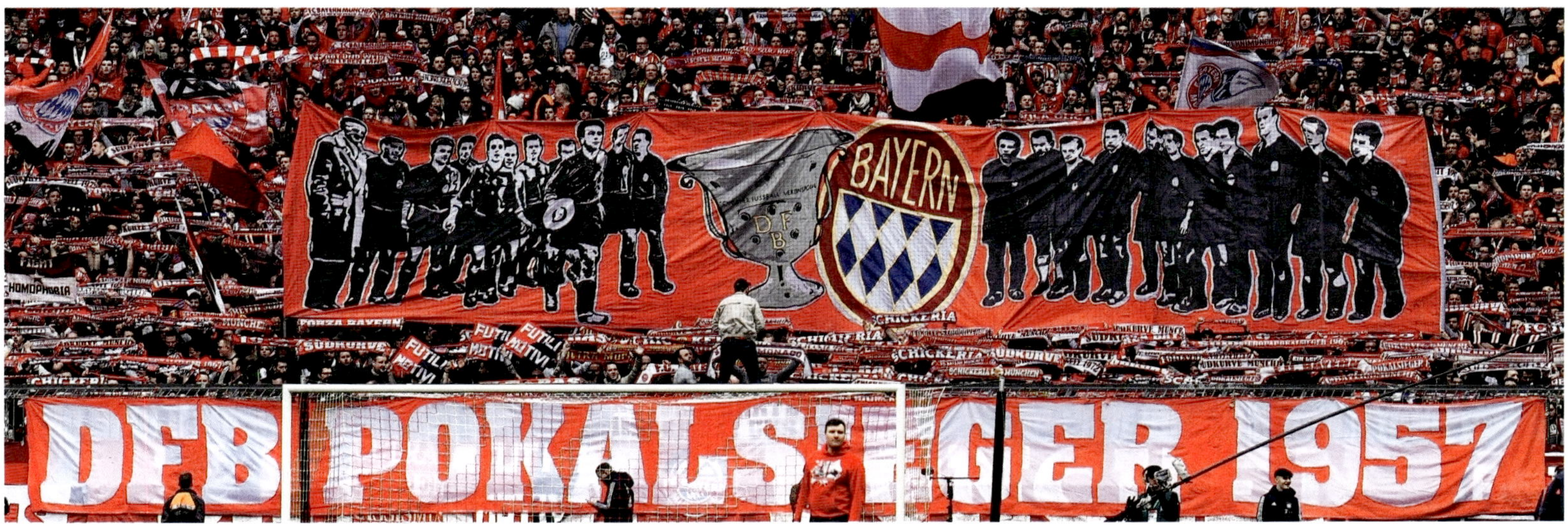

THE FAIRY TALE OF **THE BALLBOY**

When Thomas Müller was about to play his first international match in 2010, Diego Maradona, the coach of Argentina, chased him off the stage at the press conference. He thought Müller was a ballboy. Fourteen years later, a ballboy from FC Bayern really did become an international player.

In May 2024 Aleksandar Pavlović made his debut for Germany in the 0–0 draw against Ukraine. Tonsilitis kept him out of the Euros, but it was nevertheless a fairy-tale football year for a lad born in Munich who passed through all of the FCB youth teams from the under-8s onwards. At the age of 14 he was still wide-eyed when Ribéry or Müller came close. At 19 he no longer served the ball to the stars from the sidelines, but from the centre of the field. In his second Bundesliga match, in Dortmund, he set up a goal for Harry Kane. Against Augsburg and Mönchengladbach he scored himself, and in the dramatic 1–2 defeat in the Champions League semi-final away to Real Madrid he played a full ninety minutes in the famous Bernabéu. Millions of boys dreamed of this, and for him it came true. And Maradona's "ballboy" Thomas Müller praises him: "Aleks plays football the way I know it. He's gutsy."

The rise of Aleksander Pavlović continued after he missed out on the Euros. In September 2024 he scored his first goal for Germany in the 5-0 defeat of Hungary in the Nations League. "A fantastic game, very dominant", was the verdict of national trainer Julian Nagelsmann. Three weeks later he saved FCB from possible defeat against Bayer Leverkusen with a long-range shot to make the score 1-1.

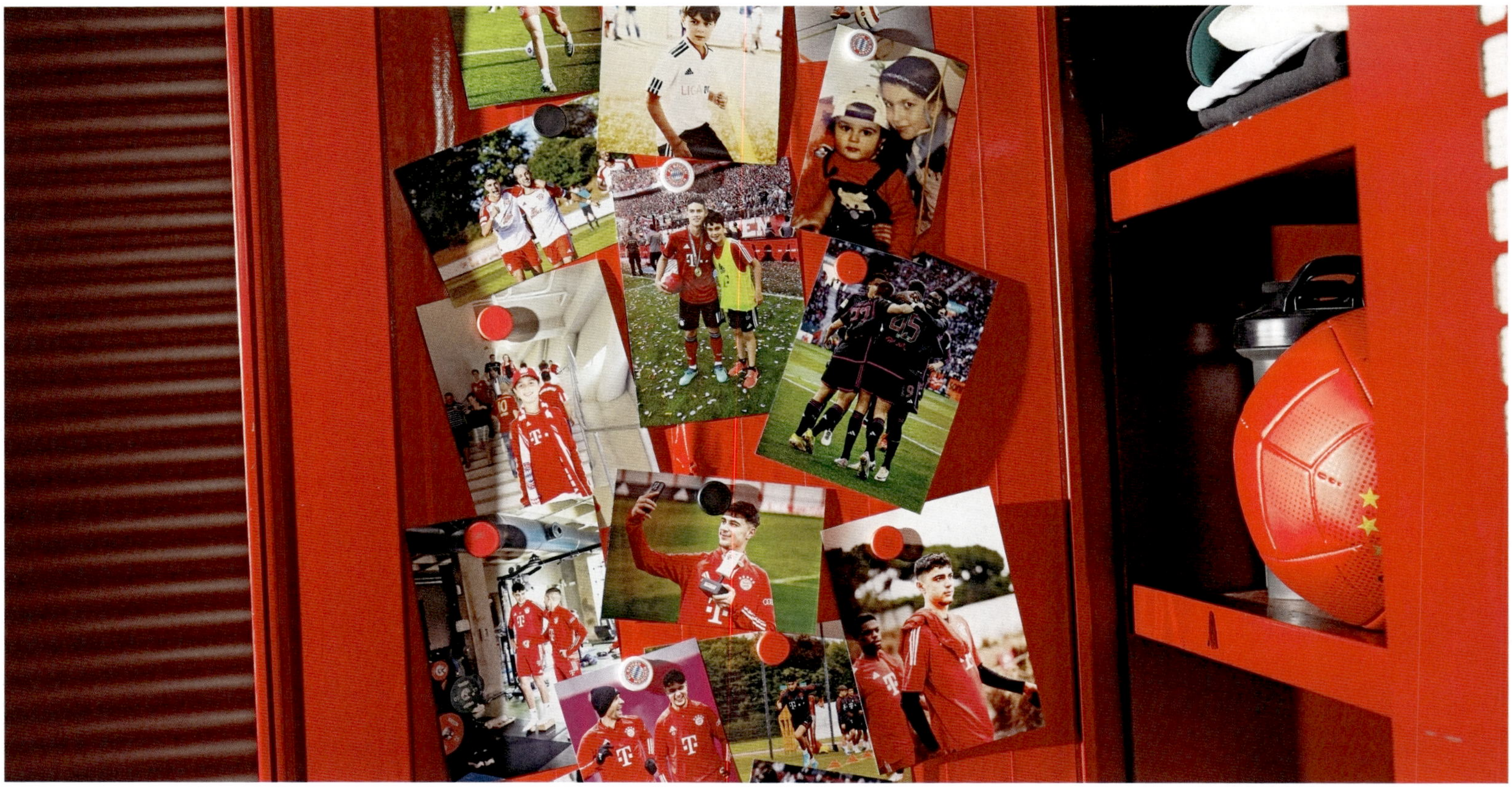

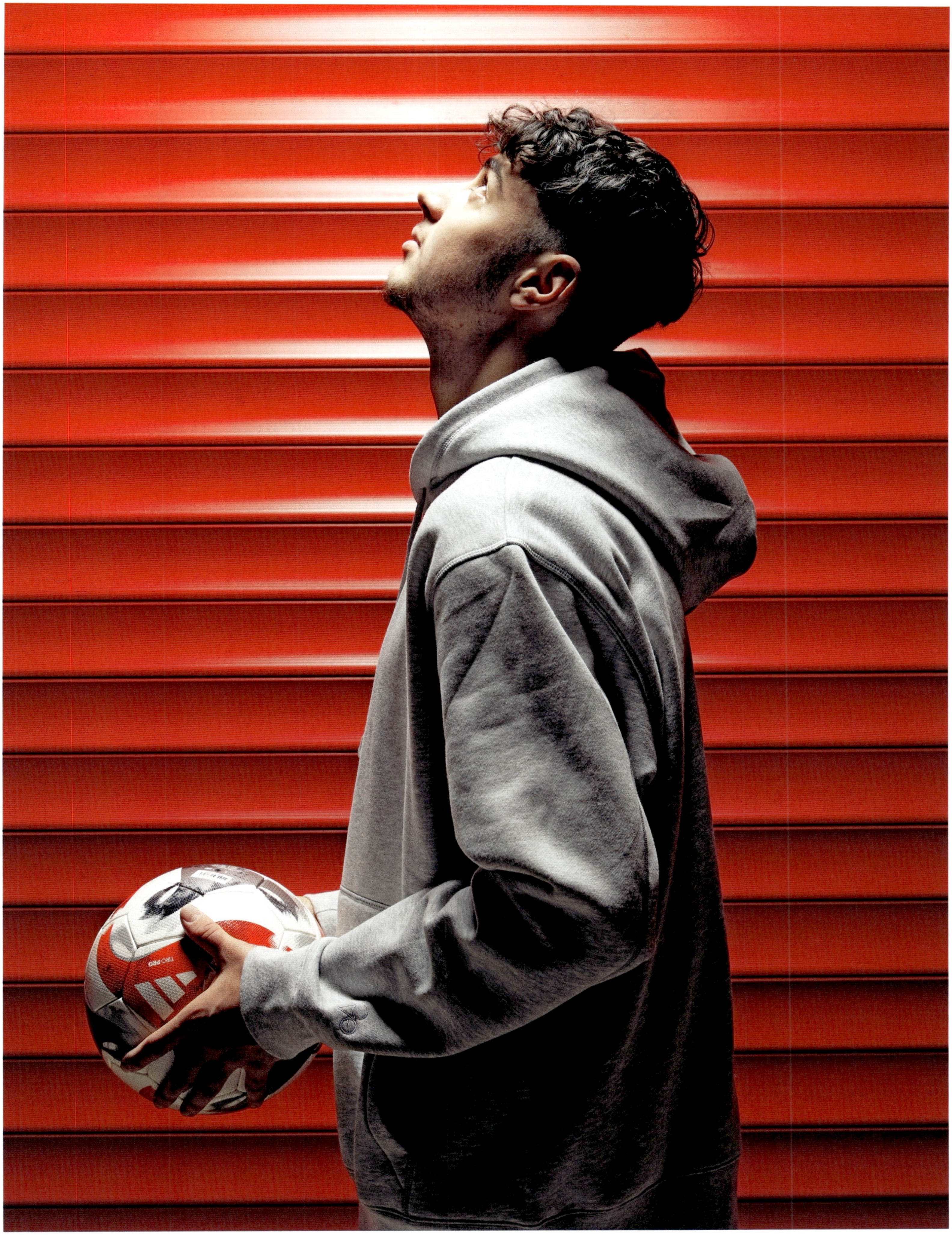

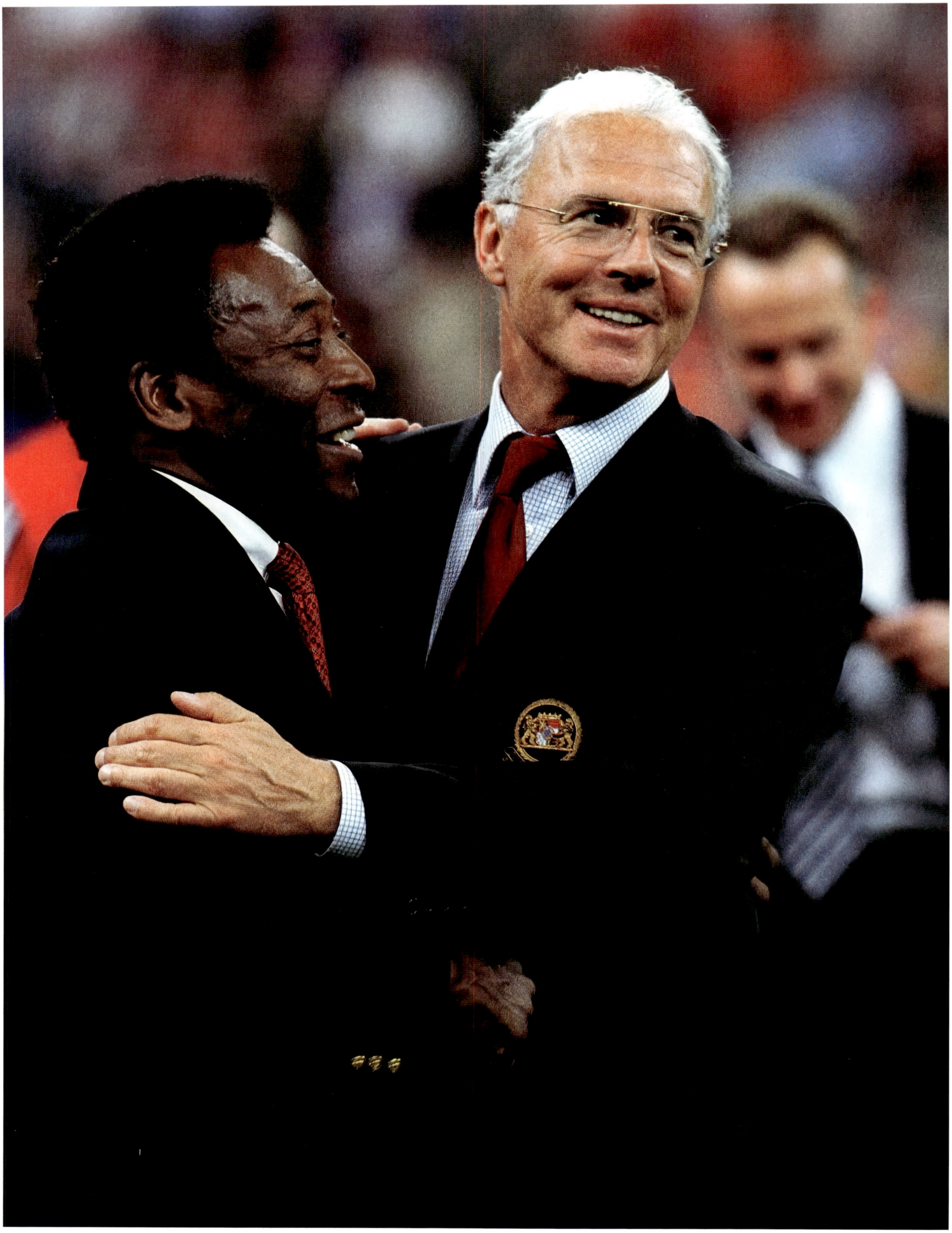

"THE KAISER" – A MAN OF THE WORLD

In New York, where he played for the Cosmos in the North American Soccer League from 1977 to 1980, in the first year with the great Pelé, Franz Beckenbauer put a lot of problems behind him. In Manhattan, high up on the balcony of his apartment on Central Park, it was all far away.

"New York opened up the world for me," he said later. "With a little bit of football on top." As "The Kaiser" he represented the New York Cosmos in an "operetta league", as critics at home ridiculed it. Warner Bros., the company that owned the team, paid him $7 million for three years. With an education as a man of the world thrown in free. His circle of acquaintances included Mick Jagger, Muhammad Ali, Robert Redford, Andy Warhol and his neighbour Liza Minelli. New York was a cosmos that gave Beckenbauer something approaching normality, even anonymity, which he no longer had in Munich. In 1980, when he returned to Germany, Frank Sinatra's last hit was released: 'New York, New York'. The lyrics almost sound as if they were written for Beckenbauer: "If I can make it there / I'll make it anywhere". When returning home he described the years in New York as "the best decision I ever took".

Look, mum, that's New York: on the twenty-first floor of the Navarro apartment hotel, high above Central Park, Franz Beckenbauer shows the Manhattan skyline to his mother Antonie. Later, with his mother and his partner, he took a carriage ride through the enormous park.

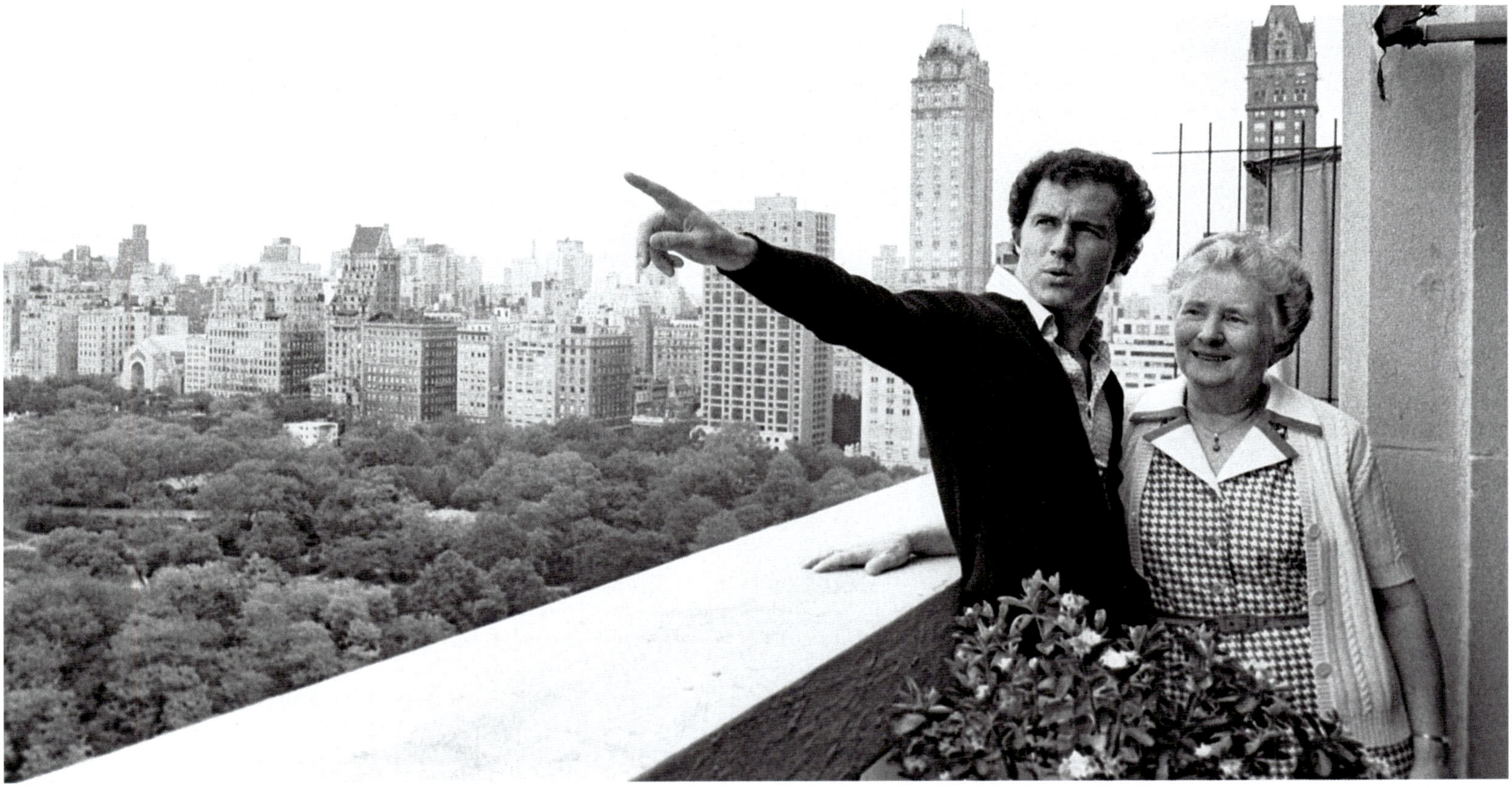

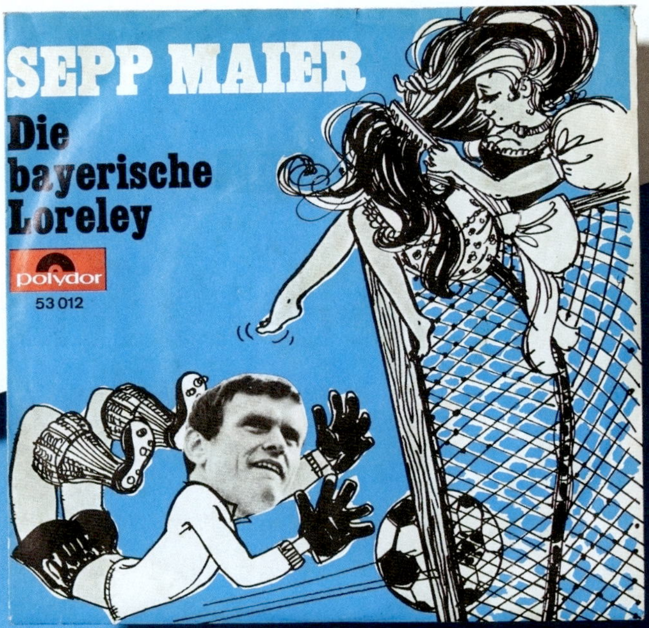
SEPP MAIER
Die bayerische Loreley
polydor
53 012

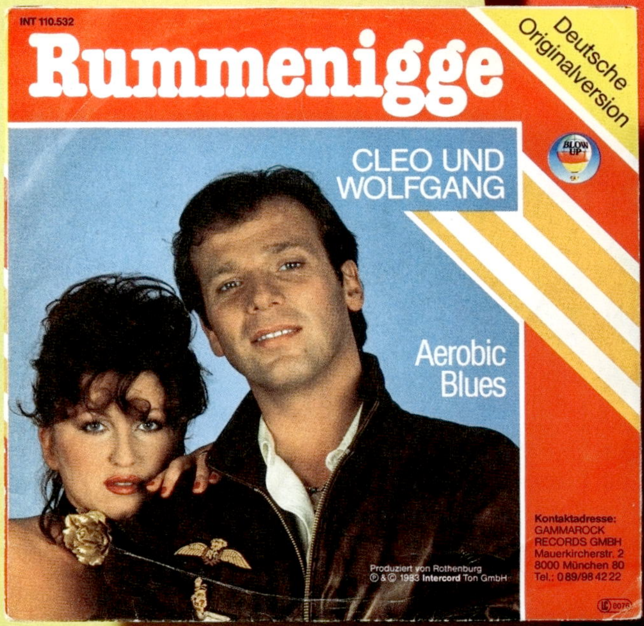
INT 110.532
Rummenigge
Deutsche Originalversion
CLEO UND WOLFGANG
Aerobic Blues
Produziert von Rothenburg
℗ & © 1983 Intercord Ton GmbH
Kontaktadresse:
GAMMAROCK RECORDS GMBH
Mauerkircherstr. 2
8000 München 80
Tel.: 089/98 42 22

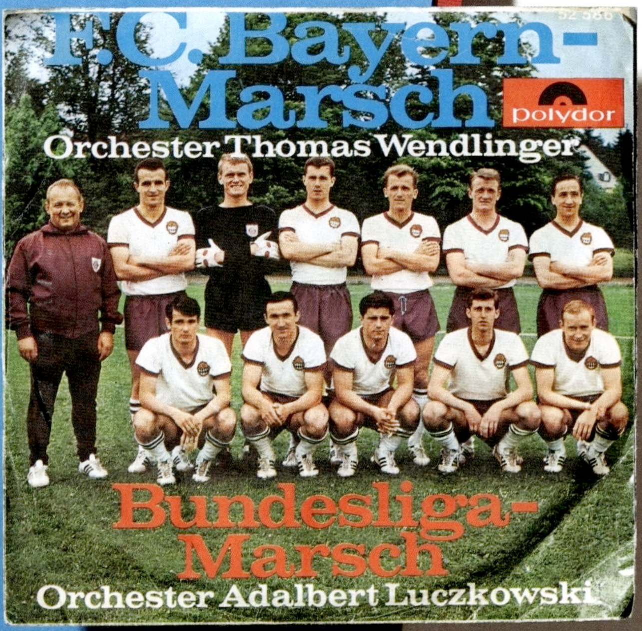
F.C. Bayern-Marsch
polydor
Orchester Thomas Wendlinger
Bundesliga-Marsch
Orchester Adalbert Luczkowski

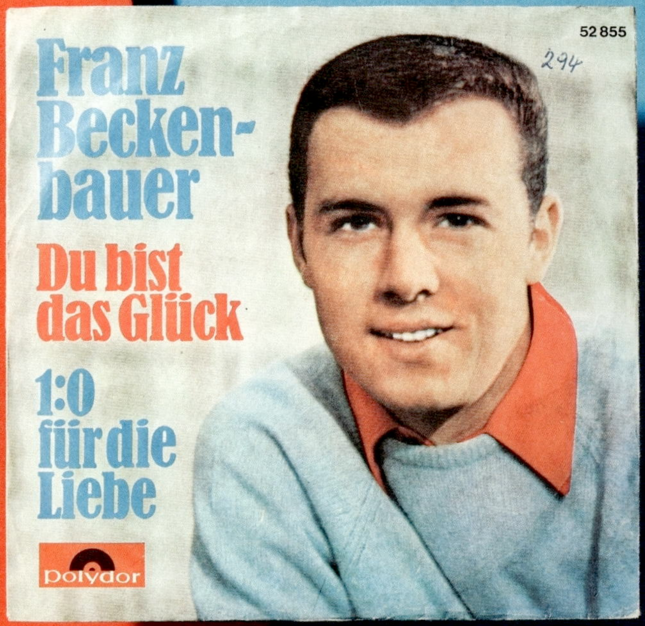
52 855
294
Franz Becken-bauer
Du bist das Glück
1:0 für die Liebe
polydor

SINGING AND DANCING **ON EVERY FOOTBALL GROUND**

It all started with Franz Beckenbauer, of course. His short career as a singer bequeathed to posterity the evergreen 'Gute Freunde kann niemand trennen' (No one can separate good friends). After that, Gerd Müller missed the target with the sentimental 'Raba Da Da', but with the follow-up singles 'Das gibt ein Schützenfest' (It's a shooting party) and 'Dann macht es Bumm' (Then it goes boom) he at least felt at home with the lyrics. And Sepp Maier tried his hand with a melodic creation called 'Die bayerische Loreley'. After that, it was usually other artists who sang about Bayern. For example Alain & Denise with their Rummenigge hit 'Sexy Knees', which admired more than just the knees: "He's so strong, Rummenigge, Rummenigge all night long, He's so tall, he's so blond, Two long legs and all beyond." In 1975 Udo Jürgens sang of the great "libero": "After the game, in the dressing room / when no one is looking / you suddenly feel older / you're worn out and tired". Volker Lechtenbrink's farewell for Breitner had a pensive mood: "Paul leaves the stage". Satirically, by contrast, the band Die Ärzte sang about "Paul Breitner's afro" and Die Prinzen about Oliver Kahn ("He has the most muscular calves / And splashes with men in the baths"). And there was a real one-off titled 'Gerd Müller', a strident number by the Austrian hard-rock band Stahl.

Since those days, Bayern stars only occasionally made an appearance as pop stars – though Dante, an unforgettably good-humoured man, took the microphone in 2013. After winning the treble in Berlin, he bellowed an improvised song to the celebrating fans behind the goal. It ended up in the charts, mixed to a party-electro version: "We win championship ... and cup too".

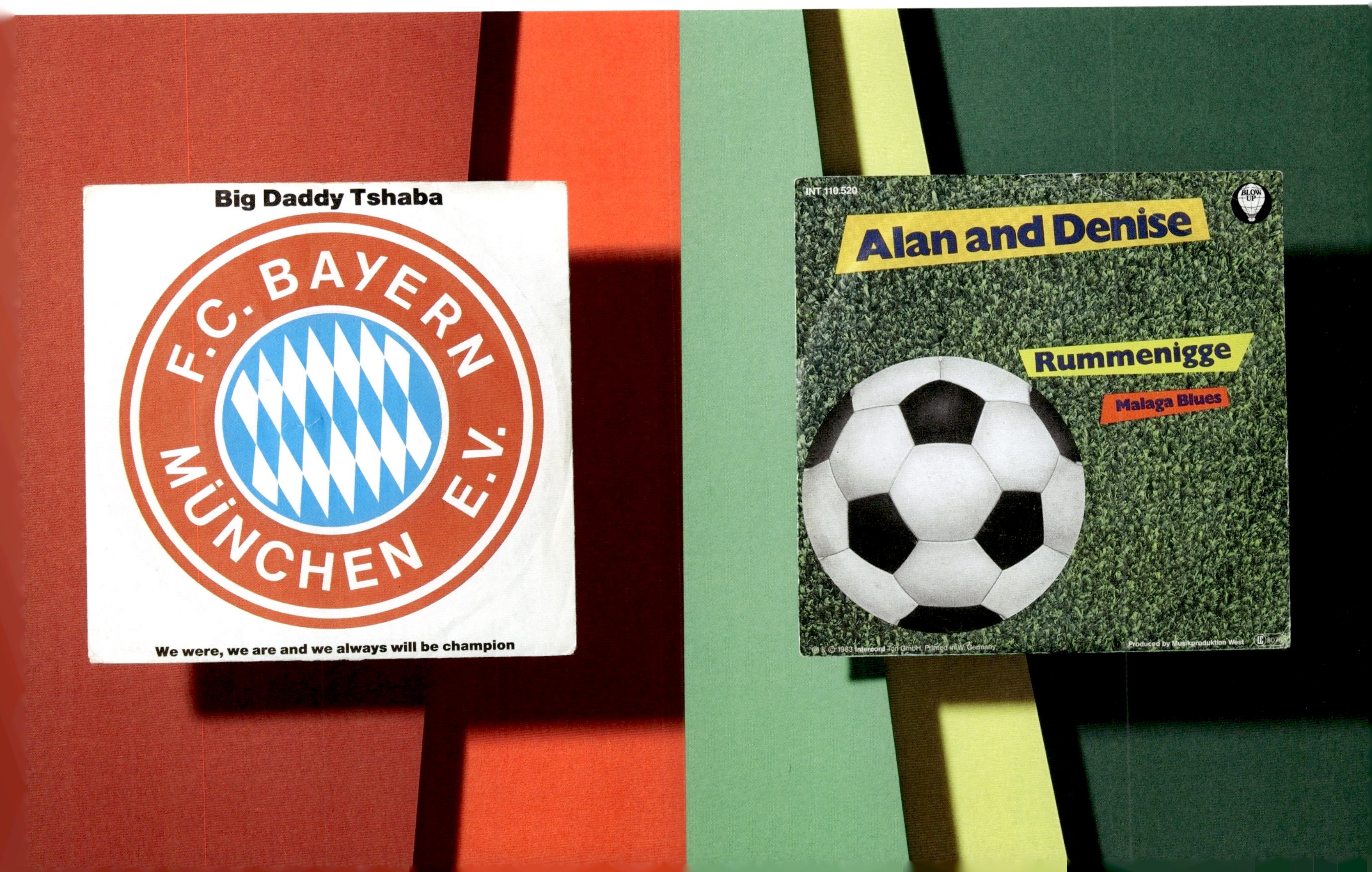

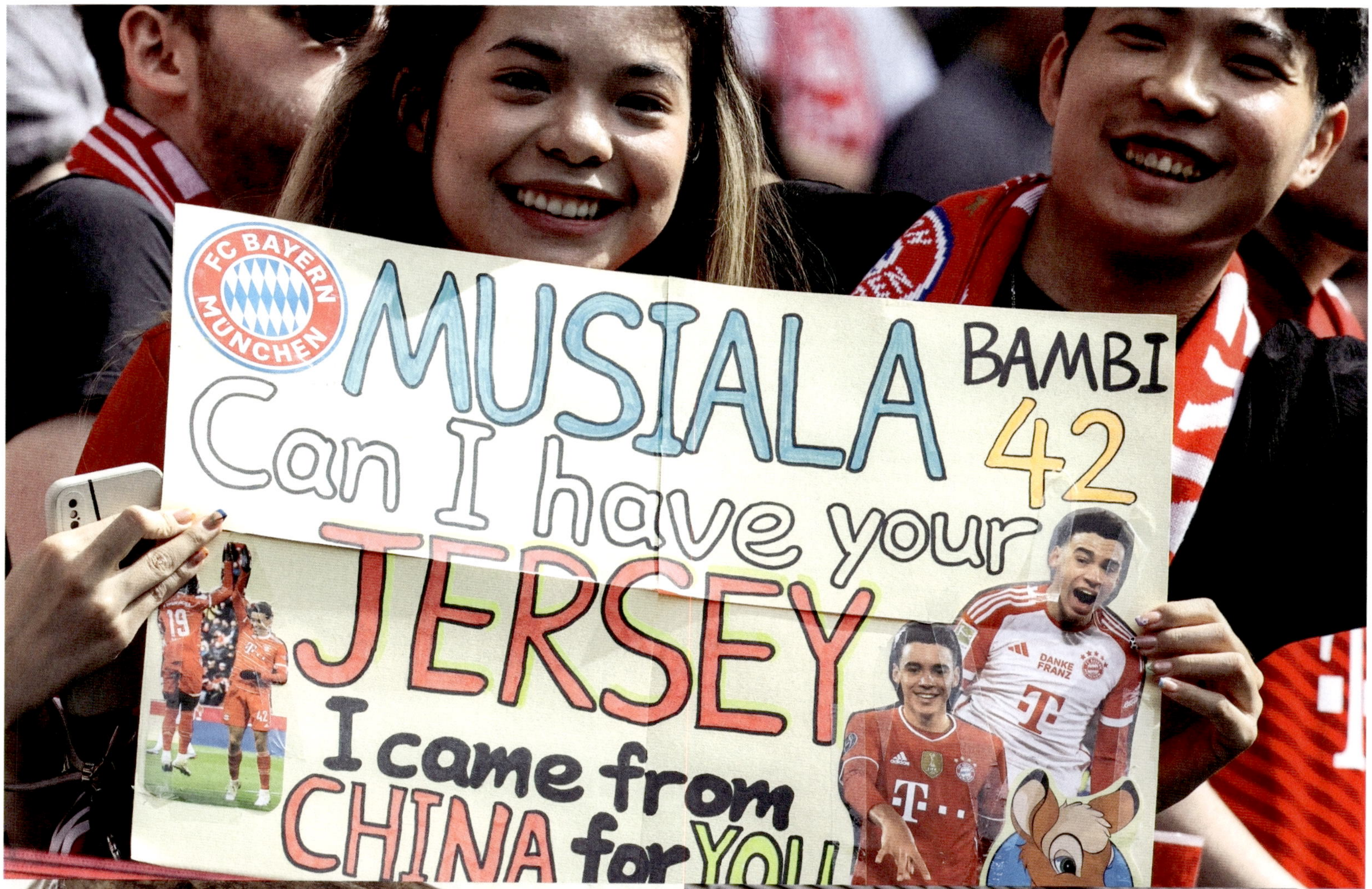
FC BAYERN MÜNCHEN
MUSIALA
BAMBI
42
Can I have your
JERSEY
I came from
CHINA for

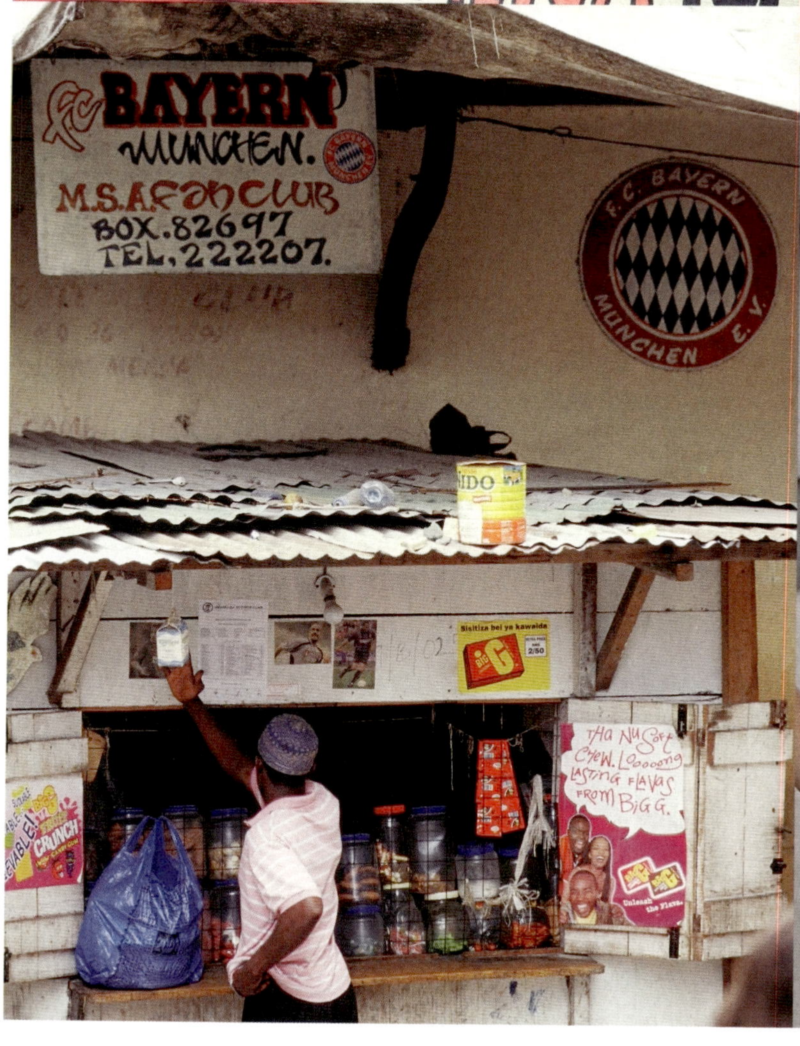
BAYERN
MUNCHEN.
M.S.A fan CLUB
BOX.82697
TEL.222207.
F.C. BAYERN MÜNCHEN E.V.

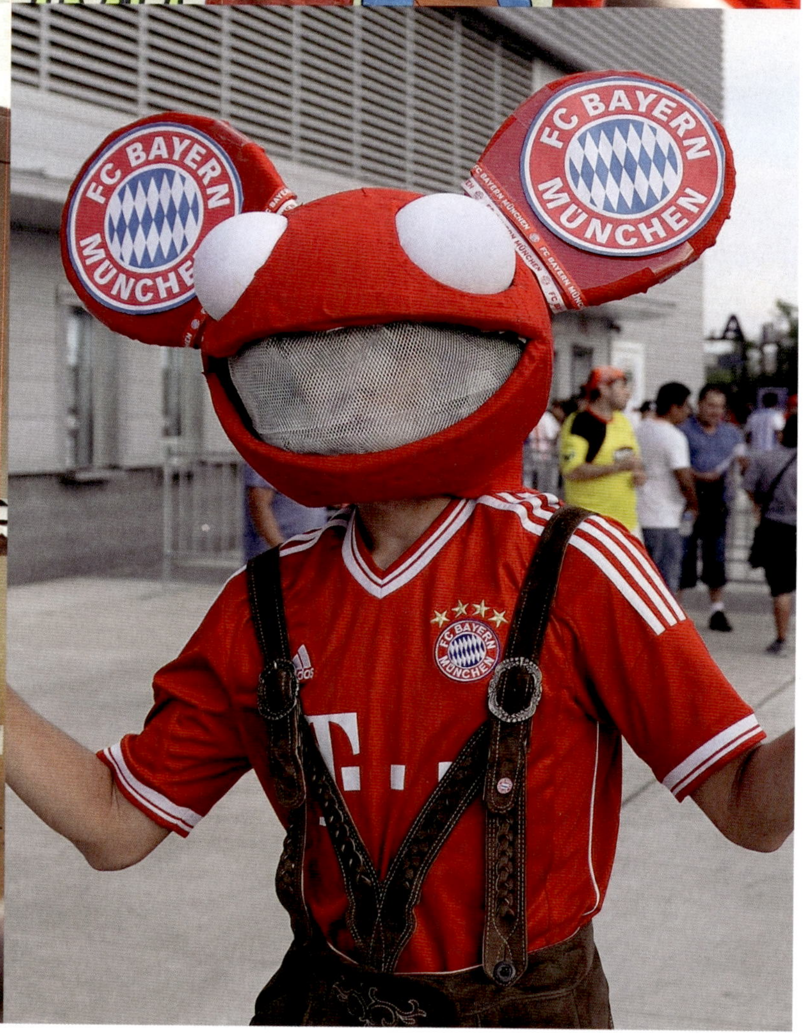
FC BAYERN MÜNCHEN
FC BAYERN MÜNCHEN

WHICH FOOTBALL TEAM **FROM MUNICH IS KNOWN** ALL OVER THE WORLD?

More than 300,000 fans in over 4,000 fan clubs, around 500 of them outside Germany, burn with match-day fever for FCB. They have names like Garden of Bayern (China) or Red Kangaroos Australia, Red-and-White Brazil or Record Champions Kazakhstan. Some love a play on words, as in Mia San Francisco, one of eighty-nine Bayern fan clubs in the USA, and Cu-Bayern, one of two in Cuba. They are active in Ukraine (Red Forest Kiev) and in Russia (The Bavarian Souls). They exist across all borders, in the whole world, on every continent except the Antarctic (even though Sepp Maier once travelled there), and even at the foot of Mount Everest (Mia San Mia Nepal): fan clubs whose members are at home far, far away from Munich – and feel nevertheless that FC Bayern is their home.

The stars of the south - for fans and fan clubs in Africa they are really stars of the north. And stars of the west for the Chinese, and stars of the east in America. But wherever you go, their aura seems to radiate across the whole of Planet Football.

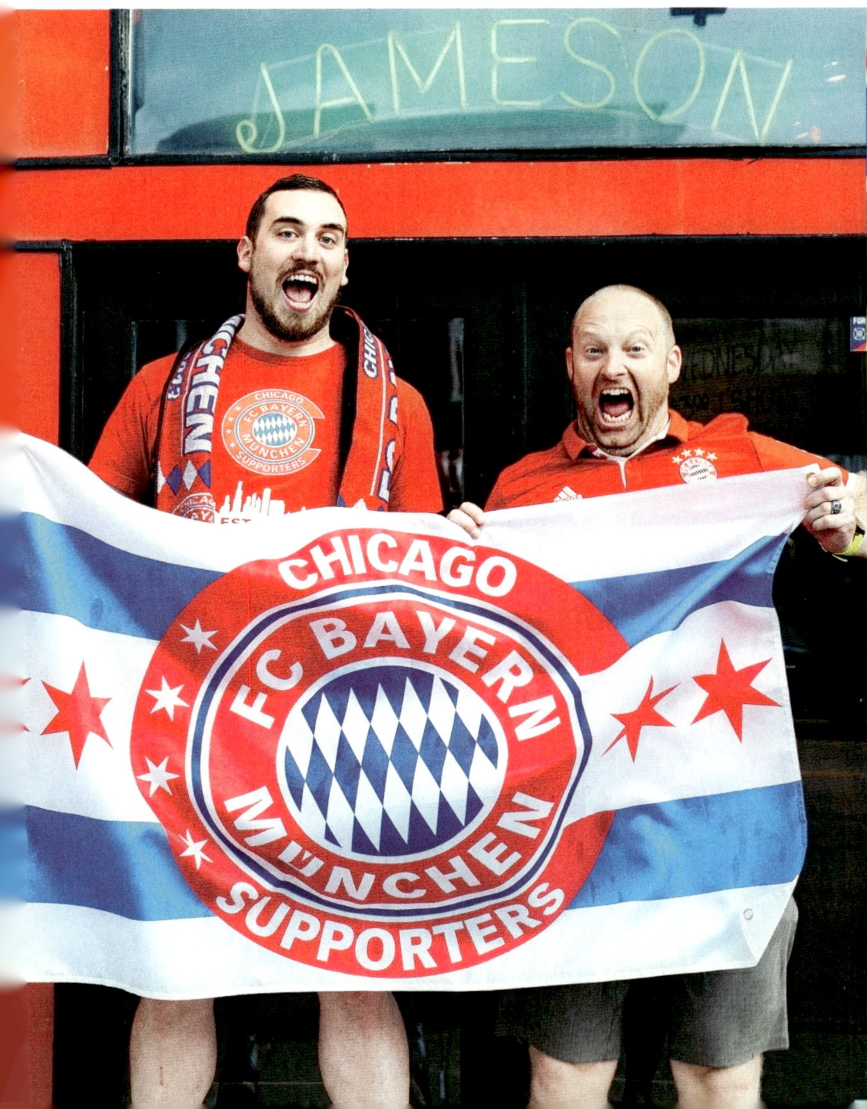

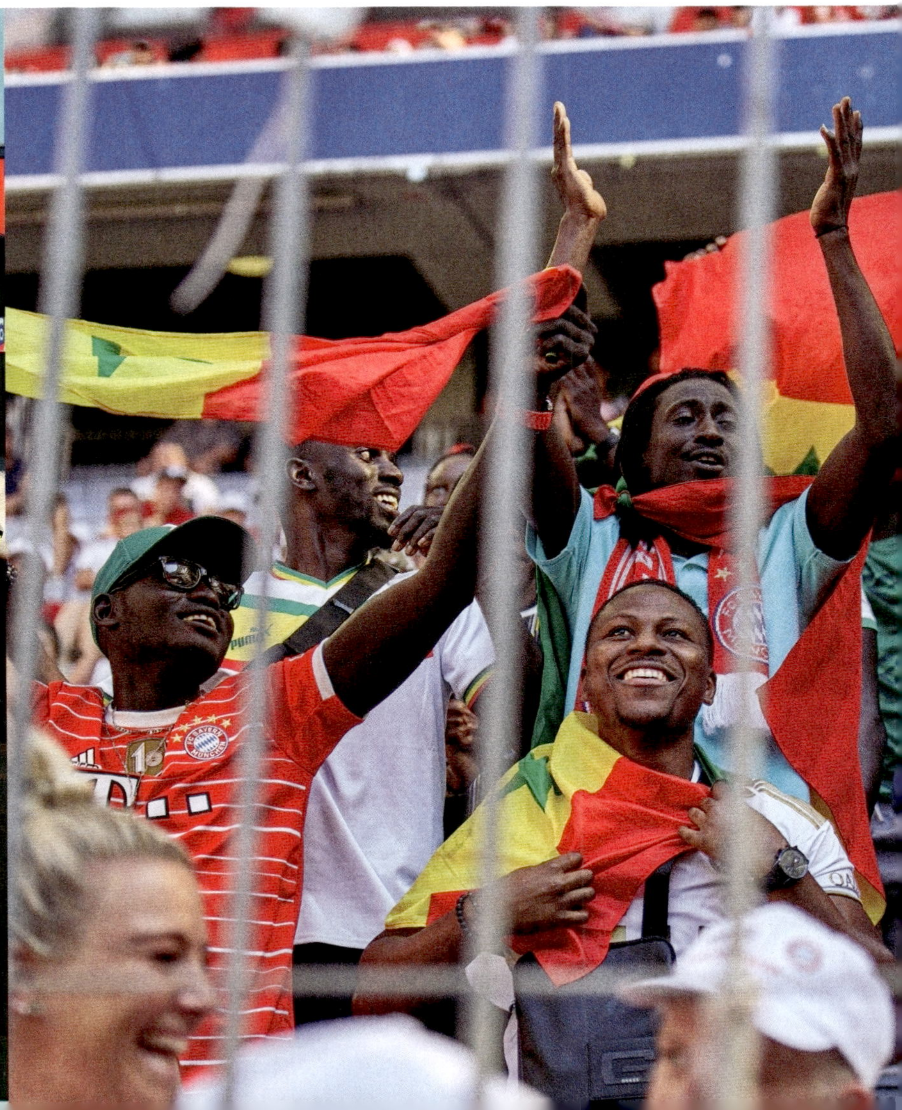

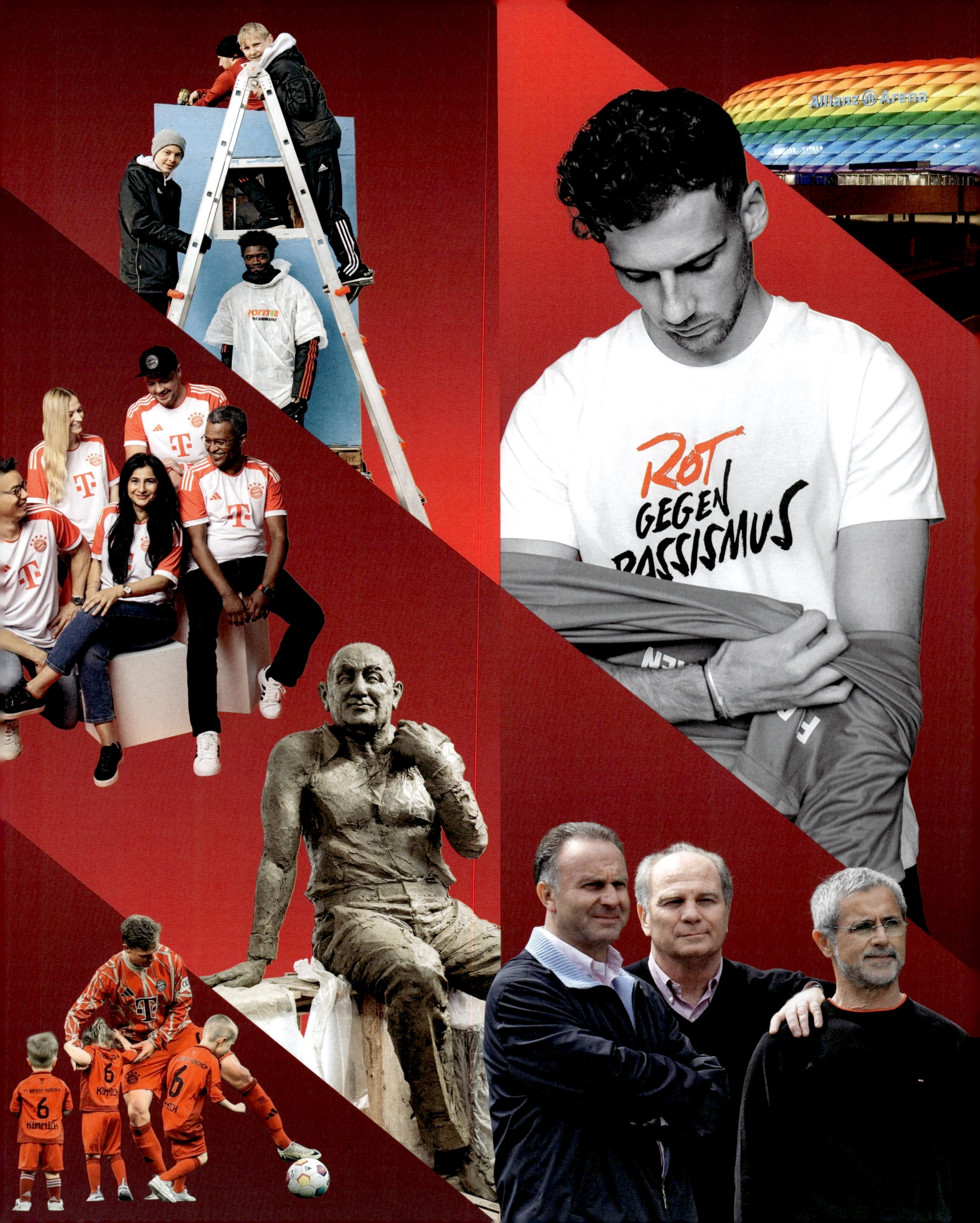
Allianz Arena
ROT
GEGEN
RASSISMUS

RESPON
SIBILITY

The motto of FCB can be interpreted in many different ways – in sport as an expression of a winning mentality. Uli Hoeness has an equally important view of it: "Mia san mia means that when you are up at the top, you also have to look down and help."

125 YEARS OF **RESPONSIBLITY**

After the tsunami in the Indian Ocean in 2004, FC Bayern donated money for rebuilding the devastated areas. And shortly afterwards founded FC Bayern Hilfe eV, a charity that is one of the pillars of social commitment at FCB. It supports individuals who are in need and organisations such as the Munich food bank and a parents' initiative for children with cancer. Former Bayern stars, too, may sometimes need help. When Gerd Müller needed "good friends", he found them in his old club. Hoeness organised rehabilitation and a new career start at FCB, where Müller had a new role for fifteen years as an assistant trainer for the amateurs. Others were assisted too, for example Sepp Maier and Lars Lunde following serious accidents.

The club has particular responsibility, partly in its own interests, for the health of the current players. Since the time of the coach Gyula Lóránt, who allegedly tried to convince the young doctor Hans-Wilhelm Müller-Wohlfahrt that "the best way to push back a slipped cartilage is to hit it with the corner flag", medical care at FCB has progressed by light years. The popular myth that players' contracts prohibit them from skiing ceased to be true decades ago – this is a matter within the players' own responsibility.

Exchanging passes with committed professional players such as Leon Goretzka, the club takes a stand in societal issues, combatting hate and intolerance, for example with the Red against Racism campaign. This includes training up-and-coming players at the Campus in engagement for society. And not least, in remembering the victims of the Nazi period. The club commissioned an independent study of its own past by the Institut für Zeitgeschichte (IfZ, Institute for Contemporary History). The result was that, in place of much that was previously believed, the club now takes a more differentiated view about its own role in the Nazi years. "FC Bayern did indeed have a considerable number of Jewish members whom – in contrast to many football clubs – it did not immediately expel after 1933", the IfZ concluded. "But this does not mean that it was a liberal 'Jews' club' – and it was not systematically treated badly by the Nazi authorities after 1933."

The results of the study have found a place in the museum in the Allianz Arena and in the travelling exhibition "FC Bayern under National Socialism: victims, fellow-travellers, perpetrators". In its "culture of remembrance", Charlotte Knobloch, the ex-president of the Central Committee of Jews in Germany, calls FC Bayern "an absolute role model in German football".

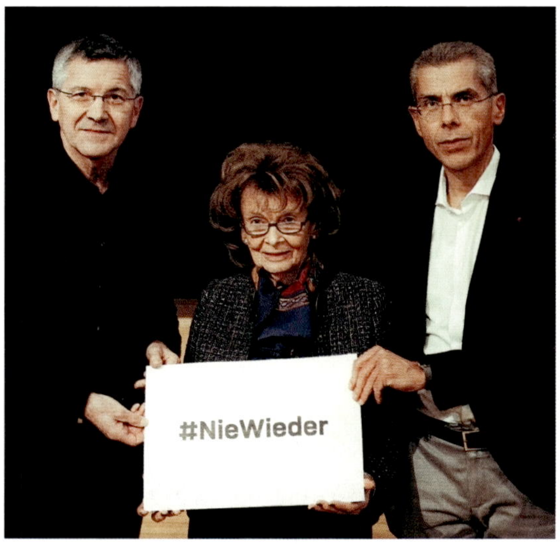

"Remembering must not become routine", appealed club president Herbert Hainer on International Holocaust Memorial Day in 2024, which FCB organised with the Israelitische Kultusgemeinde (Jewish Community) of Munich and Upper Bavaria. Its president Charlotte Knobloch explained that visitors to the Allianz Arena understand "how individual voices combine to make a loud choir - and what works in football is also what we need on the stage of society: against hate, against all extremism."

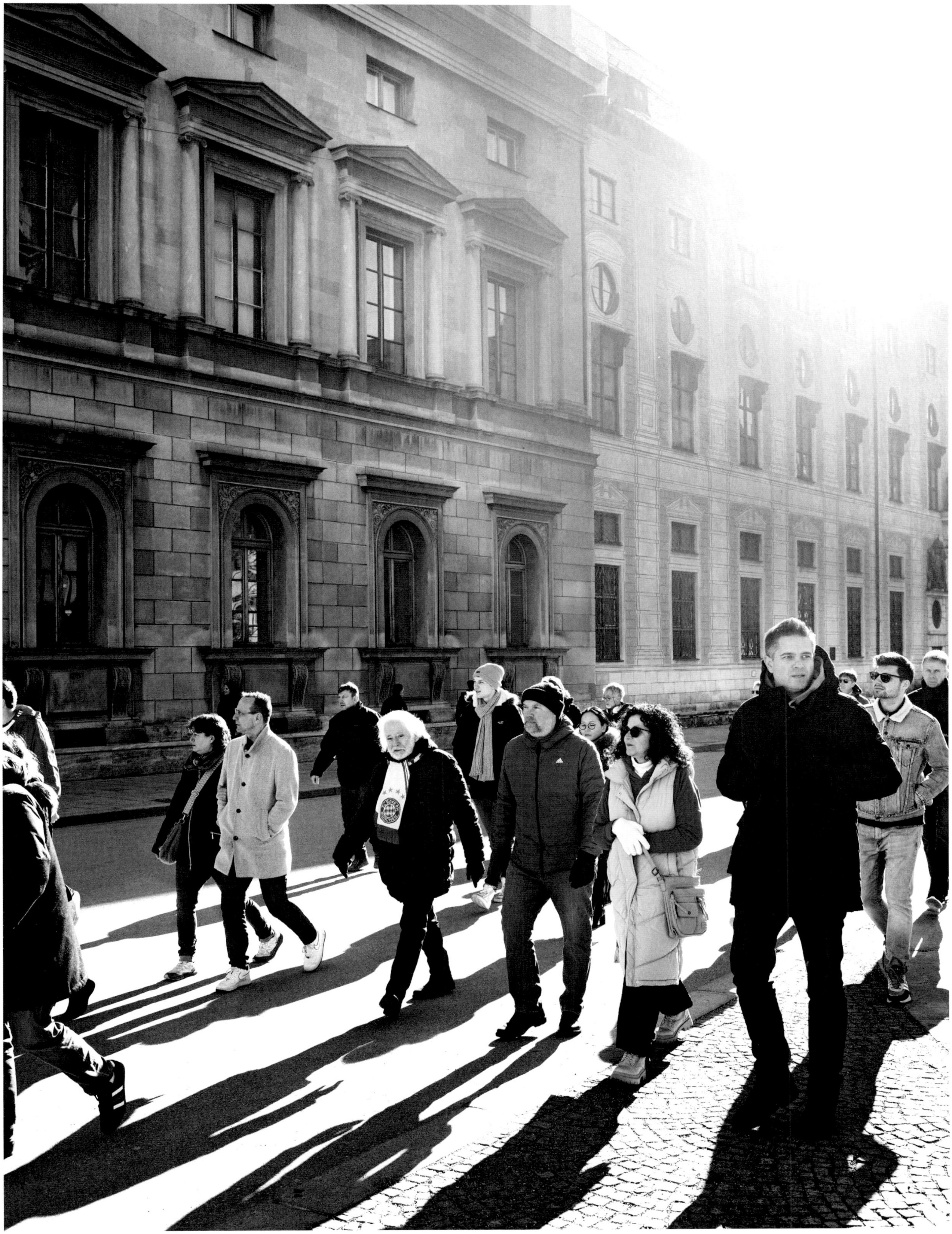

THERE FOREVER

They elevated the one-two pass between libero and goalscorer to an art form. Soon the two greatest players in FCB history will be standing together on the open space in front of the Allianz Arena.

"Without Gerd", Franz Beckenbauer liked to day, "we would still be sitting in the wooden hut on Säbener Strasse where we started out in the 1960s." Finally the two of them will take up the place that they deserve in front of an incomparable temple of football - which would probably not exist without them and their successes. In this way, the Allianz Arena is a monument to two footballers of the century.

Since 7 January 2025, the first anniversary of the death of the "Kaiser", the address of FC Bayern's stadium has been Franz-Beckenbauer-Platz no. 5. Mayor Dieter Reiter called it "a sign of the deep respect and appreciation that we feel towards Franz Beckenbauer". And FCB president Herbert Hainer declared that by means of this honour, "his memory will live on anew from match to match". On the esplanade in front of the Arena, where a statue commissioned by the Kurt Landauer Foundation already commemorates Gerd Müller, who died in 2021, Beckenbauer too will have a monument, also one and a half times life-size and cast in bronze. According to the Foundation, it will depict him "in his incomparably elegant pose as the conductor of the game".

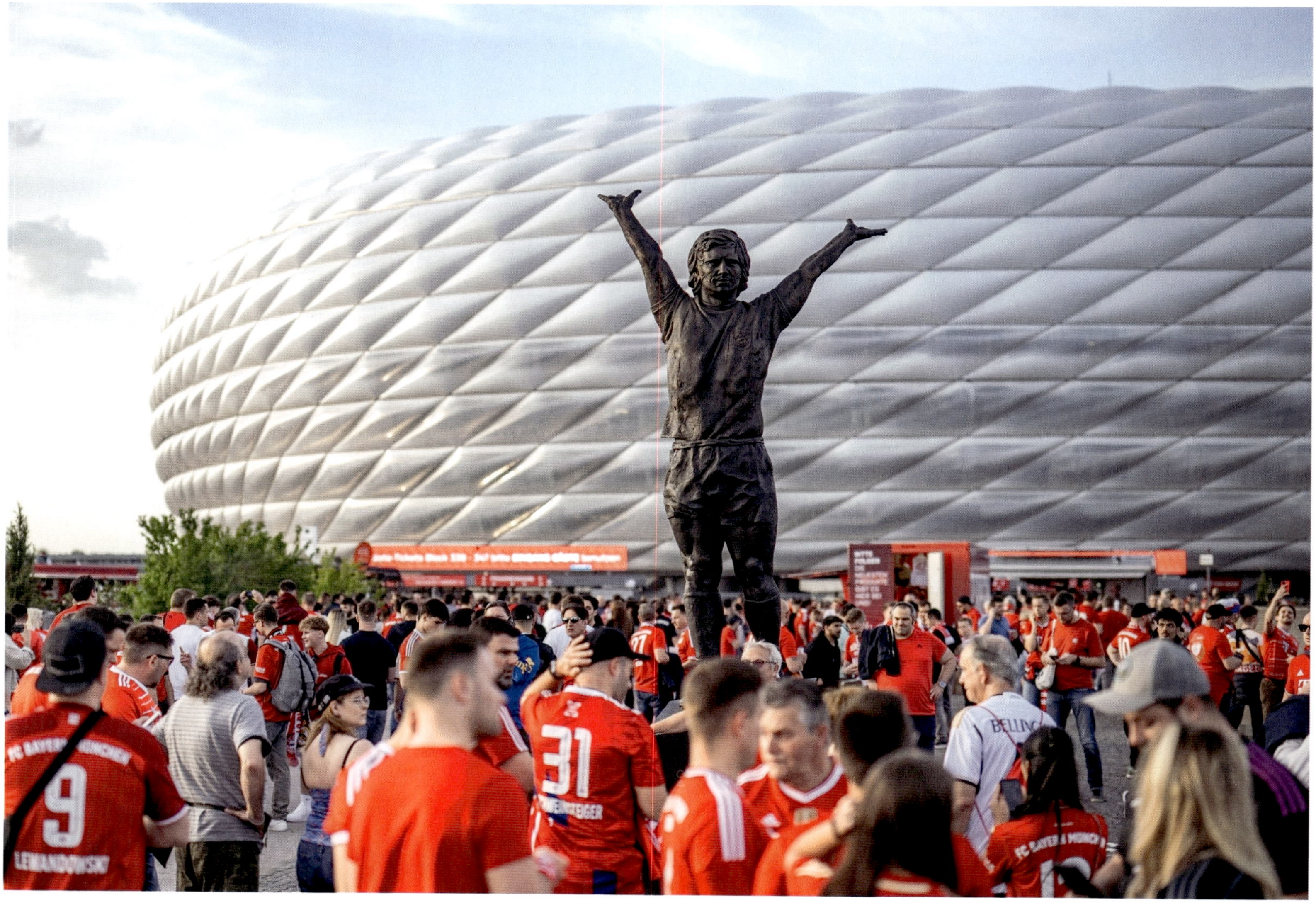

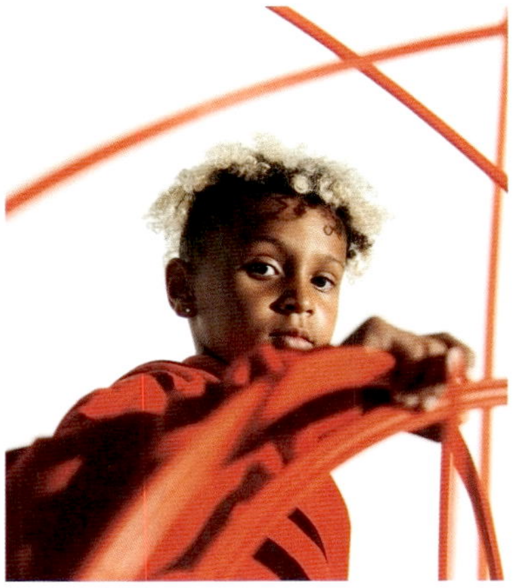

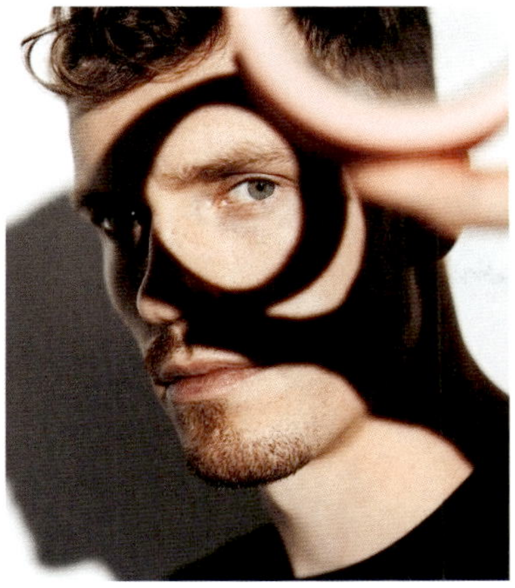

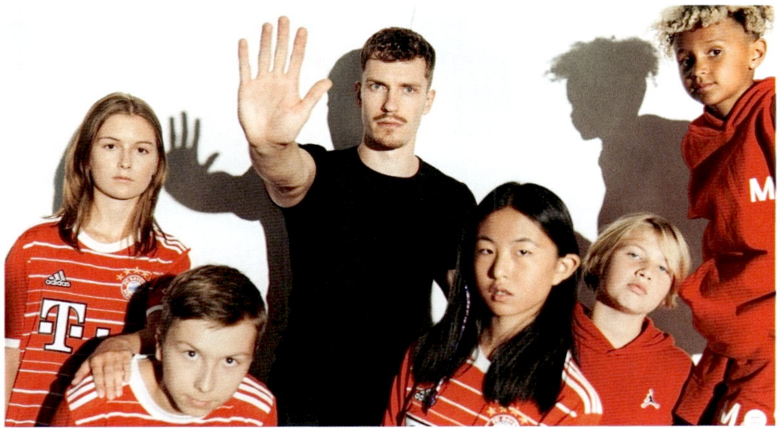

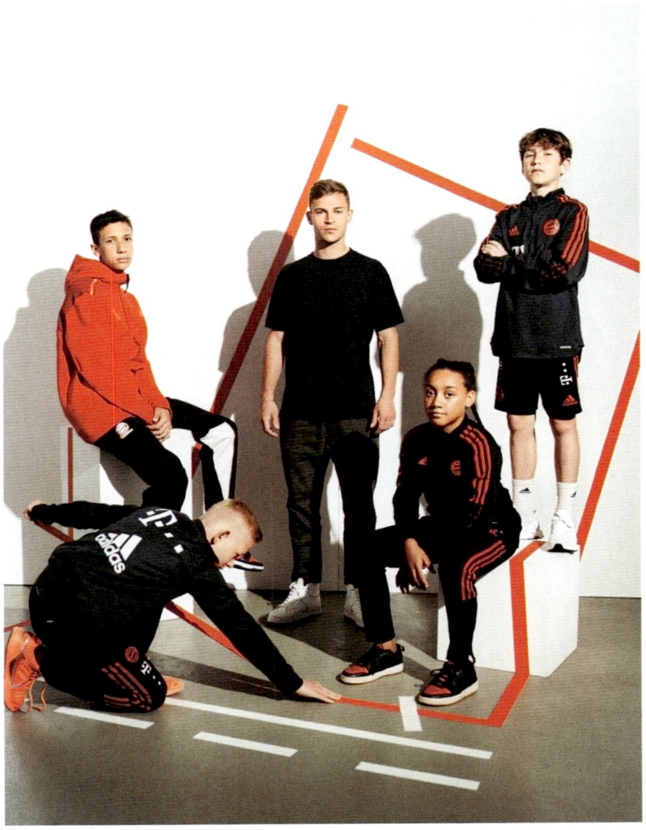

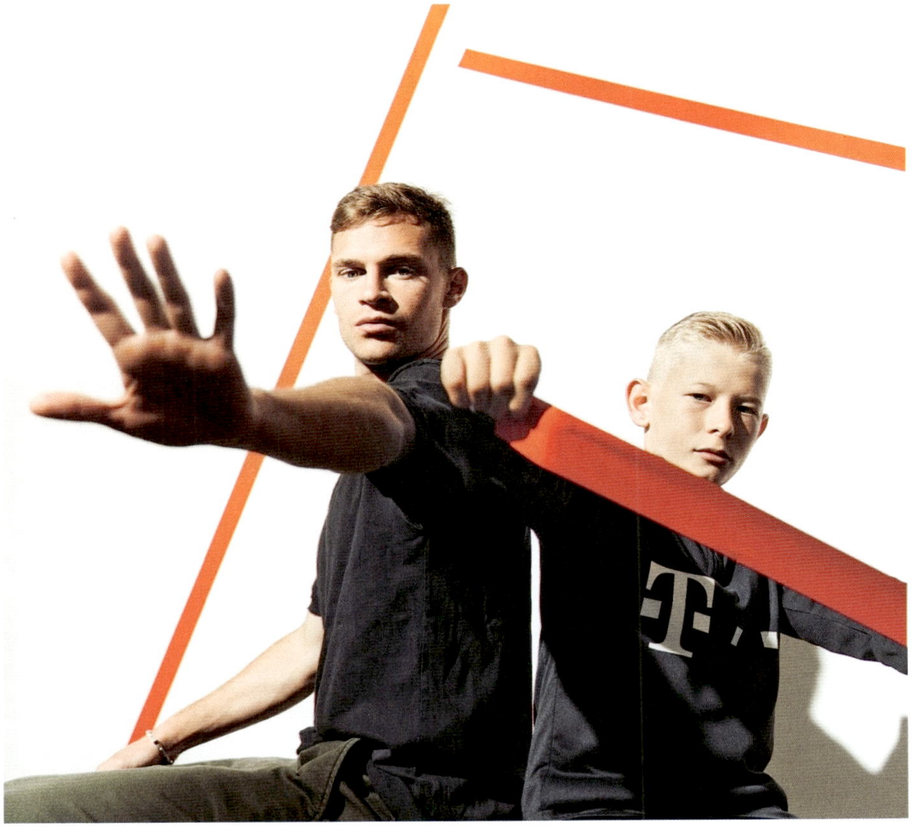

SAFEGUARDING **AND TRUST FOR** OUR CHILDREN

With “Red line – safeguard children and make them strong”, FCB has publicly taken the lead in one of the most important tasks for society, with the help of Bayern stars.

Joshua Kimmich stands up for the message “Recognise signals and take action – beyond the game”, and the basketball world champion Andi Obst, too, campaigns for the safeguarding measures that support children and young people in the club through workshops and provide recommendations for prevention and intervention in safeguarding children and young people. The current sustainability report states that “Protection of children and young people is practised all across the club at FC Bayern.” For a “culture of actively looking”, demanded by Benny Folkmann, managing director of FC Bayern eV, comprehensive structures were specially established with several child safeguarding officers, including the first such officer with full-time duties at a Bundesliga club.

WE TAKE **A STAND**

"Red against Racism" is the name for an initiative of FC Bayern across all areas of the club for diversity and against any kind of marginalisation. It is about more than printing a slogan on a shirt.

Video clips against racism, shared celebrations of shabbat as a sign of a culture of remembrance and, on the subject of inclusiveness, sign language for people with hearing handicaps: since March 2020, the Red against Racism campaign has combined elements of FCB's multifaceted social commitment. "To take a stand for diversity means engaging with the relevant societal challenges, entering into self-critical dialogue, understanding and taking action", says club president Herbert Hainer: "Especially in times when our democracy is threatened by forces that undermine it, sports must stand up and help to overcome barriers. No one should feel excluded at FC Bayern. We want to show that: We are more!"

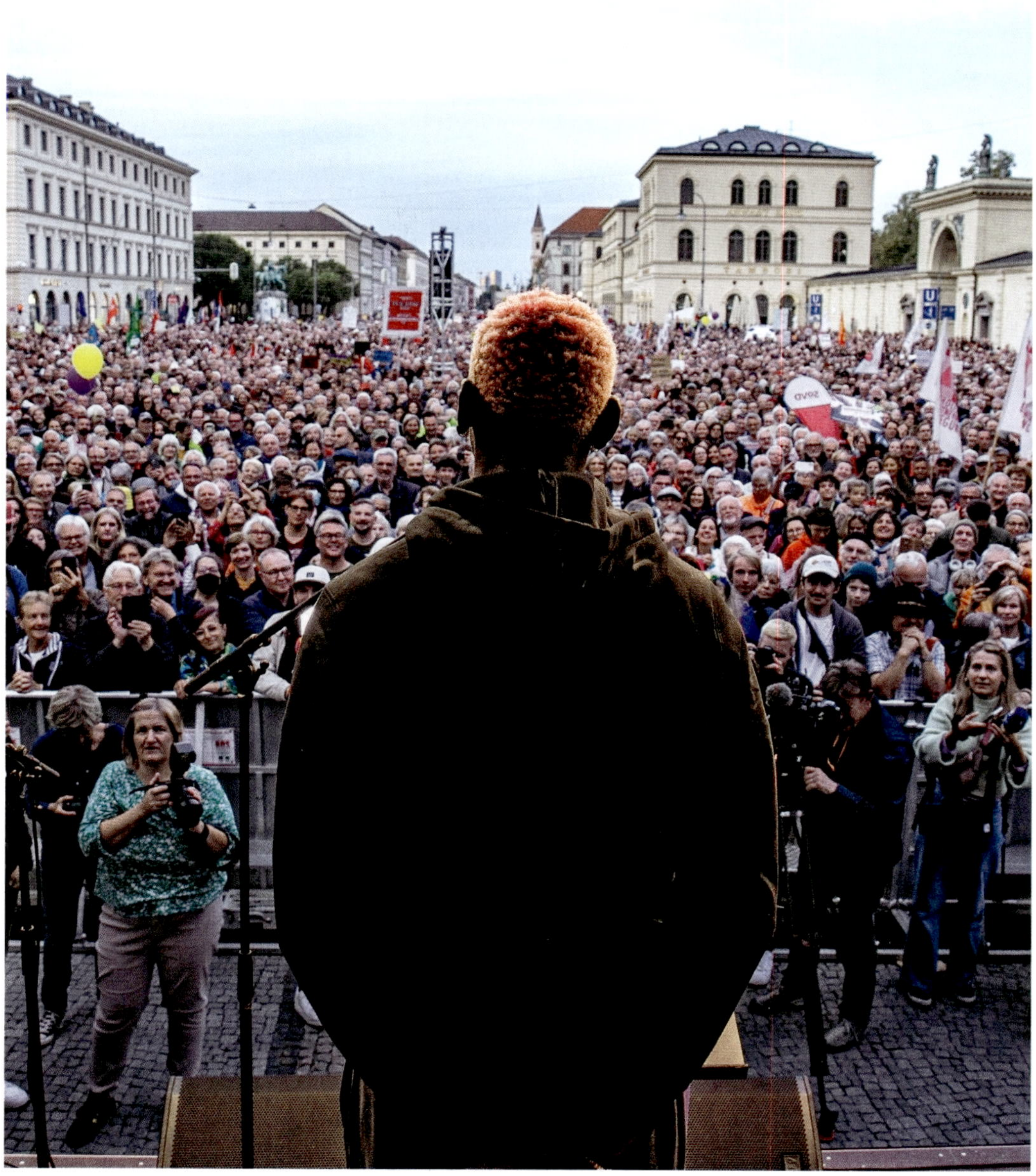

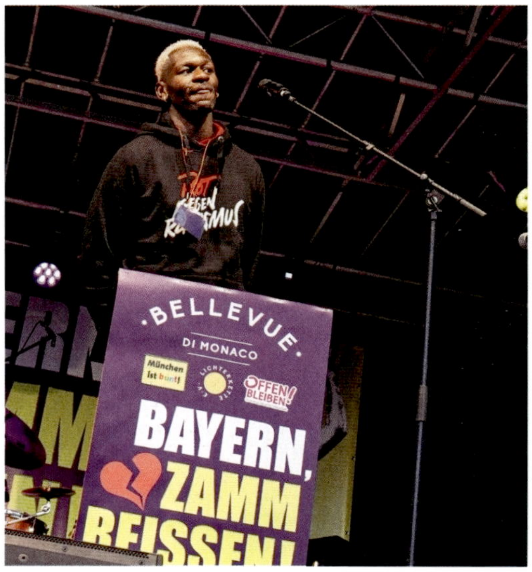

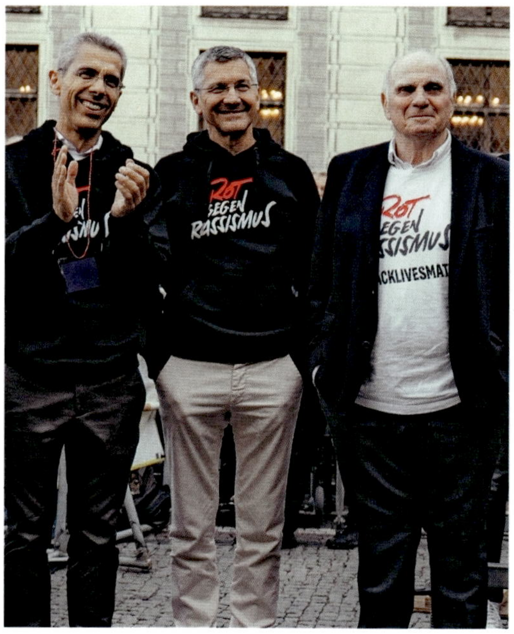

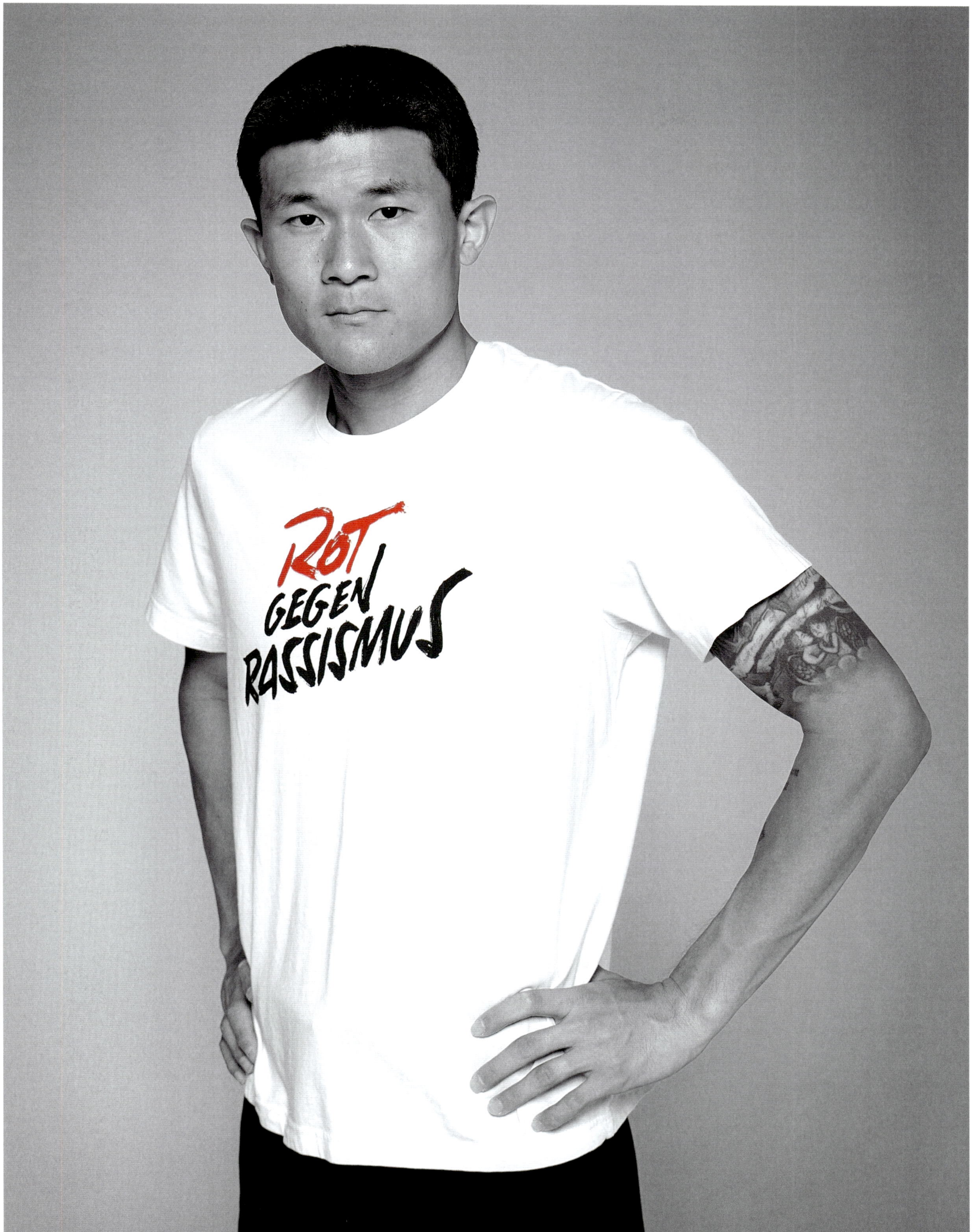
ROT
GEGEN
RASSISMUS

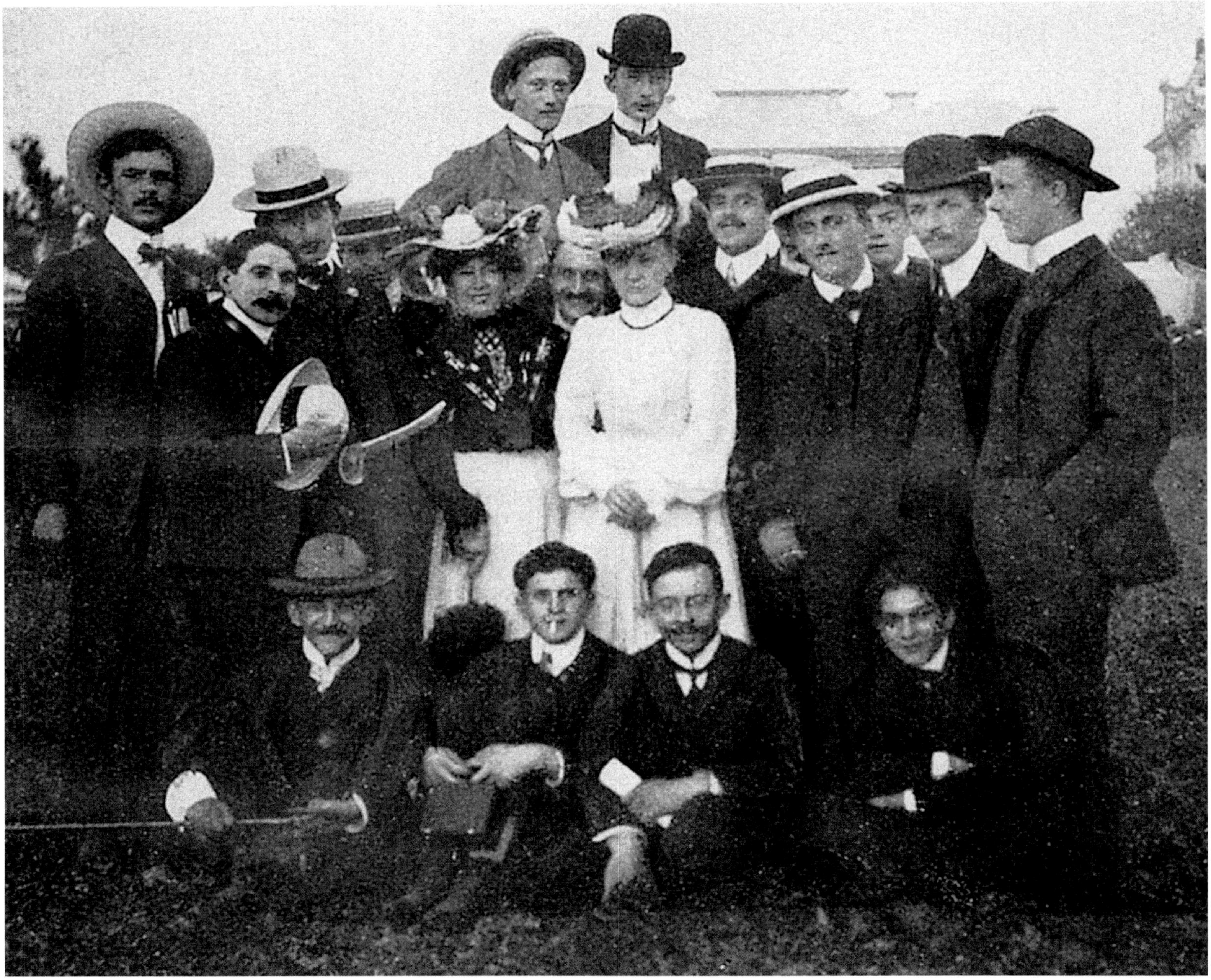

STRAW HATS **FROM SCHWABING**

A team photo with fans: the fashionable style of these early bohemian footballers seems to have scored with the ladies.

As a liberal, open club, from the very beginning FC Bayern took in footballers of every nationality and religion. However, until 1908 a school-leaving certificate was a minimum requirement for playing in the first team. The reputation of Bayern Munich as a somewhat elitist club is also reflected in the fact that the seventeen founding members included two sculptors, a photographer, an illustrator and several students – a cross-section of Schwabing, a quarter for intellectuals and artists. In appearance, these FCB footballers maintain a bohemian aura by all wearing the same French straw hats. One player called Bender was also said to have had a particularly exalted habit: he never walked onto the football pitch without a tie.

BENEFIT MATCHES – A TRADITION

For many fans in St. Pauli, Uli Hoeness was an enemy, but he didn't bear a grudge. This resulted in a first benefit match that helped the club to avoid losing its licence.

In February 2002, fresh from victory in the Club World Cup, FCB lost at bottom-of-the-table FC St. Pauli. After that, the club printed 100,000 T-shirts boasting "We beat the winners of the Club World Cup". Uli Hoeness did not buy one. But a year later, he bought a T-shirt bearing the word "Retter" (Saviour) and auctioned it for 1,500 euros. It helped St. Pauli to gain their licence to play in the third division following two relegations.

After a shameful 1–2 defeat in 2002, Hoeness gave his team a dressing-down in the bus: "Everyone thought we'll dance through this match, one, two, three. While I have a sleepless night, thirty minutes after the final whistle you're already playing cards again." In 2003 he returned with FCB, and St. Pauli, who had been relegated from the second division, earned more than 200,000 euros from tickets and T-shirts. Hoeness, until then regarded as an enemy, was cheered by the fans. "Despite all the differences" he saw a common spirit with St. Pauli and its left-wing supporters "in a strict rejection of Neo-Nazi tendencies." In the stadium he did not tolerate "any kind of Nazi propaganda or far-right radical elements. I oppose that mercilessly."

For the record-holding champions, this first benefit game started a tradition of supporting historic clubs that were short of money – and benefit matches followed at Union Berlin (2004), Darmstadt 98 (2008), Alemannia Aachen (2013), Hansa Rostock (2013), Dynamo Dresden (2015), Kickers Offenbach (2017), and 1. FC Kaiserslautern (2019). At the last two of these, Hoeness had endured two of his most embarrassing defeats as a player: 4–7 after leading 4–1 in Kaiserslautern in 1973, and 0–6 at Offenbach in 1974. But this was not a reason to refuse assistance.

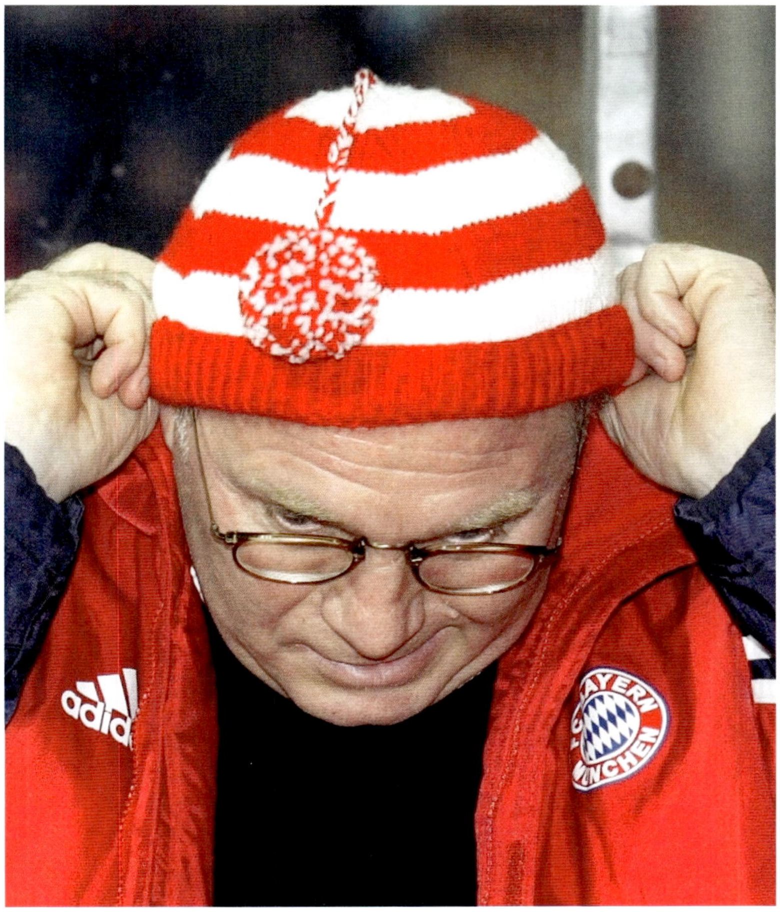

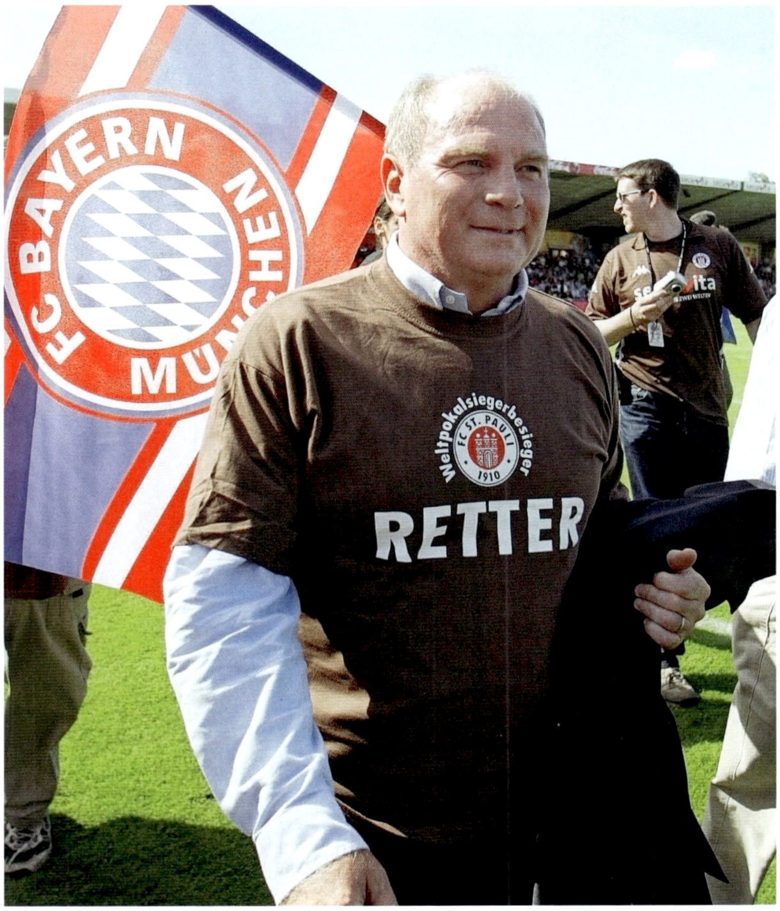

NUREMBERG – WE'RE COMING **WITH A BIKE AND FREE BEER**

1932 was a year to celebrate for Bayern Munich. But an awful year for Germany. During the global economic crisis, the unemployment rate rose to 30 per cent. In Germany more than six million people were out of work. Several hundred of them cycled to Nuremberg to be present for Bayern's first championship title.

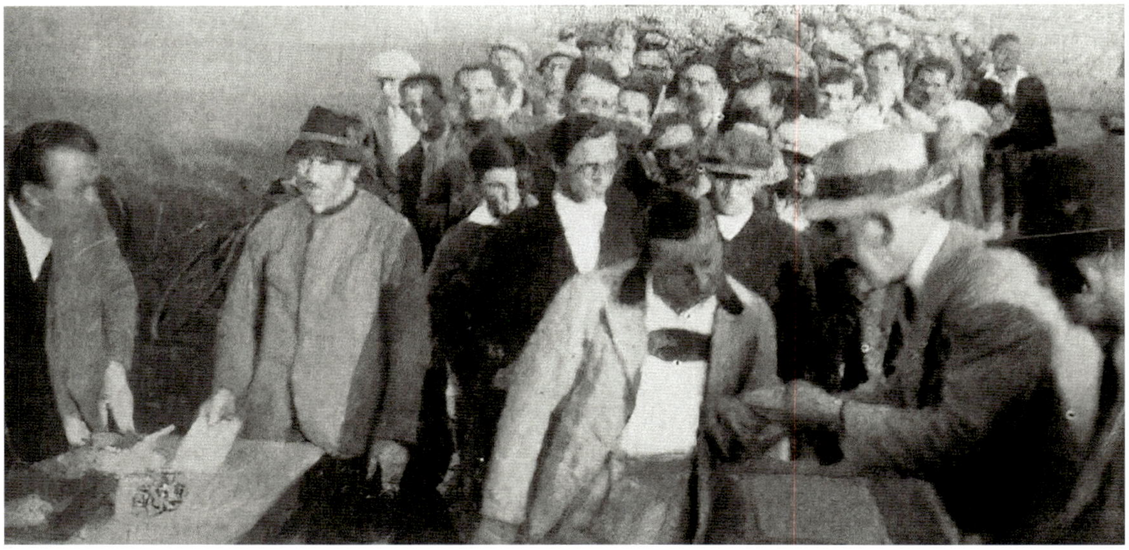

421 fans, most of them unemployed, set out on their bikes for the journey of some 180 kilometres on 12 June 1932, a scorching hot Sunday, to be part of it in the Frankenstadion. When the club heard of their intention, it paid for board and lodging for the cycling fans and donated the admission tickets. It was an unforgettable trip for them, as it was for all Bayern fans. At the end of the 2–0 win against Eintracht Frankfurt, thousands ran onto the pitch and carried the players off on their shoulders. The following day there was a parade through Munich in horse-drawn carriages, from the central station via the Stachus to the Marienplatz square and finally to a championship party in the Löwenbräukeller.

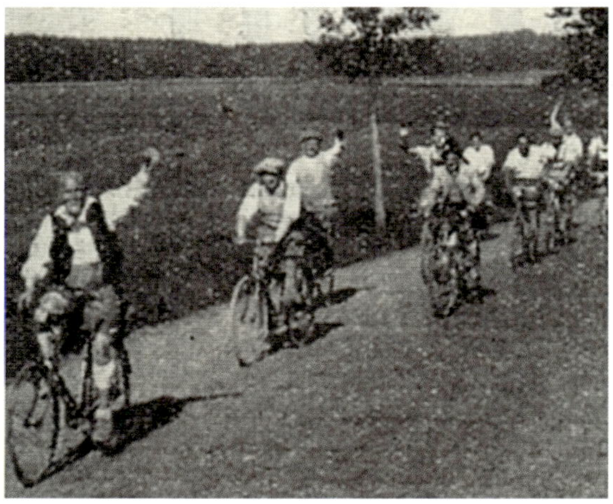

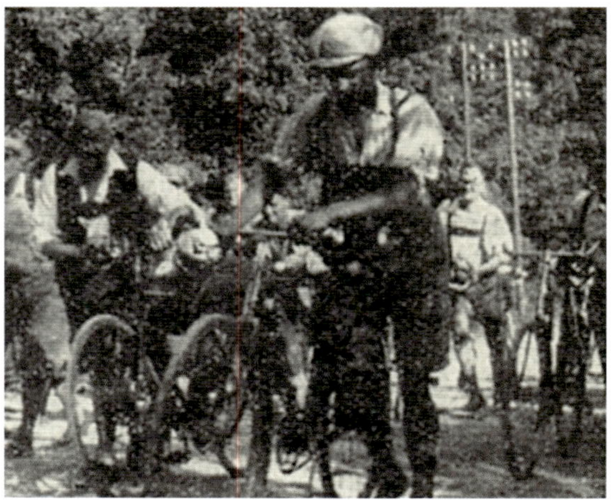

The fans cycling on the championship tour to Nuremberg in 1932 covered a distance there and back that is equal to the average distance run by a Bayern footballer in the 2023-24 season – almost 360 kilometres.

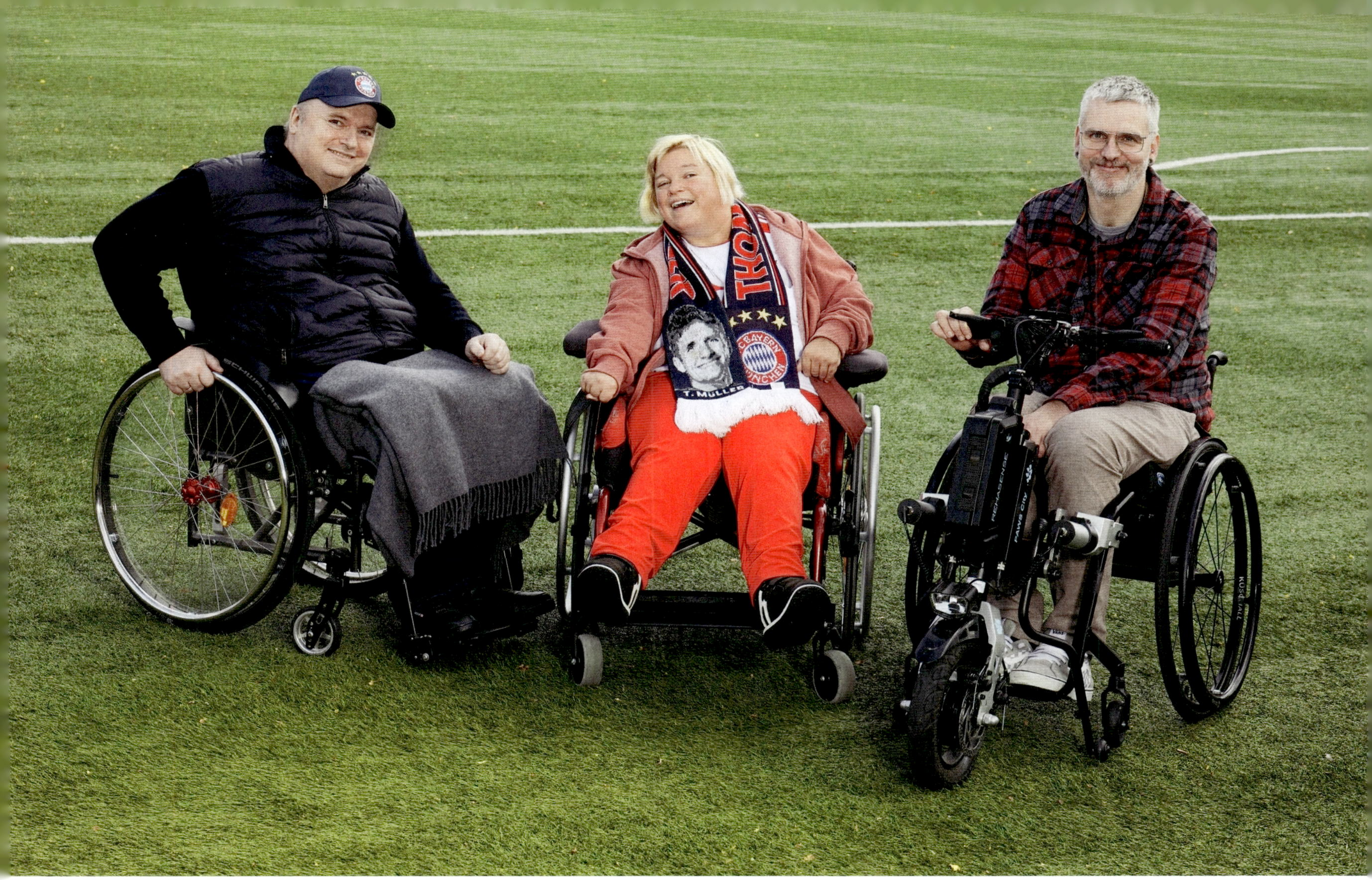

FCB WITH A CLEAR VIEW – **ROLLWAGERL 93**

Kim Krämer (right), chairman of the Rollwagerl 93 club, has been the delegate for fans with handicaps since 2015 at FCB, taking care of the interests of wheelchair users and those with impaired sight or hearing.

The members of Rollwagerl 93 were involved in planning the Allianz Arena from the very beginning – and today they are delighted about the "fantastic view of the pitch" and cheer noisily when Bayern play.

In a wheelchair (*Rollwagerl*), a good view cannot be taken for granted in most stadiums. If a goal is imminent, the other fans leap up in front of them, and people with restricted mobility often cannot see the most important moment in a football match. This is not the case in Munich, as the stadium construction takes account of their interests, which are represented by the biggest independent, inclusive fan club in Europe, with around 900 members. Thanks to their position significantly higher than the first row, the view of what is happening is always unobstructed from every one of the 227 wheelchair spaces in the Arena, in contrast to the previous situation in the Olympic Stadium. Alongside accessible parking spaces, entrances and toilets, this is one of many aspects of cooperation between the club and the fan club that have clearly improved the football experience for fans with handicaps. This has set a good example. Delegations from Brazil before the World Cup in 2014 and from Barcelona in advance of the refurbishment of the Camp Nou came to Munich for information about details of stadium accessibility.

IT'S LONELY AT THE TOP
PSG–FCB 0–1 · 2020

The Covid pandemic claimed the lives of at least 20 million people between 2020 and 2022 according to the WHO. The number of victims in Germany, allowing for uncertain cases, is estimated at 200,000. Football too went into quarantine, into a fan-free exile – and survived.

2020, of all years, the year Covid-19 brought European football to a standstill for months, cutting players off from their game and fans from the experience in the stadium – this dark year was to be the most successful in the history of FCB. Hansi Flick's team took home all six titles that were available to be won. In empty stadiums, the lifeblood of football could not flow. This did not, however, spoil the pleasure of a unique run of victories. The team celebrated uninhibitedly, especially after winning the final of the Champions League in Lisbon.

Ultimately FCB made the best of the situation, evolving innovative home training for players during the lockdown, restoring their fitness, and crushing FC Barcelona 8–2 in the shortened competition. In the final, Kingsley Coman's goal earned a 1–0 triumph against Paris St-Germain. Uli Hoeness had feared that a win would not have the same status as earlier victories in the Champions League: "A lot will be missing: the images of cheering spectators, the atmosphere in the venue for the final, the thousands of fans passing through the streets." But especially in the sad Covid year of 2020, the football played by FC Bayern gave millions of people a rare reason for undiluted joy. Even though it was not expressed in the emotional atmosphere of packed stadiums and streets, the successes of FCB in 2020 are among the very best in the history of the club.

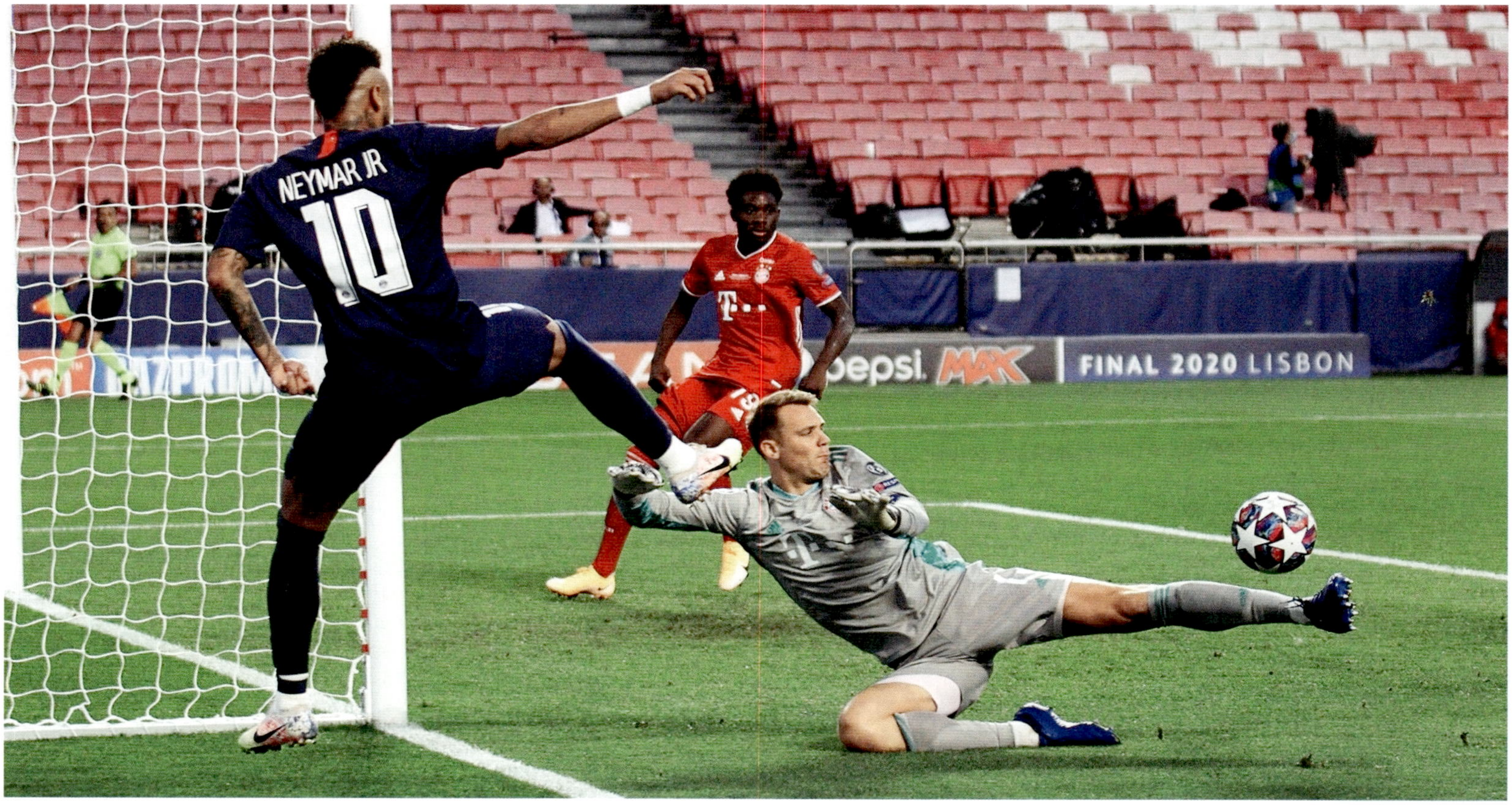

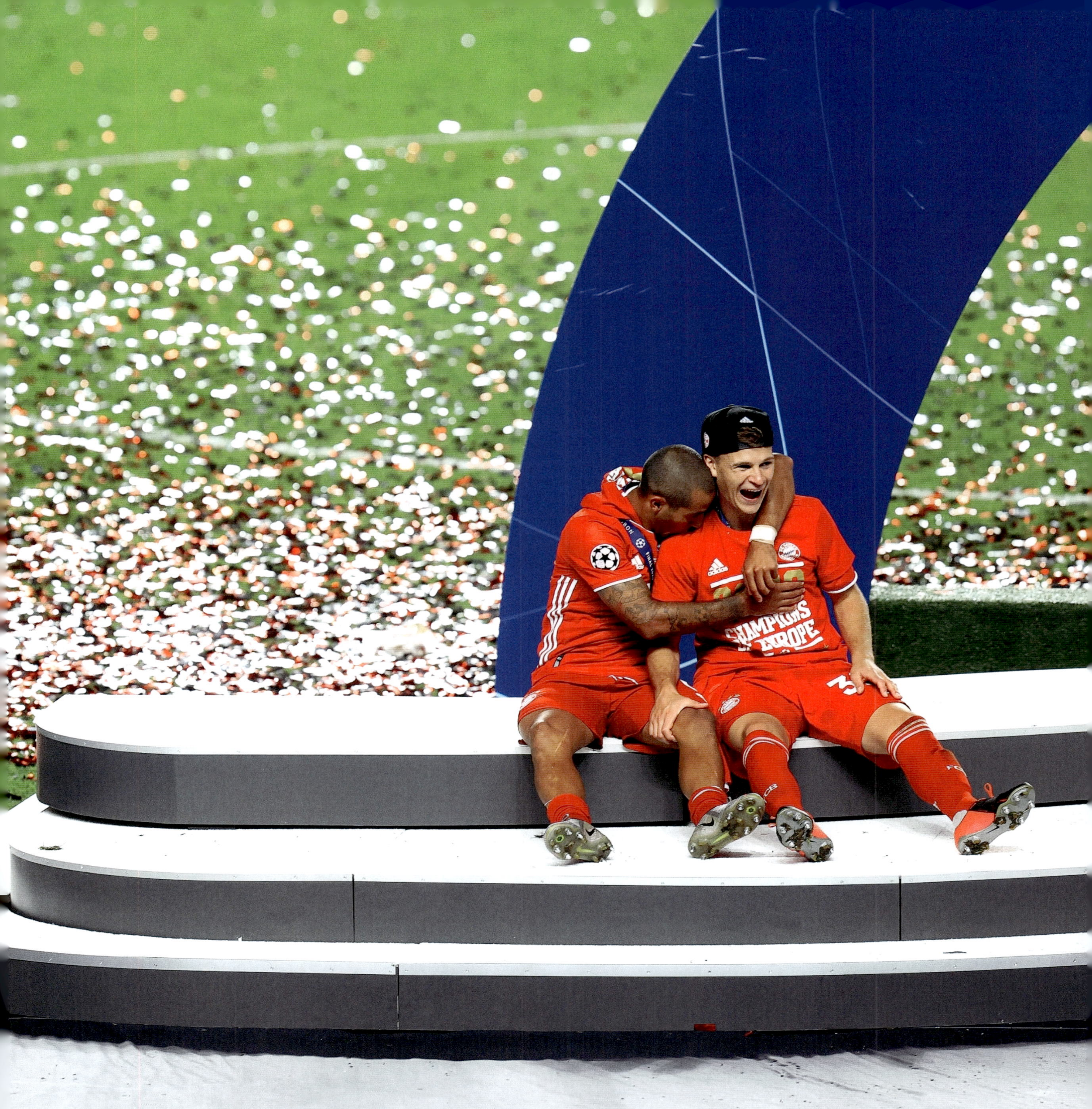

Left: "Exactly at the brief moments when Paris might have scored a goal, Manuel was there. And that is just what makes a great goalkeeper – the goalkeeper that Bayern Munich needs." This was Oliver Kahn's verdict after the final on Neuer's brilliant saves. And the titan Kahn is a man who ought to know.

To perform in front of a crowd of 65,000, to do the job: that's all part of a day's work for professional footballers. To perform well in front of 65,000 empty seats, to do the job in this situation is a real challenge. Joshua Kimmich, who later celebrated the win with his colleague Thiago, mastered the challenge with success. And set up the decisive goal with his light-as-a-feather cross to the forehead of Kingsley Coman. On this occasion, the fans could not carry their team to victory. Something different carried them forward. Kimmich put it into words as follows: "Today we felt invincible."

International successes of FC Bayern are often followed by triumphs for the German national team. Two months after winning the European Cup with FCB, Franz Beckenbauer led the German side to victory in the World Cup. And one year after the treble, Bastian Schweinsteiger and Philipp Lahm, too, had winners' medals in that competition.

AN EAGLE ON THE SHIRT – **FCB AND DFB**

Here is a quiz question for real nerds: Which FCB player represented two national teams – and scored in his first match for both of them? The answer: Gerhard Siedl. He made his debut for the Saarland in 1951. And in 1957, when the Saarland had become a state in the Federal Republic, for Germany

FCB has provided almost one hundred players for the German national team of the DFB (Deutscher Fussball-Bund; German Football Association), far more than any other club. Back in 1926 the team included its first "Bayern block". In a 4–2 win against the Netherlands, the outstanding player out of four from Bayern was Josef Pöttinger, who hit three goals. And since the time of Sigmund Haringer in 1934, with one exception at least one player from FCB was in the German side at every World Cup. In winning the final in 1974 there were no few than six of them, in 2014 as many as seven, and all three goals in the final were scored by players from FCB (Müller, Breitner, Götze). Uli Hoeness says, "When FC Bayern is strong, Germany is strong."

1958 was the only tournament without a player from FCB. The forward Erich Hahn, it is said, refused an invitation to a DFB training course, saying he had to be at the racetrack. At that, Sepp Herberger had no use for him. And Bayern soon followed suit. Against Ulm, shortly after the World Cup, Hahn limped from the pitch, seemingly injured. While his team, reduced to ten men, conceded an equaliser, he was sitting in a taxi on his way to Daglfing to the horse races. The club suspended him for fifteen matches and he left to play for Luzern. Where there is a beautiful racetrack.

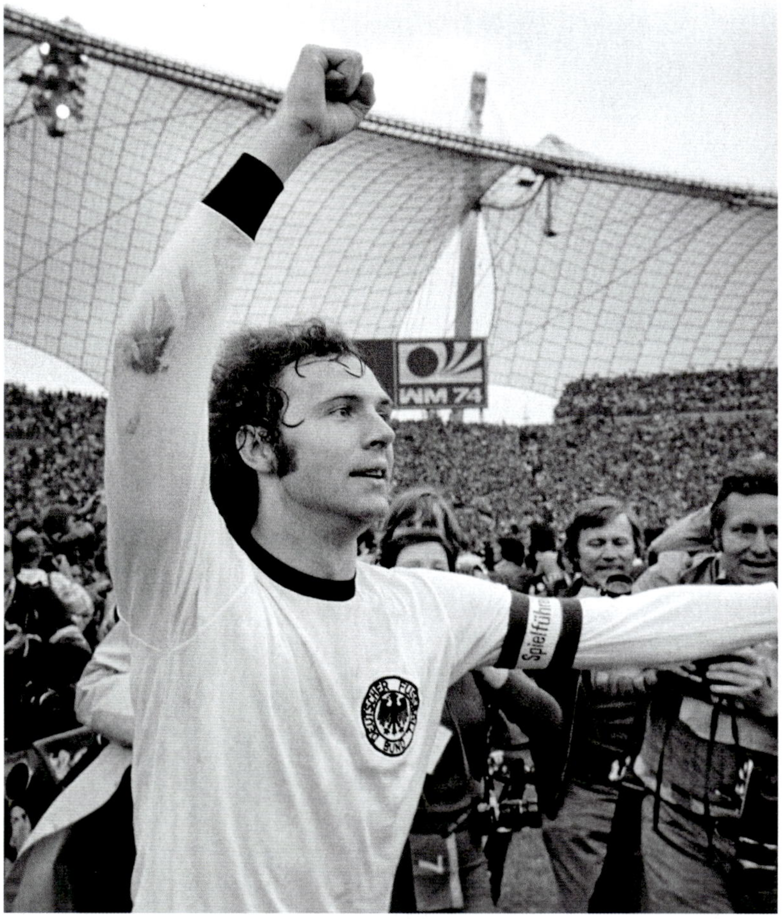

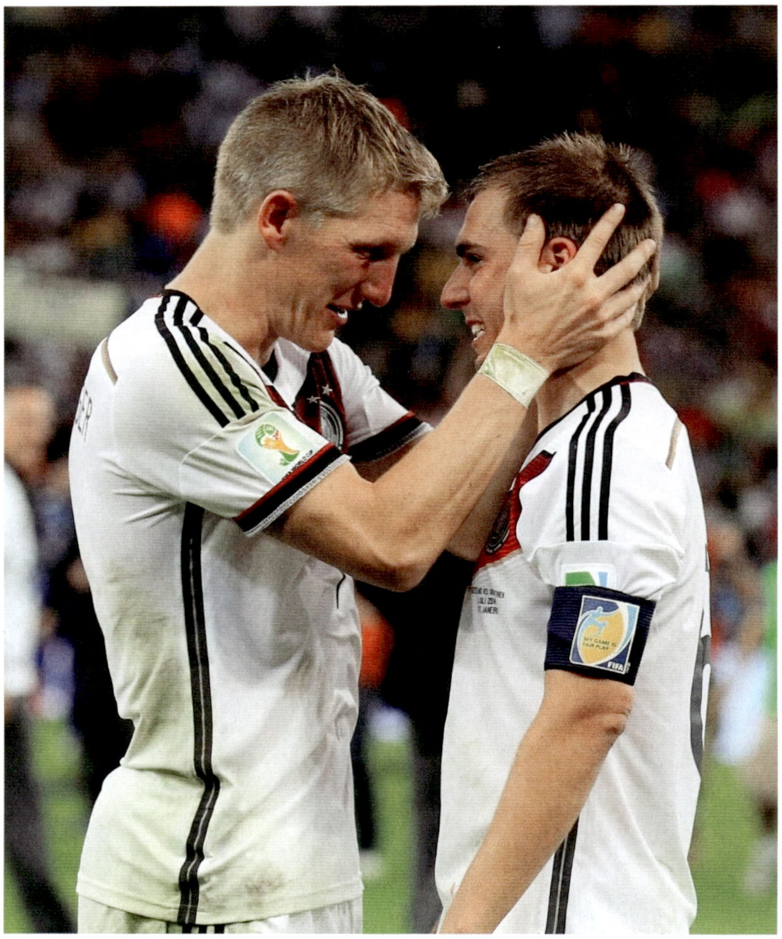

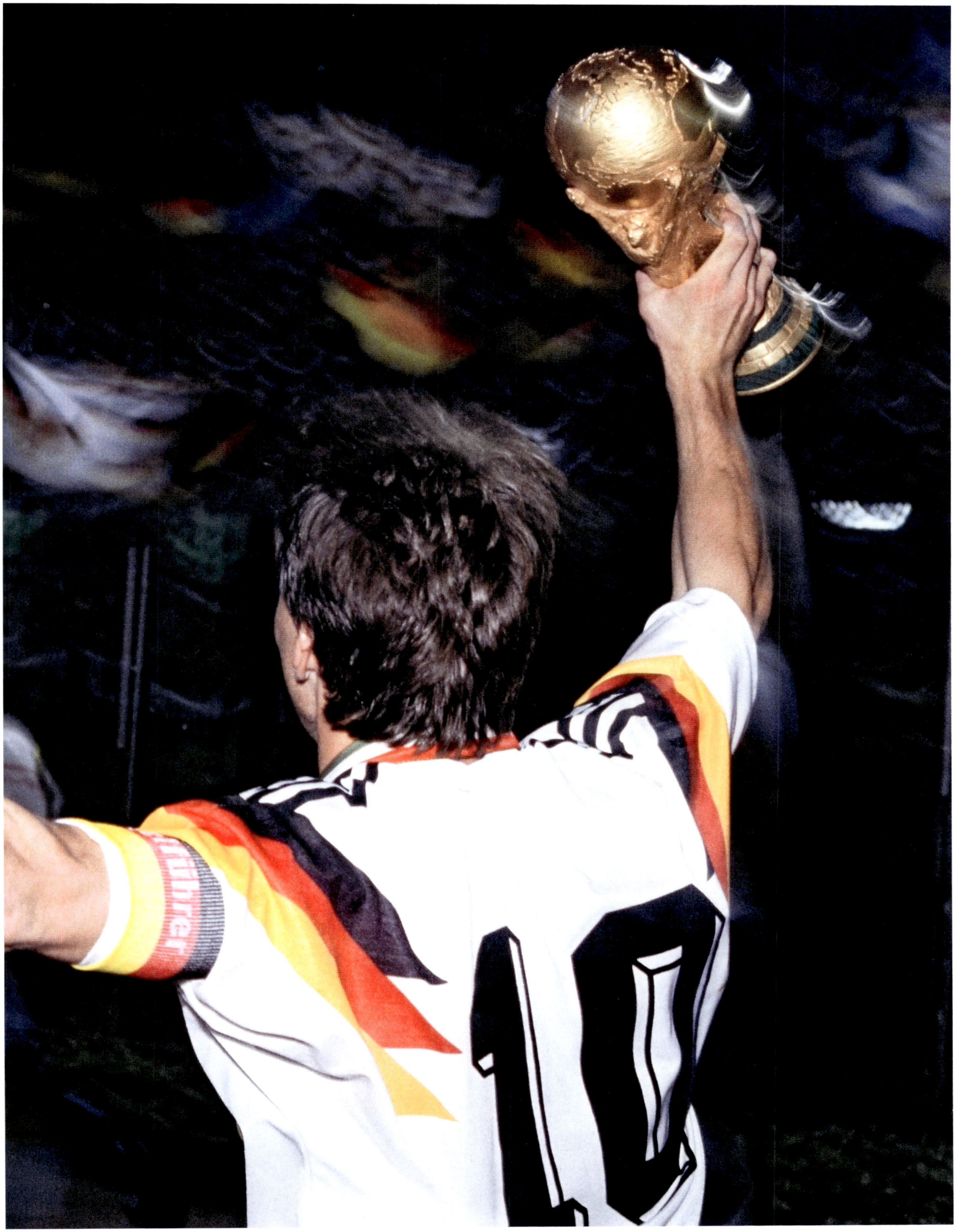

Right: With his photo series titled *Bundesliga Kathedralen*, the Munich photographer Michael von Hassel created an artistic monument to the "cathedrals of the Bundesliga", including the Allianz Arena.

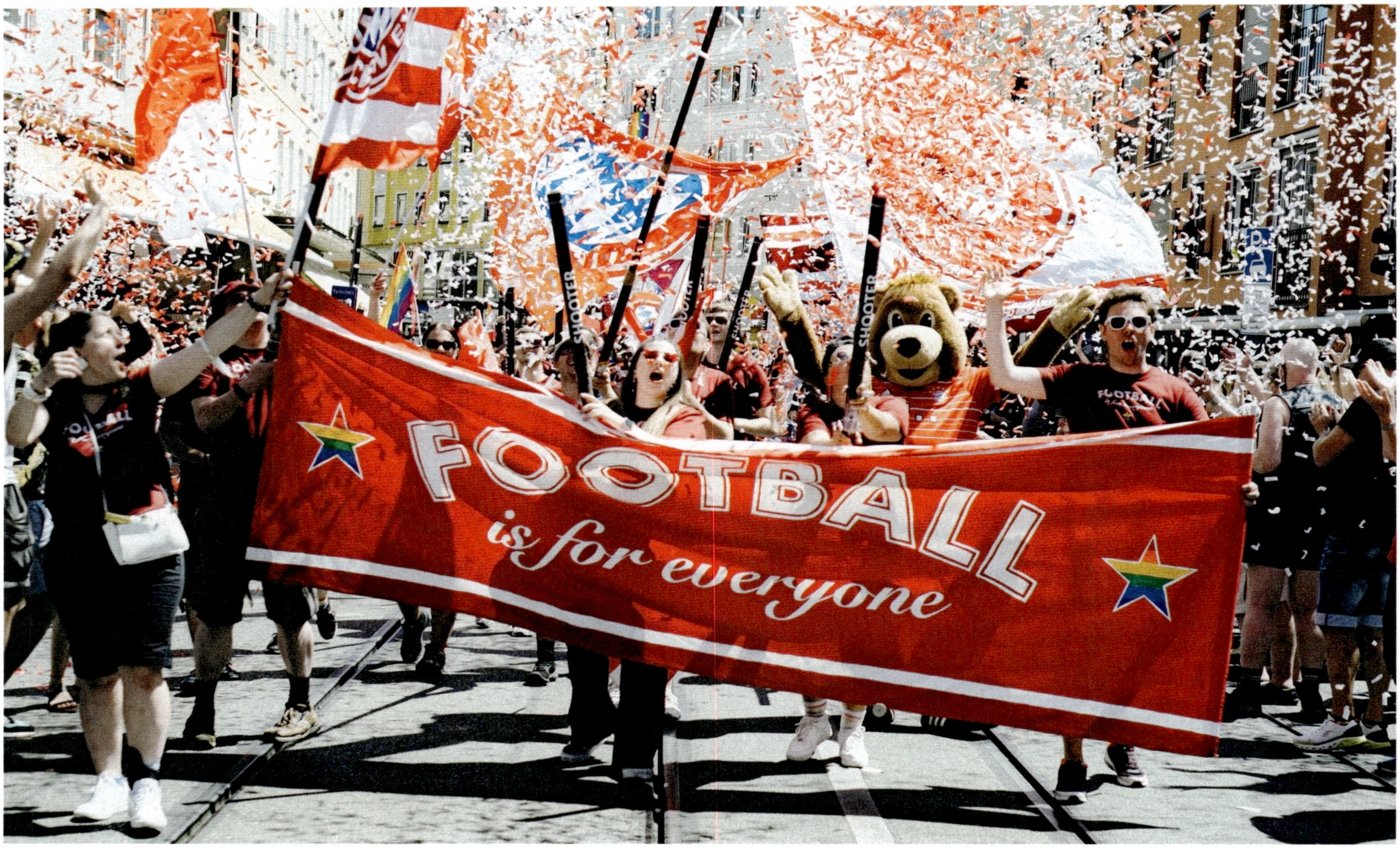

DEMONSTRATE **DIVERSITY!**

Once a year the Allianz Arena glows in the colours of the rainbow, not just in red. In this way FC Bayern shows its colours in support of tolerance and diversity on the weekend of Christopher Street Day.

On this day of worldwide celebrations and demonstrations by lesbian, gay, bisexual, transgender and in general by queer people, for years FCB has supported both the Red against Racism initiative and its QUEERPASS Bayern fan club. During the parade through Munich in 2023, watched by more than half a million spectators, the fan club displayed a banner calling for resistance against homophobia, and the following year Bianca "Jay" Rech, director of women's football at FCB, and the England international player Georgia Stanway took part. For years now, eye-catching figures in the parade have been two mascots, Berni and Mia, who are available untiringly for taking selfies. The club regularly engages in workshops and panel discussions in dialogue with QUEERPASS Bayern to draw attention to the theme of diversity.

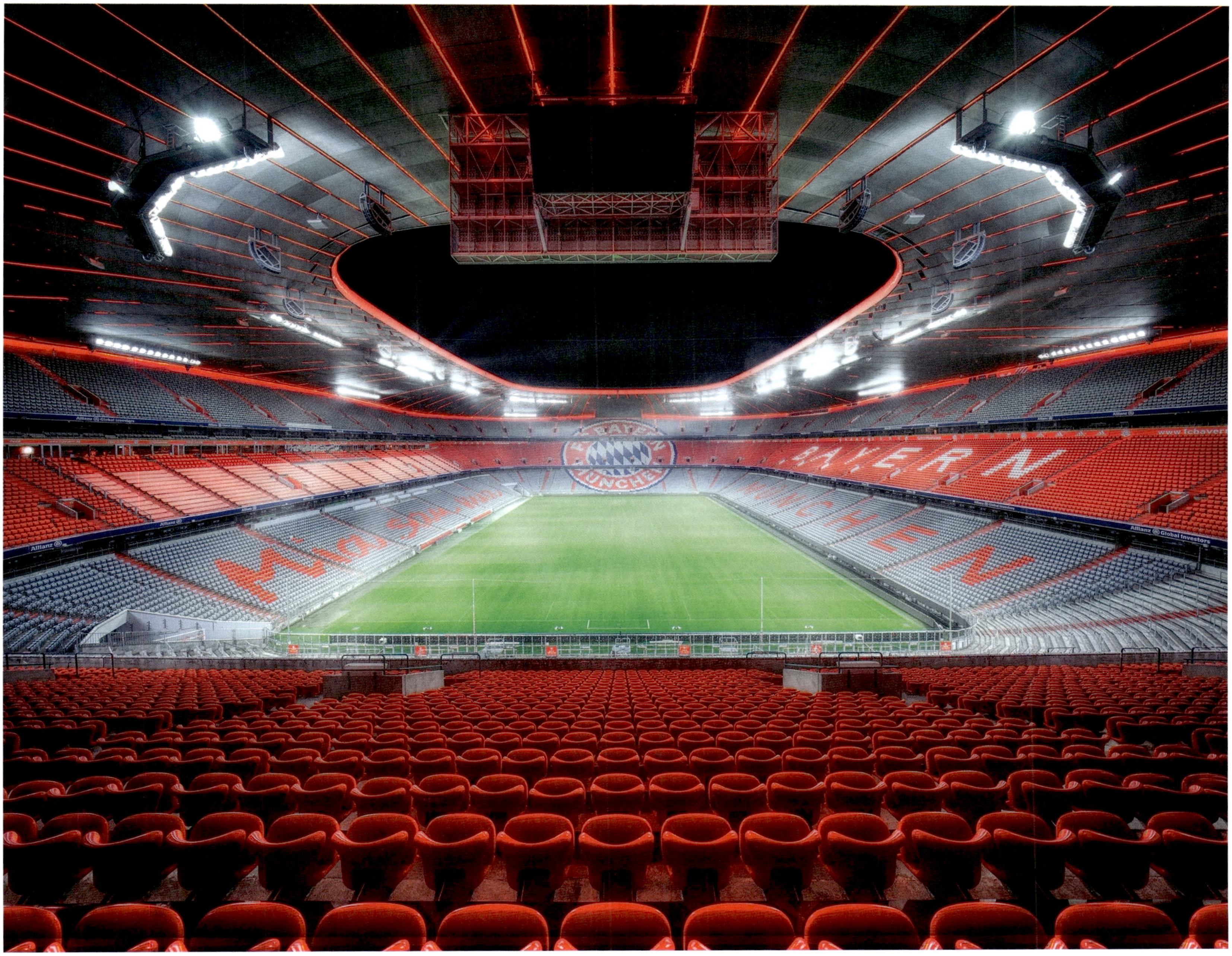

LOOK OUT! WE ARE WATCHING!

Before the European Championships in 2024, Olaf Scholz, the German chancellor, was informed in the Allianz Arena about Obacht (Look Out), the awareness programme at FC Bayern. UEFA adopted it for all stadiums in the Euros.

FC Bayern München evolved Obacht in cooperation with fans from the Südkurve and the Munich Fan Project as part of the fight against racism, violence and discrimination. It now operates for the basketballers too. The aim is to establish a "culture of looking actively" in sports venues, so that spectators look out for one another, support each other and quickly receive help. Via QR codes that are distributed around the stadium, assistance by specialists with psychological training can be summoned. "The FC Bayern family is about sticking together: everyone should feel welcome, at ease and safe," said Michael Diederich, executive vice chairman of FCB when presenting the programme. "We do not tolerate the crossing of red lines or threatening and discriminatory behaviour."

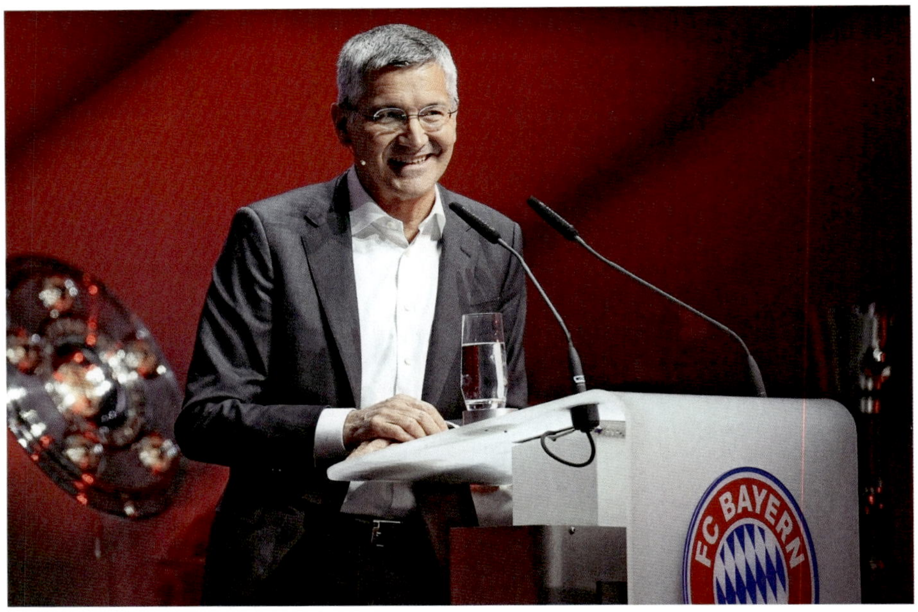
FC BAYERN

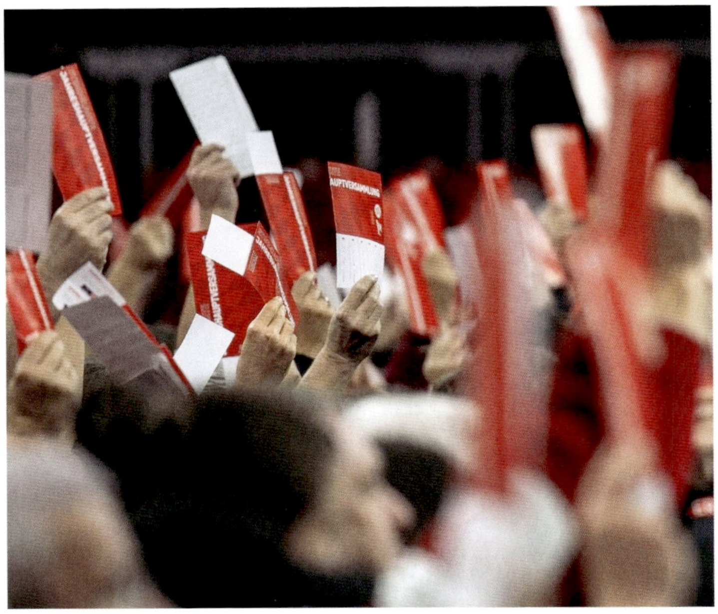

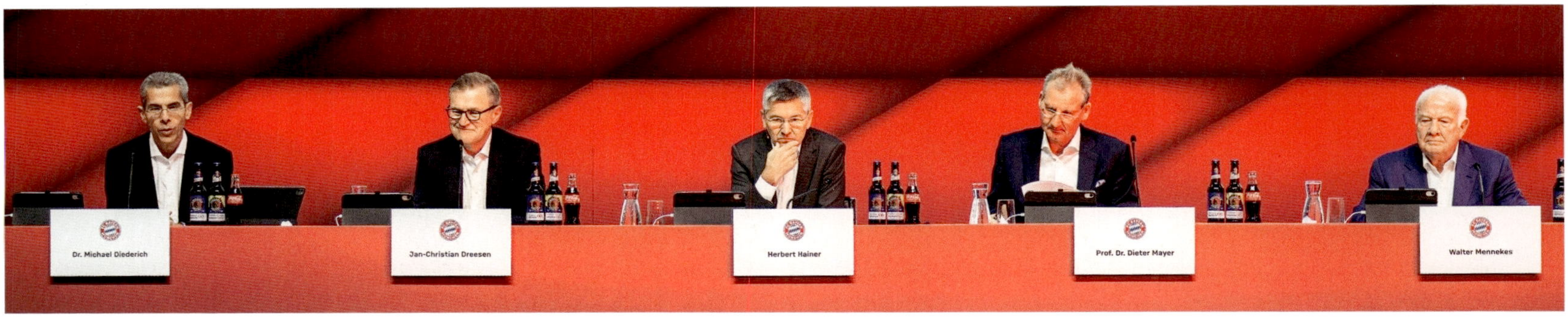
Dr. Michael Diederich
Jan-Christian Dreesen
Herbert Hainer
Prof. Dr. Dieter Mayer
Walter Mennekes

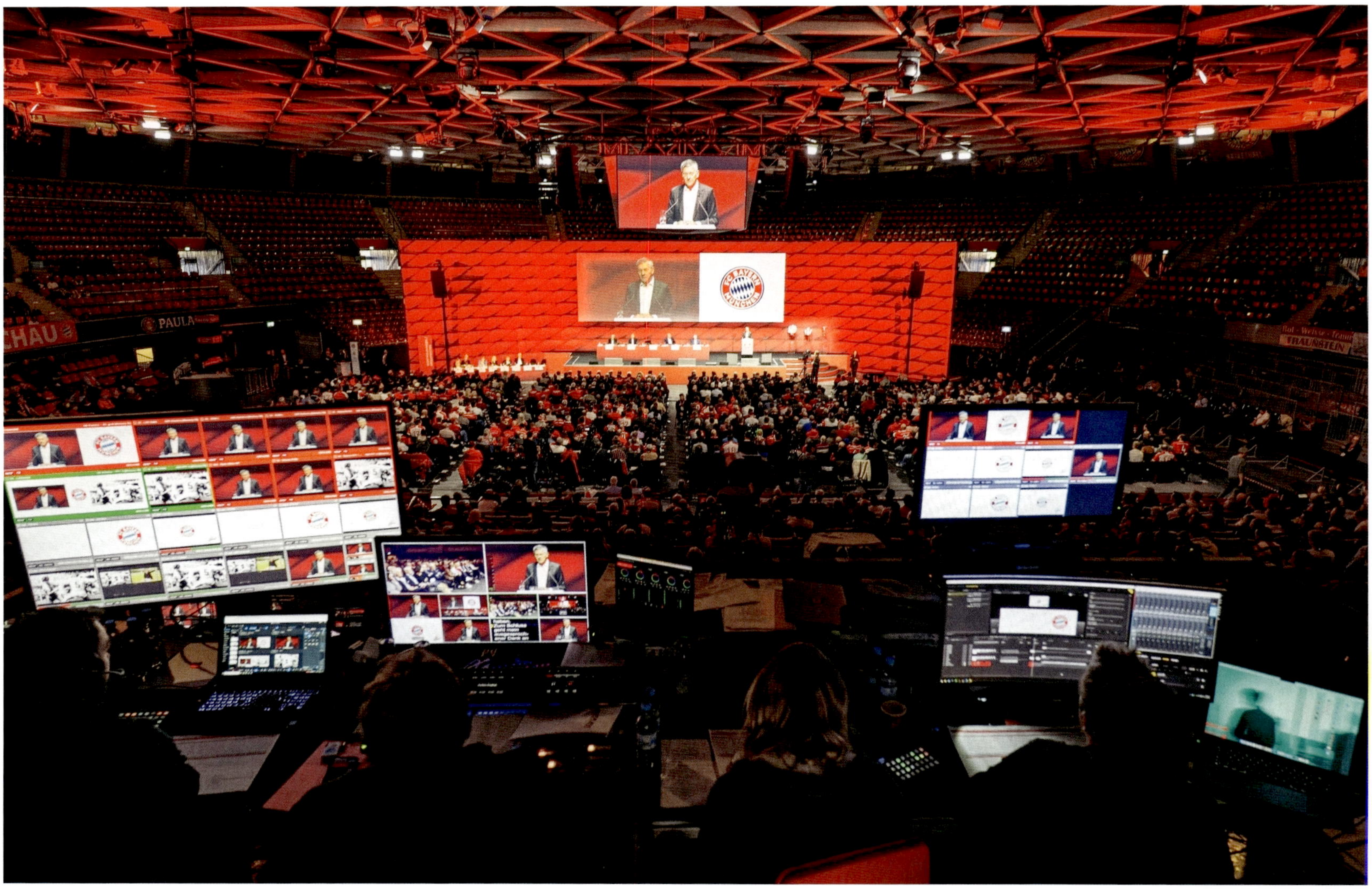

THE WORLD'S BIGGEST CLUB – **LEADERS LOOK LIKE THIS**

It began on 27 February 1900 with eleven young footballers in Café Gisela, and has grown over 125 years to be the biggest sports club in the world with 380,000 members, and a market leader in the global football business with annual revenue of almost one billion euros.

Football may have remained essentially simple since the days of the founders, but the task of managing a football club has become complex. The structure of FCB reflects this. Since 2002 the professionals have been spun off as FC Bayern Fussball AG, i.e. as a business, with the non-profit entity FC Bayern eV as principal shareholder, now with 75 per cent. The rest is held in equal parts by long-standing partners of Bayern: Adidas, Audi and Allianz, each holding 8.33 per cent. The executive board of the AG is nominated by the supervisory board, chaired by the president of FCB eV, who in turn is elected by the members of the club. While the role of the comparable committee of FCB eV, the advisory council, is largely consultative, the supervisory board of the AG must consent to all major transfers.

FCB is managed by people with a high level of business and financial know-how. Herbert Hainer, the president, was the former CEO of Adidas, the world's second-largest sportswear company, from 2001 to 2016. In 2010 he was voted Manager of the Year. The senior vice-president, Prof. Dr Dieter Mayer, is a notary and honorary professor at the Ludwig Maximilian University of Munich. The deputy vice-president, Walter Mennekes, manages a medium-sized company. Jan-Christian Dreesen, chief executive officer of FC Bayern AG, was CEO of UBS Deutschland before he moved to Säbener Strasse. His deputy Michael Diederich, who succeeded him as the board member for finance in 2023, was previously a member of the group executive committee at UniCredit Bank. And the experience of Max Eberl, the board member for sport, who passed through every team at FC Bayern from the youth to the first team in thirteen years, amounts to more than 200 matches as a professional footballer and over fifteen years as manager and sporting director in the Bundesliga.

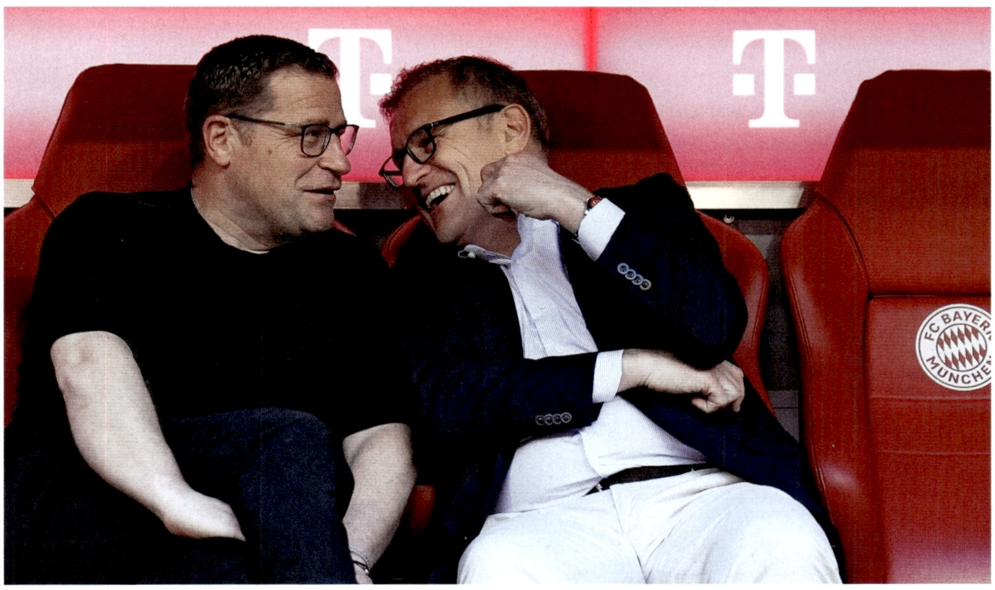

STRUCTURE · FC BAYERN MÜNCHEN eV

- President: Herbert Hainer
- Senior Vice President: Prof. Dr Dieter Mayer
- Deputy Vice President: Walter Mennekes
- Honorary presidents: Uli Hoeness, Franz Beckenbauer (†), Wilhelm Neudecker (†), Kurt Landauer (†), Siegfried Herrmann (†), Franz John (†)

EXECUTIVE BOARD · FC BAYERN MÜNCHEN AG

- Chief Executive Officer: Jan-Christian Dreesen
- Executive Vice Chairman: Dr Michael Diederich
- Board member for sport: Max Eberl

SUPERVISORY BOARD · FC BAYERN MÜNCHEN AG

- Herbert Hainer, President
- Dr Jan Heinemann, adidas AG
- Dr Gernot Döllner, Audi AG
- Dr Werner Zedelius, Allianz SE
- Uli Hoeness, Honorary President
- Thorsten Langheim, Deutsche Telekom AG
- Prof. Dr Dieter Mayer, Senior Vice President
- Dr Edmund Stoiber, Former Minister President of Bavaria
- Karl-Heinz Rummenigge, Former Chief Executive Officer of FC Bayern München AG

ADVISORY COUNCIL

- Chairman: Dr Edmund Stoiber
- Deputy: Alexandra Schörghuber
- Members: Dorothee Bär, Georg Fahrenschon, Peter Kerspe, Prof. Dr Marion Kiechle, Lars Klingbeil, Hildegard Müller, Dieter Reiter, Josef Schmid, Jochen Tschunke

The annual general meeting, a grand stage: here the executive board and presidium have presented excellent financial results (left) to the members for many years - and the Fussball AG boss Jan-Christian Dreesen (left) and sporting director Max Eberl are delighted (right).

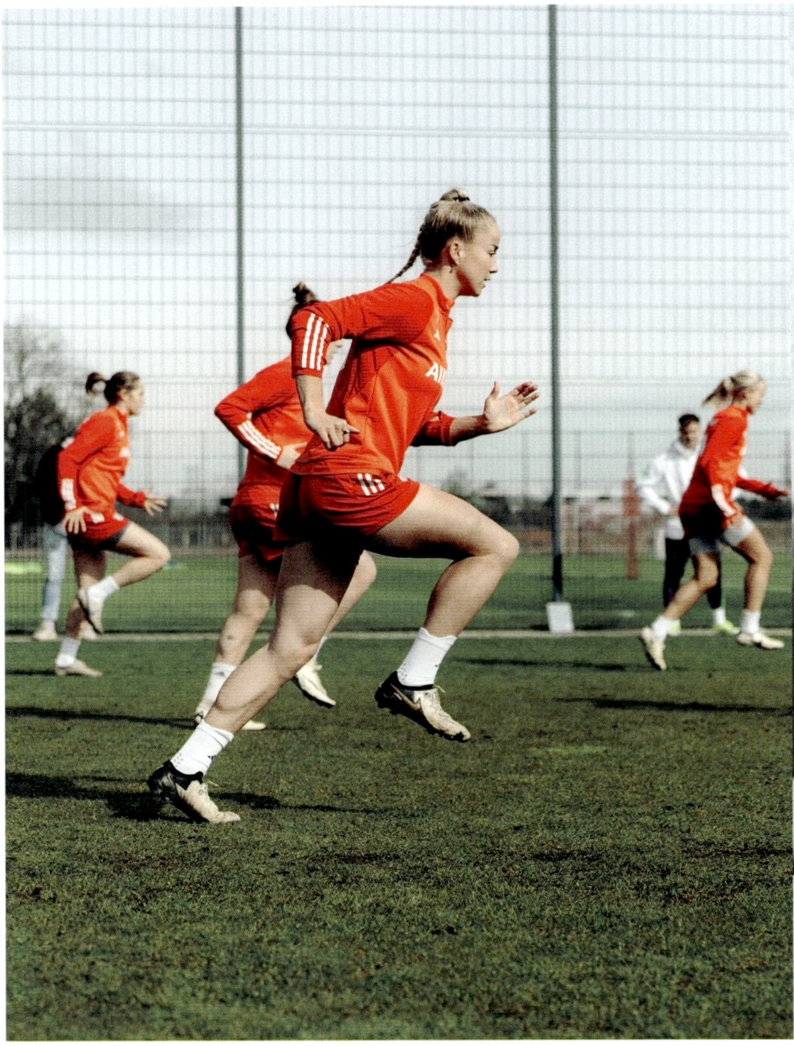

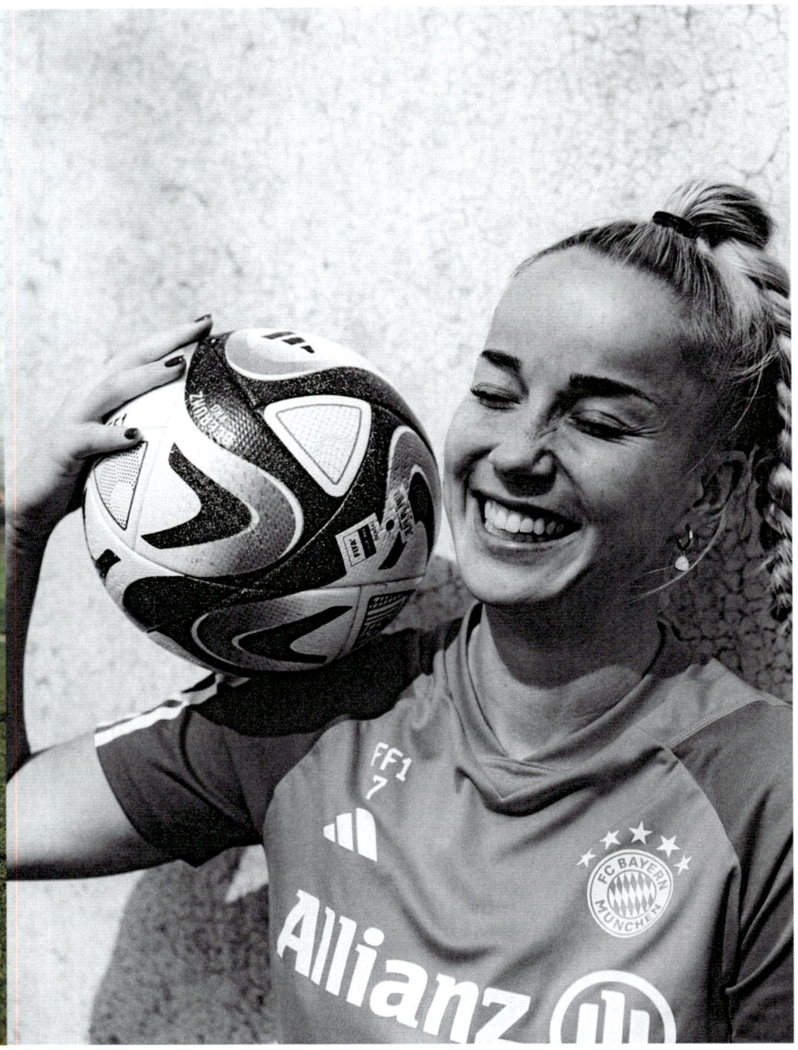

"IF YOU HOLD BACK, YOU **ACHIEVE NOTHING**"

For all their professional attitude, winners often have their very own rituals in football. For Giulia Gwinn it is the plaited hair, her trademark in every match. For this, she moves as quickly as when she is playing the ball: it takes her only five minutes to weave a plait.

A club like FCB provides its professionals with a perfect environment for top-class performances. It is equally important for them all to take responsibility for themselves and towards the team. To Giulia Gwinn, for example, this is obvious – and so is the right approach to hate speech on social media.

"I think it is cowardly to attack someone anonymously", said Gwinn, a defence lawyer, in 2024 in an interview with the FCB magazine *51*. She tries, she said, to filter social media so that "I only take out what is positive." With hateful commentaries, however, "it would be a lie to say that they have no effect on me." Taking the right attitude to such hostility is a matter for which she tries "to use all options, both on and off the field", in order "to perform as well as possible" and "to optimise everything in relation to football" – with an expert for sleep, a nutrition adviser and a coach for neuro-athletics. Mental training gives her "good strategies for keeping calm under pressure and holding on to my inner balance, for example with penalty kicks." Giulia Gwinn took the spot kick that produced the winning goal at the Olympic Games in Paris, and won bronze with the German team. Her twelfth penalty as a professional, and the twelfth that she converted. "Here I go up to the front, I don't hide. If you hold back, you achieve nothing."

ALL FIGURES AT **HIS FINGERTIPS**

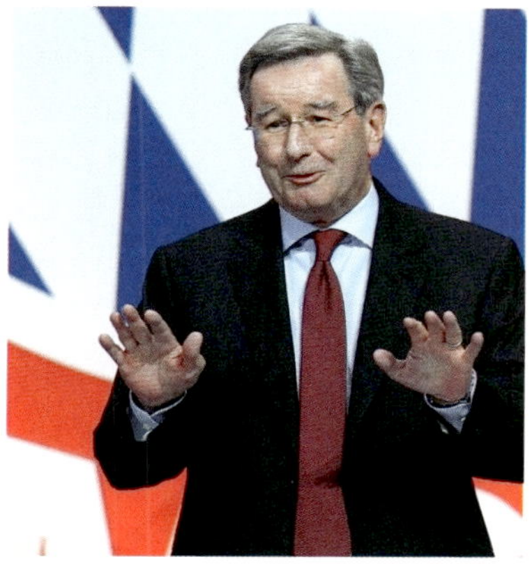

It began in 1983 with a local job advertisement. FCB was looking for a managing director. The successful candidate among 400 applicants was a young graduate in business studies, for Uli Hoeness "a stroke of luck".

Franz Beckenbauer praised him as a "financial genius", Karl-Heinz Rummenigge as "the author of FC Bayern's economic miracle": Karl Hopfner. For thirty years he was the man who made all the players' contracts watertight. Who monitored all revenue and costs with an eagle eye as head of finance and was able to announce record-breaking figures almost every season. When 99.6 per cent of the club members elected him to succeed Uli Hoeness as president in 2014, he did the job so well that two and a half years later they said farewell to him with standing ovations.

With Hopfner, who is chairman of the charity FC Bayern München Hilfe eV today, the club never made a financial loss and never borrowed money to pay for transfers. But he was not miserly – on the contrary, "Money scores goals. I am sure of that. Quality comes at a price." Thus for decades FCB has given itself the most expensive team by far in the Bundesliga – because it can afford it. Hopfner: "FC Bayern is proud that we have achieved it all ourselves."

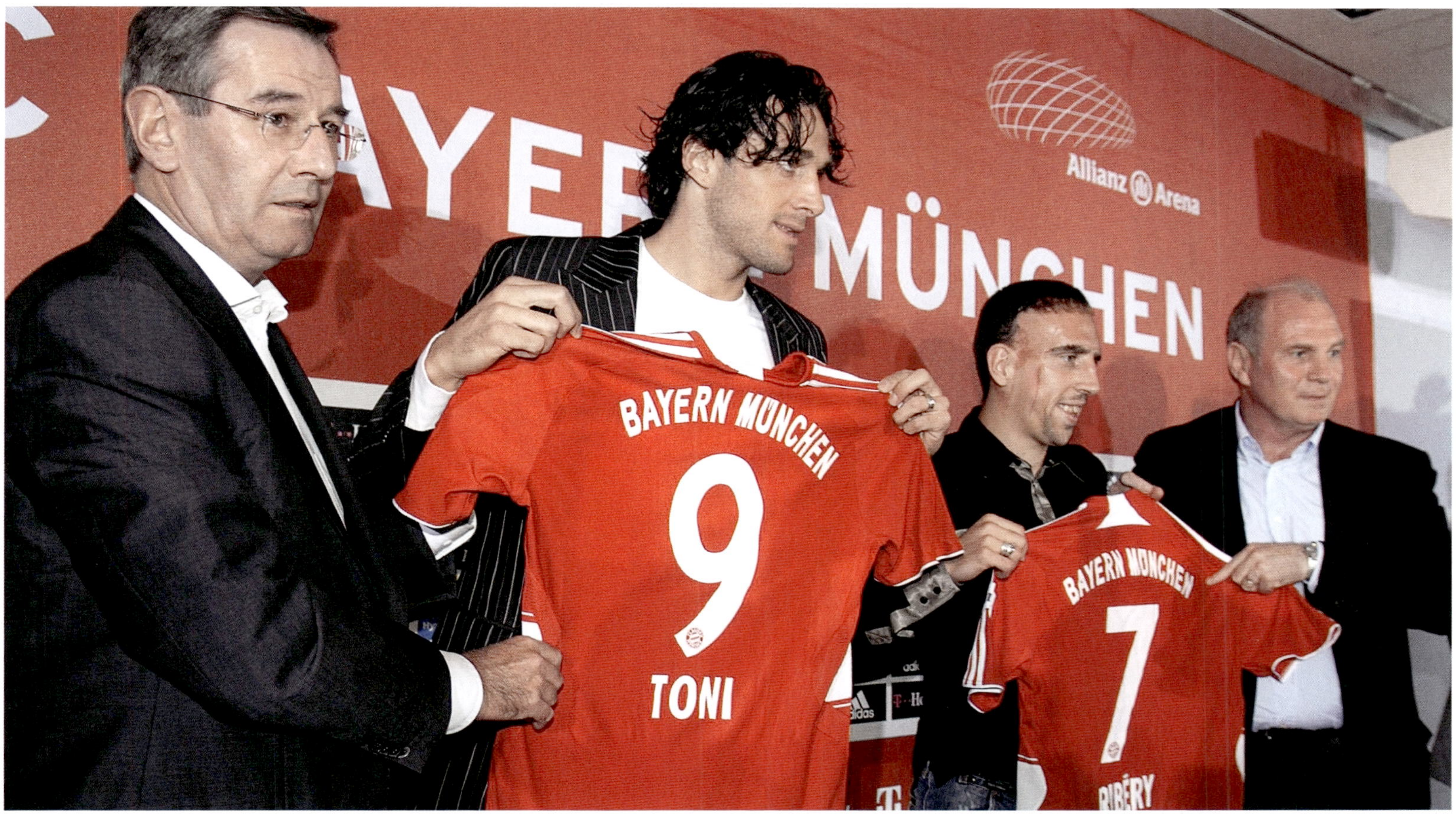

Only clubs with a competent head of finance can afford stars like these: Karl Hopfner and Uli Hoeness with Luca Toni and Franck Ribéry in 2007.

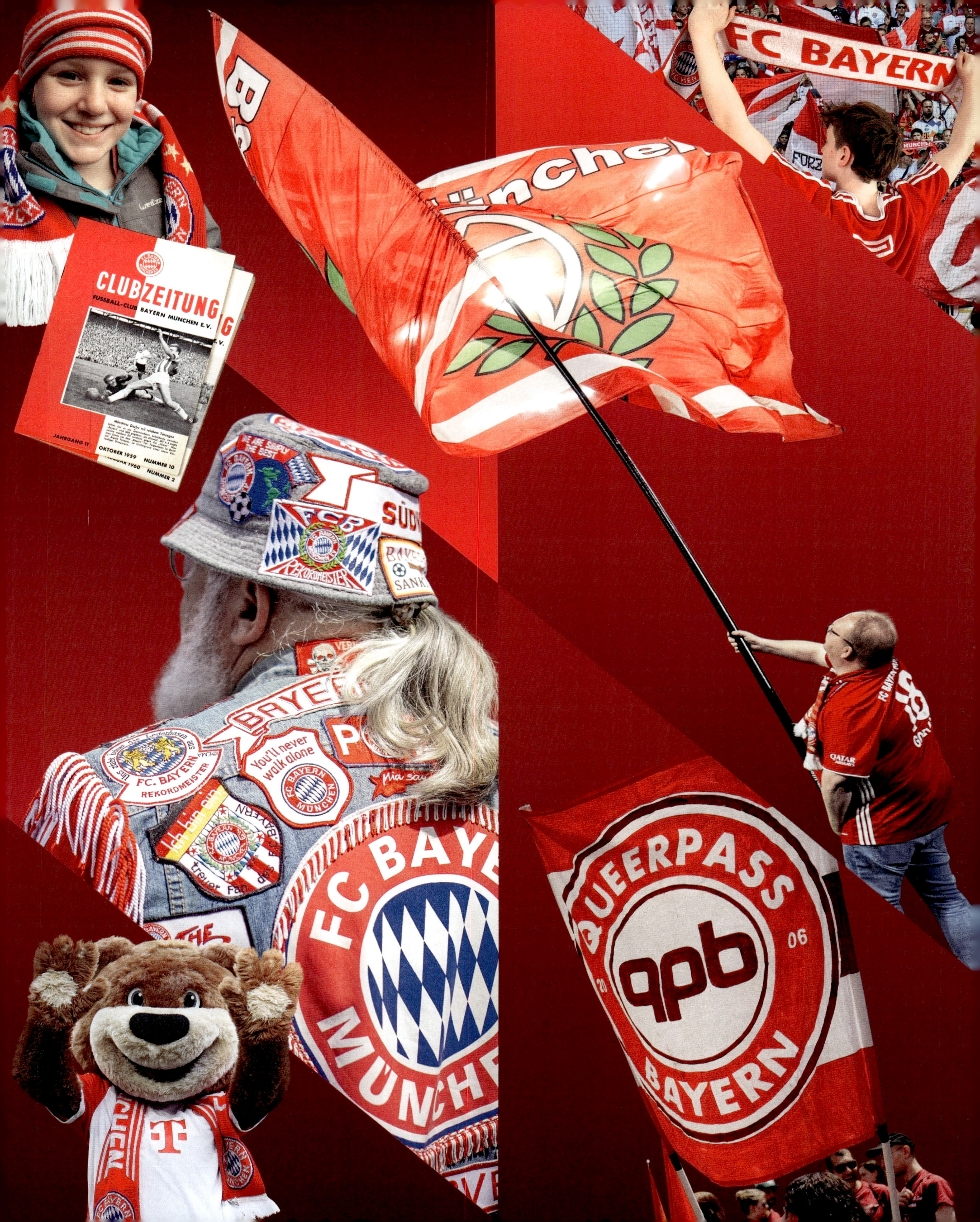
FC BAYERN
München
CLUBZEITUNG
FUSSBALL-CLUB BAYERN MÜNCHEN E.V.
OKTOBER 1959
NUMMER 10
JAHRGANG 11
FCB
REKORDMEISTER
FC. BAYERN
REKORDMEISTER
You'll never walk alone
FC BAYERN MÜNCHEN
QUEERPASS
qpb
20 06
BAYERN

RED AND WHITE

Sammy Kuffour was always a favourite of the fans. But in 2001 on Marienplatz, after winning the Champions League, he became a cult figure. With a single sentence that fans are never tired of repeating.

125 YEARS OF **RED AND WHITE**

When FC Bayern was founded in 1900, clubs in the south of Germany were not usually named after their colours. And so, in contrast to other historic clubs, for example in Essen, Oberhausen and Erfurt, the words "red and white" are not part of the name, but they are close to the heart: red and white unite the club with its members and fans, and Sammy Kuffour had expressed the culture of the club with an anthem of his own in an unmistakable way. "Red-and-white shirts, we want red-and-white shirts, red-and-white shirts, we want red-and-white shirts". Grinning, he bawled this into the microphone from the balcony of city hall to the melody of the classic Cuban song 'Guantanamera'. In the course of a century and a quarter, the colours, symbolising identification within the club and among the fans, have become an autonomous, confident factor in the development of FCB. "Red and white" stands for the interaction of FC Bayern and its loyal supporters, producing sights that are worth seeing and adorning the club as much as the numerous trophies the museum's showcases. "FC Bayern wants to be influential beyond the football pitch, to be a place to which fans and members can aim the ball," says club president Herbert Hainer, "and to be prepared for a one-two exchange of passes and for optimising things together." The board discusses supporters' wishes in regular meetings of a working group called Fandialog, specially established to attend to the needs of fans and the fan club. Furthermore, in recent years the club has produced various forums for dialogue in which Hainer and the presidium ask about the concerns of club members. Projects are often implemented jointly and the two sides give mutual support, for example in the case of the monument for Gerd Müller in front of the Allianz Arena, organised by the Kurt Landauer Foundation, to which a statue of Franz Beckenbauer will soon be added.

Moreover, the fans have taken significant action in the culture of commemoration, not least in giving back to the former club president Kurt Landauer, who was driven from office and the country, and also for a long time from memory, by the National Socialist regime, the place in history that he deserves. "I have to thank the young people, especially in the Südkurve, for engaging with Landauer so much", said Uli Hoeness. "A thank you for saying: 'We're a big club, so we're also concerned with our history.'" The Bayern fans who make the podcast *Erfolgsfans* (Success Fans) did this too. They discovered that back in 1905 goalkeeper Blome-Hamburg wrote a club song entitled 'Rot and Weiss' (Red and White): "Your voices and your glasses raise / A group united in delight / Let's sing joyfully in praise / of the colours red and white!" Sammy Kuffour enthusiastically picked up the thread almost one hundred years later.

In 2024 FC Bayern changed its logo from 2017 to comply with the rules of new legislation to improve accessibility, which specifies among other things the contrast between text and background colour; the colours in the new version of the logo are somewhat lighter and brighter.

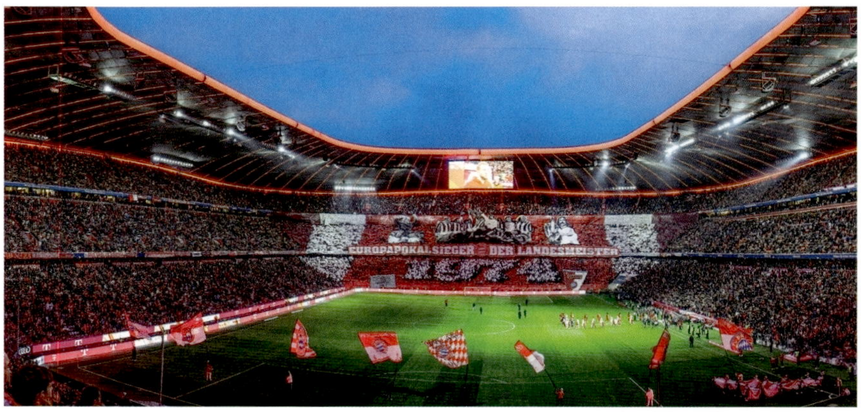

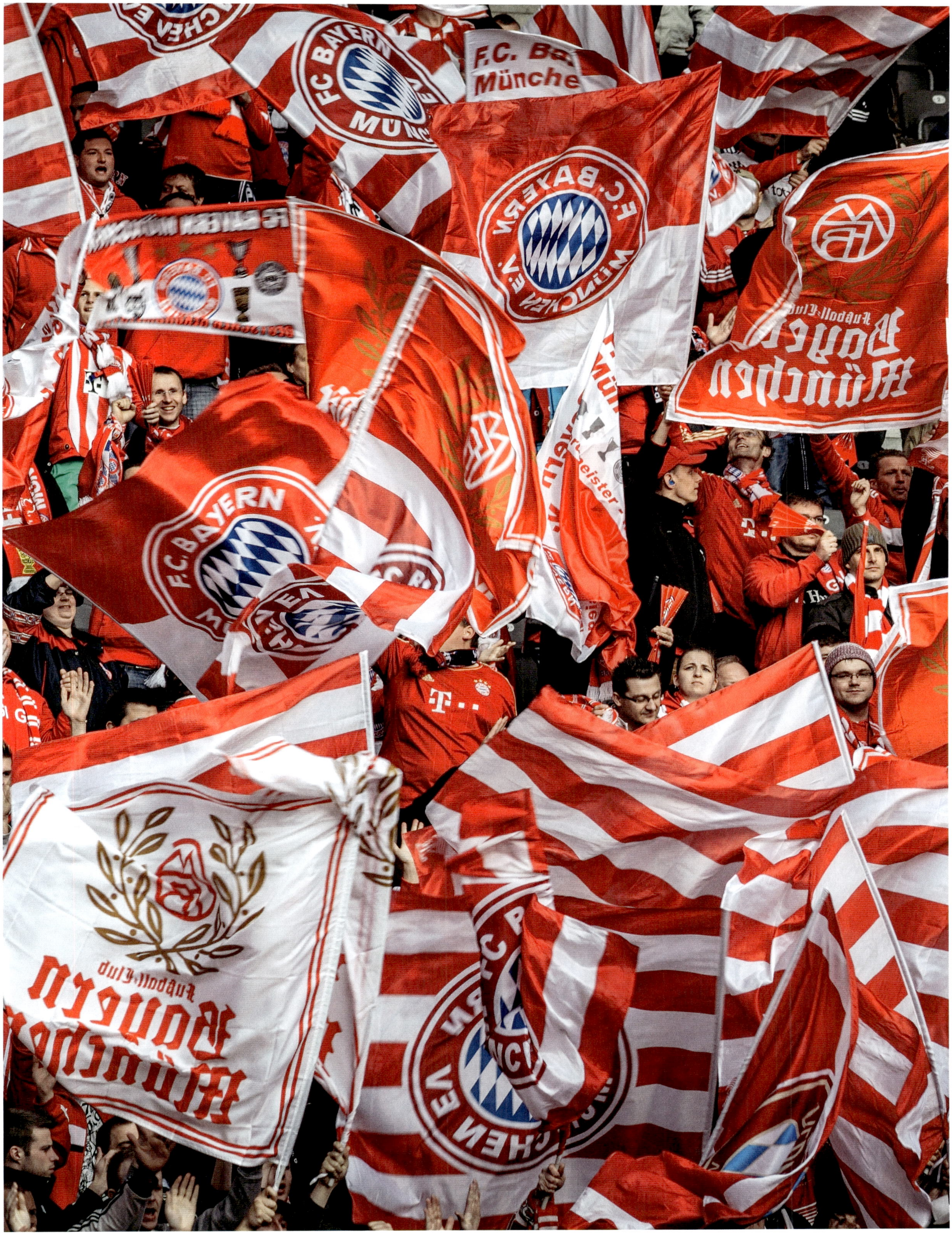
F.C.BAYERN

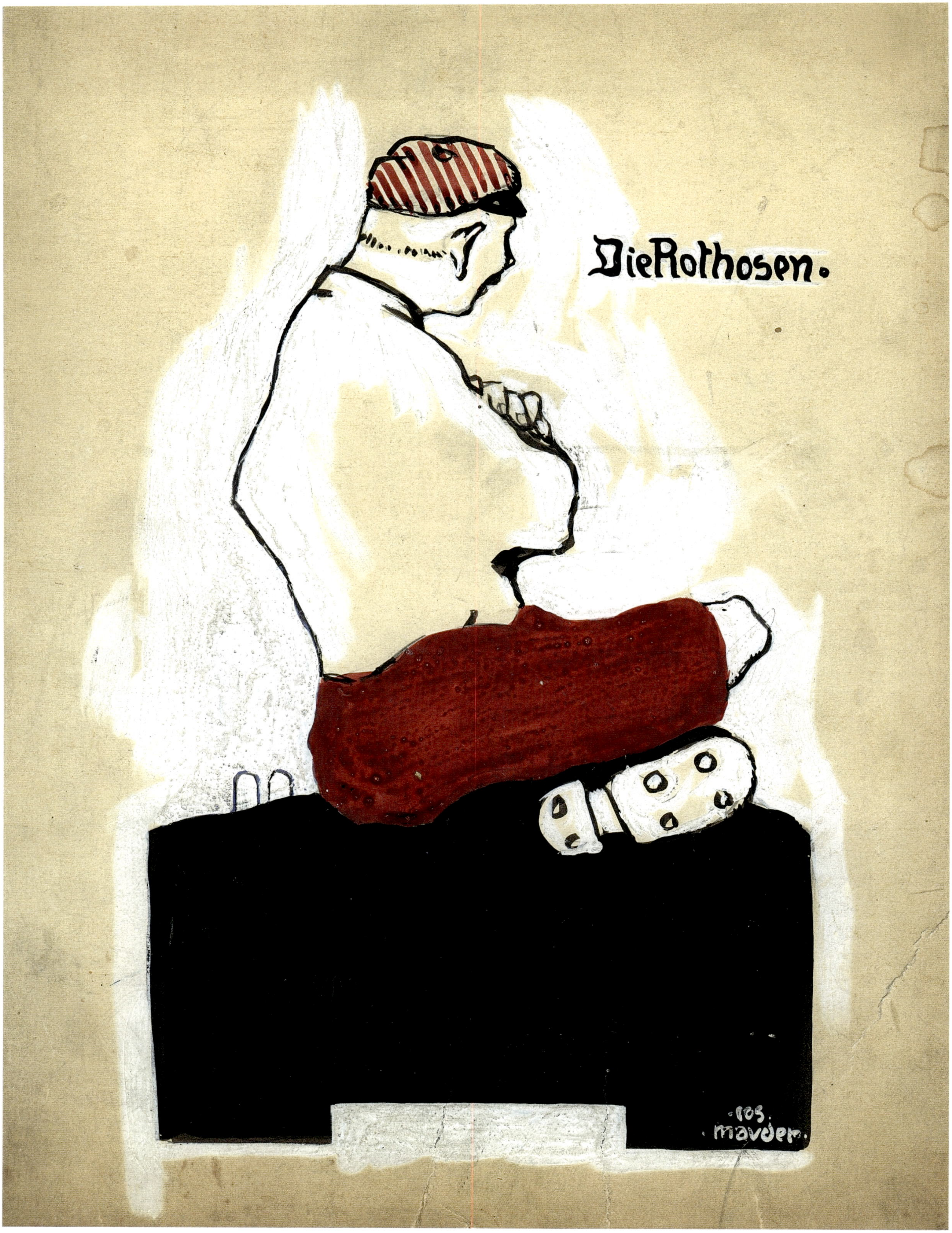
Die Rothosen.
·08.
·mavder·

THE **BIRTH** OF THE **RED** SHORTS

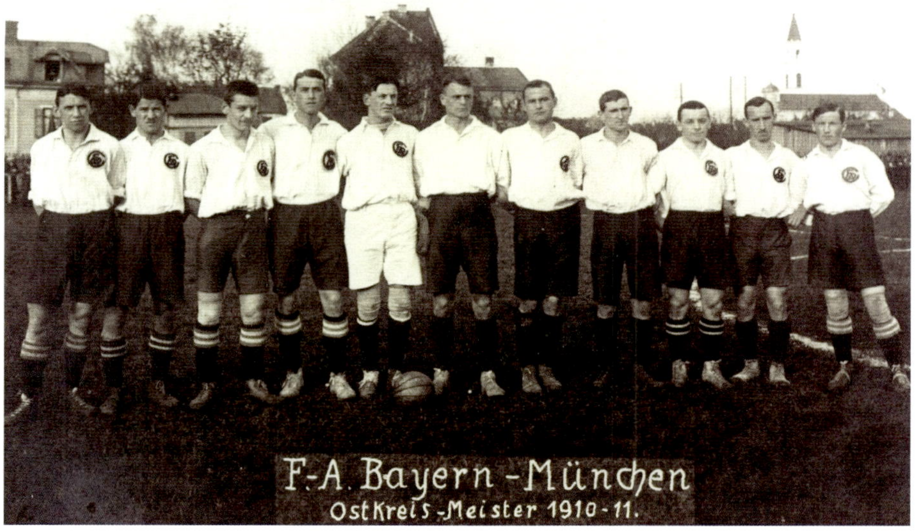

From a practical point of view, the purpose of colours in football is merely to help players find their teammates on the field and the fans in the stands see which team is which. But for the fans and their attachment to the club, the colours are much more than that. They are elemental. They are memories and emotions bound up with experiences. They are not a black-and-white film, but colour. At FCB that means red and white. Even though the beginnings were completely different.

On old photos, only two club colours are possible: black and white. Different hues could be worn, but not reproduced on photographs. In fact FCB did play in black and white for some years, until the merger with München SC led to the red-and-white combination. In this outfit the FC Bayern players posed in 1910-11 as champions of the eastern district for the black-and-white team photo.

When the brand-new club played its first match in March 1900, fielding all eleven founding members and winning 5–2 against 1. Münchner FC, they did so in a colour combination that is unthinkable today – in white and sky blue. These were the colours of the Kingdom of Bavaria and the first club colours of FC Bayern. The poet and heir to millions Alfred Walter von Heymel donated the kit. However, because white shorts do not stay white for long in football and are difficult to clean, after two years the team switched to black shorts and white shirts.

The red appeared in 1906, when FC Bayern temporarily joined the München Sport-Club, the biggest in the city, as an independent football section – benefiting from this through a rapid increase in members and teams, and a football ground with a covered stand on Leopoldstrasse. The wealthy MSC stipulated one condition, however: from that time, the FCB players had to wear wine-red shorts and silver-grey shirts. From then onwards they were called the "Red Shorts". In silver-grey shirts with collars and wine-red sleeves they won their first German championship in 1932. A retro edition of this styling did not, however, bring any luck in the Champions League final against Manchester United in 1999.

Nevertheless, sometimes a surprising change of colour does bring about a turnaround for the better. After FC Bayern failed to win at the Betzenberg Stadium in Kaiserslautern for ten years (eight defeats, two draws), causing Paul Breitner to suggest staying at home next time and "sending the points to Kaiserslautern in the post", Uli Hoeness had a better idea. In November 1983, instead of the white kit for away games, the manager put the team on the pitch in the colours of the Brazilian "Selecão": sunny yellow and blue with green stripes on the shoulders. But Kaiserslautern too played a trick with their colours, playing all in green instead of fiery red. This combination, green Kaiserslautern and yellow Bayern, produced what must be the strangest colour scheme in Bundesliga history. The skills of Brazilian football were not much in evidence, but the result vindicated Hoeness. Thanks to a deflected free kick by Klaus Augenthaler and Jean-Marie Pfaff's save against Andreas Brehme's penalty, FCB won 1–0.

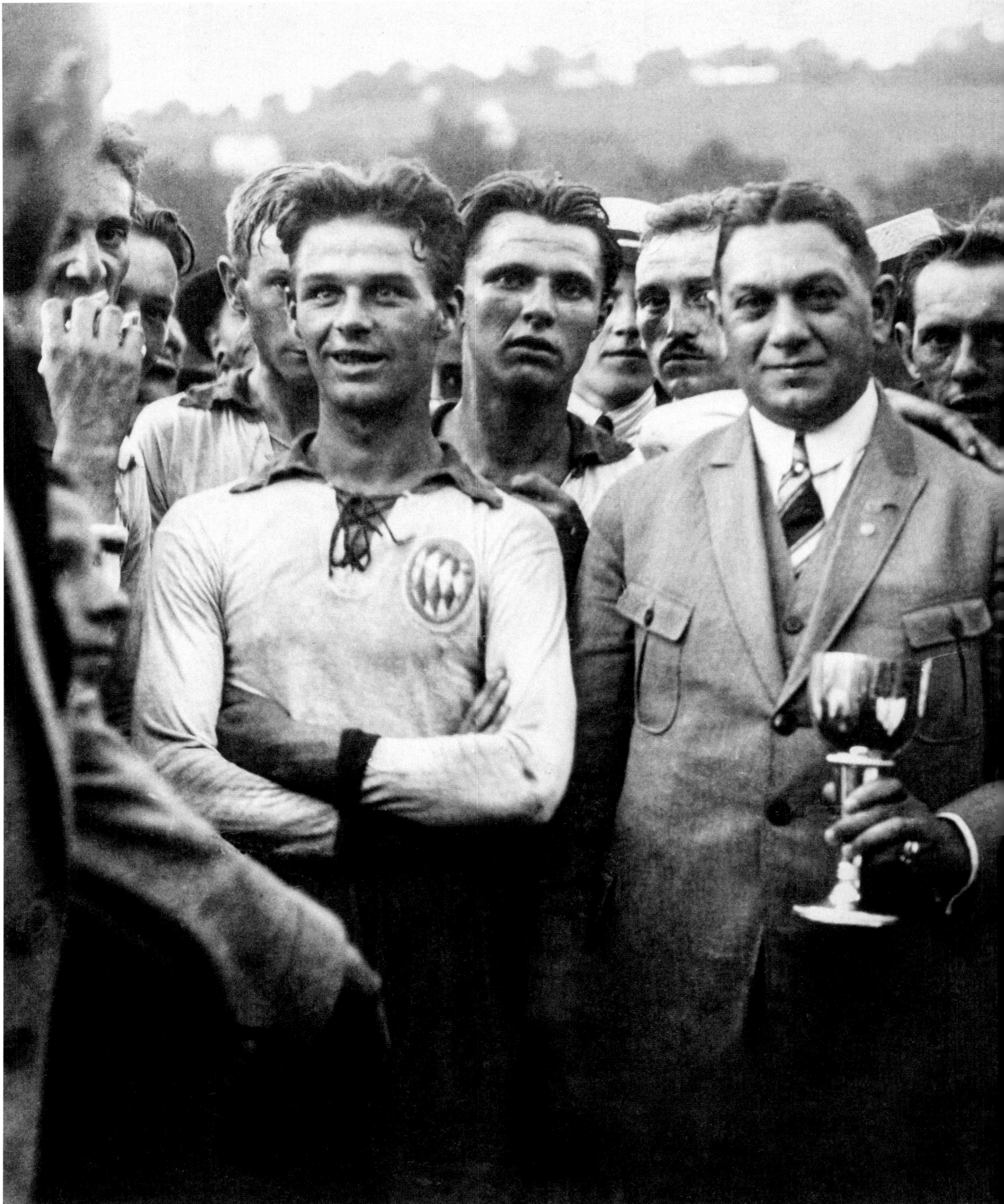

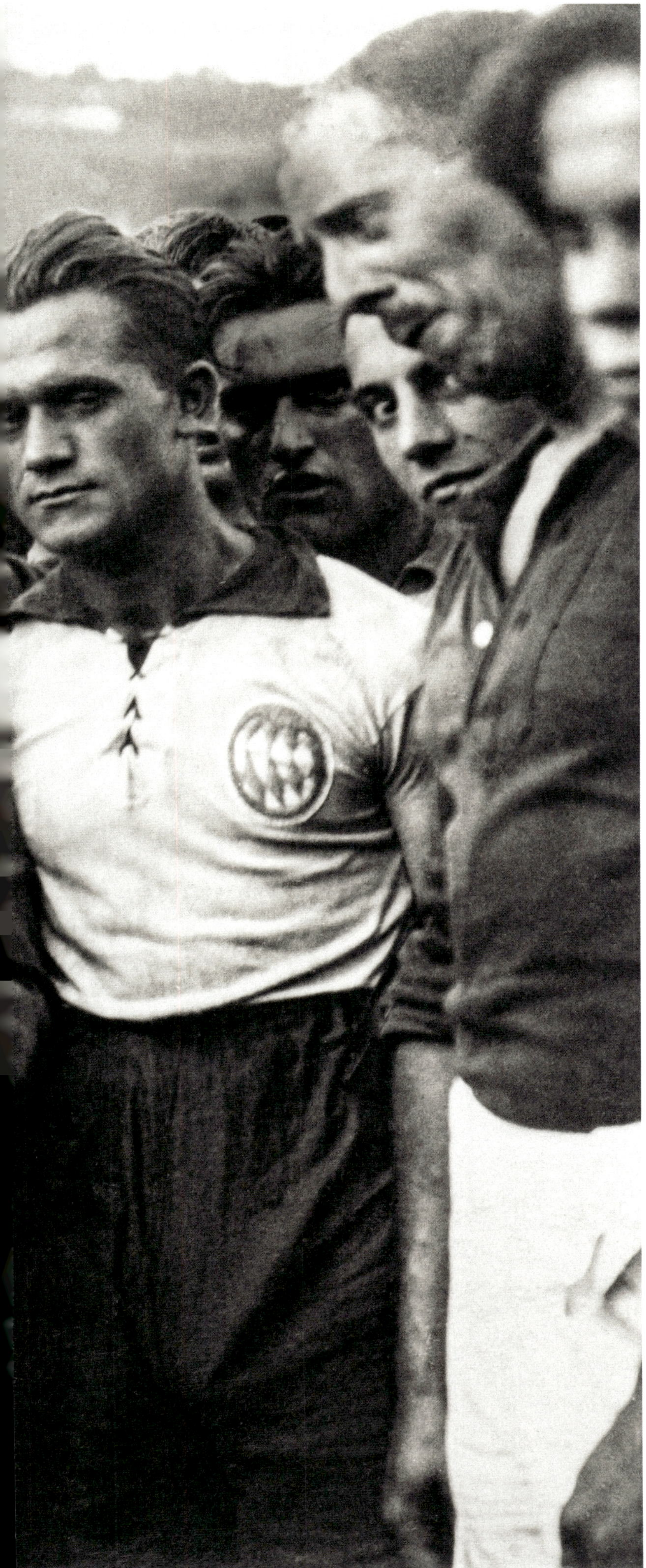

KURT LANDAUER

"FC Bayern and I belong together and are inseparable." These words were spoken by Kurt Landauer after his time in a concentration camp and flight into exile. And once again he became president of FCB, which owes much to him, not least its home on Säbener Strasse.

There Landauer sits today, cast in bronze with a view of the training grounds. He led FC Bayern from the time of the German Empire into the Federal Republic, from 1913 to 1951, interrupted only by the two catastrophes of the century – the First World War, when he fought at the front, and the years of Nazi rule that led to the Second World War. From the beginning he gave the club an international mindset. In 1919 he brought MTK Budapest, the best team on the continent, to Munich, and FCB lost 1–7, but took the fluent "Danube football" as its role model and became German champions in 1932 for the first time. A year later Hitler was in power, and Landauer resigned to avert harming the club. After thirty-three days as prisoner no. 20029 in the Dachau concentration camp, he survived by emigrating to Switzerland, while most members of his family were murdered. In 1947 he again became president of FC Bayern, lobbied the authorities to gain the training grounds on Säbener Strasse for the club, and lent it DM 5,000 from his own savings. "Inseparable" to this day.

In 1932 Kurt Landauer took Viktoria, the extremely large cup for the German champions, one metre tall with its base and weighing half a hundredweight, to bed with him in his hotel in Nuremberg. But he was pleased with small trophies, too, as the photo shows. In spite of his successes, Landauer was almost forgotten until, not least through tifos in the Südkurve and other initiatives by the fans, his life story, now the subject of a film, was brought back to mind. In 2013 he was posthumously declared honorary president.

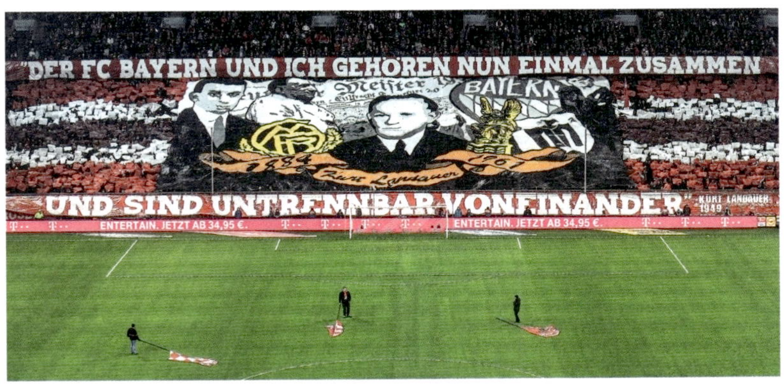

PROMOTION **AND A** LONG **MARCH**

On 26 June 1965, at 5.42 p.m. Berlin time, an 8–0 win away to Tennis Borussia sealed the eternal first-class status of FC Bayern – and triggered unusual assemblies of fans, not only in the place where it happened.

After the final whistle, hundreds of away fans stormed the pitch in the Berlin Olympic Stadium. One of them was Erich Böck from Heimhausen, who left the ground with a unique trophy: the red-and-white cotton shirt of 18-year-old Franz Beckenbauer. Today it hangs in the Bayern Museum. On the following day at Riem Airport, some 6,000 supporters welcomed the young team on their return. The airstrip was closed off due to the crush of people, but the fans broke through the barriers to the runway. And two weeks later, club president Wilhelm Neudecker fulfilled what he had promised: "If we get promotion, I'll hike round the Tegernsee." When he started out at 7.08 a.m., some 500 fans along with the team heroes Rudi Nafziger and Adi Kunstwadl joined him on the almost twenty-two-kilometre circuit of the lake. On completion, a warm meal and a band awaited. At his destination, Neudecker was tempted into making an even bigger announcement: "If we win the championship, I'll walk around Lake Constance." This did not happen, as five weeks later the Bundesliga debut for Bayern against 1860 Munich ended in a 0–1 defeat after an extremely rough game. And so FCB finished in third place in the first Bundesliga season. In 1866 the result of the derby match was the other way round, and the German champions in 1966 were not 1860 Munich but Bayern Munich.

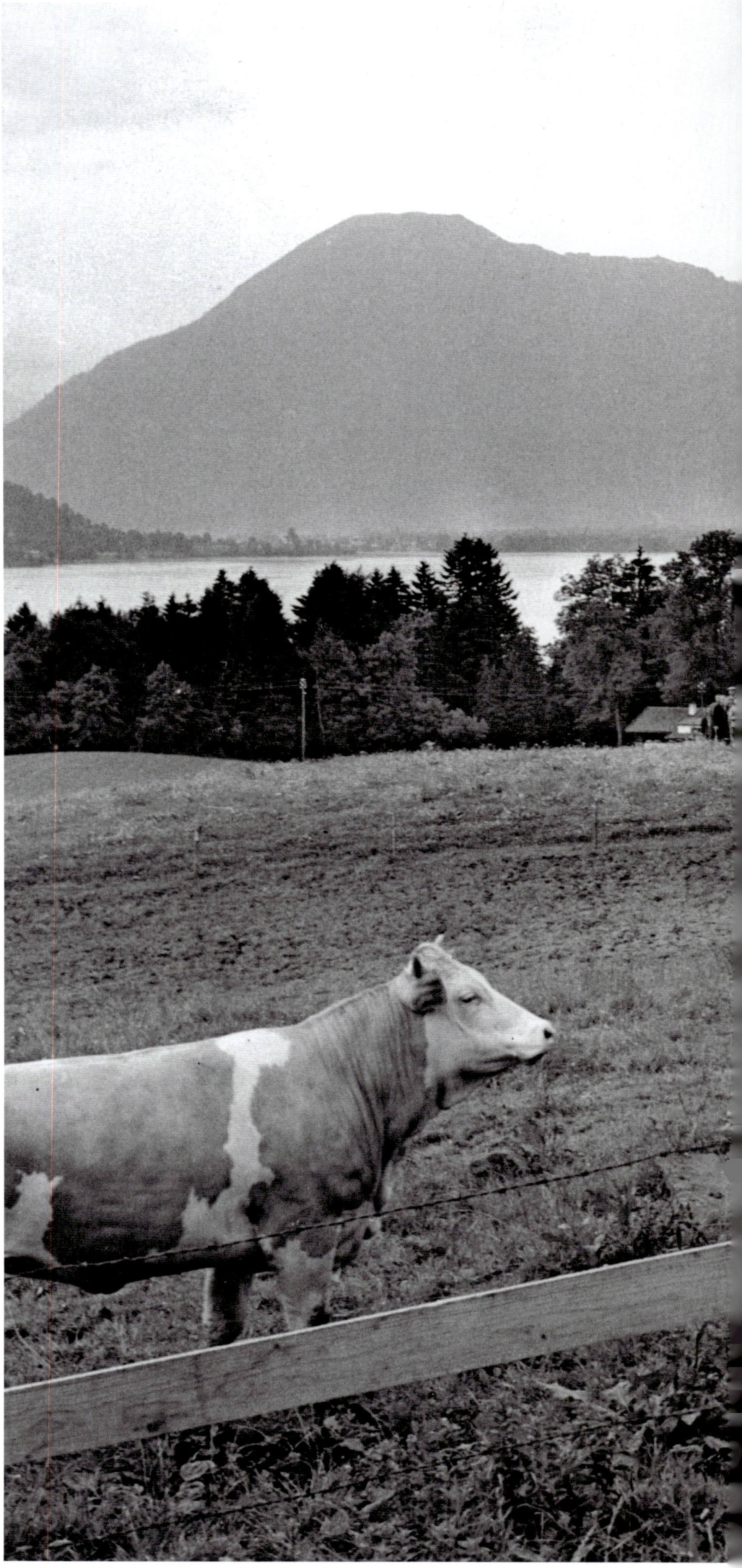

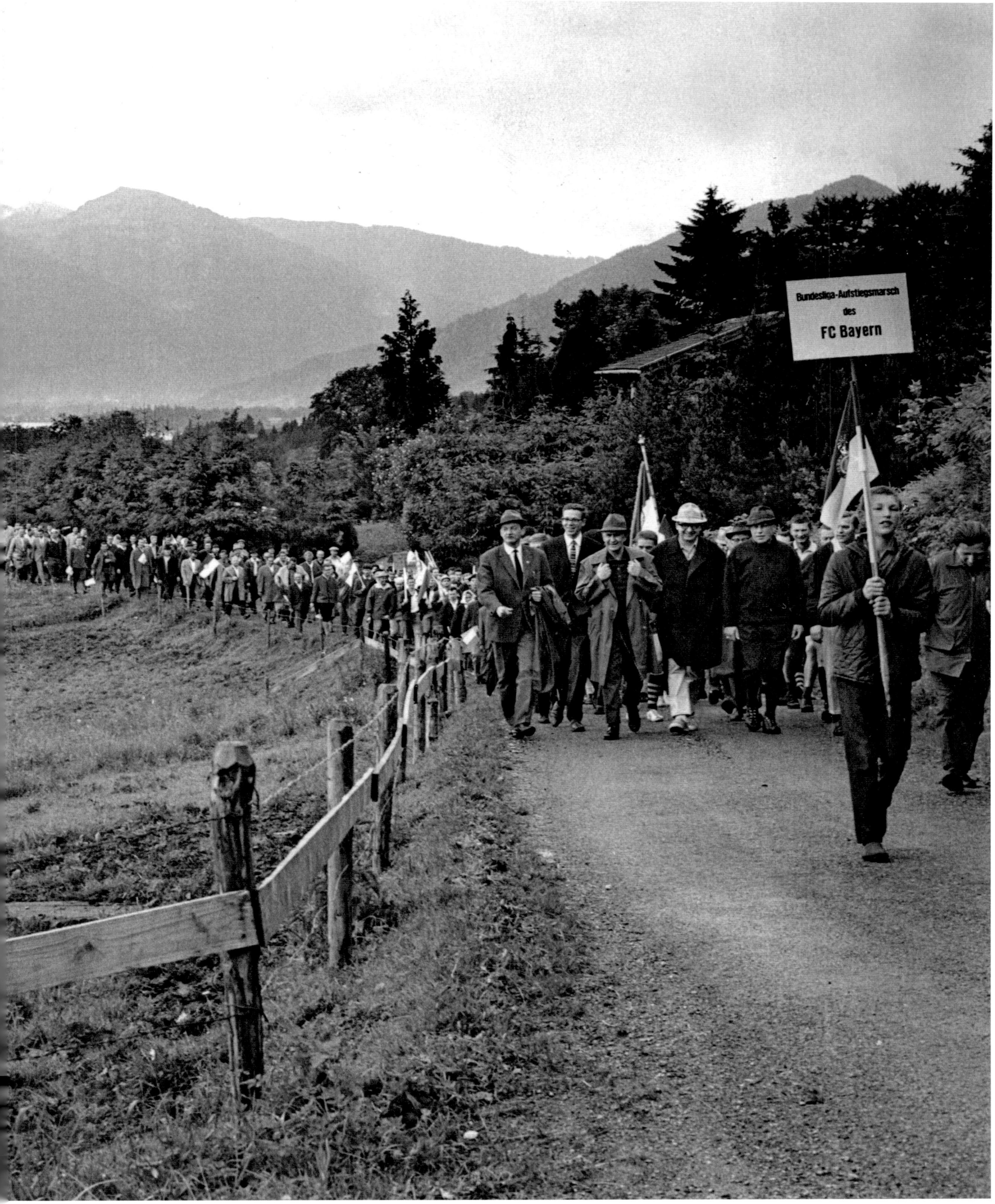
Bundesliga-Aufstiegsmarsch
des
FC Bayern

GOOD FRIENDS **ARE NEVER ALONE**

Football lets its fans share the fortune or misfortune of their club. But sometimes, in the old days in the Olympic Stadium, they wanted to take their share of more than that – the goal, the grass of the pitch, the clothes of their heroes. As a souvenir for darker days or a holy relic for a shrine at home.

Sociologists distinguish between “football-centred”, “consumption-oriented” and “experience-oriented” spectators. Or, more colloquially: scarf-wearers, success fans, ultras. The great thing is that there is a place for all of them in a football stadium.

Some have dozens of scarves or fan outfits that weigh kilos. For these people, the club is like a life partner. Others see it as an event, as entertainment – and wear everyday clothing, with a club scarf. And there are countless others who come in the most various shades of red and shirts to laugh, suffer, sing and cheer their team. And many more. Whereas the outside observer only sees the differences between all of these large and small groups, the people in the thick of it, in the temple to football, see what they have in common. These are the moments when you seem to be riding the same wave as 75,000 others in the same rhythm, overwhelmed by the tremendous energy that you feel. Football, an experience of pure vitality.

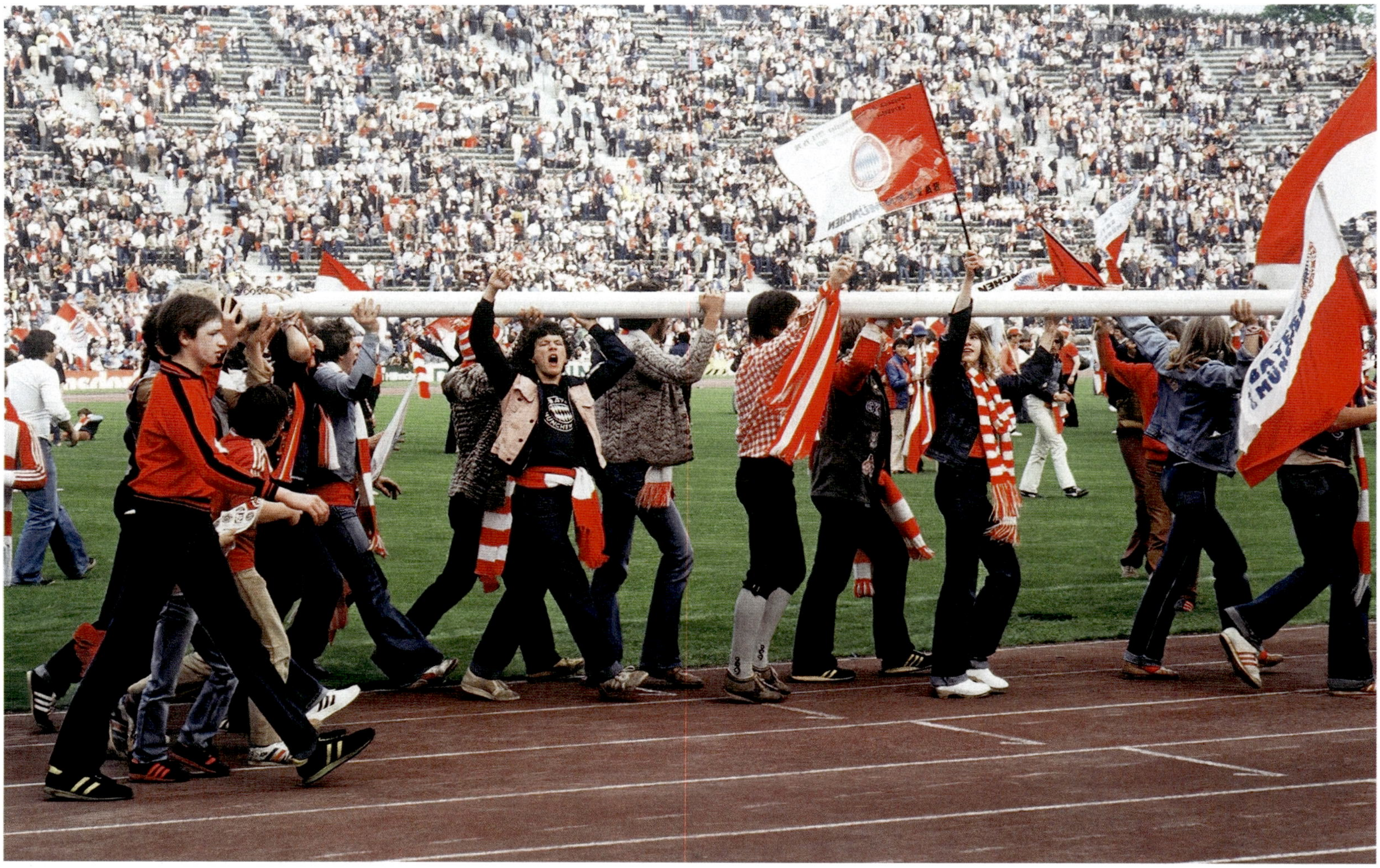

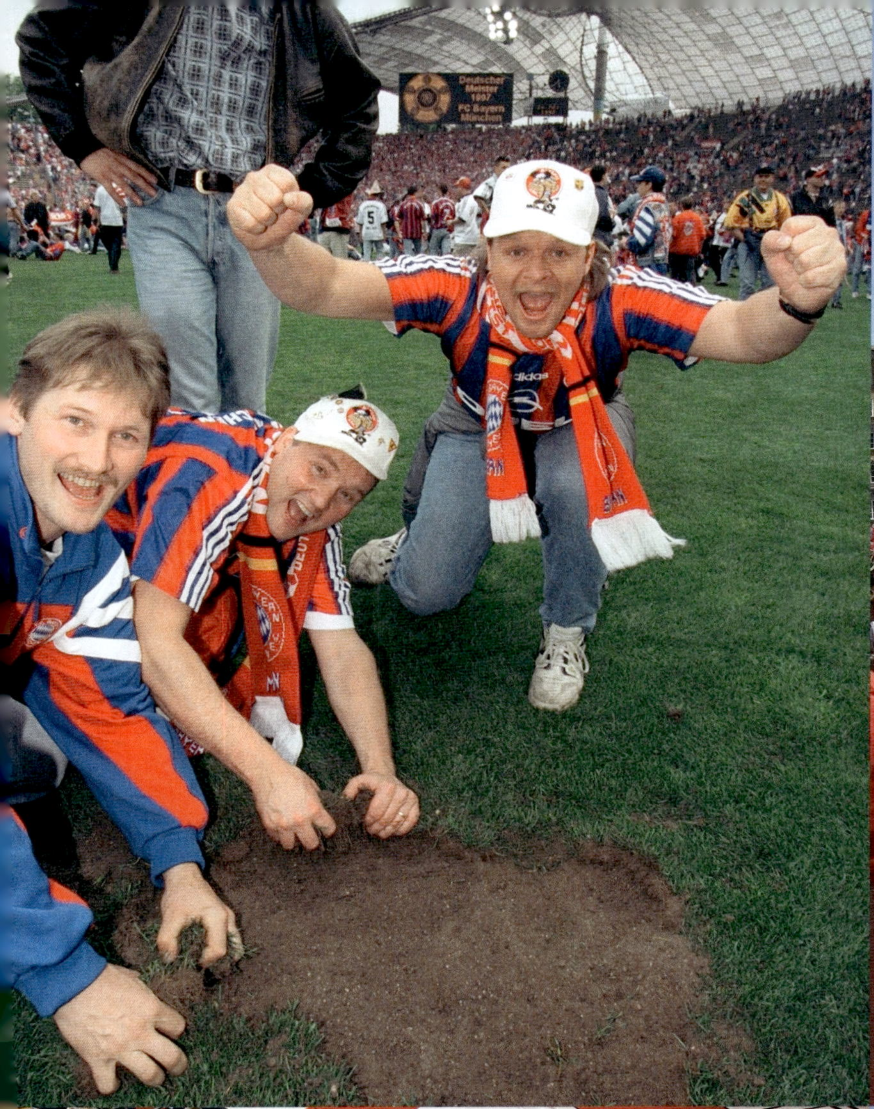

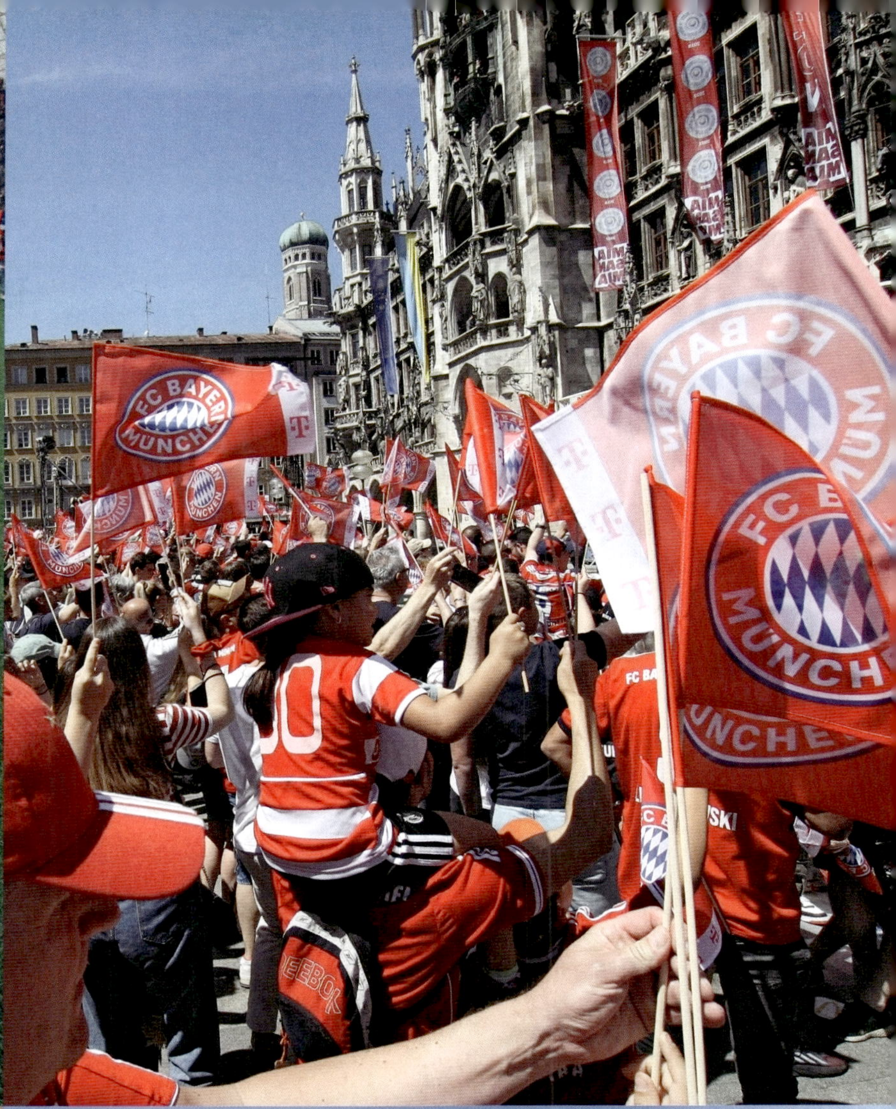
FC BAYERN MÜNCHEN

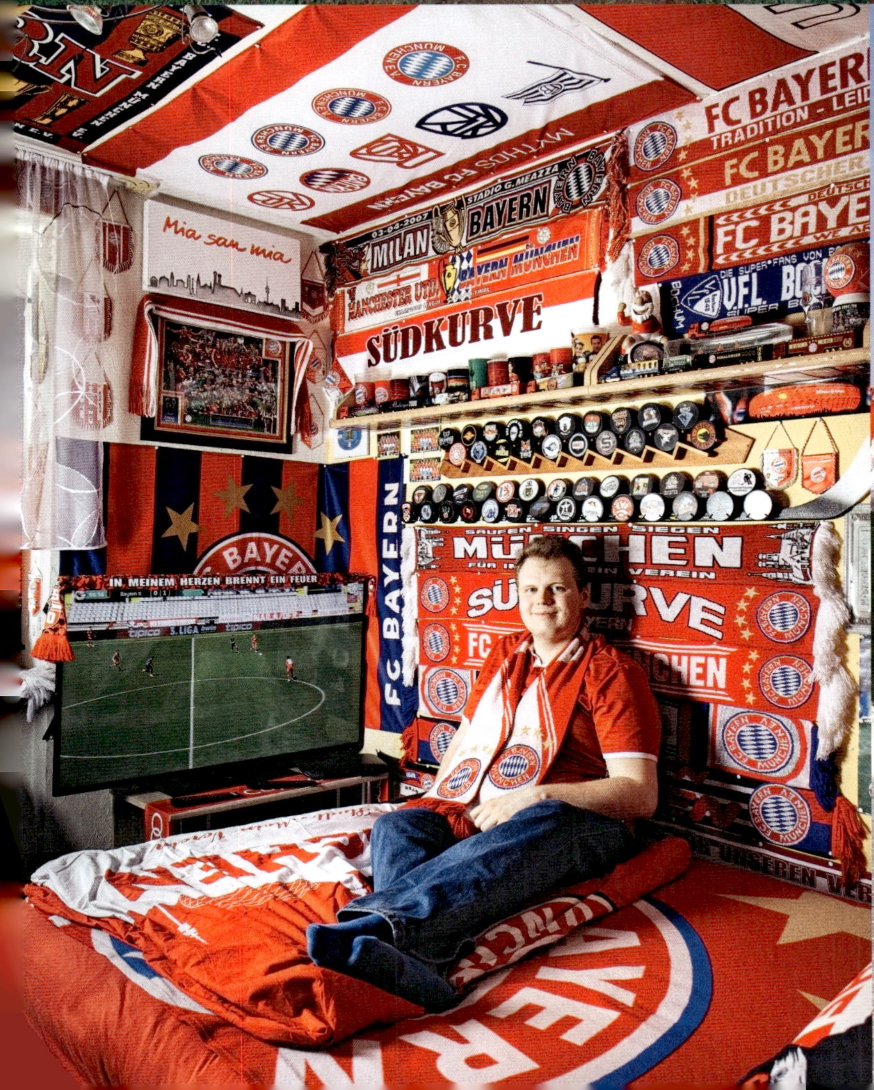
FC BAYERN
Mia san mia
MILAN
BAYERN
SÜDKURVE
FC BAYERN
IN MEINEM HERZEN BRENNT EIN FEUER
MÜNCHEN
SÜDKURVE
FC BAYERN

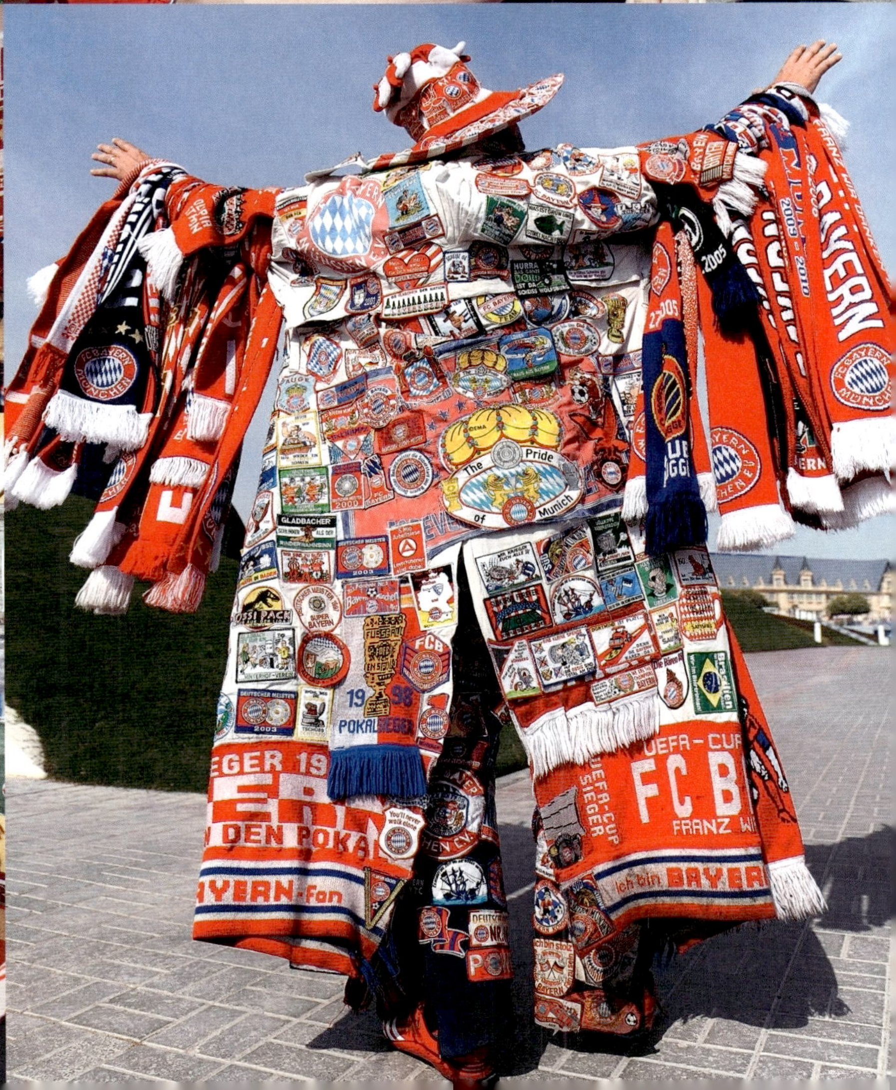
The Pride of Munich
POKALSIEGER
UEFA-CUP
FC B

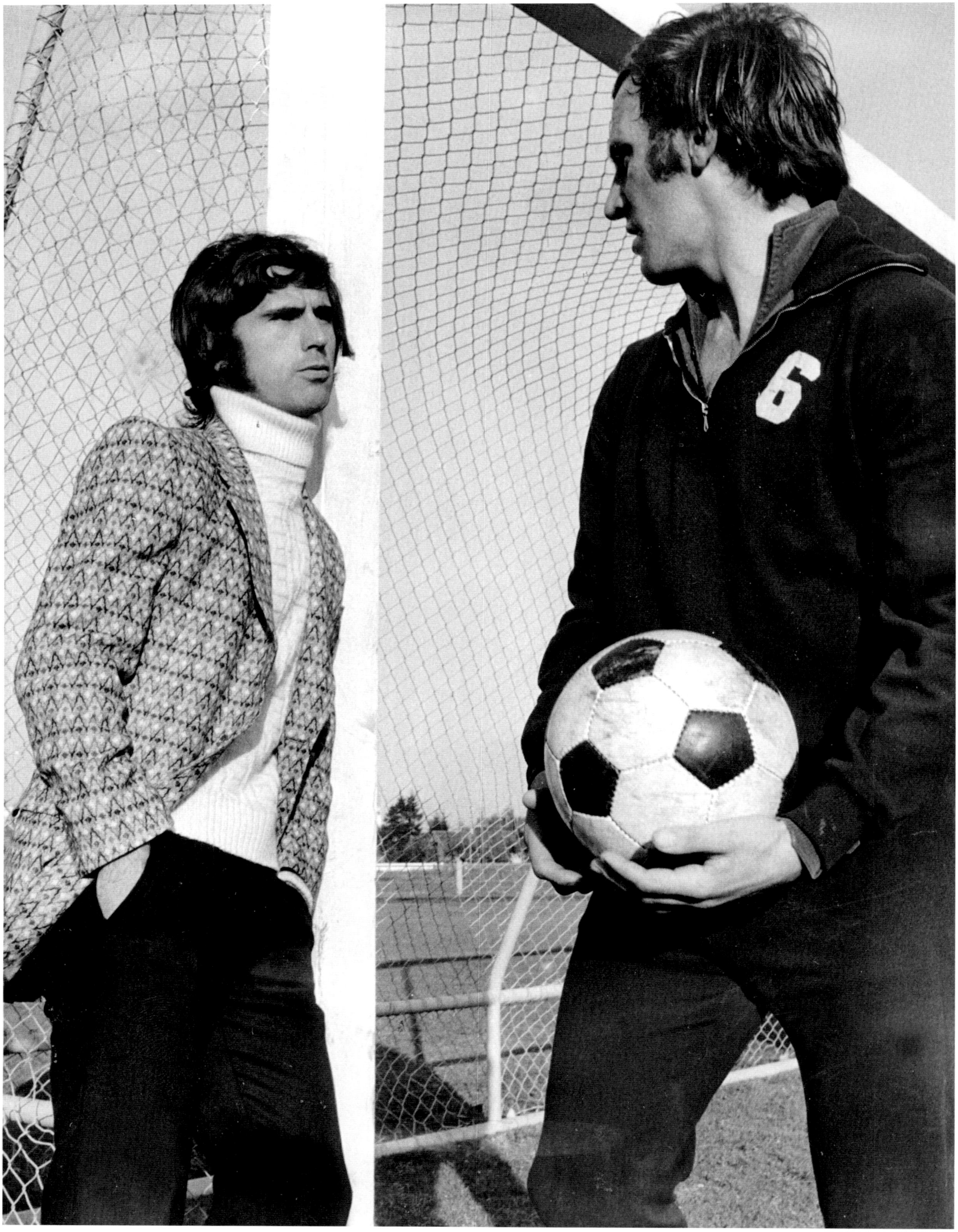

MEMBER **NO. 1** AND THE **FIRST** SCOUT

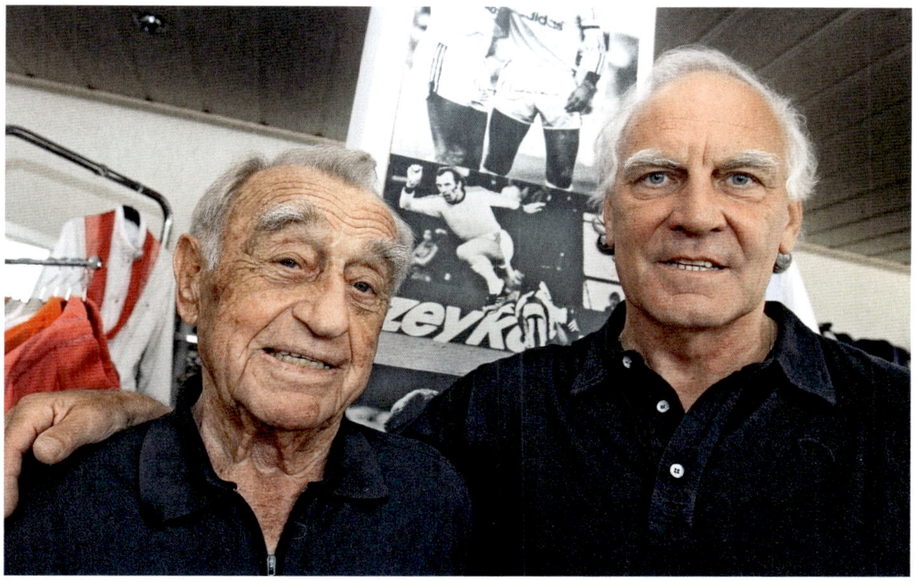

Even at the age of 90, Alexander Kotter, a “thoroughbred fan” as he called himself, never missed a match in the Allianz Arena. When he died, the president of FC Bayern attended the funeral in person. This was a matter of honour for Franz Beckenbauer, as Kotter was not a normal member. Until his death in 2007 he had membership number one, because no one had been a part of FC Bayern longer than he. But the club owed him a much greater debt: for his role as a talent-spotter.

Alexander Kotter, a master hairdresser with an eye for masterly players, was a part-time scout who discovered two FCB legends. He recommended an 18-year-old who became the world's greatest goalscorer and a 20-year-old who decided the result of three finals in European competitions: Gerd Müller and Bulle Roth.

Kotter was a master of his trade – in his Figaro Kotter salon and as head of the trade association of hairdressers in Bad Wörishofen. His wife Agnes even became national champion in competitions held by the hairdressers' association. But Kotter, who was born in Munich, achieved his true masterpiece in 1964, at a football match in Oberstdorf, when he watched an 18-year-old whom he addressed directly after the final whistle: “You're good, I'll take you to FC Bayern.” At that time he was scouting for players for a small club in the east of Allgäu, but this one was in a completely different league. And because Kotter was not only a club member at Bayern but also worked on an honorary basis as auditor on the board, his tip was noted at the highest level: take a look at this lad. Less than six months later, Gerd Müller was a professional for Bayern. The coach, Zlatko “Čik” Čajkovski, was not impressed by his physique, however, called him “fat little Müller” and left him out of the team.

After eleven matches this was too much for club president Wilhelm Neudecker, who exercised his authority. Čajkovski had to include fat little Müller, who delivered the goods straight away – and never, ever stopped. Two years later, Kotter proved once again that a simple club member with a good eye sometimes sees more than all of the scouts and more than highly paid coaches too. His recommendation brought a further exceptional player to Bayern, the 20-year-old Franz Roth. A year later, “Bulle” hit the winning goal in the final of the European Cup Winners' Cup.

Great careers in football often begin with such people, who have an eye for potential stars. Any club is fortunate to have such talent-spotters outside the structure of the club – as fans, members or part-time employees such as Jan Pienta, who formerly worked for the tax authorities. “Who is that?”, the new coach Louis van Gaal asked, and his assistant Hermann Gerland explained: “He brought most of our top players here when they were children, 12 or 13 years old. But nobody knows him. He discovered Lahm, Schweinsteiger and Müller for Bayern.” Part of what made FC Bayern what it is today were many people with a talent for spotting talent.

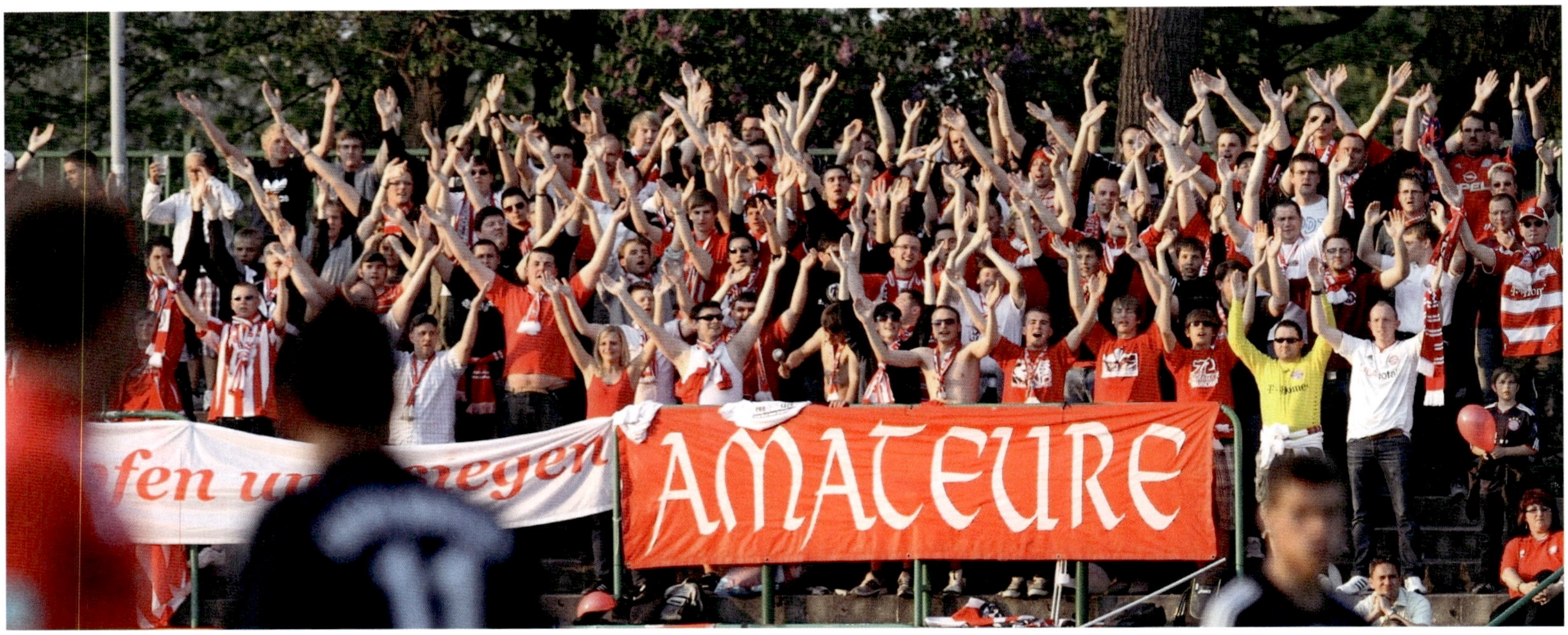

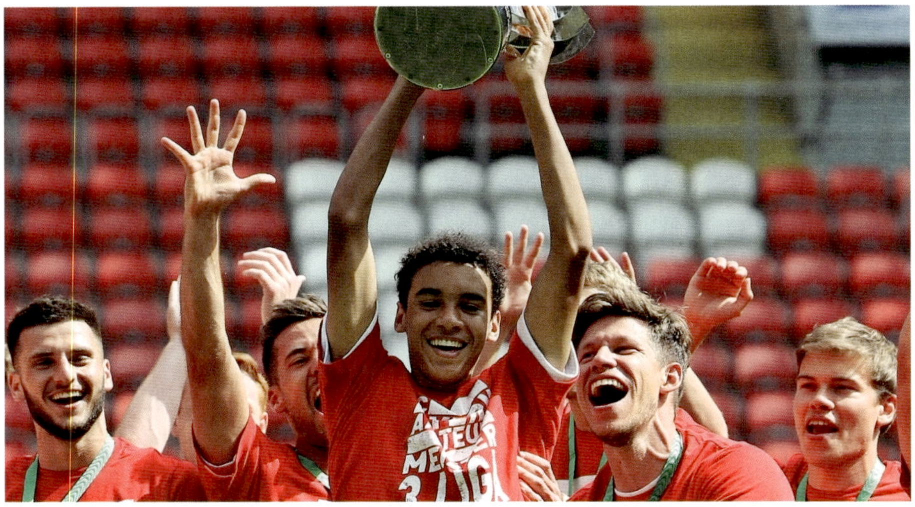

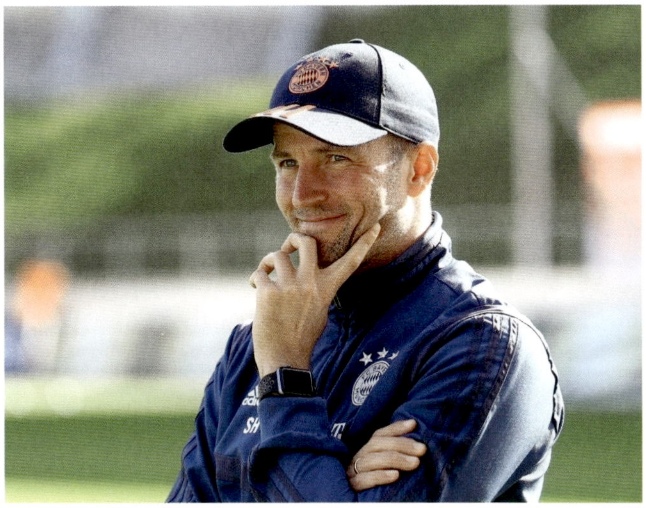

TALENT ON TOUR – **OUR AMATEURS**

In their only duel against the FCB professionals, the FCB amateurs lost 3-5 in the cup competition in 1977. But only because of Gerd Müller – who scored four times.

Once, on an August weekend in 1994, the big stars at FC Bayern were not the professionals but the amateurs. In the first round of the cup, they beat the title holders, Werder Bremen, and kicked off a series of wins.

On the following day, the FCB professionals were involved in an even greater feat of giant-killing. The Bundesliga champions were knocked out by TSV Vestenbergsgreuth. The FCB amateurs, by contrast, brought off further wins against Chemnitz and VfB Stuttgart before they were defeated in the quarter-finals by Wolfsburg. "Almost all of the players, who ultimately came from our youth A-team and turned professional, did so using the second team as a stepping stone," says Gerland, the coach at that time, of his fourteen years with the amateur side, and lists the names: "Babbel, Münch, Nerlinger, Hamann, Kuffour, Cerny, Hummels, Badstuber, Müller, Schweinsteiger, Alaba." For one of Gerland's successors, it also served as the stepping stone to a coaching career. Sebastian Hoeness, part of Bayern's amateur team that won the third-division championship in 2020, then moved to the Bundesliga and sensationally became runner-up in the championship in 2024 with VfB Stuttgart.

"FAVOURITE ANIMAL?" **LIONISED? NO! IN THE DOGHOUSE**

World stars visiting a village: there is a tradition at FCB of sending the players to fan clubs all over Bavaria in the Christmas season. "Something like this here or the Oktoberfest", said Harry Kane in Kirchweidach in Altötting district, "helps me get to know Bavarian culture." And there was plenty of that. A brass band, a a game of beer stein slinging, and as a farewell gift a snuff cannon that already reminded him of the top scorer's cannon that he won four months later for his thirty-six goals in the season. Only Emma from class 3c caught him out by asking what was his favourite animal. Kane: "A lion". Tumult amongst the onlookers, and an explanation by the moderator: lions are the animal "of the other club in Munich". Okay, then ask the question again. What's your favourite animal? Cheers for the answer: "A dog".

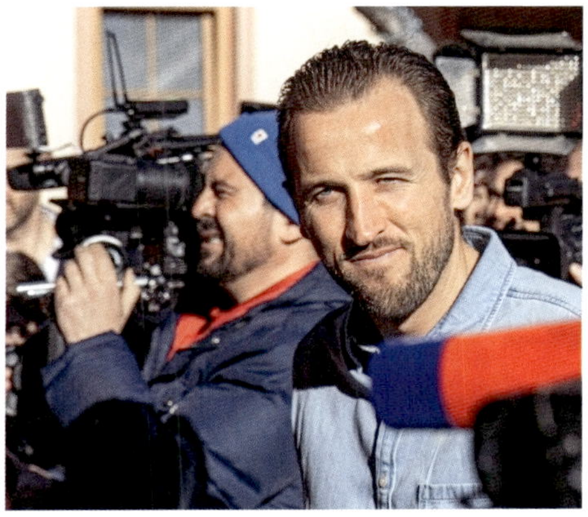

What a debut season for Harry Kane: the Golden Cannon trophy as top scorer, the Golden Boot and top marks at slinging a beer stein in the "Bavarian Olympics".

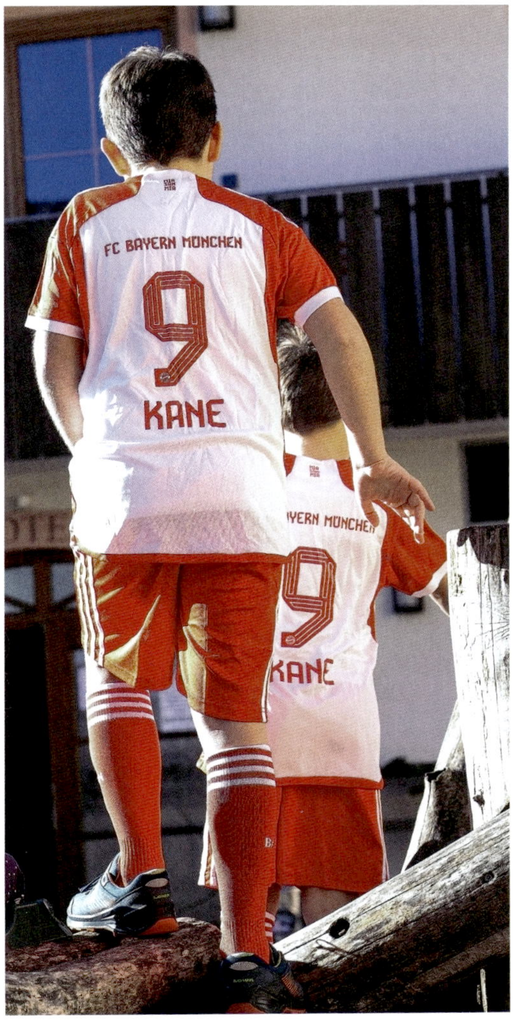

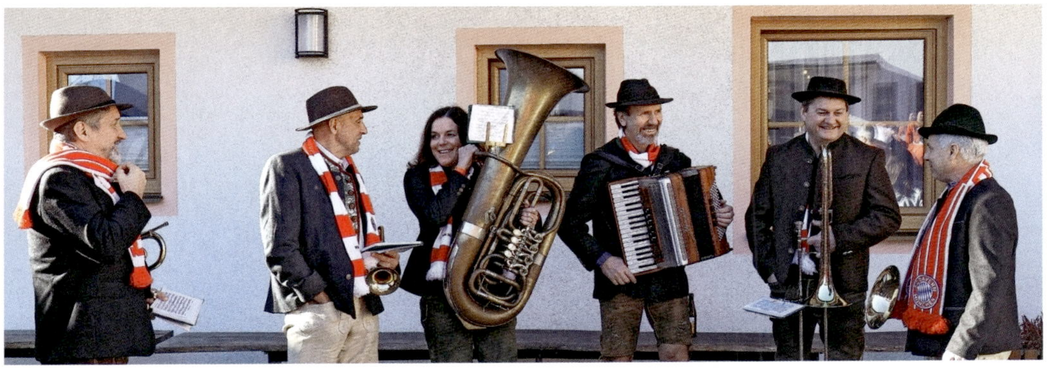

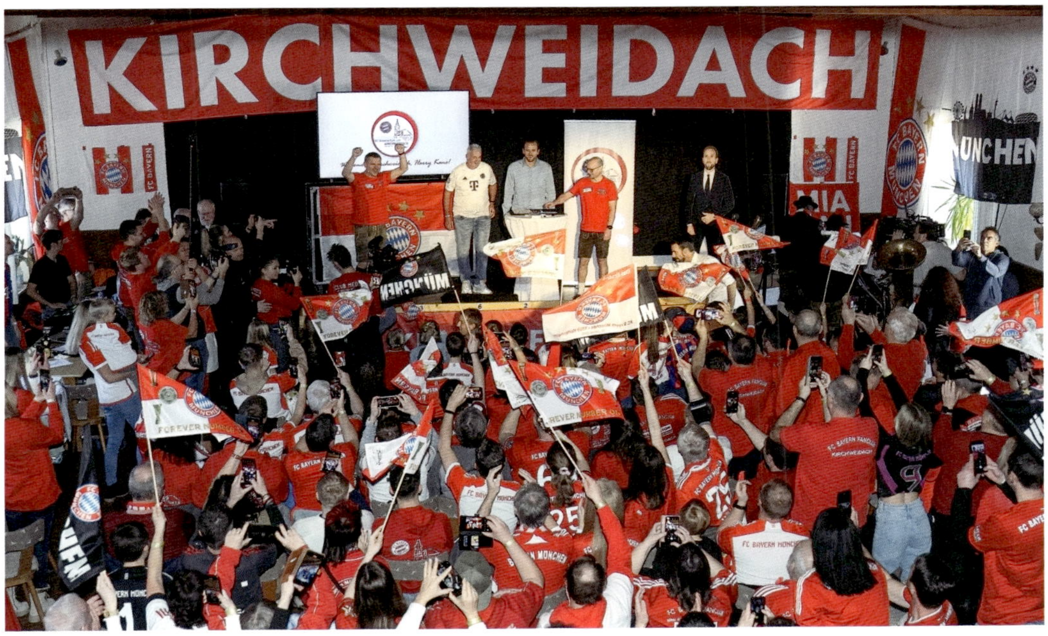

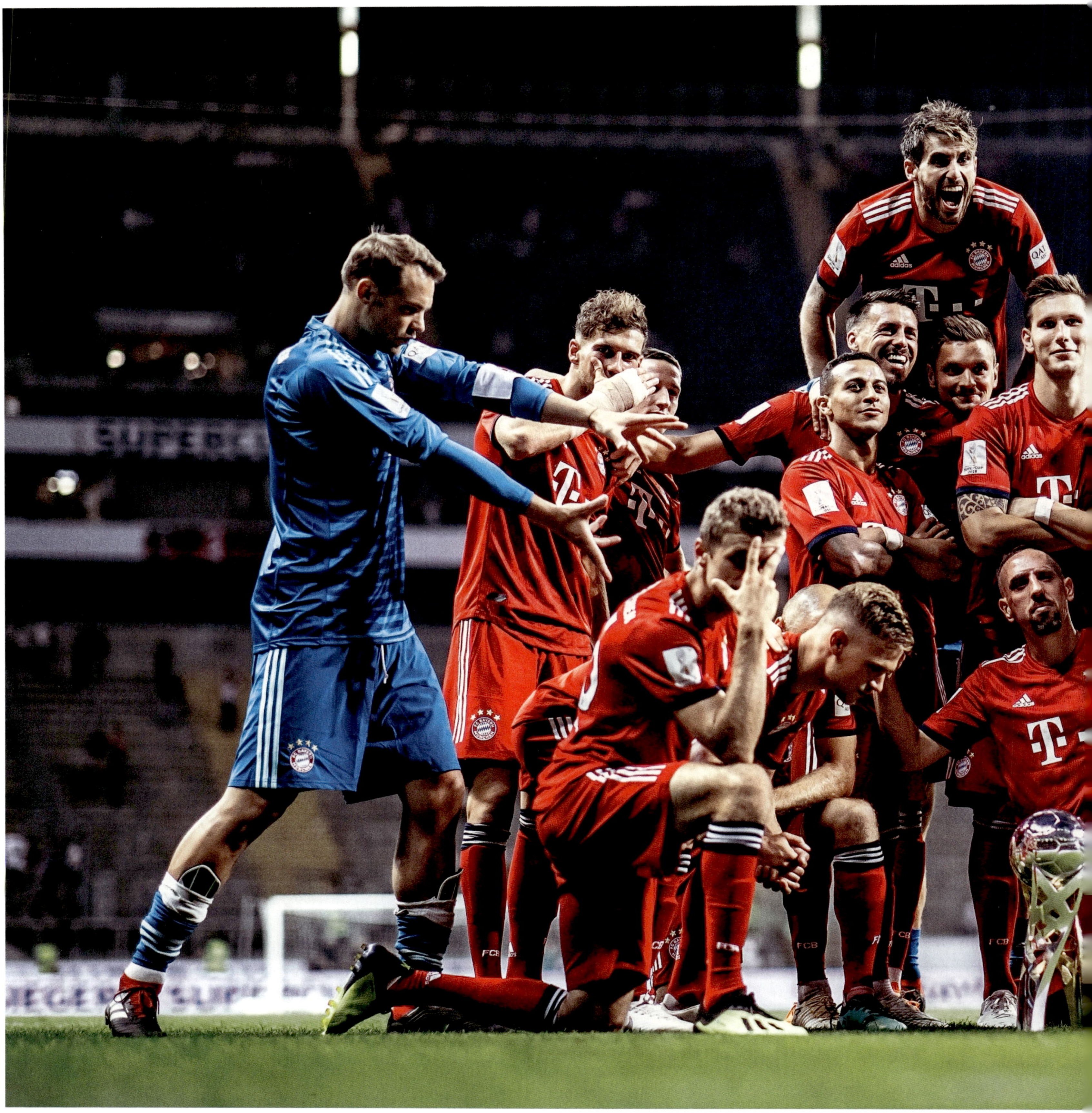

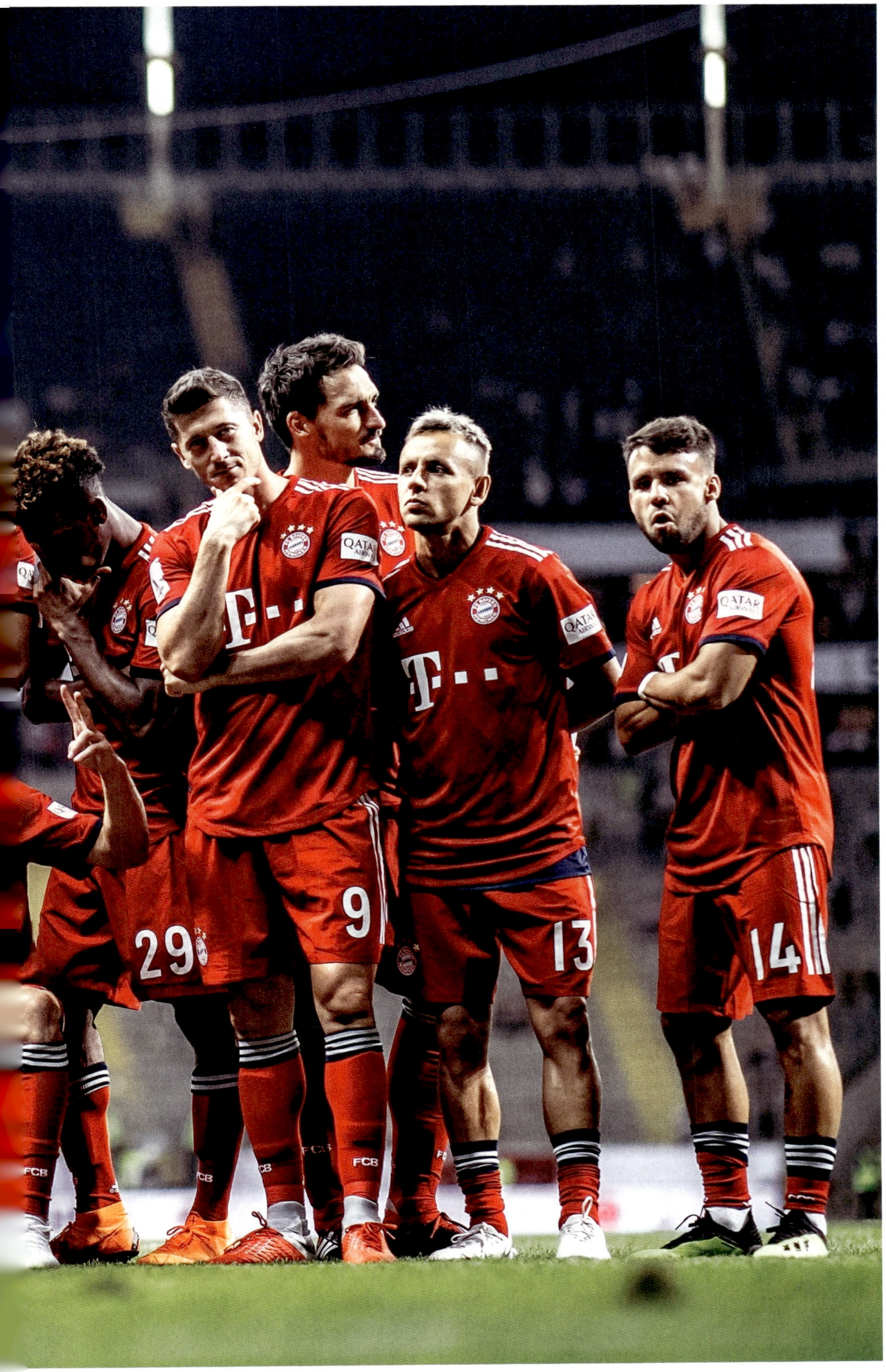

SUPER **BAYERN,** SUPER **BAYERN!**

It appeared at some stage during the treble season, this cry from the Südkurve that became the soundtrack of Bayern's greatest decade: "Super-Bayern, Super-Bayern, hey, hey!" In the gala performances of the years from 2013 to 2023 it soon echoed from every corner of the Allianz Arena. And though the fans' chants may sometimes be over-optimistic ("We'll win the European Cup / And we'll be Bundesliga champions") or not quite historically accurate ("Because for more than 1,000 years / We Bayern have been undefeated"), this one was absolutely correct. In eleven seasons, Super-Bayern brought home twenty-eight trophies: the Champions League cup twice (2013 and 2020), along with the UEFA Super Cup und Club World Championship both times, the German championship eleven times, the German DFB cup five times, and the German Super Cup (photo taken in 2018 after beating Eintracht Frankfurt 5–0) six times. That adds up to five doubles, two of which were elevated to a treble. And in one year, 2020 under Hansi Flick as coach, FC Bayern won all six available trophies. This had only ever been achieved once before, by Pep Guardiola's FC Barcelona in 2009.

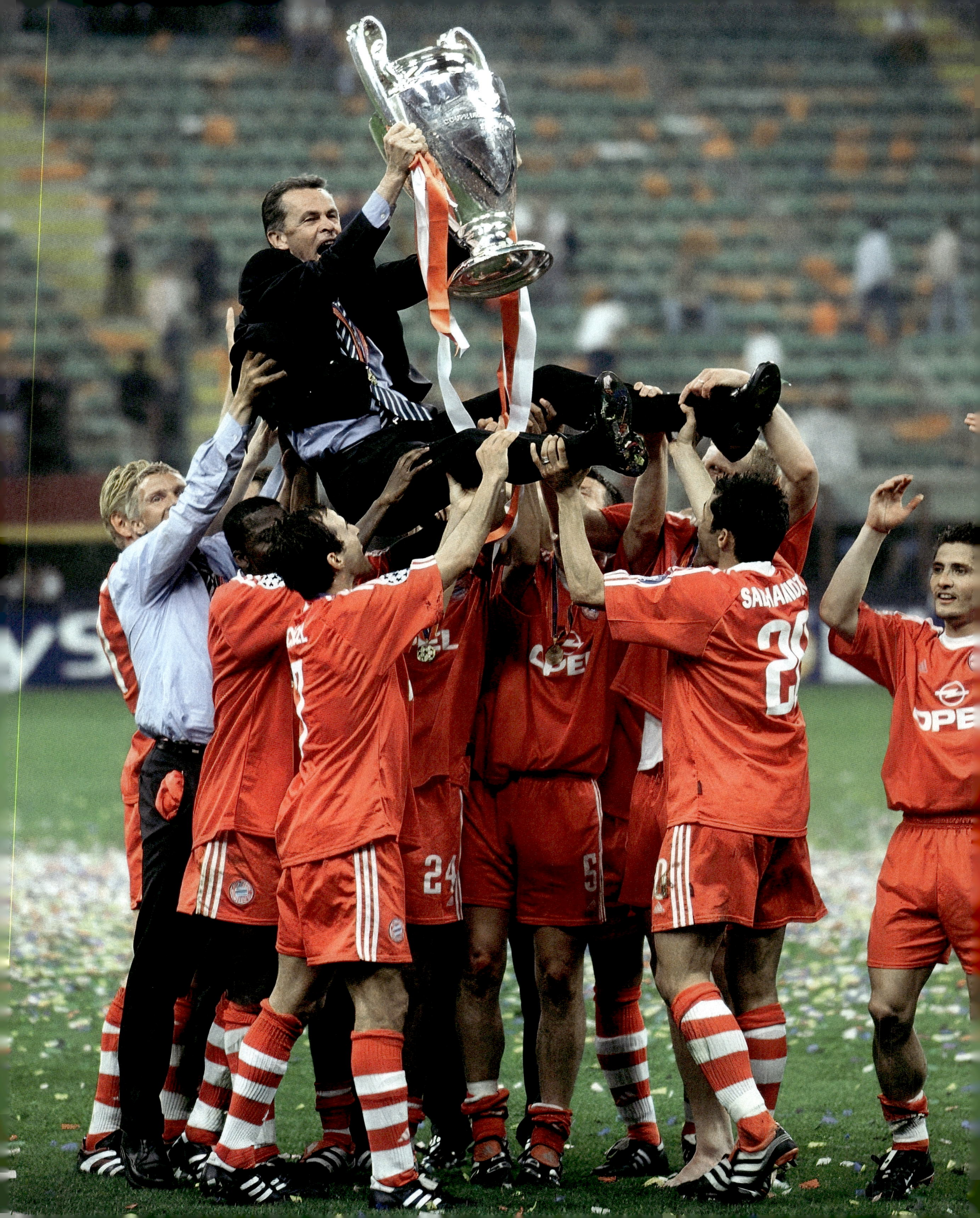

"KAHN! BAYERN!"
FCB-VALENCIA 5-4 · 2001

On working days, most Germans lie down in bed between ten and eleven in the evening. Oliver Kahn, too, lay down at this time on 23 May 2001. San Siro, Milan, just before eleven in the evening. But this was not a normal working day. It was the most important in his fourteen years as goalkeeper for Bayern.

In those minutes, between the end of regulation time and the whistle to start extra time, Kahn seemed to be the calmest person of the 75,000 in the simmering arena, lying there on the grass with all four limbs stretched out. His thoughts were "in a beautiful place where everything is completely quiet". Where he "sees himself in goal and the balls bouncing off me as I win the penalty shoot-out". After 120 minutes, as Kahn had foreseen, with no goal coming from open play in this tense final between two losing finalists – Bayern two years after the drama of added time against Manchester United, Valencia one year after being taken apart 0–3 by Real Madrid – and only two goals scored, penalties taken by Mendieta and Effenberg (with Scholl missing another), the logical end was a showdown at the penalty spot.

Two of the first four who ran up for Bayern, Paulo Sergio and Patrik Andersson, missed, but Kahn saved two penalties in succession. And he made his daydream of the evening come true by blocking the final shot by Pellegrino. At that moment the cheering exploded behind him at the Bayern end, where almost three hours earlier a legendary tifo message by the fans had declared it a "good day to make history" – a message as prophetic as Kahn himself, when he envisaged the result of the penalty shoot-out while meditating on the grass.

"This tifo", he later said, "is unforgettable for me." For twenty-five years, FC Bayern had "breathlessly chased this cup", the world's most important club trophy, as Kahn put it. "It was the last chance for this generation", and accordingly the tension ran high. But now: "Pure release. Otherwise we would have had to bear the 1999 final on our backs forever."

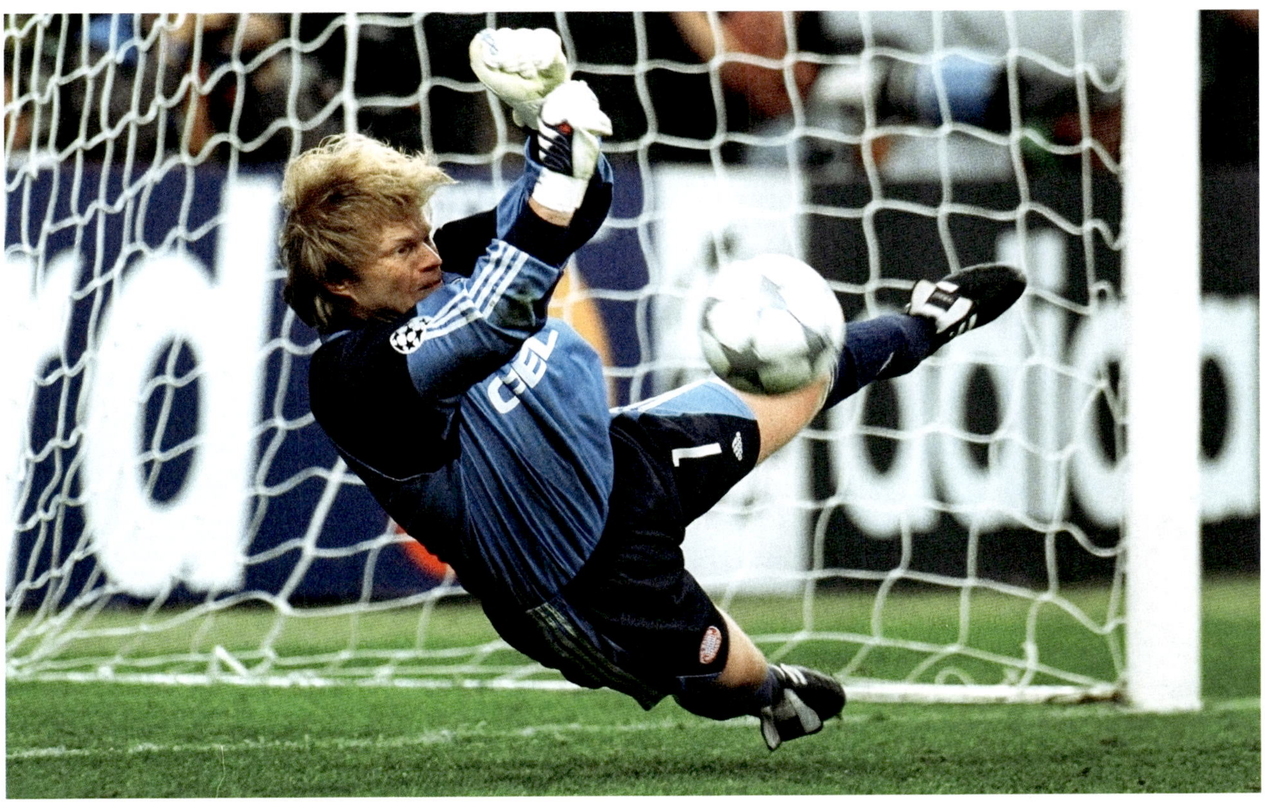

Mauricio Pellegrino is the man who, late in the evening of 23 May 2001, has to look the resolute, ready-for-anything Oliver Kahn in the eye. The Bayern goalkeeper has already saved two penalties. Pellegrino runs up - and hits the classic fearful spot kick, at half-height and a good metre away from the goalpost. Straight into a blue, one-man wall who blocks the ball. And then there is nothing but red, the colour of the winners.

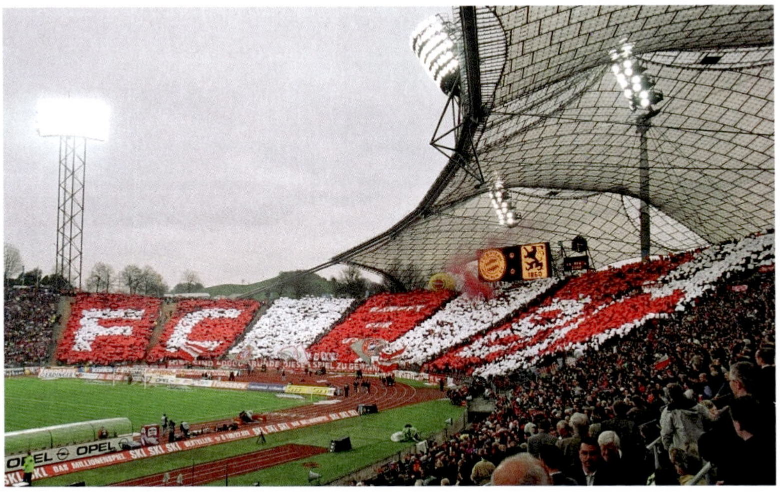

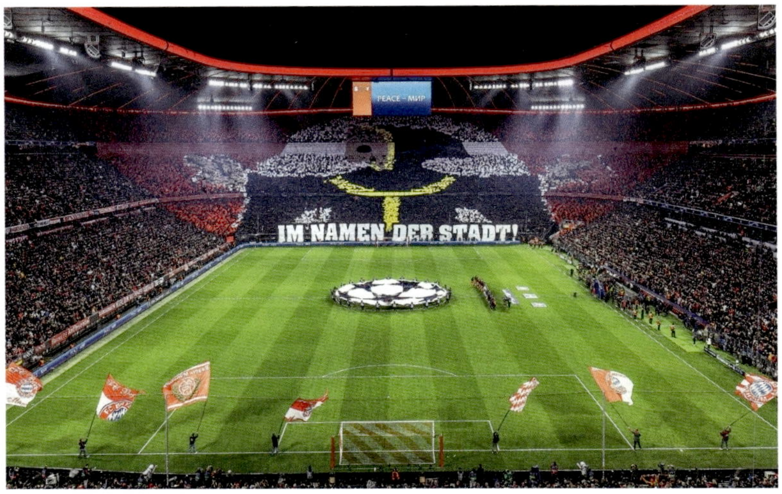

TIFO – **OUR FANS FLY** THE FLAG

Madame de Genlis is not well known among football fans. But she invented the original form of something that is familiar to all visitors to the stadium.

The governess of the Duke of Orleans' children taught her pupils to perform "tableaux vivants", living images. Paintings and tapestries represented by living persons became highly fashionable in France before the revolution. It was more or less exactly the activity that is called a "tifo" in football today: a work of art consisting of colours, surfaces, images and texts, formed by real people. While English fans have always sung, in Italy a form of visual expression evolved that conquered German stadiums too, through the ultras, who call it a "choreo" (choreography). For the Südkurve of the Allianz Arena and FCB's away games, since 2012 more than one hundred tifos have been recorded, ranging from messages of gratitude (the championship of 1932, the double in 1969) to mourning (Franz Beckenbauer, Gerd Müller) and commemoration of the victims of the Nazis. Humour also plays a part, as at the first match in Dortmund after the Wembley game in 2013, with an image of the trophy and the question "Still looking for it?"

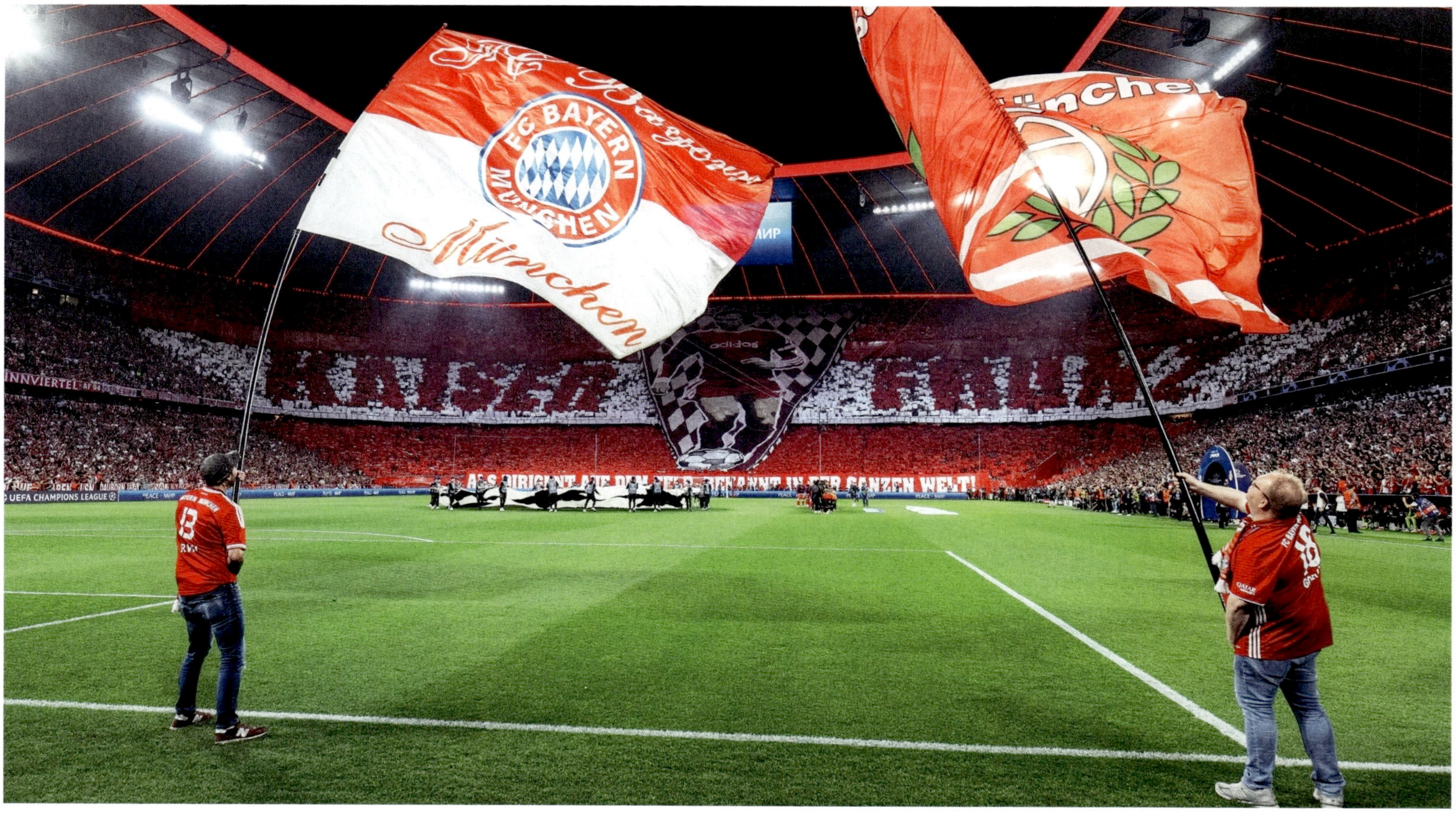

A PHILHARMONIC **FINAL ANTHEM**

In the glorious year of 2013, the club that once was FC Hollywood became FC Harmonia – not only on the football pitch, but in the concert hall too. An anthem was the accompaniment to victory at Wembley.

The maestro wore a FCB shirt with red and white stripes. Lorin Maazel conducted the Munich Philharmonic Orchestra, which performed a work especially for the final in Wembley, a blend of 'God Save The Queen', the FCB anthem and Handel's *Zadok the Priest*, the anthem of the Champions League. The choir sang: "Heading for the biggest title, the earliest champions in history, Bayern Munich were never stronger / Schweini, Müller, Lahm, Ribéry / With Jupp Heynckes at the helm, for the treble we'll wait no longer." Prophetic words, as Maazel saw for himself at Wembley as a guest of FCB.

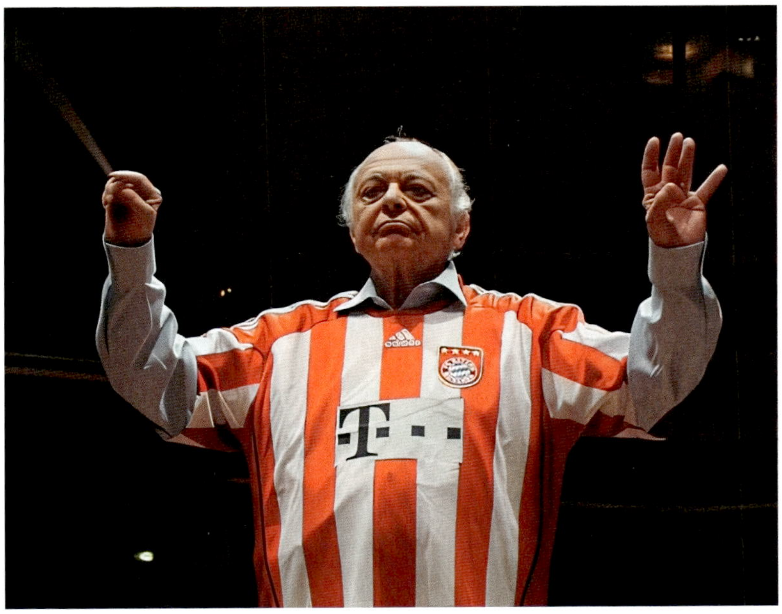

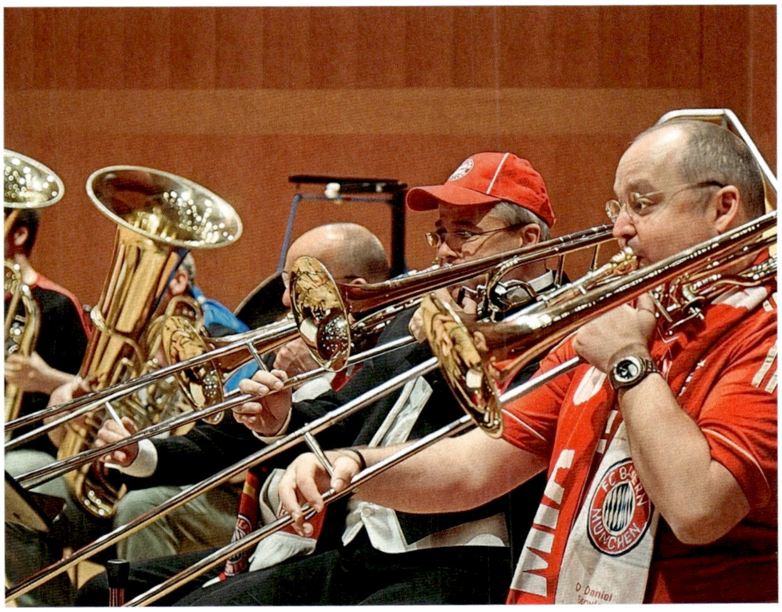

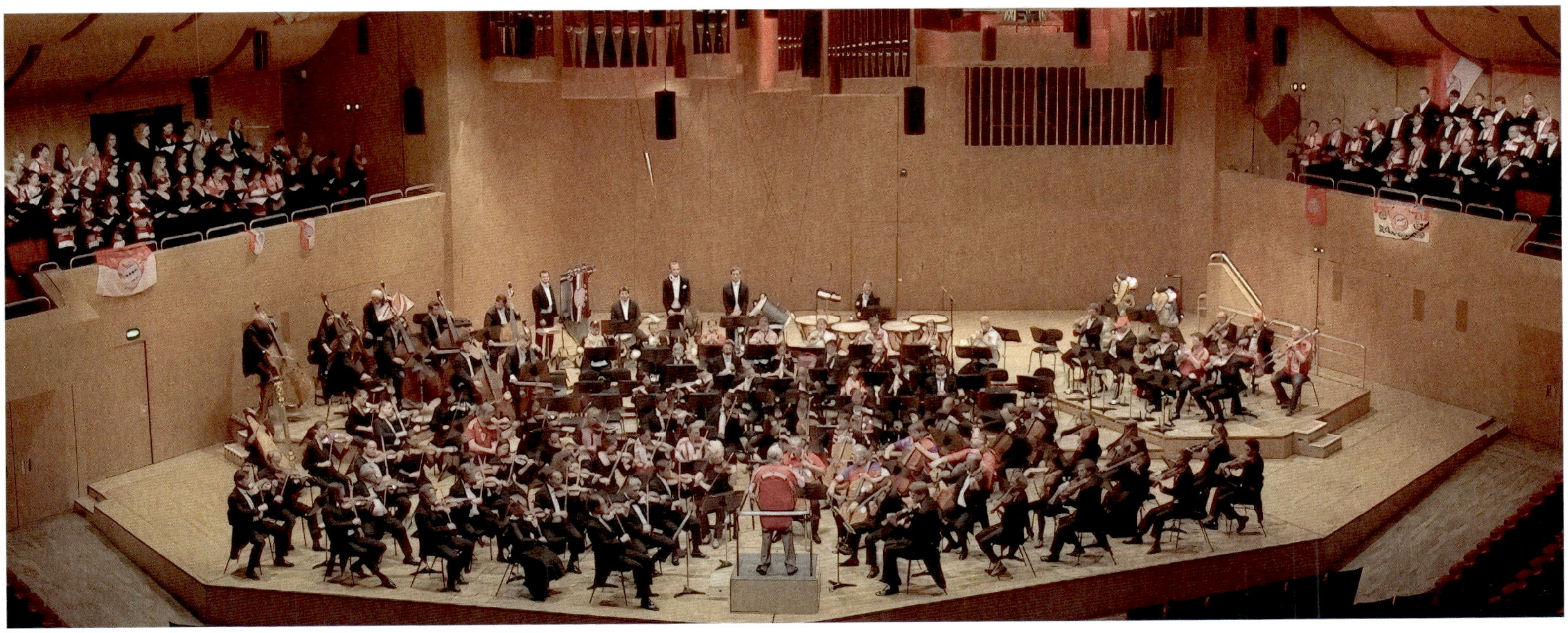

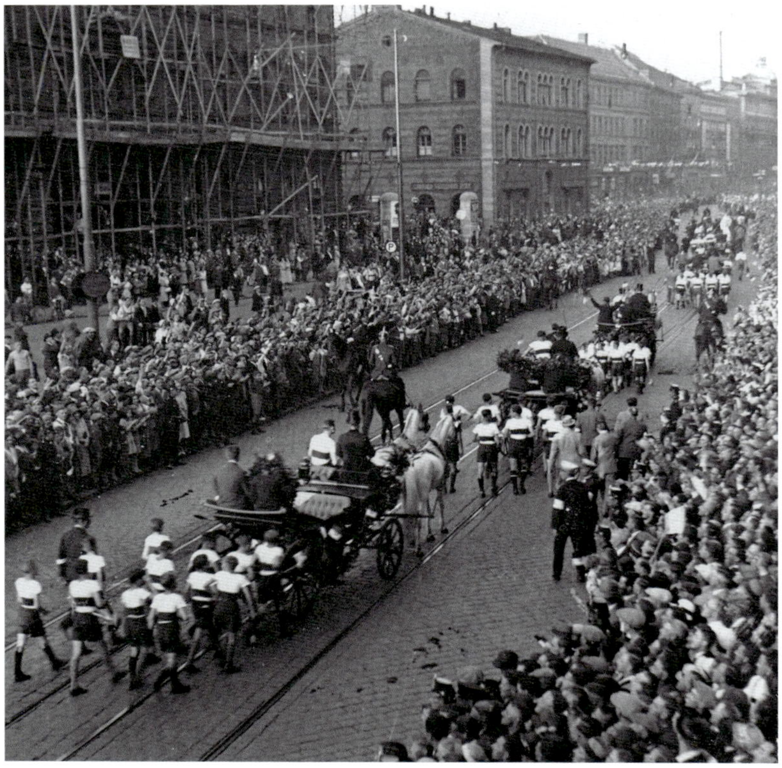

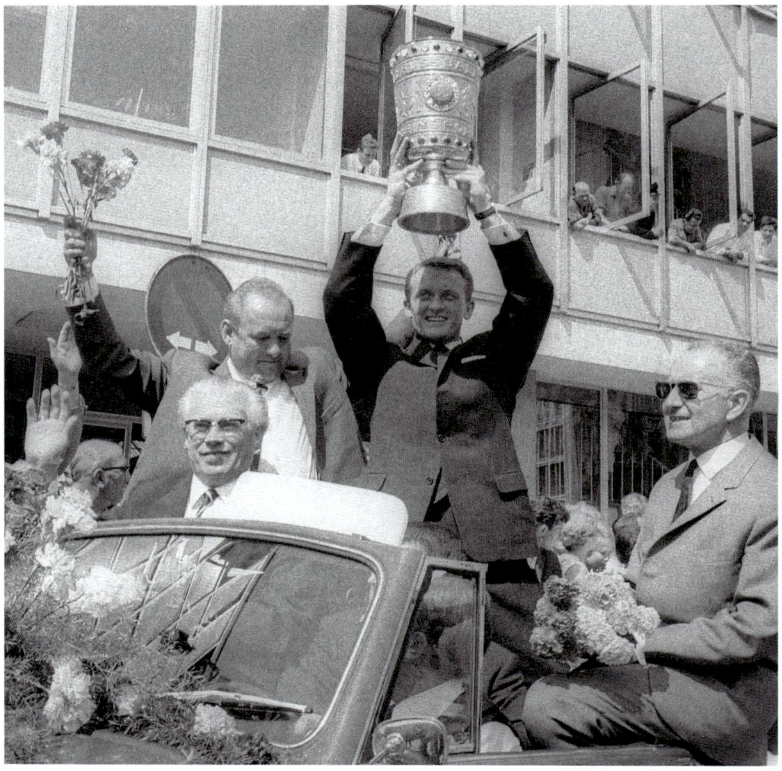

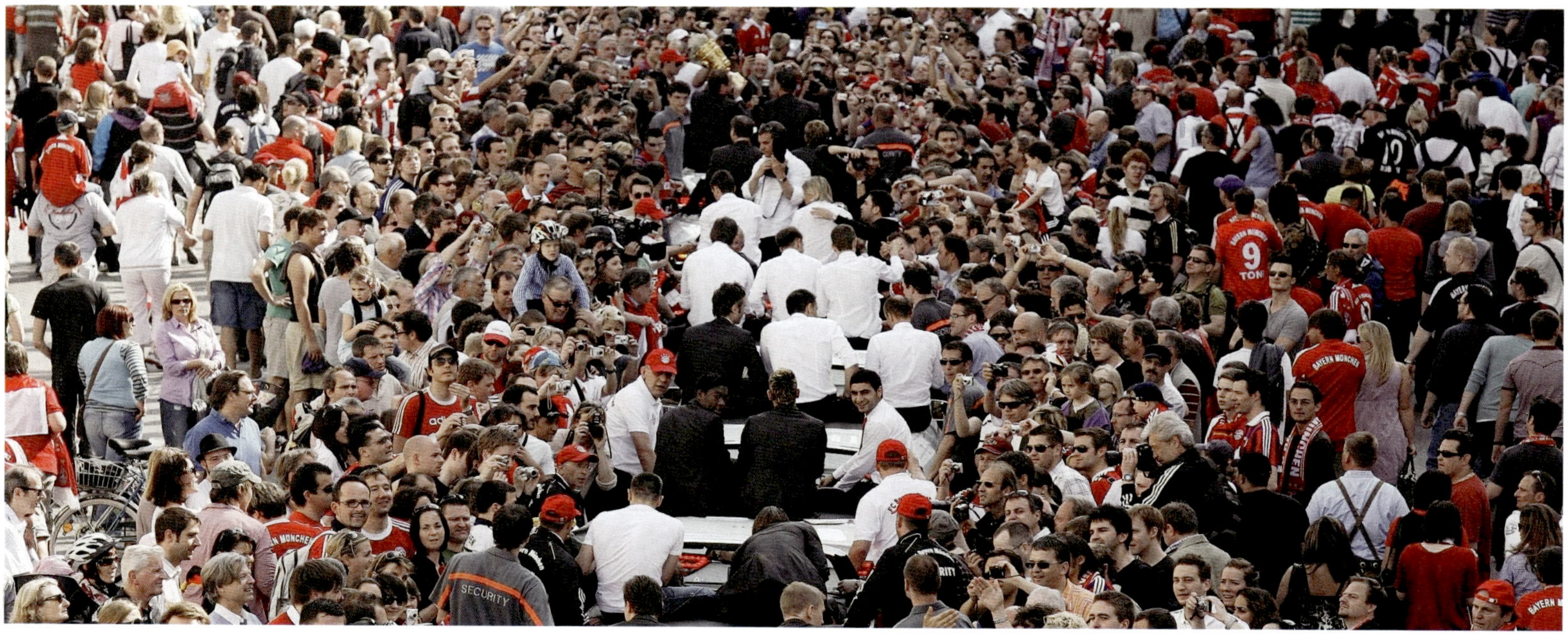
SECURITY

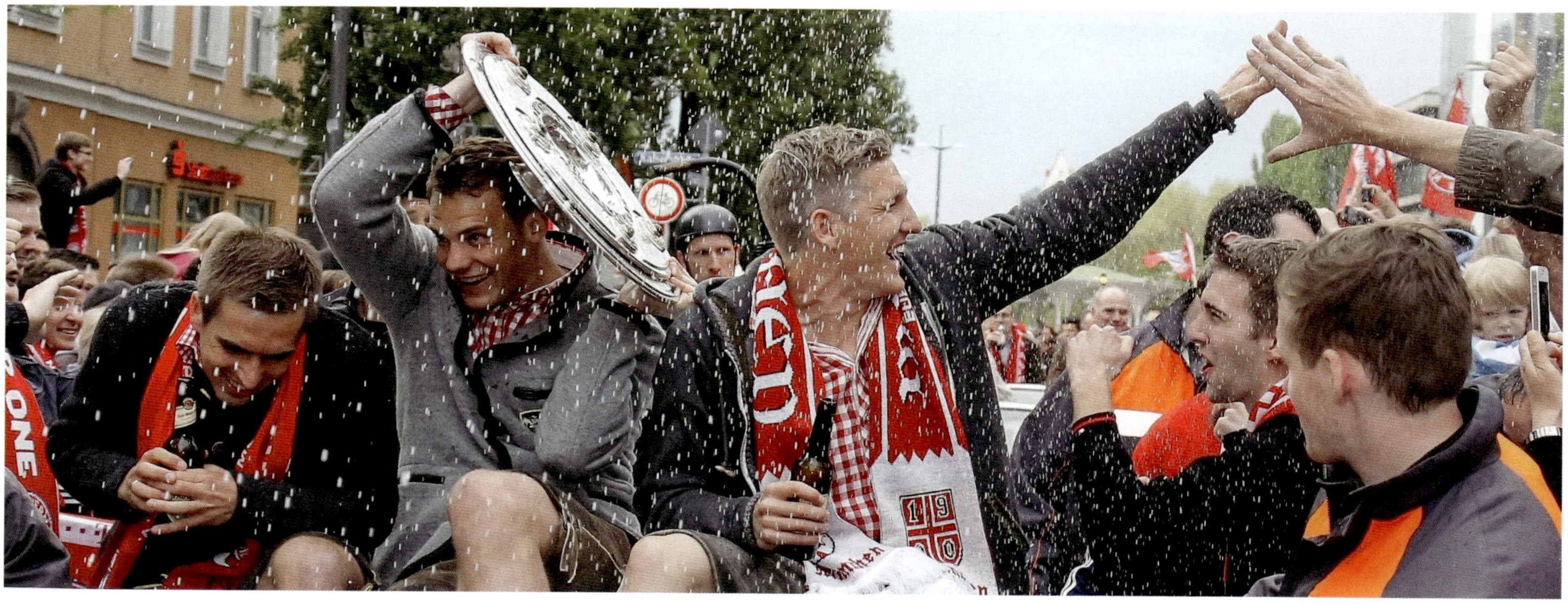

A PARADE TO **MARIENPLATZ**

Hundreds of thousands lined the streets in 1932 when FCB came home as champions. This was the start of a tradition: a parade through Munich.

In the past, the parade to Marienplatz went by horse-drawn carriage. By the time of the next big triumphal parades, the horsepower had increased in accordance with the importance of the trophy. The German cup, the DFB-Pokal, was chauffeured through the city in 1966 in a small, four-cylinder saloon car, the European Cup Winners' Cup in 1967 in a six-cylinder sports car, the European Cup in 1974 in an eight-cylinder luxury limousine. Later, when FCB had sponsors from the automotive industry, the trophy was driven past the crowds first in an Opel, then in an Audi. Cheering supporters always pressed forward to the edge of the road and finally around city hall, watching the jubilation on the balcony. And the city centre of Munich has never been as packed as in 2013, when approximately a million people wanted to see what treble-winners look like.

In the midst of the crowds, even sober-minded coaches pop up and say strange things. Jupp Heynckes, for example, who gave this promise in 1991 from the balcony of city hall: "Next year we'll win the European Cup." In a way that was true, just that the timing was a little bit inaccurate, and it took twenty-one years longer than Heynckes predicted for him to bring the European Cup back to Munich. And Louis van Gaal surprisingly turned out to be a party animal, swung a leg gracefully over the parapet and promised, as this was Mother's Day, "a big kiss from the coach of champions" to all the women in the crowd. That would have been worth repeating, but it was to be van Gaal's only appearance on the winners' balcony.

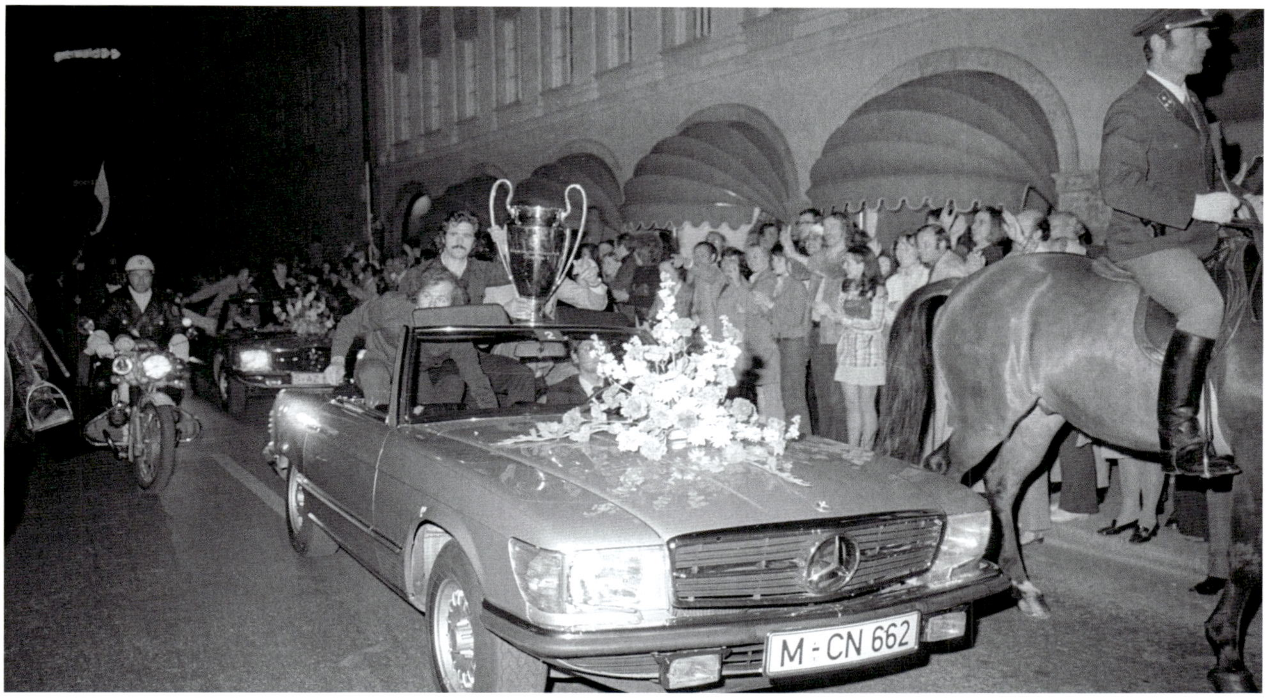

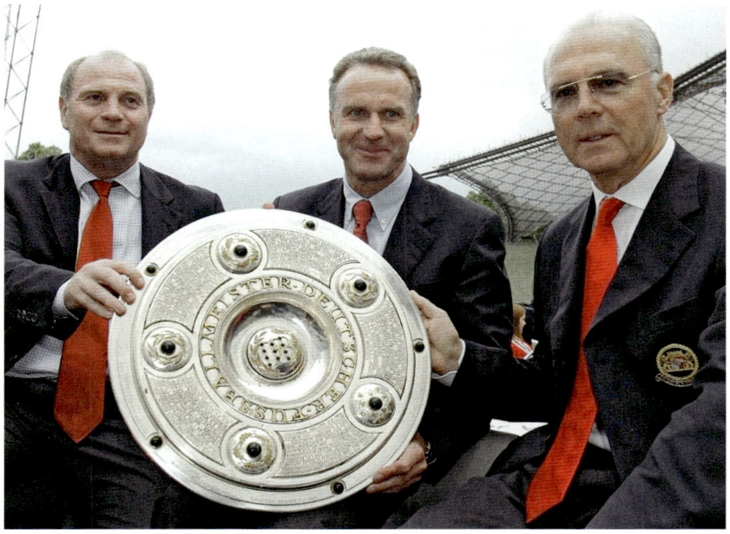

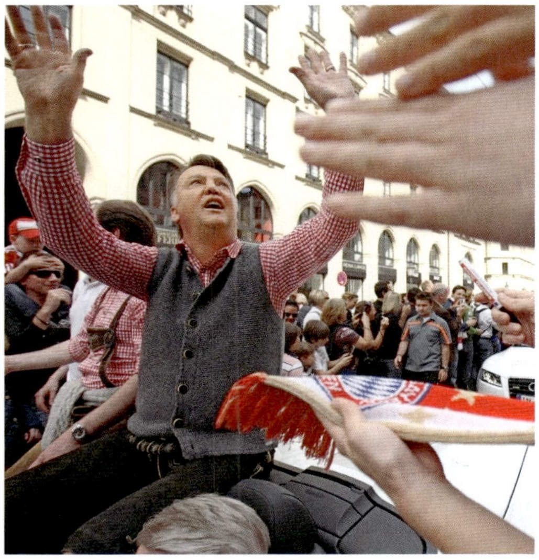

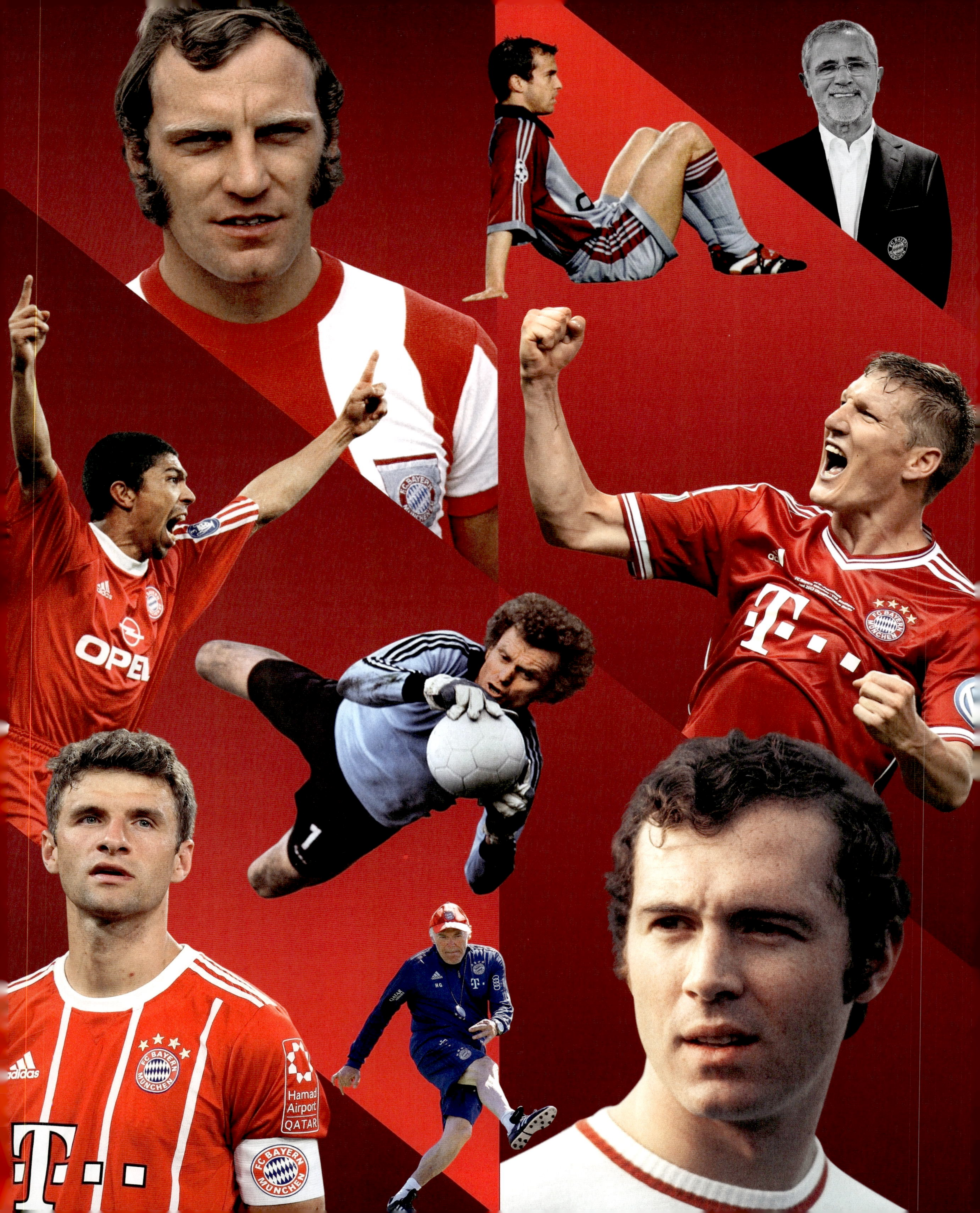

Hamad
Airport
QATAR
adidas
FC BAYERN MÜNCHEN

STARS OF THE SOUTH

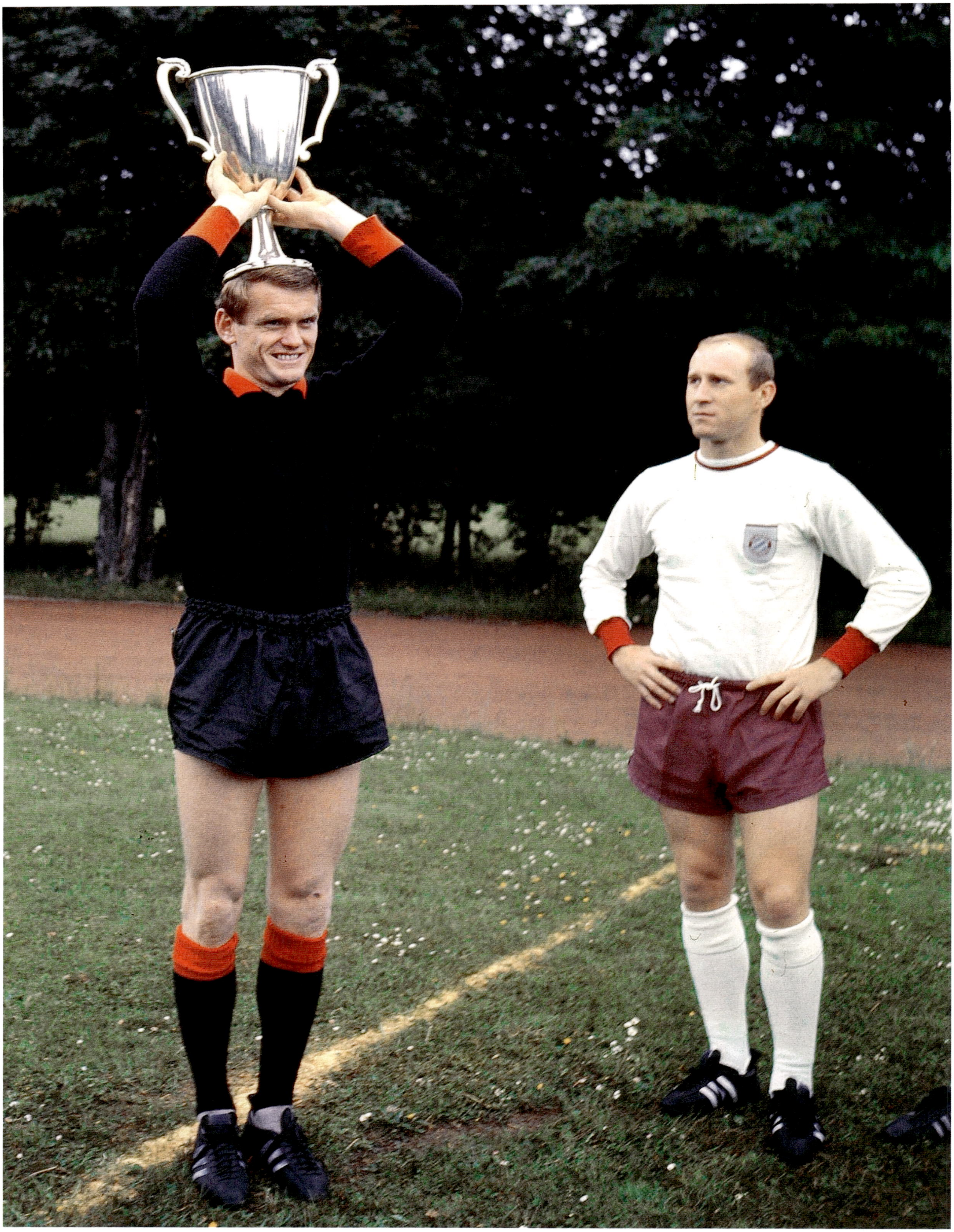

Whether he was wearing the European Cup Winners' Cup as a hat, spelling with tennis balls, using Oliver Kahn's broad chest as storage space or covering himself in muddy make-up: Sepp Maier, a sportsman and joker on and off the field, always had his fun.

SEPP **MAIER**

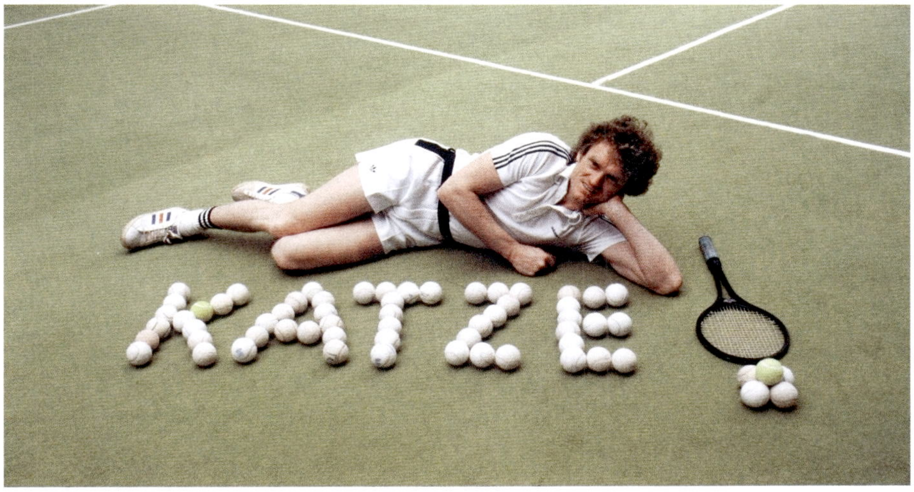

He leapt to catch ducks, hid a rabbit in the bag of the masseur Katzenmaier, and as an amateur magician "made women disappear" – Sepp Maier, the entertainer between the goal posts.

Maier, gifted at gymnastics in his childhood, brought the physical discipline of this sport to the goal of a football field. With arms like tentacles he pushed shots around the posts and plucked crosses out of the air. The sight of such slender-limbed, recklessly brave goalkeepers, often clad in plain black, is part of the footballing aesthetics of the 1970s, which many regard as the decade of the most beautiful football. Maier, whose agile flights through the penalty area earned him the nickname "the Anzing Cat", later loved to undertake long journeys, going as far as the Arctic and Antarctic in retirement.

He won the European Cup, the German championship and cup four times each, was a World Cup and European Championship winner, and Footballer of the Year three times. To hand Maier his only defeat in thirteen finals, it took another master of cunning: the Czech player Antonin Panenka, who outwitted him in the penalty shoot-out of the Euro 1976 final by chipping the ball into the middle of the goal. But the most important record for Maier was his run of 442 Bundesliga games over thirteen years without missing a single match – a record to stand for eternity. A longer series was planned, but a serious traffic accident forced him to end his career in 1979. He continued to collect major titles as goalkeeping coach of FC Bayern and the German national team – and at tennis in four German championships with Hasenbergl Tennis Club.

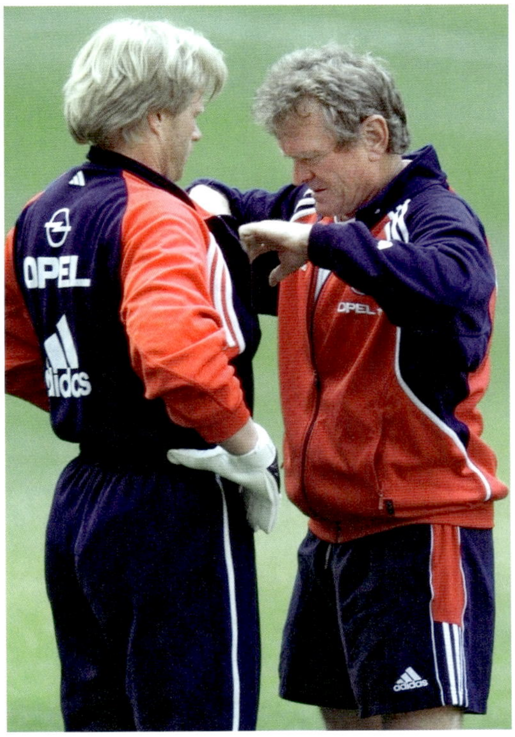

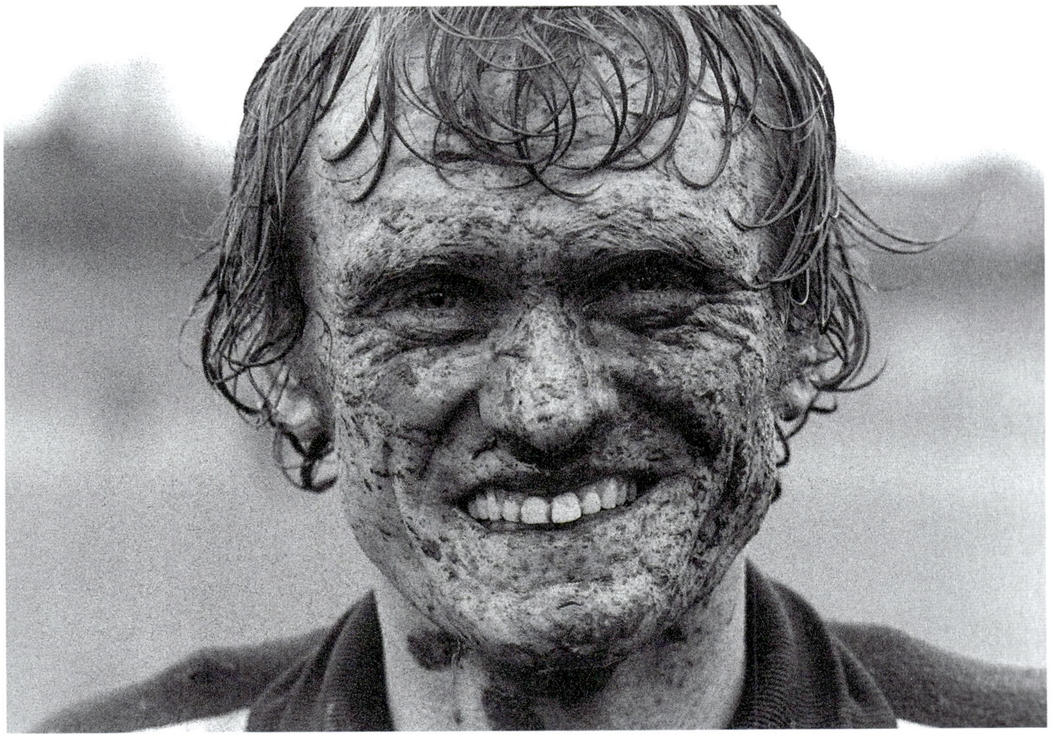

JEAN-MARIE **PFAFF**

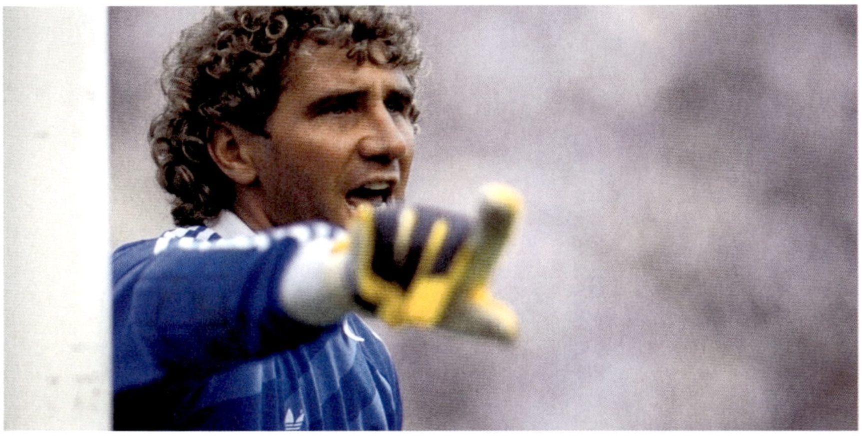

It started with a strange own goal and turned into a success story that he celebrated in song: "I was a Belgian, now I'm a Bavarian, I drink beer and eat Leberkäse with eggs."

Following a slip-up in his first match, when he deflected a throw-in by Bremen into his own net and Bayern lost 0–1, Jean-Marie Pfaff quickly made up for this with his heroics – six weeks later, for example, by saving a last-minute penalty from Manfred Kaltz when the score against champions Hamburger SV stood at 2–2, leading to a tumult that almost caused the game in the Olympic Stadium to be stopped. Or a year later in the UEFA Cup against PAOK Salonika, when he decided the longest penalty shoot-out in the history of FC Bayern almost single-handedly. Pfaff saved the Greeks' tenth penalty, then shot into the top corner himself for a score of 9–8 and was the hero of the hour. Before he came to Munich at the age of 28, Pfaff, one of eleven children from a poor Flemish family, was a semi-professional who worked in a bank in the mornings and a sports shop in the afternoon, then trained in the evening. When he left aged 34, he was "World's Best Goalkeeper" and the darling of the fans.

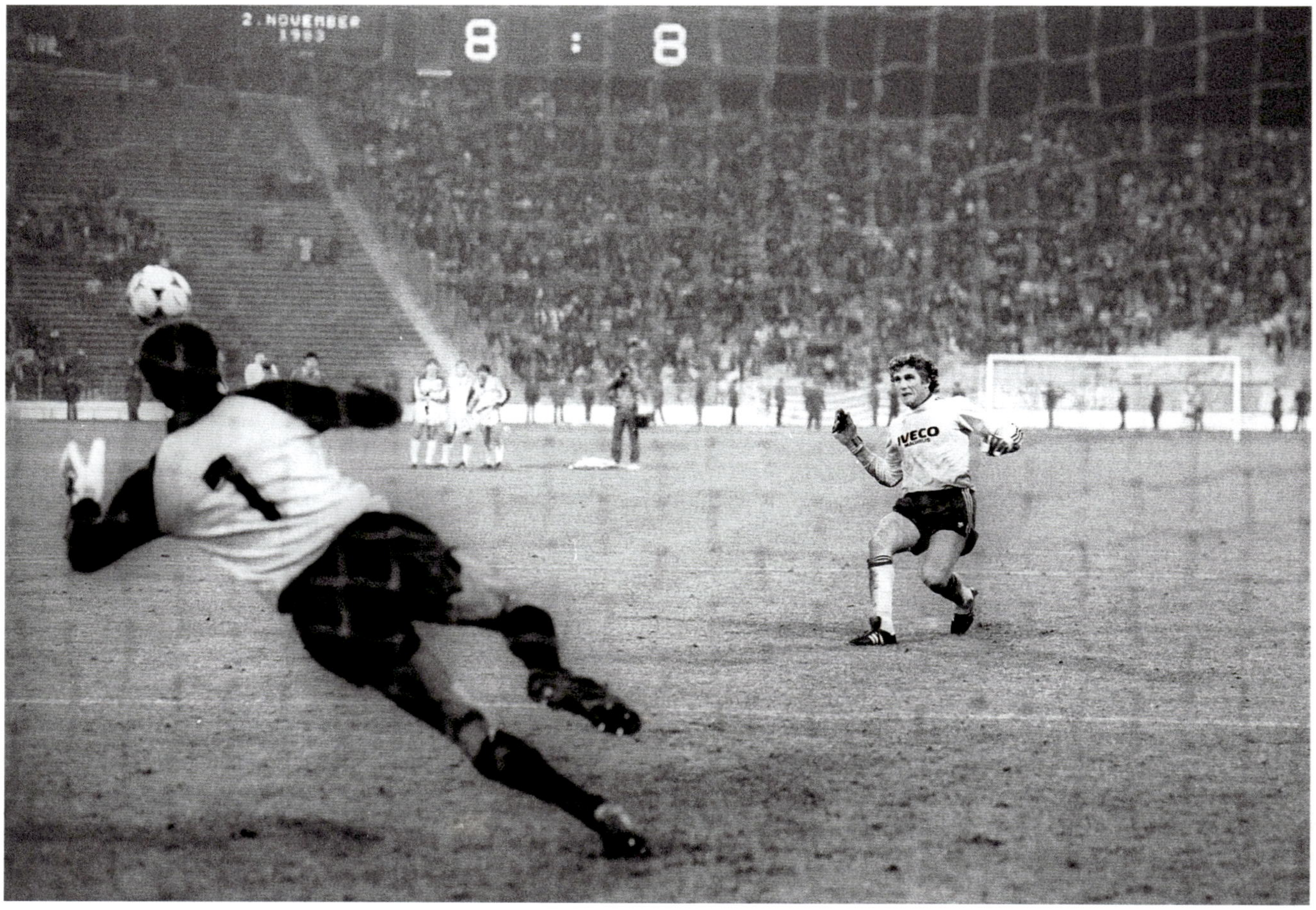

Who will take the spot kick? No outfield player in sight, but a penalty has to go in against Salonika. Where are Bertram Beierlorzer and Reinhold Mathy, the only ones who haven't taken their turn? Rummenigge hurries off and finds them in the shower. So Pfaff is the only man left - and he puts it in the net for a win. A Belgian with Bavarian genes.

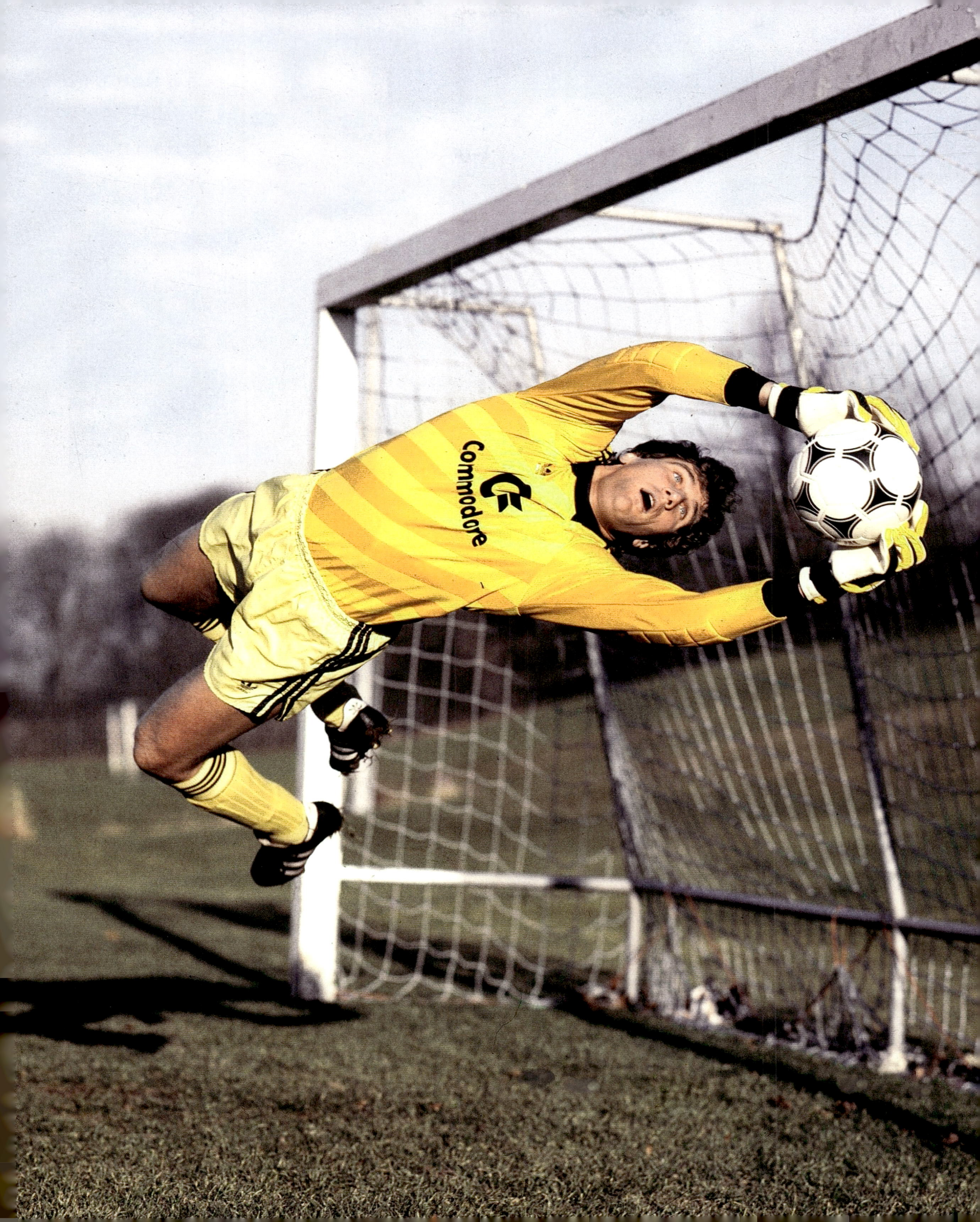
Commodore

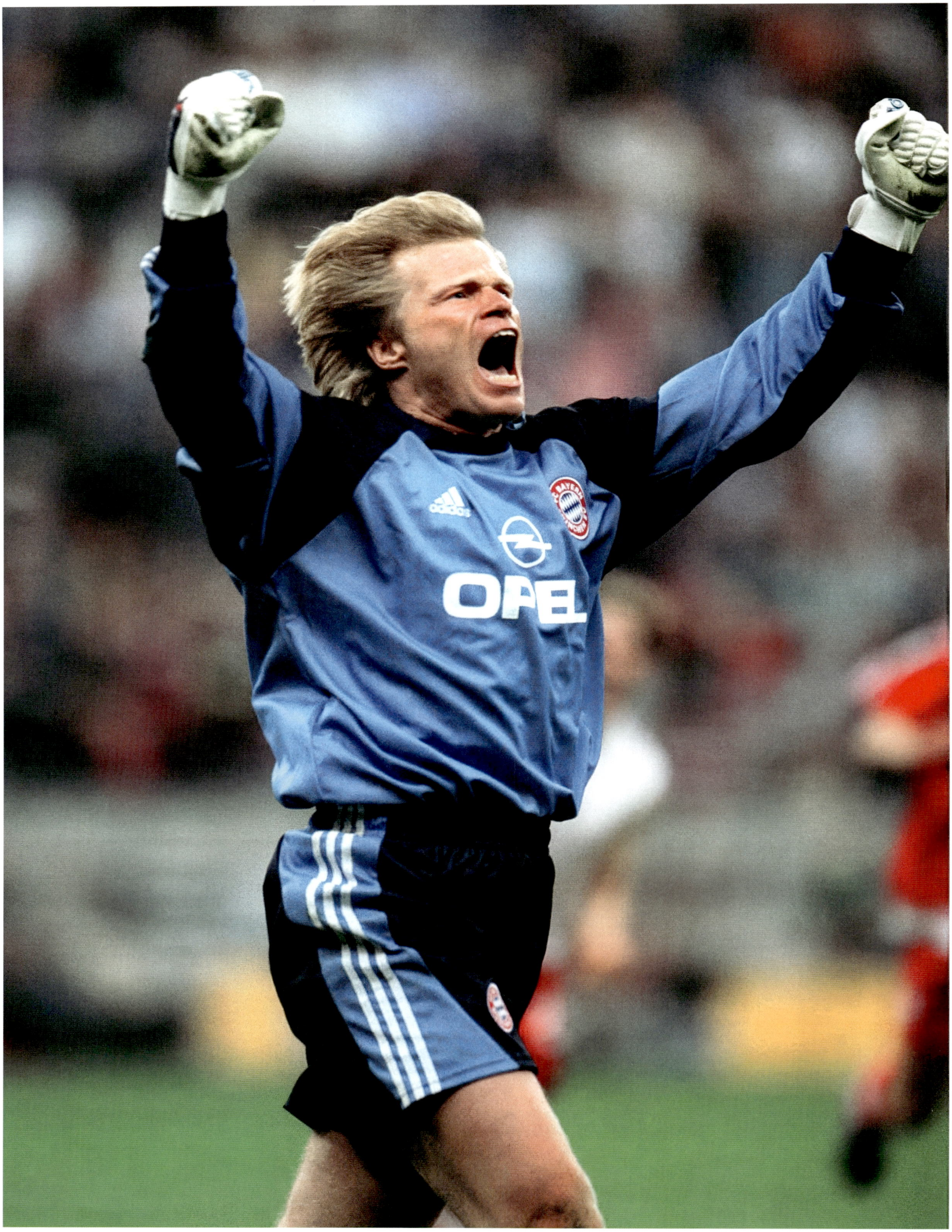
adidas
OPEL

OLIVER **KAHN**

How did a little lad from Karlsruhe become a goalkeeping giant? It started with a gift from grandad. And after that, it was all about an unstoppable will to win.

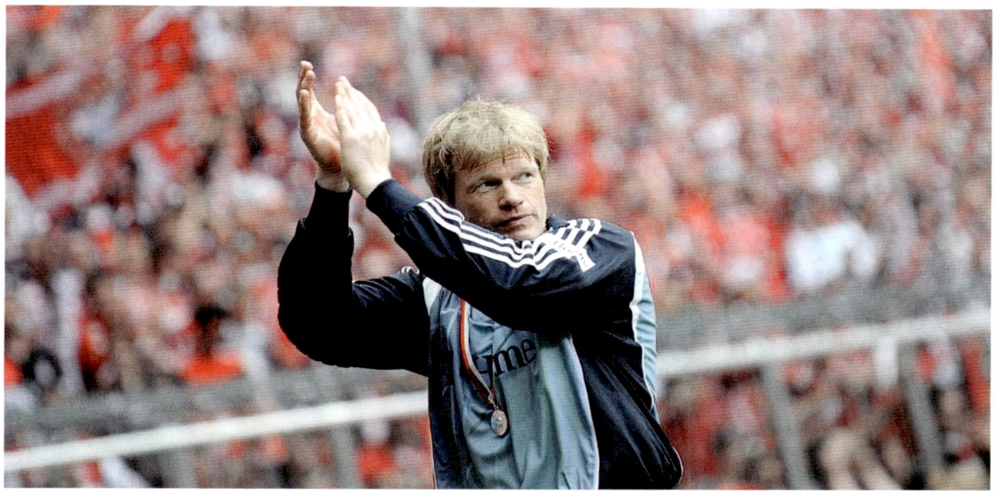

The gift was a goalie's kit, the Sepp Maier Edition, which made 7-year-old Oliver decide that his days as an outfield player were over. Twenty years later, he almost had to reverse the decision. In 1996, before the Euro semi-final against England, seven players were injured, and a shirt was embroidered "12 Kahn" for the reserve goalkeeper. He was not needed, however, so Kahn remains the last titan of the old school of goalkeeping – one of those idols who saw themselves as the final problem-solver between the goalposts rather than an eleventh outfield player.

Coached by Sepp Maier, Kahn's athletic quality, presence and aura of doggedness made him one of the most feared goalkeepers in the world – among his colleagues too, at times. When a teammate was a bit too casual, the atmosphere became frosty with a man like Kahn. After a 2–0 defeat at Schalke, Kahn spoke words that became famous: "Balls, we need balls." (He wasn't referring to footballs.) Nobody ever disagreed. After fourteen years, winning eight Bundesliga championships and triumphing in the Champions League in 2001, the three-time World's Best Goalkeeper retired in 2008. His return to Munich ended prematurely in 2023 after just under two years as chairman – but this cannot detract from his achievements as the last giant of the old school.

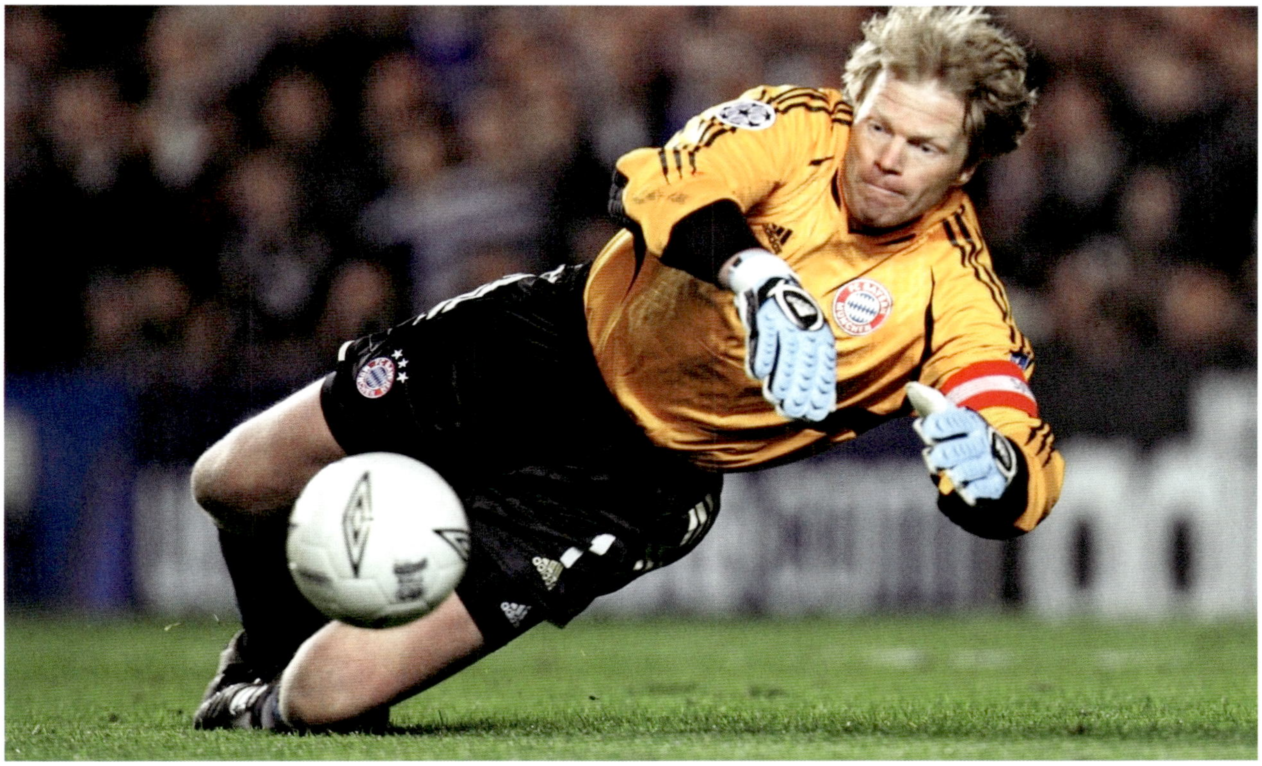

Opponents didn't like to get too close to a man like Oliver Kahn, but he took knocks himself, sometimes from teammates. Sammy Kuffour knocked him out in 1999 in Frankfurt (and FCB still won, with Michael Tarnat in goal), but two years later he reanimated Kahn with the "kiss of life" after another knockout, by Andy Cole (Manchester United). Kahn commented drily: "I wasn't conscious of his caresses."

MANUEL **NEUER**

The Südkurve, the fans at the south end, chanted “Koan Neuer” – meaning “no new one”, which is what Neuer’s name means. Louis van Gaal agreed: “I don’t need a Neuer.” How wrong they all were!

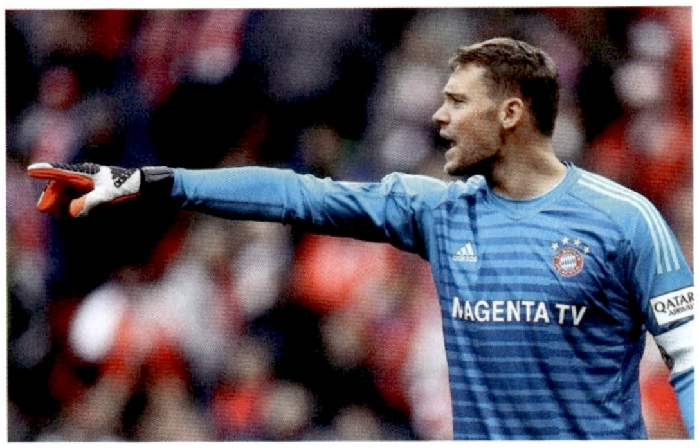

No other club has had so many World’s Best Goalkeepers as FC Bayern. The first man to be awarded the title, in 1987, played in Munich – the Belgian keeper Jean-Marie Pfaff. Oliver Kahn won the award three times. And the record, five times, is held by Manuel Neuer.

In the history of FC Bayern, no element of the team line-up can present such top-class protagonists as the goalkeeping position. World-class in forty-eight out of sixty years in the Bundesliga: fourteen years with Maier, six with Pfaff, fourteen with Kahn, fourteen with Neuer, and the story goes on. In 2011 the coach and the ultras preferred Thomas Kraft in the Bayern goal, but the management were convinced that Neuer was the man. Karl-Heinz Rummenigge enthused that “Manuel Neuer is titanium and then some. I don’t know what that alloy is called.” He needed toughness, because the man who joined from Schalke had long been a red rag for many Bayern fans – and then he became a villain for Schalke fans too. In the first duel against his old club he was booed by both sides – a bizarre drama. With typical Westphalian placidness he shut it all out, went 1,147 minutes without conceding a goal in his first season, a record for FC Bayern, won the treble in the second season, and was a World Cup winner in his third. No one laid down the benchmark for goalkeeping the way he did. For all his attachment to the Ruhr region, his home, the five-time World’s Best Goalkeeper has become a Bavarian at heart, owner of a house on Tegernsee and a tavern in the Schliersee Mountains.

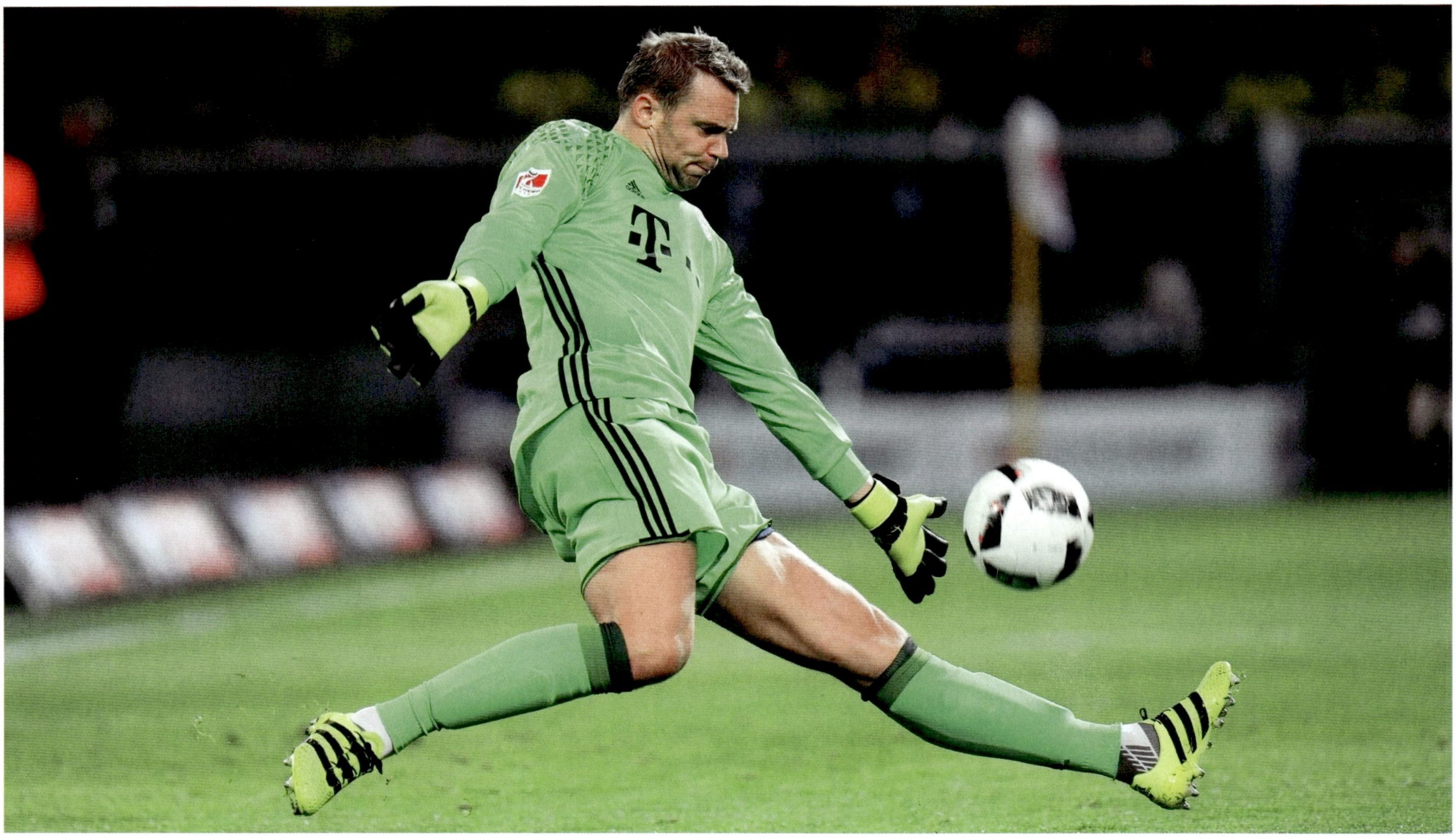

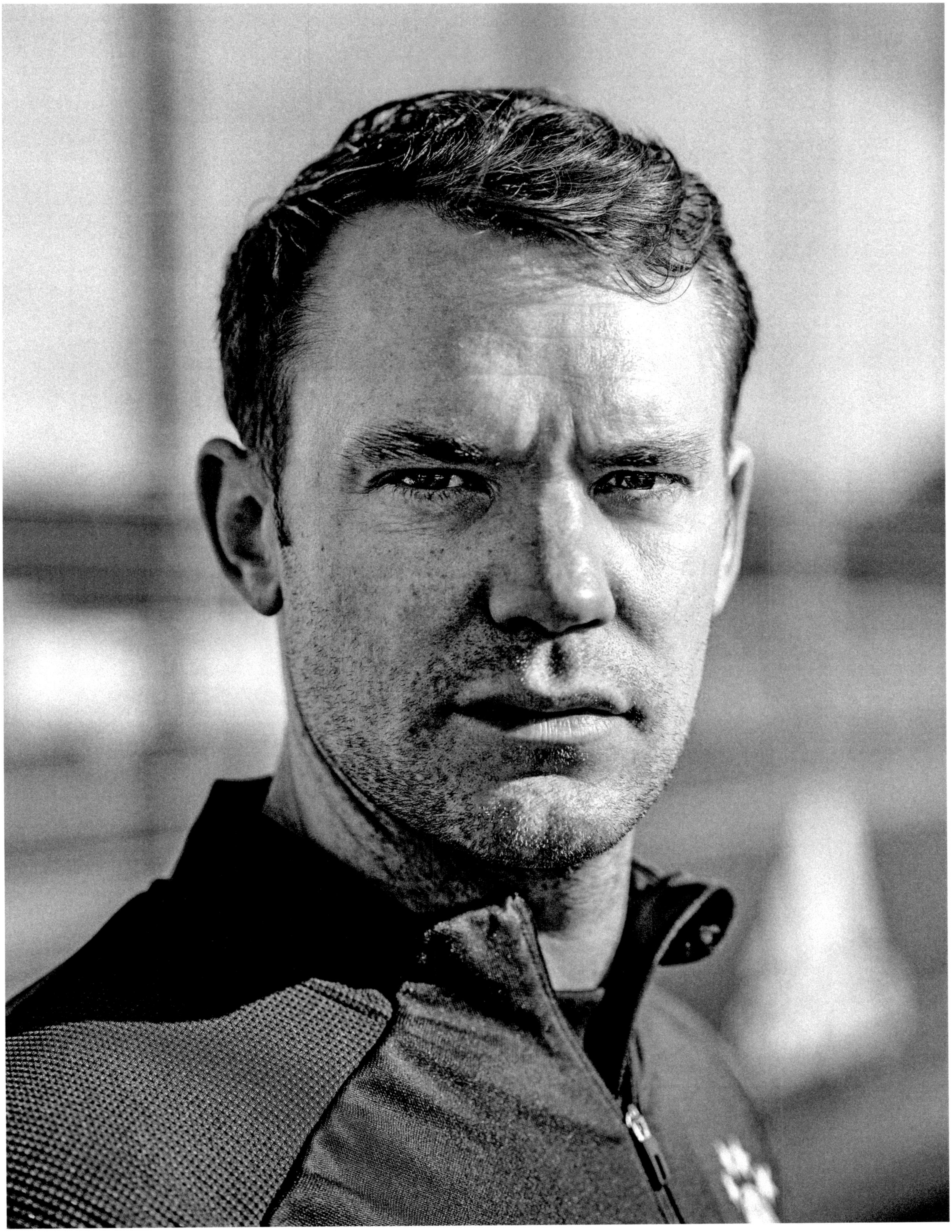

KONRAD **HEIDKAMP**

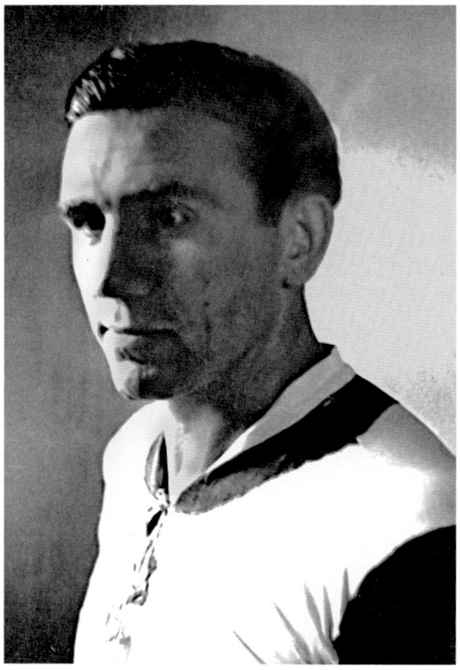

He captained the first team that won the German championship – and held together not only the defence, but the whole club in tough times.

Ludwig Hofmann, FCB's left-winger, who had a fine touch on the ball and crossed it well, was nominated for the Olympic Games in 1928. But he also had an eye for the art of defending, and during the Olympic Games in Amsterdam persuaded the Düsseldorf defender Konrad Heidkamp to come to Munich – and so played a decisive part in winning the championship in 1932, even though an injury meant that he was a spectator for the final. Captain Heidkamp put down the shutters at the back, and FCB beat Eintracht Frankfurt 2–0. Whereas Hofmann died of meningitis three years later, Heidkamp became a legend at the club. In the role of coach he kept the team together until 1945 and supplied food to the players so that they stayed with FCB. "If there had been no Conny Heidkamp", said Siegfried Herrmann, the former head of Bayern youth and vice-president, "FC Bayern would no longer exist."

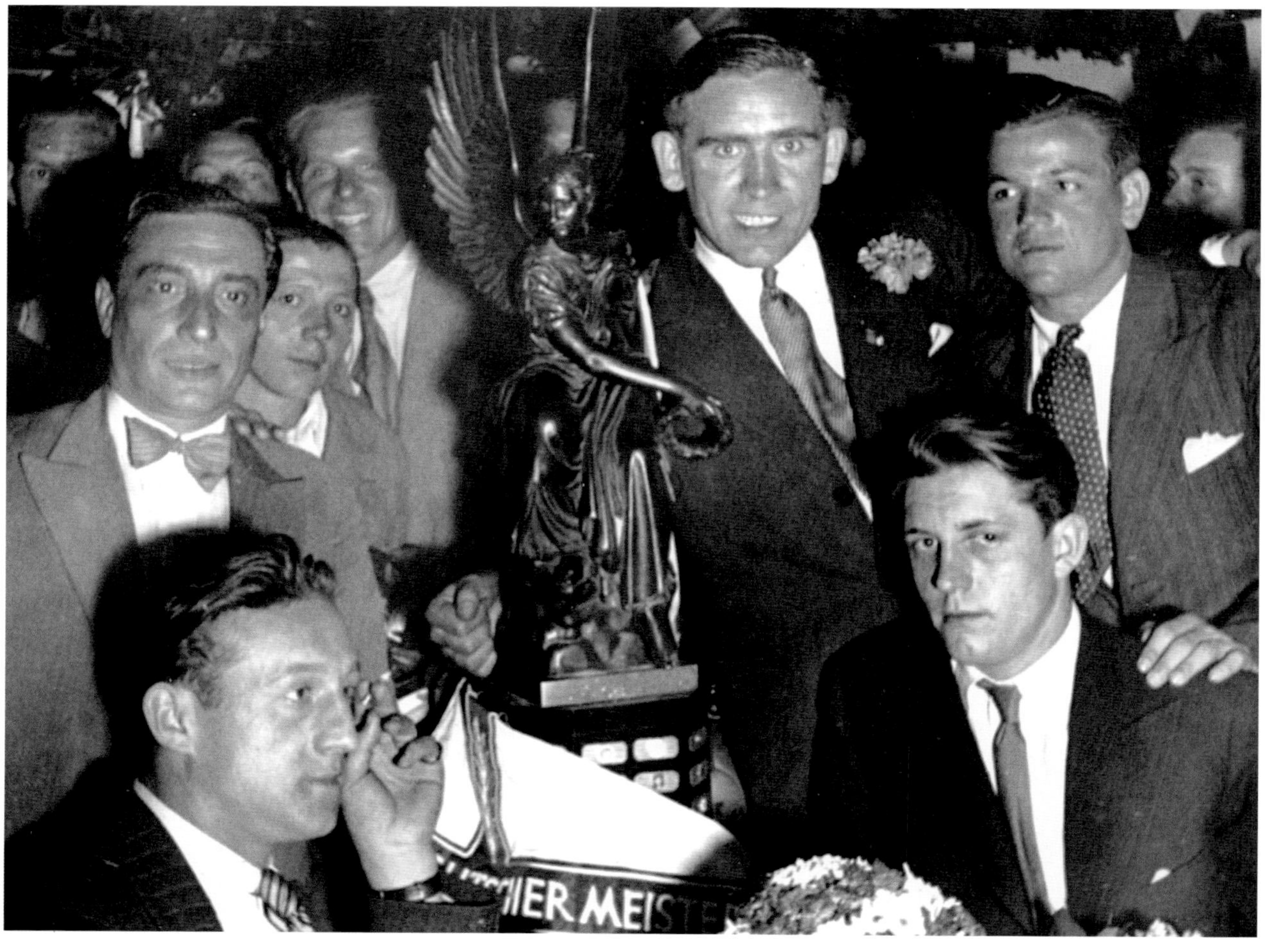

There she is: Viktoria, the championship trophy, weighing 24.6 kilos, at the banquet in 1932, between captain Conny Heidkamp and coach Richard Dombi (with a bow tie). Viktoria spent the night in bed with the club president, Kurt Landauer, and went to Düsseldorf a year later: no man was allowed to keep her. Heidkamp and his wife Magdalena brought the other pre-war trophies won by FCB through the war by taking them out of the bombed inner city of Munich to a farmer in Ascholding, where they were buried in the woods.

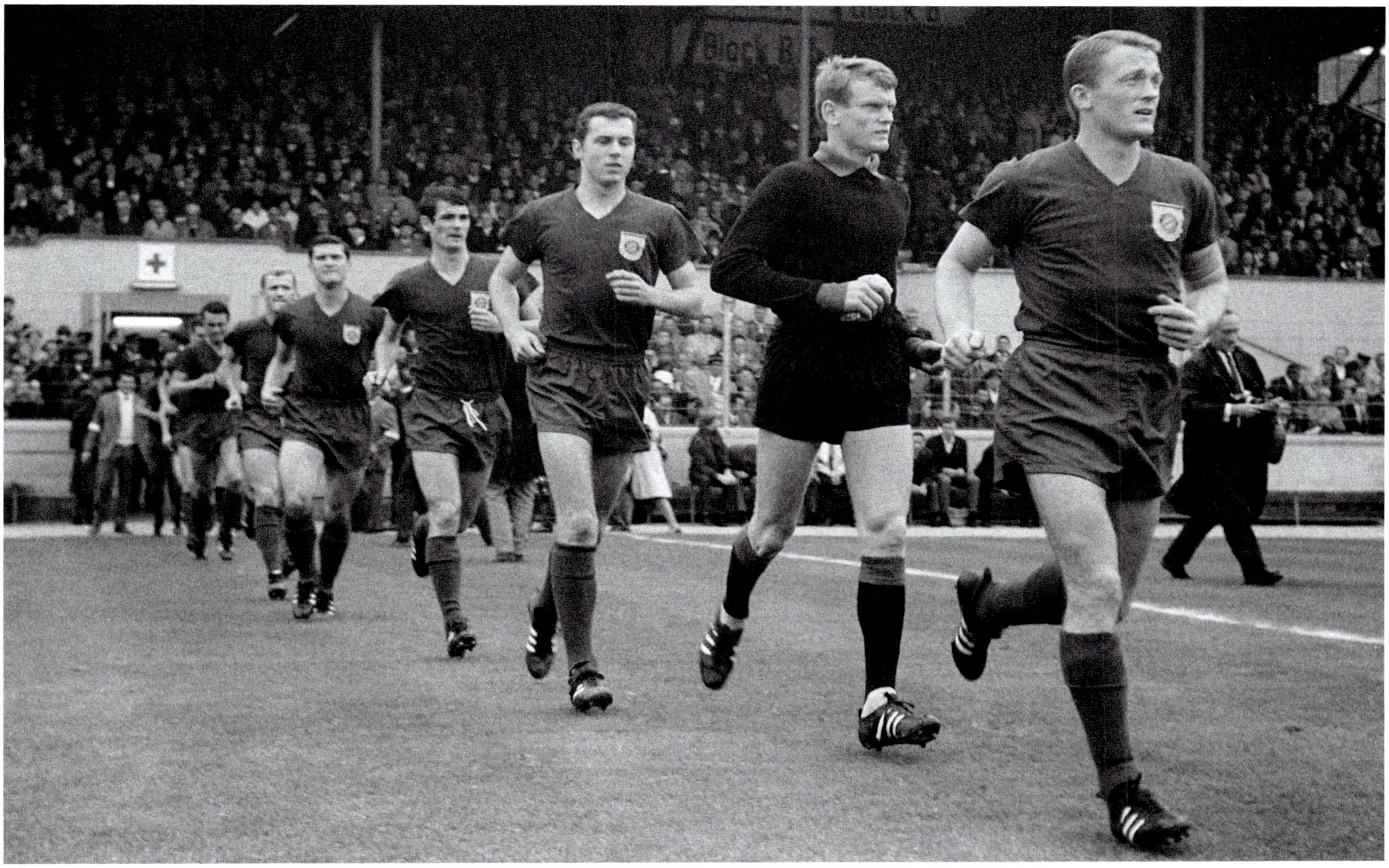

WERNER **OLK**

In 143 of his 144 Bundesliga matches, Werner Olk led the FCB team onto the pitch. The exception was his first game, when he took over the captain's armband from the injured Adi Kunstwadl.

He was such a strong jumper that they called him "the eagle of Giesing" – and he led as FCB soared high to the summit of German football.

For lack of money to buy football boots, the young eagle's career started out barefoot on dirt pitches. A stubborn defender, soon in demand, he went to FCB because the club was able to provide him with the university place that he coveted. Werner Olk was a stroke of good fortune – even as a caretaker goalkeeper, keeping a clean sheet in 1961 against 1. FC Nürnberg for eighty-seven minutes. But above all as captain for three wins in the German cup final, the European Cup in 1967 and the championship in 1969. Back then in the Swinging Sixties, they knew how to party. On returning from away games, he often ended up in a pub near the central station, where the landlord served a drink called "pole-pusher", as Olk reported. The recipe for this magic potion: wheat beer with sparkling wine.

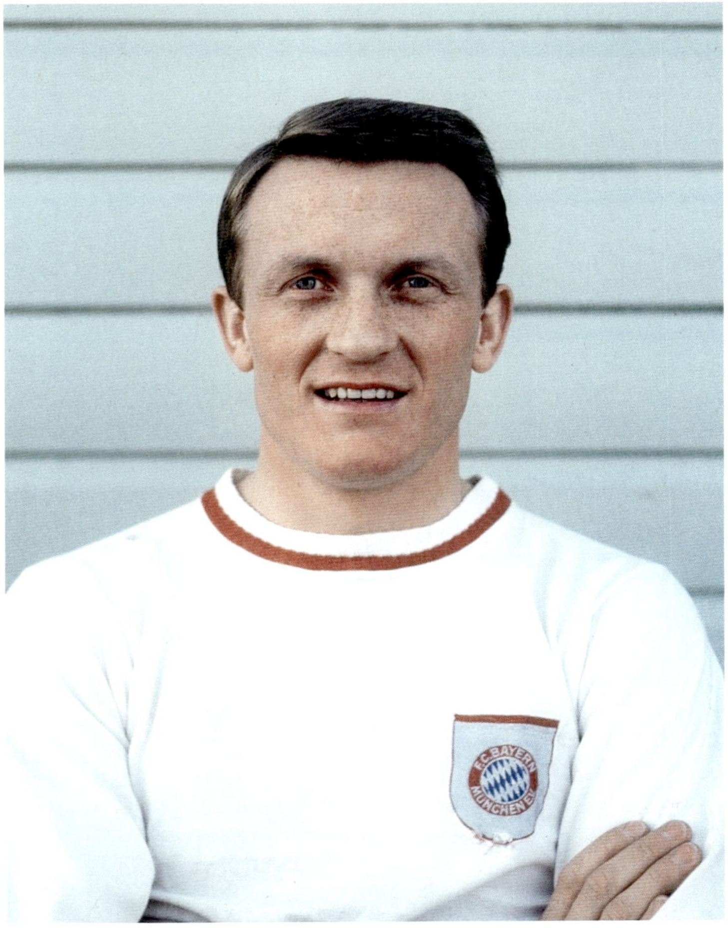

Aged only 20 he was voted "Footballer of the Year", still the youngest ever. The whole world seemed to lie at his feet: Franz Beckenbauer. But to see only his brilliance was to overlook something else: his devotion to the team, his willingness to lead, through his presence, his aura even. And his fighting spirit, too - something that was less immediately apparent in this most elegant of all players than with bruisers at the back. He was both things: Kaiser and warrior.

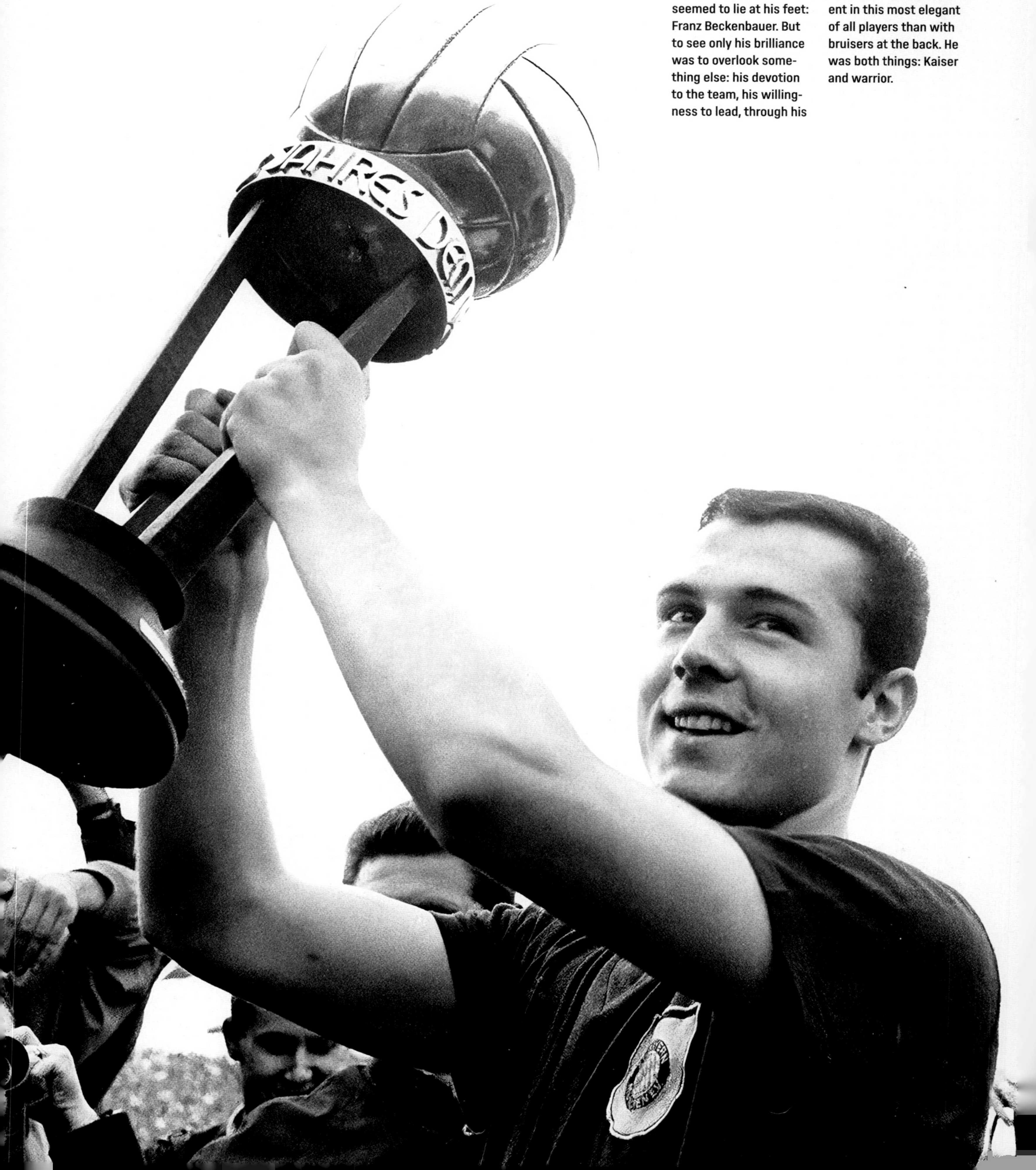

FRANZ **BECKENBAUER**

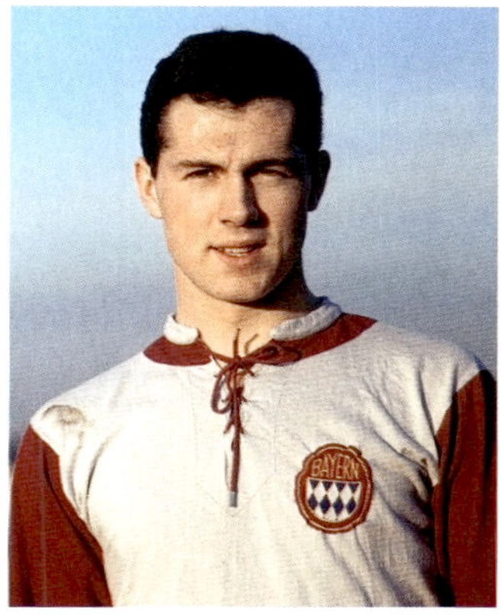

Today, if you watch old films, it still seems incomparable: this lightness of touch! How he glided, almost floated through midfield, the ball at his feet, head held high, seeing space, finding gaps, like a sleepwalker. A once-in-a-century player, from the very start.

Yet he was not only an aesthete, not just an artist; he was also a matchwinner and a team player. Udo Lattek, who coached two of the greatest, said, "Maradona was the best footballer, but an individualist. Beckenbauer was the best strategist – and a team player." But as an 18-year-old he had to prove this to his first coach. Čik Čajkovski raged, "You made of whipped cream. You no fighter. You like a straw." And at a meal in the Salvatorkeller, according to Beckenbauer, "he personally carried double portions to my table". The slim young man was successfully beefed up to become a global star. With FCB and the German national team he won everything that was there to be won. And in 1990, when he coached the world champions, to Uli Hoeness this was proof "that he can walk on water in football". Or walk on wheat beer when, in celebrating winning the championship in 1994, he kicked the ball from a beer glass into its target, a hole in a screen on the *Sportstudio* TV programme. At that time he was the Bayern coach, and remained so two years later when winning the UEFA Cup, in the position of club president at the same time.

He had it all: a genius on the field, a child of fortune as a coach, and a person who charmed and won over other people. And the public sphere always claimed him. In his last years he withdrew from the limelight, disappointed at how he was treated in public for his role in bringing the World Cup to Germany in 2006, and shattered by the death of his son Stephan, a youth coach at FCB, who died of a brain tumour at the age of 46. It was almost too much for the life of one man. Beyond his death he remains the "Kaiser", a footballer like no other.

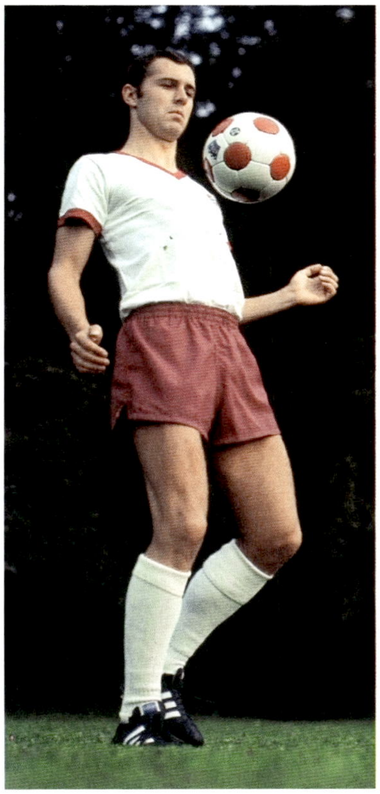

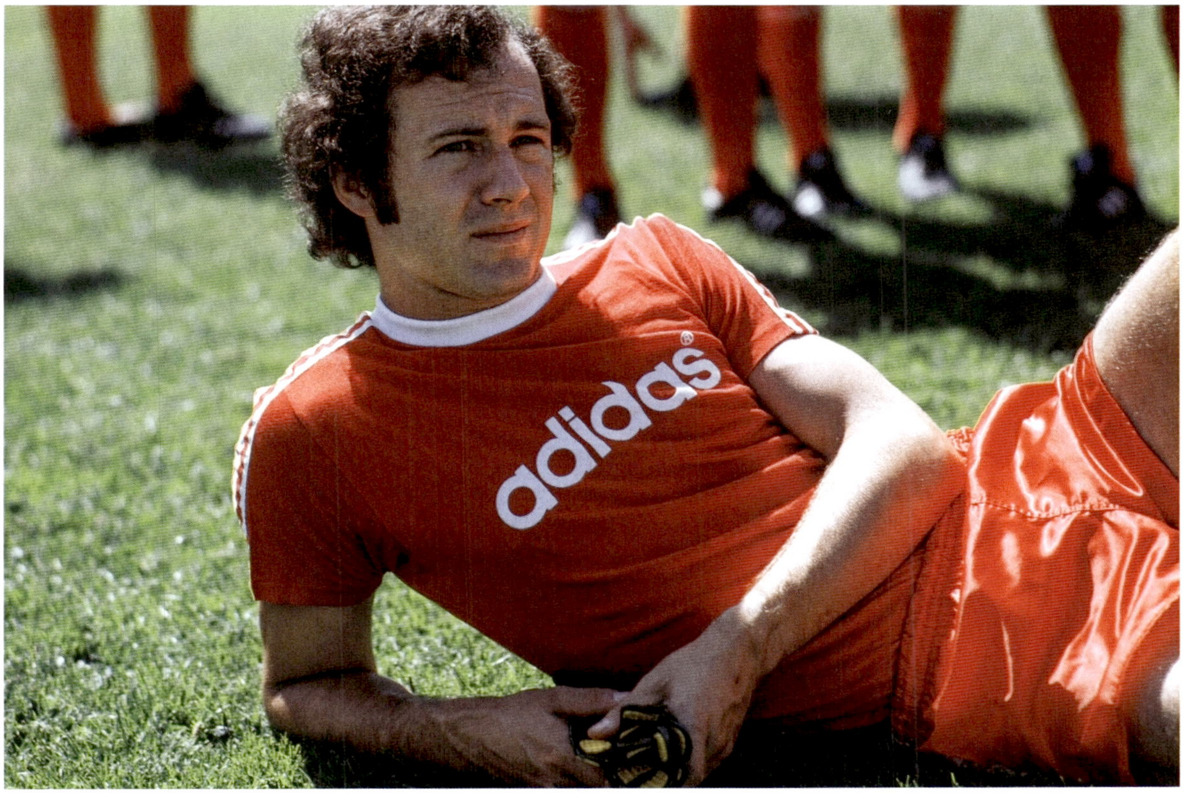

HANS-GEORG "KATSCHE" **SCHWARZENBECK**

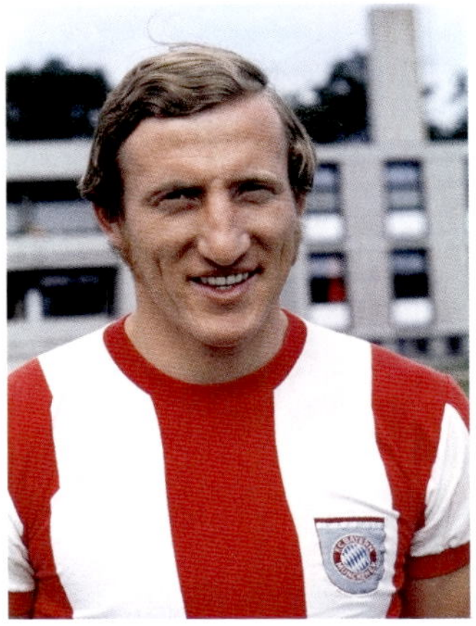

Aged only 19, he nullified Uwe Seeler in the 1967 cup final, and FCB won 4–0 against Hamburger SV. The son of an officer at Stadelheim Prison, for the next fifteen years he served the Bavarian cause by keeping opposing forwards in solitary confinement. And he scored a goal that he still has to talk about – for which he needs no more than ten words.

Even back in the days when football stars still came from the neighbourhood, nobody was living as close to FC Bayern as "Katsche". The football pitches on Säbener Strasse were in sight from his parents' home. He only ever played for FCB, from the C youth to the veterans' team. After retiring from football, he ran a stationery shop in Munich's Au for twenty-eight years, and as a pensioner still provided office supplies to FC Bayern.

He gained winner's medals in the World Cup, the European Nations Cup, the European Cup, and always played the supporting role without complaint alongside the great Beckenbauer – an unbeatable duo who could hardly have been more different. "A good combination", says Schwarzenbeck. "We had a perfect understanding." The brilliant libero and the dedicated ball-winner who covered his back – and once took the starring role himself, with a goal against Atlético in 1974 that he has described again and again since that day. He usually tells is as straight as the shot itself: "The ball went through them all, and it was in."

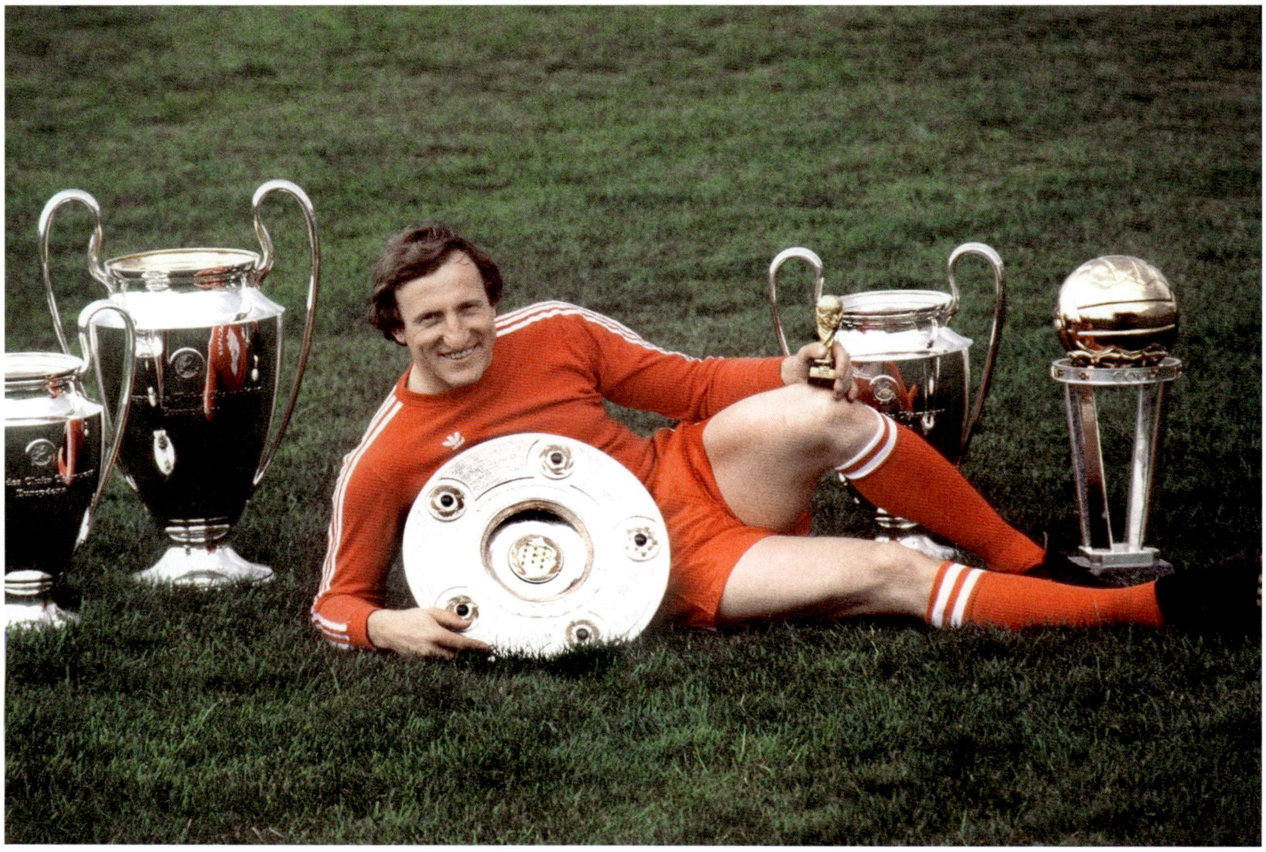

Not until his 119th match in the Bayern squad did Katsche Schwarzenbeck discover the delights of goalscoring - in 1969 in Aachen. In the 1973-74 season at the latest, when he scored seven times in the Bundesliga, more than Franz Beckenbauer ever scored in a season, Atlético might have been warned. But they weren't - otherwise one of the three beautiful cups on Katsche's patch of grass would be in Madrid today instead of in Munich.

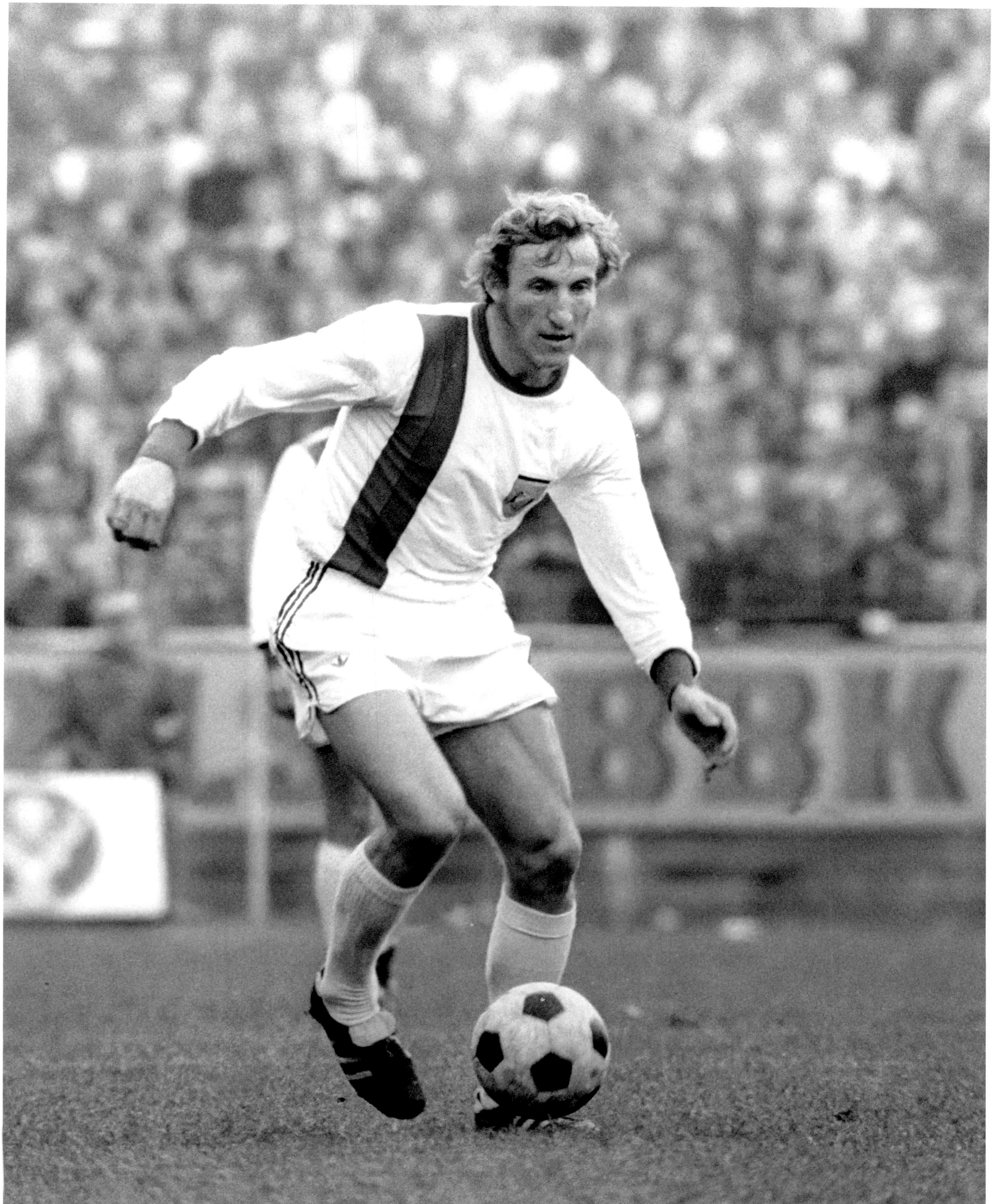

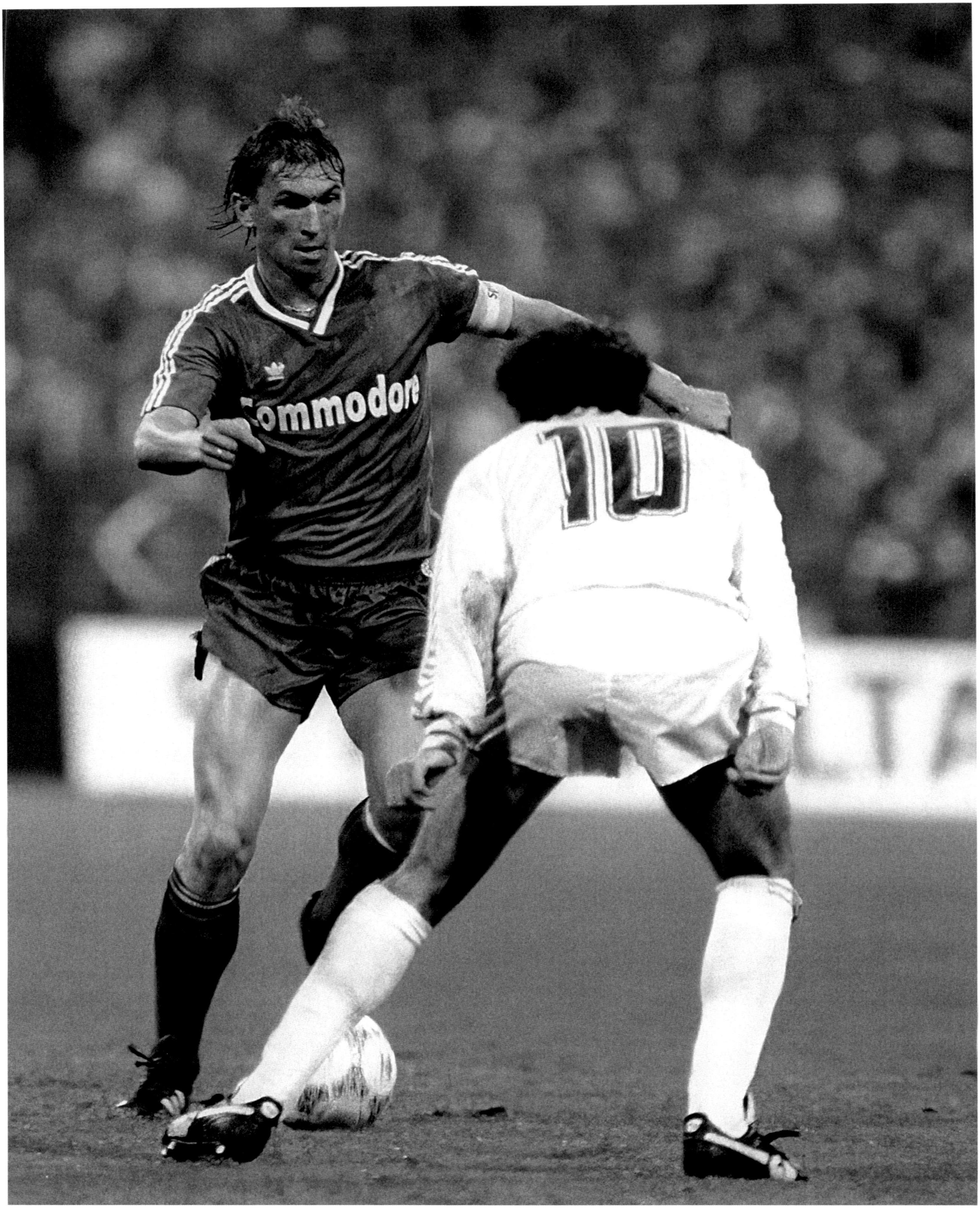
ommodore
10

KLAUS **AUGENTHALER**

After his farewell match he first of all lit a cigarette on his lap of honour in a cabriolet and ordered a wheat beer – in front of the Südkurve fans, who were celebrating their World Cup-winning "Auge".

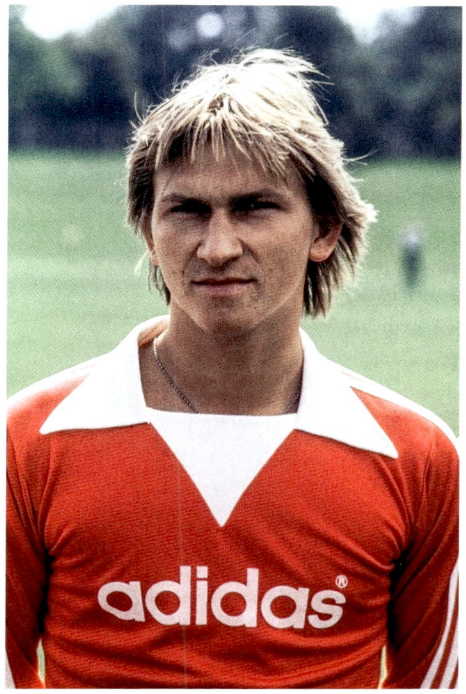

He witnessed Katsche Schwarzenbeck's legendary goal against Atlético in 1974 as a fan in Brussels. Weeks later, he went for a trial at FCB, and they took him on. It was a tough school for a teenager from Lower Bavaria. After his first game with Augenthaler, Beckenbauer complained, "I don't ever want to play with that blind man again." Bulle Roth flattened him in a training session, and Jupp Kapellmann hissed, "Go back where you came from." The assistant trainer Werner Olk made a suggestion: "You must hit back." That's what he did, "then they left me in peace". For the rest of his fifteen years as a Bayern professional, no one ever liked to go into a tackle with Auge. A hard man, a hard shot. "One day", Sepp Maier prophesied, "he'll shoot a cow dead at a hundred metres." In 1989 he took the "goal of the decade" from fifty metres out.

1989, a glorious summer day in Frankfurt. Uwe Bein chases a long ball. Casually Klaus Augenthaler outruns him, swerves round a second Frankfurt player, and trots off undisturbed. Along the way he looks up once, then again, towards the goal, and sees something that he clearly likes. Just short of the halfway line he quite suddenly strikes the ball. From fifty metres it goes over the head of the keeper Uli Stein for a fourth and winning goal. It clinches victory in the first round of the cup, is voted Goal of the Month, then Goal of the Year and Goal of the Decade. All with one single shot.

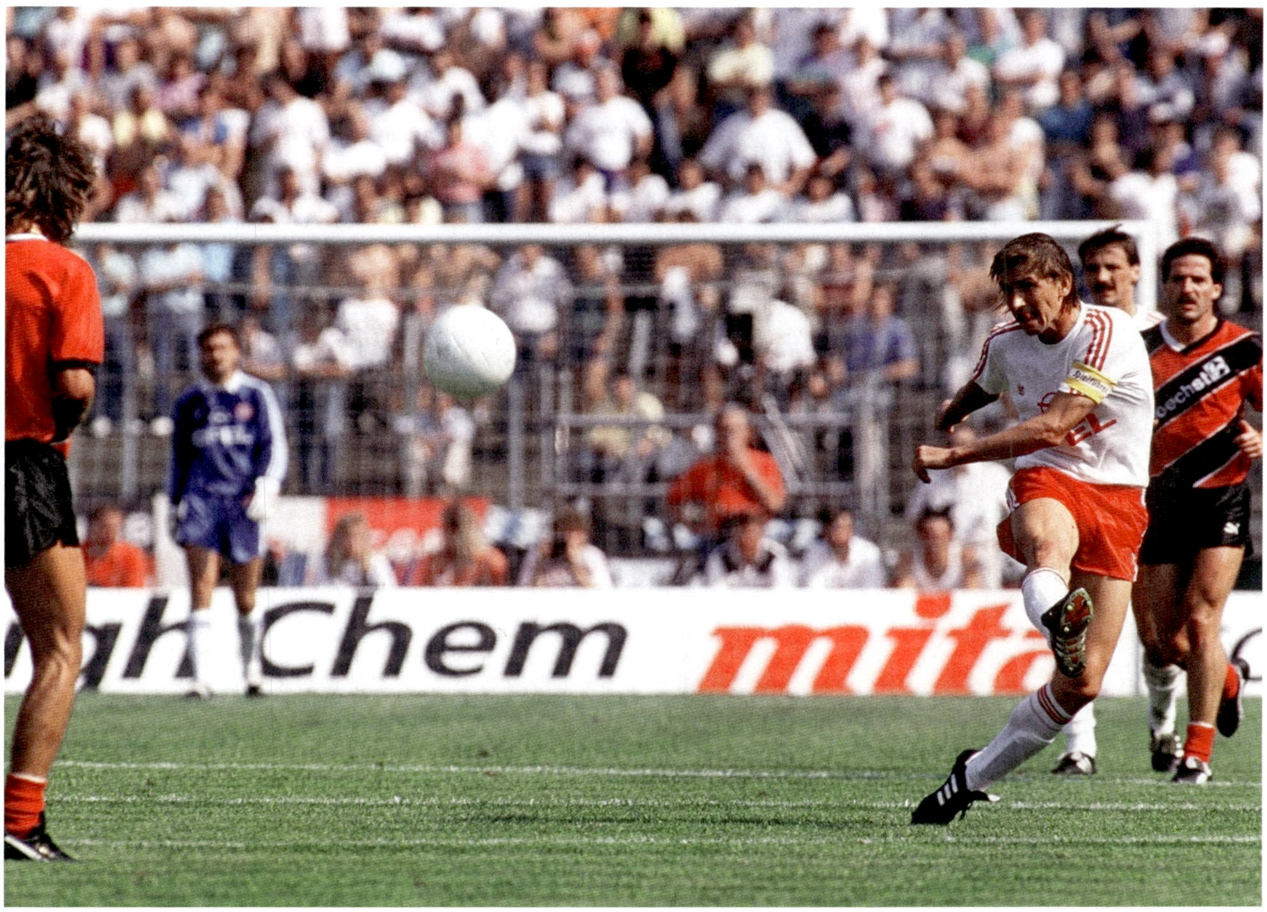

SAMMY **KUFFOUR**

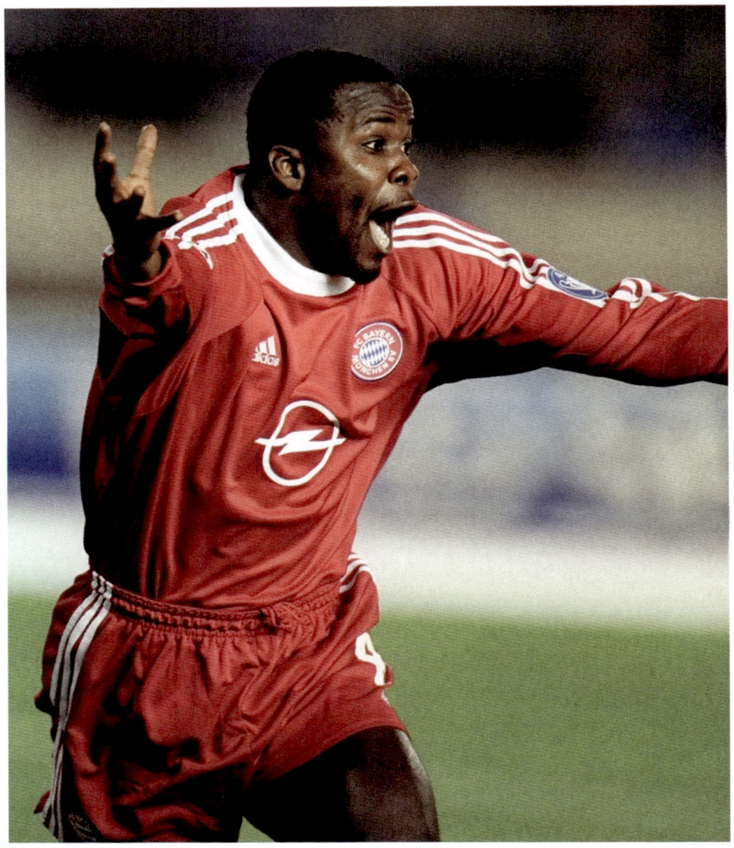

"We want the red-and-white shirt, we want the red-and-white shirt" – the words rang out across the Marienplatz square, the crowd joined in, and at the age of just 22 a club icon was born.

Hermann Gerland had discovered him at the under-16 World Cup in Australia, but was blocked by Uli Hoeness several times. He thought $500,000 was too much for a 16-year-old. Then Gerland said, "Uli, I'll go to the bank. If I get the money, I'll buy him. But then I want it back again afterwards." This persuaded Hoeness to change his mind. Kuffour arrived, and at 17 made the transition from Gerland's youth A-team to the professionals. After the dramatic final against Manchester United his tears would have melted a stone. After victory against Valencia, he grinned for days on end. And his singing on the balcony of city hall sealed the status of the beaming player from Ghana as a darling of the fans. FCB said he could not be sold, and so he stayed for more than ten years. And today he still calls Hermann Gerland "Papa".

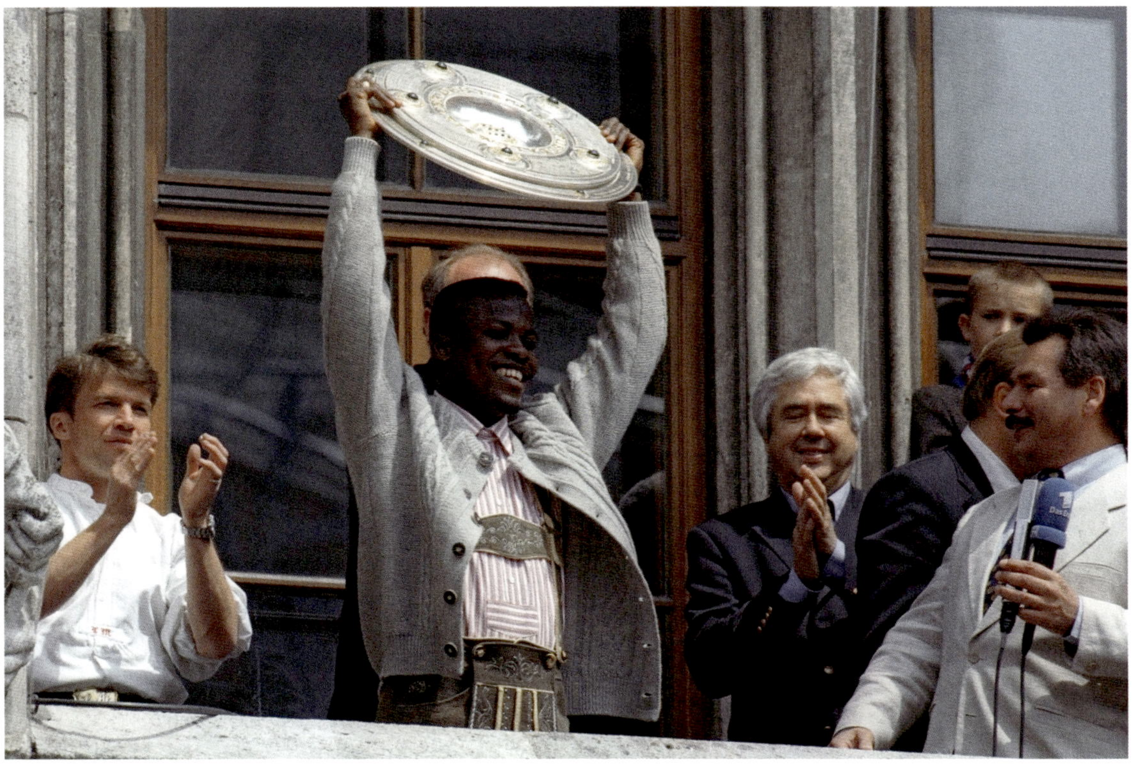

Left: He was the first African player to wear the kit of FC Bayern - and the first one to hold the trophy while wearing lederhosen. Whereas a veteran star from Ghana named Abedi Pele joined a different Munich club in 1996, wrongly thinking he had come to FCB, the young Ghanaian star Sammy Kuffour signed for the real FCB and celebrated his first championship medal at the end of the season. Five more followed, as well as the Champions League in 2001 and the Club World Cup, when he scored the winning goal (above).

Right: No number on his back here? Well, Bixente Lizarazu always had a six-pack at the front. "Liza" is considered one of the fittest players in the history of FC Bayern.

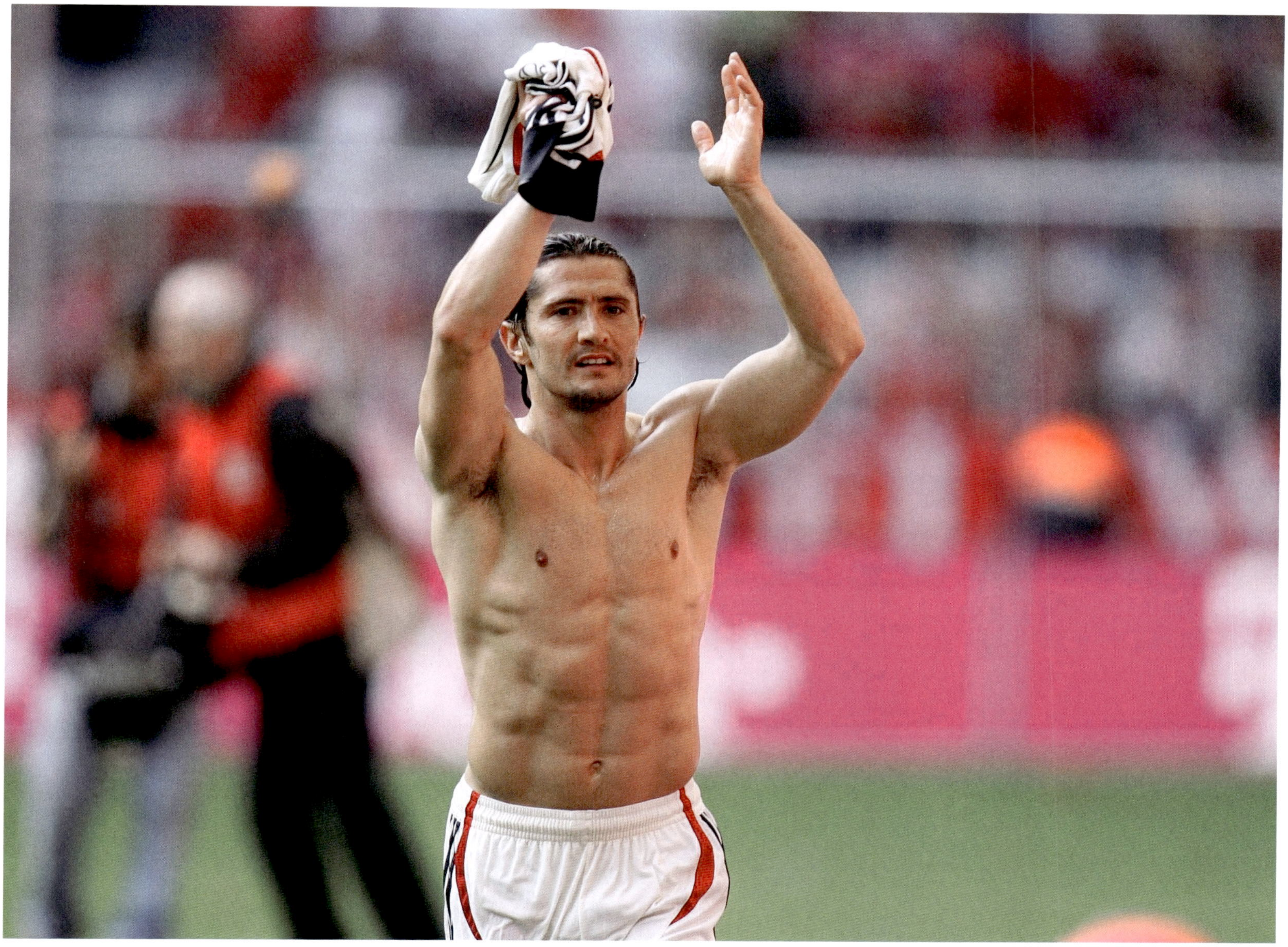

No one messes with a battling Basque. As Lothar Matthäus realised at the training ground in 1999 in a duel of two World Cup winners. He picked a fight with a smaller guy, and took a punch for his pains.

BIXENTE **LIZARAZU**

Ten years later, things could have ended up even worse between Lothar and "Liza" – who was already European champion at Brazilian jiu-jitsu in the veteran category. The hard-tackling Frenchman could be relied on for world-class quality at left back for eight and a half years, until Philipp Lahm took his place. "My life in Munich was football," he says. He won eighteen trophies with Bayern – and became the first footballer to be simultaneously a current holder of World Cup, European Nations Cup, Club World Cup and European Cup medals. As the Club World Cup competition, which Bayern won in 2001 against Boca Juniors, is no longer held, Liza will always be the only one.

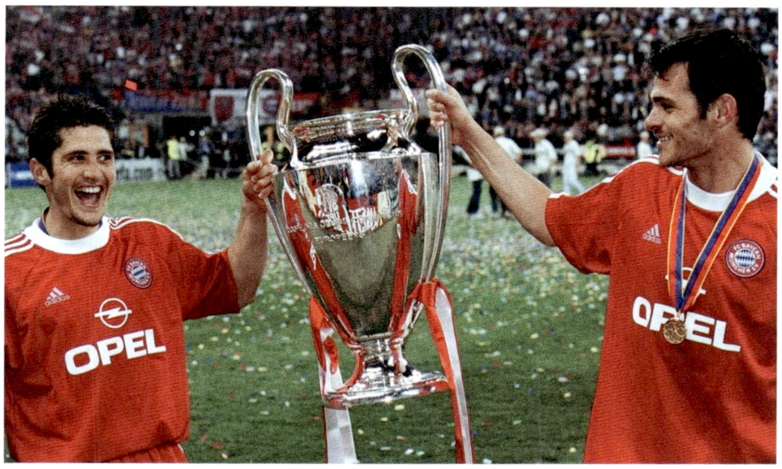

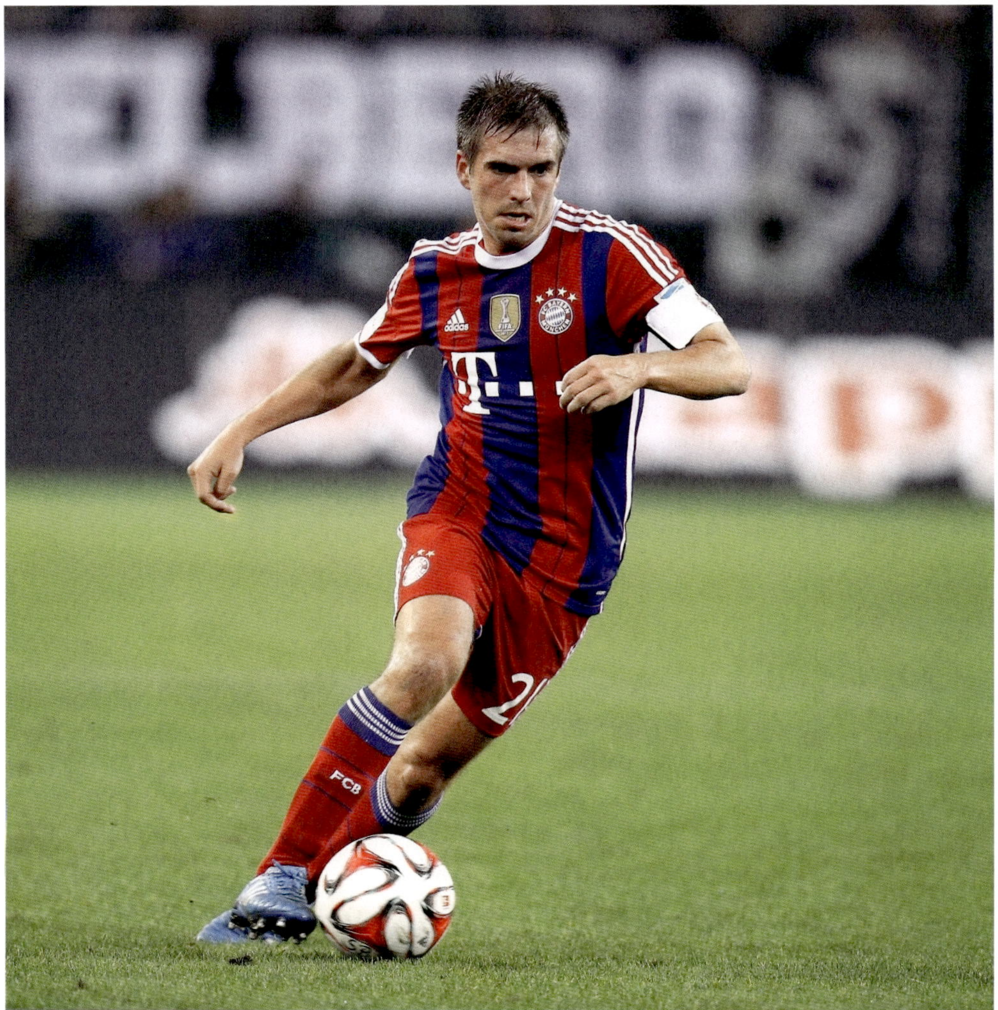

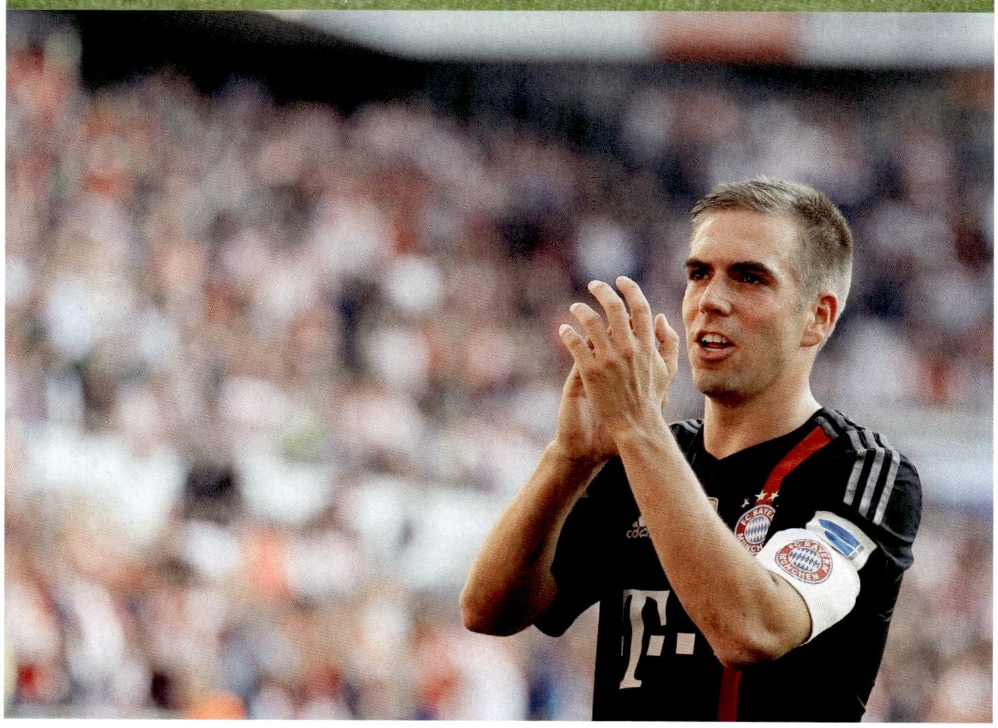

PHILIPP **LAHM**

755 matches as a professional without being sent off, and without suspension for yellow cards – as a defender. No wonder Pep Guardiola called Philipp Lahm "the most intelligent player I have ever seen".

For his model pupil, Hermann Gerland unveiled the greatest praise possible: "Watching him was like eating bratwurst for me." To begin with, however, no Bundesliga club would take him: they said he was too small. It took time to realise that Lahm was a new kind of defender, whose "sharp positional game", as he called it, neutralised his opponents. And if a tackle was needed, the main job had already been done – in the mind. That is why he almost never had to foul, which happened on average just once in every two games.

For the Bayern defence, Lahm was like a Swiss army knife. At times he switched from left to right and back again as often as a speedster on the autobahn. Then he wanted to stay on the left – but changed to the right after all, because Heynckes wanted to try out David Alaba at left back. Which was then one of the decisive steps in winning the treble. Not everyone noticed, however. In the FIFA World Team line-up of 2013, Lahm was put at left back, to his own surprise – in a position that he had not played all year.

In Philipp Lahm's immaculate career, you need a microscope to detect a serious mishap. One can be found in the cup semi-final against Dortmund in 2015, in the worst ever of the twenty-seven penalty shoot-outs in the history of FCB. Lahm, who was first up, slipped on the spot – and after him Xabi Alonso, normally equally flawless, did the same. Mario Götze's shot was saved by the keeper, and Manuel Neuer hit the bar. The result of the spot kicks: 0-2.

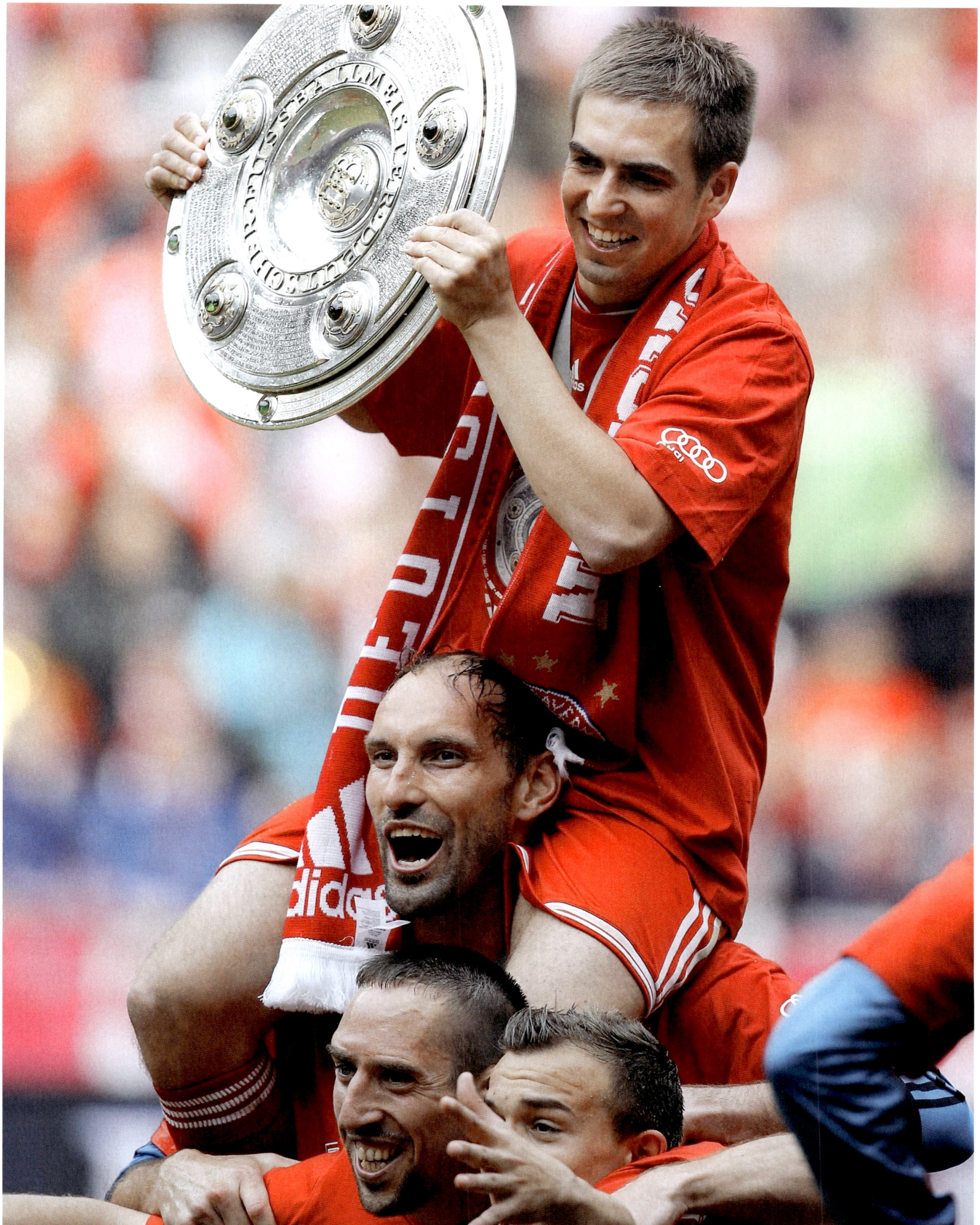

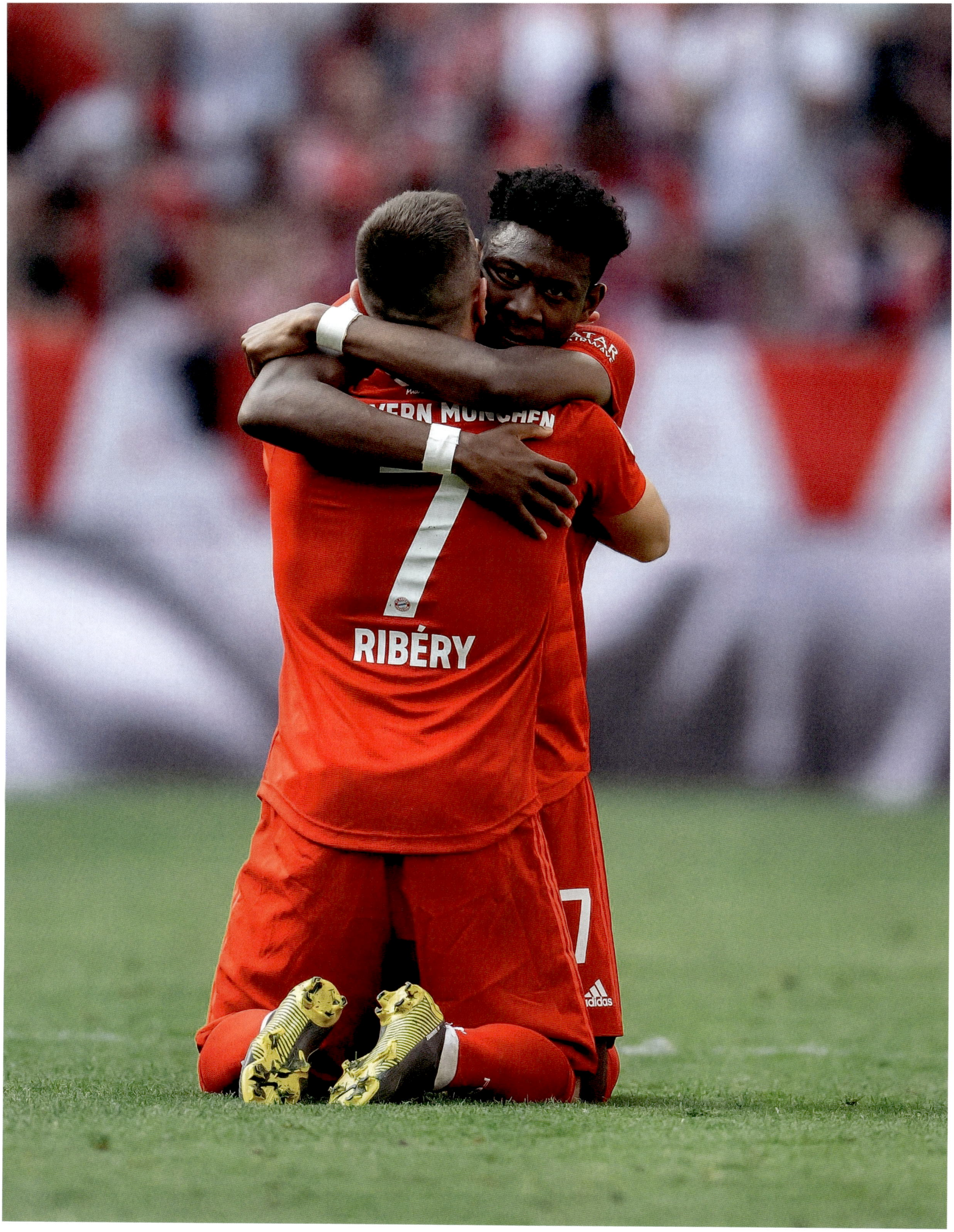
7
RIBÉRY

DAVID **ALABA**

A one-off pairing in the left lane: David Alaba and his "big brother" Franck Ribéry. With whom he loved to make jokes, to go out, and even more to put on a show with the ball. And to whom, fortunately, he listened, back then in Ribéry's Ferrari.

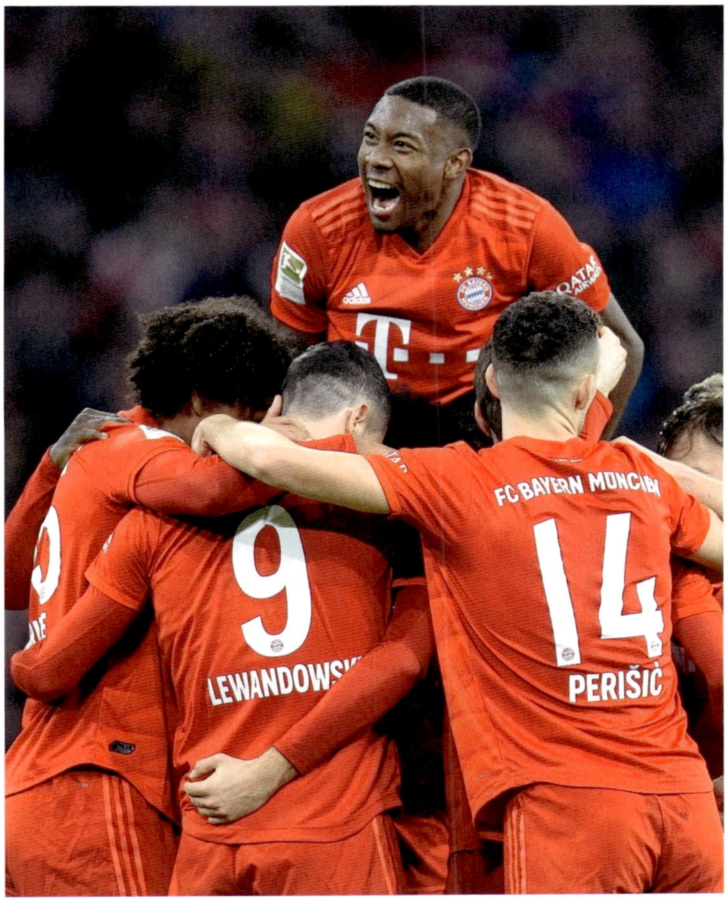

The Frenchman once picked up 16-year-old David, who was still in the Bayern school, with his racer. "As a young kid, you get wide-eyed when suddenly you're sitting next to Franck Ribéry in that kind of car. He noticed that I found this really awesome. So he said: 'David, concentrate on the football. Then the rest will follow.'" Which is exactly how it was. The funny guy from Vienna started to play a grown-up game, but at the same time was "always a young joker", as he admitted. "But I know how to hide it." At 17 he played in the Champions League, then won the first treble as a left back and the second one playing at centre back. In every match and every training session he emanates positive energy, which he explains in these words: "I think I'm always laughing inside when I play".

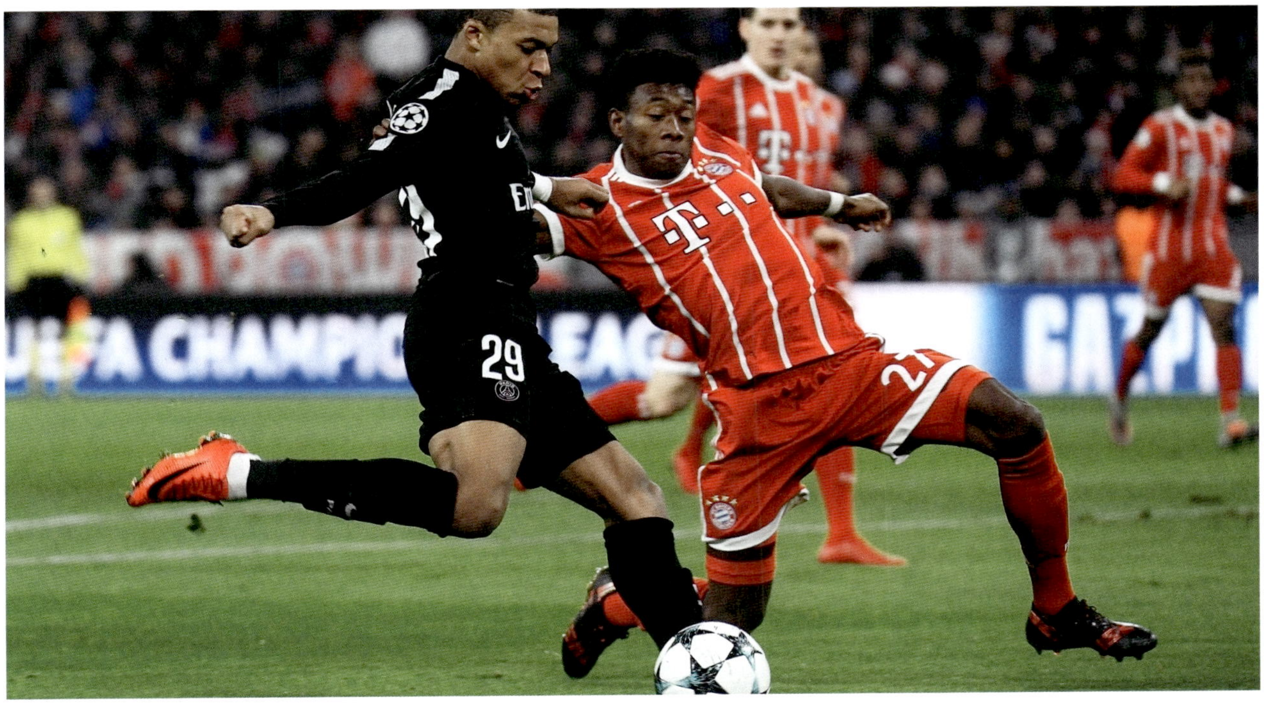

Up against world-class strikers like Kylian Mbappé or politicians like Günter Platter, David Alaba usually came up with a good answer. When Platter, regional president of Tyrol, visited the training camp of the Austrian national team in 2012, he greeted the young Bayern star in English with the words "How do you do?" At which Alaba, born in Vienna, disarmingly replied: "Fine, thanks. You can speak German to me, I'm Austrian."

FRANZ "BULLE" **ROTH**

On the day before a match, it's worthwhile being punctual. "If you didn't arrive on time after the midday rest for coffee at four o'clock, "Bulle" Roth might well have eaten all of the strawberry cake", according to Uli Hoeness. "All of it!"

"That's right", the accused confessed. "Cake was never safe in my presence. Not even on match day. I think I'm the only player who ate two pieces of cake before every Bundesliga game. Not even the coach knew that, only the manager, Schwan." So that is the source of the primeval force that gave this farmer's son from Allgäu the name "Bulle" and made him a regular in a legendary Bayern team for twelve years. He was discovered by the hairdresser Kotter, club member no. 1 at Bayern, who had already recommended the young Gerd Müller. A few weeks later – Bulle was sitting on a tractor – his mother called out "Franz, the phone, a Herr Schwan from FC Bayern." Bulle thought she was making a joke. Schwan told him to come to Munich and sign a contract. One year later, Bulle Roth scored to give FCB its first win in the European Cup.

Beware of the bull: when Roth shot the ball, it was often unstoppable. Especially in European finals. He took part in four of them with FCB, and scored the deciding goal three times: in the Cup Winners' Cup in 1967, and in the European Cup in 1975 and 1976.

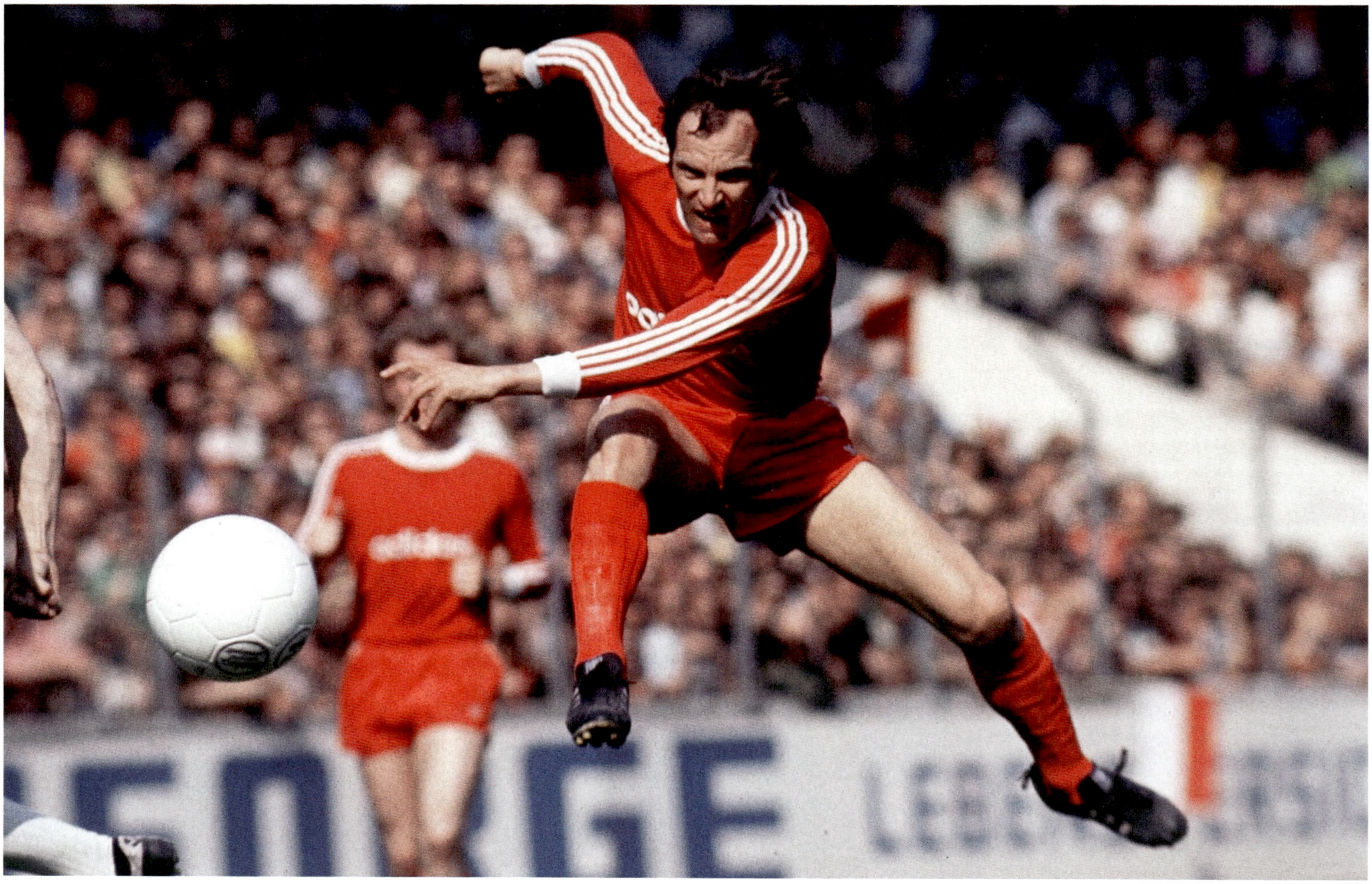

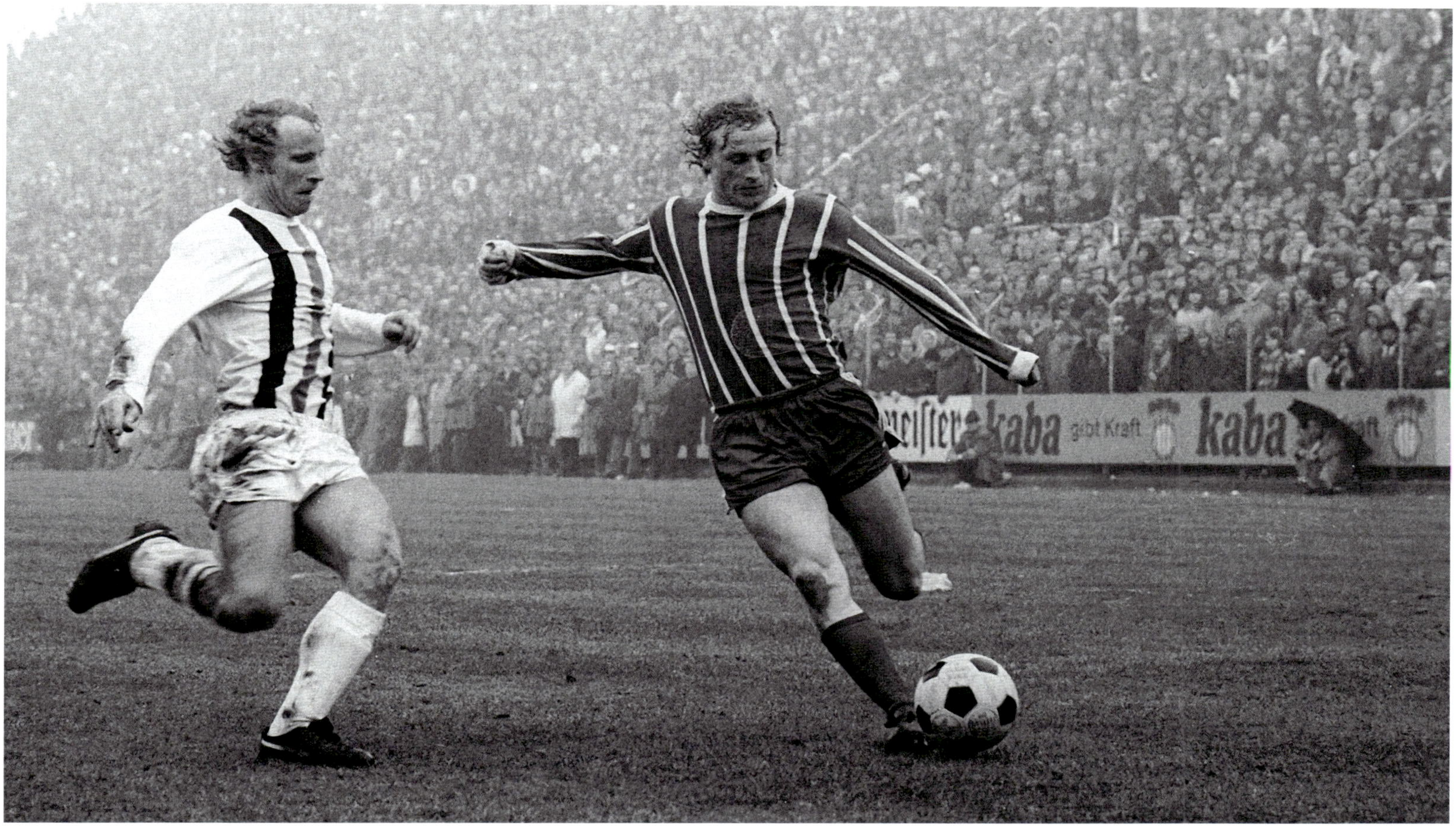

BERND **DÜRNBERGER**

For the club that was close to his heart, Bernd Dürnberger, nicknamed "Wipf" by Gerd Müller, was always committed heart and soul, whether in the Bavarian red and white or the Brazilian blue and yellow. And in 1985, instead of going to the United States to cash in at his career end, he returned to the other club of his heart: SV Kirchanschöring.

Every great team needs one: an agile, busy, reliable player, one who never envies the others who are in the limelight. Here "Wipf" surpassed everyone else – according to "Kalle" Rummenigge he was "the only Bayern player who ever earned more money with sheep's heads than from football".

One of the first songs of the group Sportfreunde Stiller went as follows: "Oh-oh, this is my dream / To be the star / Of my football team". The song is interspersed with clips from interviews with Bernd Dürnberger – who in reality never wished "to be the star". For thirteen years in 375 Bundesliga matches he cleared up at the back and served in a supporting role, never played for his country, and was the only one from the team that won the European Cup in the years 1974 to 1976 who was on the field in the 0–1 defeat against Aston Villa in 1982. Four finals in the top European tournament – a German record that was not surpassed until 2024, by Toni Kroos in his last game for Real Madrid.

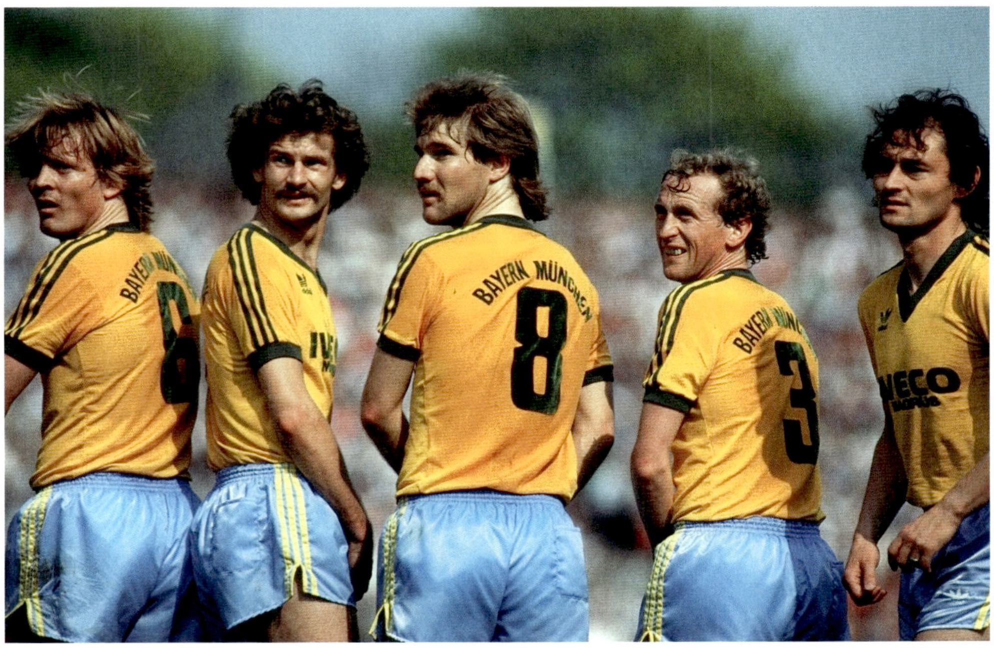

PAUL
BREITNER

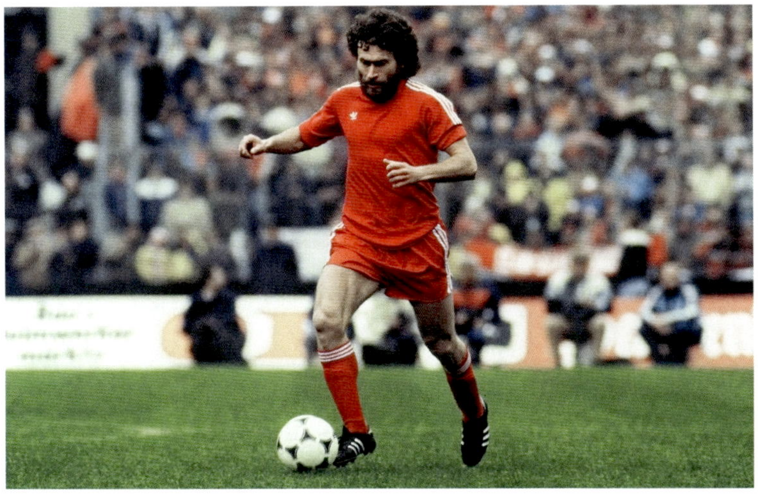

Beckenbauer played himself in *Libero*, and Schwarzenbeck had the role of a postman in *Watch Out When Schwarzenbeck Comes*, but the strangest part in a movie went to Breitner in *Potato Fritz* (aka *Montana Trap*), a German western starring Hardy Krüger.

For the role of Sergeant Stark he did not have to change his outfit, Afro hair and bushy beard, speaking sentences like this in a foreign voice: "Jenkins surely didn't run till he fell down dead just so that he could play the hero." No Bayern professional ever succeeded in as many roles as Paul Breitner. As the wild young full back or as the old "leader of the pack" in the Bayern squad and the World Cup team of 1982. As a revolutionary, anti-hero and maverick. And of course as the spokesman in the revolt against club president Wilhelm Neudecker and his preferred coach, Max Merkel.

Neudecker wanted to get rid of fractious young Breitner, who posed with Chairman Mao's *Little Red Book* in front of a poster of Che Guevara, but the team staged a rebellion. And so it was only after victory in the European Cup in 1974 that Breitner left for Real Madrid. In 1978 his old flatmate Uli Hoeness brought him back to Munich from Eintracht Braunschweig, financing the transfer fee of DM 1.75 million through a deal with the new kit sponsor, Magirus Deutz. With Breitner, success returned: champions in 1980 and 1981, cup winners in 1982. After his return he scored sixty-six goals in 146 league games, a superb record for a midfielder, before hanging up his boots in 1983 – since then he has from time to time slipped into his old role with off-field comments.

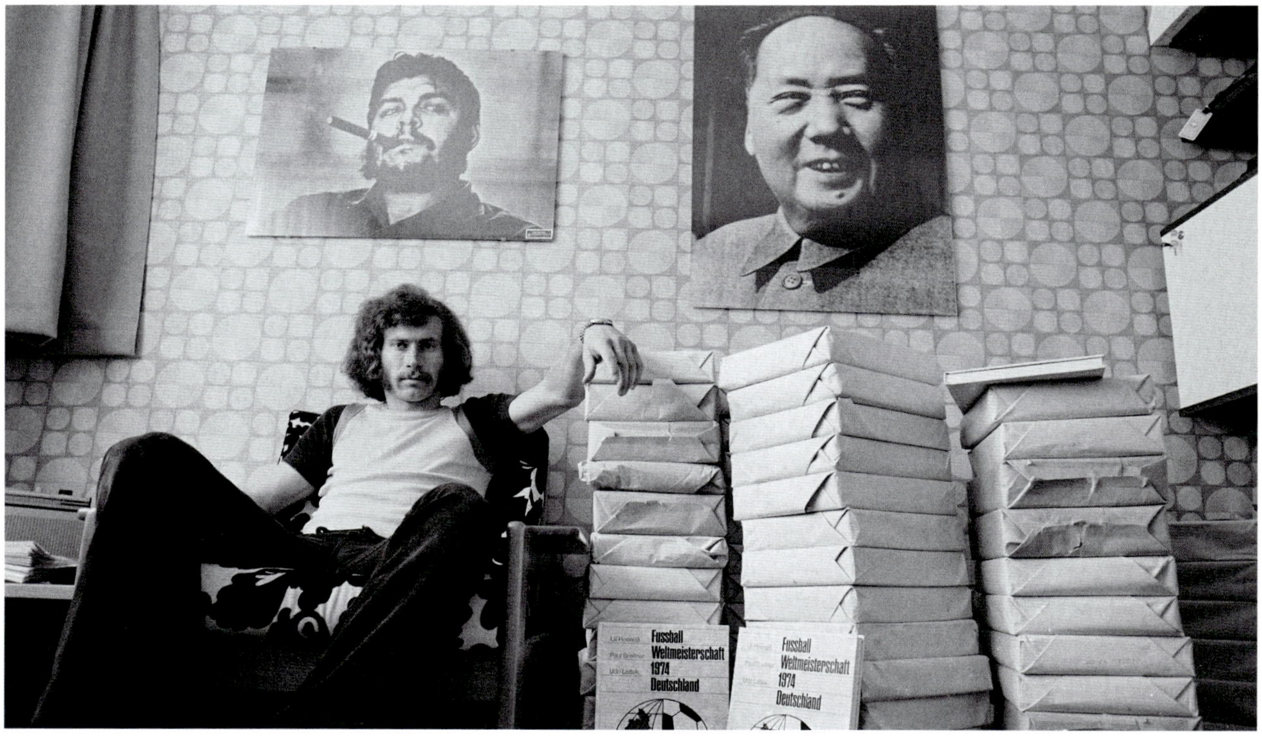

When they won the World Cup in 1974, Paul Breitner and his flatmate Uli Hoeness also set a world record – with an industrial-scale daily production of autographs that were included in their World Cup book, a total of 210,000 signatures. The pile of books may not have matched the print run of Mao's *Little Red Book*, but the two were also in demand to advertise tight-fitting white swimming trunks for a maker of menswear.

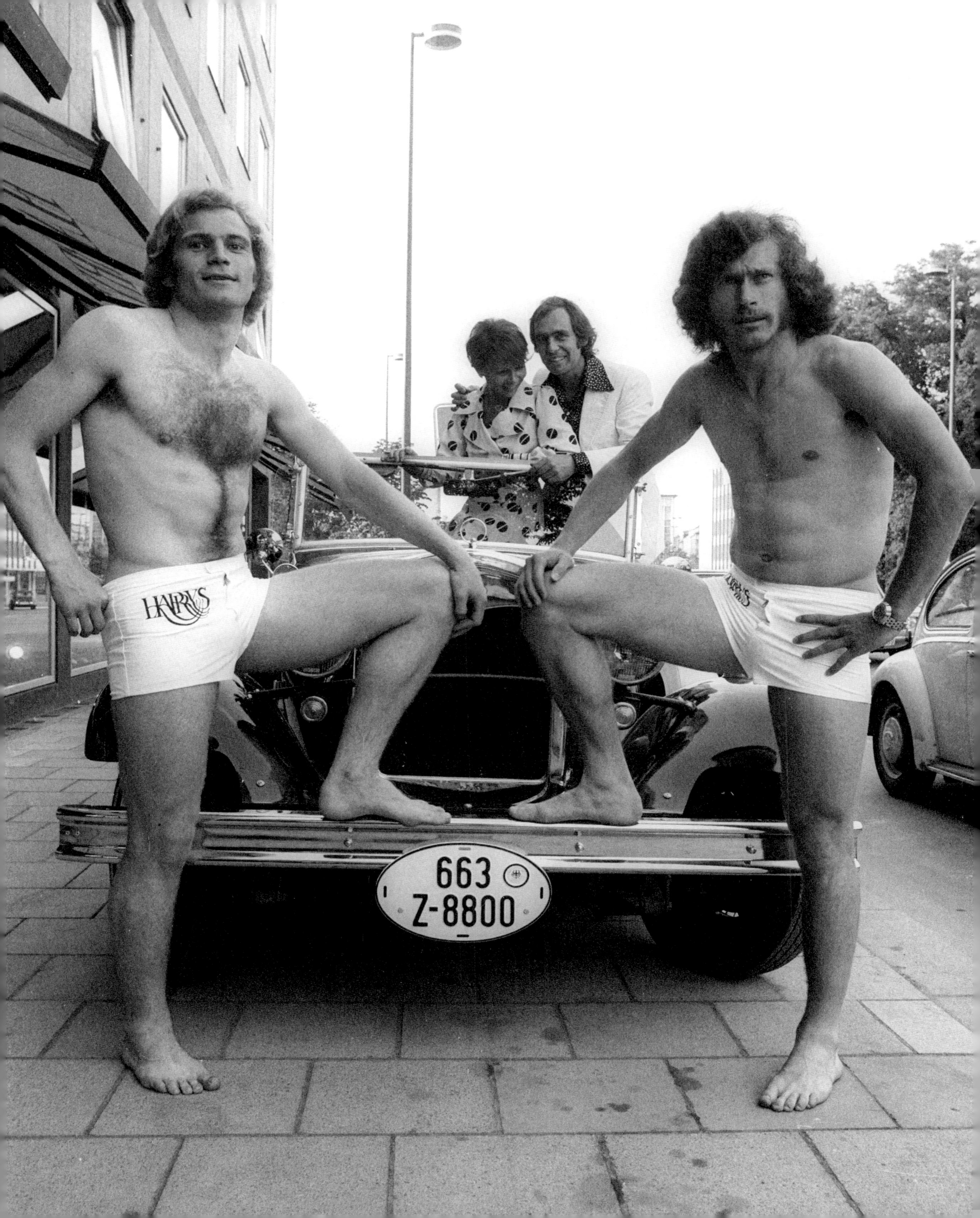
HARRYS
663
Z-8800

LOTHAR MATTHÄUS

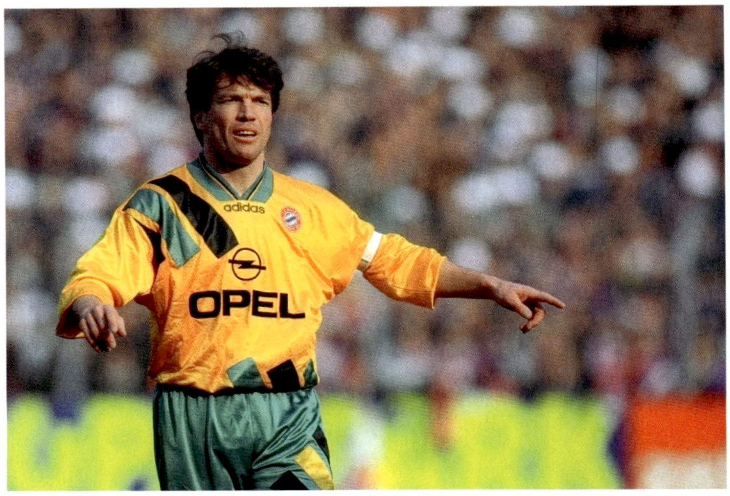

He was one of the most dynamic players that Germany ever produced. In twenty-one years as a professional, twelve of them at FC Bayern, he was a tireless playmaker – and a famous brand of trainers comes from his home town Herzogenaurach.

In his first training session on Säbener Strasse in 1984 he slide-tackled Dieter Hoeness, who came out of it with a torn ligament. Nevertheless, from the very start Matthäus was an asset for FC Bayern, with whom he won seven championship titles, the German cup three times and the UEFA Cup in 1996. During his four years at Inter Milan he captained the German national team to a World Cup victory in 1990 and was twice voted World Footballer of the Year. In 1992, now a global star, he returned to Munich and a few months later scored the Goal of the Year in Leverkusen when Mehmet Scholl hit a corner to the rear and Matthäus volleyed it under the crossbar. As a 38-year-old Methuselah of football he was selected as Footballer of the Year one more time, and was still so important to FC Bayern that he postponed his planned transfer to the US league for two months in early 2000 so that he could take part in the fixtures against Real Madrid in the second round of the Champions League. With Matthäus, FCB won 4–2 in the Bernabéu, then 4–1 in the Olympic Stadium (and without Matthäus were knocked out by Real in the semi-final). Later he fell out with Uli Hoeness, who announced that Matthäus would "not even be groundsman" at FCB. But he did just that for a fine photo: on the cover of the Bayern magazine *51* he piloted a lawnmower through the Allianz Arena.

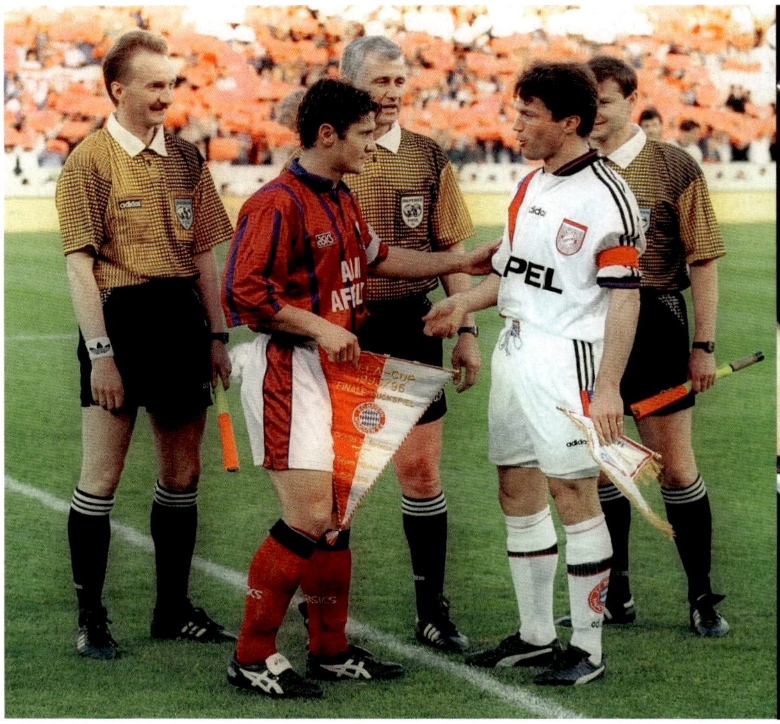

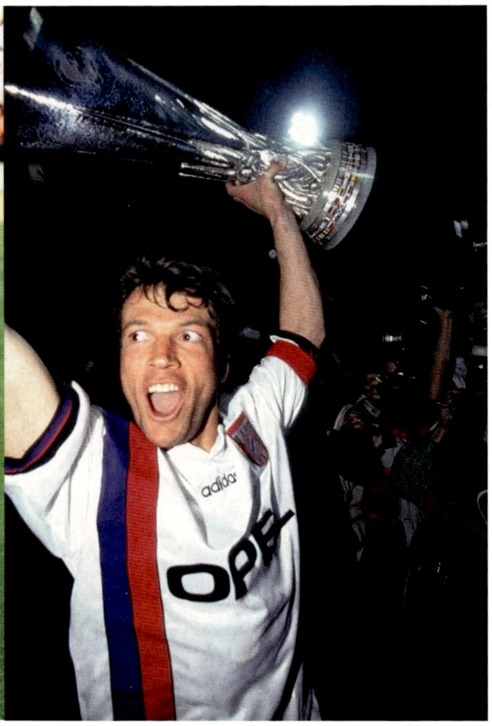

The story of Lothar Matthäus is also a tale of Bayern's kit becoming more and more colourful. In his first cup win in Berlin, against Stuttgart in 1986, he played all in red (covered by his training jacket in the celebration), after returning from Italy often in yellow and green, at the UEFA Cup victory in 1996 in white, and for the drama of 1999 in Barcelona, to match the occasion, in dreary grey.

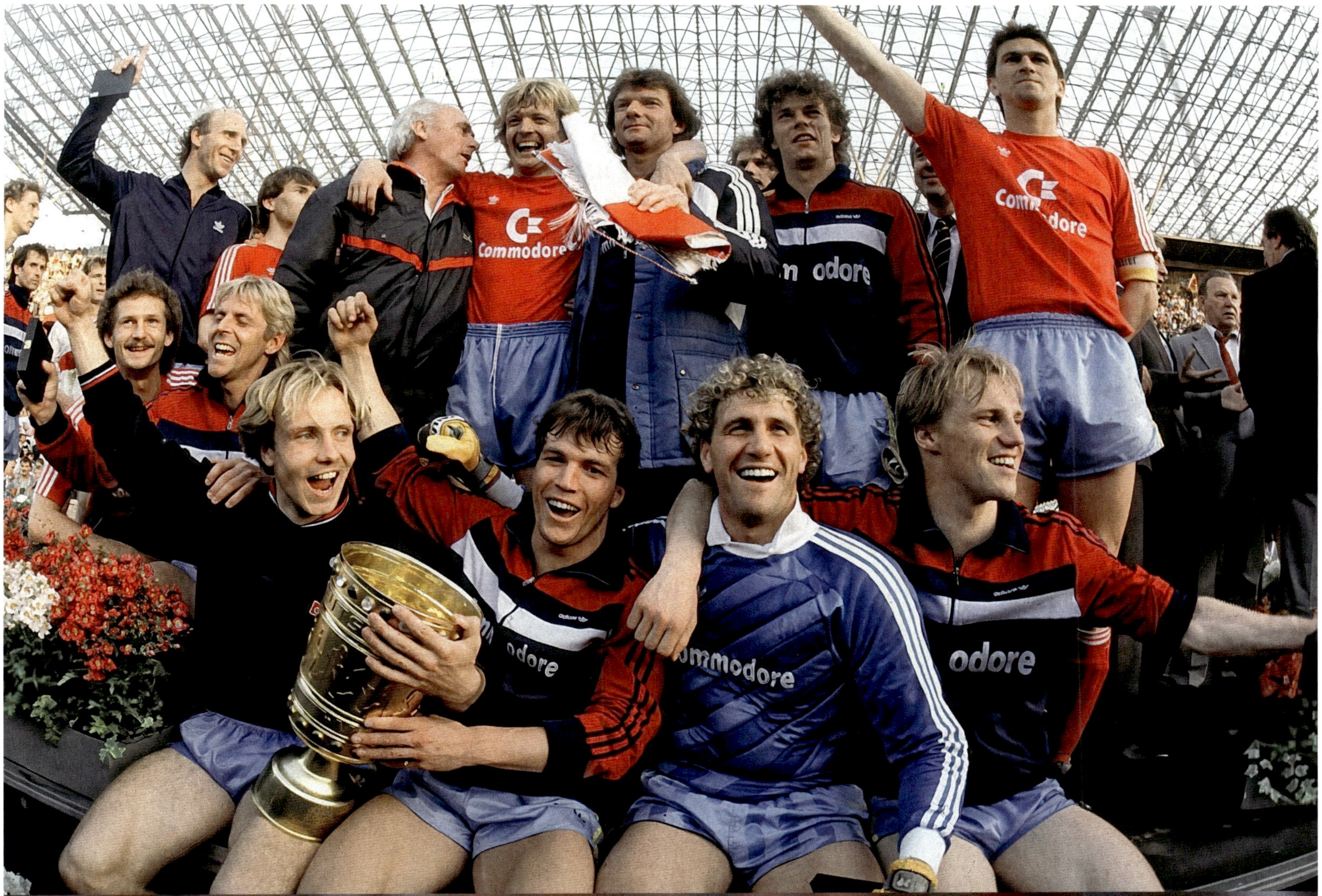
Commodore

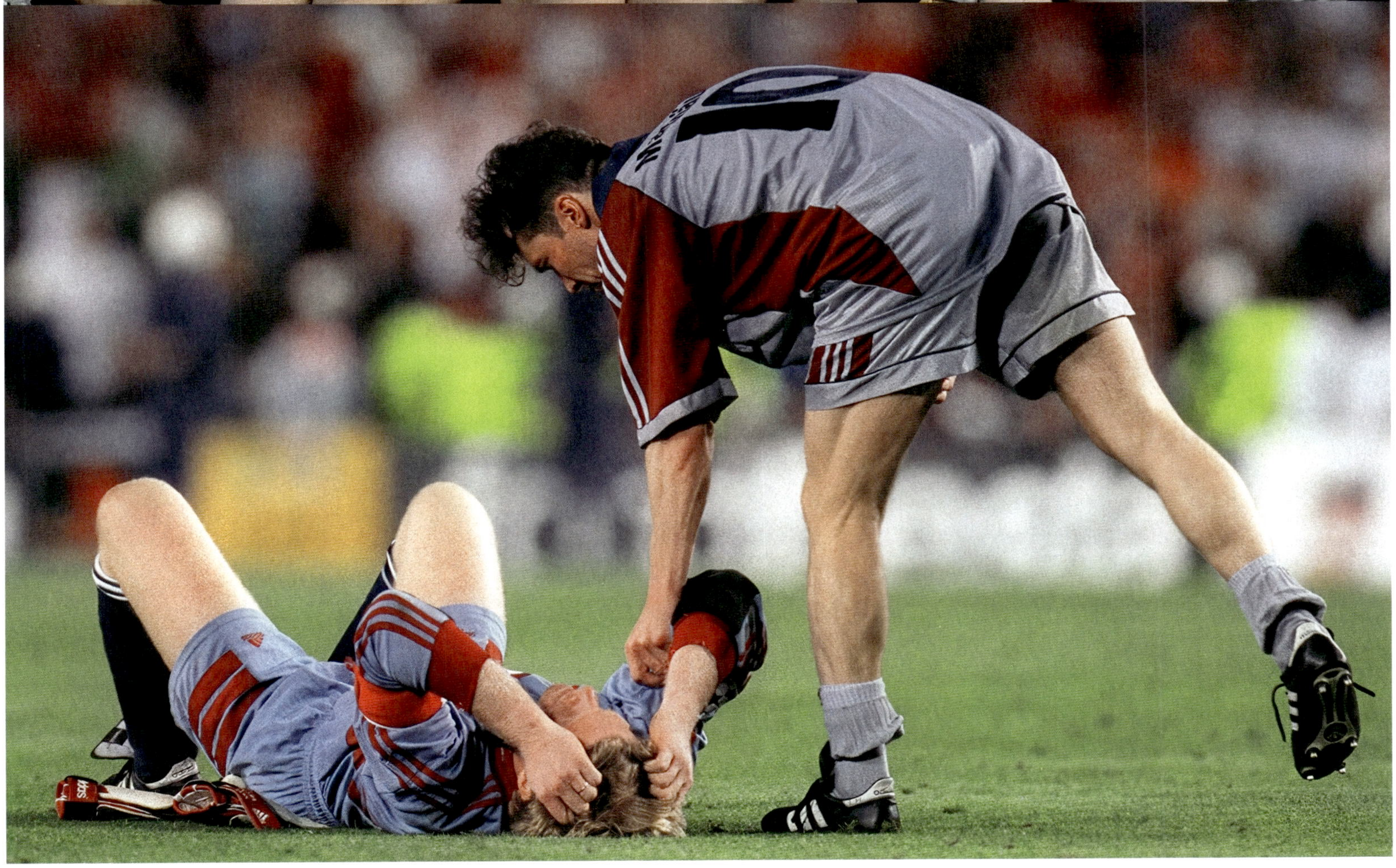
10

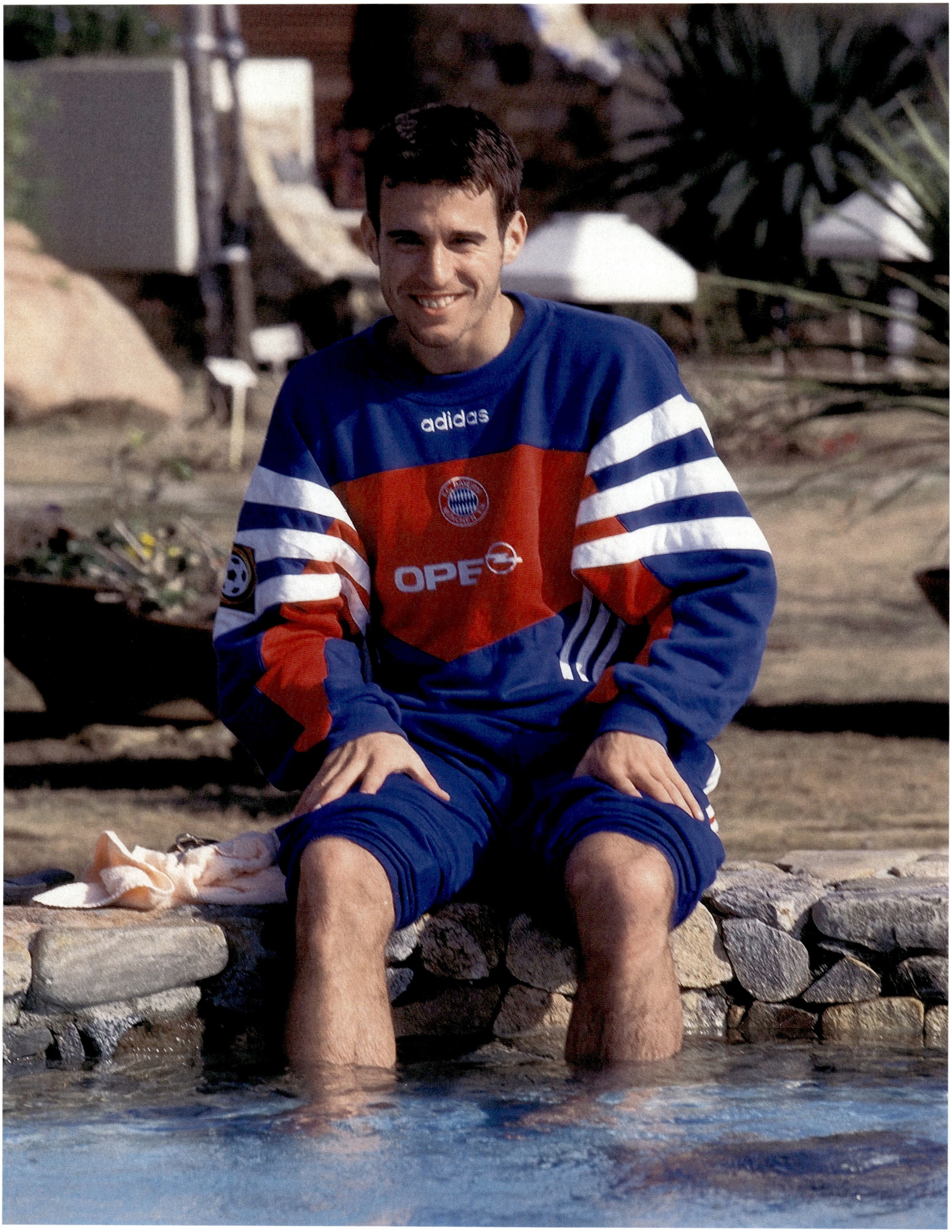
adidas
OPE

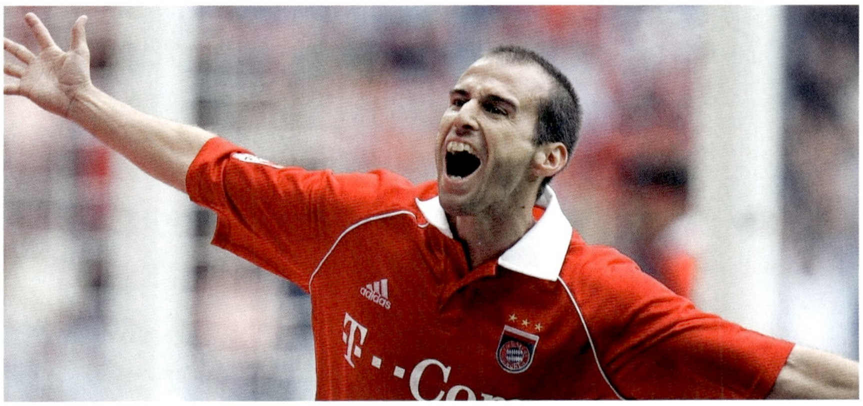

MEHMET **SCHOLL**

At a time when "fast dribbler" and "teenage star" were unknown concepts in the Bundesliga, he put life into both of these phrases.

A slender conjuror of the ball, whom Karl-Heinz Rummenigge called "the biggest talent in German football" in 1992 when he arrived in Munich, quickly became a spectators' favourite through his sparkling artistry. And he was the first teenage star at Säbener Strasse, surrounded by girl readers of the kids' magazine *Bravo* – one of the players who turned the club into "FC Hollywood" in those years. Yet he was capable of straight talking: "It's Rehhagel or me", he said, when he was at odds with the new coach. "And if they throw me out, I don't care." Scholl stayed, Otto Rehhagel left, and they won the UEFA Cup. By the time he retired in 2007 he had won every trophy that could be had with FC Bayern – except the Cup Winners' Cup, in which Bayern competed for the last time in 1985. Twenty-one titles was the grand total, first and foremost the Champions League and Club World Cup, both in 2001. As a result of several injuries he never played in a World Cup, but in 1996 he gained a winner's medal at the Euros with the German national team. For him the biggest win, however, was the club itself where he played: "My greatest success was Bayern. That I managed to play football in this circus for fifteen years without being swallowed up in that pool of sharks."

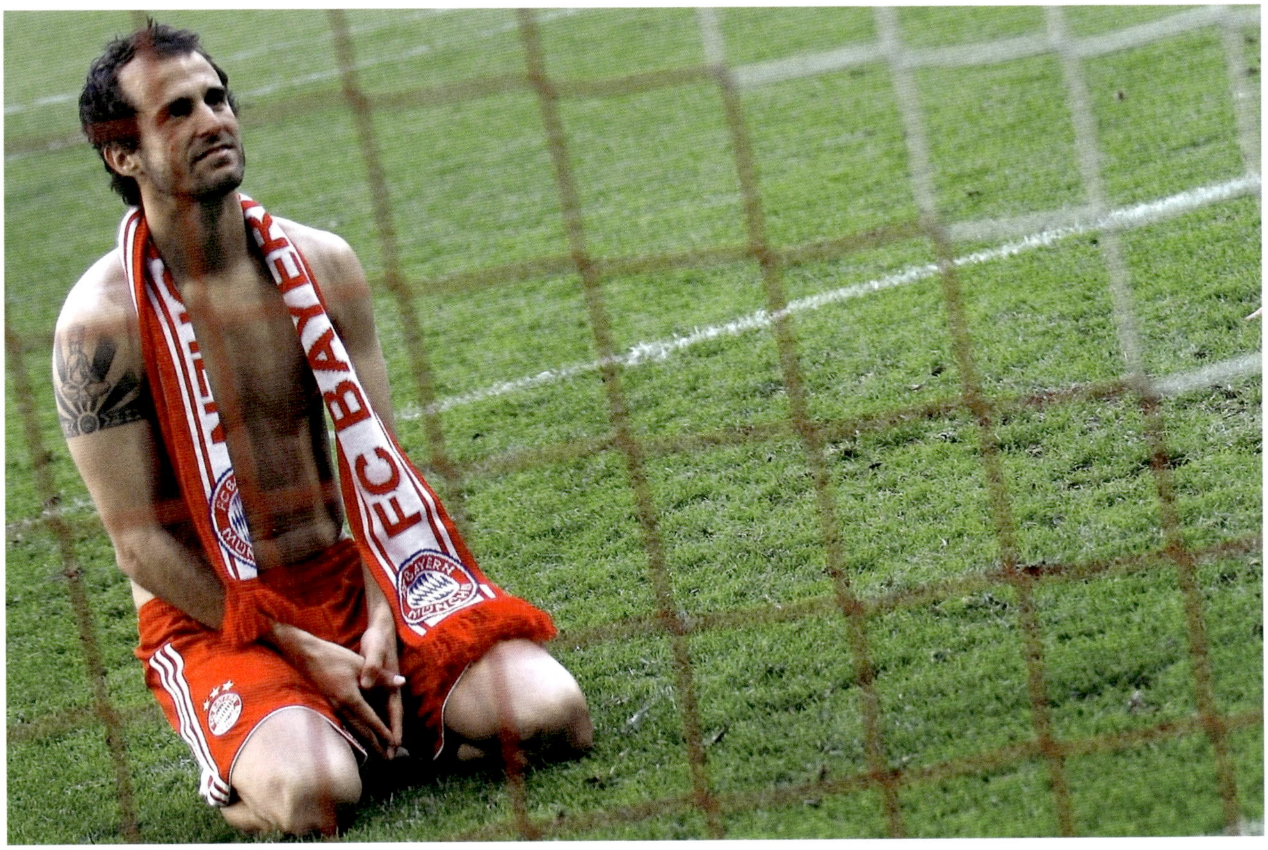

When Mehmet Scholl took a knee in front of the fans after his last match in 2007 at the age of 36, there was melancholy in the air. Fifteen years with FC Bayern, countless triumphs – yet still a feeling that, given fewer injuries, the fans might have seen much more from such stunning talent. Much like his potential successor Sebastian Deisler, who had to end his career with Bayern and in football at the age of 26, following severe depression and five knee operations, shortly before Scholl himself retired.

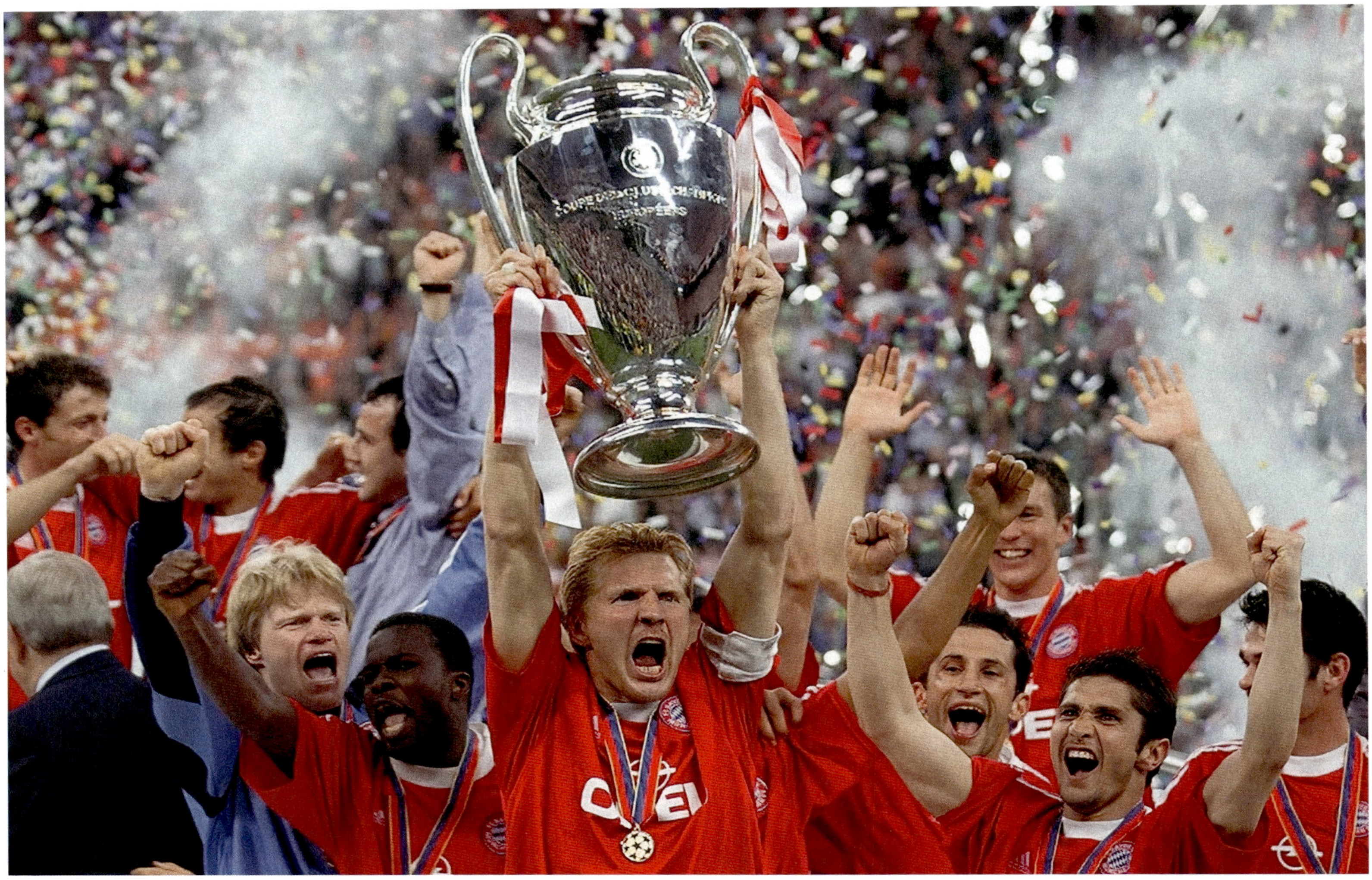

STEFAN **EFFENBERG**

There it is, part two: four days after winning the Bundesliga championship in Hamburg, Stefan Effenberg raises aloft the Champions League trophy in Milan.

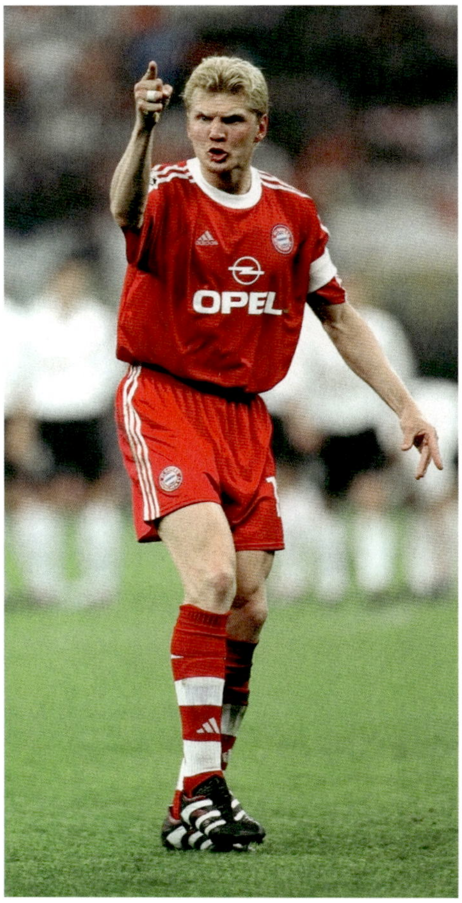

Ottmar Hitzfeld introduced the concept of the "aggressive leader" to German football. And he found a man who played in Munich for four years in such a way that the phrase might have been invented for him.

"Stefan Effenberg leads the team", said the coach. "Many players follow his lead. When others hide away, he shows himself." In top-level football today, with its networked systems and division of responsibilities, some people miss this type of player. At FC Bayern this principle worked extremely well at the turn of the millennium. Effenberg was the leader, strategist, dominator – and also an aggressor, who knew how to make an impression on opponents and drag along his own team in big games with his voice and body language, with robust toughness but also with targeted excessive toughness. In this way he led FC Bayern to a hat-trick of Bundesliga titles and in 2001 to victory in the Champions League and the Club World Cup. When he left a year later, the "aggressive leader" said, with unusual gentleness, "It all worked out, from A to Z."

JENS **JEREMIES**

The midfield is the habitat of play-makers of genius. And of hard-working distance runners, who keep things moving. Players like Bernd Dürnberger, Javi Martínez – and Jens Jeremies.

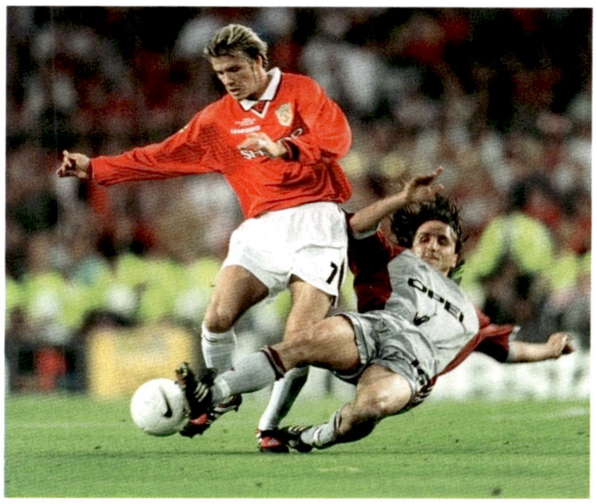

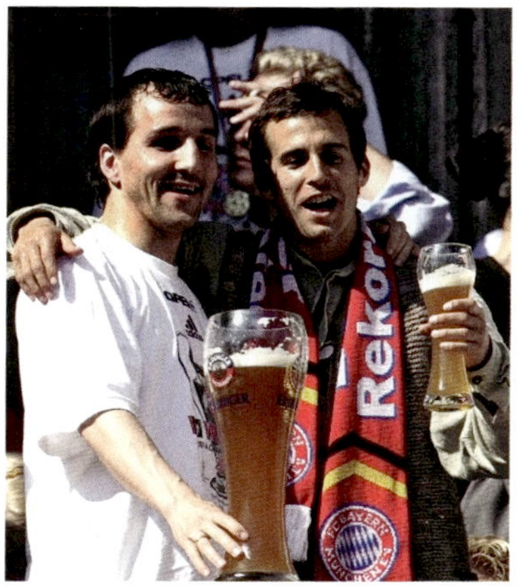

Thanks to uncompromising commitment, he became a popular figure with the fans, not an easy thing to do if you come to the club from 1860 München. He earned his status as an icon of FCB by risking his health for the club. Only twelve days after a knee operation he scored a goal for 2–1 against Real Madrid, opening the door to the Champions League final – which he missed due to another operation. He never completely got back in the groove, retired when he was 32 – and became a paying fan of Bayern. He turned down the free tickets given to ex-players and, along with friends, rented a box in the Allianz Arena.

This is quite a feat: to play for 1860 München and then become a favourite at Bayern. And as a Bayern player to remain a fan of the band Tote Hosen. For keeping faith with the band in spite of their mockery in the song 'Bayern', in 2012 he demanded "reparation" - and got it, with a concert in his party room.

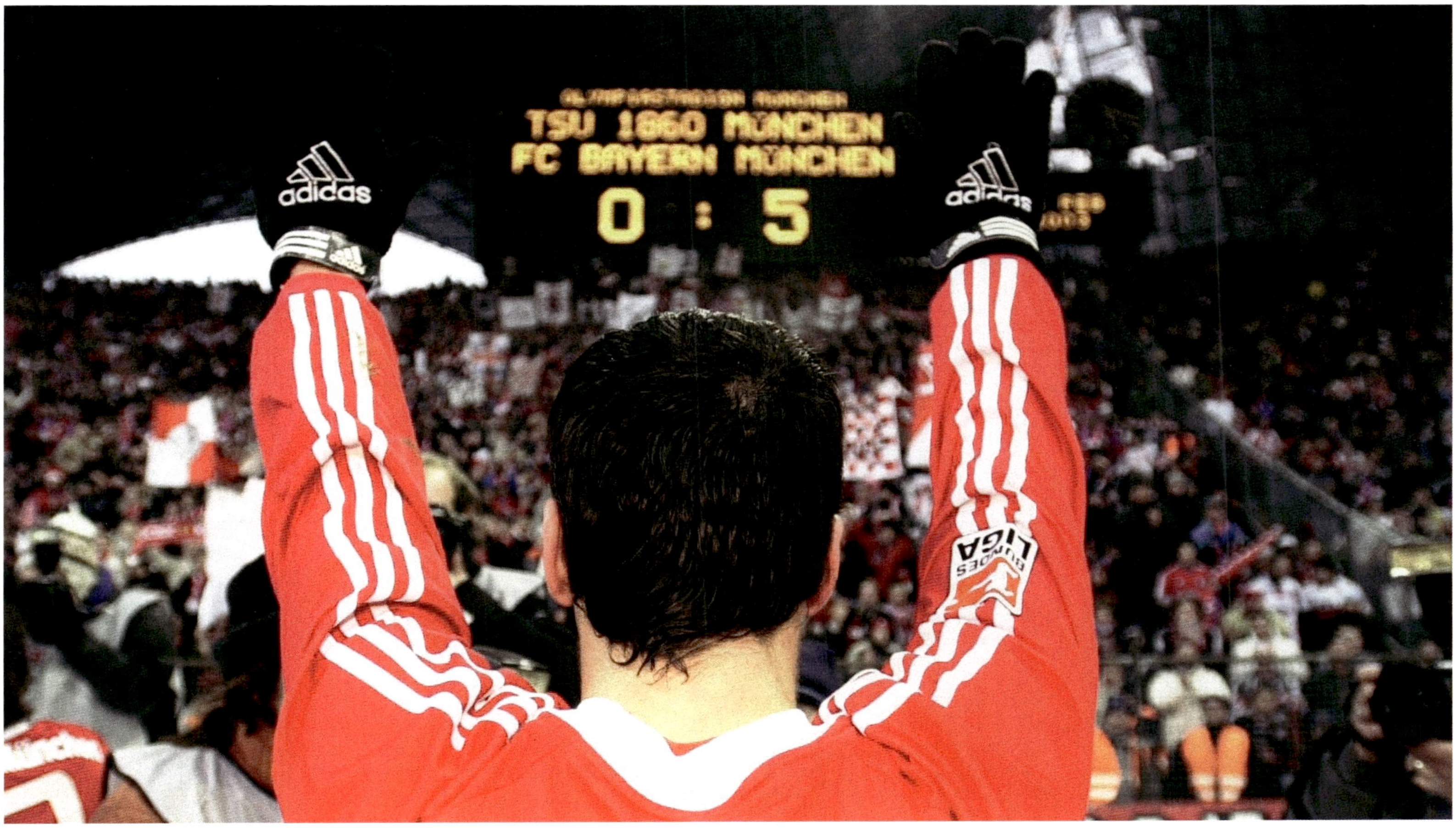

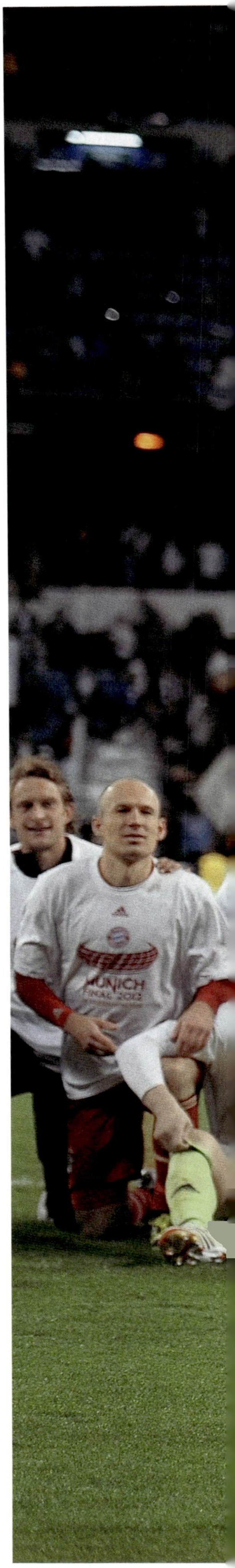

BASTIAN SCHWEINSTEIGER

He almost became a ski racer, like his friend Felix Neureuther. He would have been good enough. But football had more to offer: "First of all, you don't feel freezing. Secondly, you don't carry as much kit around. And you also don't need to get up all that early."

The football world would have missed out without "Bazi" from the mountains, who made his fortune in the big city of Munich. When Louis van Gaal brought him from the wing into central midfield, after five years as a regular in the Bayern team, Bastian Schweinsteiger seemed to have been liberated. In the middle, where quick thinking and quick reactions count, where confidence on the ball and a cool head are decisive, he flourished and became one of the most important players for the Bavarian treble in 2013 and Germany's victory in the World Cup in 2014. "The brain of the team" was how Jupp Heynckes described him. A world-class star who always stayed good-humoured, normal and down-to-earth. And did not move out to a villa in the suburbs but remained at the heart of the city, where things were happening. Passers-by could encounter him there in a café or at the Viktualienmarkt. "I am one of you" he said when, feted by the fans as a "footballing god", he spoke tearfully into the stadium microphone at his farewell match. And everyone knew that this was true.

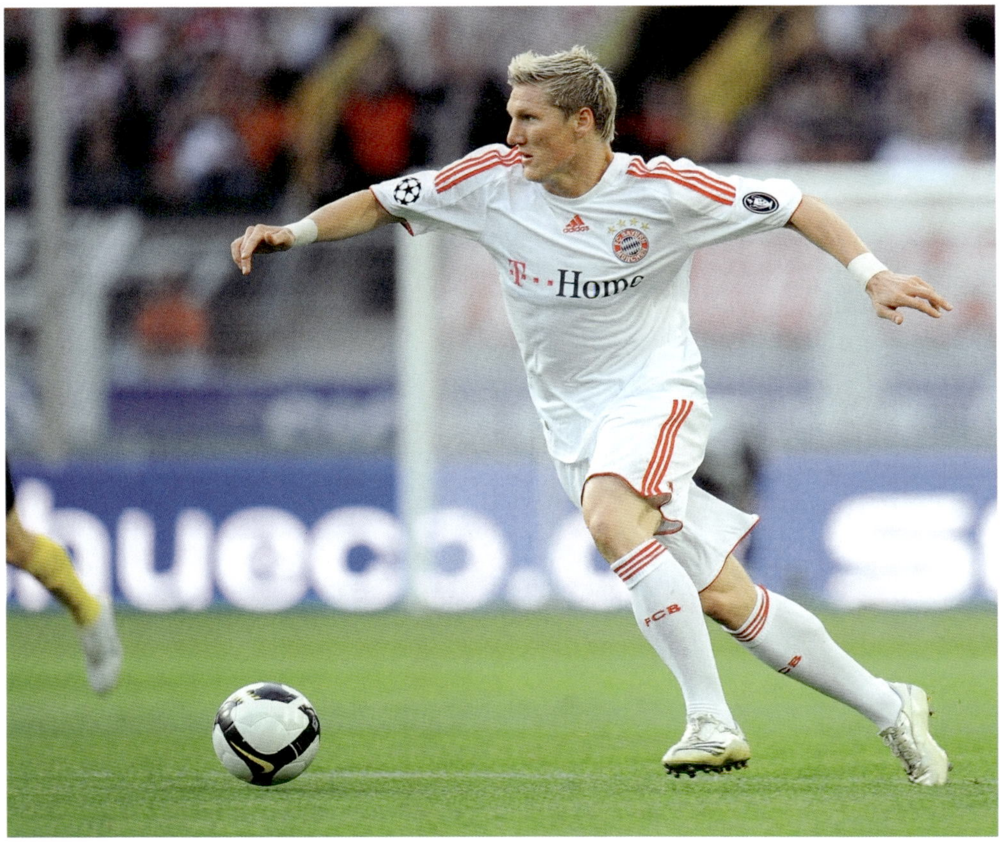

Of all the winners in the 125-year story of FC Bayern München, Bastian Schweinsteiger is the most resilient. He holds a unique record. From 18 December 2012 until 27 August 2013, FCB won every game in the Bundesliga, the cup and the Champions League when Schweinsteiger was on the pitch - over more than eight months, twenty-six times in succession. And in the match that ended this series, a 1-1 in Freiburg, Bayern were in the lead - until an injury forced Schweinsteiger to leave the field.

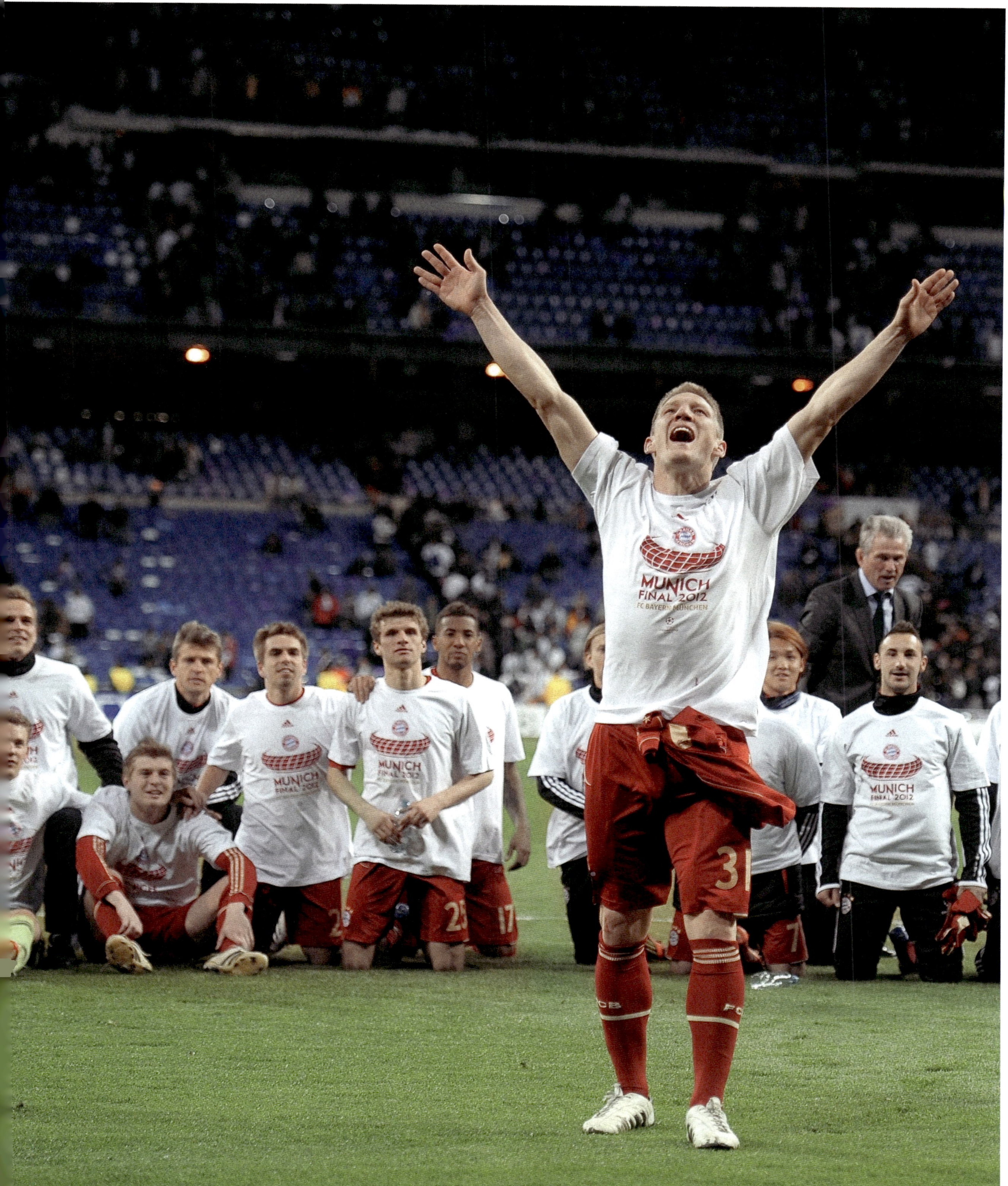
MUNICH
FINAL 2012
FC BAYERN MÜNCHEN

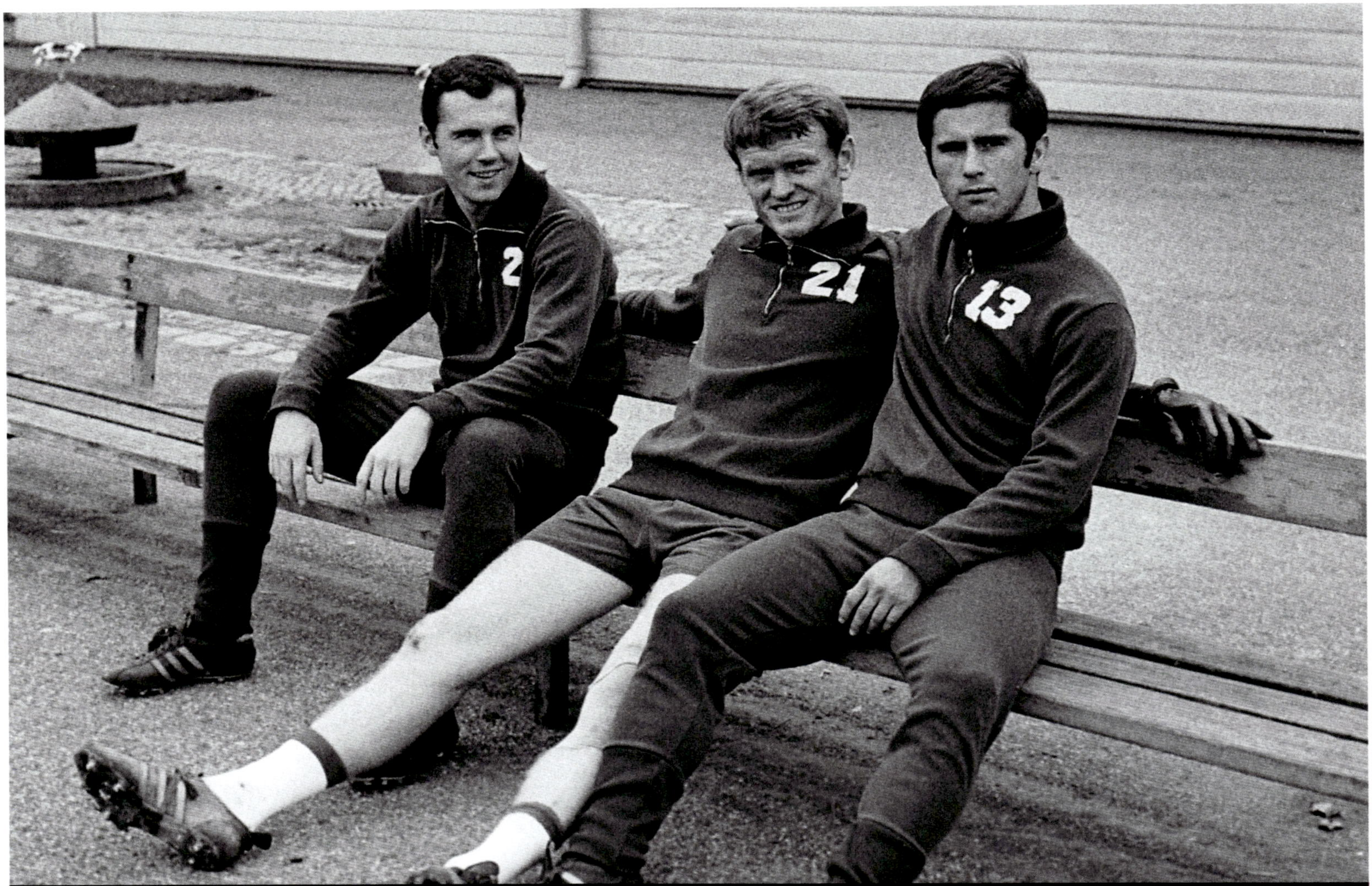

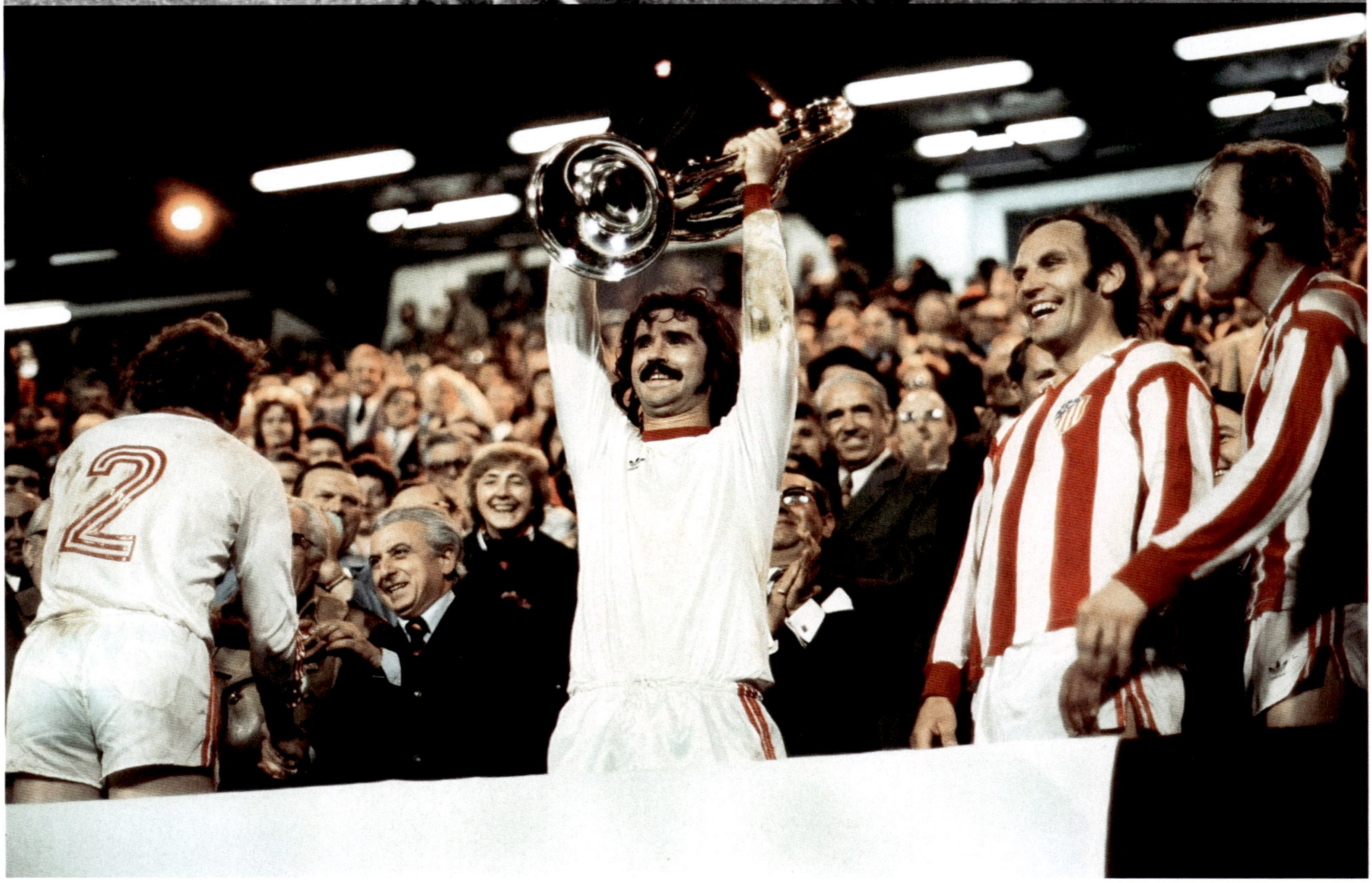

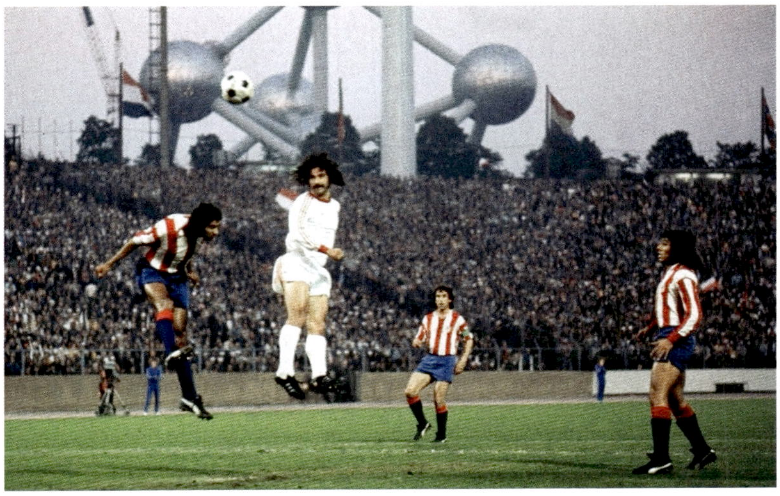

GERD MÜLLER

Everyone knows him as an incomparable goalscorer. But Gerd Müller was much more. He also shone as an engine in midfield, a man-marker – and a furniture remover.

When the powerfully built man from Nördlingen came to Munich, FC Bayern organised a part-time job for him in a furniture store to supplement his regional league salary of DM 160. So he carried a new kitchen into the apartment of Timo Konietzka – who said thank you by scoring the winning goal for 1860 München in Bayern's first Bundesliga match in 1965. In that game Müller was a man-marker who, according to *Kicker* magazine, "ideally combined defensive and attacking roles". *Sportmagazin* thought he was going "to and fro with the lungs of a horse".

Soon, however, he found his true home: the penalty area. He scored goals on a daily basis: 365 in 427 Bundesliga matches. For Bayern's double in 1969 he contributed thirty-seven of the club's sixty-nine goals. In his finest year for the national team, winning the European Nations title in 1972, in seven games he netted fourteen of the German total of nineteen. Without Müller and his scoring, the successes of FCB and the German national team would hardly have been possible in the Golden Seventies.

He was given his own special verb: to "müller". He never scored with a flourish, never played to the gallery. "Small goals count as well," he later said to the talented Bayern youngsters whom he helped along in his second football career as a coach for forwards, and recommended: "Don't simply slam it – chip it or guide it in as well." And while people somehow began to require a complicated "philosophy" for any kind of football, the theory for Gerd Müller and his goals could be expressed in one single sentence: "If you think about it, it's already too late."

There were many facets to Gerd Müller's uniquely dangerous goalscoring skill. Some of them were only known to his opponents. For example, Hermann Gerland, a defender for VfL Bochum, admired Müller's ability to "suddenly stop dead from full pace", letting his opponent run the wrong way. Or he simply let them bounce off him, as did the GDR defender Konrad Weise, who thought Müller's body "unbelievably hard". Although opponents went for him and provoked him in every possible way, Müller was only sent off once in fourteen Bundesliga years: in 1968 in Hanover, for a foul on Jupp Heynckes of all people! Despite an eight-week suspension he was still the league's top scorer.

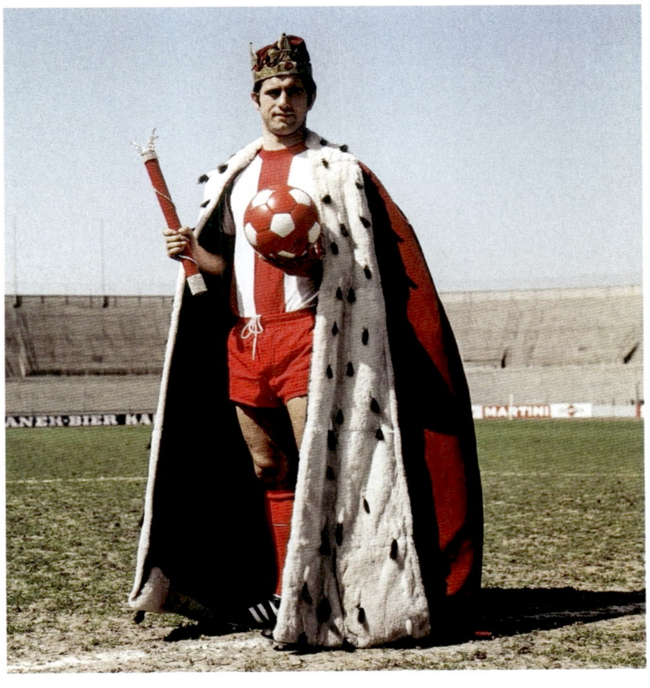

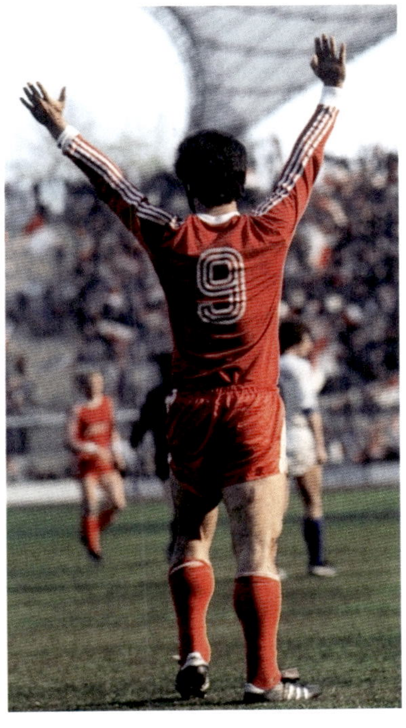

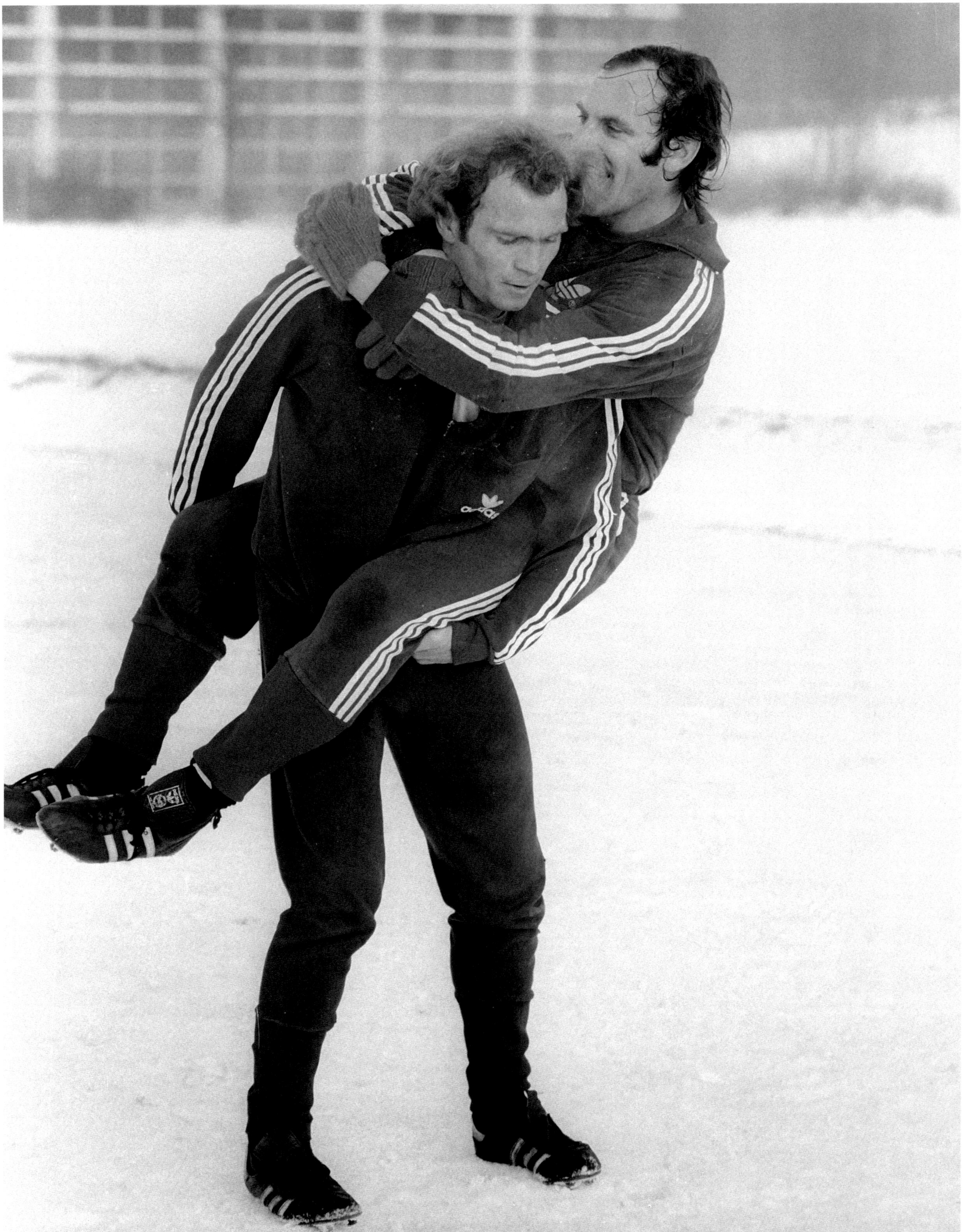

ULI
HOENESS

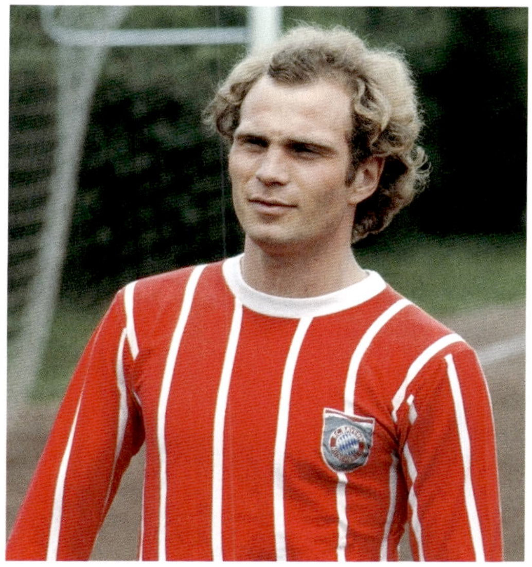

His youth-team coach thought he was “a bit slow”. He became the fastest forward of his day. Then the youngest and smartest manager in German football. He created the modern FC Bayern.

Uli Hoeness had just turned 20 when he scored the first goal in one of the most legendary victories of the German national team, a 3–1 at Wembley against England in April 1972. This was the start of a career at Formula One speed: three German championships in succession, winning the European Nations Cup, the European Cup in 1974, then twice more, and triumph in the World Cup. As a forward he was usually one step ahead of the defender, as in his greatest match, 4–0 in the repeat of a final against Atlético Madrid in 1974 – then in the manager’s role, too. After all of this sporting success, for which Hoeness toiled early in the morning while still at school on runs through the woods and later as a professional footballer with a damaged knee, in his second incarnation he faced a contest of a quite different kind.

When he moved into his empty manager’s office at the age of 27, the club revenue was DM 12 million, with debts of 7 million. Today FCB has revenues more than one hundred times higher, a stadium that has been paid for, and a legendary savings account. And it can therefore afford to buy players like his old self: lightning-fast forwards who come with nine-figure price tags in today’s football business.

At 22 he had won all of the major trophies in football and was considered the “fastest forward in Europe”. Until the Scotsman Frank Gray caught him in the bitterly contested European Cup final against Leeds United in 1975. Gray’s kick gave Uli Hoeness a severe cartilage injury and a long spell of suffering. He was out of action for half a year, played for another three years with pain and injections, and then his career was over.

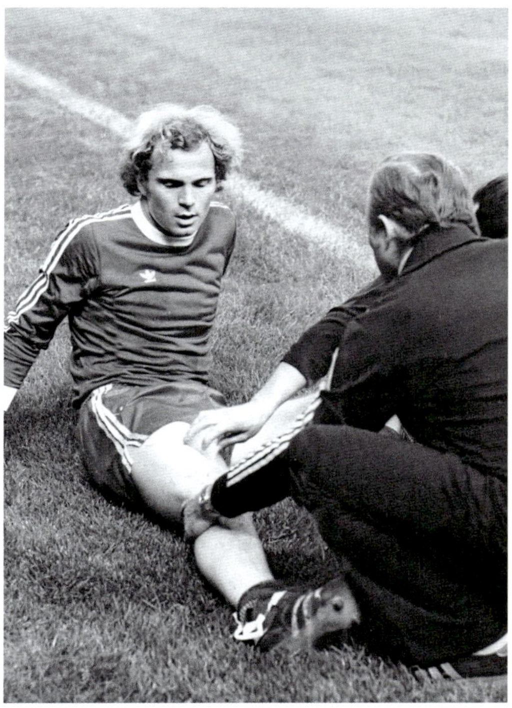

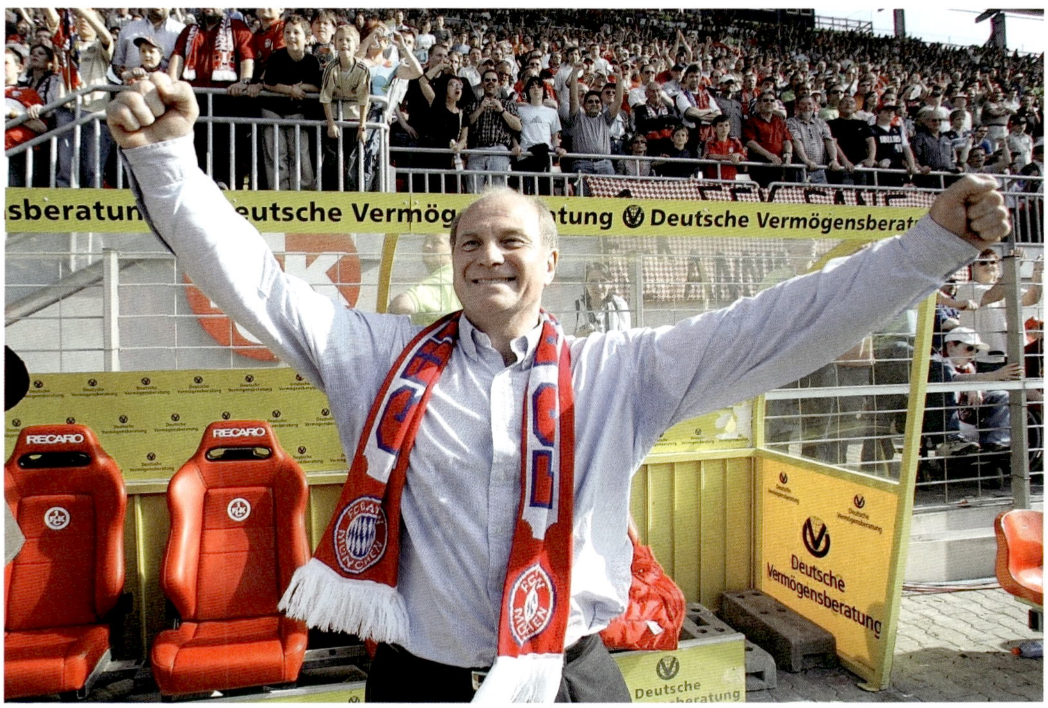

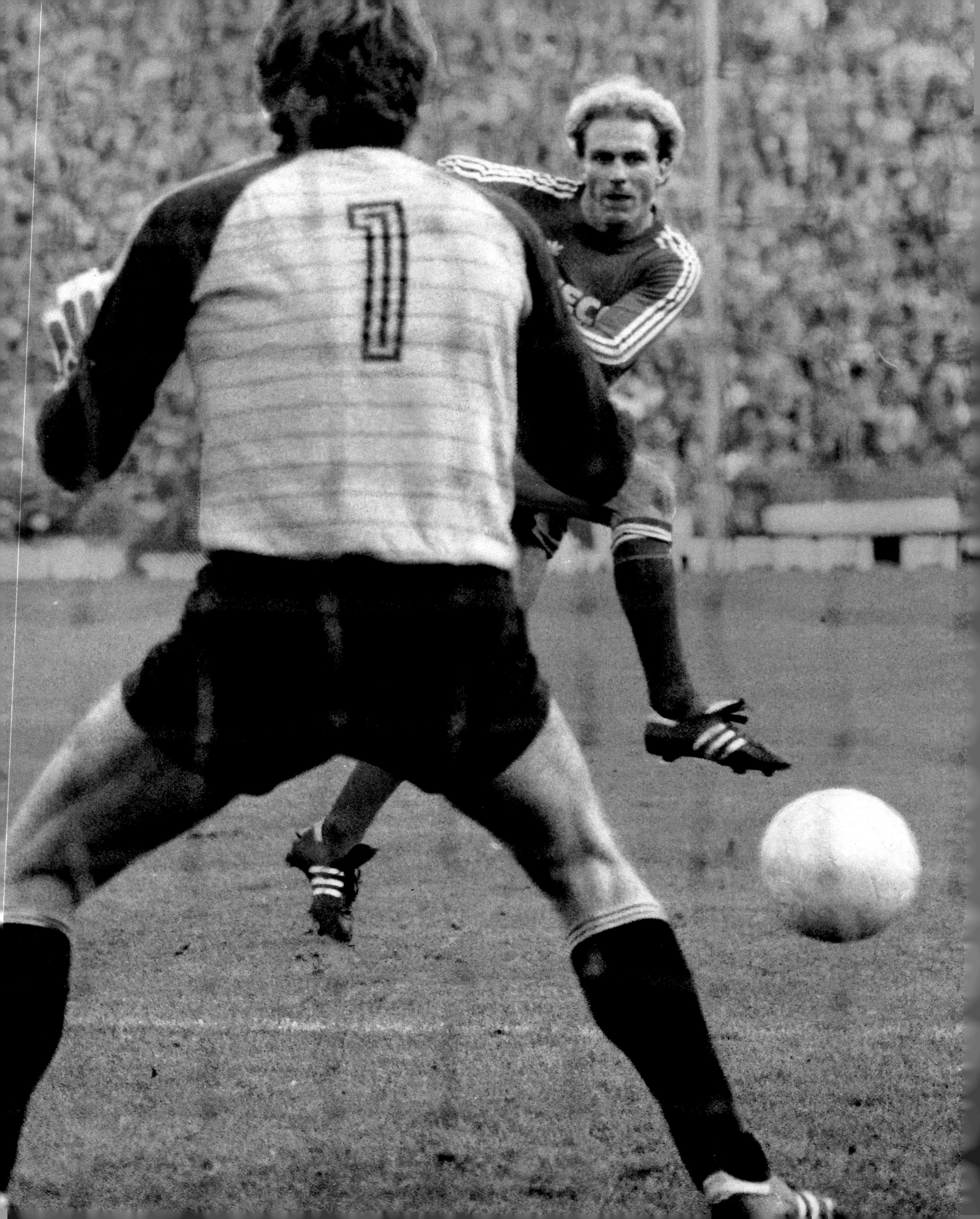
1

KARL-HEINZ **RUMMENIGGE**

In his duet with Paul Breitner, dubbed "Breitnigge" by the tabloid press, Karl-Heinz Rummenigge was at the height of his powers in the early 1980s. Twice he won the Ballon d'Or for the best player in Europe, a feat surpassed to this day only by five others: Lionel Messi (8 times), Cristiano Ronaldo (5 times), Johan Cruyff, Michel Platini and Marco van Basten (3 times each).

Germany in 1974. The VW Golf is launched, Ikea opens its first German store – and an 18-year-old bank trainee from Lippstadt gets offers from seventeen of the eighteen Bundesliga clubs.

Understandably he opted to join the champions and holders of the European Cup. The season opened with a 0–6 defeat at the hands of the promoted team Offenbach, and after Rummenigge's Bundesliga debut, FC Bayern found themselves in 18th place in the league table, for the first (and last) time in the club's history. It was one of those games, as young "Kalle" quickly learned, when you "went to the toilet for ten minutes, although you had no need", to avoid an encounter with the grim-faced manager Robert Schwan.

From then onwards, things looked up for "rosy cheeks", as they called him. In a line-up that was "satiated with success" and "no longer willing to make an effort for the Bundesliga", as he later recalled, but "was able to get things together for the highlights", in this way winning the European Cup two more times, this fast attacking player became one of the team's greatest assets – especially after the return of Paul Breitner in 1978. "Breitnigge", the dream pairing of the creator and the finisher, took FC Bayern to the championship title in 1980 and 1981, and Rummenigge was twice voted European Footballer of the Year. When he moved to Inter Milan in 1984 for DM 11.4 million, FCB's finances were in good order. The club could pay off its debts and recruit the next world-class star: the young Lothar Matthäus.

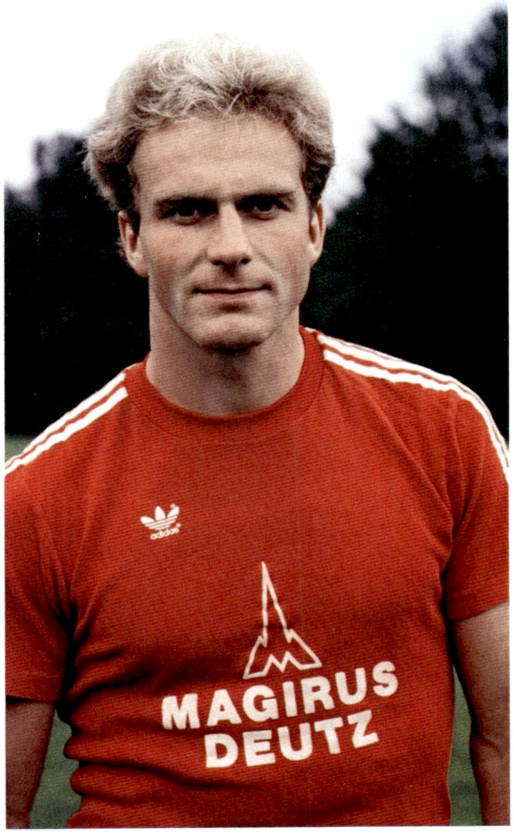

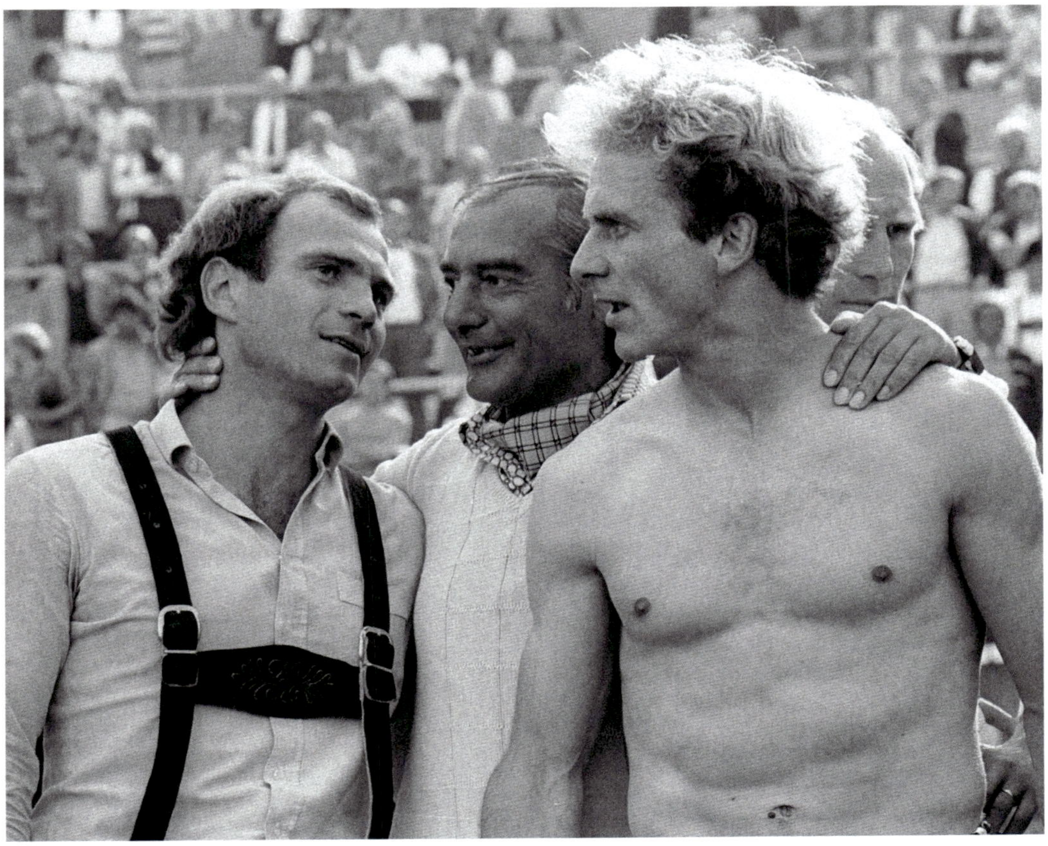

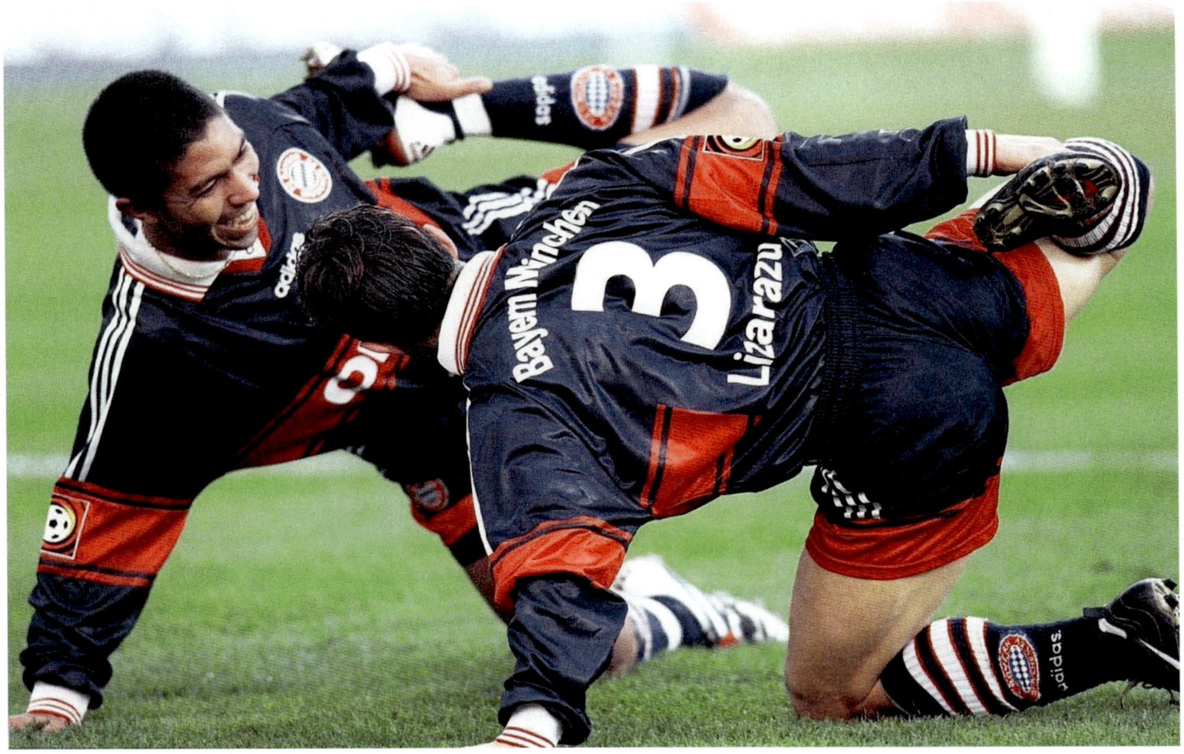

Left: A Basque and a Brazilian meet... this isn't the start of a joke, but a charming idea for celebrating a goal with synchronised gymnastics, following a 3-0 win against the reigning champions Kaiserslautern in 1998. Even in Munich, they both maintained a lasting love of the wide-open spaces of their homeland: Élber on his cattle ranch in Brazil, covering more than 10,000 hectares, Lizarazu on his surfboard in the waves of the Bay of Biscay in the Basque country.

Right: FC Bayern's first-ever top player was Willem Hesselink from the Netherlands. But a hundred years passed before more Dutchmen wore red shirts in Munich, two of them: Mark van Bommel cleared at the back, Roy Makaay scored the goals, and they celebrated it together.

GIOVANE **ÉLBER**

From the centre circle, Thomas Linke headed the ball forwards, not knowing who it was for. Somehow it reached Giovane Élber, who knew its proper place: in the goal.

And he knew where thanks were due: he kissed his knee. Twelve days before this winning goal at the Bernabéu, when he surprised the Real goalkeeper Iker Casillas with a volley, he had had an operation on his left knee. It held out, and paved the way to the 2001 Champions League final. Élber called it a "miracle". Like all Brazilians, at first he suffered from the German winter and way of life. "Here, when I go to a restaurant at ten in the evening, it's empty. As a Brazilian, I think: people will come later. But they are back at home already." Nevertheless, he became a winter-proof goalscorer, who had the best scoring ratio at FCB since Gerd Müller – and now and then he still revealed his origins, as when he scored the Goal of the Year in 1999 by outwitting the keeper in Rostock at the corner flag and netting the ball from there. Some called Élber, who likes wheat beer and lederhosen, the "German Brazilian". But in the meantime he has become an authentic German. And a Bavarian through and through.

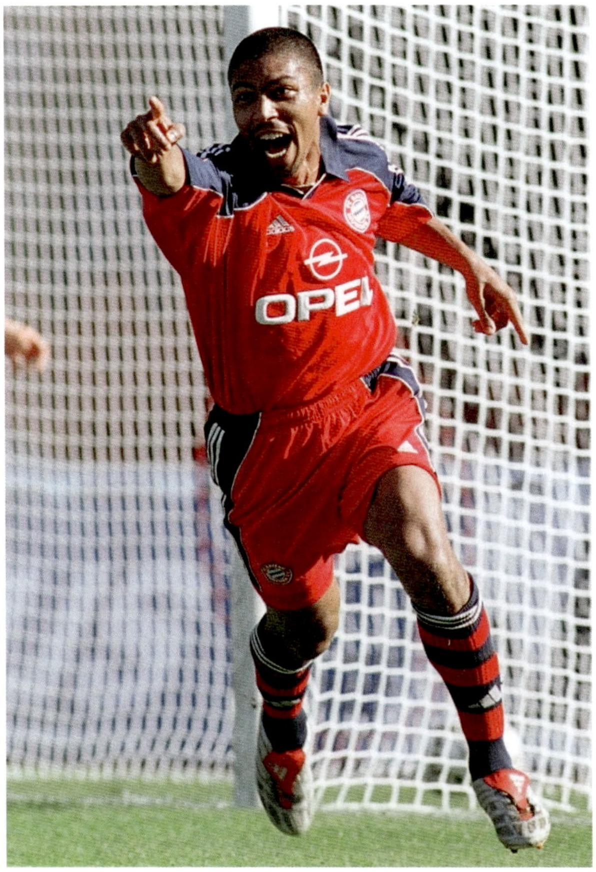

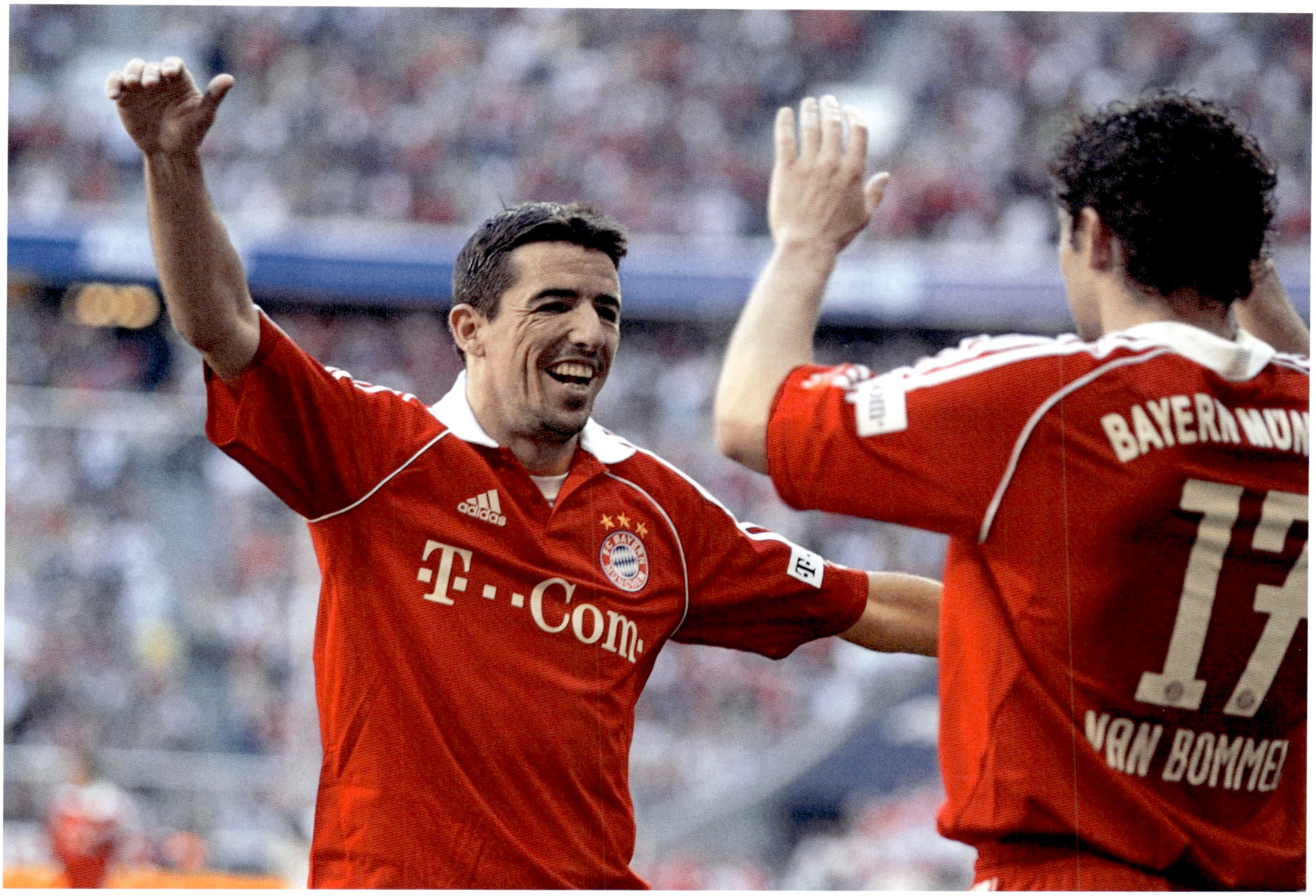

ROY **MAKAAY**

A proven method of finding players: if they were great against Bayern, they will be even greater with Bayern. The motto is: it's better to have him on our side than against us.

This began with Conny Torstensson, who almost ejected Bayern from the European Cup in October 1973 and, recruited in that winter, won the cup with them in May – and then twice more. A similar case was Roy Makaay, who scored all three goals in the Champions League preliminary round when Deportivo La Coruña won 3–2 in Munich in 2002. A year later he arrived for a price of €18.75 million, then a record-breaking transfer fee in the Bundesliga. With 103 goals in 183 matches, he paid it back. As it took Makaay in his prime statistically fewer than four attempts per goal scored, they called him "the phantom". Against Real Madrid in 2007, the phantom appeared only 10.12 seconds after the kick-off (which, strangely, Real had taken), the fastest goal in the history of the Champions League. As coach of the FC Bayern World Squad, a project that looks for young players all around the globe and prepares them for a potential professional career, Makaay searches for the phantoms of the future.

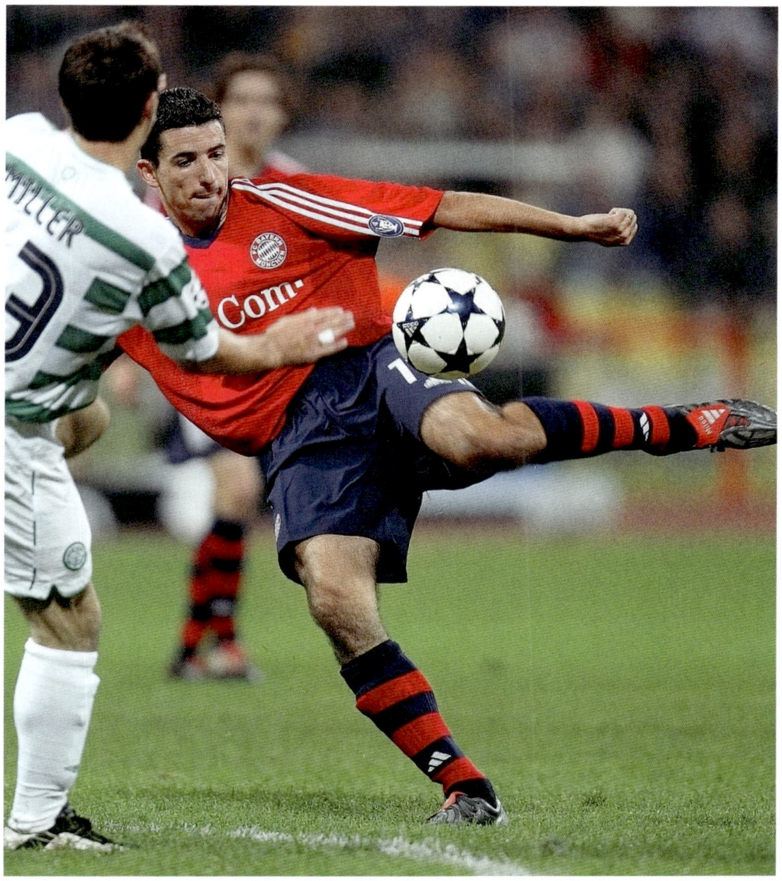

FRANCK **RIBÉRY**

For him they sang 'Oh, Champs-Elysées', though of course with the text updated. And they feted him for six words that he spoke on the balcony of city hall back in 2010: "I 'ave made five years more." They were inseparable for twelve years, the fans and their Franck.

In 2007 a funny guy came to Munich and performed pranks on his new colleagues. But what a footballer! His joy in playing, juggling, tricking and fooling his opponents sparkled in every move. Uli Hoeness took a bigger risk than ever before, paying €25 million for a character who was considered to be difficult. But he handled the man, crazy Franck, and became a kind of father figure to him. And Franck repaid this with football that shook up the Bundesliga. He cared nothing for systems – he broke them up. In this he was on his own for two years, and then Arjen Robben arrived on the other wing, a different type of person but also an impulsive player like Ribéry. What Robben did was foreseeable, but opponents were not able to prevent it. Ribéry was the personification of unpredictability. Together they provided what was needed for the team to become the "Super-Bayern" of 2013: characters, who transformed possession into a spectacle. With the kind of football that everyone wants to play as a boy.

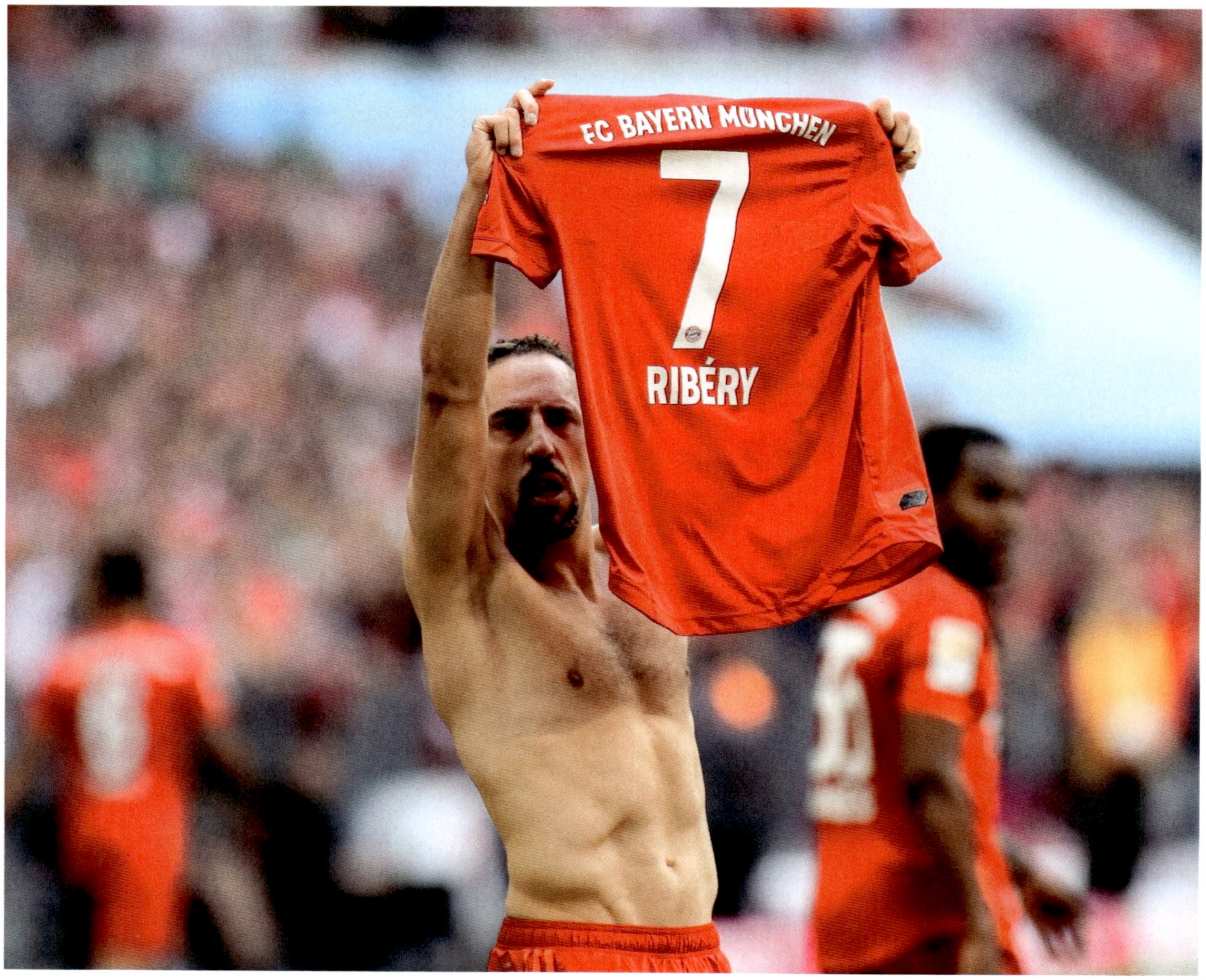

Munich, 18 May 2019, the seventy-fourth minute: Franck Ribéry scored his last goal for FC Bayern München. In farewell he tore off his shirt and held it out to the fans. Since then, opponents have been spared the pain of an aggressive little Frenchman dribbling till their legs were in knots - and his teammates at FC Bayern have been spared knots that magically appeared in their bootlaces, holes in their socks, and toothpaste under the doorknob. A sad day for everyone.

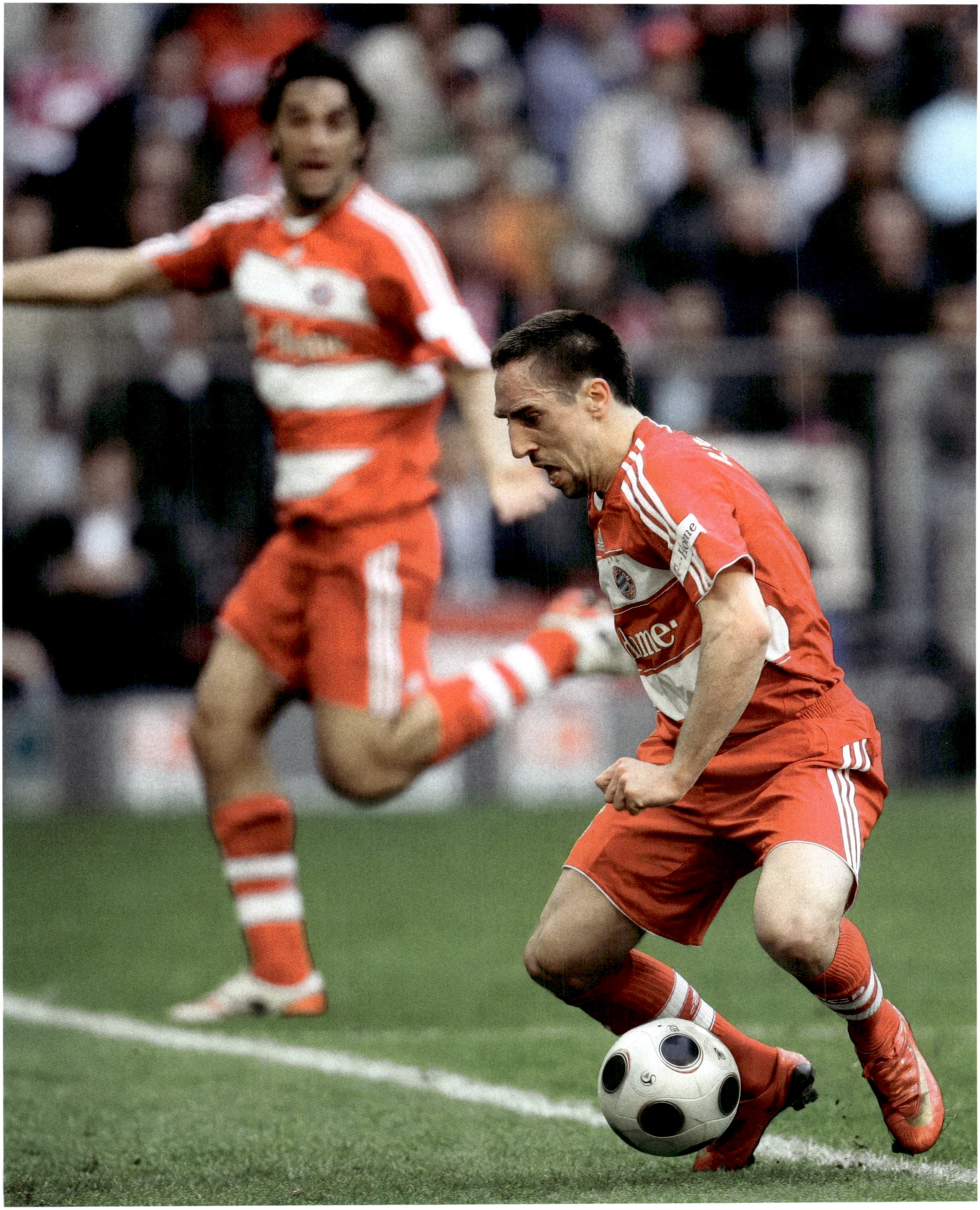

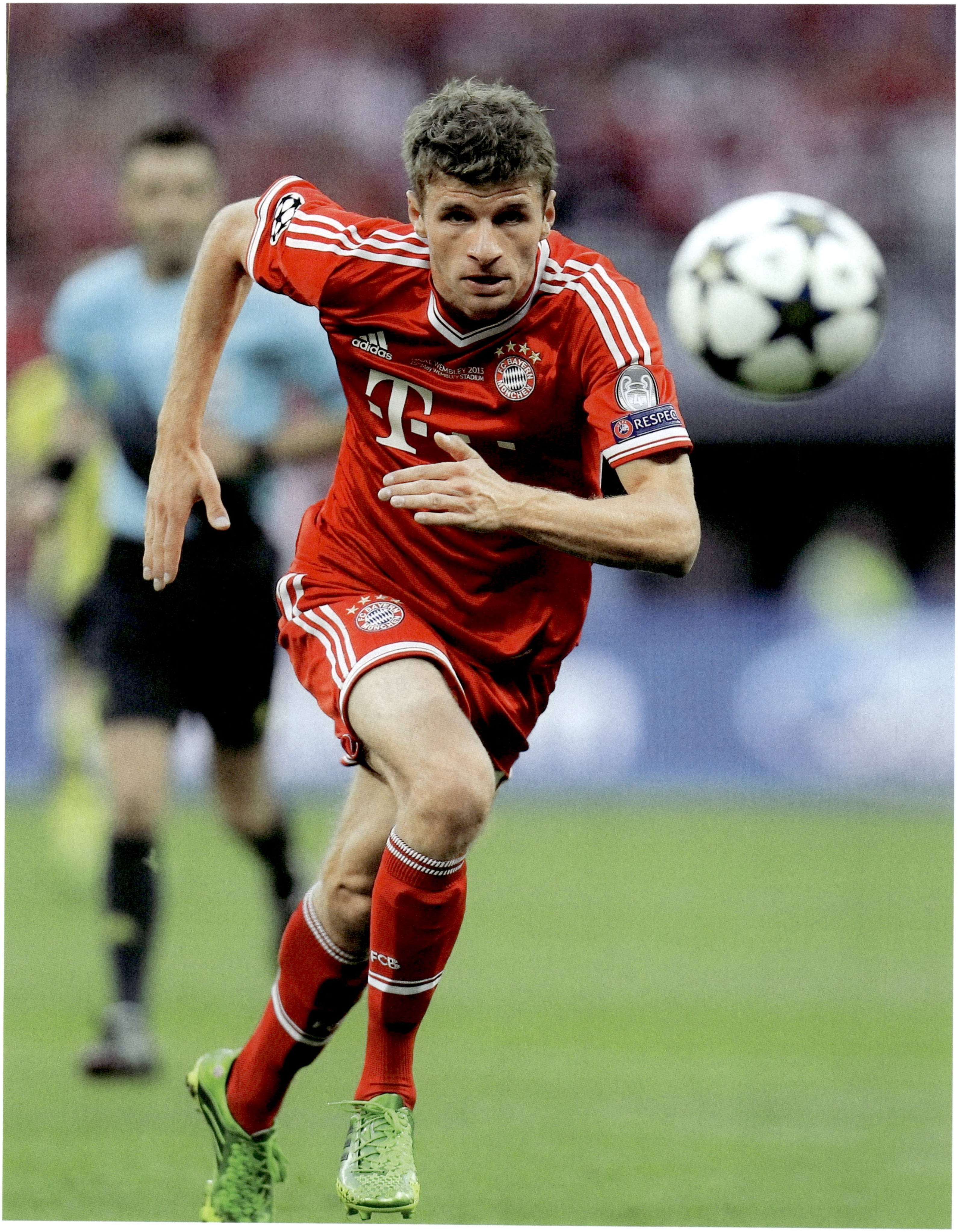
adidas

THOMAS **MÜLLER**

He is the king of assists at FC Bayern, not only with the ball. "Hold your heads up high, lads", he wrote in the team chat on the night after the home final against Chelsea: "What happened yesterday really hurts. But next year we'll hit back."

If his football career had come to nothing, "I would probably have gone to university and looked for the surprises that life has in store." But it didn't come to nothing, and for more than fifteen years he has been surprising opponents and fans with his goals and the strange paths that lead to them.

Who is Thomas Müller? This was the title of a TV documentary in 2013 that set out in search of the perfect average German with the commonest combination of first name and surname. The statistics of this person: 1.78 metres tall, 83 kilos, 43 years old. The Thomas Müller that everyone knows is completely different. Nothing like average. A World Cup winner. Although Bastian Schweinsteiger thought he looked "like a regional league player". And Müller himself? "I have rarely seen such a funny player as myself. But somehow I'm successful." No one in Germany has won more club trophies (32), more league championships (12) or more Bundesliga matches (over 350), and no one has given more goal assists (over 200). FCB decided against a further Müller record, as Karl-Heinz Rummenigge revealed to the *FAZ* book: "When we got an insane offer from Manchester United in 2015, we weren't interested for one second. Though we would have received a world-record transfer fee to go down in history." Müller was a one-off, not for sale. "If we had a genuine Bayern player carved by the religious woodcarvers in Oberammergau", says Rummenigge, "the result would be Thomas Müller."

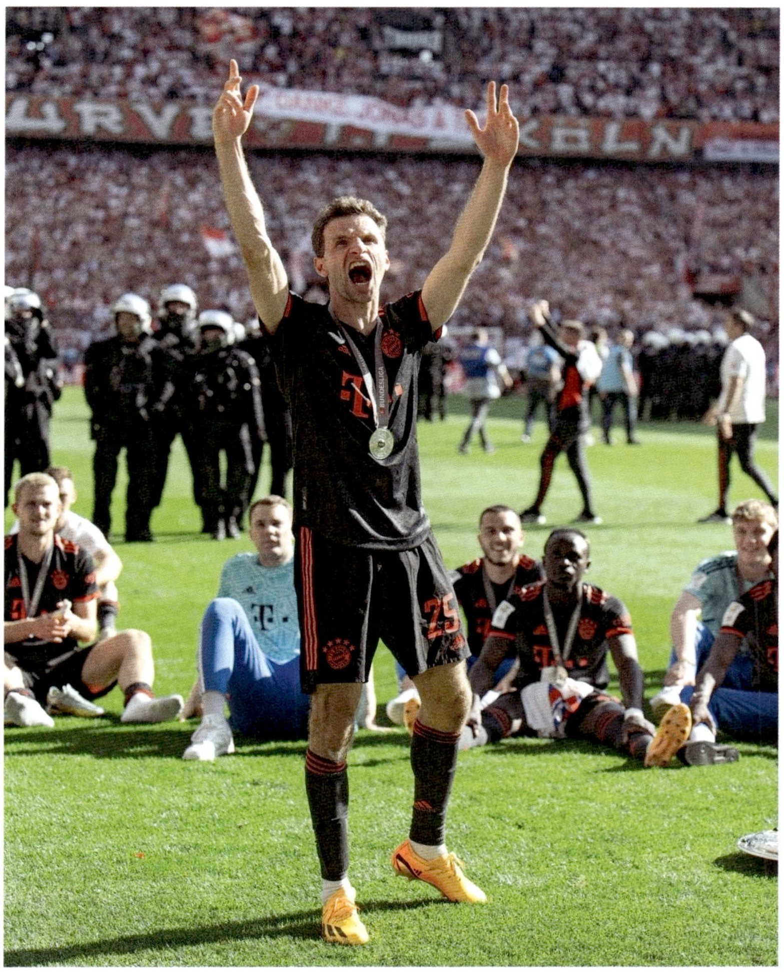

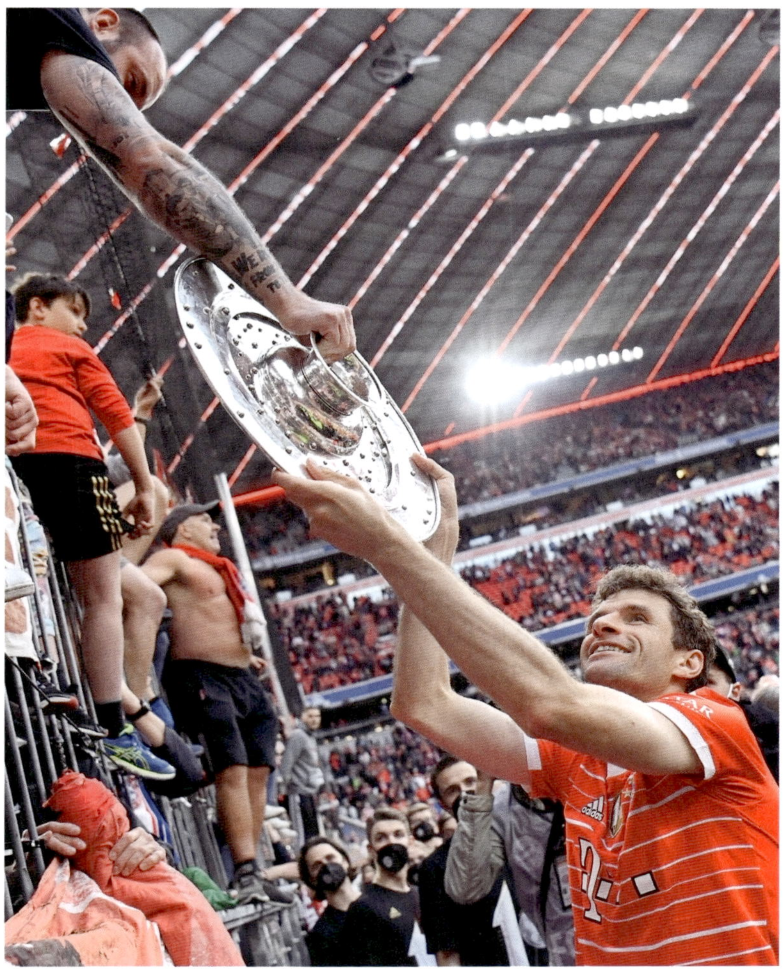

ARJEN **ROBBEN**

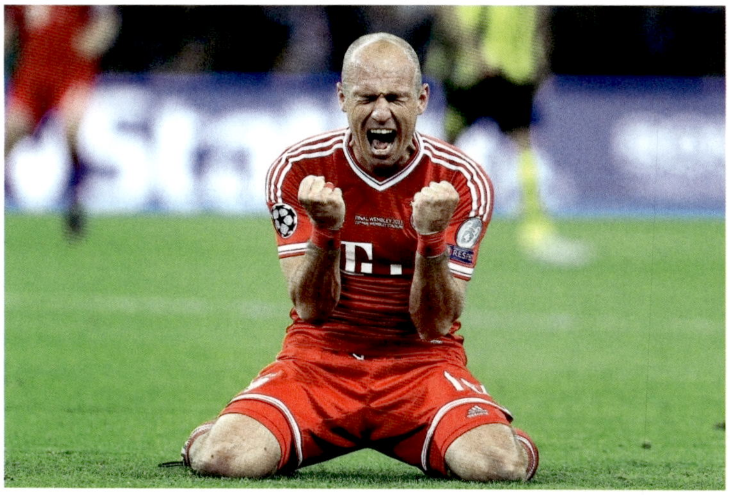

FCB had never seen a debut like it. Transferred on Friday, two turbo-goals on Saturday against the reigning champions Wolfsburg, a party atmosphere in the Arena – and a new star, who already felt "part of the history of this club" after only forty-five minutes.

He really became that, at the latest with his winning goal in the final at Wembley in 2013, but before that Arjen Robben had to overcome plenty of obstacles. After his sensational debut in 2009, after a superb first season when he cut a fine figure in long white underpants in winter, dribbling and scoring goals from the edge of the area, he was voted Footballer of the Year in Germany. The second season was overshadowed by a torn muscle, the third by a reputation for being an "ego shooter". Missed penalties against Dortmund and Chelsea cost the club the German championship and the Champions League, and set the fans against him. And then there was a slap in the face from Franck Ribéry at half-time in the semi-final against Real Madrid, after which the Bayern bosses had a tough time calming the troubled waters.

The treble year changed everything. As an individual artist, Robben was already a spectacle, a man who played as if every attack would be the last one. But under Jupp Heynckes the born soloist turned into a team player who saw a better-placed teammate, helped out in defence, won back the fans – and following Ribéry's back-heel got the opening for the goal of his life. According to Ribéry, then they "became true brothers". And stayed that way until his farewell after ten great years of "Robbery".

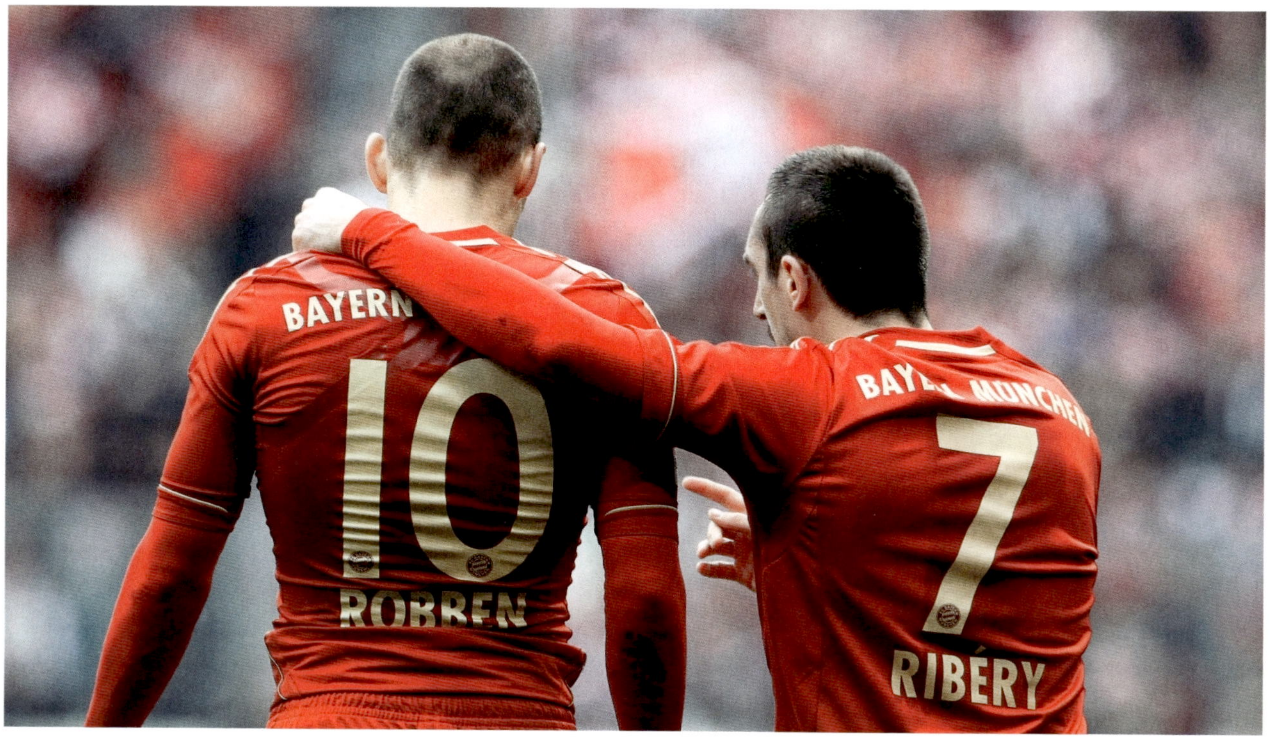

10 + 7 = 20. That's how many titles FCB won in ten years with the flying Dutchman and the cunning Gaul. Their finest co-production came in their first season, without having rehearsed it at all in advance. At Old Trafford in Manchester Ribéry chipped a corner to Robben, who was lurking outside the penalty area. And turned the perfect assist into the perfect finish, a volley into the far corner.

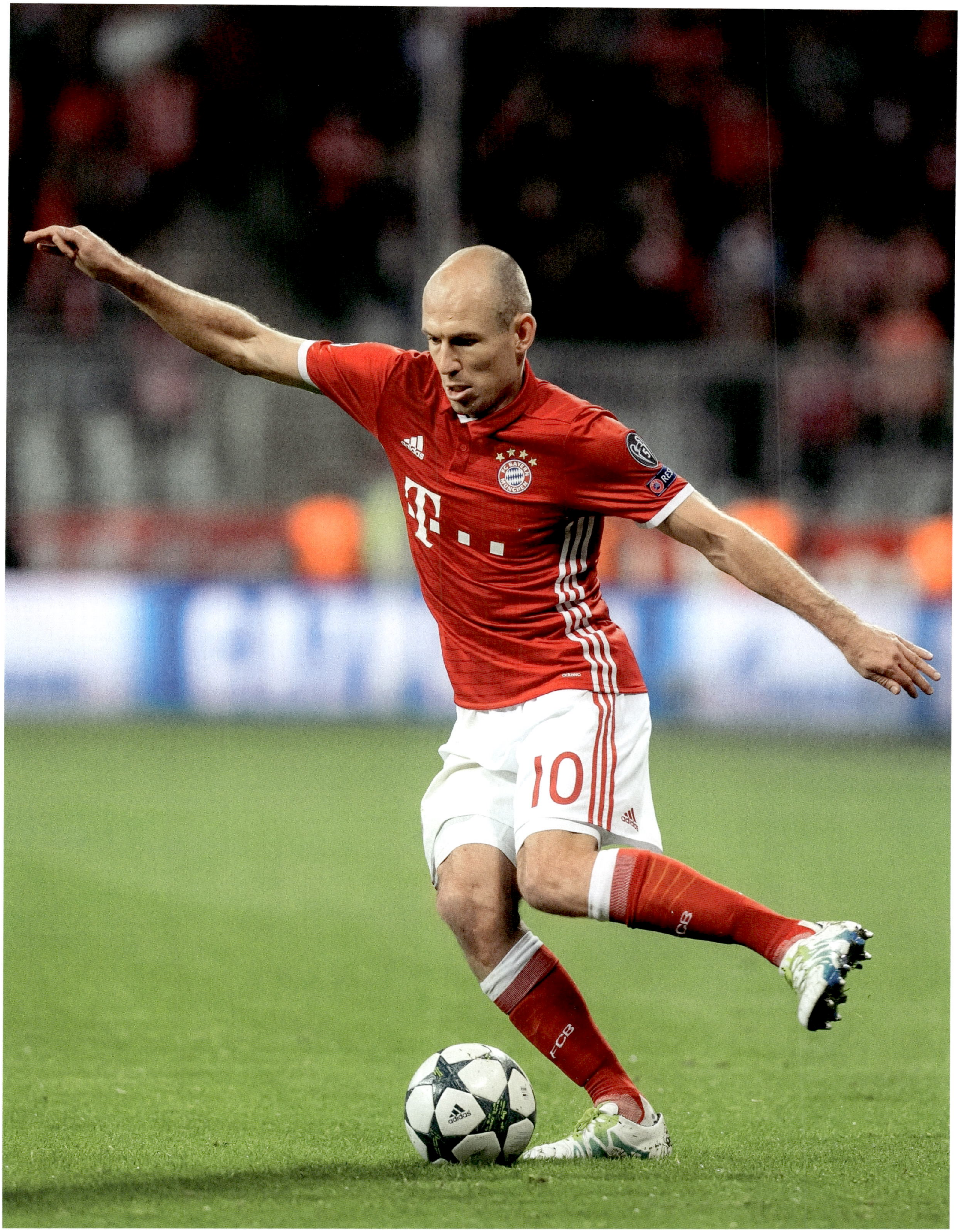
10
FCB
adidas

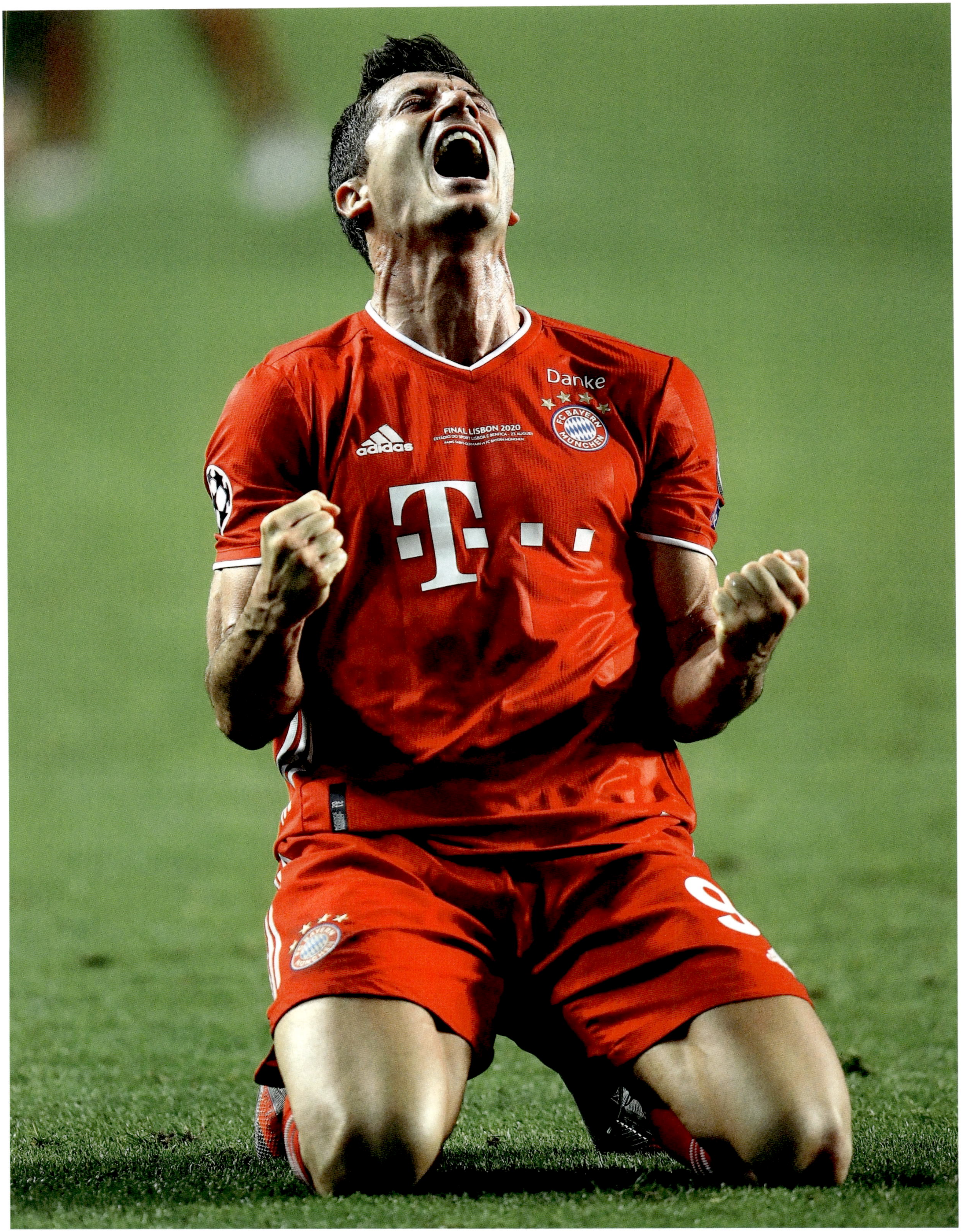
Danke
adidas
FINAL LISBON 2020

ROBERT LEWANDOWSKI

Uli Hoeness learned of Lewy's legendary five goals in nine minutes against Wolfsburg via video text on a tiny TV screen while in prison in Landsberg. With every goal that popped up, he rejoiced that Pep Guardiola had listened to him.

Fifteen goals in nine Champions League matches, the magnificent bottom line of the sensational 2019-20 season. Only in the final against PSG did he fail to score, but still went down on his knees to celebrate. But Lewy's favourite opponent was always his old team: in sixteen league games against Borussia Dortmund he hit twenty-three goals - and Dortmund only scored fifteen.

When Lewandowski came from Dortmund in 2014, he fitted into the usual pattern of poaching by Bayern, who always wanted the best footballers available, especially if they can weaken their closest rivals in that way. But the question was whether he would get on well with the star coach, who liked to replace the classic centre forward with the "false" number nine, with a midfielder disguised as a forward. It took a little time, but sooner or later Pep realised that Hoeness and company had recruited the right man for him. And that here he had acquired a completely new type of player, two things in one: a genuine number nine and a false one, who could both set up a move and finish it. In eight years at Bayern, the Pole became possibly the most skilful centre forward of all time. And a goal machine, for whom not even the supposedly unsurpassable season's record set by Gerd Müller was out of reach – a record that Lewandowski broke with forty-one goals and honoured with the words "4EVER GERD" on his shirt.

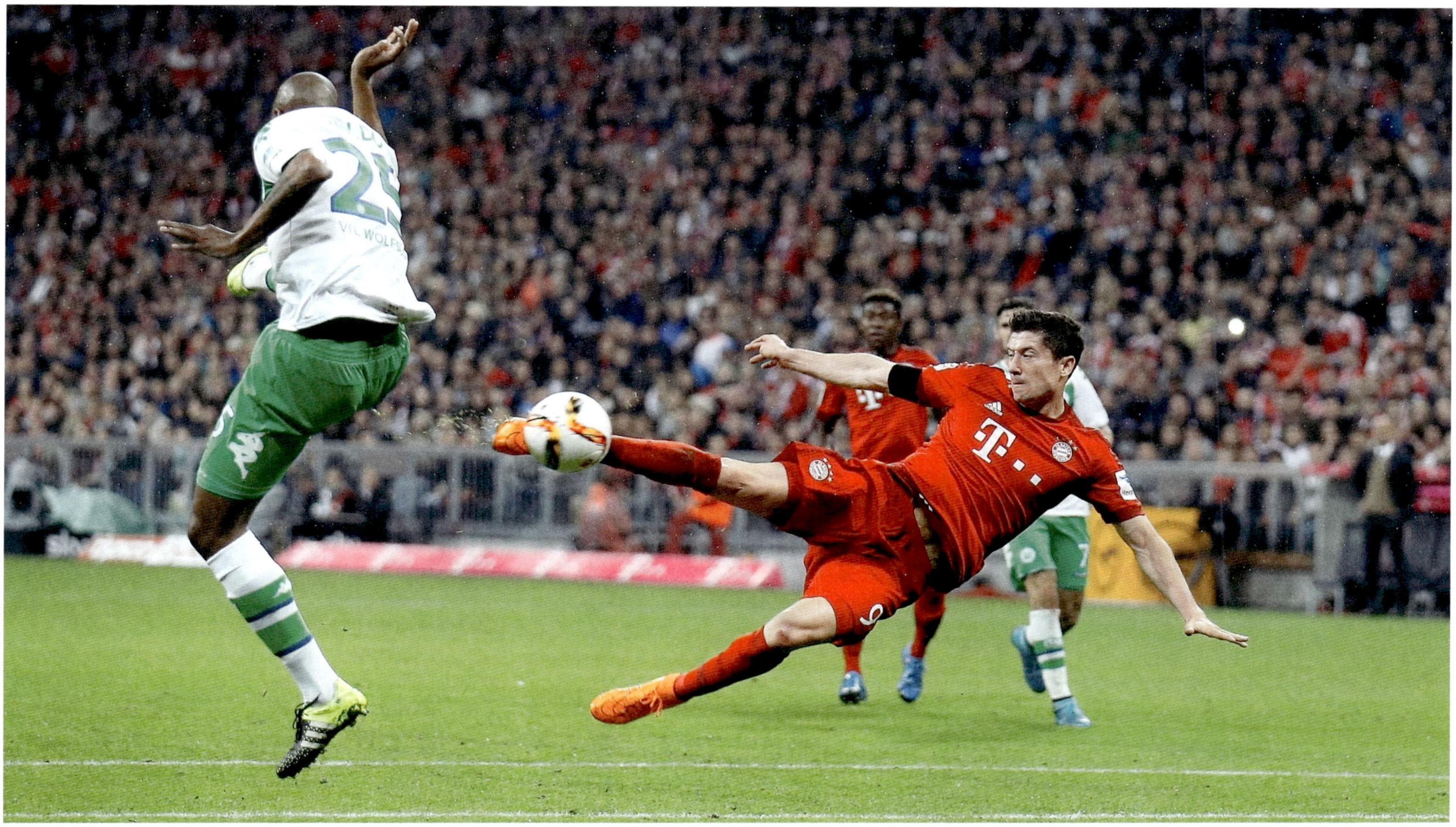

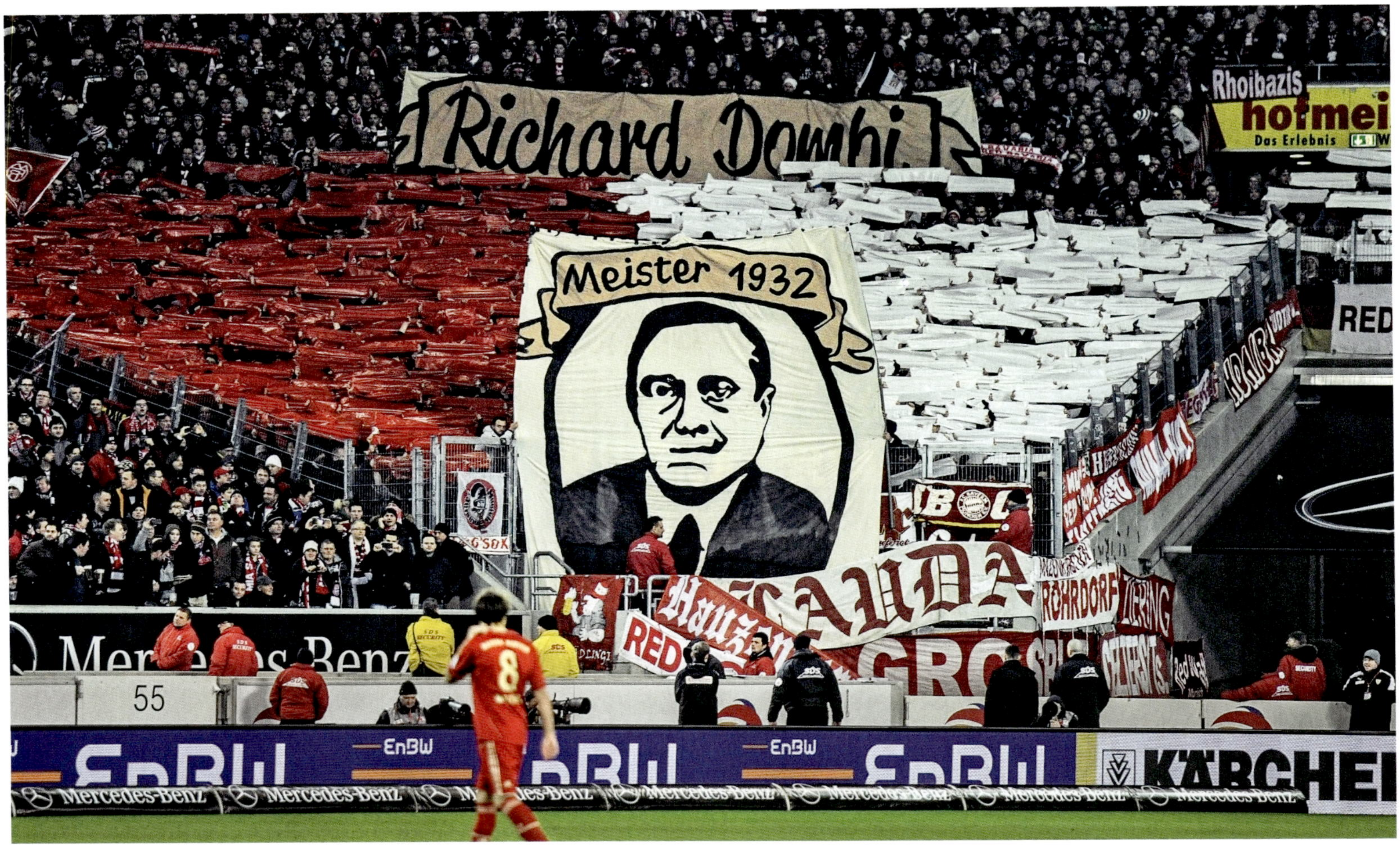

RICHARD "DOMBI" **KOHN**

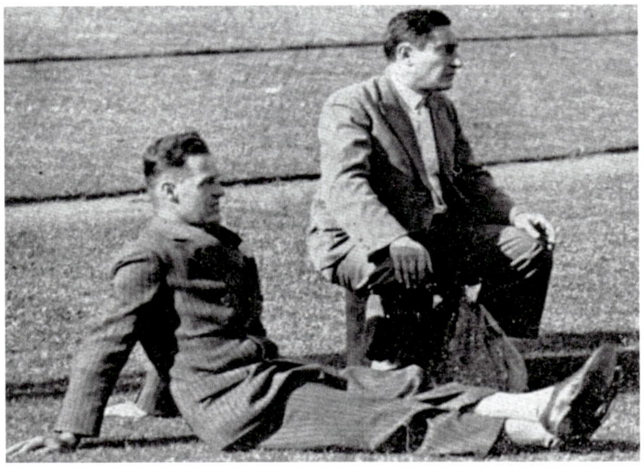

The first man who coached FCB to the league championship was also managing director of the club – and the players' masseur. However, in 1932 the board gave him instructions to restrict his massages "only to treatment for the 1st and 2nd team". Shortly afterwards, the team won the championship.

Dombi not only had several roles, but also several names. Born in Vienna under the name Richard Kohn, as a player he called himself "Little" and as a coach "Dombi", meaning "eminence" in Hungarian. At Bayern he continued the influence of the "Danube football" that was expressed in a stylish manner of playing when FCB won the final against Eintracht Frankfurt in 1932.

Dombi was considered one of the most expensive but also the most modern coaches of his day. His drills concentrated on ball control in a tight space when pressed by the opposition. The players were meant to learn to handle this in training, so that they would be relaxed in the game itself – which is what trainers are in principle still trying to do almost a hundred years later.

FCB's first championship win is regarded as the last success for Jews in German football. President Kurt Landauer fled to Switzerland. Otto Beer, head of the youth team, was deported to Kaunas, Lithuania, and murdered. The coach Dombi (on the right in the photo) survived in the Netherlands, where he won the championship twice with Feyenoord. Since 1997 a street in Rotterdam has been named after him.

ZLATKO "ČIK" **ČAJKOVSKI**

The diminutive, round Croat, a world-class player in the 1950s, brought both success and fun to Bayern's football.

In training sessions he always joined in at the end, picked the best players for his team, and "carried on with the game until he had won", said Sepp Maier. "So we always let him win." The young squad learned a lot from him, especially technique and tricks – but less of tactics. Čik let them get on with it – and that is what they did: promotion, winning the cup, winning the European Cup. And he pocketed the bonuses that he had already cleverly negotiated for all of this success when Bayern were still in the regional league.

Five in a row and the joker: Dieter Brenninger (on the right on the railing) was known as "Wucki", but Čik, whose real name was Zlatko, heard it as "Mucki", and that name stuck to this day. For his grandchildren, Brenninger is "Mucki grandad". And Gerd Müller (centre) was called "fat little Müller" by his tall, slim coach – he had a sense of humour.

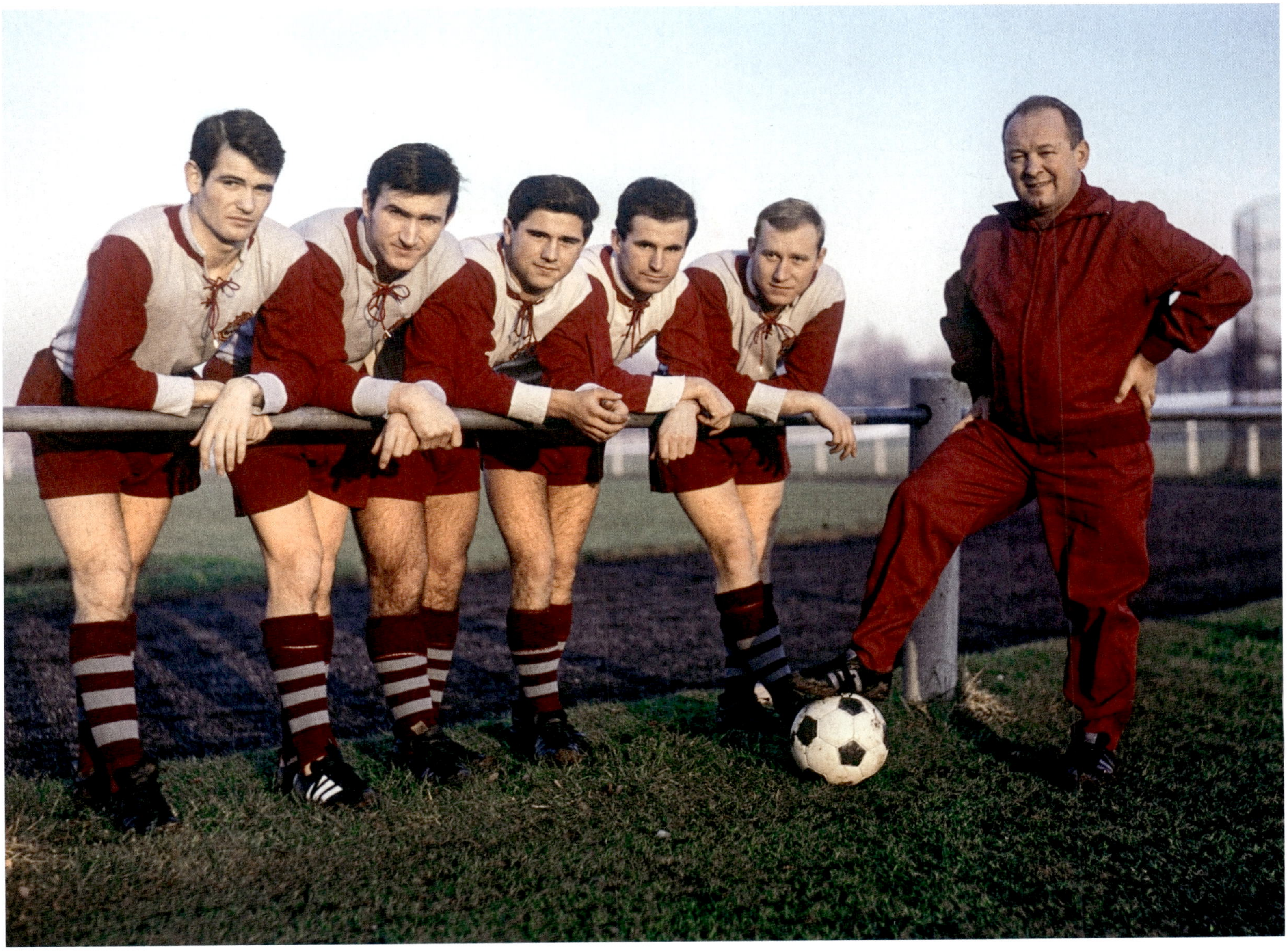

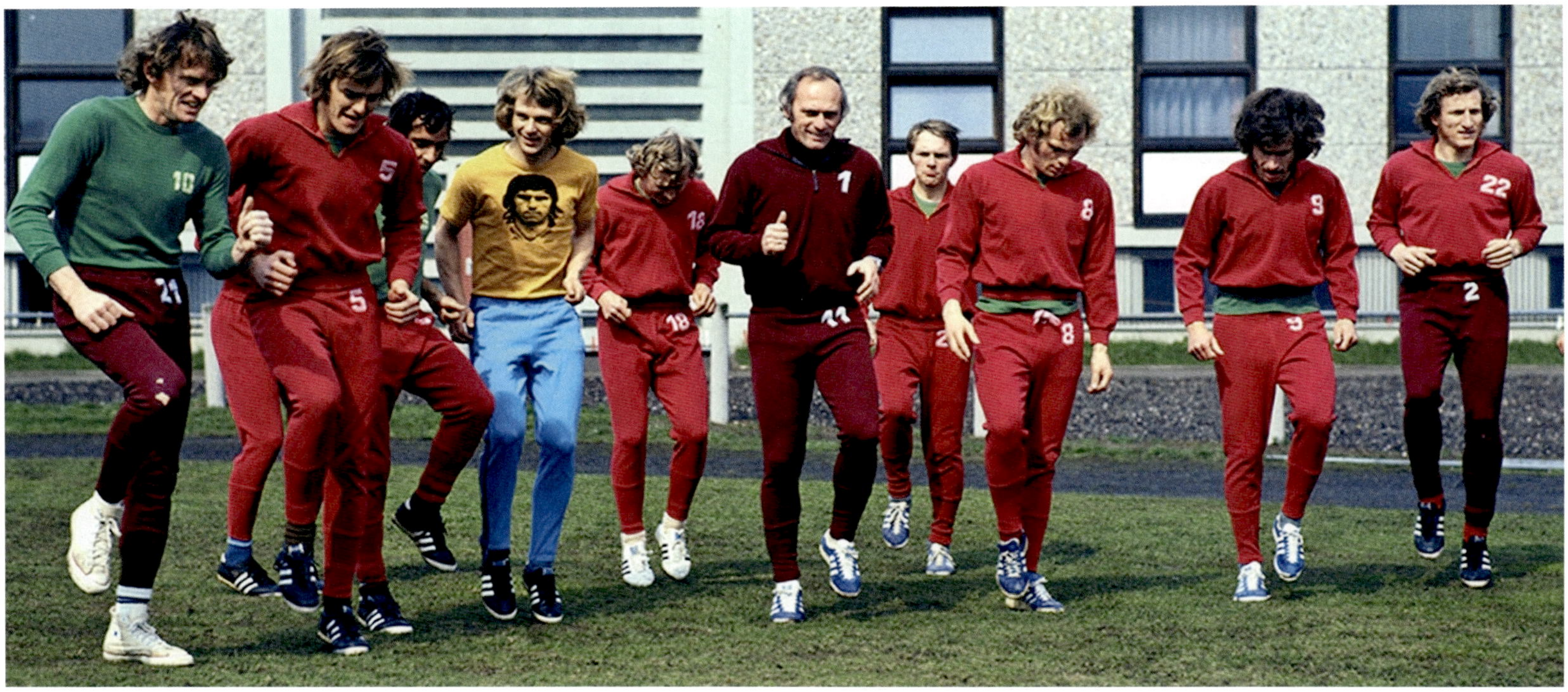

UDO **LATTEK**

In March 1970 the telephone rang in Munich newspapers and news agencies – someone from FCB was on the line. There was a new coach. For some journalists, the name had to be spelt out: Lattek, Udo, 35 years old.

In the case of a certain Guardiola a few years later, the news was broken in a somewhat different way – a presentation to more than 200 journalists, streamed live all over the world. But it was not the Pep show, but the brief announcement of Lattek that heralded the most successful coach's career in Bundesliga history. Lattek won eight league championships, six of them in two spells with Bayern, plus the European Cup in 1974. He was never considered a great tactician or even a football visionary, but he knew what made a team tick. He was "like a twelfth man" according to Sepp Maier. "I never thought of him as a coach, but more as a mate." When Lattek came across players in a disco although they were banned from going out, he said, "Now I'm going to count to 25,000, and if anyone is still here, there will be trouble."

"A farmer's son, coming from nowhere", is how Udo Lattek saw himself. "I owe everything to football." At FC Bayern he was the first to win titles in series: FCB won at least one trophy in every one of his eight years as trainer.

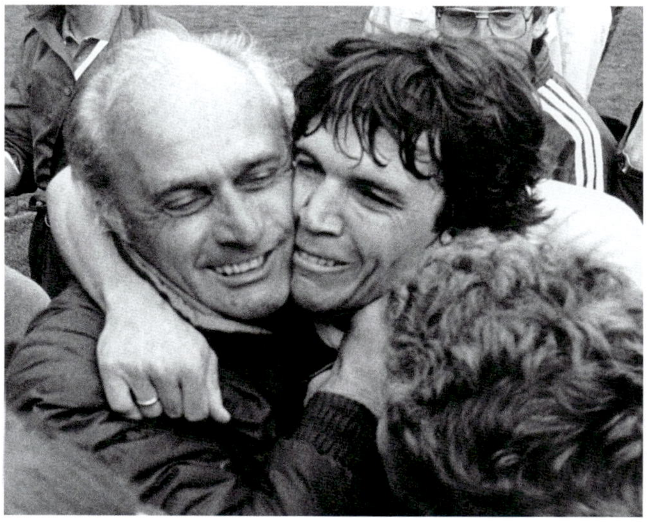

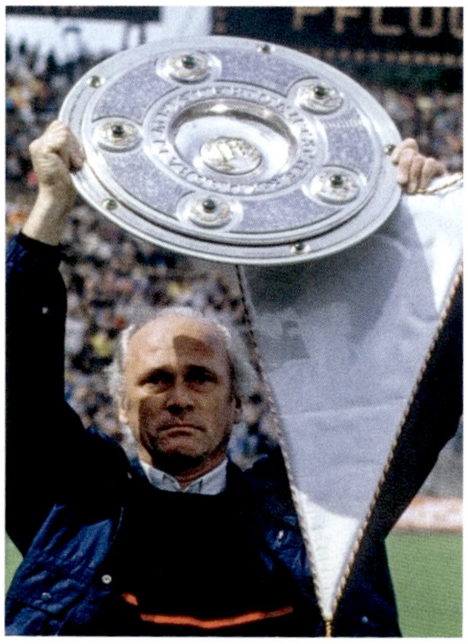

DETTMAR **CRAMER**

He was a walking map of global football, engaged in development work in more than eighty countries. But his "best times", he said, were his three years in Munich, with a unique record: the Club World Cup once, the European Cup twice, but never the German championship.

The short, wiry "football professor" did not always have an easy time with the fans, the media and his club president Neudecker, who said, "In the end we'll all have academic qualifications, but no points." And then he posed for a photo taken by Beckenbauer's girlfriend Diana Sandmann, in the style of a general with a bicorn hat. This gave him the nickname "Napoleon", but for Cramer that was no more than a "carnival joke".

At FCB Cramer was helped by his long-standing friendship with Franz Beckenbauer, whom he had once saved from being thrown out of the German national youth team (the association officials thought the young star was unacceptable because he fathered a child out of wedlock at the age of 18). Twelve years later "Kaiser Franz" repaid the trust that his wedding witness Cramer had shown. And Cramer succeeded in getting the best out of a team that was resting on its laurels, at least in big games. Here the "professor" also revealed his pragmatic traits: before the 1976 final against AS Saint-Étienne, he plied the nervous young star Rummenigge with two glasses of cognac. It helped.

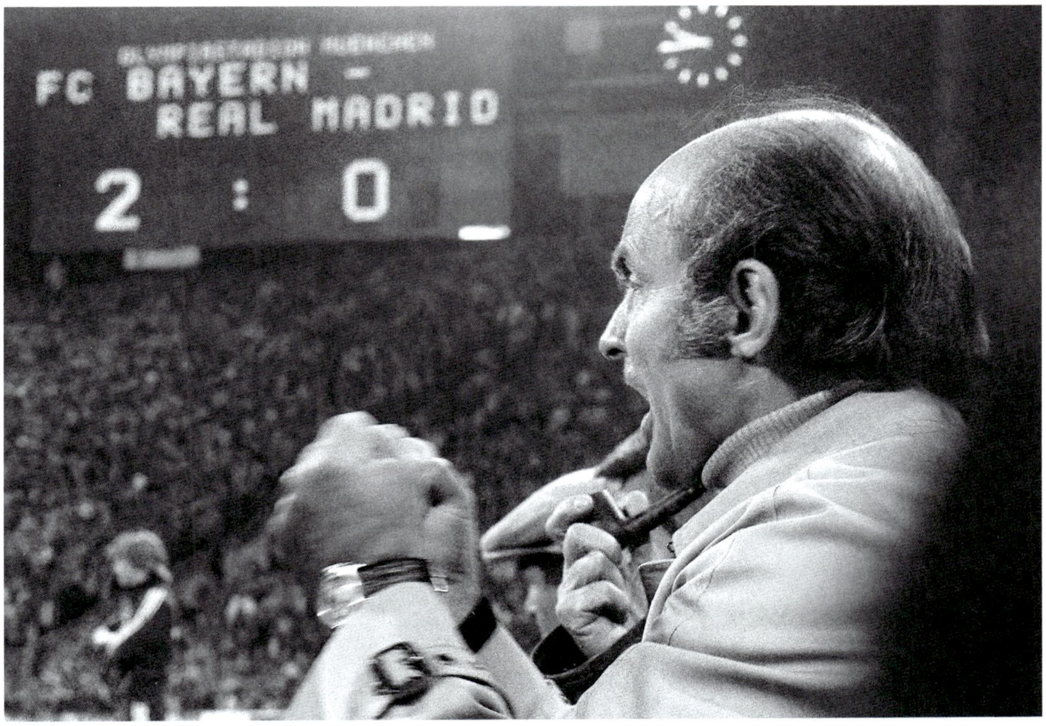

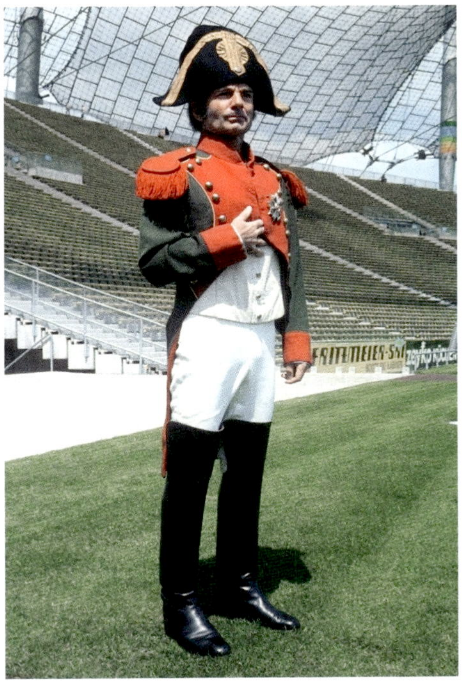

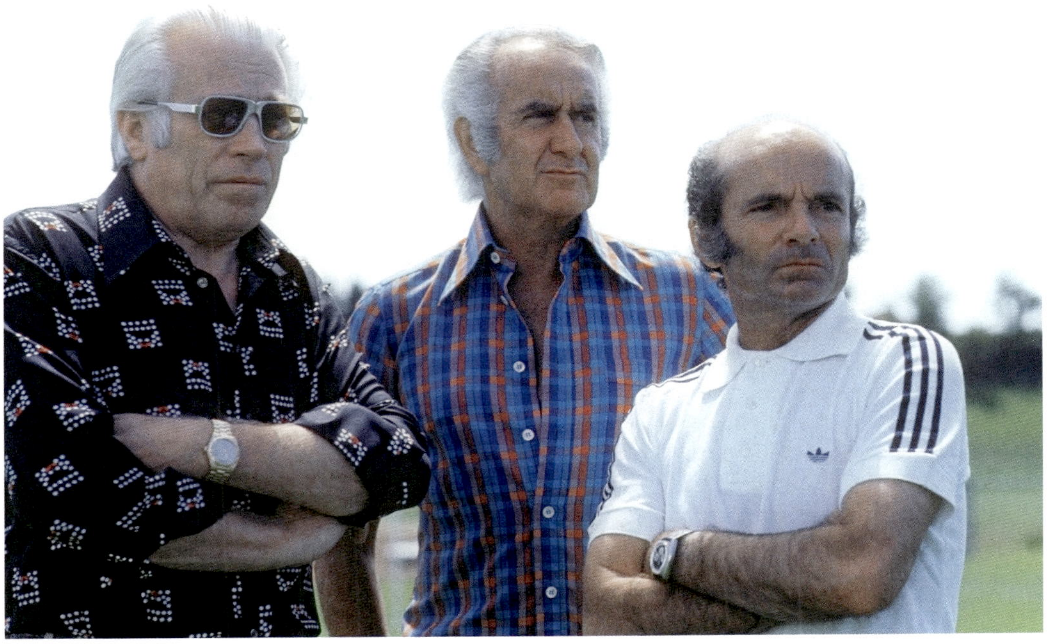

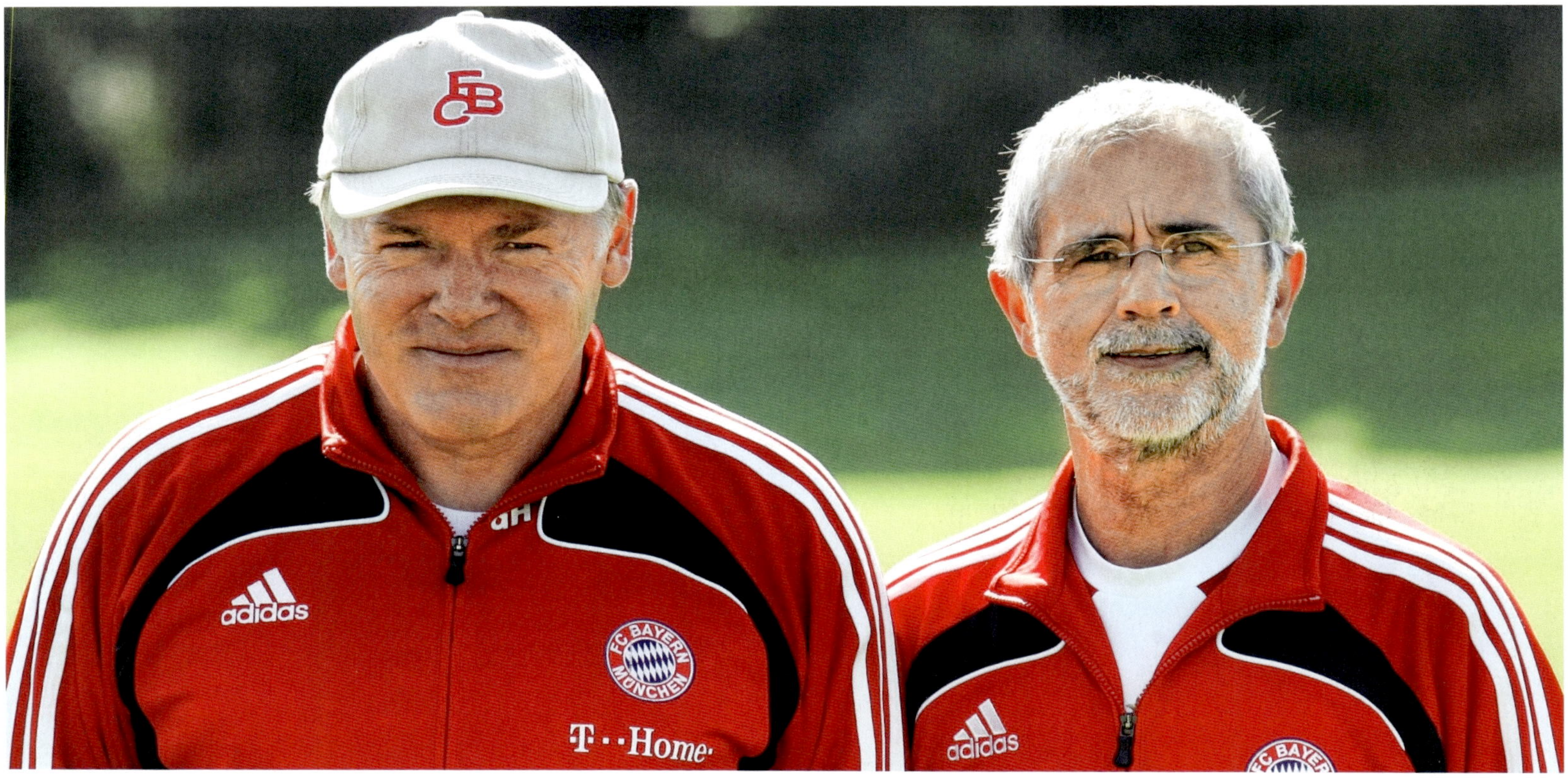

HERMANN **GERLAND**

He is what the Germans like to call *Urgestein*: "bedrock". In the case of Gerland, the toughest trainer ever, it fits almost literally. He made the players hard as rock. They hated it, and later understood. Thomas Müller, for example: "Thanks, Tiger. Every kick in the arse was a goal."

No one was a Bayern trainer for longer: twenty-five years. He was never the front man, but always there, in the place where the foundations for success were laid. Youth A-team, the reserve team, then assistant to van Gaal, Heynckes, Guardiola and Flick. The years of glory with the "best coaches in the world", as he said, were a great joy for him: "They could say to me: Stay at home, you'll get paid. And I would say: Keep the money, I don't want to stay at home." Gerland was not only the world's most successful assistant coach, but also – and this is more important to him – a man who always sought and did what was best for hundreds of talented youngsters. Some of them had what it took to be world champions – for example Philipp Lahm and Thomas Müller, for whom he battled against Uli Hoeness, or Bastian Schweinsteiger, who often did crazy things when he was young. "Then he got a rocket from me. And afterwards I drove home and thought about how we were once just like that." For others the right course was to look for an alternative to professional football early on. Tiger told the truth to everyone.

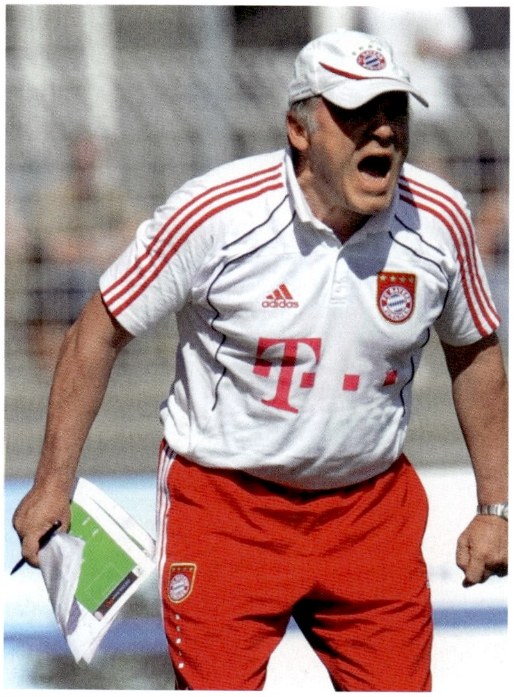

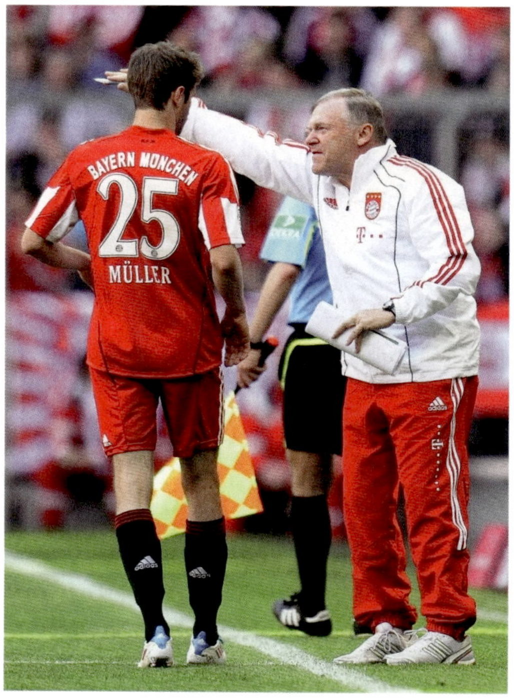

Beware of the volcano: players who don't give their all can brace themselves for a verbal eruption from Hermann Gerland. Especially after the ultimate deadly sin in Tiger's world: losing the ball and not running back for it. But there is a different side to Gerland, above all where his two Müllers are concerned: Gerd, his assistant of many years, and Thomas, his apprentice made good. Of these two goal-getters he speaks in the most enthusiastic terms possible for a former defender.

LOUIS VAN GAAL

He had his own theory about why the chemistry was not right between him and the bosses of Bayern: "It's always a problem to work with former players." By contrast, he was not unpopular with the spectators. From the balcony of city hall, after winning the double, he called out: "You are the best fans in the world!" And he became the only person who ever addressed them with the formal German "Sie" instead of the informal "Du".

One single win was all he lacked for a first Bayern treble, in the final against Inter Milan. Even so, his first and only full season was one of the best in the history of FC Bayern. One year after their tactical catastrophe in the 0–4 in Barcelona, with creative training, strict discipline and plenty of courage, van Gaal succeeded in making FCB one of the European greats again. But "King Louis" also had self-confidence in spades, and vehemently stood up for his own opinions and theories. As a result of poor results, in his second season he and the club parted ways. There is no question, as Uli Hoeness confirmed, that his achievement was to lay the foundations for a superb decade at Bayern: "I give a lot of credit to Louis for initiating a great footballing culture here."

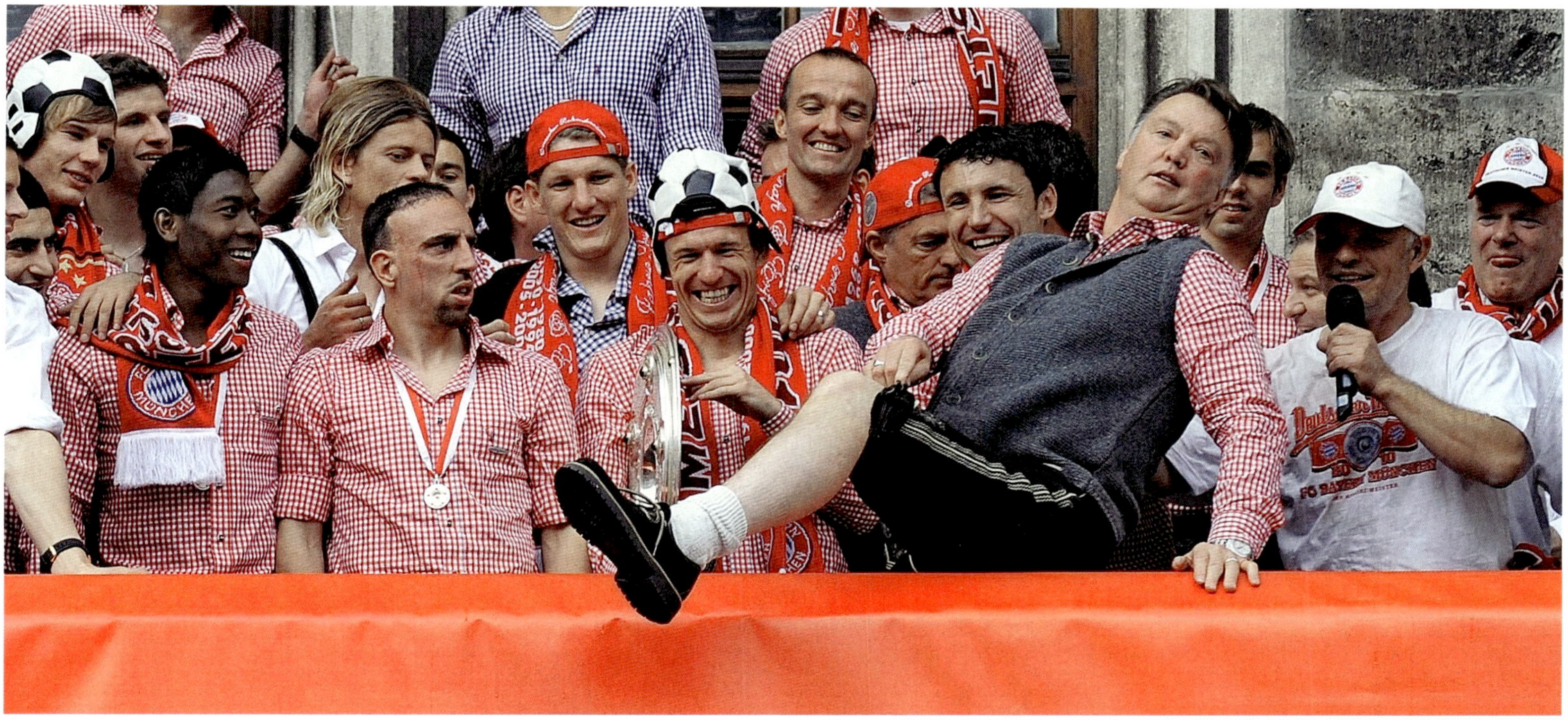

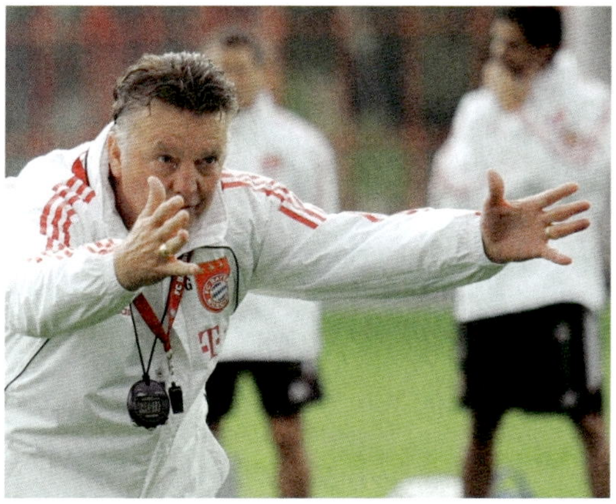

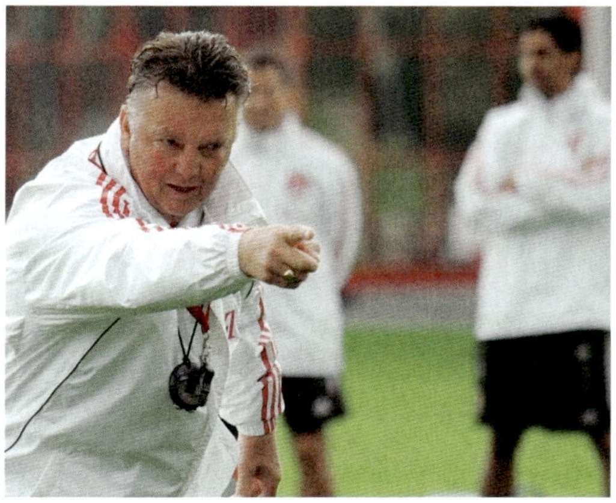

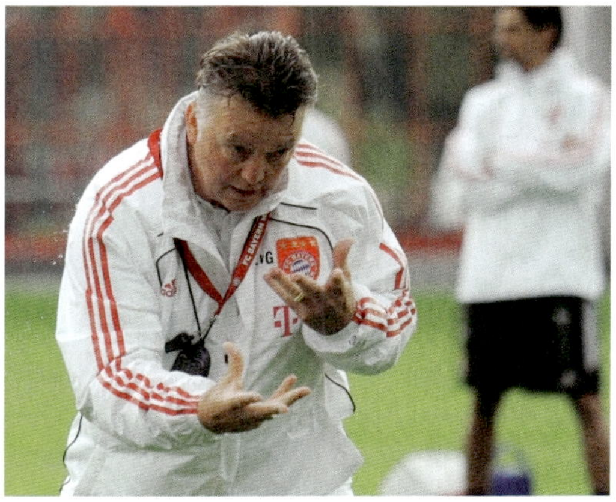

JUPP HEYNCKES

Firing him in 1991 was, said Uli Hoeness, "my biggest mistake". Luckily it was possible to reverse the decision later, no less than three times. And Jupp Heynckes became the most loyal and highest-achieving trainer in FCB's history.

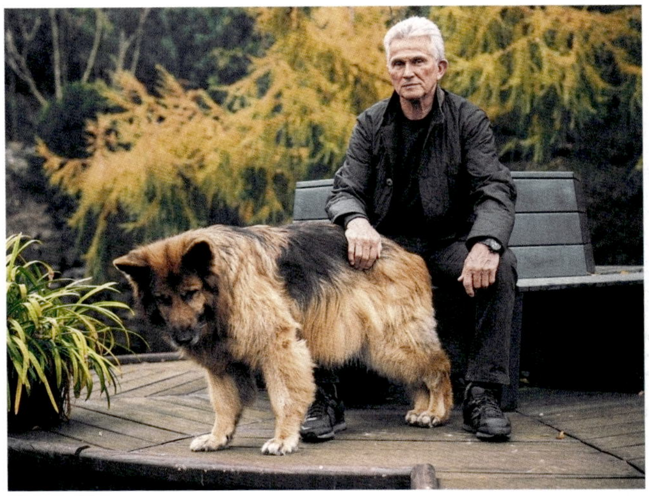

What a career! 1,038 games in the Bundesliga, fifty-three years between his first match, as an unknown young professional footballer, and the last one, as a world-famous coach – and twenty-nine years between his first league championship trophy with Bayern in 1989, and his fourth and last in 2018. Records, every one, probably for all time. And all of this is overshadowed by Jupp Heynckes' masterpiece, the treble season of 2012–13, when "Super-Bayern" fulfilled almost to perfection his ideal of a football team: "Like chess with chess pieces that move themselves – and do it intuitively." Heynckes achieved this through obsession about detail, discipline and at the same time intelligent man management, thanks to which there was no moaning by the players on the bench, no one sitting in the stands and taking offence, no bad feeling – never. Especially with Heynckes himself. When it was already clear that Pep Guardiola would take over in the summer, Heynckes concentrated an untameable energy in himself and the team in an unprecedented way for the sake of the greater cause. Later Uli Hoeness said, with tongue in cheek, that Heynckes had developed this ambition simply to make his point to everyone one more time.

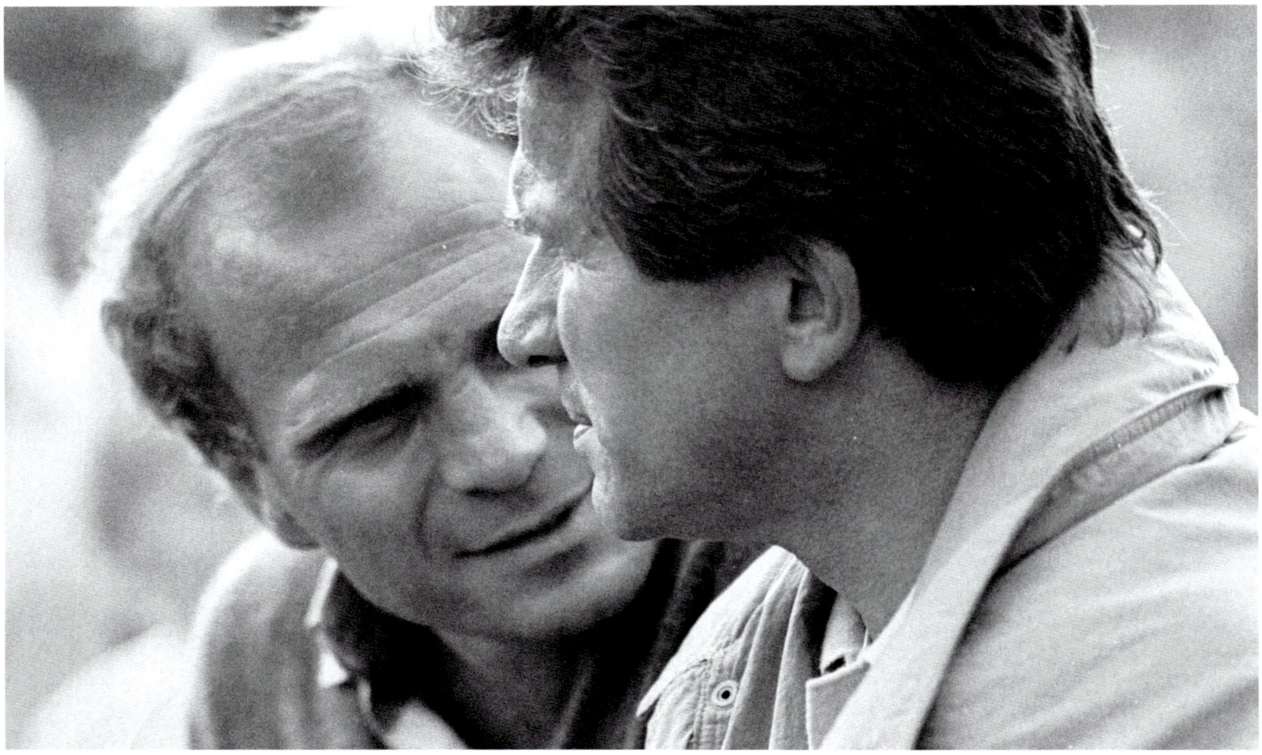

Firing Jupp Heynckes in 1991 was "my biggest mistake", Uli Hoeness said later. He brought him back three times, following the dismissals of Klinsmann, van Gaal and Ancelotti. Heynckes delivered the goods every time - and departed in 2018 shortly after his 72nd birthday, retiring for good to his home region, the Lower Rhine, the oldest trainer in the history of the German league to win the championship.

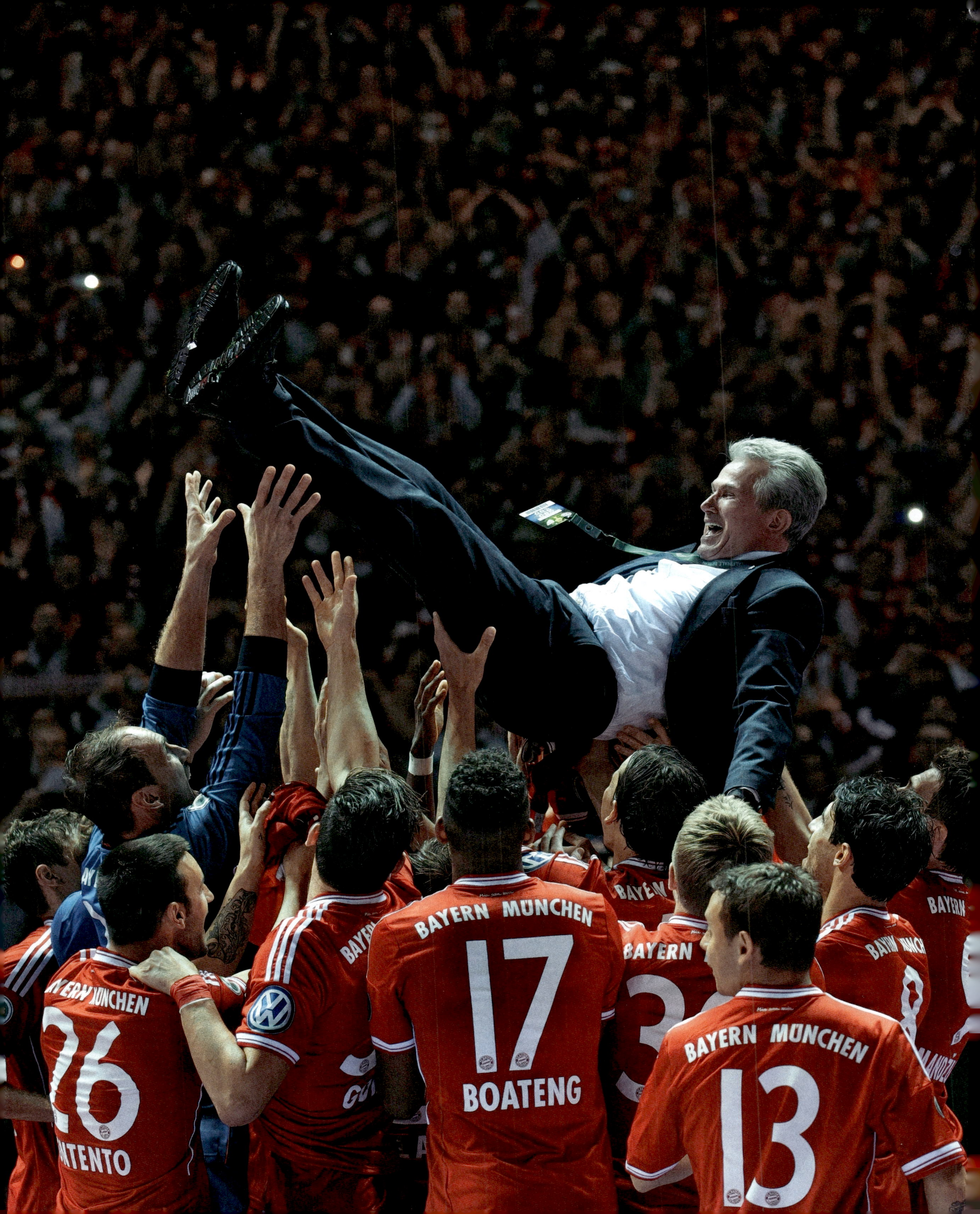
BAYERN MÜNCHEN
17
BOATENG
BAYERN MÜNCHEN
13
26
BAYERN

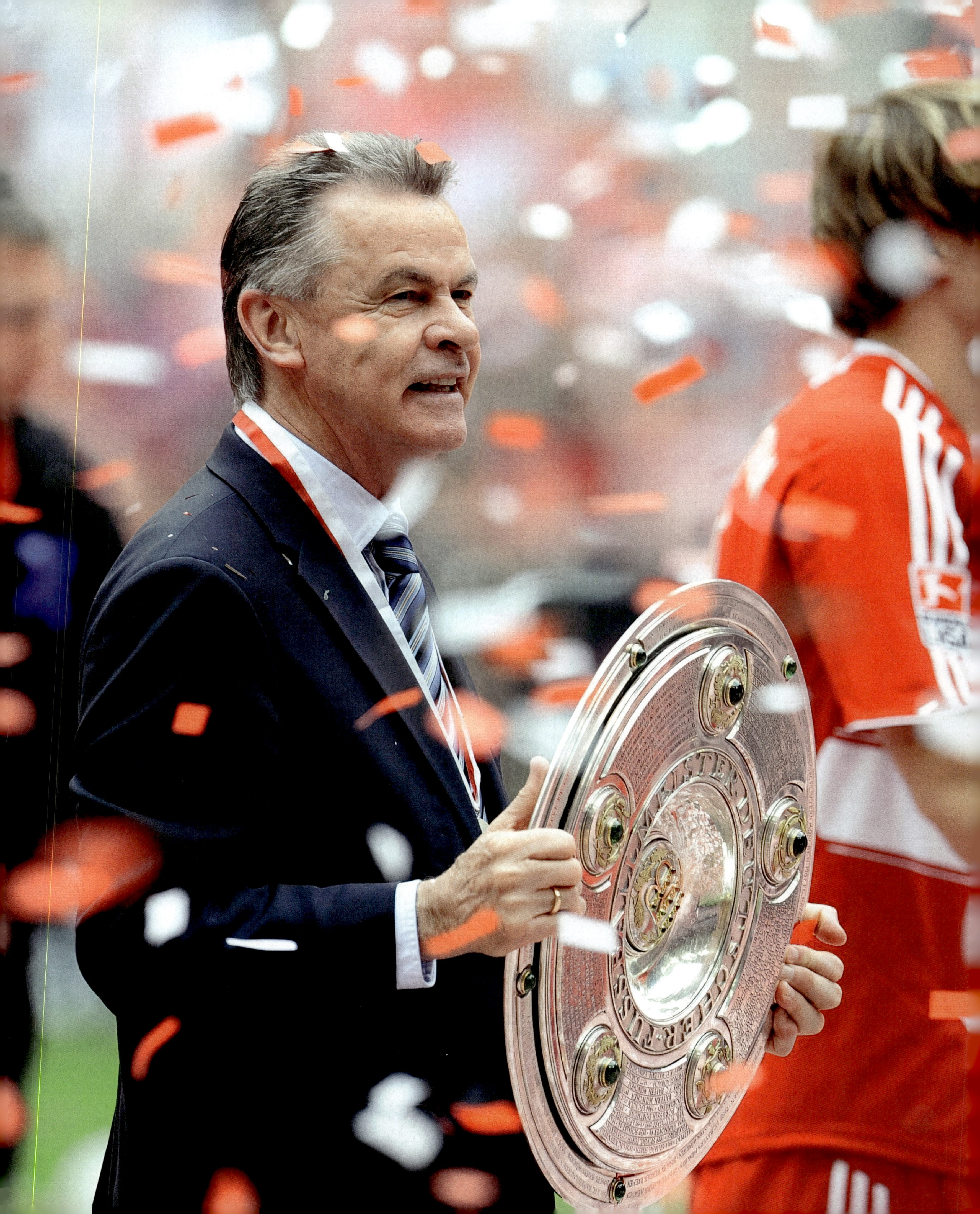

OTTMAR **HITZFELD**

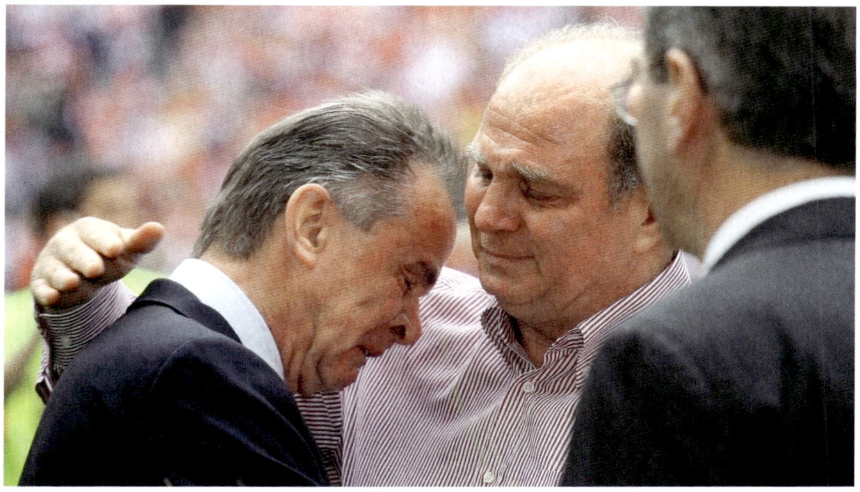

To this day he holds a scoring record for the second division of the Bundesliga: six goals in one match, scored in 1977 in an 8–0 win for VfB Stuttgart against Regensburg. But he was a record holder above all as a coach.

With twenty-five club trophies, Ottmar Hitzfeld is the most successful German coach by some distance. Probably his greatest achievement was not a major victory but after the "mother of all defeats", as he called the traumatic 1–2 against Manchester United in 1999. "Everyone was completely devastated, but as a coach it's your job to put down new markers. I thanked the team. They played well, we were better than them, it was fate. I said: We have to set our course, we have to stick together." For Karl-Heinz Rummenigge it was Hitzfeld's clarity and empathy "that contributed to our winning the cup two years later against Valencia."

Every morning when he came to the changing room, Hitzfeld shook his players' hands. It is just a detail, but a characteristic one for his style of leadership. In a respectful way he set standards in the tough business of football. But he also stored up a lot inside himself. After six years at Bayern, his energy was spent. He took an open approach to his burn-out, sought professional help and returned two and a half years later to FCB and coached them to the championship again in 2008, for the fifth time. No farewell was more tearful than his. "It was always important to me to have recognition as a human being," was his conclusion. "It's not possible to act the tough guy all the time."

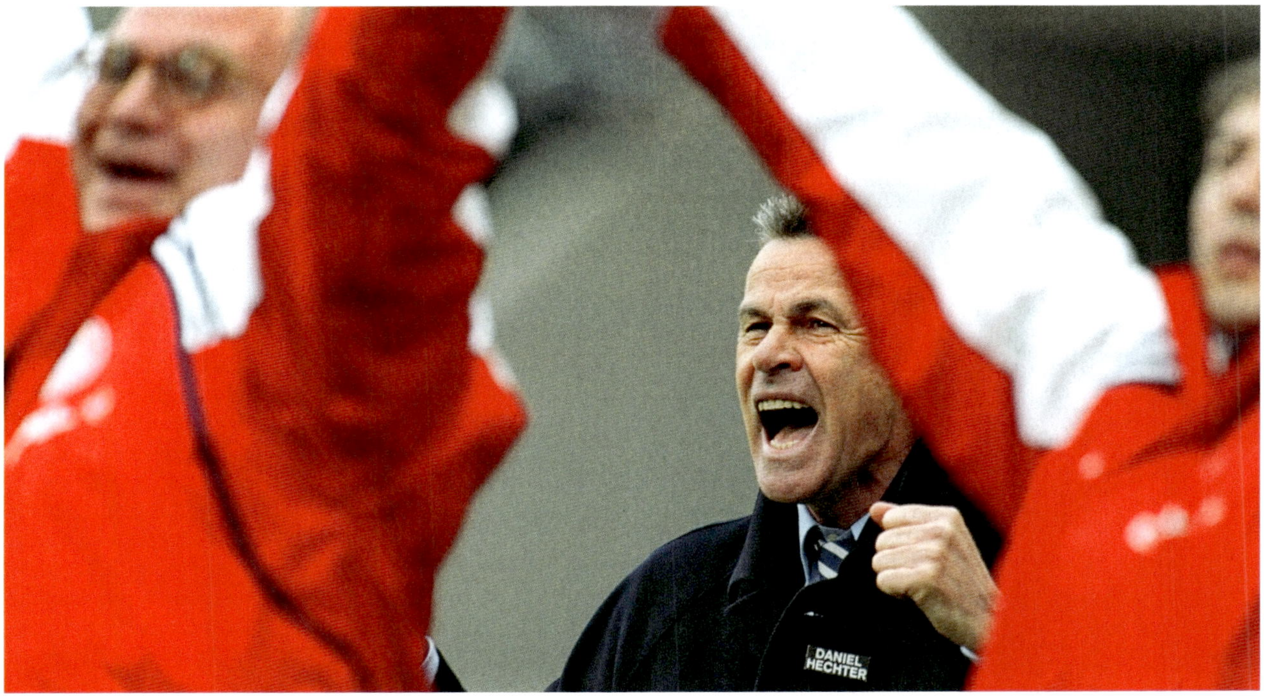

If there has been a Bayern coach who deserves the appellation "gentleman", it must be Ottmar Hitzfeld. Formerly a mathematics teacher, towards his football pupils he showed a blend of respectful distance and emotional approachability. On his return to FCB in 2007, said Hasan Salihamidžić, when the trainer came into the dressing room, "the sun rises". When he left for good a year later, it rained tears.

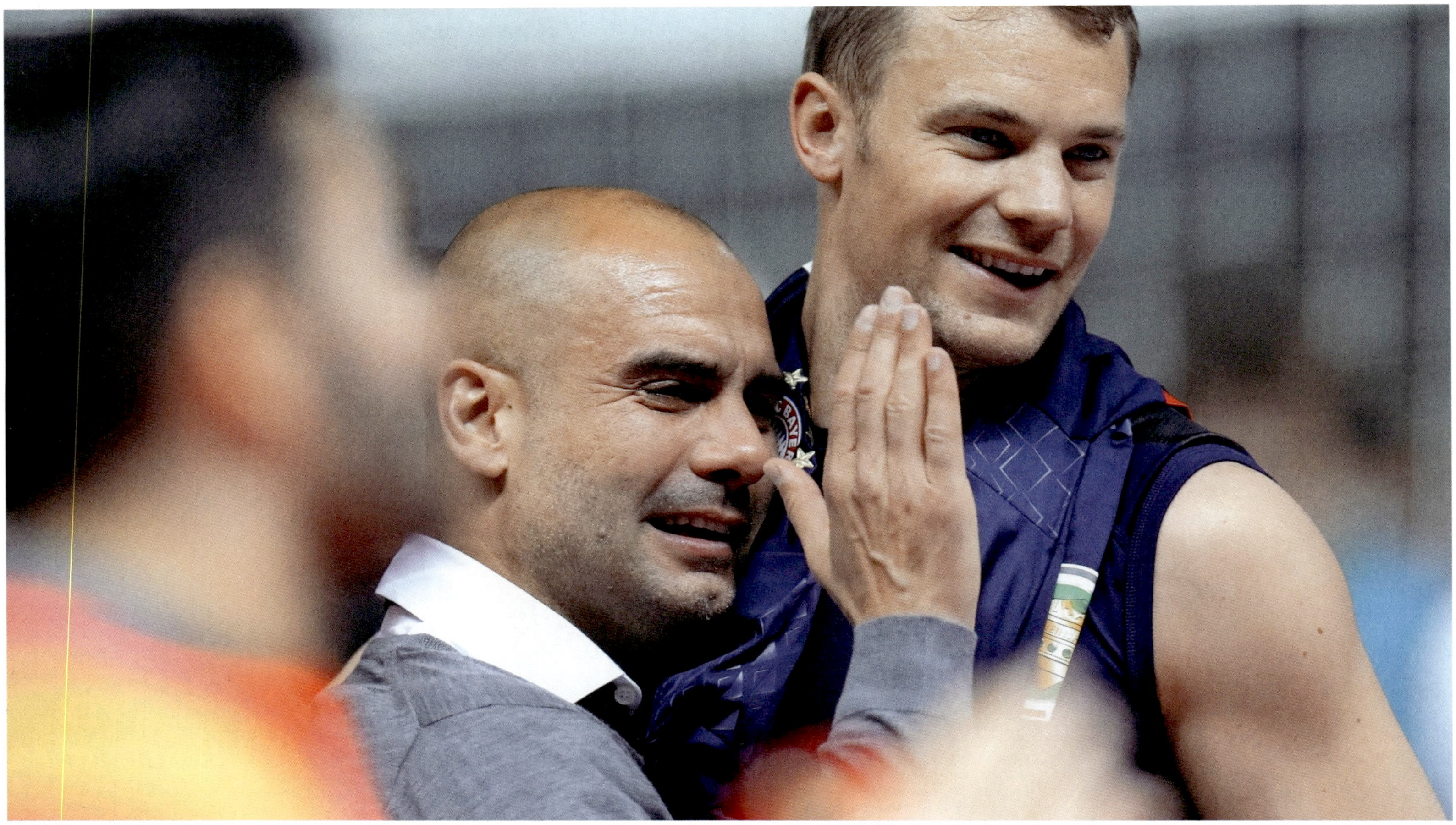

PEP **GUARDIOLA**

The twenty-first century was the age of "superheroes" – not only on the cinema screen, but also on the training ground. Pep Guardiola had the training pitch covered up so as not to reveal his secrets. He created a post-treble team of unsurpassed footballing skill that gained everything except the greatest accolade.

He brought a new aura to the coaching job. No brooder on the bench but a choreographer on the line, perfecting moves and positions – and not even split pants could hold him back. At his very first Champions League away game, a 3–1 win at Manchester City, Bayern retained possession of the ball with fifty-eight passes in succession. When they won 3–1 against Hertha BSC in Berlin in March, they had two epoch-making records: the earliest league championship, in only the twenty-seventh match, and the nineteenth successive victory. Three years of Pep meant three championship titles, two victories in the German cup, countless brilliant games, and the semi-final of the Champions League three times. He turned Bayern into the world's best team at possession football, who could only be stopped just before the final by teams from Guardiola's homeland: Real Madrid, FC Barcelona and, with particular bad luck, Atlético Madrid. After a fantastic performance and a ratio of 33–7 shots at goal, Guardiola said farewell, "happy and proud".

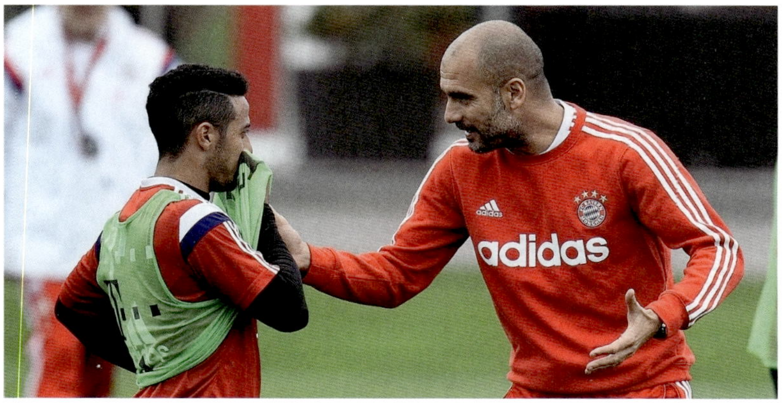

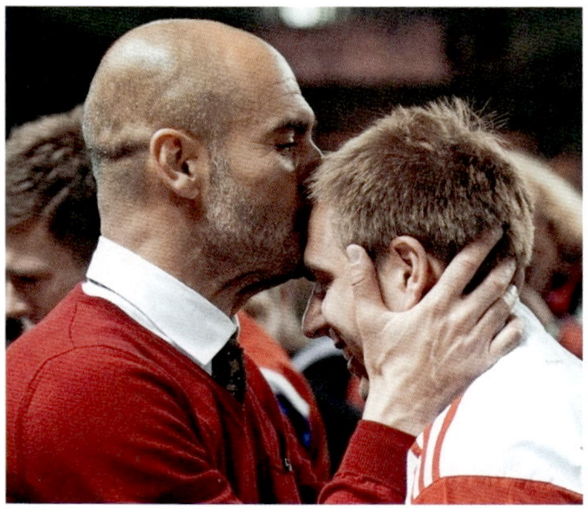

There has probably never been a trainer who was such an active fan of his own players. He hugged, kissed and praised them whenever he could, and elevated some with the superlatives top-top or even "top-top-top player". The affection was mutual. In three years with Pep, the players became fans of their own coach. So did the bosses at Bayern. They all wanted to keep him - in vain.

HANSI **FLICK**

In the dreary Covid year he led FCB to a unique series of wins and titles.

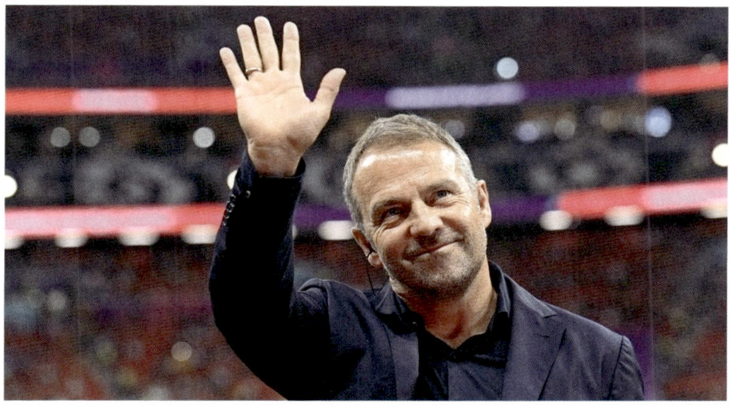

Three years after FC Bayern and Hansi Flick parted company, they had a reunion in October 2024 that ended painfully for Flick's former club. In the Champions League, Vincent Kompany's side lost 1-4 against Flick's new team, FC Barcelona.

From February to September 2020, Flick's line-up won twenty-three matches in succession, more than any professional German team before. In doing so, they won five trophies: the German championship and cup, the Champions League, the German Super Cup and the UEFA Super Cup. The FIFA Club World Cup in December made it the maximum possible, a one-off event in the history of the club. Flick, who gained a championship medal four times with FCB, seemed unable to put a foot wrong. Even the Covid pandemic could not take the team out of its stride – on the contrary, a smart plan for home training during the lockdown led to a superior level of fitness after the restart of the season in the Champions League final stages, for example in an 8–2 against FC Barcelona. Even though it was not possible to celebrate these successes with the fans, FCB's winning streak gave millions of people a rare outburst of joy in difficult times. In the following season he gained "only" one title, the championship. In the end, the club parted with Hansi Flick, who became coach of the German national side – and in that position attained hardly any of the success that seemed to be taken for granted at FCB.

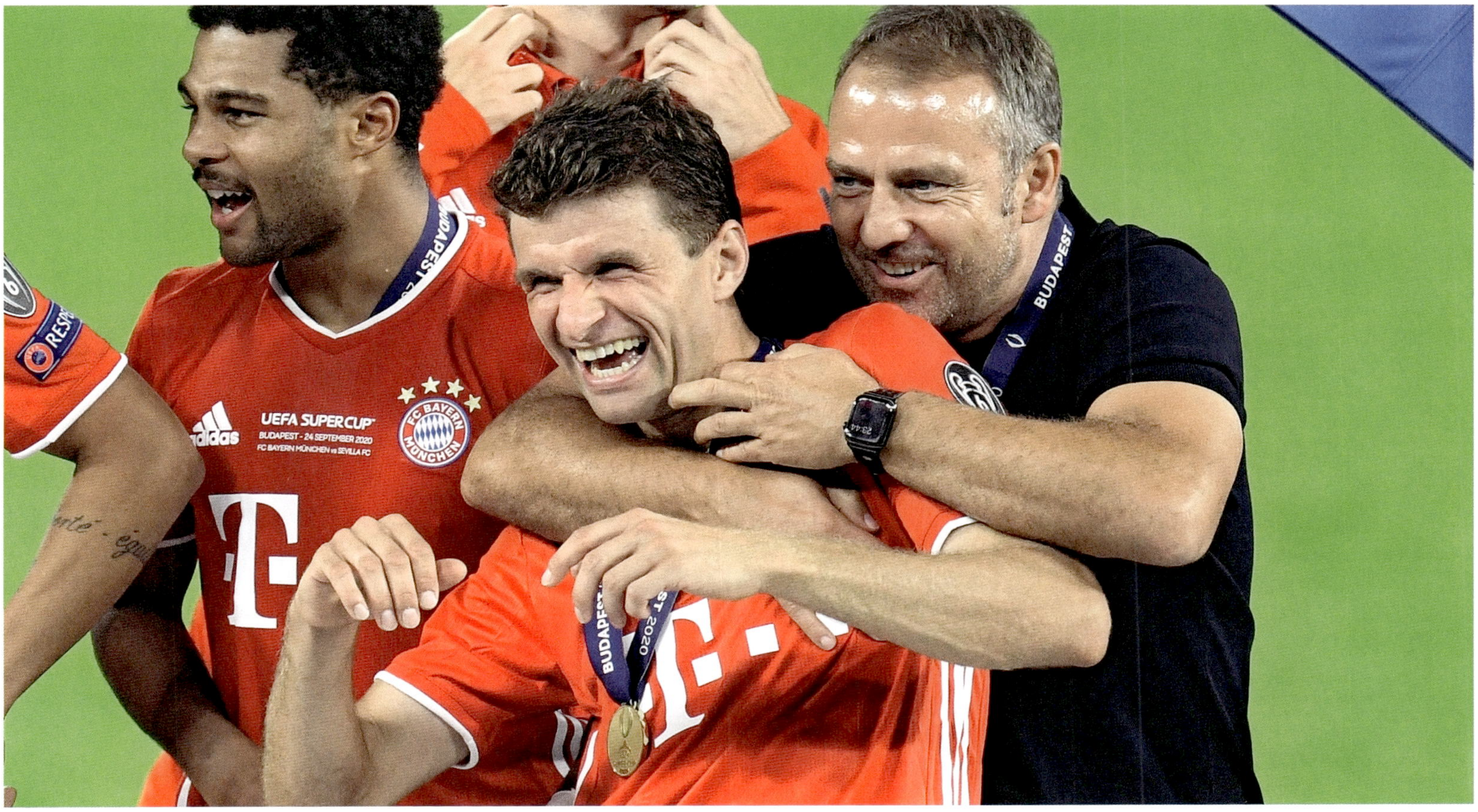

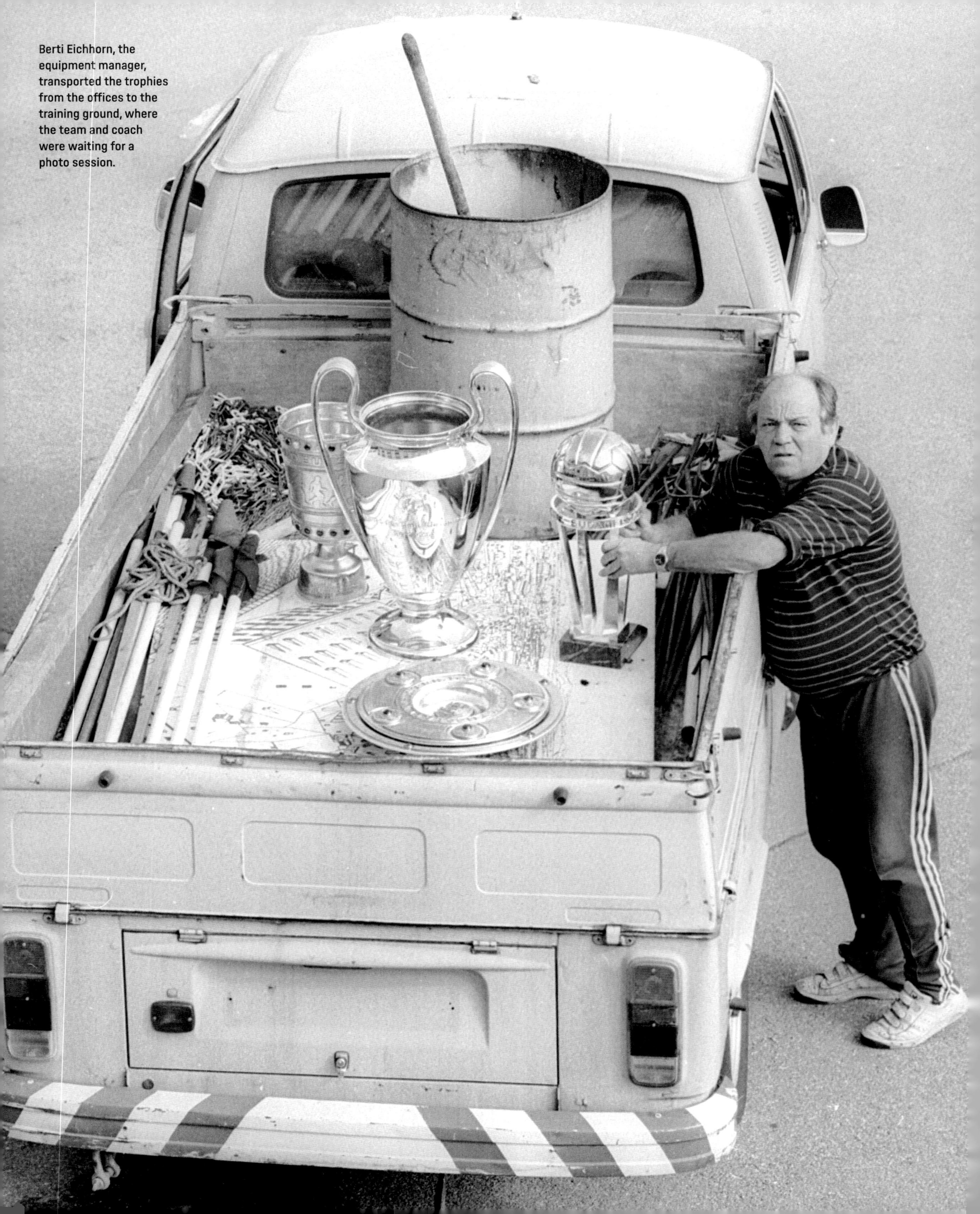

Berti Eichhorn, the equipment manager, transported the trophies from the offices to the training ground, where the team and coach were waiting for a photo session.

125×FCB

FC Bayern München eV
Säbener Str. 51-57
81547 München

Date of founding:
27 February 1900

Sections:
- Football, male licensed players affiliated as FC Bayern München AG
- Basketball
- E-sport
- Handball
- Skittles
- Chess
- Referees
- Senior football
- Table tennis

Former sections:
baseball, ice hockey, gymnastics, rugby

Main shareholder of FC Bayern München AG, owning 75 per cent

Owner of FC Bayern Campus

Sole shareholder in FC Bayern München Basketball GmbH

1

Shields and players' badges are emblems of FC Bayern, known worldwide, symbols of passion, success and tradition. Players and fans wear the logos with pride and represent the club's values all over the globe.

SHIELDS

1901–1902 | 1902–1906 | 1906–1919 | 1920–1924 | 1924–1953

1954–1970 | 1970–1997 | 1997–2002 | 2002–2017 | since 2017

BADGES

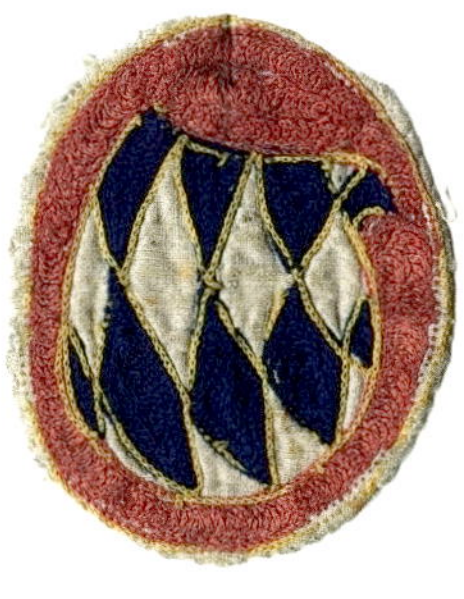

1923

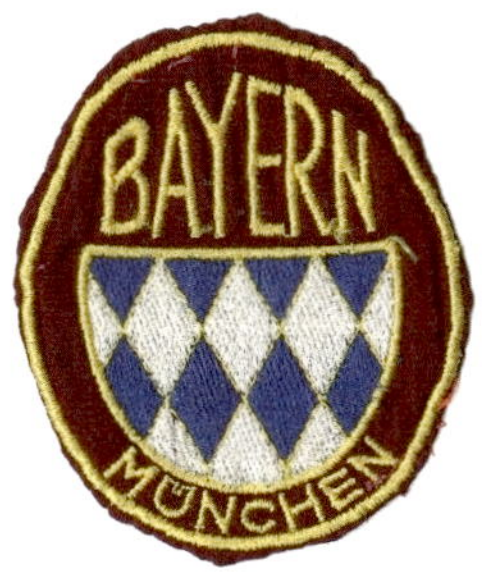

1950s

Over the history of FCB, the club logo has changed with the times. When the club was founded in 1900, its colours were at first blue and white. This had already changed to red and white by 1906 as a condition of the merger with the Münchener Sport-Club. The Bavarian diamond pattern was initially part of the FCB logo, but as a symbol of the club's home soon adorned the players' badges. The design of the logo was most recently altered in 2017 and remains with slight colour adjustments to this day.

2 SWAPPING **SHIRTS**

In red, white, black, silver, even in yellow - in the course of the club's history, FC Bayern players have taken the field in kits of many different colours. Some shirts are closely connected with special moments and stories. One of the most unusual was worn by Bayern players when

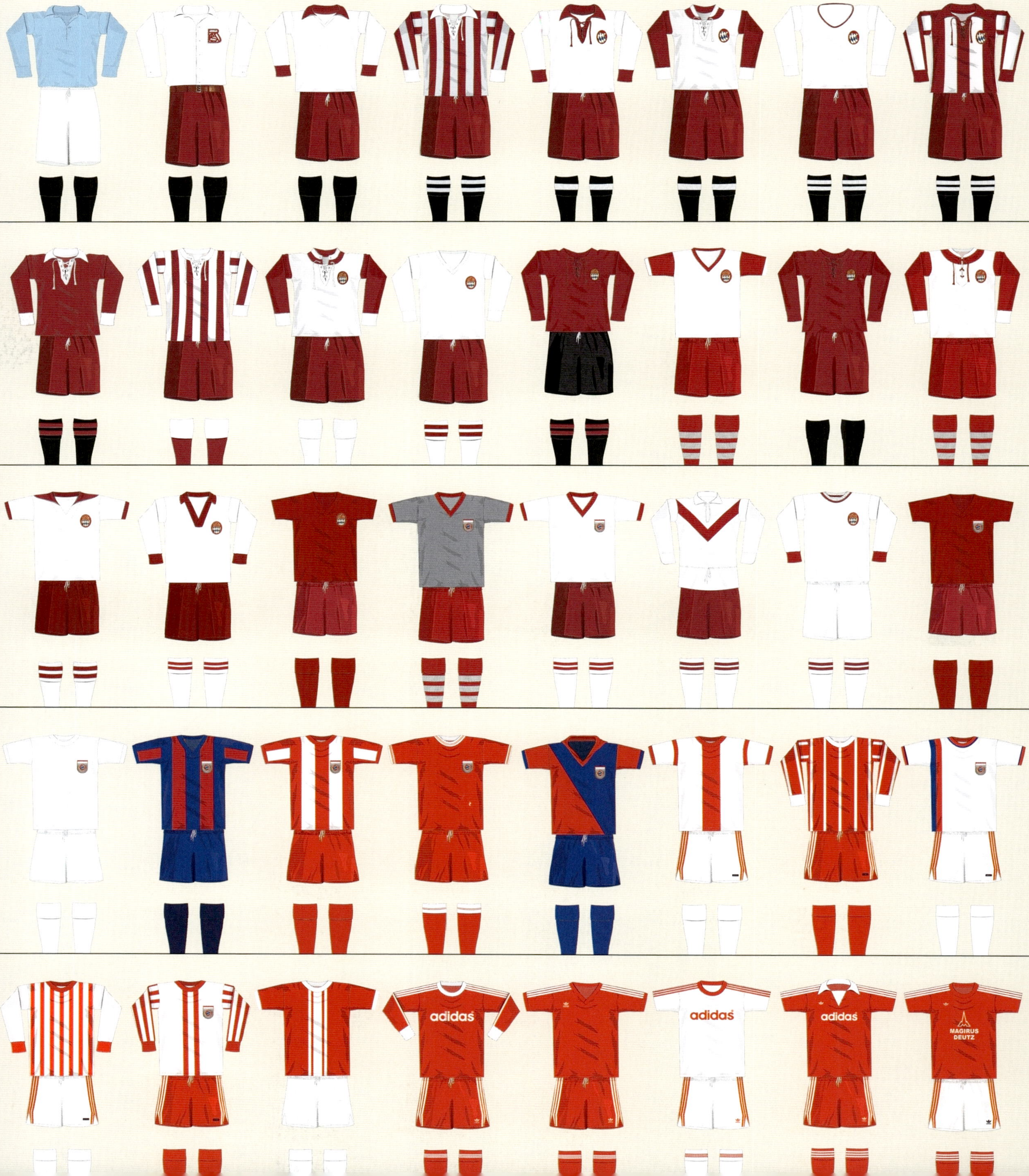

they beat 1. FC Köln 2-0 in 2001. As the equipment manager had left the white kit for away games back in Munich, they played the match wearing their white warm-up jackets over the red home kit. The entire range of players' kits over 125 years can be admired in a book republished for the club anniversary: *Alle Bayern-Trikots. Von 1900 bis heute* (Every Bayern Shirt: From 1900 to the Present) by Raimund Simmet, a Munich hairdresser and Bayern fan whose illustrations keep the collection constantly up to date.

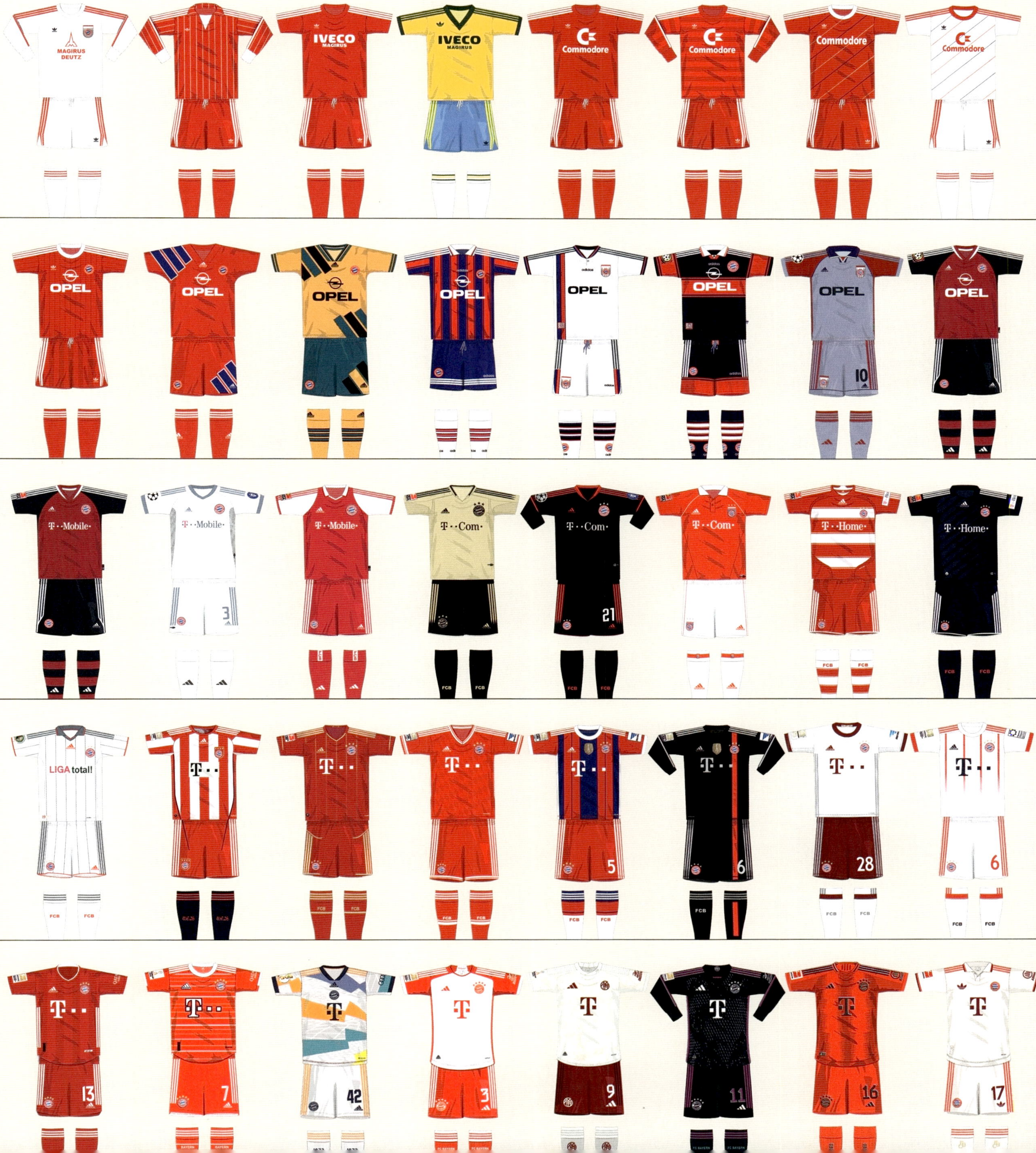

SERIAL **CHAMPIONS**

3

2013-2023
FC Bayern München

1999-2001
FC Bayern München

1985-1987
FC Bayern München

1972-1974
FC Bayern München

It's unbelievable, but true: eleven championships in a row between 2013 and 2023. A major part in all of these triumphs was played by Manuel Neuer, the captain, and Thomas Müller, the quintessential Bayern player, who were involved every time.

4 MIA SAN **MORE AND MORE**

382,000
2024

Since 2006 the number of members has more than tripled. Club president Hainer: "This shows the strength of FC Bayern, that this club constitutes a home for many people and that people all over the world can identify with the club and its values."

120,000
2006

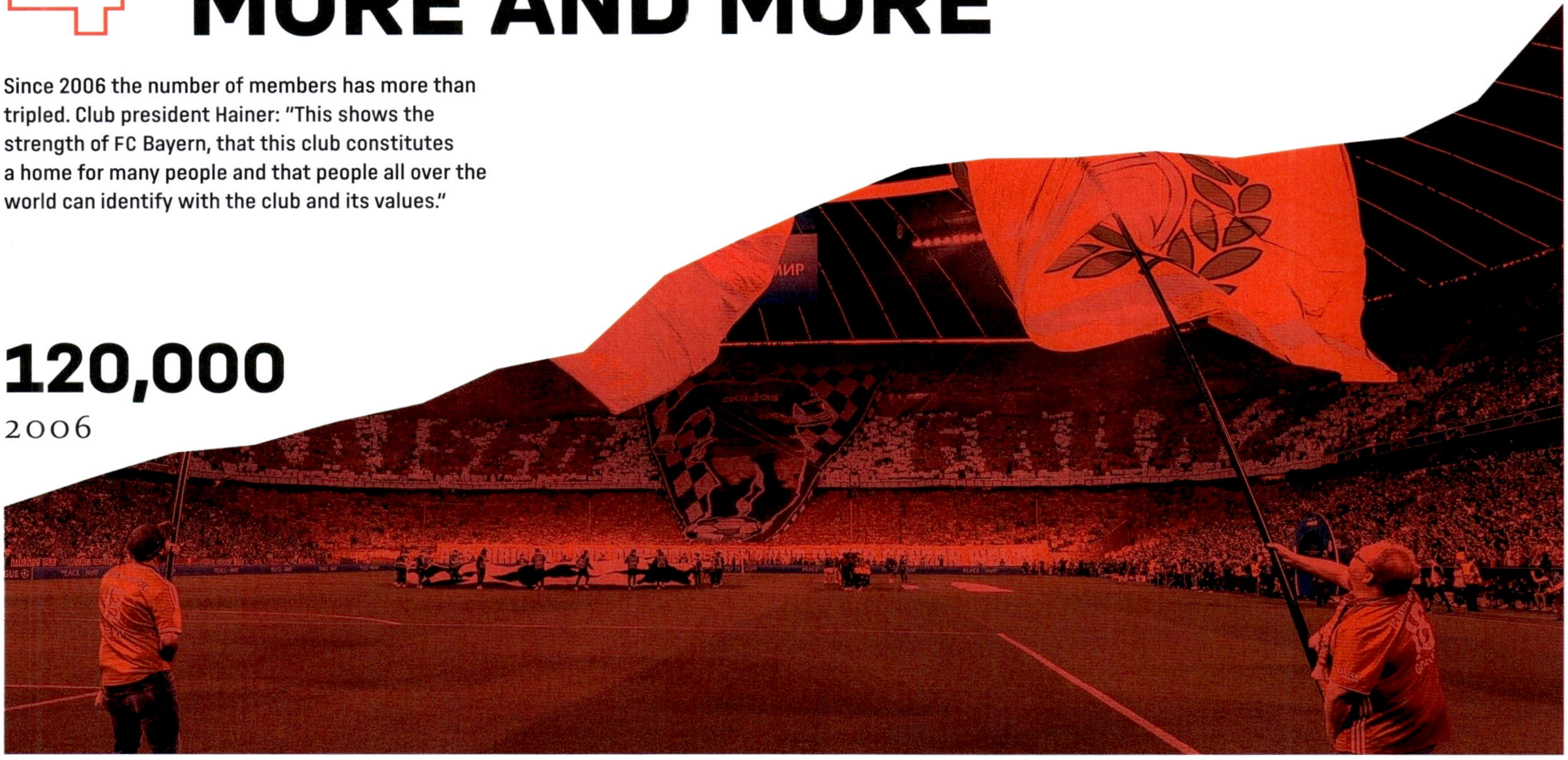

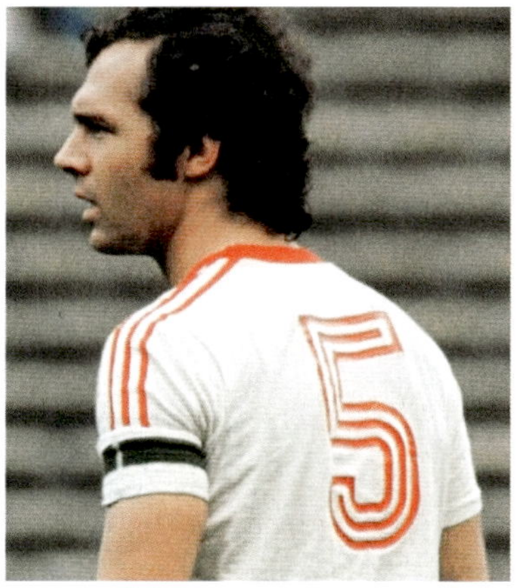

5

He always wore the number 5 shirt on the pitch. According to a decision by the members in 2024, FC Bayern will honour Franz Beckenbauer by not giving this number again to any other player. Since the first anniversary of the death of the "Kaiser", the open space in front of the Allianz Arena has been named Franz-Beckenbauer-Platz. Giving the stadium an unbeatable address: Franz-Beckenbauer-Platz 5.

6 A RECORD! **91 POINTS**

With 91 points from a possible maximum total of 102, the winners of the most German championships set a Bundesliga record in the treble season of 2012-13. The goal difference, too, was a new best: +80 (98-18). An equally unique achievement is that Jupp Heynckes' team did not concede a single goal from a counter-attack in the whole season.

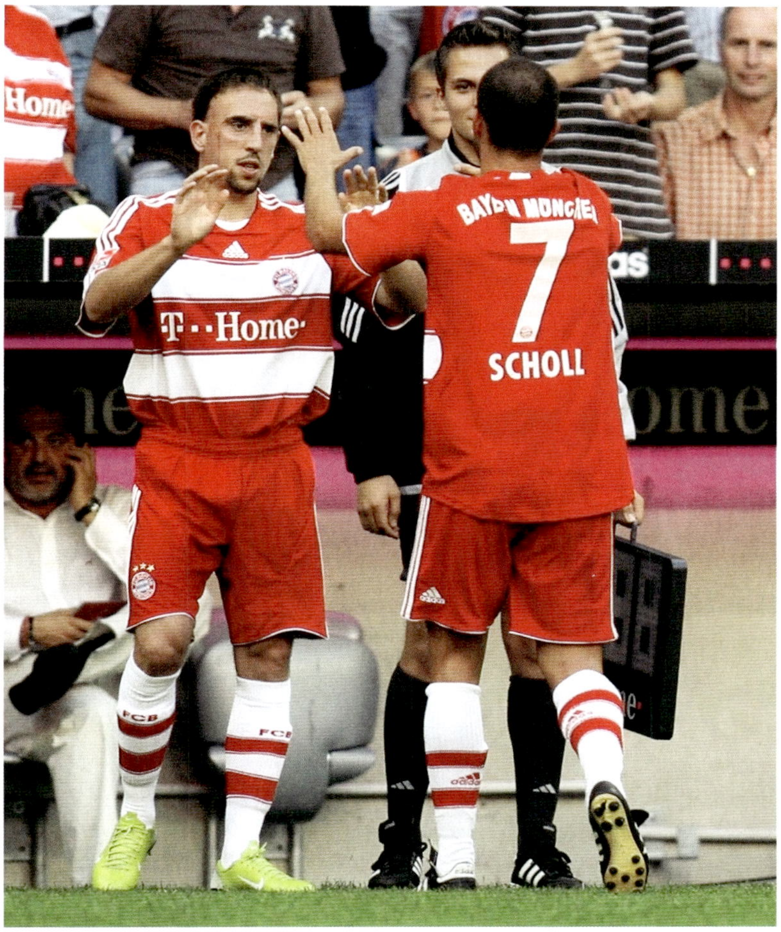

7 After the era of Mehmet Scholl, to honour him it was decided that shirt number 7 would not be worn again. However, Scholl agreed with the management to make his number available again for Franck Ribéry.

8 1970 was a milestone for red-and-white women's football (below: the first openly shown training session). In that year the first section for women's football at FC Bayern was established and the previous prohibition of women's football by the German association was lifted.

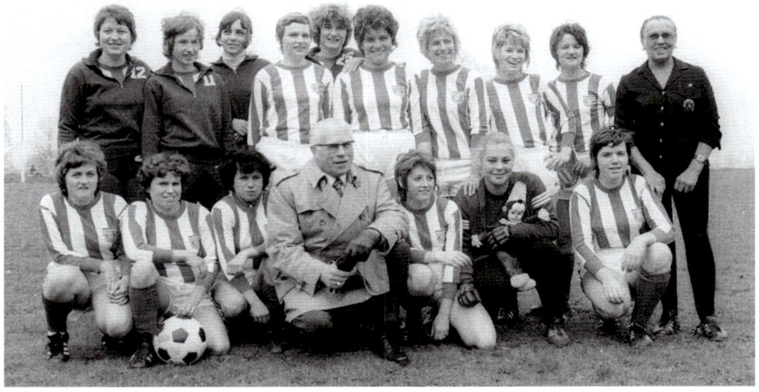

9 Gerd Müller's sole sending-off in the Bundesliga: in 1968 after a foul on Jupp Heynckes. Despite an eight-week ban, he was still the league's top scorer.

10 Lothar Matthäus did not get the number 10 shirt until he returned to Bayern in 1992. He brought it with him from his time at Inter Milan. Before that he played for FCB for four seasons with the number 8 on his back.

11 Eleven World Cup finals in succession with at least one FCB player on the field (a selection): '82 Breitner, '86 Matthäus, '90 Augenthaler, '94 Jorginho, '98 Lizarazu, '02 Kahn, '06 Sagnol, '10 Robben, '14 Lahm, '18 Tolisso, '22 Coman

12 What a battle! 2001 in Dortmund (1-1), twelve cards shown to FC Bayern players: red for Stefan Effenberg, a second yellow leading to red for Bixente Lizarazu, and eleven more yellow cards. Dortmund got one red and two yellow cards.

13 The same thirteen players took the field for the whole season in 1968–69 and won the championship. The other extreme: Schalke's in 2020–21, when thirty-nine players were used.

14

In 2014, seven FCB players were World Cup winners: Manuel Neuer, Jérôme Boateng, Philipp Lahm, Toni Kroos, Bastian Schweinsteiger, Thomas Müller and Mario Götze. No country ever won a World Cup final with more players from a single club.

15

FC Bayern in 1914: above, wearing a suit, William James Townley, after Charles Griffith the second full-time coach from England.

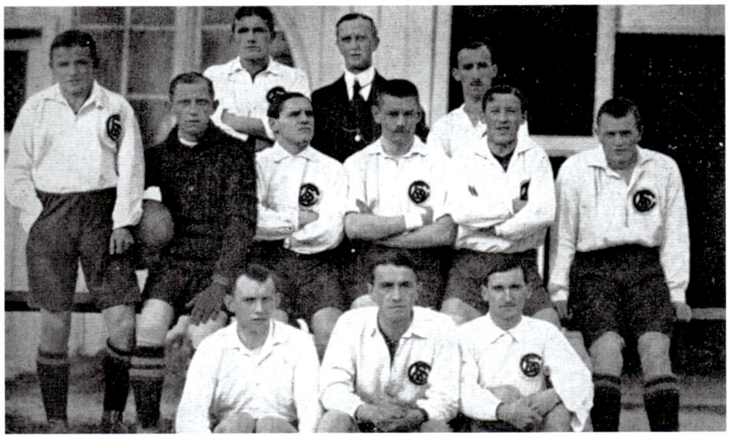

16 The longest unbroken goalscoring streak: Gerd Müller scored at least once in sixteen successive matches in the 1969–70 season.

17 With Manuel Neuer in goal in the 2015-16 season, FCB conceded only seventeen goals in thirty-four Bundesliga matches. This remains a record. In the previous season, the team kept a clean sheet twenty-two times.

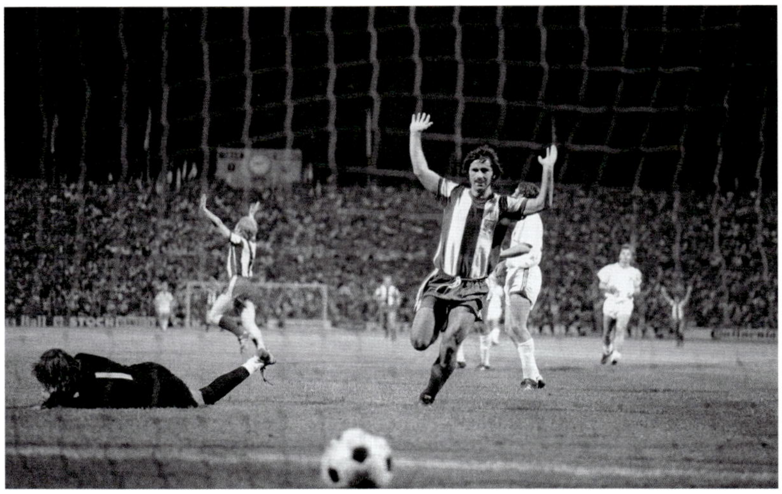

18 In every one of the eighteen Bundesliga matches against Bayern in his career, whether with Stuttgart, BVB Dortmund, Hannover or Hertha Berlin, Fredi Bobic always played on the losing side.

19 In the 2013-14 season, Bayern won nineteen matches in succession - a Bundesliga record! The team secured the championship well before the end of the season, in March. In the history of the Bundesliga, no team has ever won the championship so early.

20 MÜLLER = #1 **365 BL-GOALS**

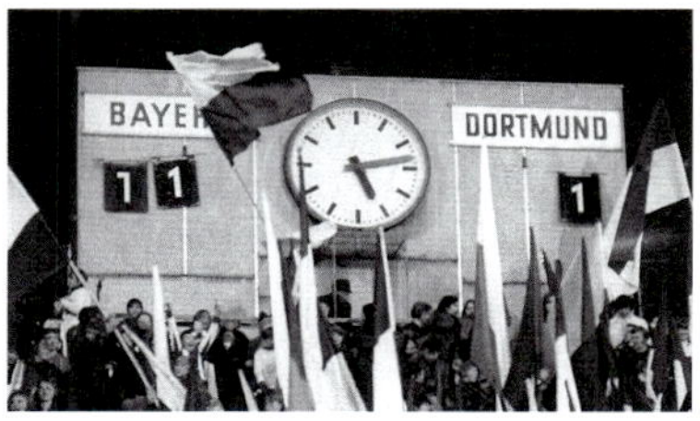

21 In November 1971 the biggest winning margin of all time was shown on the scoreboard in the Grünwald Stadium: 71-1. When the score stood at 11-1 against Dortmund, the scorers ran out of number-one signs and had to find a creative solution. To this day it was the biggest Bundesliga win for FCB.

22 On 6 February 1958 the plane carrying the Manchester United team crashed at Riem airport in Munich. Twenty-three passengers died, including eight players. Bobby Charlton survived and gained a winner's medal in the World Cup eight years later. Since 1960 the Munich Clock in Old Trafford has served as a reminder of this dreadful moment. In Munich, FCB commemorates the disaster with a memorial stone and a glass case at the site of the crash - a place of pilgrimage for fans from all over the world.

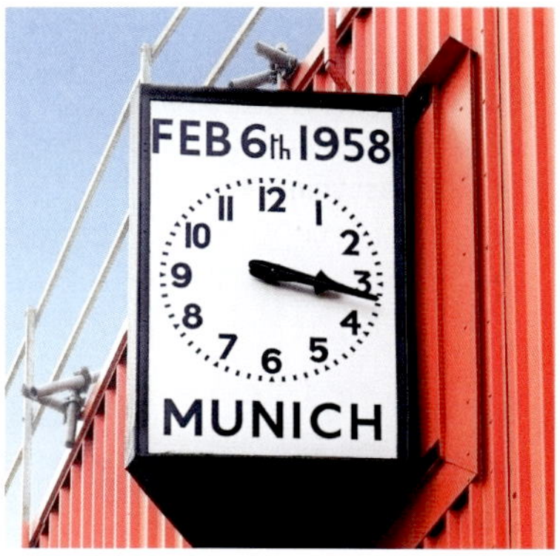

23 POOL **PARTY**

"Baptised" by Klaus Augenthaler, manager Uli Hoeness celebrates winning the German championship in 1989 in the recuperation pool of the Olympic Stadium, four weeks after a legendary discussion in the TV studios with Christoph Daum, the coach of 1. FC Köln.

24 In the arithmetical average after fifty-nine Bundesliga seasons, Bayern have won their matches by 2.25 goals to 1.09. In 35.9 per cent of the games they did not concede a goal.

25 The club was top of the league after 42.8 per cent of all match days and on 52.5 per cent of the last days of the season - i.e. were champions more than half of the time.

26 More record-breaking statistics from the Bundesliga: Bayern were awarded a penalty in 17.8 per cent of their matches (and scored from 79.7 per cent). Gerd Müller holds the unwelcome record for the most penalties missed: 12. And Jérôme Boateng for the most penalties conceded, a total of 14.

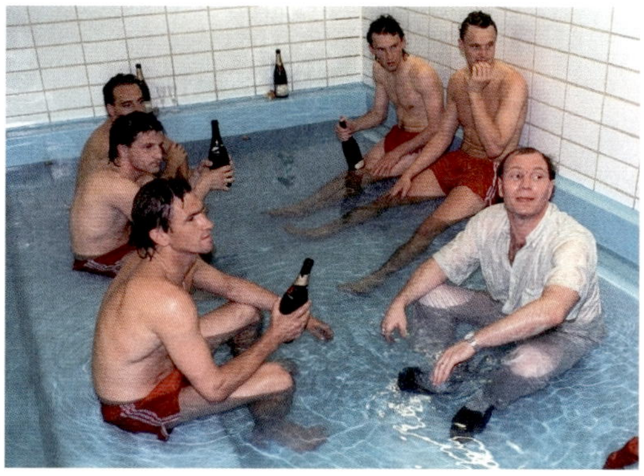

GERMAN CHAMPIONS, A COMPARISON (AS OF 2024)

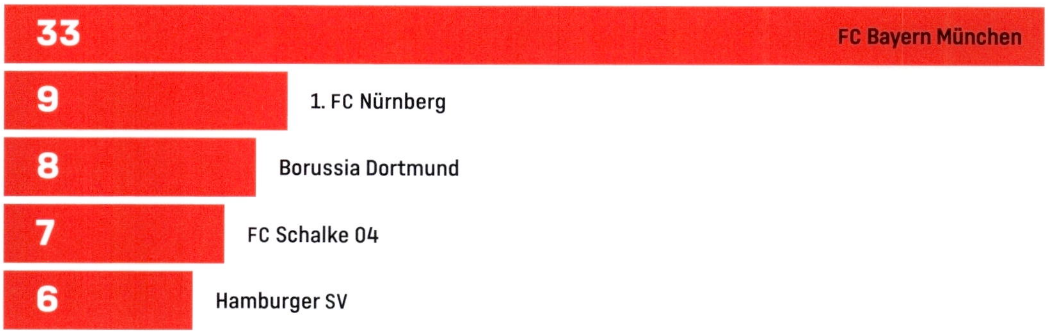

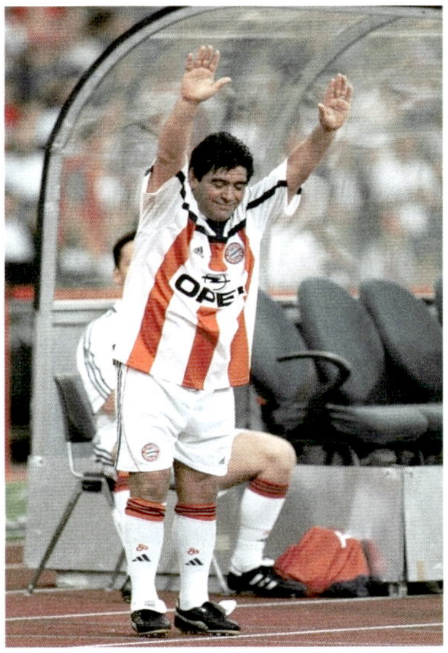

27 Uli Hoeness wanted to sign Diego Maradona at one time, but the Argentinian only played in an FCB shirt once, in the year 2000 in a farewell match for Lothar Matthäus. Twenty years later, on the occasion of his death, club president Herbert Hainer said, "To see Diego Maradona play was to be fascinated. His genius on the ball remains outstanding to this day. FCB mourns with the world of football one of the greatest players in history."

28 "Bulle" Roth – his nickname characterises his playing style: true passion and unstoppable energy, a tireless worker in midfield whose goals decided no fewer than three European Cup finals.

29 When the club was founded in 1900, training took place on the municipal park at Schyrenplatz. The first two matches were played by the founding members on this field in Untergiesing in Munich.

30 "That's not football, it's the Uwe Seeler tradition team, old men's football!" Following Franz Beckenbauer's speech at the banquet after the Champions League match at Olympique Lyon on 6 March 2001, FCB did not lose another game, winning twice against Manchester United and Real Madrid, and winning the Champions League trophy in the final against Valencia.

31

"The most important thing for me is memories, the best thing you can have." Bastian Schweinsteiger.

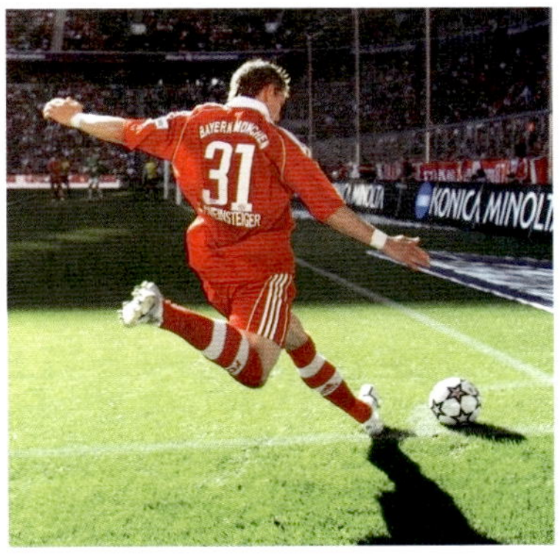

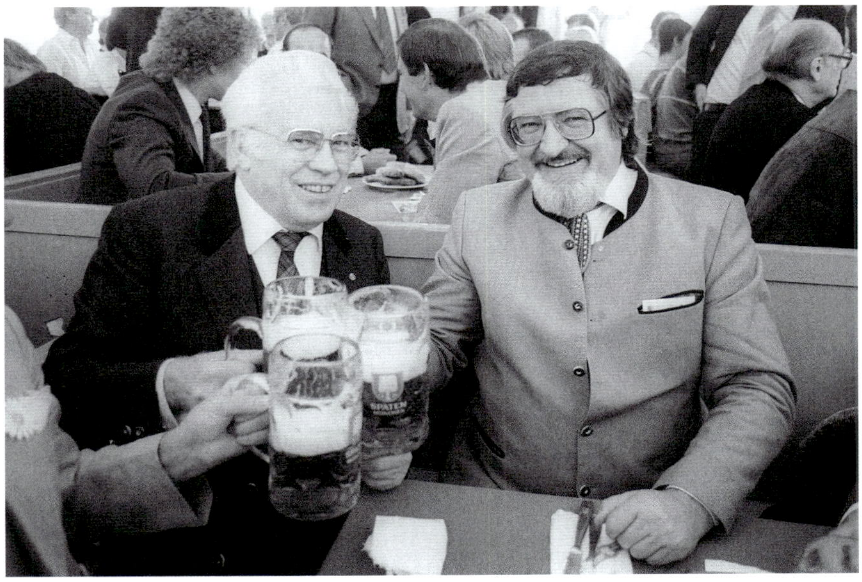

32 "¿Habla español?" Goalkeeper Pepe Reina, Claudio Pizarro, Javi Martínez, Juan Bernat, Xabi Alonso and Thiago Alcantara on the substitutes' bench in 2015 against Hertha BSC. "Thiago or nobody": Guardiola knew precisely which players he needed for his football.

33

The Oktoberfest in 1983: honorary president Wilhelm Neudecker and president Willi O. Hoffmann, who introduced the tradition that the Bayern professionals should show up at the Oktoberfest every year. In lederhosen, of course. Despite this, he always took a certain pride in his nickname "Champagne Willi".

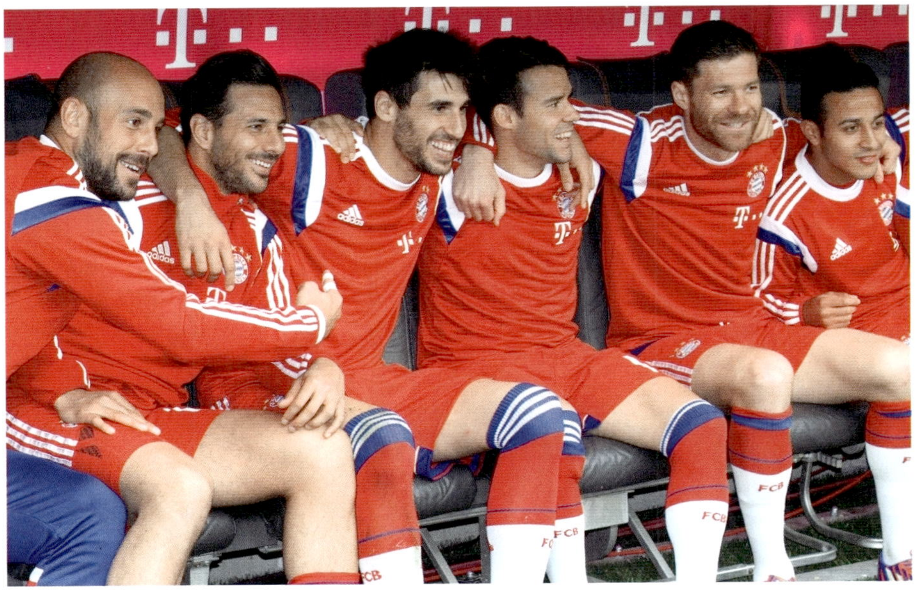

34 No other winner of the German championship had such a large lead on the thirty-fourth and last day of the season as FC Bayern in 2012–13: twenty-five points.

35 Following the relegation of Hamburger SV in 2018, FC Bayern is the club with the longest continuous period playing in the Bundesliga – since 1965.

36 The FCB chess section was not established until 1980, but quickly won nine German championships and a victory in the European Cup. Since the mid-1990s, it has put its focus on sport with mass appeal.

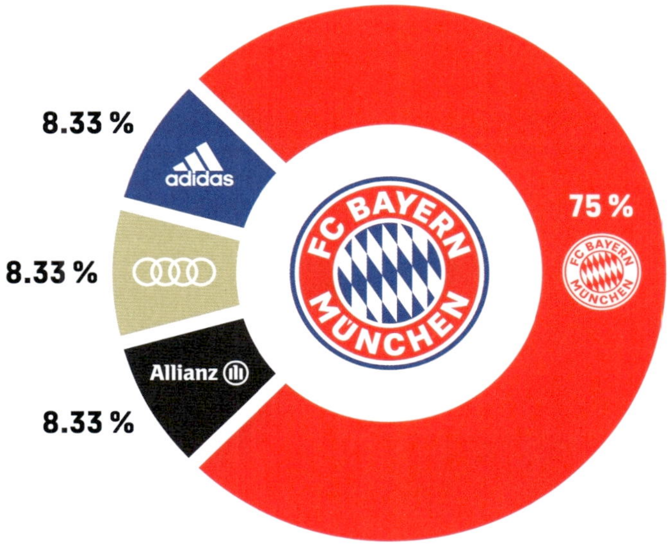

37 FC Bayern München eV is the main shareholder of FC Bayern München AG, with a 75 per cent stake.
38 Three long-term partners of FCB hold 8.33 per cent each: adidas AG, Audi AG and Allianz SE.
39 Around 4,100 fan clubs with almost 320,000 members - the fans of FC Bayern (2024).
40 In 2001 Oliver Kahn wanted to take the free kick for 1-1 against Hamburger SV himself.
41 Franz John, the first president of FCB, worked for the ducal Bavarian court photographer.
42 Since 1988 players of FC Bayern have visited fan clubs at Christmastime.
43 For the premiere of the Christmas visits, 150 of the then existing 260 fan clubs put in an application.
44 Arjen Robben is the author of three children's books that were published in the Netherlands.
45 Approximately one in five spectators at the Allianz Arena live in the city of Munich.
46 FCB: a positive win-loss ratio against 56 of the 57 BL teams (exception: Stuttgarter Kickers).
47 Max Gablonsky, FCB's first international player, withdrew his entry for the 1912 Olympic games.
48 The anthem for a goal: "Can Can", from Jacques Offenbach's *Orpheus in the Underworld*.
49 "He saved my skin." U2 front man Bono on Doc Müller-Wohlfahrt.
50 Each season fifty kilos of laundry have to be sent to Säbener Strasse to be washed.
51 FC Bayern Munich has published its own club magazine since 1906.
52 In 59 seasons, FCB has played against fifty-seven of the fifty-eight Bundesliga clubs - but not against Preussen Münster.

53

§ 1 of the club constitution: The club's name is "Fußball-Club Bayern München e.V."…. The club colours are red and white.

54 The purpose and mission of the club is to promote sport. In addition, the physical education and character formation of young members is a special aim according to the club constitution.

55 The club FC Bayern Munich provides a sporting home for children, young people and adults, regardless of their origin, skin colour, faith, gender, sexual orientation or social status.

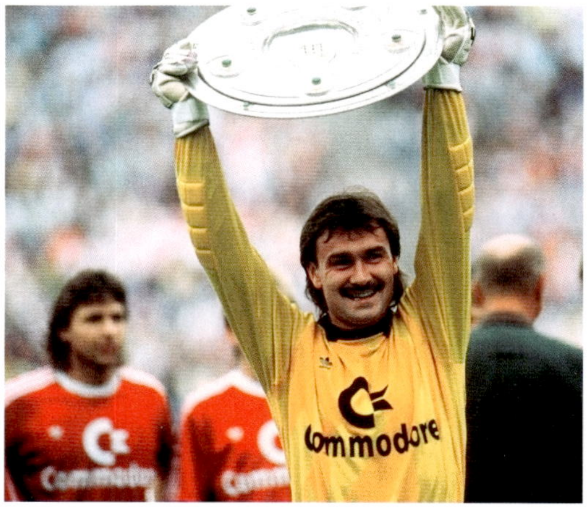

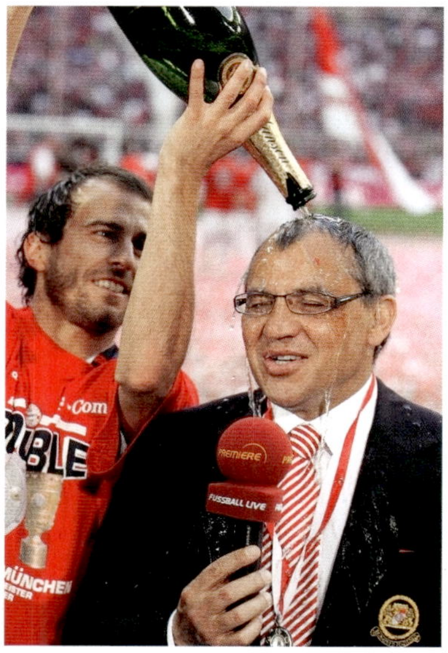

56 A champagne shower from Mehmet Scholl for the coach and two-time winner of the double, Felix Magath, whose nickname was "Quälix" – see no. 111.

57 Only four men have received the two most important trophies in football, the European Cup and World Cup, in the role of captain: the French player Didier Deschamps, the Spanish player Iker Casillas - and two from Munich: Franz Beckenbauer and Philipp Lahm.

58 'Stern des Südens' (Star of the South) is the only song by the composer Willy Astor that made it into the charts: in the first six months after release, it reached over 100,000 sales. He wrote the lyrics with the stadium announcer Stephan Lehmann.

59 Raimond Aumann played in a Bayern youth team, then kept goal for them in the Bundesliga 216 times, won the German championship six times and in 1990 the World Cup too. After his playing career he headed the organisation of fans and fan clubs for many years, then took on the job of training the legendary team.

60

A WHEAT BEER CAROUSEL

Was the special shape of a wheat-beer glass the source of inspiration? Franz Beckenbauer, then coach of FCB, kicked a ball from a full glass of wheat beer into the lower target hole of the "goal wall" at the championship celebrations in 1994 on *Sportstudio* of the ZDF TV channel.

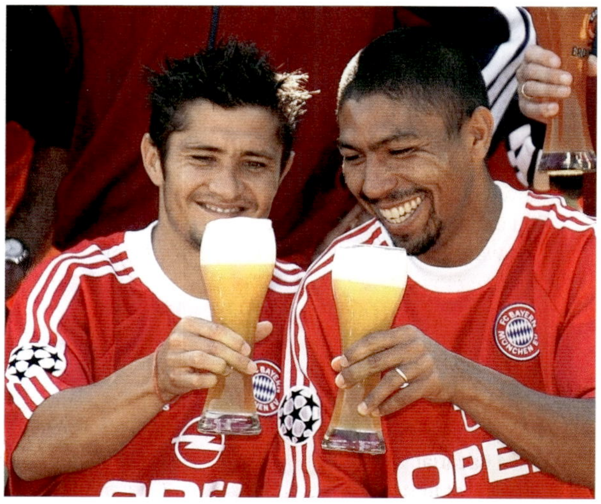

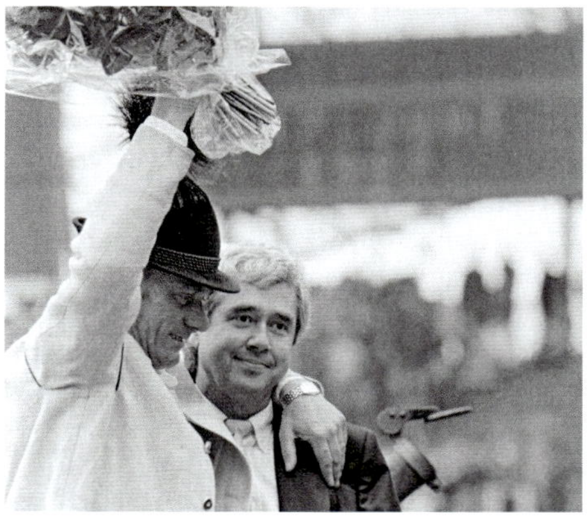

62 "That was the best decision of my life." Arjen Robben on his move to FC Bayern. He came from Real Madrid in 2009.

63 Of the 600 "goals of the month" since 1971, 63 have been scored by players from FCB, with Karl-Heinz Rummenigge (6) and Gerd Müller (5) hitting the most.

64 "Sometimes it was tougher than the negotiations themselves", said Fritz Scherer about the card games in the presidium room.

65 "People say of me that I can't stand losing, and that's true." President Herbert Hainer, like Uli Hoeness the son of a butcher.

61 When Fritz Scherer arrived at FC Bayern München in 1979 as treasurer, his aim quickly became clear: "No debts ever again!" Now an honorary vice-president, for many years he pursued this aim untiringly, first as treasurer, then as president and finally as vice-president.

66 Start early: three quarters of all FC Bayern München fans support the club in their childhood. Ideally this is a lifelong love.

67 The *Munich Football Guide* was published until the late 1980s. The little book revealed to autograph hunters the private addresses of the FCB players.

68 "Chasing Bayern is like planting lettuce in the desert." Christoph Daum

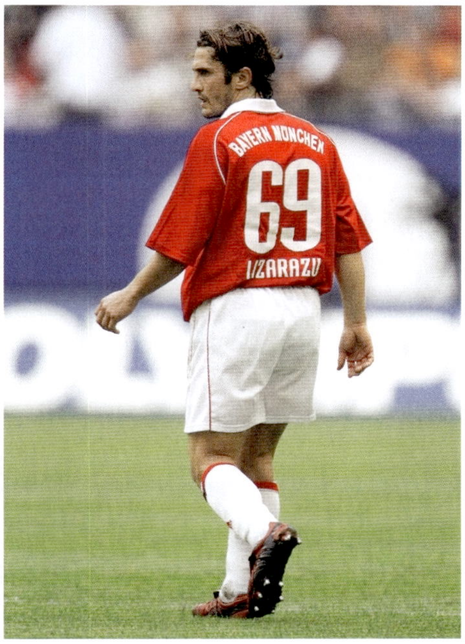

69 The year when Bixente Lizarazu was born: 1969. And 69 is the highest shirt number in the history of FCB.

70 Of all the trophies that they could win in international professional football and in Germany, FC Bayern only lacks one: second-division champions. But for that, FCB would first have to be relegated.

FCB AND **1860**

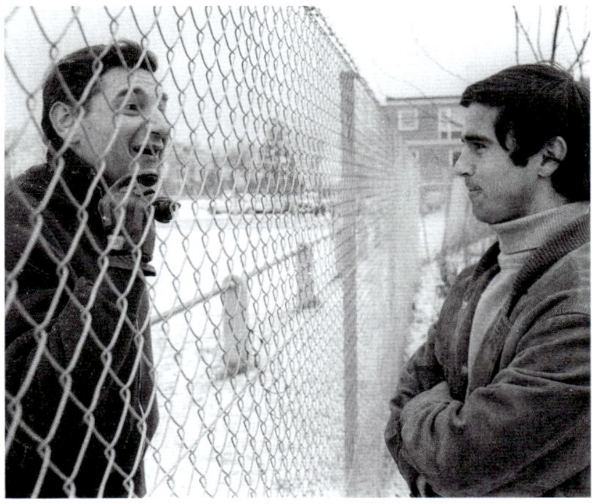

Left: 1860 goalkeeper Petar Radenković and Gerd Müller - not much separates the two clubs (650 metres) and yet they are so far apart. Below: Franz Beckenbauer in front of his parents' house in Giesing.

71 FCB was undefeated in fifteen derby games in succession from 1978 until 1999 (9 wins, 6 draws).
72 In the 1999-20 season Bayern lost twice, but still won the championship.
73 FCB won all of the derby matches in the new millennium: nine wins out of nine against 1860 Munich, "the Lions".
74 As a youth player, Philipp Lahm opted for Bayern because there were too many holes in the goal fence at 1860.
75 In 1931 the Lions lost the final of the German championship, and in 1932 Bayern won the title.
76 "It's as if Mozart and Beethoven were playing in one band." Max Merkel on Beckenbauer/Müller.
77 "Bin i Radi, bin i Depp ('idiot'), the king is Maier Sepp". The FCB goalkeeper's answer to Radenković's song.
78 A cup drama in 2008: Ribéry saved FCB from a penalty shoot-out with a retaken penalty kick.
79 FCB won 1-0 in a cup match in 2008, the 164th and today still the last Munich derby. What a pity!
80 "His whole being is from Giesing", says Walter Beckenbauer about his brother Franz.
81 From Grünwalder Strasse over to Säbener and into the fans' hearts: "Wiggerl" Kögl, Jens Jeremies, Andi Görlitz.
82 "That was a bit like Upper Giesing against Lower Giesing," said Beckenbauer about a drawn derby.
83 The first derby: 2 September 1902 - Bayern in blue, 1860 in red, the result: 3-0.
84 The first Bundesliga derby: 14 August 1965 - 1860 won the match 1-0 and the championship, Bayern won the cup.
85 After taking over shares in the Arena for €11 million, in 2006 Bayern saved the Lions from insolvency.
86 The overall record since the Second World War in 70 games: 38 wins for Bayern, 16 draws, 16 defeats.
87 Gerhard König, 1860: "I waited till the referee was looking away, then I hit Franz."
88 "It wasn't a hard blow", said König. He left 1860 at the age of 15, and Franz became the "Kaiser".
89 "In the Bavarian league, it's well-known…": FCB fans still sing about the Lions' relegation in 1982.
90 A 1-5 defeat in the derby in 2001 was the trigger for firing the coach Lorant (10th place in the league table).

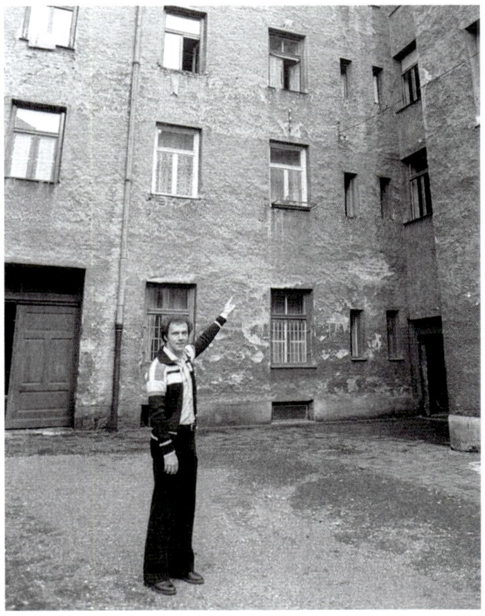

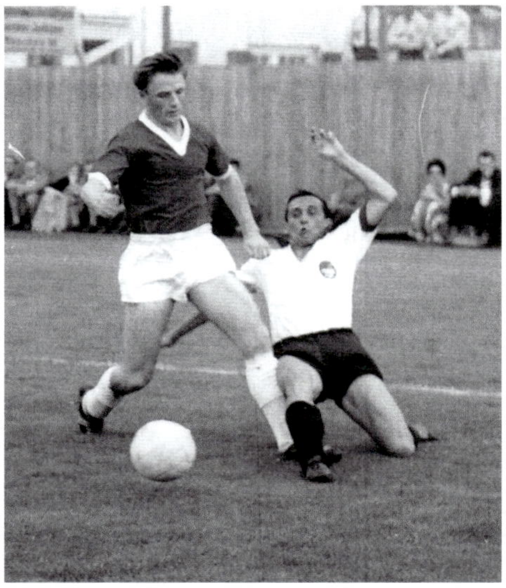

92 93

Six FCB players achieve a world first with the 1974 World Cup victory: being world champions, European champions, winners of the European Cup and national champions at the same time.

Wilhelm Simetsreiter's pace and goalscoring ability earned him a nomination for the 1936 Olympics in Berlin. Germany lost to Norway in the quarter-finals, but the FCB left winger became friends with the star of the games, Jesse Owens. He used a photo of them together as an autograph card for the rest of his life.

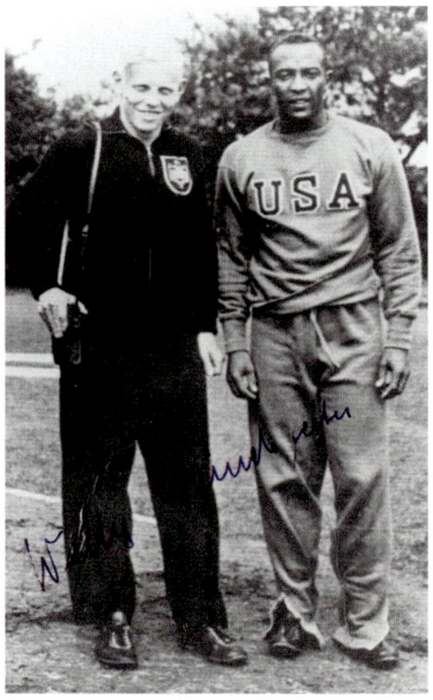

91 In the pre-Bundesliga history of FC Bayern there were many stars. Among those who will never be forgotten are Emil Kutterer, Josef Pöttinger, Sigmund Haringer, "Jackl" Streitle, "Lutte" Goldbrunner, Gerd Siedl (above in a friendly match between FCB and Manchester United in 1959), "Bertl" Moll, Ernst Nagelschmitz, Willi Giesemann, Erich "Witsche" Hahn, "Stopsi" Brandmeier, Kurt Sommerlatt, Karl Mai, Otto Schweitzer, Árpád Fazekas and Wiggerl Landerer.

94 "The older players often speak with a strong Bavarian accent, and I don't understand them. Then I simply nod." Michael Ballack's recipe for success in Munich.

95 At TSV Pähl, the club of his youth, Thomas Müller is known not only as a winner of World Cup and Champions League trophies but also for his team's goal difference at the end of the 1998-99 season: 175-7.

96 "FC Bayern keeps you young and agile." Club member number one, Heiner Jüngling, a member since the year of his birth, 1939, and almost always present in the Arena.

97 Gerd Müller and Franz Beckenbauer, arm in arm with Mick Jagger before the final of the European Cup in Glasgow in 1976. Back then, UEFA had a special rule for a hat-trick of victories: a club that won the trophy three times in a row was allowed to keep it permanently. It worked out.

98 In 2000 the distance between joy and tears was a mere 17 kilometres: in the Olympic Stadium FCB celebrated winning the championship while Leverkusen, in Unterhaching, mourned their failure to win a title thought to be surely won.

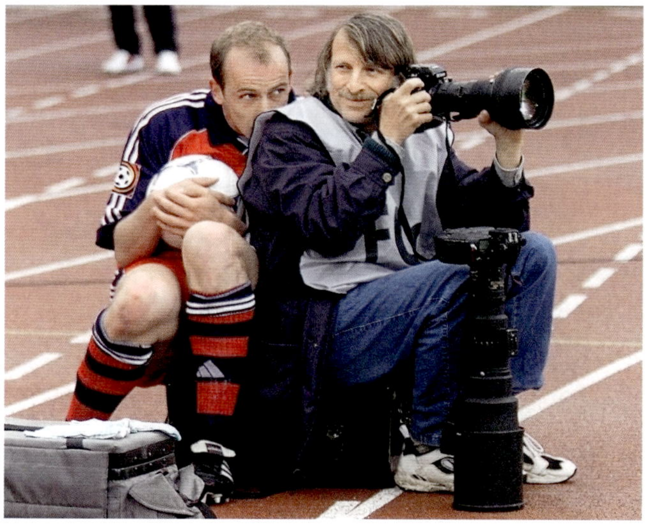

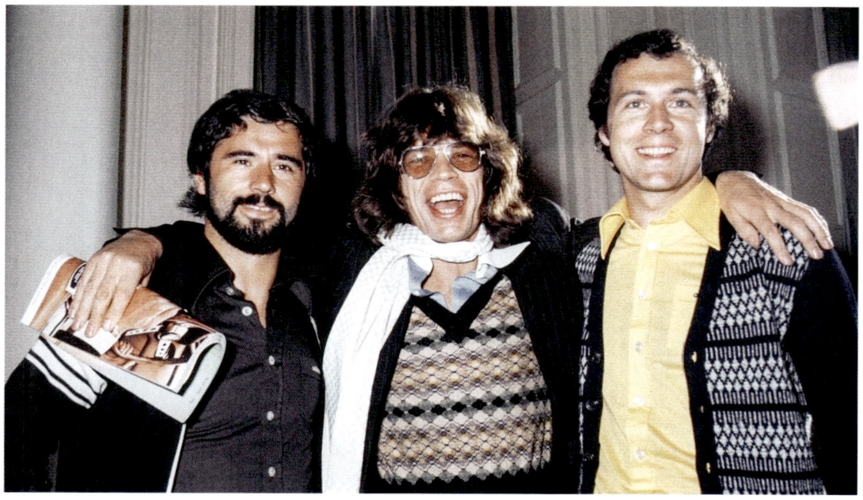

99 HIDE AND SEEK

"I ran so fast today that no camera could capture me." Mario Basler, known for brilliant free kicks, corners and dribbling, was equally an expert for unforgettable comments, for example: "Mister, I've got a body like Schwarzenegger" (to Giovanni Trapattoni). Today he estimates his market value at 150 million.

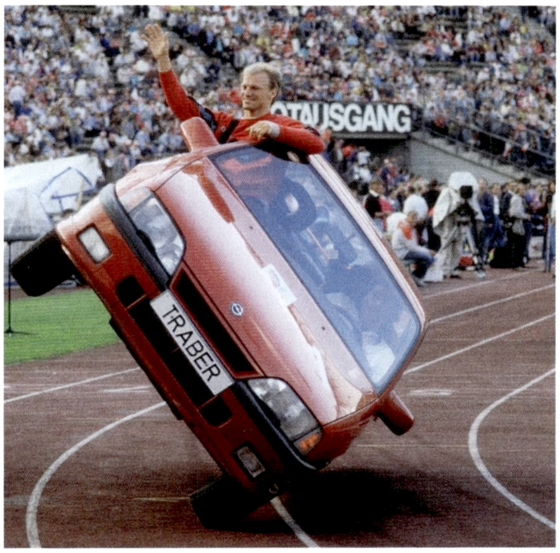

100 HANSI SAYS GOODBYE

Hansi Pflügler, who played for FC Bayern at youth, amateur and professional level (276 Bundesliga matches) and was a World Cup winner in 1990, became head of the FCB Outlets department at the end of his active career in 1992 and played a decisive part in the success of FCB merchandising.

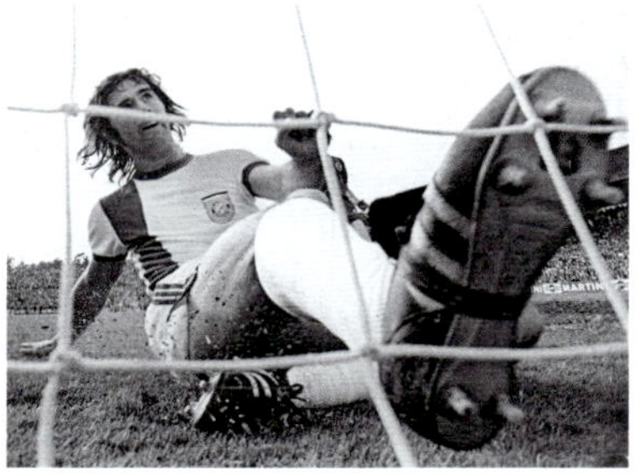

101 Only Bayern have ever managed a three-figure tally of Bundesliga goals. In 1972, in the 5–1 win over Schalke, they scored goals number 97 to 101 of the season. And in 2020 they fell only one goal short of this record.

102 In December 2016 Thiago Alcántara passed the ball into the run of a teammate, as he thought - but it was the figure of a Father Christmas on an animated advertisement at the edge of the pitch.

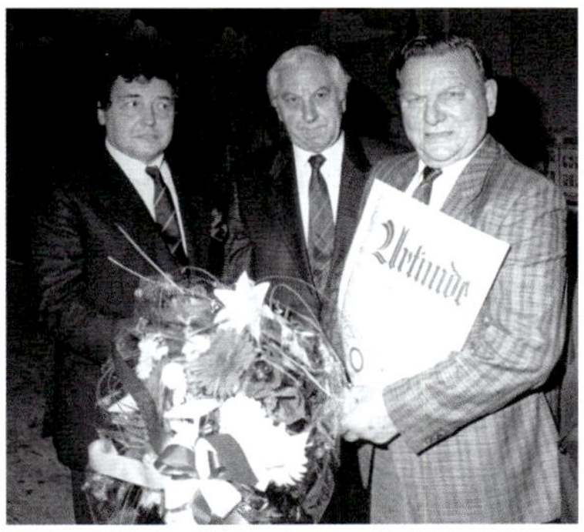

105 Personalities who made their mark on FCB as secretary, treasurer, head of department or vice-president (from left to right): Kurt Hegerich, Hans Schiefele and Karl Pfab. Below: honorary vice-president Bernd Rauch, the "club builder", with responsibility for the Allianz Arena, the Campus and the professionalisation of the basketball section.

103 Five top-scorers in the World Cup, from the past and the present, played for FC Bayern or are still hunting goals for the club: alongside the two Müllers, Gerd (1970, ten goals) and Thomas (2010), they are Miroslav Klose (2006), James Rodríguez (2014) and Harry Kane (2018).

104 The long-standing captain Klaus Augenthaler is the highest-scoring defender in the history of Bayern Munich. In 546 games for the club, "Auge" hit 76 goals.

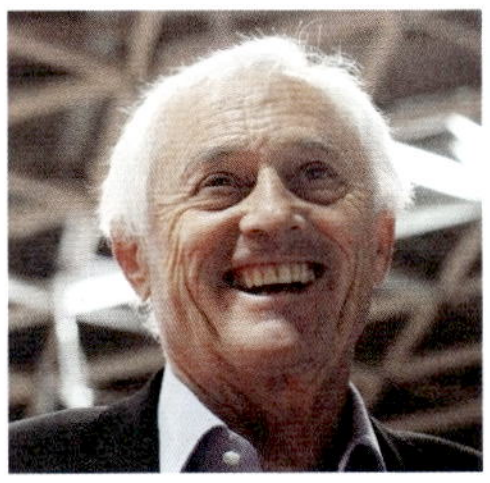

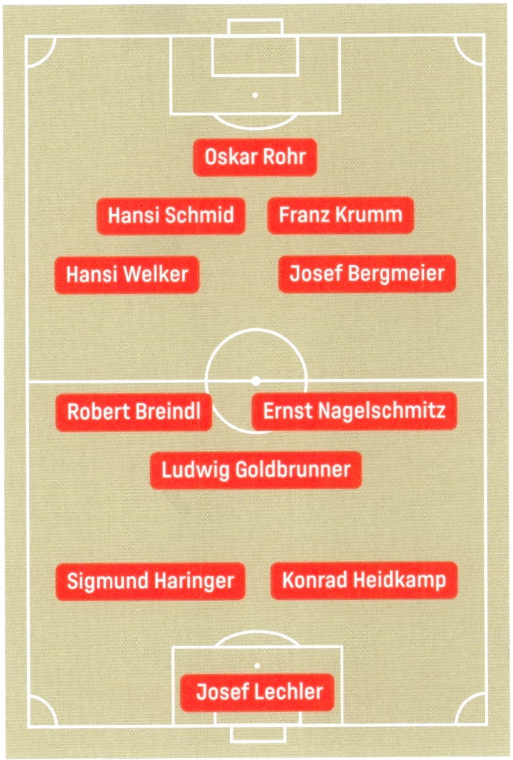

106 THE FIRST TEAM OF CHAMPIONS

On 12 June 1932 in Nuremberg, the team coached by Richard "Dombi" Kohn beat Eintracht Frankfurt 2-0. The goals were scored by Oskar Rohr (36th minute, penalty) and Franz Krumm (75th). With a first championship win began the rise of FC Bayern to become the most successful club in Germany. At left: the team line-up.

107 "Bayern Bazi": indefatigably in action from 1993 to 2004, before being sent into retirement by Berni in the last season played in the Olympic Stadium.

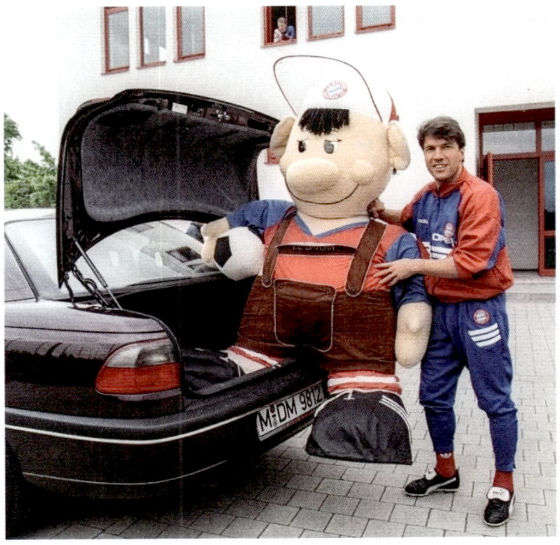

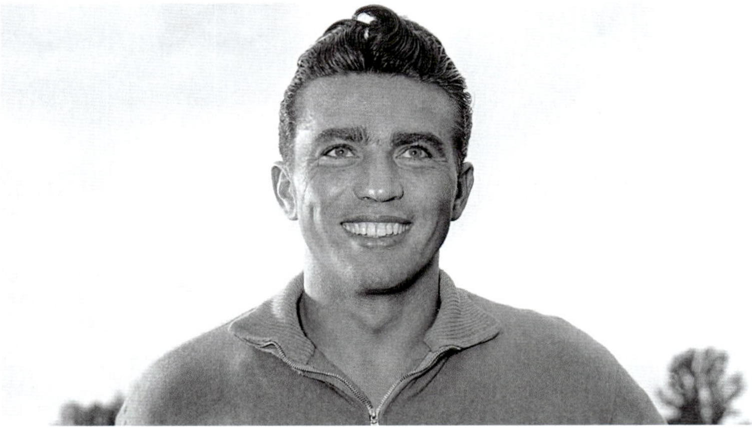

108 On the way to victory in Bern in 1954: the defender Hans Bauer, the club's first winner of the World Cup. Three years later: the German cup as team captain!

109 From a global point of view, FC Bayern today has more than 60 million fans. In Germany almost 8 million people support FCB.

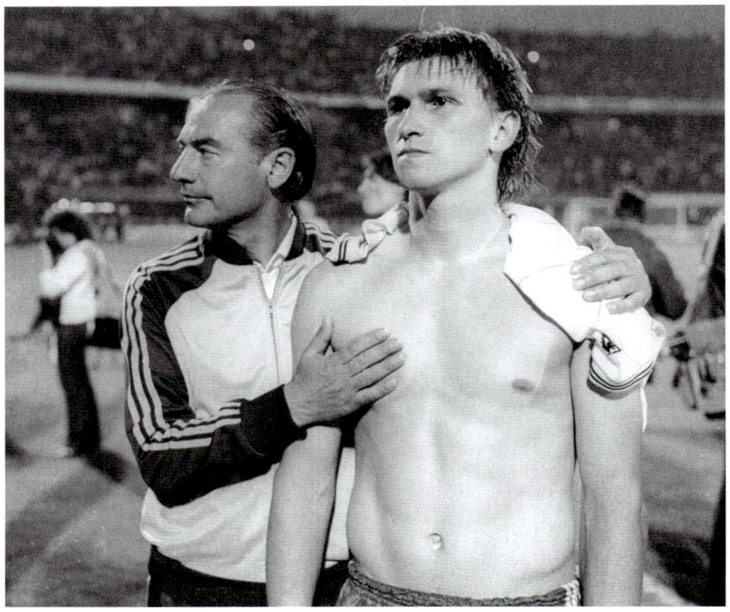

110 PÁL CONSOLES

In the early 1980s, as coach of FC Bayern Munich, Pál Csernai took the club back into the world's elite. With FCB he won the German championship in 1980 and 1981, and the DFB cup in 1982. In the same year, he and Bayern reached the final of the European Cup, but lost 0-1 to Aston Villa. Gyula Lóránt, for whom he worked as assistant coach at first, is regarded as a pioneer of the zonal marking that is standard today.

111 In 2004 the coach Felix Magath used the Wallberg, a mountain on Tegernsee (1,722 metres), as a training ground. The defender Thomas Linke said, "We were just told we'll run till someone says stop - and unfortunately that only happened at the cross on the summit."

112 "I give my heart for you, I live for Bayern, I'll never let you down." Sung in the Südkurve for the first time in 2011, with a melody borrowed thanks to friendship with the ultras of the Italian third-division team SS Sambenedettese.

113 "Yesterday in Kiev, tomorrow in Vienna, standing together we are great! We are from Munich, we are Bayern, we are always the ones who can celebrate!" A firm part of the repertoire since 1995 (a match against IFK Göteborg).

114 Stefan Effenberg collected an impressive total of 114 yellow cards in his Bundesliga career, a record that no one has equalled.

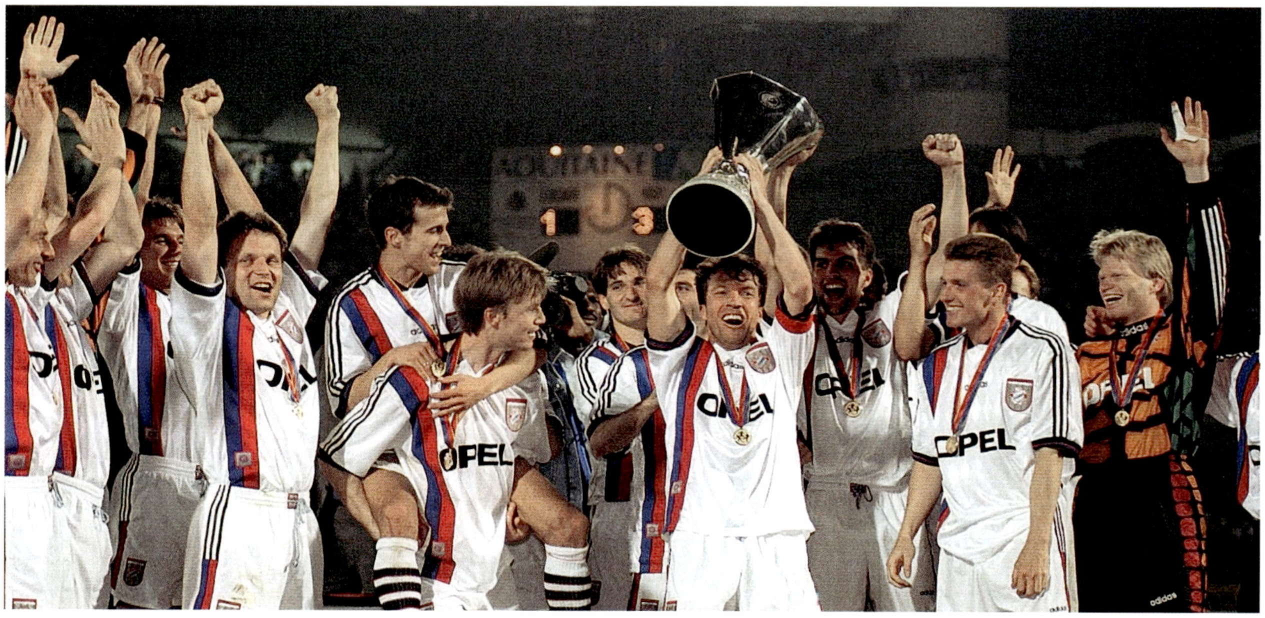

115 Until 1976, thirteen finals ended in no defeats at all for FCB. This later changed, at least in international matches, after 1982 (0-1 against Aston Villa) and 1987 (1-2 against Porto). Twenty long years after the last triumph in the European Cup (1-0 against Saint-Étienne), on 15 May 1996 FC Bayern brought the UEFA Cup home to Munich for the first time. Bayern won a final again, against Girondins Bordeaux (first and second legs: 2-0 / 3-1).

116 Along with Gerd Müller they were the dream attack for FCB in the 1960s. In 1965 they celebrated promotion to the Bundesliga together, and won the German DFB cup in 1966, the European Cup Winners' Cup and the DFB cup in 1967, and the first double in the club's history in 1969: Dieter "Mucki" Brenninger (left), who scored 110 goals in 276 matches, and Rainer Ohlhauser, who scored 186 times in 286 matches.

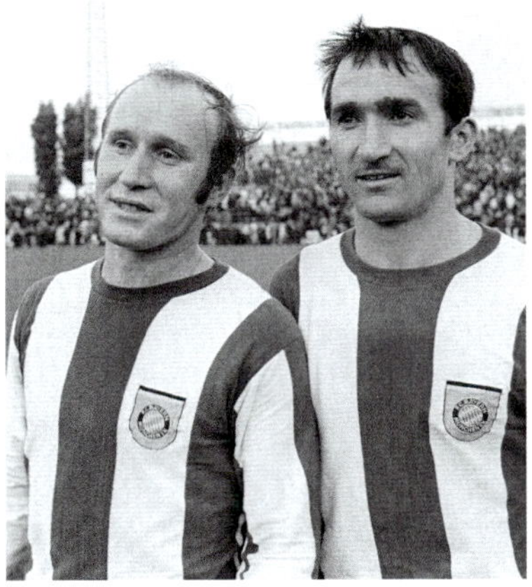

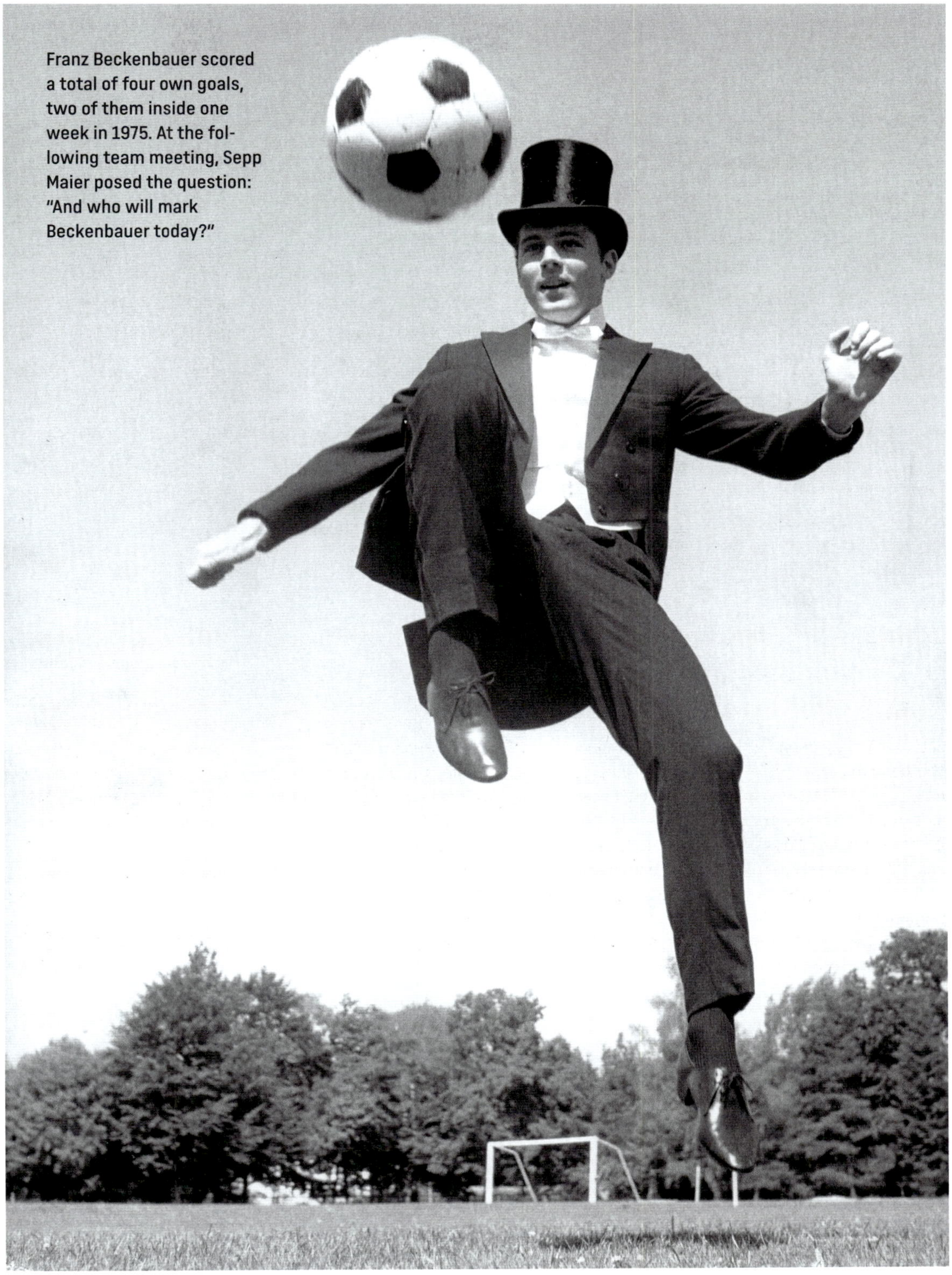

Franz Beckenbauer scored a total of four own goals, two of them inside one week in 1975. At the following team meeting, Sepp Maier posed the question: "And who will mark Beckenbauer today?"

117 The referee section at FC Bayern has existed since 1919 and currently has 150 referees, including nine women. To this day the section is an established part of the club, and has evolved into one of the largest referees' departments in any club in Germany.

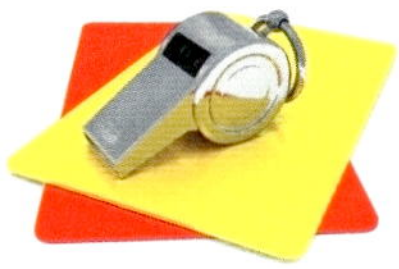

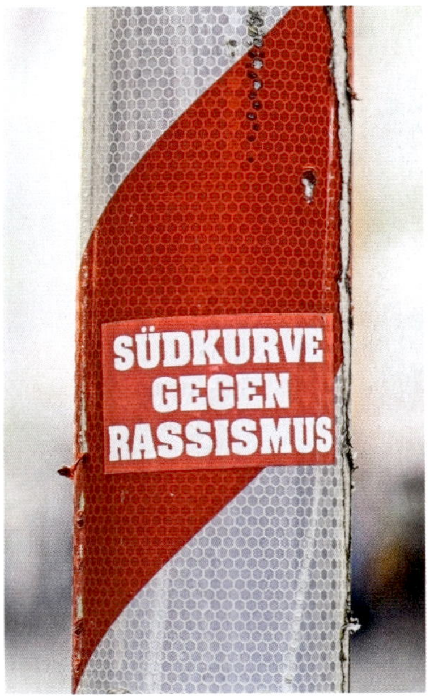

118 Ultras against racism: "Munich is open to the world and multicultural, and FC Bayern has always been like that."

119 The average number of spectators in the Olympic Stadium was 39,380. The lowest number was registered for a match in the UEFA Cup against Aarhus in 1979, when 3,000 watched a 3-1 win.

120 Well-known interpreters of songs about Franz Beckenbauer: Udo Jürgens with 'Libero' and Peter Alexander with the 'Kaiser Franz-Marsch'.

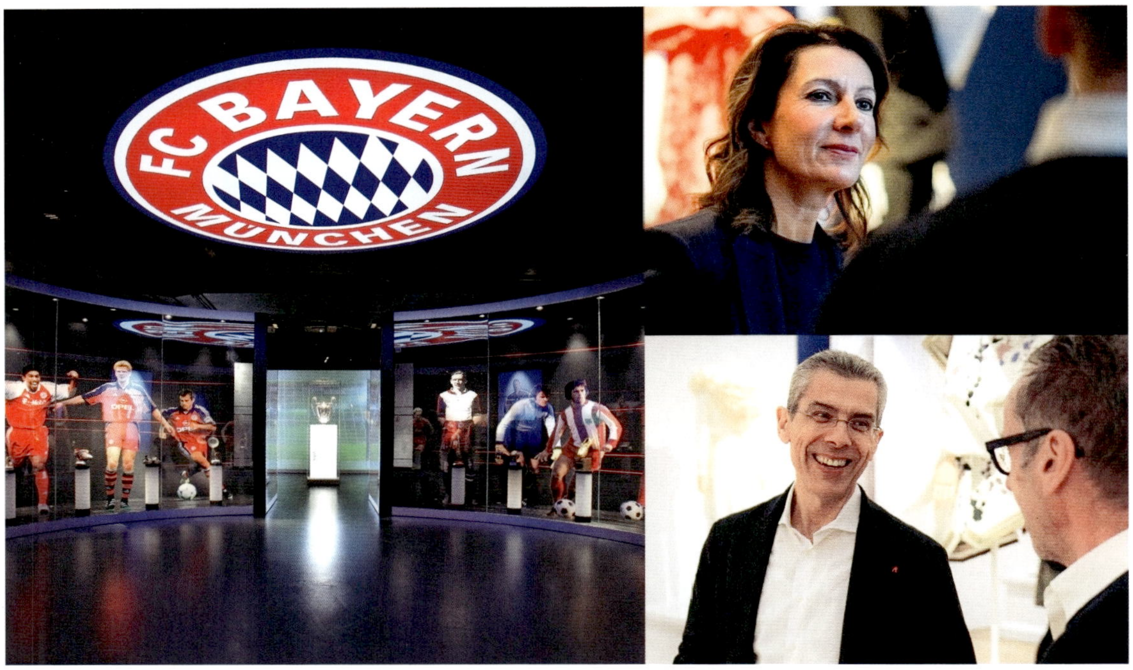

121 The team at the FC Bayern Museum says thank you! "More than 500,000 visitors in the 2023-24 season make it one of the most-visited museums in Munich", says Petra Leufstedt, the museum director. By the way: under the motto "Munich Match", the museum and the Kunsthalle München are starting a cooperation that will link more closely these two leading institutions in the museum scene and at the same time create attractive incentives. As part of this cooperation, visitors can save 20 per cent of the admission price in the other museum by means of the "Show your ticket" system. Board member Michael Diederich and Petra Leufstedt tried it out for themselves at the Kunsthalle in the centre of Munich.

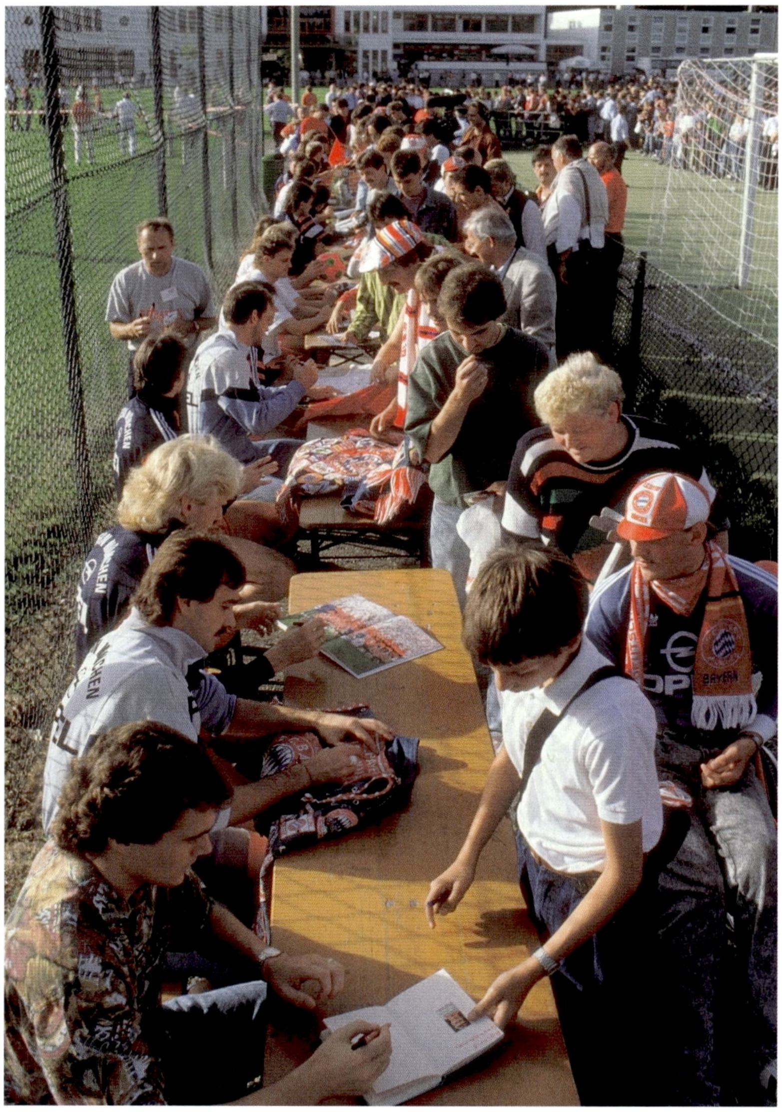

122

UP CLOSE

Signing autographs in the open air in 1990 - the Bayern players patiently put their signatures on scarves and shirts: at the front Roland Grahammer, Raimond Aumann and Stefan Effenberg. Today Harry Kane and company sign almost 10,000 autograph cards every year. For organisational reasons it is no longer possible to queue for this, so now the cards can be ordered and then sent off.

123 Franz with a moustache – in spite of club president Neudecker's view that "a footballer's neck and face should be free from hair". He shaved it off again only six months later, for a good cause.

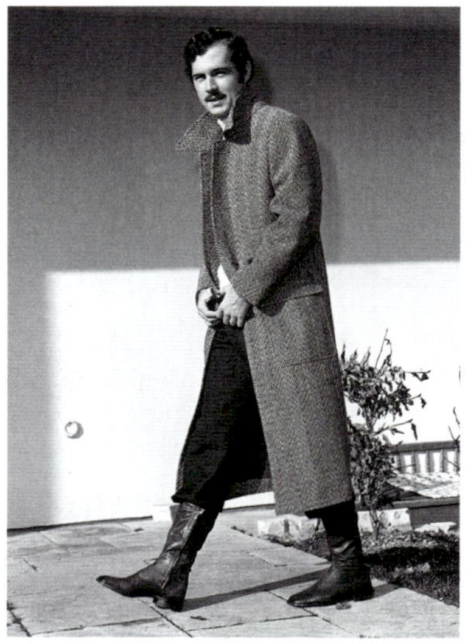

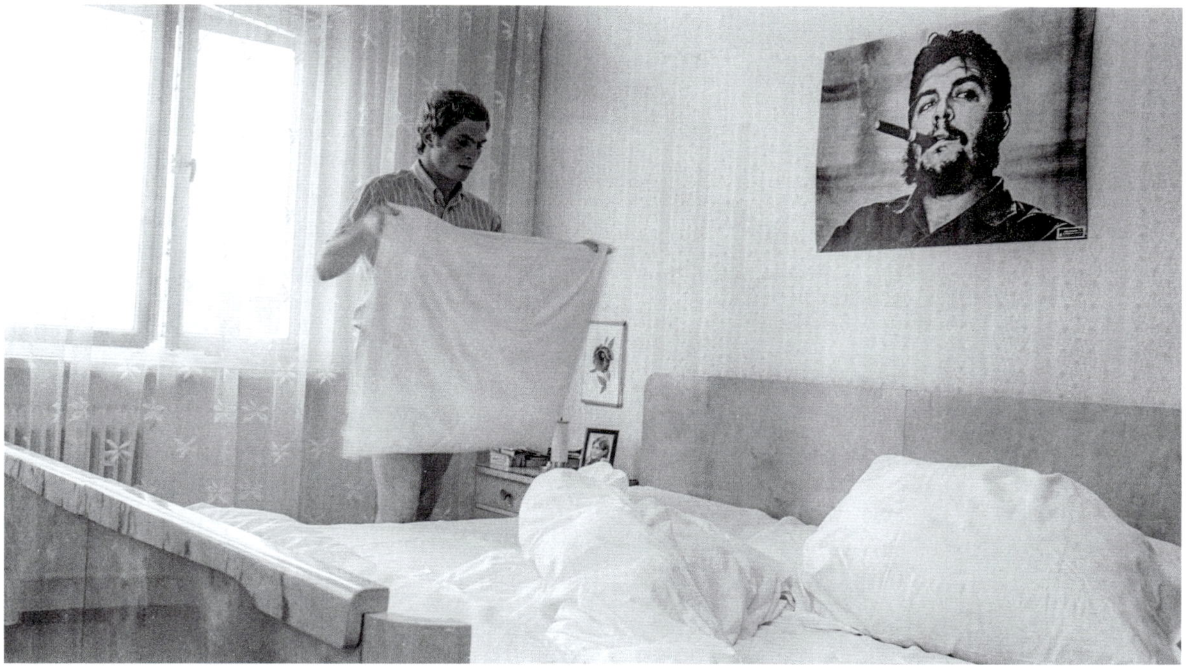

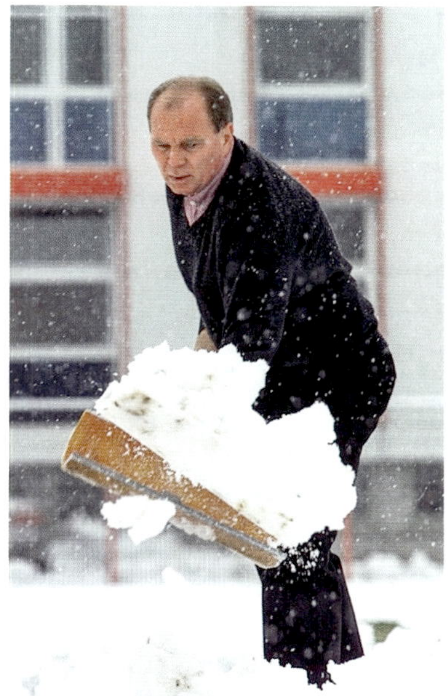

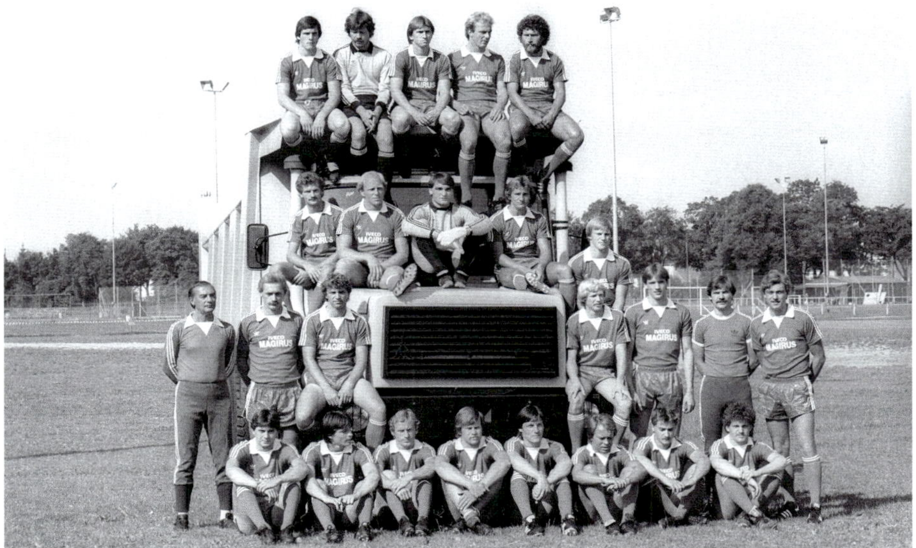

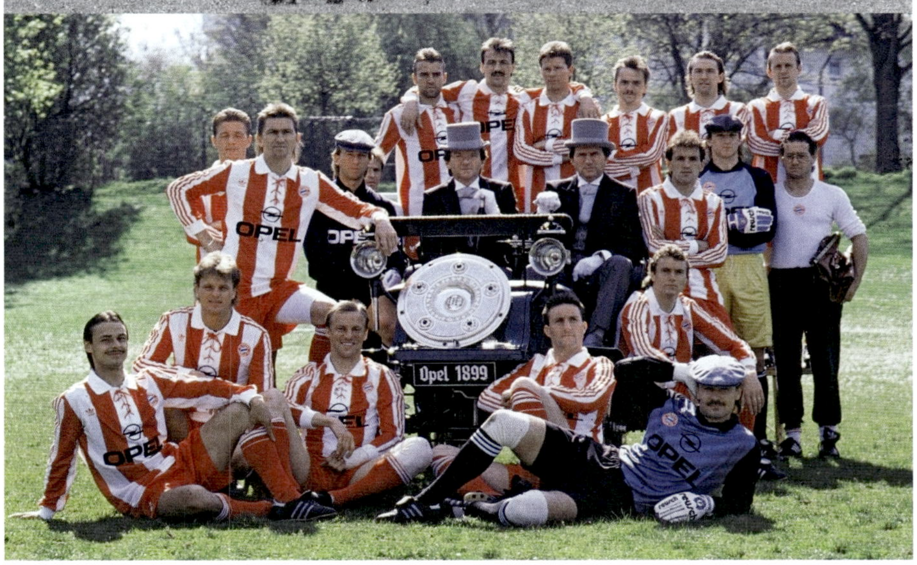

124 Uli Hoeness was always a man to roll up his sleeves and work, whether making beds in shared accommodation with Paul Breitner or shovelling snow on Säbener Strasse. And he appreciates it when others do the same. "I was fifteen, living in the FCB youth house", says Bastian Schweinsteiger. "It was December, and we kids had to clear snow from the pitches." And were amazed when Hoeness gave each of them fifty deutschmarks for their work.

125

STAY STILL! CHEESE!

On 6 April 1974, for the first time in their history, Bayern played in the Olympic Stadium with the name of a sponsor on their shirts. "Adidas" in large letters adorned the kit worn by Franz Beckenbauer and company. Since then, the shirts have advertised for Magirus Deutz, Iveco, Commodore, Opel and Telekom, with T-Com, T-Home and T-Mobile, and sometimes the sponsors had special requests when team photos were taken.

A member of Penguin Random House Verlagsgruppe GmbH
Neumarkter Strasse 28 · 81673 Munich
produktsicherheit@penguinrandomhouse.de (The above information is mandatory information according to GPSR)

A Library of Congress Control Number is available.
A CIP catalogue record for this book is available from the British Library.

Project management FC Bayern München:
Hans-Peter Renner
Copy-editing FC Bayern München:
Hans-Peter Renner and Andreas Werner
Editorial support FC Bayern München: Max Breitner, Alexa Gattinger, Michael Hellstern, Simon Mellar, Georg M. Mooshofer, Moritz Münch, Laura Nicolaiciuc, Adriana Wahl, Tina Woith

Book concept: Christian Rieker, Curt Holtz, Florian Frohnholzer
Editorial direction Prestel: Curt Holtz
Translation from German: John Sykes
Copy-editing: Jonathan Fox
Design and typesetting, image selection:
Florian Frohnholzer, Sofarobotnik, Augsburg & Munich
Image acquisitions: Marco Fertig, Interfoto/Visual Experts
Origination: Reproline Mediateam, Munich
Printing and binding: aprinta druck GmbH, Wemding
Paper: Magno Volume

MIX
Paper | Supporting responsible forestry
FSC
www.fsc.org
FSC® C004592

Penguin Random House Verlagsgruppe FSC® N001967

Printed in Germany

ISBN 978-3-7913-9344-5

www.prestel.com

Credits: p. 2: FC Bayern München; p. 7: FC Bayern München (2), FC Bayern München Museum; p. 8: IMAGO / Frinke; p. 9: IMAGO / ActionPictures; p. 10: IMAGO / Günther Schneider; p. 11: FC Bayern München; p. 12: IMAGO / Sven Simon; p. 13: FC Bayern München; p. 14: FC Bayern München; p. 15: FC Bayern München; p. 16: IMAGO / Ulmer/Cremer; p. 17: IMAGO / Fred Joch; pp. 18–19: picture alliance / Rzepka; p. 20: Julian Baumann; p. 21: IMAGO / Eisele; p. 22: FC Bayern München / Marco Donato; p. 23: Fritz Beck; pp. 24–25: Steffen Eirich; pp. 26–27: picture alliance / Frank Hoermann /Sven Simon; p. 28: IMAGO / Fred Joch; p. 29: IMAGO / Ulrich Wagner; pp. 30–31: IMAGO / Uwe Kraft; p. 32: FC Bayern München / Marco Donato; p. 33: IMAGO / DeFodi; p. 34: IMAGO / Werek; p. 35: Fritz Beck; p. 36: Getty Images / Lennart Preiss; p. 37: IMAGO / Kicker/Eissner, Liedel; p. 38: IMAGO / Fred Joch; p. 39: IMAGO / Revierfoto; p. 41: Sebastian Arlt; p. 42: FC Bayern München Museum; p. 43: Bernd Ducke; p. 44: IMAGO / HJS; p. 45: picture alliance / Peter Kneffel; p. 46: IMAGO / ActionPictures; p. 47: IMAGO / HJS; p. 48: Christian Kaufmann; p. 49: FC Bayern München; p. 50: IMAGO / Horstmüller, IMAGO / Uwe Kraft, IMAGO / MIS, IMAGO / Kicker/Eissner, IMAGO / Ulmer, Getty Images / Christof Stache; p. 52: Amelie Niederbuchner; p. 53: FC Bayern München; p. 54: Julian Baumann, IMAGO / MIS; p. 55: IMAGO / MIS; p. 56: IMAGO / Jan Huebner; p. 57: IMAGO / MIS; p. 58: Getty Images / Bongarts; p. 59: Getty Images / Bongarts; p. 60: IMAGO / Moritz Müller; p. 61: IMAGO / Revierfoto, IMAGO / Imago Images; p. 62: Daniel Delang, FC Bayern Museum, IMAGO / Sportfoto Rudel; p. 63: Dominik Gigler, Lara Freiburger, FC Bayern Museum; p. 64: IMAGO / Werek, IMAGO / Team2, Christian Kaufmann; p. 65: IMAGO / Thomas Exler; p. 66: IMAGO / Philippe Ruiz; p. 67: IMAGO / sportworld; p. 68: IMAGO / Werek; p. 69: IMAGO / Werek, IMAGO / Fred Joch; p. 70: Matthias Ziegler; p. 71: IMAGO / foto2press; p. 72: IMAGO / Werek, IMAGO / Fred Joch (2); p. 73: IMAGO / Kicker/Liedel; pp. 74–75: Hans Rauchensteiner; p. 76: FC Bayern Museum (5), IMAGO / Sven Simon; IMAGO / Lackovic; Getty Images / Stuart Franklin, Julian Baumann, IMAGO / Stepniak, IMAGO / Werek, p. 78: IMAGO / MIS; p. 79: Jens Utzt; p. 80: IMAGO / Contrast; p. 81: IMAGO / Alternate, IMAGO / Sven Simon; p. 82: IMAGO / Contrast; p. 83: ClubNr.12 (Gregor); p. 84: IMAGO / Werek; p. 85: IMAGO / Fred Joch; pp. 86–87: FC Bayern Museum; p. 88: IMAGO / Pressefoto Baumann, IMAGO / Horstmüller; p. 89: IMAGO / Sven Simon; p. 90: Bernd Ducke; p. 91: Bernd Ducke, Amelie Niederbuchner; p. 92: IMAGO / Horstmüller; p. 93: IMAGO / Sven Simon; p. 94: IMAGO / Poolfoto; p. 95: IMAGO / Fred Joch, pp. 96–97: Getty Images / A. Beier; p. 98: IMAGO / Lackovic, IMAGO / Werek, IMAGO / Sven Simon, IMAGO / kolbert-press, IMAGO / Eibner, picture-alliance / SZ Photo, IMAGO / Ulmer/Teamfoto, IMAGO / Sammy Minkoff, FC Bayern München; p. 100: FC Bayern München Museum; p. 101: Carlos Blanchard; p. 102: FC Bayern Museum; p. 103: picture-alliance/dpa; p. 104: IMAGO / MIS, p. 105: IMAGO / Ulmer/Cremer; p. 106: IMAGO / Kicker/Eissner, IMAGO / Fred Joch; p. 107: Getty Images / Alexander Hassenstein; IMAGO / Westend61; p. 108: IMAGO / Beautiful Sports (2), IMAGO / Lackovic, 3XN Architects; p. 110: IMAGO / Beautiful Sports, FC Bayern München; p. 111: IMAGO / Sven Simon; pp. 112–113: FC Bayern München Museum; p. 114: FC Bayern München / Simon Mellar; p. 115: IMAGO / Fred Joch, IMAGO / ActionPictures (2), Daniel Delang; p. 116: IMAGO / Sven Simon; p. 117: Dirk Bruniecki, IMAGO / Sven Simon, IMAGO / Fred Joch; p. 118: IMAGO / Fred Joch, IMAGO / Lackovic, IMAGO / Ulrich Wagner (2), IMAGO / Fotostand; p. 119: IMAGO / Ulrich Wagner, FC Bayern München; p. 120: IMAGO / MIS (2); p. 121: Stephie Braun; p. 122: IMAGO / Arnulf Hettrich, IMAGO / Fred Joch, IMAGO / Kicker/Metelmann, IMAGO / ANP, IMAGO / Chai v.d. Laage, IMAGO / MIS, IMAGO / Eibner, IMAGO / Werek, Getty Images / Joahnnes Simon; p. 124: Robert Fischer, FC Bayern München; p. 125: Matthias Ziegler; p. 126: IMAGO / Fred Joch (2); p. 127: IMAGO / Fred Joch; p. 128: IMAGO / ActionPictures; p. 129: FC Bayern München Museum, Kurt Landauer Stiftung; p. 130: Witters; p. 131: IMAGO / Fred Joch; p. 132: IMAGO / DeFodi, IMAGO / Sven Simon; p. 133: IMAGO / Michael Weber, IMAGO / Ulrich Wagner, IMAGO / Ulmer/Teamfoto; p. 134: IMAGO / Fred Joch; p. 135: FC Bayern München / Simon Mellar, IMAGO / Kicker/Liedel; p. 136: picture alliance / dpa; p. 137: IMAGO / Ulmer, IMAGO / Horstmüller; p. 138: Markus Burke; p. 139: Markus Burke; p. 140: IMAGO / BSR Agency; p. 141: IMAGO / Werek; pp. 142–143: Sarah Führbringer (6); p. 144: IMAGO / Ulmer, IMAGO / Thomas Frey, IMAGO / Lackovic; p. 145: FC Bayern München / Marco Donato, IMAGO / ActionPictures; p. 146: Getty Images / Miguel Villagran, FC Bayern München / Marco Donato, Amelie Niederbuchner, Fritz Beck, IMAGO / ActionPictures, IMAGO / FC Bayern München, IMAGO / MIS (2), FC Bayern Museum; p. 148: FC Bayern München; p. 149: Daniel Delang; p. 150: Getty Images / Sebastian Widmann; p. 151: FC Bayern München / Julian Baumann; p. 152: FC Bayern München / Lukas Steinbauer, FC Bayern München (2); p. 153: FC Bayern München; p. 154: FC Bayern München Museum; p. 155: IMAGO / Avanti, IMAGO / Ulmer; p. 156: FC Bayern München Museum (3); p. 157: Sebastian Arlt; p. 158: IMAGO / Poolfoto UCL; p. 159: IMAGO / Poolfoto UCL; p. 160: IMAGO / Chai v.d. Laage, IMAGO / Werek; p. 161: IMAGO / Laci Perenyi; p. 162: Daniel Nguyen; p. 163: Michael von Hassel; p. 164: IMAGO / kolbert-press, IMAGO / MIS (3), p. 165: IMAGO / Revierfoto; p. 166: Amelie Niederbuchner (2); p. 167: IMAGO / Sven Simon, IMAGO / kolbert-press; p. 168: Daniel Nguyen, IMAGO / Revierfoto, IMAGO / ActionPictures, IMAGO / Moritz Müller, Florian Frohnholzer (2), FC Bayern München Museum, IMAGO / Matthias Koch; p. 170: IMAGO / MIS; p. 171: Reinaldo Coddou; p. 172: FC Bayern München Museum; p. 173: FC Bayern München Museum; pp. 174–175: Jüdisches Museum München / Nachlass Kurt und Maria Landauer; p. 175: picture alliance / sampics/Stefan Matzke; pp. 176–177: FC Bayern München Museum; p. 178: IMAGO / Sven Simon; p. 179: picture-alliance / dpa, IMAGO / Ulmer/Cremer, Anna Aicher, IMAGO / IPA Photo; p. 180: IMAGO / Werek; picture-alliance / dpa; p. 182: IMAGO / Picture Point LE, IMAGO / Karina Hessland, IMAGO / Jan Huebner; p. 183: IMAGO / Eibner (4); pp. 185–186: Getty Images / Simon Hofmann; p. 186: IMAGO / Pressefoto Baumann; p. 187: IMAGO / Kolvenbach; p. 188: IMAGO / kolbert-press, IMAGO / Matthias Koch, IMAGO / Werek; p. 189: Münchner Philharmoniker (3); p. 190: FC Bayern München Museum, IMAGO / MIS, IMAGO / Werek, IMAGO / ActionPictures; p. 191: IMAGO / ActionPictures, IMAGO / Sven Simon, IMAGO / Fred Joch, p. 192: IMAGO / PanoramiC, IMAGO / Frinke, Witters (2), Getty Images / Marco Donato, Getty Images / Jamie McDonald, IMAGO / ActionPictures, IMAGO / Ulmer, IMAGO / Fred Joch; p. 194: IMAGO / Werek; p. 195: IMAGO / Sven Simon, IMAGO / Fred Joch, picture alliance/AP Images; p. 196: IMAGO / Kicker/Liedel, IMAGO / Werek; p. 197: IMAGO / Fred Joch; p. 198: IMAGO / Team2; p. 199: IMAGO / ActionPictures, IMAGO / Ulmer; p. 200: IMAGO / Eibner, IMAGO / Team2; p. 201: FC Bayern München / Simon Mellar; p. 202: FC Bayern München Museum (2); p. 203: IMAGO / Werner Otto, IMAGO / Horstmüller; p. 204: IMAGO / Sven Simon; p. 205: IMAGO / Kicker/Metelmann (2), IMAGO / Sportfoto Rudel; p. 206: IMAGO / Frinke, IMAGO / Sven Simon; p. 207: IMAGO / Ferdi Hartung; p. 208: IMAGO / Ferdi Hartung; p. 209: IMAGO / Sven Simon, IMAGO / Werek; p. 210: IMAGO / Fred Joch, IMAGO / HJS; p. 211: IMAGO / Ulmer, IMAGO / BSR Agency; p. 212: IMAGO / Eibner, IMAGO / Laci Perenyi; p. 213: IMAGO / Laci Perenyi; p. 214: IMAGO / photoarena/Eisenhuth; p. 215: IMAGO / Jan Huebner, IMAGO / MIS; p. 216: IMAGO / Sven Simon; p. 217: IMAGO / Kicker/Liedel, IMAGO / Ferdi Hartung; p. 218: IMAGO / Sven Simon, Bayerische Staatsbibliothek/stern-Fotoarchiv/Peter Thomann; p. 219: IMAGO / Fred Joch; p. 220: IMAGO / Pressefoto Baumann, IMAGO / Contrast, picture-alliance / DPPI; p. 221: IMAGO / WEREK, IMAGO / Sven Simon; p. 222: IMAGO / HJS; p. 223: IMAGO / photoarena/Zumpe, IMAGO / Ulmer; p. 224: IMAGO / Uwe Kraft, IMAGO / Ulmer; p. 225: IMAGO / Sven Simon (2), IMAGO / Uwe Kraft; p. 226: IMAGO / Ulmer; p. 227: IMAGO / MIS; p. 228: IMAGO / Colorsport, SZ Photo / WEREK; p. 229: IMAGO / Kicker/Metelmann, IMAGO / Horstmüller, IMAGO / Colorsport; p. 230: IMAGO / Fred Joch; p. 231: IMAGO / Frinke, IMAGO / Horstmüller, IMAGO / Ulmer; p. 232: IMAGO / WEREK: p. 233: IMAGO / Ferdi Hartung, picture-alliance / WEREK; p. 234: IMAGO / Team2 (2); p. 235: IMAGO / MIS, IMAGO / Eisele; p. 236: IMAGO / Ulrich Wagner; p. 237: IMAGO / ActionPictures; p. 238: IMAGO / Norbert Schmidt; p. 239: IMAGO / Ulmer, IMAGO / MIS; p. 240: IMAGO / Shutterstock, picture-alliance / REUTERS; p. 241: IMAGO / photoarena/Eisenhuth; p. 242: IMAGO / ABACAPRESS; p. 243: Getty Images / Boris Streubel; p. 244: FC Bayern München Museum, IMAGO / MIS; p. 245: IMAGO / Horstmüller; p. 246: IMAGO / Fred Joch, picture-alliance / Holger Hollemann, IMAGO / Fred Joch; p. 247: IMAGO / Sven Simon, IMAGO / Horstmüller, IMAGO / WEREK; p. 248: IMAGO / Gerhard König, IMAGO / Plusphoto, IMAGO / WEREK; p. 249: IMAGO / Ulmer, IMAGO / Lackovic; p. 250: IMAGO / MIS, Thomas Fähnrich; p. 251: IMAGO / Camera4; p. 252: IMAGO / Ulmer, p. 253: IMAGO / Kolvenbach, IMAGO / Team2; p. 254: IMAGO / Sven Simon, IMAGO / Annegret Hilse, IMAGO / ActionPictures; p. 255: IMAGO / Sven Simon (2); p. 256: IMAGO / Fred Joch; p. 257: FC Bayern München Museum (2); pp. 258–259: Raimund Simmet; p. 260: IMAGO / Magic, IMAGO / Matthias Koch; p. 261: FC Bayern München Museum, IMAGO / Ulmer, IMAGO / WEREK; p. 262: IMAGO / Imagebroker, IMAGO / Fred Joch, IMAGO / WEREK (2); p. 263: IMAGO / ActionPictures, IMAGO / Lackovic, IMAGO / Alternate; IMAGO / WEREK; p. 264: IMAGO / Sven Simon (2), IMAGO / Eisele; p. 265: IMAGO / WEREK (2), IMAGO / Claus Bergmann, picture-alliance / Pressefoto Rudel; p. 266: IMAGO / Pressefoto Baumann, Getty Images / Brian Morgan/Popperfoto, Family Simetsreiter/Gaßner, IMAGO / Otto Krschak; p. 267: IMAGO / Lackovic, IMAGO / Frinke, IMAGO / Fred Joch, IMAGO / Kicker/Eisner, IMAGO / Ferdi Hartung; p. 268: IMAGO / Fred Joch, IMAGO / WEREK; p. 269: IMAGO / Panthermedia, IMAGO / Rust, IMAGO / MIS, IMAGO / Sven Simon; p. 270: IMAGO / Sven Simon, IMAGO / WEREK, FC Bayern München Museum; p. 271: IMAGO / Fred Joch (3), IMAGO / Horstmüller; cover: FC Bayern München